Marxian Legal Theory

The International Library of Essays in Law and Legal Theory
Series Editor: Tom D. Campbell

Schools

Natural Law, Vols I & II *John Finnis*
Justice *Thomas Morawetz*
Law and Economics, Vols I & II *Jules Coleman and Jeffrey Lange*
Critical Legal Studies *James Boyle*
Marxian Legal Theory *Csaba Varga*
Legal Reasoning, Vols I & II *Aulis Aarnio and Neil MacCormick*
Legal Positivism *Mario Jori*
American Legal Theory *Robert Summers*
Law and Language *Fred Schauer*
Sociological Theories of Law *Kahei Rokumoto*
Rights *Carlos Nino*
Law and Psychology *Martin Levine*
Feminist Legal Theory, Vols I & II *Frances Olsen*
Law and Society *Werner Krawietz*
Contemporary Criminological Theory *Francis Cullen and Velmer Burton*

Areas

Criminal Law *Thomas Morawetz*
Tort Law *Ernest Weinrib*
Contract Law, Vols I & II *Larry Alexander*
Anti-Discrimination Law *Christopher McCrudden*
Consumer Law *Iain Ramsay*
International Law *Martti Koskenniemi*
Property Law, Vols I & II *Elizabeth Mensch and Alan Freeman*
Constitutional Law *Mark Tushnet*
Procedure *Denis Galligan*
Evidence and Proof *William Twining and Alex Stein*
Company Law *Sally Wheeler*
Privacy, Vols I & II *Raymond Wacks*
Administrative Law *Denis Galligan*
Child Law *Harry Krause*
Family Law, Vols I & II *Harry Krause*
Welfare Law *Peter Robson*
Medicine and the Law *Bernard Dickens*
Commercial Law *Ross Cranston*
Environmental Law *Michael Blumm*
Conflict of Laws *Richard Fentiman*
Law and Religion *Wojciech Sadurski*
Human Rights Law *Philip Alston*
European Community Law, Vols I & II *Francis Snyder*
Tax Law, Vols I & II *Patricia White*
Media Law *Eric Barendt*

Legal Cultures

Comparative Legal Cultures *Csaba Varga*
Law and Anthropology *Peter Sack*
Hindu Law and Legal Theory *Ved Nanda*
Islamic Law and Legal Theory *Ian Edge*
Chinese Law and Legal Theory *Michael Palmer*
Socialist Law *W. Butler*
Japanese Law and Legal Theory *Koichiro Fujikura*
Law and Development *Anthony Carty*
Jewish Law and Legal Theory *Martin Golding*
Legal Education *Martin Levine*
Civil Law *Ralf Rogowski*

Future Volumes

Labour Law, African Law and Legal Theory, Postmodernism and Law, Law and History, Law and Ethics and Cumulative index.

Marxian Legal Theory

Edited by

Csaba Varga

Scientific Adviser, Hungarian Academy of Sciences

NEW YORK UNIVERSITY PRESS
REFERENCE COLLECTION

Manufactured in Great Britain

First published in the U.S.A. in 1993 by
NEW YORK UNIVERSITY PRESS
Washington Square
New York NY 10003

Library of Congress Cataloging-in-Publication Data
Marxian legal theory / edited by Csaba Varga.
p. cm. — (The International library of essays in law and legal theory. Schools ; 9)
"New York University Press reference collection."
Includes bibliographical references and index.
ISBN 0-8147-8772-X
1. Law and socialism. I. Varga, Csaba, 1941– . II. Series.
K357.Z9M36 1992
340'.1—dc20 92-36109
CIP

Contents

PART IV CONTEMPORARY ISSUES

PART V PERSPECTIVES FOR SOCIO-LEGAL ANALYSIS

PART VI LAW AND IDEOLOGY

PART VII FINAL ACCOUNT

Acknowledgements

The editors and publishers wish to thank the following for permission to use copyright material.

Academie serbe des Sciences et des Arts for the essay: Zdravko Grebo (1985), '"Kelsenism" and Marxism', in Radomir Lukic (ed.) *La métodologie du Droit*, in *Académie serbe des Sciences et des Arts*, Conférences Scientifiques, **28**, Classe des Sciences Sociales No. 5, pp. 113–31.

American Journal of Jurisprudence for the essay: William Leon McBride (1970), 'Marxism and Natural Law', *The American Journal of Jurisprudence*, **15**, pp. 127–53.

Annual Review of Sociology for the essay: Steven Spitzer (1983), 'Marxist Perspectives in the Sociology of Law', *Annual Review of Sociology*, **9**, pp. 103–24. Reproduced, with permission, from the Annual Review of Sociology, Vol. **9**, Copyright © 1983 by Annual Reviews Inc.

Australian Journal of Law and Society for the essay: Peter Fitzpatrick (1983), 'Marxism and Legal Pluralism', *Australian Journal of Law and Society*, **1**, pp. 45–59.

Basil Blackwell for the essay: Richard Kinsey (1978), 'Marxism and the Law: Preliminary Analyses', *British Journal of Law and Society*, **5**, pp. 202–27.

Duncker & Humblot GMBH for essays: Eugene Kamenka (1987), 'Lukács and Law', *Rechtstheorie*, **18**, pp. 516–23 and Wieslaw Lang (1976), 'Law and Morality from a Marxist Point of View', *Rechtstheorie*, **2**, pp. 137–52.

Harcourt Brace Jovanovich Limited for essays: Kálmán Kulcsár (1980), 'Ideological Changes and the Legal Structure: A Discussion of Socialist Experience', *International Journal of the Sociology of Law*, **8**, pp. 61–81; Peter Schöttler (1986), 'Friedrich Engels and Karl Kautsky as Critics of "Legal Socialism"', *International Journal of the Sociology of Law*, with the Introduction of the translator, Iain Stewart, **14**, pp. 1–32; Csaba Varga (1981), 'Towards a Sociological Concept of Law: An Analysis of Lukács' Ontology', *International Journal of the Sociology of Law*, **9**, pp. 159–76, and R. Warrington (1981), 'Pashukanis and the Commodity Form Theory', *International Journal of the Sociology of Law*, **9**, pp. 1–22.

Eugene Kamenka (1983), 'A Marxist Theory of Law?', *Law in Context*, **1**, pp. 46–72. Copyright © Eugene Kamenka.

K. Kulcsár (1963), 'The Historical Concept in the Science of Law of the XXth Century', *Acta Juridica Academia Scientiarum Hungaricae*, **1**, pp. 1–40. Copyright © K. Kulcsár.

Kluwer Academic Publishers for the essay: Li Changdao (1980), 'The Old Law Cannot Be Critically Inherited, It Can Only Be Used as a Mirror', *Review of Socialist Law*, **No. 3**, **6**, pp. 287–91. Reprinted by permission of Kluwer Academic Publishers.

Law and Society Association for essays: Alan Hunt (1985), 'The Ideology of Law: Advances and Problems in Recent Applications of the Concept of Ideology to the Analysis of Law', *Law and Society Review*, **19**, pp. 11–37, and Alan Stone (1985), 'The Place of Law in the Marxian Structure–Superstructure Archetype', *Law and Society Review*, **19**, pp. 39–67. Reprinted by permission of the Law and Society Association.

Osteuropa–Recht for the essay: Michael Jaworskyj (1960), 'Soviet Critique of the "Bourgeois" Philosophy of Law', *Osteuropa–Recht*, **6**, pp. 11–34.

Rivista Internazionale di Filosofia del Diritto for the essay: Csaba Varga (1979), 'Rationality and the Objectification of Law', *Rivista Internazionale di Filosofia del Diritto*, **4**, pp. 676–701.

M.E. Sharpe Publisher for the essay: L.S. Mamut (1968), 'Questions of Law in Marx's *Capital*', *Soviet Law and Government No 4*, **6**, pp. 3–10. Reprinted by permission of M.E. Sharpe, Inc., Armonk, New York 10504.

Studies in the Theory and Philosophy of Law for the essay: Jerzy Kowalski (1985), 'Idea of Equality and the Law', *Studies in the Theory and Philosophy of Law*, **1**, pp. 21–5.

I. Szabó (1976), 'The Notion of Law', *Acta Juridica Academiae Scientiarum Hungaricae*, **18** (3–4), pp. 263–71, and I. Szabó (1972), 'The Social Limits of Law', *Acta Juridica Academiae Scientiarum Hungaricae*, **14** (3–4), pp. 231–43. Copyright © I. Szabó.

The University of Chicago Press for the essay: William Leon McBride (1975), 'The Concept of Justice in Marx, Engels, and Others', *Ethics*, **85**, pp. 204–18. Copyright © The University of Chicago Press.

Jerzy Wróblewski (1976), 'Problems of Legality in Marxist Theory', *Archiv für Rechts- und Sozialphilosophie*, **62**, pp. 497–515. Copyright © Jerzy Wroblewski.

Every effort has been made to trace all the copyright holders, but if any have been inadvertently overlooked the publishers will be pleased to make the necessary arrangement at the first opportunity.

Series Preface

The International Library of Law and Legal Theory is designed to provide important research materials in an accessible form. Each volume contains essays of central theoretical importance in its subject area. The series as a whole makes available an extensive range of valuable material which will be of considerable interest to those involved in the research, teaching and study of law.

The series has been divided into three sections. The Schools section is intended to represent the main distinctive approaches and topics of special concern to groups of scholars. The Areas section takes in the main branches of law with an emphasis on essays which present analytical and theoretical insights of broad application. The section on Legal Cultures makes available the distinctive legal theories of different legal traditions and takes up topics of general comparative and developmental concern.

I have been delighted and impressed by the way in which the editors of the individual volumes have set about the difficult task of selecting, ordering and presenting essays from the immense quantity of academic legal writing published in journals throughout the world. Editors were asked to pick out those essays from law, philosophy and social science journals which they consider to be fundamental for the understanding of law, as seen from the perspective of a particular approach or sphere of legal interest. This is not an easy task and many difficult decisions have had to be made in order to ensure that a representative sample of the best journal essays available takes account of the scope of each topic or school.

I should like to express my thanks to all the volume editors for their willing participation and scholarly judgement. The interest and enthusiasm which the project has generated is well illustrated by the fact that an original projection of 12 volumes drawn up in 1989 has now become a list of some 60 volumes. I must also acknowledge the vision, persistence and constant cheerfulness of John Irwin and the marvellous work done by Mrs Margaret O'Reilly and Mrs Sonia Bridgman.

TOM D. CAMPBELL
Series Editor
The Faculty of Law
The Australian National University

Introduction

Marxian legal theory has never been an 'ordinary' trend or current or school of theorizing on legal issues in the sense or the way in which, for instance, legal positivism, natural law thinking or the sociology of law have been.

In the middle of the past century, the teaching of Marx and his comrades radiated all over Europe in total repudiation of the tendencies that were then on the agenda in Western European economic, social as well as political development. The annihilating criticism, which was cumulative in effect, was categorical indeed, reminding one both of the sarcasm of the prophets of the Old Testament and of the determination and finality of the Last Judgement of the New Testament. As to its methodology, it may have followed a Jewish tradition of thinking and writing, certainly more alive in theology than in other, markedly worldly, fields, having more features in common with a mass of commentaries, comments and marginalia superimposed on one another in an incomprehensible way, than with any systematic exposition. As a matter of fact, the eschatological undertone of the categoricality of Marxism, both early and mature, was hardly counterbalanced by its claim definitively to cover anything and everything science and scholarship had ever been able to discover or explain since civilization began.

To put it briefly, from the beginning Marx's personal vision of Marxism amalgamated positive knowledge with ideology and *weltanschauung* on the one hand, and a political platform as well as a party programme (set up for guiding practical action on a daily basis but also amidst particular or exceptional circumstances) on the other.

The outcome that such a variant to theorizing on eternal grand topics related to the vocation of humanity and the destiny of world history could offer was, first, the intellectual challenge it continuously evokes (thanks to the great number of methodological ideas and theoretical insights it has sparkingly borne out). Also it offers a mixture destined to be used partly as a surrogate for positive religion and partly as a catechism to draw upon of axiomatic and expected responses to all kinds of questions that could be raised either in theory or in practice.

Although Marxism has, since the time of its inception, professed a deep commitment to the idea of evolution, even the formative thought of the Founding Fathers proved to be closed to a surprisingly large extent. In their rhetoric, Marx and Engels insisted, within the perspective of evolution, on everything being process-like, open-textured and, as such, multi-chanced. Only later and tacitly was it revealed, from the analysis of the answers they offered, that what they actually meant to convey was, in the final analysis, an exception to the rule.

It may be surprising to learn that, from their youth, law served as a favourite subject for both Marx and Engels from which they learned to take a stand, to argue for or exemplify what they had in mind. The same holds for early disciples (like Ferdinand Lassalle) as much as for late adepts (like Georg von Lukács). In fact, law must not have been a specific or difficult job to them. After all, it manifested the juristic logic of how to develop and present ideas and argue for claims – a pattern which was the fashion of the day. Not by chance,

Marx was a law graduate from Berlin; as columnists, Marx and Engels were also used to debating social and political issues in terms of law. Even the fundamental paradigm they introduced, notably the economy conceived of as a basis for the social superstructure which, in turn, serves it as a mere instrument by corresponding at all times to it, got exposed by the instance of law. Law was the master paradigm – a servant of the economic imperative of which it was considered to be an outgrowth.

In any case, the question remains unanswered whether or not Marxism has developed genuinely philosophical disciplines testing the evidence of on-going times as do ontology, epistemology, aesthetics and so on. Notwithstanding, we may take it for granted that Marxism has failed in developing a theory of law of its own which deserved the word. Marxism, as an amalgam of differing inspirations, methodological assumptions, theoretical insights and practical considerations, was largely applied only to questions related to law.

The fact that Marxism was born under an unlucky star and had but fragmented interest in law marginalized its applicability from the very beginning, predestining the limited impact it would have both on law and on theorizing upon law.

Its fertilizing effect may have first been exerted on European history at a period when the wishful preparation for the international revolution was, for many, the number one preoccupation of the day. The Golden Age spanned from the Founding Fathers' formative years, via the *fin de siècle* moods and expectations, to the manipulation of World War I events, their side-effects, consequences and the aftermath. This resulted in a theory facing immediate challenges in the present which had to revolutionize constituencies to meet and overcome them. By a Philosophy of History inspiration, even if purely eschatological in nature, it was Predemption and Utopia that prevailed as substitutes for reality – stronger than reality; therefore, also finally able to transcend, annihilate and destroy reality.

According to scholarly opinions, mostly from Western observers frequently not without a touch of sympathy for leftism, this was the generation of truly Marxian ideas which paved a new path in the history of social sciences. For that matter, the path in question was predetermined by the will of power and the wish to provoke through World Revolution, a new turn in history rather than by any theoretical consideration. This is why none of the paths and achievements set out by grand theories of Marxism was able to survive conditions that might have been instrumental to inspiring them, notwithstanding the fact that the age was characterized by names of great intellectual strength like Karl Liebknecht, Anton Menger, Georg von Lukács, Karl Renner and Ernst Bloch.

The kinds of encounters and attempts at realization Marxism experienced later on can be divided into two groups. For the first, revolutionary conditions supplied the ideological frame for the issue of law; this was an intellectual exercise of formulating a programme of radical renewal for legal policy. For the second group, Marxism was only referred to as a methodological frame for inspiring a new theoretical start by fostering critical approaches.

In the first case, it was the Bolshevik revolution in Russia and the early experience of bolshevizing the region, especially in the short-lived Hungarian Soviet Republic, that set the model. The pattern was enlarged when the Soviet Union ended World War II as a winning power, imposing its rule on Eastern Central Europe and Eastern Europe and, step by step, also in parts of Asia, Africa and even in Central America.

Needless to say, even the zeal of the new Jacobins could not succeed in forcing a breakthrough in the humanities. Law was not an exception, either. In most cases, the revolutionary enterprise involved intellectuals with purely abstract ideas about society, who were filled with the firm will to elevate society to a stage never dreamt of. Reporting on his impressions of Georg Lukács, commissar of the people in exile in Vienna in 1929, Thomas Mann considered him basically a 'thoroughly intellectual man who played, believed he had to play, a political role at a time when catastrophic conditions offered transitory social zealots the possibility of trying out their ideas experimentally on the living body of the people, trying out the order in which they believed.'[1]

As is known, the first decades of Soviet construction were in fact rich in promising new attempts at theorizing. Perhaps it is sufficient to refer to the works of M.A. Reisner, P.I. Stuchka, as well as E.B. Pashukanis. In contrast, the triumph of Stalinism in legal ideology, expressed by the imposition of A.Ja. Vyshinskii's legal concept on the scholarly community at the meeting of the Institute of State and Law of the Soviet Academy in 1939, meant a full stop to (and practically a deadly reprisal against) any sign of further innovation.

The theoretical perspective of what has officially been called the 'Marxist-Leninist Theory of State and Law' has not changed strikingly since. A few characteristic features of Soviet Marxism in law can be listed as follows:

- priority is given to political and ideological considerations;
- assumptions of legal positivism, the prevailing professional ideology, are taken as axiomatic stepping-stones in theory;
- socialist normativism remains supreme and unchallenged;
- because power factors are granted preference (which is called 'dialectics'), no specifically legal considerations can be taken independently;
- Marxism's self-assertion is only weakly counterbalanced by aggressively blind universalization, which is unjustifiably extrapolated as a world-wide, ahistorical eternal condition;
- Marxism becomes isolated by getting bogged down in its own tradition;
- the ideology rejects any otherness by ignoring approaches (anthropology, sociology, political science, linguistic philosophy), methodologies (analytical, logical, systems theoretical) and authorities (outside the control of agents of 'actually existing socialism') which differ from its own, and treat them, if at all, with scornful criticism.

Such an intellectual climate cannot be favourable to any genuine development in scholarship. Only small scope has ever been allowed the issue since. Consequently, the appreciation of their results is a function of the prior phase they have overcome. By way of illustration, let me quote one instance. The great turning point, achieved since the rise of Vyshinskii which opened theoretical vistas towards sociology, was in fact a debate revolving around the question of how to understand the definition of law Vyshinskii had accepted in 1939. Its main arguments held that (1) Vyshinskii accepted what had only been customarily established as law, and that (2) legal relationships were the exclusive forms of the practical realization of the workings of law. So the debate went on to explore whether relationships established in a way other than as 'realizations of "the" law' and 'fulfilment of "socialist legality"' (e.g. issuing from judicial practice, which the doctrine of mechanical jurisprudence, then prevailing, excluded from official recognition) could be regarded as law-generating components.[2]

As to the literature, one can of course find an abundance of outstanding names and magisterial works. The present situation is, however, rather unfair. For the underlying conditions which have prevailed for Marxists since the early 1920s have themselves been rather unfair. To name but a few, these have included political domination, complete isolation, no access to international journals and symposia, scarcity of domestic publishing in foreign languages, preference for Russian (and especially Muscovite) institutions, practical destruction of cultures differing from the Byzantic one (particularly in the Baltics, as well as in Armenia and Georgia). All these indicate future lines of research which may surprise us with achievements worthy of further consideration and study.

In the countries which were made satellite to the Soviet Union after World War II, Moscow exported Marxism in a form reduced to a Byzantine, state-controlled religious surrogate. Marxism was imposed as the last word of scholarship at the uppermost stage of human civilization. In practice, the reception of the Soviet pattern also meant the destruction of national identities and traditions, ignorance of their academic past and its institutional framework. The Soviet pattern was visible even in minute details of both everyday life and in the professions. The chair system at universities, the selection of state days, the reorganization of journals, the storing of food by the army – nothing, including titles, formalities, uniforms and directions of use – was exempted. Academic freedom was discontinued; even the few academic survivors had no option but to change into proletarian clothing.

This brutal imposition process was a general condition. But the actual depth to which Soviet domination could provoke genuine change differed slightly. Those countries most vulnerable to getting thoroughly Sovietized had themselves been in want of a modern legal culture (e.g. Mongolia and Albania) or had a Byzantine past in common with their colonizing power (e.g. Bulgaria, Romania, as well as Serbia).

As to Central Europe, the Soviet occupation zone of Germany was dramatically Sovietized. It was perfected to such a point that not even contemporary German scholarship can respond to local arguments. Almost the same isolation was enforced on Czechoslavakia after the crushing of the Prague Spring movement in 1968.

Happily enough, Poland and Hungary have remained a different case. Historically speaking, Poland has had a flourishing tradition in social thought and methodology, particularly strong in formal logic and conceptual analysis. In consequence, Poland was quite successful in preserving relative 'otherness' in intellectual fields, by accepting Marxism in politics and ideology, but keeping it aside in domains where scholarship was felt to be at stake. That is, national pride and tradition were used as barriers to save scientific thought. The chance of intellectual survival in Hungary was less promising. A small country with a handsome number of universities, Hungary has had an established tradition mostly in social science theory inspired from new Kantianism. Even so, the humanities in Hungary could not withstand the army of new Bolshevik academics, including Georg Lukács and his comrades, who argued that they were laying the foundations of modern social theory instead of a narrowly German approach. Step-by-step Marxism became the only vehicle of scholarship in the humanities.

Finally, as to China, North Korea, Vietnam and Cuba, as well as further countries in Asia and Africa at one time exposed to revolutionary upheaval but later fallen into chaos and disaster (Cambodia, Ethiopia and Afghanistan), information is too sporadic and scant to substantiate any judgement. One cannot even say whether the lack of information is to blame or whether legal theorizing is missing. Or is it simply that legal thought is wedged in a non-European context.

In the Western hemisphere, Marxism has at all times been well received, though only as a peripheral force. In the interwar period, the encounter of legal scholarship with Marxism was mostly dedicated to surveying what had been going on in Soviet Russia. Considering the fact that the Communist theory of law was of poor quality and its criticism was also politically biased, critical attitudes seldom led to any theoretical advance.

The case differed after the death of Stalin when Marxism became a fashionable subject in the West. Outstanding theoretical results were achieved, reminding one of the intellectual strength of the classical Golden Age of Marxism. Marxian legal theory, dealt with as a special topic, as a trend of social philosophy as well as a chapter in the history of ideas, became widely acknowledged as an academic subject. Finally, it was transformed into a discipline with specialists in the field.

In the English-speaking world, it was at a relatively late stage of development that interest in Marxian legal theory ultimately arose. Professional specialization in the field has, however, remained the privilege of only a few scholars. For the bulk of interest is mostly attached to some special consideration: this may be the methodological choice it offers or the political sympathy it is motivated by. Sometimes it is the particular discipline or topic that offers the scope for such special consideration.

In sum, contemporary interest in Marxian legal theory is both divided and particularized to a considerable extent.

Until recently, in that part of the world which was called 'actually existing socialism', Marxian legal theory was nothing but the function of Soviet rule – until the Soviet empire itself fell apart. Marxian legal theory, forced as a strait-jacket, came to be imposed (for want of anything better) in countries where it was meant to replace deep-rooted culture in law and philosophy (in Poland, Hungary, as well as the Czech and Moravian lands). In other places, where culture had been hindered from transcending grassroots levels, it became a panacea or a substitute for culture, influencing both conceptual and institutional patterns.

In the Western hemisphere, Marxism has never gone beyond mirroring certain particular interests. Marxism has appeared as an umbrella or methodological prop for trends like critical studies, deconstructive analysis, feminist theory or the theory of modernization.

At the present stage of development of theorizing on law in Marxism, the perspectives are extremely difficult to draw. In the English-speaking world as well as in Western Europe, Marxism may remain one of the fashionable patterns, evergreen in its potential to challenge minds. As one of the prime embodiments, as well as the methodological and conceptual reserve, of critical analysis, it may well in the future foster investigations, especially into the social complexity of law and the nature of the social totality in which legal enterprise is embedded. Although political sympathy, nostalgia as well as being the last hope for meeting revolutionary expectations (mostly in countries where social revolution has been aborted or transformed into a compromise) may have disappeared as motifs of the easy success and world-wide spread of Marxism (especially earlier in this century), it cannot be denied the chance to readapt and respond to new challenges.

What is most probable, however, is that its Soviet variant will be ousted from the intellectual map and that, in response to past abuses, its cultivation will be less feverish, if not discontinued, within the satellite orbit for awhile. As a matter of fact, such a course could even be favourable for the future of Marxian legal theorizing. In the long run, it may advance Marxism to leave behind Soviet-type degeneration and subservience to discredited politics. In this way, Marxism will be given the chance to reformulate its critical methodology, instead of propounding the Utopia it once was its cherished dream to impose upon reality.

Notes

1. Cf. A. Mádl and J. Györi (eds) (1977), *Thomas Mann und Ungarn, Essays, Dokumente, Bibliographie*, Budapest: Akadémiai Kiadó, 339–40.
2. For a survey of the debate, reminiscent of the classical clash between legal positivism and sociology of law in Germany in 1916–17 [collected in Stanley L. Paulson (ed.) (1992), *Hans Kelsen und die Rechtssoziologie*, Auseinandersetzungen mit Hermann U. Kantorowicz, Eugen Ehrlich und Max Weber, Aalen: Scientia, forthcoming], see Csaba Varga (1967), 'Quelques problèmes de la définition du droit dans la théorie socialiste du droit' in *Archives de Philosophie du Droit*, **12**, Paris, Sirey, 189–205.

Selected Bibliography

1. Introduction and Reference

1.1. Bibliographies

Fitzpatrick, Peter and Rüegg, A. (1987), 'Marxisme en recht: een bibliografie van de Engelstalige literatuur', *Recht en Kritiek*, No. 1, 73–83.

Fitzpatrick, Peter and Rüegg, A. (1987), 'Marxismo y derecho: una bibliografia de la literature en lengua inglesa', *Critica Juridica*, No. 5, 169–83.

1.2. Seminal Post-Classic Contributions

Bloch, Ernst (1986), *Natural Law and Human Dignity*, Cambridge (Massachusetts): MIT Press, 323 pages.

Il 'Socialismo giuridico' (1974–75), Ipotesi i letture, I–II, in *Quaderni Fiorientini per la storia del pensiero giuridico moderno*, Nos. 3/4, Mailand: Giuffrè, 1041 pages.

Renner, Karl (1949), *The Institutions of Private Law and Their Social Functions*, transl. A. Schwarzschild, introd. O. Kahn-Fruend, London: Routledge and Kegan Paul, reprinted 1976, 307 pages.

1.3. The Assessment of Seminal Post-Classic Contributions

Christensen, Ralph (1987), *Freiheitsrechte und soziale Emanzipation*, Ernst Bloch's Kritik der marxistisch-leninistischen Rechtstheorie, Berlin: Duncker & Humblot, 254 pages [Schriften zur Rechtstheorie, Heft 122].

Conclin, W.E. (1985), 'The Legal Theory of Horkheimer and Adorno', in *Windsor Yearbook of Access to Justice*, 230–57.
Haaß, Bernhard (1990), 'Justizkritik bei Karl Liebknecht der Begriff "Klassenjustiz"', *Zeitschrift für Rechtssoziologie*, **11**, 120–36.
Hörner, Hans (1977), *Anton Menger*, Recht und Sozialismus, Frankfurt am Main, Bern, Las Vegas: Peter Lang Verlag, xl + 217 pages [Europäische Hochschulschriften, Reihe II: Rechtswissenschaft, Band 179].
Pocar, V. (1970), 'Diritto e legislazione nel pensiero sociologico di Karl Renner', *Rivista internazionale di filosofia del diritto*, **47**, 425ff.
Reich, Norbert (1972), 'Anton Menger und die demokratische Rechtstheorie', *Recht und Politik*, Vierteljahreshefte für Rechts- und Verwaltungspolitik, **8** (3), 93ff.
Sawer, G[eoffrey] (1961), 'Law as Socially Neutral: Karl Renner', in G[eoffrey] Sawer (ed.), *Studies in the Sociology of Law*, Canberra: Australian University Press.

1.4. General Collections in and on Marxian Legal Theory

Guastini, Riccardo (ed.) (1980), *Marxismo e teorie del diritto*, Antologia di scritti giuridici, Bologna: Il Mulino, 272 pages [Il pensiero moderno/Diritto].
Lukic, Radomir [D.] (ed.) (1978), *Sur la philosophie du droit,* [papers in English, French and Serbian], Belgrade, 657 pages [Académie serbe des Sciences et des Arts: Classe des Sciences sociales].
Marx et le droit moderne (1967), Paris: Sirey, x + 391 pages [Archives de Philosophie du Droit, 12].
Reich, Norbert (ed.), (1972), *Marxistische und sozialistische Rechtstheorie*, Frankfurt am Main: Athenäum, 235 pages [Studien und Texte zur Theorie und Methodologie des Rechts, Band 12].
Rottleuthner, Hubert (1975), *Probleme der marxistischen Rechtstheorie*, Frankfurt am Main: Suhrkamp, 514 pages.

2. Soviet Marxism

2.1. Works

Cerroni, Umberto (ed.) (1964), *Teorie sovietiche del diritto*, Milano: Giuffrè, li + 320 pages [Civiltà del diritto, 7].
Hazard, John N. (ed. and introd.) (1951), *Soviet Legal Philosophy*, transl. Hugh W. Babb, Cambridge (Massachusetts): Harvard University Press, xxxvii + 465 pages [Twentieth Century Legal Philosophy Series, 5].
Iavich, L.S. (1963), 'A Contribution to the Question of the Methodology of Jurisprudence', *Soviet Law and Government*, **2** (2), 11–16.
Jawitsch, L. (1981), *The General Theory of Law*, Moscow: Progress.
Kerimov, D.A. (1963), 'Liberty, Law and the Legal Order', *Northwestern University Law Review*, **58**, 643–56.
Pashukanis, Evgeny B. (1978), *Law and Marxism, A General Theory*, transl. Barbara Einhorn, ed. Chris J. Arthur, London: Ink Links, 195 pages.
Pashukanis, Evgeny B. (1980), *Selected Writings on Marxism and Law*, transl. Peter B. Maggs, ed. Piers Beirne and Robert Sharlet, New York: Academic Press, xvii + 374 pages.
Rappoport, Anatol (1927), *Die marxistische Rechtsauffassung*, Riga: Selbstverlag, 54 pages.
Strogovich, M.S. (1966), 'Problems of Methodology in Jurisprudence', *Soviet Law and Government*, **4** (4), 13–22.
Stuchka, P.I. (1964), *Izbrannye proizvedeniia po marksistko-leninskoi teorii prava* [Selected Contributions to the Marxist-Leninist Theory of Law], Riga: Latvian State Publishing House [in Italian translation: Petr I. Stuchka (1967), *La funzione rivoluzionare del diritto e dello Stato i altri scritti*, introd. and transl. Umberto Cerroni, Torino: Einaudi, xlvi + 545 pages [Nuova biblioteca scientifica Einaudi, 16].

2.2. Criticism of Trends of Western Legal Thought

Protiv sovremennoi pravovoi ideologii imperializma [Against the Legal Ideology of Contemporary Imperialism] (1962), Moscow: Inostrannaia Literatura.

Radev, Ja[roslav] and Tumanov, V. (eds) (1983), *Problemi gossudarstva i prava v sovremennoi ideologitsheskoi bor'be* [The Problems of State and Law in the Contemporary Ideological Fight], Sofia: Nauka i izkustvo; Moscow: Juriditscheskaia Literatura, 206 pages.

Tumanov, V.A. (1969), 'Contemporary Anti-marxism and the Theory of Law', *Soviet Law and Government*, **8** (1), 3–20.

Tumanov, V[ladimir] A. (1974), *Contemporary Bourgeois Legal Thought*, Moscow: Progress [in French: *Pensée juridique bourgeoise contemporaine*, Appréciation marxiste des conceptions fondamentales, Moscow: Edition du Progrès, 392 pages].

3. Socialist Satellite Marxism

3.1. Works

Basta, Danilo N. (1990), 'Grenzen und Schwierigkeiten der Menschenrechts kritik von Karl Marx', *Rechtstheorie*, **21**, 106–16.

Ceterchi, Ioan and Popescu, Sofia (1984), 'Droit et valeur', *Revue roumaine des Sciences sociales: Série de Sciences juridiques*, **28**, 13–20.

Cosmovici, Paul (1978), 'Traits spécifiques du concept du droit relevés par la science juridique de Roumanie', *Revue roumaine des sciences sociales: Série de Sciences juridiques*, **22**, 51–63.

Cuper, J. (1987), 'Types of Metascientific Reflection in Marxist-Leninist Science of State and Law', in *Law, Culture, Science and Technology*, Prague: Ceskoslovensky Komitet IVR, 102–28.

Eörsi, Gyula (1979), *Comparative Civil (Private) Law*, Law Types, Law Groups, the Roads of Legal Development, Budapest: Akadémiai Kiadó, 651 pages.

Földesi, Tamás (1989), 'Esquisse d'une possible conception marxiste de la justice', *Rivista internazionale di filosofia del diritto*, **66**, 24–57.

Grahn, W[erner] and Wagner, I[ngo] (1975), 'Legal and Social Equality from the Marxist Point of View', *Law and Legislation of the German Democratic Republic*, No. 1, 31–45.

Grahn, Werner (1979), *Die Rechtsnorm*, Eine Studie, Leipzig: Sektion der Rechtswissenschaft [der] Karl-Marx-Universität Leipzig, 175 pages [Schriftenreihe Methodologie der marxistisch-leninistischen Rechtswissenschaft, Heft 6].

Haney, Gerhard (1987), 'Der materialistische Rechtsbergriff (Ein Diskussionsbeitrag)' in *Festschrift für Erich Buchholz*, 1, Berlin: Humboldt-Universität, 62–71.

Klenner, Hermann (1977), 'The Marxist Conception of Human Rights', *Retfaerd*, No. 6, 8–20.

Klenner, Hermann (1983), 'Marx gegen/für Menschenrechte', *Rechtsfilosofie en Rechtstheorie*, No. 2, 107–12.

Klenner, Hermann (1984), *Vom Recht der Natur zur Natur des Rechts*, Berlin: Akademie-Verlag, 234 pages.

Klenner, Hermann (1986), 'Soziale Voraussetzungen der Rechtsphilosophie' in Eugene Kamenka, Robert S. Summers and William L. Twining (eds), *Soziologische Jurisprudenz und realistische Theorien des Rechts*, Berlin: Duncker & Humblot, 52–67 [Rechtstheorie, Beiheft 9].

Klenner, Hermann (1991), 'Was bleibt von der marxistischen Rechtsphilosophie?', in *15th World Congress on Philosophy of Law and Social Philosophy*, Plenary Lectures, Göttingen: no publisher, 113–31 [reprinted in Werner Maihofer, Gerhard Sprenger (ed.) (1992), *Praktische Vernunft und Theorien der Gerechtigkeit*, Stuttgart: Franz Steiner Verlag [in press] [Archiv für Rechts- und Sozialphilosophie, Beiheft 50].

Kowalski, Jerzy (1982), 'The Notion of Law' in Paul Trappe (ed.), *Contemporary Conceptions of Law*,

Wiesbaden: Franz Steiner Verlag, 385–94 [Archiv für Rechts- und Sozialphilosophie, Supplementa, I. 2].
Kulcsár, Kálmán (1961), 'Some Problems of the Sociology of Law', *Acta Juridica Academiae Scientiarum Hungaricae*, **3**, 227–38.
Lang, Wieslaw (1977), 'John Rawl's Theory of Justice: A Marxist Rejoinder' in *Law and the Future of Society*, Warsaw: Institute of State and Law [of the] Polish Academy of Sciences; Polish Section of [the] International Association of Philosophy of Law and Social Philosophy, 67–93.
Lang, Wieslaw (1979), 'Marxism, Liberalism and Justice' in Eugene Kamenka and Alice Erh-Soon Tay (eds), *Justice*, London: Arnold, 116–48 [Ideas and Ideologies].
Lang, Wieslaw (1981), 'Law and Politics', in *Memoria del X congreso mundial ordinario de filosofia del derecho y filosofia social*, 2, México: Universidad Nacional Autonóma de México, 261–75.
Lang, Wieslaw (1983), 'Recht und Sittlichkeit vom marxistischen Standpunkt aus betrachtet', *Rechtstheorie*, 155–80.
Lotze, Lothar (1992), 'Wege und Irrwege der marxistischen Rechtstheorie', *Archiv für Rechts- und Sozialphilosophie*, **78**, 396–406.
Lukic, Radomir D. (1964), 'La giustizia e l'objectività del Diritto', *Rivista Internazionale di Filosofia del Diritto*, **41**, 687ff.
Lukic, Radomir [D.], (1974), *Théorie de l'État et du Droit* [1951], trad. Marc Djidara, Paris: Dalloz, 600 pages [Collection 'Philosophie du Droit', 13].
Naschitz, Anita [M.] (1965), 'Wert- und Wertungsfragen im Recht', *Revue Roumaine des Sciences sociales: Série de Sciences juridique*, **9**, 3–23.
Opalek, Kazimierz (1970), 'The Relations between the Social and Economic Development and Development of Law' in *Rapports polonais présentés au huitième Congrès international de Droit comparé*, Wroclaw, Warsaw, Kraków, Gdansk: Ossolineum, 133–45.
Opalek, Kazimierz (1971), 'Law as Social Phenomenon', *Archiv für Rechts- und Sozialphilosophie*, **57**, 37–55.
Opalek, Kazimierz (1974), 'The Conception of Human and Civic Rights and Duties: Its Origin and Character', *Archivum Iuridicum Cracoviense*, **7**, 47–63.
Opalek, Kazimierz (1977), 'Law and Politics', *Archivum Iuridicum Cracoviense*, **10**, 16–29.
Peric, Berislav (1981), 'Problem of Coercion in Law', in *Memoria del X Congreso Mundial Ordinario de Filosofia del Derecho y Filosofia Social*, 7, México: Universidad Nacional Autónoma de México, 183ff.
Peschka, Vilmos (1967), 'Rechtsquelle und Rechtserzeugung', *Acta Juridica Academiae Scientiarum Hungaricae*, **9**, 175–85.
Peschka, Vilmos (1980), 'Ideologische Vorurteile über das Verhältnis zwischen Wirtschaft und Recht', *Acta Juridica Academiae Scientiarum Hungaricae*, 22, 259–74.
Peschka, Vilmos (1980), 'Typus und Analogie im Recht', *Archiv für Rechts- und Sozialphilosophie* **66**, 85–101.
Peschka, Vilmos (1982), *Die Theorie der Rechtsnormen*, Budapest: Akadémiai Kiadó, 266 pages.
Peschka, Vilmos (1982), 'Some Aspects of the Relation between Law and State', *Acta Juridica Academiae Scientiarum Hungaricae*, **24**, 287–96.
Peschka, Vilmos (1985), 'Equity as Correction of Legal Justice' in Jan M. Broekman, Kazimierz Opalek and Djangir A.A. Kerimov (eds), *Social Justice and Individual Responsibility in the Welfare State*, preface Carl Wellman, Stuttgart: Franz Steiner Verlag Wiesbaden, 38–40 [Archiv für Rechts- und Sozialphilosophie, Beiheft 24].
Peschka, Vilmos (1987), 'Das Recht und die Ästhetik' in Werner Krawietz and Walter Ott (eds), *Formalismus und Phänomenologie im Rechtsdenken der Gegenwart*, Festgabe für Alois Troller zum 80. Geburtstag, Berlin: Duncker & Humblot, 343–50.
Peschka, Vilmos (1989), *Die Eigenart des Rechts*, Budapest: Akadémiai Kiadó, 199 pages.
Peschka, Vilmos, 'Wider die missverstandene marxistische Rechtstheorie', 11–18.
Péteri, Zoltán (1966), 'Die Kategorie des Wertes und das sozialistische Recht', *Wissenschaftliche Zeitschrift der Friedrich-Schiller-Universität Jena: Gesellschafts- und Sprachwissenschaftliche Reihe*, **15** (3), 427–29.
Péteri, Zoltán (ed. & introd.) (1968), *Aktuelle Probleme der marxistisch-leninistischen Staats- und*

Rechtstheorie, Material der Konferenz der Staats- und Rechtstheoretiker der europäischen sozialistischen Länder, Budapest: Magyar Tudományos Akadémia Állam- és Jogtudományi Intézete, 327 pages.

Péteri, Zoltán (1978), 'The Notion of Positive Law' in Imre Szabó and Zoltán Péteri (eds), *Comparative Law – Droit comparé*, Budapest: Akadémiai Kiadó, 57–71.

Péteri, Zoltán (ed.) (1984), *Legal Theory – Comparative Law*, Studies in Honour of Professor Imre Szabó, Budapest: Akadémiai Kiadó, viii + 464 pages.

Péteri, Zoltán (1989), 'Perspectives for a Socialist Axiology of Law', in Erhard Mock and Csaba Varga (eds), *Rechtskultur – Denkkultur*, Stuttgart: Franz Steiner Verlag Wiesbaden, 96–105 [Archiv für Rechts- und Sozialphilosophie, Beiheft, 35].

Przetacznik, Franciszek (1977), 'The Socialist Concept of Human Rights: Its Philosophical Background and Political Justification', *Revue Belge de Droit International*, **13**, 238–78.

Samu, Mihály (1988), 'Historicity of Law – Basic Aspect of Socialist Legal Theory' in S[tavros] Panou, G[eorg] Bozonis, D[emetrios] Georgas and P[aul] Trappe (eds), *Philosophy of Law in the History of Human Thought*, Stuttgart: Franz Steiner Verlag Wiesbaden, 168–73 [Archiv für Rechts- und Sozialphilosophie, Supplementa II].

Szabó, Imre (1963), *Die theoretische Fragen der Auslegung der Rechtsnormen*, Berlin: Akademie-Verlag, 19 pages [Sitzungsberichte der Deutschen Akademie der Wissenschaften zu Berlin: Klasse für Philosophie, Geschichte, Staats-, Rechts- und Wirtschaftswissenschaften, 2/1962].

Szabó, Imre (1963), 'Quelques questions de la théorie socialiste du droit', *Annales Universitatis Scientiarum Budapestinensis de Rolando Eötvös nominatae: Sectio Iuridica*, **4**, 141–70.

Szabó, Imre (1970), 'Lénine et le droit', *Revue internationale de Droit comparé*, 675–86.

Szabó, Imre (1973), *Les fondements de la théorie du droit*, Budapest: Akadémiai Kiadó, 340 pages.

Szabó, Imre (1974), 'Les fonctions sociales du droit', in Luis Legaz y Lacambra (ed.), *Die Funktionen des Rechts*, Wiesbaden: Franz Steiner Verlag, 63–84 [Archiv für Rechts- und Sozialphilosophie, Beiheft Neue Folge, 8].

Szabó, Imre (1977), 'Les perspectives fondamentales de la liberté et de l'égalité' in Carl Wellman (ed.), *Equality and Freedom*, Past, Present and Future, Wiesbaden: Franz Steiner Verlag, 9–15 [Archiv für Rechts- und Sozialphilosophie, Beiheft Neue Folge, 10].

Szabó, Imre (1981), *Karl Marx und das Recht*, Vorträge, Berlin, Akademie-Verlag, 128 pages [Staats-und Rechtstheoretische Studien, 10].

Szotáczky, Mihály (1970), 'Le problème de la continuité et discontinuité dans l'évolution du droit', *Archivum Iuridicum Cracoviense*, **3**, 25–43.

Szotáczky, Mihály (1971), 'Socialist Law and Justice, in Mihály Szotáczky (ed.), *Current Problems of Socialist Jurisprudence*, Pécs, 33–42 [Studia Iuridica auctoritate Universitatis Pécs publicata, 76].

Szotáczky, Mihály (1979), 'Die Gerechtigkeit als Wertmaßstab des Rechts', *Wissenschaftliche Zeitschrift der Freidrich-Schiller-Universität Jena: Gesellschafts- und Sprachwissenschaftliche Reihe*, No. 1, 79–85.

Szotáczky, Mihály (1986), 'Axiologische Betrachtung und Rechtsgeltung' in Csaba Varga and Ota Weinberger (eds), *Rechtsgeltung*, Stuttgart: Franz Steiner Verlag Wiesbaden, 73–78 [Archiv für Rechts- und Sozialphilosophie, Beiheft 27].

Varga, Csaba (1969), 'Lenin and the Revolutionary Law-Making', *International Journal of Contemporary Law*, No. 1, 1982, 47–59.

Varga, Csaba (1976), *Codification as a Socio-historical Phenomenon*, Budapest: Akadémiai Kiadó, 1991, viii + 391 pages.

Varga, Csaba (1976), 'The Relative Autonomy of Formal Rational Structures in Law: An Essay in the Marxist Theory of Law', *Eastern Africa Law Review*, A Journal of Law and Development, **8** (3), 245–60.

Varga, Csaba (1980), 'Chose juridique et réification en droit: Contribution à la théorie marxiste sur la base de l'Ontologie de Lukács', in *Archives de Philosophie du Droit*, 25, Paris: Sirey, 385–411.

Varga Csaba (1981), 'Rechtssetzung als Objektivationsprozess: Rechtsphilosophische Fragen vom sozialphilosophischen Sicht'' in *Filosofia del Derecho y Problemas de Filosofia Social*, Memoria del X Congreso mundial ordinario de filosofia del derecho y filosofia social, 4, México: Universidad Nacional Autonóma de México, 91–103 [Instituto de Investigaciones Juridicas, Serie G: Estudios doctrinales, 57].

Varga, Csaba (1983), 'Towards the Ontological Foundation of Law (Some Theses on the Basis of Lukács' Ontology)', *Rivista internazionale di filosofia del diritto*, **60**, 127–42.
Varga, Csaba (1985), *The Place of Law in Lukács' World Concept*, Budapest: Akadémiai Kiadó, 193 pages.
Varga, Csaba (1985), 'Domaine "externe" et domaine "interne" en droit', *Revue Interdisciplinaire d'Etudes Juridiques*, No. 14, 25–43.
Varga, Csaba (1985), 'Reflections on Law and on Its Inner Morality', *Rivista internazionale di filosofia del diritto*, **62**, 439–51.
Varga, Csaba (1986), 'Macrosociological Theories of Law: From the "Lawyer's World Concept" to a Social Science Conception of Law' in Eugene Kamenka, Robert S. Summers and William Twining (eds), *Soziologische Jurisprudenz und realistische Theorien des Rechts*, Berlin: Duncker & Humblot, 197–215 [Rechtstheorie, Beiheft 9].
Varga, Csaba (1988), 'Anthropological Jurisprudence? Leopold Pospisil and the Comparative Study of Legal Cultures' in *Law in East and West*, On the occasion of the 30th anniversary of the Institute of Comparative Law [of the] Waseda University, Tokyo: Waseda University Press, 265–85.
Varga, Csaba (1988), 'Law as History?' in S[tavros] Panou, G[eorg] Bozonis, D[emetrios] Georgas and P[aul] Trappe (eds), *Philosophy of Law in the History of Human Thought*, Stuttgart: Franz Steiner Verlag Wiesbaden, 191–98 [Archiv für Rechts- und Sozialphilosophie, Supplementa II].
Varga, Csaba (1990), 'Law as a Social Issue', in Slawomirz Wronkowska and Macieja Zielinski (eds), *Szkice z teorii prawa i szczególowych nauk prawnich*, Poznan: Uniwerszytet im. Adame Mickiewicza, 239–55 [Uniwerszytet im. Adame Mickiewicza w Poznaniu: Seria Prawo, 129].
[Wert und Recht] (1979), [a special issue of] *Wissenschaftliche Zeitschrift der Friedrich-Schiller-Universität Jena*, 28.
Wróblewski, Jerzy (1978), 'The Philosophical Problems of Legal Theory in Marxist Interpretation', *Archivum Iuridicum Cracoviense*, **11**, 41–58.

3.2. Survey

Seidler, Grzegorz L. (1967), 'Marxist Legal Thought in Poland', *Slavic Review*, **26** (3), 382–94.
Varga, Csaba (1986), 'Current Legal Theory in Hungary', *Current Legal Theory*, **4** (1), 15–21.
Wróblewski, Jerzy (1976), 'State and Law in Marxist Theory of State and Law', *Wayne Law Review*, **22**, 815–39.

3.3. Criticism of Trends of Western Legal Theory

Borucka-Arctowa, Maria (1979), 'The Conception of Legal Consciousness as a New Approach to the Problems of Natural Law', in Adam Lopatka (ed.), *Contemporary Conceptions of Law*, Warsaw: Institute of State and Law [of the] Polish Academy of Sciences, 153–70.
Mollnau, Karl A. (1974), *Vom Aberglauben der juristischen Weltanschauung*, Berlin: Akademie-Verlag.
Naschitz, Anita M. (1966), '"Le problème du droit naturel" à la lumière de la philosophie marxiste du droit', *Revue roumaine des Sciences sociales: Série de Sciences juridiques*, **10**, 19–40.
Peschka, Vilmos (1961), 'Die existentialistische Rechtsphilosophie', *Acta Juridica Academiae Scientiarum Hungaricae*, **3**, 17–56.
Peschka, Vilmos (1965), 'Der Psychologismus in der modernen bürgerlichen Rechtstheorie', *Acta Juridica Academiae Scientiarum Hungaricae*, **7**, 207–44.
Peschka, Vilmos (1973), '"Idealtypen" der Rechtssoziologie von Max Weber', *Acta Juridica Academiae Scientiarum Hungaricae*, **15**, 263–83.
Peschka, Vilmos (1974), *Grundprobleme der modernen Rechtsphilosophie*, Budapest: Akadémiai Kiadó, 235 pages.
Peschka, Vilmos (1977), 'Das bürgerliche rechtstheoretische Denken in der ersten Hälfte des XX. Jahrhunderts', *Acta Juridica Academiae Scientiarum Hungaricae*, **19**, 1–29.
Péteri, Zoltán (1960), 'Gustav Radbruch und einige Fragen der relativistischen Rechtsphilosophie', *Acta Juridica Academiae Scientiarum Hungaricae*, **2**, 113–60.

Péteri, Zoltán (1966), 'Influence of Natural Law on Positive Law' in Zoltán Péteri (ed.), *Études en droit comparé*, Budapest: Akadémiai Kiadó, 45–60.
Szabó, Imre (1964), 'Droit et nature des choses selon la théorie socialiste du droit (Pays de l'Est)', *Annales de la Faculté de Droit de Toulouse*, Fasc. 1, 141–56.
Szabó, Imre (1979), 'Marxismus und Naturrecht', *Archiv für Rechts-und Sozialphilosophie*, **65**, 503–20.
Tumanov, V.A. (ed.) (1969), *Kritika sovremennoi burzhuaznoi teorii prava* [Criticism of Contemporary Bourgeois Theory of Law], transl. from Hungarian [1963], preface L.S. Jagodovskoi, Moscow: Progress, 288 pages.

4. Contemporary Western Marxism

4.1. Works

Añón Roig, Mario José (1991), 'Agnes Heller: el lugar del derecho en el paradigma de las objectivaciones sociales', *Sociologia del Diritto*, **18** (1), 85–110 [abstract in English: p. 219].
Arthurs, C.J. (1976–77), 'Towards a Materialist Theory of Law', *Critique*, **7**, 31ff.
Atienza, Manuel (1983), *Marx y los Derechos Humanos*, Madrid: Editorial Mezquita, 280 pages.
Beirne, Piers and Quinney, Richard (eds) (1982), *Marxism and Law*, New York: Wiley, xiv + 381 pages.
Blom, Raimo (1979), 'On the Foundations of the Materialistic Theory of State and Law', in *European Yearbook in Law and Sociology*, 1978, The Hague: Nijhoff, 81–95.
Bobbio, Norberto and Treves, Renato (1978), 'Teoria del diritto e sociologia del diritto in Marx', *Sociologia del Diritto*, **5** (2), 279ff.
Brimo, Albert (1977), 'Le dépérissement du droit dans la théorie marxiste du droit et de l'Etat' in *Mélanges offerts à Georges Burdeau*, Paris: Librarie Générale du Droit et de Jurisprudence, 235–52.
Cain, Maureen and Hunt, Alan (eds) (1979), *Marx and Engels on Law*, New York, London: Academic Press, 281 pages.
Cerroni, Umberto (1962), *Marx e il diritto moderno*, Roma: Editori Riuniti, 233 pages; enlarged 3rd ed., (1972), 300 pages [Universale, 14]. For a German translation, see *Marx und das moderne Recht*, Frankfurt am Main: Fischer Taschenbuch Verlag, 1974, 264 pages [Texte zur politischen Theorie und Praxis, 6520].
Collins, Hugh (1982), *Marxism and Law*, Oxford: Clarendon Press; New York: Oxford University Press, viii + 159 pages.
Conde, Remingo (1968), *Sociedad, Estado y Derecho en la filosophia marxista*, Madrid: Editorial Cuadernos para el dialogo, S.A., 232 pages.
Edelman, Bernard (1973), *Ownership of the Image*, Elements for a Marxist Theory of Law, transl. Elizabeth Kingdom, introd. Paul Q. Hirst, London, Boston: Routledge and Kegan Paul, 1979, xii + 217 pages.
Eklund, Per (1974), *Rätten i klassenkampen*, En studie i rättens funktioner, [no place]: Tidens Förlag, viii + 416 pages.
Farrell, Martin Diego (1989), *Analisis critico de la teoria marxista de la justicia*, Madrid: Centro de Estudios Constitucionales, 71 pages [Cuadernos y Debates, 17].
Gabel, Peter (1980), 'Reification in Legal Reasoning' in Rita J. Simon (ed.) and Steven Spitzer (guest ed.), *Research in Law and Sociology, A Research Annual*, 3, Greenwich (Connecticut): The JAI Press, 25–51.
Geras, N. (1985), 'The Controversy about Marx and Justice', *New Left Review*, No. 150, 47–85.
Gil, Antonio Hernandez (1970), *Marxismo y positivismo logico*, Sus dimensiones juridicas, Madrid: Rivadeneyra, 173 pages.
Guastini, Riccardo (1974), *Marx dalla filosofia del diritto alla scienza della società*, Il lessico giuridico marxiano (1842–1851), Bologna: Il Mulino, 542 pages [Saggi/Il Mulino, 142].
Higi, Peter (1988), *Sein und Sollen in der marxistischen Rechtstheorie*, Unter Berücksichtigung des marxistischen Wissenschaftsverständnisses, Zurich: Schulthess, xxiv + 328 pages.

Hirst, Paul (1979), *On Law and Ideology*, Atlantic Highfields, New Jersey: Humanities Press, 181.
Hunt, Alan (1981), 'Marxism and the Analysis of Law' in Adam Podgórecki and Christopher J. Whelan (eds), *Sociological Approaches to Law*, London: Croom Helm, 91–109.
Hunt, Alan (1983), 'Marxist Legal Theory and Legal Positivism', *Modern Law Review*, **46**, 236–43.
Kamenka, Eugene (1982), 'Marxism, Economics and Law' in J.L. Curiel (ed.), *Memorie del X Congreso Mundial Ordinario de Filosofia del Derecho y Filosofia Social*, VII, Mexico: Universidad Nacional Autónoma de México, 49–72.
Kamenka, Eugene and Tay, Alice Erh-Soon (1971), 'Beyond the French Revolution: Communist Socialism and the Concept of Law', *University of Toronto Law Journal*, **21**, 109–40.
Lascoumes, Pierre and Zander, Hartwig (1984), *Marx du 'vol de bois' à la critique du droit*, Karl Marx à la 'Gazette rhénane': naissance d'une méthode, Paris: Presses Universitaires de France, 283 pages [Philosophie d'aujourd'hui].
Leser, Norbert (1980), 'Marx and Freud', *Archiv für Rechts- und Sozialphilosophie*, **60**, 363–87.
Mandel, Michael (1986), 'Marxism and the Rule of Law', *University of New Brunswick Law Journal*, **35**, 7–33.
Milonavonic, Dragan (1989), *Weberian and Marxian Analysis of Law*, Development and Functions of Law in a Capitalist Mode of Production, Aldershot: Avebury, viii + 223 pages.
Norton, A. (1982–83), 'Marx, Engels and Pashukanis on Law', *Natal University Law Review*, **3** (1–2), 161–90.
Paul, Wolf (1974), *Marxistische Rechtstheorie als Kritik des Rechts*, Intention, Aporien und Folgen des Rechtsdenkens von Karl Marx – eine kritische Rekonstruktion, Frankfurt am Main: Athenäum, viii + 184 pages [Studien und Texte zur Theorie und Methodologie des Rechts, Band 16].
Paul, Wolf (1988), 'Die zwei Gesichter der marxistischen Rechtstheorie' in Arthur Kaufman, Ernst-Joachim Mestmäcker and Hans F. Zacher (eds), *Rechtsstaat und Menschenwürde*, Festschrift für Werner Maihofer zum 70. Geburtstag, Frankfurt am Main: Klostermann, 329–54.
Phillips, Paul (1980), *Marx and Engels on Law and Laws*, Oxford: Martin Robertson, xi + 238 pages.
Planty-Bonjour, G. (ed.) (1986), *Droit et liberté selon Marx*, Paris: Presses Universitaires de France, 223 pages.
Reich, Norbert (1973), *Marxistische Rechtstheorie*, Historische und aktuelle Diskussionen und Tendenzen, Tübingen: J.C.B. Mohr, 39 pages [Recht und Staat in Geschichte und Gegenwart, 420/421].
Reine Rechtslehre und marxistische Rechtstheorie (1978), Symposium, Wien: Manz, 218 pages [Schriftenreihe des Hans Kelsen-Instituts].
Ripepe, Eugenio (1987), *Alla ricerca della concezione marxista del diritto*, Con un'appendice in terma di crisi nel e del marxismo, Torino: G. Giappichelli, 395 pages.
Sarotte, Georges (1969), *Le matérialisme historique dans l'étude du droit*, Paris: Editions du Pavillon, 311 pages.
Stoyanovitch, K[onstantin] (1960), 'La Règle de droit dans la doctrine marxiste et néo-marxiste' in *Archives de Philosophie du Droit*, 5, Paris: Sirey, 188–207.
Stoyanovitch, K[onstantin] (1963), 'La théorie marxiste du dépérissement de l'État et du droit' in *Archives de Philosophie du Droit*, 8, Paris: Sirey, 125–43.
Stoyanovitch, K[onstantin] (1964), *Marxisme et droit*, Paris: Librarie Générale du Droit et de Jurisprudence, iii + 406 pages [Bibliothèque de Philosophie du Droit, I].
Stoyanovitch, K[onstantin] (1974), *La pensée marxiste et le droit*, Paris: Presses Universitaires de France, 197 pages [Collection SUP: Le Juriste, 4].
Sugarman, David (ed.), (1983), *Legality, Ideology and the State*, London: Academic Press, xiv + 304 pages [Law, State and Society Series, 11].
Sumner, Colin (1979), *Reading Ideologies*, An Investigation into the Marxist Theory of Law and Ideology, New York: Academic Press, 313 pages.
Sumner, C. (1981), 'The Rule of Law and Civil Rights in Contemporary Marxist Theory', *Kapitalstate*, **9**, 63–92.
Tay, Alice Erh-Soon and Kamenka, Eugene (1959), 'Karl Marx's Analysis of Law', *The Indian Journal of Philosophy*, **1**, 17–38.
Troller, Alois (1983), 'Erkenntnistheoretische Parallele von Widerspiegelungstheorie und Phänomenologie im praktischen Rechtsdenken' in *Conceptions contemporaines du droit*, 3, Wiesbaden:

Franz Steiner Verlag, 51–66 [Archiv für Rechts- und Sozialphilosophie].
Tushnet, M. (1983), 'Is There a Marxist Theory of Law?' in Roland Peenock and John W. Chapman (eds), *Marxism*, New York: New York University Press, xv + 342 pages [Nomos, XXVI].
Wagner, Heinz (1976), *Recht als Widerspiegelung und Handlungsinstrument*, Beitrag zu einer materialistischen Rechtstheorie, Cologne: Pahl-Rugenstein Verlag, 195 pages [Kleine Bibliothek: Politik, Wissenschaft, Zukunft, 70].
Waldron, Jeremy (ed.) (1987), *Nonsense Upon Stilts*, Bentham, Burke and Marx on the Rights of Man, London and New York: Methuen, 236 pages.
Weyl, Monique and Weyl, Roland (1972), *Idéologie juridique et lutte de classe*, Paris: Centre d'études et de recherches marxistes, 30 pages [Les Cahiers du centre d'études et de recherches marxistes, 100].

4.2. Survey

Greenbert, David F. and Anderson, Nancy (1981), 'Recent Marxisant Books on Law: A Review Essay', *Contemporary Crises*, **5**, 293–322.
Jeffrey, W. Jr. (1983), 'Marxist Theory and Law: An Essay Review of Three Books', *Review of Socialist Law*, **9**, 35–53.
Jessop, Bob (1980), 'On Recent Marxist Theories of Law, the State, and the Juridico-political Ideology', *International Journal of the Sociology of Law*, **8**, 339–68.
Kamenka, Eugene (1983), 'Three Marxist Theories of Law', in *Conceptions contemporaines du droit*, 4, Wiesbaden: Franz Steiner Verlag, 455–63 [Archiv für Rechts- und Sozialphilosophie].
Krygier, Martin (1983), [review on Collins' book], *University of New South Wales Law Journal*, **6**, 238–46.
Villey, Michel (1966), 'Un ouvrage récente sur Marx et le droit [Umberto Cerroni: Marx e il diritto moderno]' in *Archives de Philosophie du Droit*, 9, Paris: Sirey, 329–37.

4.3. Criticism upon Soviet and Satellite Marxism

Balbus, Isaac D. (1977), 'Commodity Form and Legal Form: An Essay on the Relative Autonomy of Law', *Law and Society Review*, **11**, 571–88.
Bodenheimer, Edgar (1952), 'The Impasse of Soviet Legal Philosophy', *Cornell Law Quarterly*, **38**, 51–72.
Brunner, Georg (1971), 'Naturrecht und Sowjetideologie', *Anales de la Catedra Francisco Suarez*, **11**, 47–88.
Cerroni, Umberto (1969), *Il pensiero giuridico Sovietico*, Rome: Editori Riuniti, 260 pages.
Coccopalmiero, Domenico (1984), *Dogmatismo e storicità del marxismo*, Politico e diritto nell'esperienza comunista, Mailand: Giuffrè, ix + 213 pages [Università degli Studi di Trieste].
[Debate on continuity] (1980), *Review of Socialist Law*, **6**, by Eugene Kamenka, 261–74, as well as by Münzel, 275–79, with transl. of Lin Ronguian, 280–6.
Desolre, Guy (1976), 'Théorie "pure" et théorie marxiste du droit: Le débat entre Hans Kelsen et les juristes de l'Est', *Revue des Pays de l'Est*, Nos. 1–2, 83–117.
Dorsey, G.L. (1967), 'Post-Stalin Soviet Jurisprudence', *International Lawyer*, **1**, 378–91.
Fogelklou, Anders (1986), 'Continuity and Change in Soviet Legal Thought after Stalin: The Concept of Law', *Nordic Journal of Soviet and East European Studies*, **3** (3–4), 1–40.
Fogelklou, Anders (1990), 'Paa Spaning efter Raettstaten: Det nya Raettstankandet i Sovietunionen [In Search for the Rechtsstaat: New Legal Thinking in the Soviet Union]', *Retfaerd*, No. 51, 4–24.
Fuller, Lon L. (1949), 'Pashukanis and Vishinski: A Study in the Development of Marxist Legal Theory', *Michigan Law Review*, **47**.
Ginsburgs, George and Ginsburgs, Herta (1976), 'Thoughts on Soviet Legal Theory: On Reading Reich and Reichel's *Introduction*', *Review of Socialist Law*, **2**, 57–61.
Kamenka, Eugene (1965), 'The Soviet View of Law', *Problems of Communism*, **14** (2), 8–16.

Kelsen, Hans (1955), *The Communist Theory of Law*, New York: Praeger; London: Stevens, viii + 203 pages.
Kühne, D. (1985), *Der marxistisch-sozialistische Rechtsbegriff*, Eine kritische Stellungnahme, Berlin, Munich: Duncker & Humblot.
Lamsdorff-Galagne, Vladimiro (1969), *El Concepto de Justicia en el marxismo soviético actual*, Santiago de Compostela: Porto y Cia. Editores, S.L., 165 pages [Biblioteca Hispanica de Filosofia del Derecho, 2].
Lapenna, Ivo (1964), *State and Law*, Soviet and Yugoslav Theory, London: University of London – The Athlone Press, xi + 135 pages.
Ludwikowski, R.R. (1987), 'Socialist Legal Theory in the Post-Pashukanis Era', *International and Comparative Law Review*, **10**, 323–42.
[Marxism and the Law] (1985), [a special issue of] *Columbia Journal of Transnational Law*, **23** (2), 217–444.
Mazurek, Per (1985), 'Marxistische und sozialistische Rechtstheorie' in Arthur Kaufmann and Winfried Hassemer (eds), *Einführung in die Rechtsphilosophie und Rechtstheorie der Gegenwart*, 4th ed., Heidelberg: Müller, 327–43 [Uni-Taschenbücher, 593].
Mullin, N. (1980), 'Pashukanis and the Demise of Law: An Essay Review', *Contemporary Crises*, **4**, 433–38.
Norrie, A. (1982), 'Pashukanis and the "Commodity Form Theory": A Reply to Warrington', *International Journal of the Sociology of Law*, **10**, 419–38.
Petev, Valentin (1989), *Kritik der marxistisch-sozialistischen Rechts- und Staatsphilosophie*, Berlin: Duncker & Humblot, 161 pages [Münsterische Beiträge zur Rechtswissenschaft, 37].
Pfaff, Dieter (1968), *Die Entwicklung der sowjetischen Rechtslehre*, Cologne: Verlag Wissenschaft und Politik, 286 pages [Abhandlungen der Bundesinstitute für ostwissenschaftliche und internationale Studien, Band XIX].
Powell, S.J. (1967), 'The Legal Nihilism of Pashukanis', *University of Florida Law Review*, **20**, 18–32.
Ripllès, Antonio Quintano (1950), 'Filosofia y Ciencia del Derecho Sovieticas', *Revista General de Legislacion y Jurisprudencia*, Marzo, Madrid: Institut Editorial Rens, 33 pages.
Stoyanovitch, K[onstantin] (1965), *La philosophie du droit en U.R.S.S.*, 1917–1953, Paris: Librairie Générale de Droit et de Jurisprudence, 284 pages [Bibliothèque de Philosophie du Droit, IV].
Tozzi, Antonio (1960), 'Appunti intorno della dottrina comunista del diritto e dello Stato: M.A. Reisner' [offprint from] *Studi in memoria di Lorenzo Mossa*, Padova: Casa Editrice dott. Antonio Mizari, 28 pages.
Tozzi, Antonio (1962), 'Appunti intorno alla teoria communista del diritto e dello stato (La reazione e al formalismo giuridico in un articolo di P. Yudin)' in *Studi in memoria Giovan Battista Fungioli*, Mailand: Giuffrè, 785–816.
Troller, Alois (1986), *Das Rechtsdenken aus bürgerlicher und marxistisch-leninistischer Perspektive*, Zurich: Schulthess, 80 pages.

Part I
Origins

[1]

Theory of Law

Sovetskoe gosudarstvo i pravo, 1967, No. 12

L. S. Mamut

QUESTIONS OF LAW IN MARX'S CAPITAL

(On the 100th Anniversary of Volume I)

In connection with the publication of the first volume of Capital, Engels wrote: "In the years that capitalists and workers have existed on earth, no book has appeared that is as important for workers as the one that now lies before us." (1) These words continue to be valid today. The past century, the central event of which was the triumphant Great October Socialist Revolution in Russia, has been marked by the triumph of Marxism. Life is confirming the correctness and timeliness of the major conclusions of Capital. The dialectical materialist concept of the state and law that was set forth in it has also withstood the test of time.

Marx's work of genius continues to serve the proletariat in its practical struggle for the social reshaping of the world. It continues to be an inexhaustible spring of knowledge feeding the development of advanced social thought.

Soviet jurists have long and fruitfully made use of Marx's creative heritage, including many of the theoretical postulates of Capital, in resolving key problems of jurisprudence that are important in perfecting law as an effective means of guiding the processes occurring in society. In the legal and sociological literature, it is the question of law as a system of universally binding rules of behavior (norms), established by the state, that has had the most detailed investigation. But at the same time, in Marx's writings (particularly in Capital), other aspects of that exceedingly complex and multidimensional phenomenon, the law, have been studied. The study of Capital makes possible a clearer notion of these aspects and sides of the law and, thereby, a fuller disclosure of its nature and mechanism of action. Some of Marx's views on the law, as set forth in Capital, are dealt with briefly in the present article.

Law as a Social Relationship

The bourgeois society analyzed in Capital is regarded by Marx as a set of historically con-

The author is a Senior Research Associate at the Institute of State and Law of the USSR Academy of Sciences.

crete systems of relationships endowed with the corresponding institutions [instituty, uchrezhdenii] and ideology. Marx also singles out law as a specific relationship; in accordance with the practice of that day, he calls it the legal relationship.

The pattern of legal relationships was interpreted variously in the scholarship of Marx's day. Some theoreticians held that legal relationships are connections among persons defined by rules of law. (2) Others, including Hegel, did not at all consider the fact of regulation by a legal norm to be a necessary point of departure for a legal relationship. "Law is a relationship among men in their capacity as abstract persons." (3).

In investigating the connection among commodity owners in Capital, Marx adopts that construction of law which holds it to be a relationship in which the establishment of a norm by legal prescription is not an absolute requirement for the existence of a relationship at law. (4) For him, law in a society of commodity producers is a relationship that develops out of the economic system; it takes shape among free and autonomous persons, and its distinguishing features are abstractness, equality of the parties (sides), and its volitional character. (5)

Marx ascribes enormous importance to a principle that combats all idealism in jurisprudence: legal relationships are not to be explained on the basis of themselves and not from the evolution of the human spirit. The womb from which they spring is "civil society." He returns to this notion repeatedly. "Every form of production," writes Marx in his introduction to the Critique of Political Economy, "gives rise to its own legal relations." (6) In the preface to the same work, it is emphasized that legal relations are "rooted in the material relationships of life." (7) In Capital it is clearly stated that economic relationships determine the content of legal relations. (8) Finally, in the Critique of the Gotha Programme, special emphasis is placed on the fact that legal relations arise out of the relationships of production. (9)

A necessary condition for the shaping of law as a relationship is the attainment of a level of maturity by the social community at which its participants already enjoy a certain freedom. Specifically, in evaluating the position of the parties in commodity exchange — a realm in which legal relationships are most sharply marked — Marx calls them (the parties) "free individuals." (10) To be able to dispose of oneself and one's things is the meaning of freedom (in the context under consideration here). If an individual is not free, it is impossible for him to enter into a legal relation. Institutions, Marx notes, accurately describe as a slave (in other words, an object of legal intercourse) one who cannot acquire things for himself in exchange, (11) i.e., one who does not dispose of himself and his things.

In order for law to take on the form of a stable relationship, it is not enough for individuals to possess a certain freedom: they must also be autonomous personalities, formally independent of each other. In the evaluation, cited above, of parties to commodity exchange, Marx also calls them "independent commodity owners." Such individuals were inconceivable in "the socio-productive organisms of antiquity," which rested upon underdevelopment of the "individual man, who had not yet torn free of the umbilical cord of natural clan ties with other persons, or from direct relationships of dominance and subjection." (12) Such individuals were unknown to "gloomy European medievalism." At that time, all were dependent: "serfs and feudal lords, vassals and suzerains, the secular and the priests. Personal dependence here characterizes both the social relationships of material production and the spheres of life based upon it." (13)

At the moment when a legal relation begins, there occurs (outside the consciousness and wishes of men) a process of abstraction from the distinctive, individual, unique characteristics of the person.

The first materialist explanation of the abstractness of legal relations was provided in Capital. It derives not from a dubious recognition of persons as formally free and mutually independent, but from the essence, the regularities of commodity production. Every day and every hour it surmounts the differences among the innumerable types of concrete labor; it "removes" and erases this diversity in the form of abstract universal labor that creates value, i.e., is embodied in a commodity. Commodity owners are merely the personification (embodiment) of the commodity, and as such they are condemned to lose their own personal "I"; they are condemned to transformation, in the arena of "civil society," into "abstract" people.

The abstractness of a legal relation places upon it the imprint of a relationship of equality. As the result of abstraction from the economic, political, spiritual and other properties of the individual, people become wholly comparable values. Accordingly, they are measured by a single criterion that is identical for all, and the role of criterion is played by the fiction of a formally free and formally independent personality. The subjects at law are equal to each other solely as that type of personality. Equality of the parties has not and cannot have any other meaning in a legal relation. It is erroneous to derive the equality of the parties in relationships under the law in purely logical fashion from the abstractness of the legal relation. The ultimate source of this equality is the spontaneous equating, by the social process of commodity production, of non-uniform amounts of labor, that obviously emerges in the exchange of commodity products. To the equating of types of labor that differ in quality, which occurs objectively deep in the system of commodity production, there corresponds, at the surface of life, an equality among participants in legal intercourse.

The notion of law developed in Capital as of a relationship of external, formal equality is summed up by Marx in the Critique of the Gotha Programme. The nature of law consists in the application of an equal scale: "...but unequal individuals (and they would not be different individuals if they were not unequal) can be measured by a single standard only to the degree that they are regarded from an identical viewpoint, are considered only in one specific aspect." (14)

In his polemic with Dühring, Engels directed attention to the fact that it is useless to talk about law "without touching on the question of so-called free will." (15) The legal relation is a volitional one in the first place because the prerequisite for that relation is the capacity of subjects to select a variant of behavior that is expedient for them, and to dispose of themselves and their things in accordance with the decision they have taken.

Capital offers a comprehensive substantiation of the view stated briefly in The German Ideology and The Communist Manifesto: the individual's will is determined by material interests; the source of those interests is, in the final analysis, the place held by the individual in the system of social production. The will of one party in a legal relationship is free of compulsion by the other: he is motivated by his own needs and strivings. However, these are not the product of his imagination; they are imposed on him by the laws of the functioning and development of that socioeconomic system within which he functions.

For convenience in familiarizing ourselves with the principal aspects of the legal relation, we have had recourse to viewing each aspect in isolation from the others. But it would be hopeless to attempt, by this technique, to reconstruct an integrated picture of law as a relation in all its complexity. It is necessary that the unity of all the characteristic details of law be carefully considered and that their dialectical interaction be traced.

The legal relation performs a very important task: it mediates a diversity of different (primarily material) social relationships which, to be realized, demand expression through law. However, the capacity of law as a relation to be the shell of other connections in society flows from its abstractness, as a consequence of which law preserves its "neutrality" with respect to the content of the relationship being mediated and does not change this relation itself.

Marx understood law as a relation to be a form of production relations, but one that is not fused with the latter, is not dissolved in them. Law is, least of all, their internal organization or an inseparable mode of their existence. It is merely that another phenomenon, different from it, is expressed in the law, namely, the economic relation. The legal relation is not absorbed by production relations; it is disposed over them and forms an element of the legal superstructure.

A legal relation, which over a given time segment gradually separates itself from economic relations, depends in its movement upon the social relations that give it birth and condition it. Law is incapable of subjecting them to itself and of dictating to them the direction and rates of development. It seems to us that it is precisely this that Marx asserts in the Critique of the Gotha Programme, in criticizing the idealist thesis of the Lassalleans to the effect that production relations can be regulated by the categories of law. However, Marx nowhere says that the evolution of law will mechanically repeat the stages traversed by production relations. On the contrary, within the confines of general dependence upon the economic system, the development of law has its distinctive features and regularities. (16)

Marx's interpretation of law as a relationship that is engendered and conditioned by the economic structure of society does not in any way testify that Marx denied or underestimated the vast importance of the rules of law and normative acts of a state.

The Individual and the Law

The object of Capital was to discover the economic law of motion of capitalism. This law does not exist other than in the actions of members of bourgeois society. Marx investigates the behavior of the subject to the degree that the latter is the creator and bearer of social relations, behind which the economic law that governs them stands, invisible. The stimuli, content, and limits of the behavior of the subject are determined by his social essence. In accordance with the formula of Marx's sixth thesis on Feuerbach, that essence is "the totality of social relationships." Among the complex of qualities constituting the essence of man as a social being, there is that which Marx identifies as the law.

In his rough drafts for Capital, Marx writes of the right to property belonging to the individual, which initially rested upon his own labor. Capitalist production transforms the capitalist's property right into the right to the product of another, the right to appropriate the labor of another without giving an equivalent in exchange. (17)

The concept of the integral connection between law and the individual as "social man" emerges more explicitly in Marx's analysis of the conflict between the rights of the capitalist and those of the worker. "The capitalist effectuates his right as buyer when he seeks to lengthen the working day as far as possible, and the worker effectuates his as seller when he seeks to limit the working day to a given normal level. Consequently, an antinomy emerges here: right is counterposed to right.... In the conflict between two equal rights, it is strength that wins." (18)

When, in the Critique of the Gotha Programme, he deals with the question of the principles of distribution of goods among individuals in the period of transition from capitalism to communism, Marx says that at that stage "the right of the producers is proportional to the amount of labor they contribute." (19)

The social qualities of the individual (one of them is right in the aspect in which we are now considering it) are inevitably shaped in the course of his practical participation in the life of society. They emerge as the consequence of the refraction, in the essence of the individual, of the totality of social connections.

The content and volume of the right possessed by a person (or a collective) are conditioned by the features of that historical community within which the person (or collective) lives and functions. Therefore, Marx emphasizes, "right can never be higher than the economic structure and the cultural development of society conditioned by it." (20) Through the system of interests, the economic structure exercises dominant influence upon the shaping of the relationships of law.

The tendencies that set the tone in social development imperiously demand that right find its external expression, that it become objectivized. Touching upon the question of the relationship between the economic position of the workers and their civil rights, Marx pointed to the fact that the capitalist mode of production presupposes a worker who is personally free, and rests upon his personal freedom. (21)

Unlike the feudal system that preceded it, the bourgeois system is interested to some extent in cultivating man's social properties and in producing him as a man of somewhat richer qualities and associations. (22) From this it also follows that activation of the rights of the individual is dictated by the objective needs of, above all, the mode of production itself and the society erected thereupon, and not by anybody's philanthropy. This is a fundamental social need, the satisfaction of which favors the development of society and protects it against stagnation and degeneration.

Capital and the related works contain a mass of statements by Marx addressed to the bourgeois ideologists of the 17th and 18th century, who preached faith in the "natural rights" of man. In this connection, a clarification of Marx's attitude toward the doctrine of natural law is of interest.

The doctrine of "natural law," which exercised, in point of fact, a great influence both upon jurisprudence and bourgeois political economy and various trends in Utopian Socialism, suffers from at least two faults. In the first place, it is shot through with anthropologism. Man is regarded in it as an isolated atom distinct from society.

The proponents of the school of "natural law" adhered to the viewpoint that the right of an individual is an attribute with which he is endowed by the simple fact of having been born (from "nature," from "substance"), apart from society and any connection with the social environment. Criticizing the mode of thought of ideologists of the school of natural law, which erroneously understood the essence of man and the meaning of the rights adhering to him, Marx demonstrates that the real essence of the individual is not at all abstract and characteristic of the individual taken separately. On the contrary, the essence of man, according to Marx, coincides with those social relationships of which he is a part and which dictate his modus operandi.

In the second place, this doctrine is metaphysical through and through. In the words of Marx, to 18th century prophets, man of that century is conceived of "not as the result of history but as its point of departure because, in accordance with their view of human nature, the individual who is in accord with nature is regarded by them not as having developed historically, but as given by nature itself." (23) A historically determined (to be more exact, a bourgeois-democratic) set of individual rights and freedoms is elevated by them to the level of natural, non-transient, absolute values. In Capital, Marx exposes the exploitative substrate and the employment by the bourgeoisie, in their own interests as a class, of these "eternal" values.

The Social Role of Legislation

The laws of the state are the means whereby individuals are subordinated to the principal conditions of production in a given society, and the various forms of intercourse arising out of them. Much space is given in Capital to the problem of laws of the state, to legislation.

According to Marx, a law is an official, universally binding rule, proceeding from the state and having the function of regulating men's social behavior. In its origin, a law is the child of material relationships of production. Legislation merely formalizes the demands of economic relationships, records and thereby simply recognizes facts. Marx, in refuting the juridical world view of Proudhon, wrote: "Under the patriarchal system, under the caste system, under the feudal and guild system, the division of labor in society as a whole was carried out in accordance with definite rules. Were those rules established by some lawgiver? No. Initially called into existence by the conditions of material production, they were made into laws only after a considerable lapse of time." (24) The material relation is produced by the objective existence of some human community; the law expresses and guarantees that relation.

In Capital, Marx again turns to the idea he expressed in The Poverty of Philosophy, when he speaks of the fact that in precapitalist systems "the separation of one craft from another first develops naturally, then crystallizes, and finally is fixed in law." (25) In a generalized form, this idea of Marx's appears as follows: "If a form has existed for a certain length of time, it takes root as a custom and tradition and finally gains sanction as positive law." (26) In these judgments, Marx formulates his central idea on the matter of the nature of law, to wit: what is erected into law and becomes its content is simply a particular aspect of the system of social relationships that has objectively come into being.

There can be no doubt that Engels employed Marx's observations on the genesis of law as his point of departure (in his work On the Housing Question) in his classical description of the process whereby a law arises: "At some very early stage in the development of society, the need arises to encompass, under a general rule, the acts of production, distribution and exchange of products that are repeated from day to day.... This rule, first expressed as a custom, then becomes a law." (27) Consequently, social life stands in need of normative regulation of men's deeds, and it works out stereotypes of human intercourse that take on the form of objectively given norms of human behavior. The lawgiver, in expressing his will, sanctions these norms and makes them universally binding externally.

The degree to which the acts issued by the state appear to correspond with the historically established system of relations among men (i.e., how effective and implementable they are) depends upon the state. Marx writes that laws acquire economic meaning and real force only when the aspect of the order of social relations approved, sanctified, and expressed in them is in harmony with the social mode of production.

It is in the interest of the strata dominant in society that the state of things that suits them be formalized as law. Marx illustrates the procedure of "erection into law" by the example of the adoption of a number of England's Factory Laws: "These petty edicts regulating the time, extent and breaks in labor...developed gradually out of these relationships as natural laws of the contemporary mode of production. Their formulation, official recognition, and enunciation by the state were the result of a prolonged class struggle." (28)

Bourgeois legislation can be correctly understood only in the light of the class struggle unceasingly in progress between the capitalists and proletarians. This is particularly true of what is termed social legislation, which in Marx's day amounted primarily to state regulation of labor in capitalist enterprises and to legislation on the political liberties of the working class.

The history of bourgeois society, states Marx, demonstrates irrefutably that in the absence of constant pressure on the part of the laboring population, the exploiting classes themselves would never have adopted such laws on their own initiative. The more organized and powerful the pressure of the workers, the more yielding is the bourgeoisie and the more ready is its government to make concessions. Contrary to its desires, "Parliament repealed the laws against strikes and trade unions under the pressure of the masses." "The cruel laws against coalitions (in England — L. M.) fell in 1825, when the behavior of the proletariat became threatening." (29)

Marx ascribed much importance to the successes of the proletariat in the field of legislation. And this is why: the workers attain by means of a universal act of legislation what they could hardly have gained by a multiplicity of isolated individual efforts. (30) A law in accordance with the interests of the workers, extracted from capital, is a convenient means of protecting the physical and intellectual interests of the working class. The law on the ten-hour working day, issued in England in June 1847, for example, was regarded by Marx as a fundamental victory for the proletariat, for this was the first time that the political economy of the bourgeoisie openly capitulated to the political economy of the working class. When it overcomes political passivity and fights for such laws, the proletariat does not at all strengthen the state power hostile to it. On the contrary, in each given concrete instance, it turns the power aimed and employed against it into its own weapon.

The law of the state is born in the trouble of fierce class struggle. But the class struggle does not, of itself, create juridical laws. The issuance under capitalism of certain acts of legislation (in particular, factory legislation) was regarded by Marx as society's first attempt to influence, in conscious and planned fashion, the changing character of its process of production. (31)

According to Marx, the need for such influence is called forth for two sorts of reasons: on the one hand, because of cooperation on a vast scale, and the joint use of implements of labor, particularly machines. Legislation injecting itself into the realm of the economy is just as necessary a fruit of large-scale industry as cotton yarn, spinning jennies, and the electric telegraph. On the other hand, the intervention of the law is dictated by the effort to restrain "excessive evildoing" on the part of the masters of the factories, mines, mills, and means of communication, and to prevent a destructive exhaustion of all the physical and mental energy of the proletarians, upon whose exploitation the capitalist system rests.

Conscious manipulation of individual social processes, which is engaged in by the bourgeoisie with the aid of laws issued by the state, is by no means evidence that ideologists and leaders of capitalism have penetrated into the secret of the regularities governing the functioning and development of capitalist society and have mastered these regularities.

The legislative regulation engaged in by the bourgeoisie is confined within the tight limits of the private-property regime of entrepreneurship, marked by the brand of slavery of an exploitative system. Marx aptly dubbed this kind of legislative regulation a "capitalist caricature" of that genuine administration of social processes that the ever more socialized and enormous productive forces of society imperiously demand. When the laboring masses break the chains of the bourgeois relationships and institute "an alliance of free men, working with commonly held means of production and expending their individual labor powers in planned fashion, as a single social labor power," (32) i.e., when the principles of socialism triumph, only then will juridical laws fully become, in the hands of man, implements of conscious social control.

Footnotes

1) K. Marx and F. Engels, Soch., Vol. 16, p. 240.

2) See System des heutigen Römischen Rechts, by Friedrich Karl von Savigny, Vol. I, Berlin, 1840, p. 333.

3) G. Hegel, Philosophische Propädeutik, Stuttgart, 1927, p. 217.

4) Suffice it to recall Marx's point to the effect that possession (which is incomparably older than laws of the state) already constitutes "the simplest legal connection."

5) In advancing this proposition, we base ourselves primarily on the ideas formulated by Marx in Capital, Vol. I, Chapter II, and Vol. III, Chapter XXI, and also in the "Chapter on Capital" of his first draft of Capital, as well as upon other sources.

6) Soch., Vol. 12, p. 714.

7) Soch., Vol. 13, p. 6.

8) Soch., Vol. 23, p. 94.

9) Soch., Vol. 19, p. 16.

10) Soch., Vol. 23, p. 407.

11) See Marx, Grundrisse der Kritik der politischen Ökonomie, Berlin, 1953, p. 157.

12) Soch., Vol. 23, p. 89.

13) Soch., Vol. 23, p. 87.

14) Soch., Vol. 19, p. 19.

15) Soch., Vol. 20, p. 115.

16) Soch., Vol. 12, p. 736.

17) Grundrisse der Kritik der politischen Ökonomie, p. 361.

18) Soch., Vol. 23, p. 246.

19) Soch., Vol. 19, p. 19.

20) Ibid.

21) Soch., Vol. 26, Part III, pp. 448-449.

22) Grundrisse der Kritik der politischen Ökonomie, pp. 312-313.

23) Soch., Vol. 12, pp. 709-710.

24) Soch., Vol. 4, pp. 153-154.

25) Soch., Vol. 23, p. 369.
26) Soch., Vol. 25, Part II, p. 357.
27) Soch., Vol. 18, p. 272.
28) Soch., Vol. 23, p. 292.
29) Soch., Vol. 23, p. 751.
30) Soch., Vol. 16, p. 198.
31) Soch., Vol. 23, p. 492.
32) Soch., Vol. 23, p. 88.

[2]

International Journal of the Sociology of Law 1986, **14**, 1–32

Friedrich Engels and Karl Kautsky as Critics of "Legal Socialism"

PETER SCHÖTTLER
University of Bremen, Federal Republic of Germany

Translated by
IAIN STEWART*
University of Hull, U.K.

Translator's Introduction

Having established, they believed, a form of socialism grounded in a historical and materialist science, Marx and Engels felt able to contrast earlier socialism as 'topian'. Schöttler draws our attention to a 'forgotten and repressed' controversy of the late 1880s in which Engels, assisted by Kautsky, pursues the distinction firmly into the sphere of the legal. What Engels and Kautsky say is highly relevant to current debates on 'rights' and 'critical legal studies'.

Already in the *Anti-Dühring*, Engels, with Marx's approval, touches on the scientific/utopian distinction with some reference to law, regarding demands for 'equality' (Engels, 1878, pp. 127–8). From a historical–materialist standpoint, equality is possible only with the abolition of classes: the proletarian

*This article appeared in 1980 as "Friedrich Engels und Karl Kautsky als Kritiker des 'Juristen-Sozialismus' ", in *Demokratie und Recht*, 3–25. In making this English translation I have been helped both by the author, who has made a few amendments to the original, and by the French translation by Vincent Jerewsky, (1982) *Procès*, **9**, 145–77. A concluding section on relevance to modern German politics, and in consequence a few earlier lines, have been omitted. For quotations, existing translations have been used where possible, sometimes with amendment. Quotations from 'Juristen-Sozialismus' itself are referenced to Marx and Engels, *Werke* (Engels & Kautsky, 1887b), as 'JS'. It has been translated in full in 1977 by Piers Beirne, as 'Juridical Socialism', in *Politics and Society*, **7**, 203-20. Emphases are original or by Schöttler. All other notes are by Schöttler; many of the original notes have been incorporated in the text. The original masculine mode of speech in some quoted passages has been retained. Marx and Engels, *Werke* are referenced as 'MEW', the *Collected Works* as 'MECW'. (Translator)

Numerous notes have been retained in this translation, despite this journal's usual ruling against extensive footnotes. [Ed.]

0194-6595/86/010001+32 $03.00/0

demand for equality is therefore 'more far-reaching' than the bourgeois demand, which envisages only their harmonisation. Thus the proletarian demand for equality differs from the bourgeois demand not merely in degree but in kind. Yet, Schöttler notes, the difference is not yet clear and it remains uncertain whether and, if so, how the proletarian demand could take a legal form.

The matter is stated more clearly, Schöttler argues, a decade later, in another intervention on behalf of the left wing of the Social Democratic Party: the article "Legal Socialism". Here, Engels and Kautsky review Anton Menger's book *The Right to the Full Proceeds of Labour, Historically Presented.* Whereas Dühring invited socialism back into metaphysics across the whole range of thought, Menger specifically attempts a 'legal reworking of socialism', as a peaceful path of legal reform. Thus Engels and Kautsky have to distinguish scientific and utopian socialism specifically in relation to law.

They suggest that the passage from feudalism to capitalism involves a passage from a 'theological' to a 'legal' world outlook which is the 'classic' world outlook of the bourgeoisie. To them, Menger exemplifies a utopian–socialist variant of the legal world outlook — both generally, in his idea of a 'legal reworking' and particularly in his view that socialism is the realisation of certain 'fundamental rights', such as that to 'the full proceeds of labour'.

Engels and Kautsky might then have rejected not only belief in legal ideology but all dealings with law. However, they characterise this as a reaction of the disappointed utopian. To the scientific socialist, class struggle is fundamentally economic but also political and legal, so that political struggle, including the making of legal demands, is a tactical requirement. Engels and Kautsky insist that making legal demands cannot be a strategy *and* that it must be a tactic.

They specify that the relation of utopian–socialist to bourgeois legal demands is (as Schöttler formulates it) only *symmetrical*, while that of scientific–socialist legal demands is *asymmetrical.* Utopian socialism only reproduces bourgeois forms; scientific socialism supersedes them, with demands that are of a different kind and put forward in a different kind of way. Schöttler finds an example in an article by Engels on Britain.

As Schöttler notes, the principle of asymmetry is still stated only broadly and needs to be refined and concretised. And, although Engels and Kautsky discuss only pre-revolutionary action, the principle is also relevant to the period of transition from political to overall revolution — in search of a new 'socialist legality' (cf. Hipkin, 1985) — as well as to the period, or at least the idea, of communist society. For the asymmetry of tactical prescriptions, in the pre-revolutionary and transitional periods, presumably must be grounded in strategic prescription.

However, consistently with Marx's 'Critique of the Gotha Programme' (Marx, 1875) and with Engels' contention in the *Anti-Dühring* that the future socialist society will see administration no longer of persons but only of things (Engels, 1878, pp. 307, 333), Engels and Kautsky do not advocate 'socialist' law or rights. They speak only of socialist 'legal demands' whose 'legal' character remains bourgeois.

Yet a strategic prescription may be implied by Marx's and Engels' expressivist and anti-dominatory concept of human personality and social relations, which is both wholly different from the concept underlying existing ideas of law or rights (Mészáros, 1980) and, by that same token, impossible to finalise in advance of the relations that can give rise to fully socialised consciousness. Thus a strategic prescription can, and in Marx and Engels does, appear as a favouring of fuller expressivity. Albeit that even today that preference remains, quite dangerously, less clearly formulated that it could be (Lukes, 1985).

Although he cites 'Legal Socialism' only on the strategy/tactics distinction, Campbell (1983, 1985), basing himself in a favouring of expressivity, progresses toward an asymmetrical strategic concept of rights, from which he derives asymmetrical tactical concepts. But his argument remains, as he says, 'relatively utopian' (Campbell, 1985, p. 20): for his paradigm of socialist society is mainly a negative image of capitalist society and the continuum between these positive and negative poles does not, as he believes, embrace Marxism (cf. Hirst, 1985). Accordingly he produces valuable ideas on a tactical concept of rights without making a good case for a strategic concept. And, in querying a need for a strategic concept of *rights*, one must remember that Marxism can develop its concepts through critique not only of capitalist consciousness as such but also of such feudal consciousness as it preserves (cf. Raes, 1984).

This perspective counters the reificatory, evolutionist view (cf. Stewart, 1981) in which the idea of 'the administration of things' is understood in an instrumental way, to provide a *technocratic* strategic prescription. Yet it does not share Habermas's tendency (Sumner, 1983) to revert toward iusnaturalism.

Engels' and Kautsky's argument is implicitly both expanded and contracted by Lukács. He rejects 'both the cretinism of legality and the romanticism of illegality' (Lukács, 1920, p. 270), characterising illegal action as merely tactical. But he also contracts the argument, by not allowing for tactical legal *demands*.

For the transitional period, such contraction is a programme for new oppression — a point that leads E. P. Thompson to reverse that contraction and even to add an insistence on defending some bourgeois legal provisions (see Fine, 1984, pp. 169–89). Although Engels and Kautsky discuss only new legal demands, their argument seems not to exclude holding, if one may so restate Thompson, that the workers' movement must tactically defend bourgeois legal institutions so far as they correspond to asymmetrical legal demands that it would otherwise have made. This restatement may move toward the asymmetry for which some of Thompson's critics have asked (Hunt, 1981; Sumner, 1981). A similar extension could be developed for preservations and some inn-

4 *Engels, Kautsky and 'Legal Socialism'*

ovations in the transitional period. In either period, the bourgeois provisions introduced or maintained would often involve rights. Though one would always have to heed Engels' and Kautsky's warning that the demands must vary conjuncturally and must not be erected, as with Menger, into a new legal philosophy.

Moving from 'ought' to 'can', the prescriptive value of the principle of asymmetry depends on its descriptive value in investigating whether asymmetrical legal demands actually can be formulated. However, the descriptive aspect of Engels' and Kautsky's argument — broadly, concerning legal ideology — is very obscure. Schöttler traces this partly to a contradiction between, on one side, their anti-determinist idea that historical materialism only 'helps' the workers' movement, in a learning process that begins with the spontaneous overcoming of illusion, so that critical 'inversion' is thus not merely negation, nor only negation of negation, but involves a practical spontaneity, and, on the other, some frequently deterministic phrasing. Schöttler suggests that the basic view offers a more materialistic conception of the logic of working-class struggle than that provided in the *Anti-Dühring* and proposes directions of further clarification, drawing on Althusser, Brecht and Pêcheux to indicate how ideology is not monolithic but may be 'perforated' by critical factors (concerns similar to those of Sumner, 1979).

Although Engels and Kautsky are not very clear what they mean by a 'legal (*juristische*) world outlook', still less by 'classic', and even by 'law', they do pose the question of a legal *ideology*. This takes us beyond the middle-level concept of 'fetishism' and suggests that Marx's distinction between idealist and reificatory fetishism (cf. Cohen, 1978, pp. 115ff.) does not imply such a close analogy between commodity and 'legal' fetishism as Renner, Pashukanis, and others have assumed. Rather, Engels and Kautsky hint at a continuity of form from Christian iusnaturalism into legal positivism, or at least an analogy between positive–legal and religious meanings — a point common to both some bourgeois and some early Soviet jurists.

Engels' and Kautsky's 'article of occasion' thus clarifies a road toward a sociology of law in which actors are seen as bearers of an ideology composed of dominatory prescriptions — forms, however, that are contradictory precisely because they are not entirely false or bad. We can be grateful to Schöttler for lifting a 'repression' in Marxist jurisprudence. His argument is important not only in the West but also as the Soviet and Chinese régimes place increasing stress on formal legality.

References

Campbell, T. (1983) *The Left and Rights.* Routledge and Kegan Paul: London.

Campbell, T. D. (1985) Philosophy, Ideology and Rights. *Legal Studies*, **5**, 10–20.

Cohen, G. A. (1978) *Karl Marx's Theory of History. A Defence.* Clarendon Press: Oxford.

Engels, F. (1878) *Anti-Dühring* (1975). Lawrence and Wishart: London.
Fine, B. (1984) *Democracy and the Rule of Law*. Pluto Press: London.
Hipkin, B., Ed. (1985) *Socialist Legality International Journal of the Sociology of Law*, **13**, no. 2 (special issue).
Hirst, P. Q. (1985) Socialist legality. *Economy and Society*, **14**, 113-27.
Hunt, A. (1981) The politics of law and justice. *Politics and Power*, **4**, 3–26.
Lukács, G. (1920) Legality and illegality. In *History and Class Consciousness* (1971). Merlin Press: London.
Lukes, S. (1985) *Marxism and Morality*. Clarendon Press: Oxford.
Marx, K. (1875) Critique of the Gotha programme. In *The First International and After* (Fernbach, D., Ed.) (1974). Penguin: Harmondsworth.
Mészáros, I. (1980) Marxism and human rights. In *Understanding Human Rights* (Falconer, A. D., Ed.). Irish School of Ecumenics: Dublin.
Raes, K. (1984) The ethics of anti-moralism in Marx's theory of communism. *Philosophica*, **34**, 23–84.
Stewart, I. (1981) Sociology in jurisprudence: the problem of 'law' as object of knowledge. In *Law, State and Society* (Fryer, B. et al., Eds). Croom Helm: London.
Sumner, C. (1979) *Reading Ideologies. An Investigation into the Marxist Theory of Ideology and Law*. Academic Press: London.
Sumner, C. (1981) The rule of law and civil rights in contemporary marxist theory. *Kapitalistate*, **9**, 63–91.
Sumner, C. (1983) Law, legitimation and the advanced capitalist state: the jurisprudence and social theory of Jürgen Habermas. In *Legality, Ideology and the State* (Sugarman, D., Ed.). Academic Press, London.

IAIN STEWART

Preliminary

In this essay I will examine a little noticed text that appeared in 1887, in *Die Neue Zeit*, under the title 'Legal Socialism' (*Juristen-Sozialismus*). Its authors, not named at the time, were Friedrich Engels and Karl Kautsky. I would like to show that in this modest 'article of occasion' are developed theoretical theses that differ notably from comparable passages in the *Anti-Dühring* and contain another, I think more materialist, conception of 'ideological class struggle' — more exactly, of the 'logic' of proletarian class struggle.*

*This essay originated in 1976 and was first presented to the seminar of M. Pêcheux in Paris, after which it went through several revisions. A very much longer version appeared in 1977, together with the first publication of 'Legal Socialism' in Dutch, in the journal *Recht en Kritiek* (Nijmegen). For critique and discussion, I have to thank the Bochum workshop '*Positionen*' and also, particularly, E. Balibar, M. Pêcheux, G. Plumpe, J. Kolckenbrock–Netz, K.–H. Ladeur and F. O. Wolf.

6 *Engels, Kautsky and 'Legal Socialism'*

A controversy forgotten and repressed

In 1842-43, the law student Marx found himself, as he said later, for the first time 'in the embarrassing position of having to discuss what is known as material interests' (Marx, 1859, p. 19). Then in 1886, three years after Marx's death, it was the aged Friedrich Engels who found himself in the embarrassing position of having to join battle with the 'so-called scientific lawyers' in order to defend the theory developed in the interval by Marx and himself, against the attempt at a 'legal reworking'.

What was the issue? In the autumn of 1886, Cotta, in Stuttgart, published a book with the title '*The Right to the Full Proceeds of Labour, Historically Presented (Das Recht auf den vollen Arbeitsertrag in geschichtlicher Darstellung)*' [1]. What this was, judging by the literature cited, was a thoroughly well-informed, if also pithy, summary of the history of social ideas, from William Godwin to the present. Particularly unusual, however, was the book's programme, which the author, Dr Anton Menger, a professor of laws at the University of Vienna [2], stated in his preface as follows:

> "*The object of the present essay is to rework (bearbeiten)* the basic ideas of socialism from a legal standpoint [...]. Not until socialist ideas slough off the interminable economic and philanthropic disquisitions that form the main content of socialist literature, and are transformed into sober legal concepts, will practical statesmen be in a position to recognise how far the prevailing legal order may be reformed in the interest of the suffering masses of the people. In this *legal reworking of socialism* I glimpse the most important task of legal philosophy in our time; its correct solution will be an essential contribution toward accomplishing the indispensable alterations of our legal order along the path of *peaceful reform*" (Menger, 1886*b*, p. cxiii).

After briefly referring to the inadequate research on socialist history of theory, thus further underlining his own effort 'to draw directly from the original sources', he added:

> "The almost absolute ignorance of English and French socialism, especially of the older period, has contributed not a little to the disproportionate esteem which the works of Marx and Rodbertus currently enjoy in Germany. If, thirty years after Adam Smith's work on the wealth of nations appeared, someone had again 'discovered' the theory of the division of labour, or if today a writer were to put forward Darwin's theory of development as his own intellectual property, he would be taken for an ignoramus or a charlatan. Only in the domain of social science [...] can one conceive of this sort of attempt being successful. *In this work I will furnish proof that Marx and Rodbertus have borrowed their most important socialist theories from earlier English and French theorists, without naming the sources of their views.* Indeed, I have no hesitation in declaring that Marx and Rodbertus, whom some are so keen to present as the creators of *scientific socialism*, in depth and thoroughness are far surpassed by their predecessors" (Menger, 1886*b*, pp. cxiv–v).

Menger thus pursued a double objective: he wished (1) to undertake a 'legal reworking of socialism' and (2) to furnish proof that Marx's (and Rodbertus' ...) theory is basically no more than a poor plagiarising of earlier socialist authors.

The significance of this publication, which was an immediate sensation [3], was thus obvious: in rejecting as groundless the 'economic' critique of earlier socialism propounded by Marx and Engels, and going so far as to accuse Marx of 'charlatanism', but on the other hand seeking to establish proof of a relatively autonomous tradition of *legal* social criticism, Menger intervened more or less openly in the struggles between tendencies within the labour movement (on the situation of social democracy in the 1880s see Engelberg, 1959, and Lidtke, 1966). His political conclusion too, that class struggle should be replaced by legally pursued 'peaceful reform', could only provide theoretical reinforcement for the position of the right, anti-Marxist wing in the SPD and in particular the *Reichstag* fraction. In the period of the so-called 'leniency' of the Anti-Socialist Law, this wing — partly relying on the old Lassallean 'legal humbug' (cf. Marx, 1875, pp. 347–8) — supported a pragmatic strategy of reform, which took Bismarckian 'state socialism' *at its word* and laid the 'main stress of the labour question neither on free association nor on the struggle between capital and labour, but on *legislation*' (*Berliner Volksblatt*, no. 17, 1884; quoted in Engelberg, 1959, p. 93). After the new onset of repression early in 1886 and the drastic restriction of the possibilities of struggle within the law, the reformists certainly had to stay more firmly in the background with regard to theory, but it was quite clear that they had in no way revised their opinions. The Marxist polemic on the relationship between reform and revolution accordingly continued unabated — until finally, at the Party Conference in St Gallen (October 1887), the right suffered a severe defeat (cf. Engelberg, 1959, pp. 130ff.). But, as it turned out, this defeat did not prove at all lasting ...

Only against the background of this controversy can one understand the social-democratic journal *Neue Zeit*, already in February 1887, hence just a few months after Menger's book had appeared, going into the book in detail and publishing a scathing review with the title 'Legal Socialism' (Engels and Kautsky, 1887*a*) [4].

Only many years later did it become known that the actual author of this *anonymous* position statement was no less than Friedrich Engels, who insisted on answering Menger's provocative attack personally. Owing to illness, however, he was not able to complete the text, so that Kautsky had to take on the final editing. Although the article was not republished in Engels' lifetime, there is no reason to suppose that the 'General' was not satisfied with the final version. Nor can it now be established whether it was Kautsky's collaboration that led to the article appearing anonymously or whether, rather, Engels was afraid that an 'official' reply would give too much credence to Menger [5]. It is certain, at any rate, that until the appearance of the French translation in 1904

8 *Engels, Kautsky and 'Legal Socialism'*

the true authorship of this text remained unknown even in Marxist circles [6].

Though the immediate motive for Engels' intervention was the severe attacks on Marx that quickly began in the press [7], he was, as already in the polemic against Dühring, compelled to give the matter close attention himself, which meant setting against his opponent's theoretical considerations his own positions and theses, at least in outline. So came about a text which, despite its brevity — Engels was not only ill in body but also occupied with editing *Capital!* — was far more than a mere 'sketch': in his hands, critique of the Viennese professor's 'socialism' became a fundamental settling of accounts with any legal ideology as well as — in outline — with legalistic forms of thinking within the labour movement itself [8].

Before looking more closely at this controversy between Engels & Kautsky and Menger, I would like briefly to sketch its later reception.

In the years that followed, Menger's book — as with other of his publications — was an immense publishing success. It went through several editions and was translated many times. Within a short period, the hitherto unknown Austrian jurist advanced to become the best known representative of an entire tendency in 'socialist' criticism of law. His 'legal socialism' found lively echo not only in Germany but also in other European countries [9]. The immediate influence of this position within the labour movement cannot yet be evaluated precisely, in the absence of the required research, but it cannot have been very small, if one takes as just one indication that, a few years after the controversy in *Neue Zeit*, the SPD felt able to summon the 'famous Viennese legal scholar' to state the justification for its electoral demands (quoted in Müller, 1975, pp. 37ff.). It can also be added that, while in his day Menger was continuously opposed by the majority of his fellow specialists as a naïve outsider, one can observe in the Federal Republic, over the last few years, a tendency to style him the forerunner of a social-democratic 'legal politics' (*Rechtspolitik*) (see, among others, Reich, 1972*a*).

By comparison, the effects of Engels' and Kautsky's little text were far smaller. Its resonance in the SPD is unknown. Moreover, *Neue Zeit* with its print run at that time of 2500 had anyway only a relatively small influence on the ideological attitude of the masses of the SPD membership. At any rate, the discussion was not carried further: Menger himself, who had earlier seen fit to declare that 'any criticism leaves him cold — he pays attention only to that of *N[eue] Z[eit]*' (Adler, 1886*b*, p. 25), considered that an answer to the anonymous article would be undignified, since it 'enters far too little into the decisive questions of literary history to make a scientific polemic possible' (Menger, 1886*b*, p. 84).

So what eventually happened? Was there not, albeit very late, a serious discussion after Kautsky had made this unusual text available to *Mouvement Socialiste* in 1904? From that moment, certainly, the article was 'known', but one has to observe with astonishment that, e.g., the adherents of the left, such as Rosa Luxemburg, never noticed it, even though it could have provided her with valuable ammunition for her criticism of social-democratic opportunism. Lenin himself, who in the course of his extensive visits to libraries had got hold of Marx's and Engels' most inaccessible texts to work on them, appears in this case to have overlooked something [10].

The *first* to place any special value on the article 'Legal Socialism' were the Soviet legal theorists of the twenties. Confronted in practical terms with the question of law, in the dramatic conditions of the October Revolution and War Communism, not only Marx's 'Critique of the Gotha Programme' but also 'Legal Socialism' served them as theoretical underpinning for the thesis that in socialism/communism there could be *no* 'new law' [11] and 'the struggle against the bourgeois legal view of the world' represented 'a task of pressing importance for the jurists of the Soviet Republic' (Pashukanis, 1929, p. 33). In addition, there was disunity over whether the legal forms continuing in existence and temporarily necessary ought to be fixed and systematised as 'transitional law' (Stuchka) or whether that itself should already be criticised as an indication of a revolution frozen in mid-course (Pashukanis) [12]. If one reads the publications of that period carefully, one can readily see that they pick out only a few aspects of 'Legal Socialism', while the text's core problematic, the labour movement's contradictory relation to law and to legalistic ideology, has not yet been effectively assimilated.

How this first, Leninistic phase of an alleged 'legal nihilism' ended is well known. In the conditions of the Stalinist terror, which lauded itself as the 'triumph of legality' (Vyshinsky) [13], the questions that Engels and Kautsky or Stuchka and Pashukanis had raised became the trademarks of an 'alien' ideology. The just-rediscovered text thus had to sink anew into obscurity.

Let us, by way of conclusion, cast a further glance at modern commentaries. It is hardly surprising that, in the non-Marxist camp, this text has been dismissed as an 'extremely polemical' document on controversies of the moment (Martiny, 1977, p. 458; see also Ramm, 1975, p. 8). Also, however, legal theorists living under 'real socialism', who cite 'Legal Socialism' *on occasion*, barely work it into their own arguments. The reason is obvious: while the text by Engels & Kautsky advocates the thesis that Marxism and legal ideology are *incompatible*, there is nonetheless an interest in creating the impression that there exists an autonomous 'socialist legal ideology'. Since however one cannot deal with Engels as with Pashukanis, one tries to pin the verdict of 'legal nihilism' on the latter and quite simply to 'overlook' Engels' topic — i.e. to falsify it, in that one maintains that it is directed merely against an 'exaggerated' emphasis on law and not against legal ideology as such. Thus we read:

> "In reality, the critique of legal ideology as a world outlook did not prevent Marxism from founding a theory of law and its relationship to other vital social phenomena — economics, the state, classes in society, politics, education and culture. Nor has Marxism ever denied the necessity for a

> education and culture. Nor has Marxism ever denied the necessity for a juridical standpoint, for a juridical design for studying the social milieu. It criticised the juridical outlook not because it operated with legal postulates, but because the postulates had been *exaggerated* out of all proportion to the detriment of other approaches essential to an understanding of the mechanism of public life" (Tumanov, 1974, p. 39).

Thus defused, 'Legal Socialism' can eventually become 'respected' as a 'classic' text and be called upon to legitimate a particular politics (cf. Mollnau, 1974). Only very rarely and in passing is it even conceded that, with respect to the *factuality* of any 'socialist law', the core of Engels' argument would simply be *obsolete* [14].

In the Federal Republic too there are authors who broadly accept this interpretation (cf. Wagner–Beck, 1976). Others, on the contrary, seek to take up the critical impulse of 'Legal Socialism' in a contemporary context, in the struggle against legal-positivistic views (cf. Negt, 1973), or indeed to employ it in elaborating a Marxist strategy under the conditions of bourgeois *Rechtsstaat* relations [15]. Moreover: there can be no question of an assimilation corresponding to the text's theoretical significance and reflecting its specificity, seeing that outside specialist circles it is completely unknown [16]. In other countries, to my knowledge, the situation is similar, partly because even now there are no accessible translations.

Reading an 'article of occasion'

The article by Engels and Kautsky falls into four sections. It begins with a short sketch of the historical development of 'world outlooks' from the Middle Ages to the present. This is followed by the confrontation with Menger — first with his 'legal-philosophical' conception of history, then with his reduction of socialist theories to specific 'basic rights' (to exist, to work and to the full proceeds of labour). Lastly Engels & Kautsky come to what appears to them to be the real point of Menger's work – the accusations against Marx and the distortion of his theoretical views. At the end follows a short résumé, to indicate the political consequences of legal socialism and the position of German social democracy with regard to legal demands.

The critique of Menger in the two central sections contains several interesting arguments, which however, for the sake of brevity, I can refer to only in abbreviated fashion, so that I can go on to concentrate on the, in my opinion, more important passages concerning general theory at the beginning and at the end.

(1) In their reply Engels & Kautsky work out first of all the *difference* between a historical–materialist and a legal world outlook (Menger appearing as representative for the latter kind). Their starting point is Menger's assertion that socialism should not be tied to particular economic presuppositions but should depend solely on the existence of a 'socialist legal consciousness'. This

would be why from the declining Roman Empire, with its extreme 'centralisation of the means of production' and its 'defective social relations', followed not a socialist but the medieval legal order. Engels and Kautsky, to the contrary, recall such classic Marxist theses as the objective necessity of particular economic or, indeed, politico-legal structures under concrete historical conditions. For historical materialism the issue is not at all a consciousness of the 'legal legitimacy' of 'states of affairs, modes of appropriation, social classes', but solely their 'contemporary historical justification'. Since, for Marx, law 'always only reflects the economic conditions of a particular society', consequently it comes into consideration 'only in an entirely secondary way' (JS*, p. 501). Certainly in some respects the argument here is not always free from evolutionistic echoes; nonetheless it is unmistakeably clear that historical investigations must go beyond the 'legal horizon', because they do not allow themselves to be forced into a 'legal Procrustean bed' (ibid.).

(2) For Engels and Kautsky, Menger's method, of reducing all socialist theories to 'legal–philosophical postulates', or 'basic rights', so as to be able then to set them side by side and compare them, obliterates the respective theories' historical particularity and empties their concepts of their specific, contextually defined content. Thus Menger can 'overlook' Marx's theoretical innovations and instead foist on him an 'economically embellished' legal philosophy, including the utopian claim to the 'full proceeds of labour'.

(3) Menger's accusation that Marx had plagiarised the English socialists and especially William Thompson (1775–1833), whom he characterises as the true 'originator' of the theory of surplus value, is based on a false reading, affected by 'legal spectacles', which assimilates two incompatible concepts: 'additional value' as value added to raw material by the expenditure of labour upon it and 'surplus value' as congealed 'surplus labour' [17]. Engels & Kautsky however — as also often in other writings [18] — stress in this connection not just the novelty of Marx's analysis, which seeks the conditions of exploitation not in an unjust form of distribution but in the capitalist relation of production, but rather that the very assumption that Marx could have formulated legal claims within his theory is mistaken: 'Nowhere (has Marx) made claim to a 'right to the full proceeds of labour'', *because* 'in his theoretical writings above all he does not raise legal demands of any kind' (JS, p. 501). Behind this *separation* in principle of scientific analysis and political legal demands (which, as we shall see, in no way excludes raising legal demands *on the basis* of scientific analyses) stands the thesis that the break that Marx executes, in the mid-1840s, with the 'obvious' in bourgeois philosophies of law and history was possible only from a *non-legal* standpoint: Marxism and legal philosophy — however the latter may declare itself to be 'socialist' — are epistemologically incompatible (cf. also JS, p. 509).

Let us now examine more closely those sections where Engels and Kautsky

* *'Juristen–Sozcialismus'*

define *positively*, so to speak, the relationship among 'scientific socialism', the labour movement and legal ideology. On the first pages of their article one finds a sort of 'tableau' which sketches the historical succession of various 'world outlooks' and in the process introduces some astonishing formulations of the rise of the proletarian world outlook. One reads here first of all, on the 'bourgeois world outlook':

> "This outlook was a secularisation of the theological. Into the place of dogma, of divine law, stepped human *law* — into that of the Church, the *state*. Economic and social relations, which earlier had been imagined to be created by the Church and dogma, because sanctioned by the Church, were now imagined to be founded on law and created by the state. *Because commodity exchange* on a societal scale and in its full development, particularly through the giving of advances and credit, *developed contractual relations of reciprocity* and accordingly required *universally valid rules*, which could be laid down only by the community — *legal norms* established by the state — *one fell into the illusion* that these legal norms arose not out of economic facts but from formal establishment by the state. And because competition, the basic form of trade of free commodity-producers, is the greatest equaliser, *equality before the law* became the main battle cry of the bourgeoisie. The fact that the struggle of this newly aspiring class against the feudal lords and the absolute monarchy then protecting them had, like every class struggle, to be a political struggle, a struggle for possession of the state, and had to be organised around *legal demands* contributed to reinforcing the legal world outlook" (JS. pp. 492–3).

Under these *ideological* conditions (the economic and political prerequisites are taken as read) there developed in class struggle the first signs of proletarian consciousness:

> "As for its part, the bourgeoisie, in its struggle against the aristocracy, had dragged the theological world outlook along with it for some time, by way of adherence to tradition, so *the proletariat in the beginning took over the legal way of seeing things from its opponent and sought in it weapons against the bourgeoisie.* The first forms of proletarian party, as well as their theoretical representatives, remained entirely on the legal 'basis of right (*Rechtsboden*)', except that they put together for themselves a *different* basis of right from that of the bourgeoisie. On one side the demand for *equality* was *extended*, so that legal equality was to be *complemented* by social equality; on the other, from Adam Smith's propositions that labour is the source of all wealth but that the product of labour must be shared with the landowner and the capitalist the conclusion was drawn that this sharing was *unjust* (*unrecht*) and had to be either abolished or modified in favour of the worker. But the *feeling* that this leaving the question on the merely legal 'basis of right' in no way made it possible to eliminate the evil conditions created by the bourgeois-capitalist, and particularly by the modern large-scale industrial, mode of production, already led the most important minds among the earlier

> socialists — Saint–Simon, Fourier and Owen — to abandon the legal-political sector *altogether* and to declare *all political struggle* to be fruitless" (JS, p. 493).

Engels & Kautsky find that socialist ideological resistance has taken up two basic positions:

— on one side, a tendency toward a purely 'political' socialism, which in succession to Babeufism, though especially Jacobin humanism, is oriented to a radical 'revolution from above'; one may give as a typical example of this the 'social state' approach of Louis Blanc, whose concept of a 'Ministry of Labour', or of 'organisation of labour', as Marx said, aimed straight towards an emancipation of the proletariat '*alongside* the bourgeoisie' (Marx, 1850, p. 56);

— on the other side, a tendency toward a purely 'economic' socialism, oriented entirely to the anticipatory and (partly) model-setting reorganisation of socio-economic conditions, ignoring the real *political* conditions of possibility and especially evading the class struggle with respect to the existing relations of production; this school of thought is that treated in the *Manifesto* as 'critical-utopian socialism and communism', which indicates both their merits and their weaknesses, and where it is said of the systems of 'Saint-Simon, Fourier, Owen, and others' that:

> "they reject all political, and especially all revolutionary, action; they wish to attain their ends by peaceful means, and endeavour, by small experiments, necessarily doomed to failure, and by the force of example, to pave the way for the new social Gospel" (Marx & Engels, 1848, pp. 514–5).

Just as the first tendency attempts only to 'extend', 'complement' and turn *against* the dominant order, the discovered categories of the bourgeois legal world outlook, the second undertakes to turn the categories of classical political economy *against* the capitalists, thus to combat them 'with their own weapons' (Engels, 1885, p. 96). Both tendencies, naturally, mark out only extreme positions, between which can be located numerous variants and intermediate positions of economic, political, and legal critique(s) of bourgeois society. Yet what is important for Engels and Kautsky is not a complete description of the various socialistic theoretical blueprints but the proof of their ideological *complementarity*:

> "Both views were *equally insufficient* to *express adequately* and *sum up completely* the working-class emancipatory movements thrown up by the prevailing economic conditions. The demand for equality, no less than that for the full proceeds of labour, lost themselves in *irresolvable contradictions* as soon as they were given detailed legal formulation and left *the heart of the matter* — the transformation of the *mode of production* — more or less *untouched*. The rejection of *political* struggle by the great utopians was at the same time a rejection of *class struggle*, thus of the *sole*

> possible mode of action of the class for whose interests they were speaking. *Both* outlooks abstracted from the historical background, to which they owed their existence; *both* appealed to feeling: the one to the *feeling of rightness* (*Rechtsgefühl*), the other to the *feeling of humanity* (*Menschlichkeitsgefühl*). *Both* clothed their demands in the form of *pious wishes*, of which one could not say why they ought to be fulfilled at that very time and not a thousand years earlier or later" (JS, p. 493).

If thus both — one could also say, all — forms of early socialism are banished to the realm of *utopia*, this is *not* because they were unable to perform any service for the rising labour movement [19] but because, over and above all the divergences between them, there is one divergence that they have in common, namely that they can leave the terrain of bourgeois ideology only by the method of Baron von Münchhausen, who pulled himself out of a bog by a tuft of his own hair. The 'mystifying' presence of legal ideology either holds out a kind of 'new law' — hence provides for the *continuity* of law and its ideological effects — or operates a purely *symmetrical* inversion (hence the maxim of law, 'The form is all, the content nothing', is voluntaristically replaced with its counterpart, 'The content is all, the form nothing'), whose practical consequences imply a political loss of reality. In *both cases* it is still a matter of 'pious wishes': the legal illusion continues in force.

In a concluding passage, to this false opposition between 'political' and 'economic' *utopian* socialism Engels & Kautsky oppose the basic principle of a quite different, yet thoroughly possible, 'proletarian world outlook':

> "*The working class*, which was stripped of all ownership in the means of production by the changing of the feudal mode of production into the capitalist mode and is constantly being recreated in this hereditary state of propertylessness by the mechanism of the capitalist mode of production, *cannot express its condition of life exhaustively within the bourgeoisie's legal illusion. It can discern this condition of life fully itself only if it looks at things in their reality, without legally tinted spectacles. Marx has helped it to do this*, with his materialist conception of history, by proving that all legal, political, philosophical, religious etc. ideas that human beings have are derived, in the last instance, from their economic conditions of life, from their mode of production and of exchanging products. Thus the situation of the proletariat — its life, its struggle — was provided with the corresponding world outlook; *to the workers' lack of property could correspond only a lack of illusion in their minds.*" (JS, p. 494).

With this confrontation, legal illusion v. proletarian lack of illusion, is defined an ideological *class opposition*, which has a specific form of existence: the bourgeoisie depend on the existence of such legal institutions as property, contract, and so on as material and ideological guarantee of the relations of production that they dominate; the working class, on the other hand, has no objective interest in the continued existence of capitalist exploitation or of the codes that serve especially to legitimate that order as 'order' and of the ideology that functions in terms of those codes' rules.

As Engels and Kautsky have stressed, this *objective* interest gets as far as 'lack of illusion' yet never so far as effectively to break through the 'legal horizon' (Marx, 1875, p. 347) prevailing in bourgeois society, since the mystifying character of law does not lie merely in ideas (is not a mere 'disguising') but has a *material* form of existence; it realises itself materially in capitalist production/circulation, i.e. constantly *reproduces* itself anew in the social relation 'law'. *Every* individual is necessarily a *legal subject* and only a Crusoe (or a Münchhausen ...) could pull himself out of that. Consequently every attempt to criticise capitalist relations of production with the categories of 'justice' and 'injustice' (*Recht und Unrecht*) must founder on commodity production's form of appearance, since, as Marx maintains expressly in *Capital*:

> "The justice of transactions between agents of production consists in the fact that these transactions arise from the relations of production *as their natural consequence*" (Marx, 1883, p. 460) [20].

To be able to snap the 'invisible threads' that bind worker to capitalist and at the same time hold the workers prisoner in the obviousness of their 'independence' and 'freedom', requires particular *conditions*, which can be reduced neither to a legal nor to a moral 'critique' of the current state of affairs. And, contrary to all ideas of a simple act of 'liberation', of the proletariat 'consciously' stepping out of the bourgeoisie's political–ideological magic circle, the question is not of one but of *two* conditions, of a *double* prerequisite, which can be realised only in a complex process. In contrast to many passages by Marx and Engels themselves [21], in the text before us *this very complexity* of the development of proletarian ideology or proletarian 'class consciousness' is expressed with astonishing clarity.

The *first*, hence the most important condition of possibility of seeing things 'without legally tinted spectacles', of 'discerning' them 'exhaustively' and 'fully', according to Engels & Kautsky, is *scientific analysis* — as Marx, "by proving that all legal, political, philosophical, religious etc. *ideas* that human beings have are derived, *in the last instance*, from their economic *conditions of life*", has revealed for the first time. The 'lost connection' (Engels, 1888, p. 617) between legal ideology and the bourgeois mode of production had also first to be *recognised in its necessity*, through which the proletariat could quit the bourgeois 'basis of right' not just apparently but *really* — and indeed in favour of a new, until then unknown (and unthinkable) '*ideology of lack of illusion*' [22] which — one can say — is characterised by the fact that ever and anew it breaks not only with the illusions of the *homo oeconomicus* of political economy and the *homo rationalis* of philosophical theory of knowledge but also with those of the *homo juridicus (et moralis et politicus)* of legal ideology (cf. Althusser, 1975, p. 169).

At the same time however, Engels & Kautsky mention a *second* indispensable prerequisite for the constituting of proletarian ideology. Even if they provide no lengthy explanation of this second aspect, it is unmistakeably present in their text — even though only through a single word: 'helped'. Marx had *helped* the working class toward a new ideology — not presented them with it in fixed and finished form, for them to adopt (or decline), to re-recognise themselves in it (or not). The constituting of a specific proletarian ideology is thus to be conceived neither after the Feuerbachian model of a 'becoming conscious' nor after the Hegelian model of a teleologically guaranteed transition from 'object' to 'subject', nor, finally, after the model of a simple 'importing' of theory into the working class (Kautsky). And this on grounds that cohere both with the particular character of Marxist science [23] and with the particular character of the until then theoretically unknown (and today still poorly known) proletarian ideology.

Engels and Kautsky give roughly the following explanation. The break between the old legal and the new proletarian 'world outlook' is *above all*, though *not exclusively*, to be traced to the existence of the *science* founded by Marx (hence: *without* this new science the constituting of the new ideology is impossible, though on the other hand this does not mean any 'supersession' of ideology *within* science). The authors speak expressly here only of Marxism's *assistance* regarding the 'proletarian world outlook', *hence presuppose* that the proletariat has already managed *beforehand* to derive from its own class practice *elements of disillusionment*, which enter into this new world outlook. Indeed they also explain the failure of the early socialist systems from their inability 'to express adequately [...] the working-class emancipatory movements' already *in existence*, in that they ideologically dismiss or at least leave out of account the real and 'sole possible mode of action of the class for whose interests they were speaking', namely the *class struggle*. To put this another way: with the purely scientific analysis and critique of currently existing ideological relations, the real, practical, and massive supersession of these is not yet achieved (nor prospectively guaranteed) and the prerequisite for constituting the new ideology is in no way provided. This is the case *only if and when* there occurs a *connection* of Marxist science with the *spontaneous* 'world outlook' of the working class — Engels and Kautsky speak here of 'the situation of the proletariat — its life, its struggle'. In this way, scientific theory *supports* the real class struggle, which is bound up with the proletariat's existence, in such a way that the proletariat can develop a way of seeing that will 'exhaustively' express its own class situation [24].

The thesis of the at once both complex and contradictory connection of Marxist theory with the spontaneous ideology of the proletariat, however, still remains, of itself, abstract and formal, so long as the real historical movement of the 'transition', or 'transitions', from bourgeois to proletarian ideology is not reappraised and analysed. Engels' and Kautsky's formulations, however, plainly exclude both an evolutionistic and a voluntaristic explanation: the emergence of the proletarian ideology is to be conceived *neither* as mere 'putting into scientific form' (*Verwissenschaftlichung*) *nor* as resulting from a 'great leap' out of *the* ideology into *the* science. Rather, the question is of a *long continuing* ideological class struggle, a proletarian *learning process* structured by defeats and victories, partial successes and phases of stagnation [25]. That this struggle is in principle *open* is underlined by the following postscript:

> "Understandably, the struggle between the two world outlooks continues, and not only between proletariat and bourgeoisie but also between free-thinking workers and those still dominated by old tradition." (JS, p. 494).

Just as little as the proletarian ideology can be traced back monocausally to a single 'origin' (e.g. 'the' economy or 'the' science) so little is the process of its being constituted in class struggle ever finished. It continues not only as struggle between classes but also *within* the working class and the labour movement itself: its 'entry' is the 'merging' of Marx's (revolutionary) science with the (revolutionary) labour movement — and thus, finally, the socialist revolution.

At this point a brief *interjection* is required. In my view, the foregoing reading of the introductory section of 'Legal Socialism' is certainly legitimate and well founded, but it in no way gets round the problem that throughout this text one can also find a certain *evolutionistic tendency* which on a superficial and uncritical reading may obliterate the innovative aspects. To take just two examples: (1) the form of the 'tableau' [26], not least among various finalistic expressions and metaphors, may point to a teleological conception of history. The 'sequence' of ideologies would then conform to a 'plan', so to speak, that predetermined all specific transitions and transformations as variants of a unitary 'logic', as constantly *analogous* processes. A class, in these terms, 'creates' its 'double', which each time 'inverts' the ruling class's ideology, so as finally — in the synthesis of this three-step — to reach a consciousness of itself. In the mean time, the formations 'overtaken' lose their historical 'justification'; they become parasitic, and so on; (2) a further problem is presented by the tremendously fuzzy expression 'world outlook' (*Weltanschauung*), which, as is well known, Marx and Engels nowhere define unambiguously. It thus permits dangerous theoretical associations and confusions. While, for example, on one side Engels & Kautsky distinguish expressly between 'proletarian world outlook' and scientific 'conception of history', a few pages later they suddenly describe Marx as 'the founder of the proletarian world outlook' (JS, p. 500). The proletariat's independent 'contribution' has vanished; science and ideology become identical. As we know, in the history of the labour movement, taking the idea of 'scientific ideology' and the evolutionistic concept of history together has more than once served to legitimate economistic and/or voluntaristic strategies. This holds not only for Stalin (cf. Lecourt, 1976, who analyses the operation of a normatively functioning 'scientific world outlook') but also — why deny this contradiction? — for the aged Engels himself [27].

18 *Engels, Kautsky and 'Legal Socialism'*

Nevertheless, I think, the evolutionistic tendency in 'Legal Socialism' is not dominant, but rather is dominated by the text's main tendency, which is materialistic. To put this more simply: a traditional terminology is frequently used to suggest or state new problems that contradict an evolutionistic idea of class struggle. Thus, e.g. it is expressly said that the 'proletarian world outlook' does *not* arise from a mere 'socialisation' or 'proletarisation' of the bourgeois world outlook (albeit that the latter is spoken of only as a 'secularisation' of the theological world outlook); its conditions of emergence follow not an evolutionary but a complex dialectic [28]. And while it is maintained, of the transition to the bourgeois world outlook, that its material form of existence (law, state and so on) steps simply 'into the place' of feudal structures (a schematic thesis indeed ...), *nothing* 'analogous' is said at all about the apparatuses and practices of the labour movement: trade unions and workers' parties do not 'take the place' of bourgeois institutions, do not take over their functions of domination. That, admittedly, Engels & Kautsky mark this difference only indirectly, namely by a silence, is scarcely surprising: the missing answer to this question in terms of the new material forms of realisation of proletarian ideology was one of the central *unsolved* problems of the Second International.

At any rate, the text has more to say, in its concluding passages, on another, nowadays still politically explosive problem: the question of the function and form of *legal demands* in political class struggle.

Menger had maintained that one could bring about an alteration of the social order only by formulating certain 'basic rights'. Although Engels & Kautsky severely criticise this approach as such, they do not decline in principle to draw up legal demands of their own:

> "This is [...] not to say that socialists will abstain from putting forward certain legal demands. *Without such, an active socialist party is impossible* — or any political party *at all.* The claims deriving from the common interests of a class can be realised *only* by that class capturing political power and endowing its claims with universal validity in the form of *laws. Every struggling class therefore has to state its claims in the forms of legal demands within a programme.* But, in the course of social and political reorganisation, the claims of every class change: they are different in every country, according to its characteristics and the degree of its social development. Accordingly, the legal demands of individual parties too, notwithstanding any agreement as to the final goal, cannot be entirely the same for every period and for every people. They are a variable element and will be revised from time to time, as one can observe in the socialist parties of different countries. What is taken into account in such revisions is the *actually existing relations*; however, it has not occurred to any of the current socialist parties to turn its programme into a *new philosophy of law*" (JS, p. 509).

Engels' & Kautsky's thesis therefore runs: there is indeed *no* proletarian or socialist legal ideology (just as there can be no *socialist philosophy of law*), but there are proletarian, or socialist, *legal demands*, and these are necessary, nay indispensable, if the proletariat wishes to articulate its interests *politically* in opposition to the bourgeoisie and the bourgeois state. The political class struggle includes making legal demands. This is not a merely tactical question but a necessity grounded in the 'actually existing relations' — unless one abstains from the class struggle itself and contents oneself with 'pious wishes' (though in this case too the class struggle goes on 'from above' *and* as spontaneous resistance of the exploited classes).

This raises the fundamental question of the *difference* between the bourgeoisie's legal demands and those of the proletariat. Or are all legal demands *similar*, so that their encounter always repeats only the eternal negotiatory situation of contract, with the consequence that this eternal repetition can only contribute to the reproduction of capitalist relations? Let us recall here the sentence quoted a while ago:

> "*The fact that the struggle* of this newly aspiring class [the bourgeoisie (P.S.)] against the feudal lords and the absolute monarchy then protecting them had, *like every class struggle*, to be a political struggle, a struggle for possession of the state, and had *to be organised around legal demands* contributed to *reinforcing* the legal world outlook" (JS, pp. 492–3).

One cannot avoid remarking that these aims stand in patent contradiction to the necessity, stated elsewhere, of a non-legal, namely proletarian, world outlook. For how, especially, is a non-legal position to be conceived, if the class struggle itself, owing to the necessity, implicit in it, of raising legal demands, must lead to 'reinforcement' of the bourgeois world outlook and thereby of the existing state of affairs?

Since Engels and Kautsky evidently do not adopt a 'syndicalist' position, which abstains from *any* politics as corrupting and sees a way out of the integrating mechanisms of the bourgeois state only in 'pure' economic struggle, one could conclude that the general necessity of legal demands results with sheer inevitability in a strategy of 'law-abiding and gradual revolution'. This (it may also be said, still exceedingly relevant) interpretation has however the disadvantage that it would contradict the criticism of 'Legal Socialism' developed earlier, indeed would revert back past it. Thus one must search for *another* 'solution', neither apolitical nor law-abidingly reformist, that will answer the question: how is it possible for the proletariat's political class struggle, although conducted with legal demands, to lead not to a reinforcement (reproduction) but to an alteration (transformation) of the actually existing relations of production?

In the course of their article, Engels and Kautsky give a few indirect indications on this:

(1) The working class must formulate their programme and their legal demands not on the basis of a 'philosophy of law' but on that of the 'actually existing relations' (JS, p. 509). Here the primacy of *practice* is stressed, but

also the necessity of a rigorous, illusionless *analysis* of reality, since capitalist relations can never be adequately *discerned* through the 'tinted spectacles' of the dominant ideology (JS, p. 494).

(2) Engels & Kautsky say in addition what they do *not* understand as the revolutionary formulation of legal demands: a mere *inversion* of bourgeois demands or claims in favour of the proletariat. That would be to leave untouched 'the heart of the matter — the transformation of the mode of production' (JS, p. 493). At the same time they reject the complementary reaction of simply *refusing to make* legal demands, although they stress that in earlier times this position was represented by the '*most important* minds' and the '*great* utopians' (JS, p. 493). Stated positively, this dissociation from the legal, or utopian, illusions of early socialism (of which it is said, at the same time, that they continue among workers 'still dominated by old tradition'!) implies that the revolutionary labour movement finds itself materially *coerced* into raising legal demands. Nonetheless it is *never sufficient to take the bourgeoisie at their word*, i.e. at *their* word; rather (to stick with this by no means accidental metaphor — see further, the final section, below) one must struggle for *other words*, or other meanings of words. This however is to say nothing other than that the labour movement for its part must also struggle 'about words' — only it does not come upon these words fully cast (so that it would be sufficient for it to 'turn them the right way up', unless it then loses its speech ...) but must (in its 'propaganda') struggle with *other* words, *alter* words, so that its struggle is not a bourgeois struggle with the signs inverted but an entirely different struggle, with entirely different aims.

The decisive points to which these indications refer may be summed up in two short *theses*:

(1) The revolutionary labour movement must put forward *different* legal demands from those of the bourgeoisie.

(2) The revolutionary labour movement must put forward its legal demands *in a different way* from the bourgeoisie.

These two points belong together: when all is said and done, that of *adequacy* and that of *difference* coincide — i.e., in the practice of the class struggle [29].

Nevertheless this does not yet answer adequately the question of how legal demands [30] function in the ideological struggle. In particular the issue remains open, *why* the proletariat should be in a situation to conduct its class struggle in this way. Engels and Kautsky therefore conclude their train of thought with the assertion:

> "in the course of social and political reorganisation, the claims of every class change; they are different in every country, according to its characteristics and the degree of its social development. *Accordingly*, the legal demands of individual parties [...] cannot be entirely the same for every period and for every people. *They are a variable element*" (JS, p. 509).

The evident dissimilarity among legal demands might thus be quite simply a consequence of the diversity of history itself (in which case no further differentiation between bourgeois and proletarian demands is needed). It has surely to be said that this curious argument offers no *theoretical* solution (apart perhaps from a reformist reading that might see in it a confirmation of a 'national path' ...), since the statement that the 'claims [...] change', that 'legal demands' are 'a variable element', and so on, is nothing but a platitude, a 'bad infinity' (Althusser, 1965, p. 126) that is intended to fake an argument of proof that actually will never commence.

With this manifest weakness, however, 'Legal Socialism' *ends*! The problem of the *asymmetrical* forms of proletarian politics, as of the corresponding — simultaneously 'different' and 'correct' — demands, is, indeed, looked at from all sides — even, indirectly, posed. But the underlying 'dialectic' is not really explained; rather, in the end it is again relativistically 'superseded', i.e. suppressed. Since, however, *this* question overdetermines the whole analysis, it may be not least because of this flaw that the innovatory aspects of the text can so easily have been overlooked.

What then is *lacking* in this text? To my mind, the missing element is nothing other than a materialist concept of *ideology* and of ideological class struggle (the word does not appear anywhere; the expression 'world outlook' cannot take the place of the *concept*). Seeing, however, that since 1886 the Marxist concept of ideology has been developed further and critically differentiated — not least under pressure of the experiences of socialist construction and disintegration, and of the crisis of the communist movement, it seems to me to be possible, leaning on the works of Althusser and Pêcheux [31], to propose for discussion a *hypothesis* toward answering the problem that Engels and Kautsky left open:

—That the proletariat, or the labour movement, can put forward within the bourgeois 'legal horizon' asymmetrical legal demands that do not inevitably 'reinforce' the conditions of existence of the dominant legal ideology but tend to 'perforate' it (Brecht), coincides with a discursive mechanism that so operates that the 'subject-form' (Althusser, 1973, p. 95) constitutive for the structure of bourgeois ideology through the effect on one side of Marxist science and on the other of proletarian class struggle, although *not* superseded, tends to get *perforated*, so that non-subjective statements ('proletarian ideology') and non-legalistic legal demands ('proletarian politics' under capitalist conditions) become possible. This 'integration' — never concluded, but rather always to be renewed, always finding itself in question — of historical and materialist knowledge about the real causes of law and the real mode of functioning of legal ideology *within* the necessary ideological forms of political struggle must/can trigger off a '*disidentification effect*' (Pêcheux, 1975) regarding the cornerstones of the dominant ideology ('law', 'state', 'society'), whose 'obviousness' can be put in question from the class position of the proletariat *without* these political actions, which have to be carried out with 'the tools to hand in the existing state of affairs', necessarily meaning an 'acceptance' of that state of affairs [32].

This hypothesis is of course very abstract and general: it needs checking and amending in historical and theoretical analyses [33]. But at least to indicate what it can mean, to set out the issue of legal demands from the non-legalistic standpoint of historical materialism, I will add two brief examples.

A first example is afforded by a newspaper article by Engels himself, in which, in 1881, he embarked on a revision of the English trade unions' classic motto 'A fair day's wage for a fair day's work' (Engels, 1881; the quotations that follow are from this work. Engels analyses here the social reality hiding behind the 'equality' of the labour contract and notices a 'peculiar sort of fairness', if:

> "according to political economists, wages and working days are fixed by competition, fairness seems to require that both sides should have the same fair start on equal terms. But that is not the case. The Capitalist, if he cannot agree with the Labourer, can afford to wait, and live upon his capital. The workman cannot. He has but wages to live upon, and must therefore take work when, where, and at what terms he can get it. The workman has no fair start. [...] The fairness of political economy, such as it truly lays down the laws which rule actual society, that fairness is all on *one* side — on that of Capital."

The legal demand for 'a fair day's wage', then, does not stand up to a materialist analysis of the asymmetrical structure of social class relations. 'In the race with Capital, Labour is not only handicapped, it has to drag a cannonball riveted to its foot.' Engels concludes:

> "Let, then, the old motto be buried for ever and replaced by another:
> POSSESSION OF THE MEANS OF WORK — RAW MATERIAL, FACTORIES, MACHINERY — BY THE WORKING PEOPLE THEMSELVES."

A second example is offered by the classic controversy between Bernstein and Luxemburg. In Bernstein's view, social formations are to be judged 'not according to their technological or economic foundations, but according to the fundamental principle of their *legal institutions*' (Bernstein, 1899, p. 96). Thus for him it was settled that, for social democracy, an orientation to legal change should come first and the capitalist wage system *as a legal* system should be abolished step by step. Luxemburg, on the other hand, had grasped the Marxist thesis that the wage system as such is *not a legal relation at all*, even if it necessarily works with legal forms. 'In our whole system of law one cannot find a single statutory formula for the class domination of today', she wrote:

> "so how is one to supersede wage slavery in stages 'by the road of statute' if the statutes say nothing at all about it? Bernstein, who wants to get

going on the work of statute reform, to prepare an end for capitalism along that road, finds himself in the situation of the Russian policeman who, according to Uspensky, told of his thirst for adventure: 'Quickly I grabbed the fellow by the collar, and do you know what happened? The damned fellow didn't *have* a collar!' " (Luxemburg, 1898, pp. 74–5; Uspensky was a Russian revolutionary writer).

Luxemburg thus characterises with precision the legalistic chimera of reformist struggle, which wants to take capitalism by the collar of its statute books and in the end must admit that they are only made of paper ...

'Legal Socialism' and the '*Anti-Dühring*'

In what follows, some conclusions from this reading of 'Legal Socialism' will be confronted with another, much more frequently quoted text by Engels: the *Anti-Dühring* of 1878.

The passage relevant here is to be found in Chapter 10, in the famous section on *equality*:

> "from the moment when the bourgeoisie emerged from feudal burgherdom, when this estate of the Middle Ages changed into a modern class, it was always and inevitably accompanied by its shadow, the proletariat. And in the same way bourgeois demands for equality were accompanied by proletarian demands for equality. From the moment when the bourgeois demand for the abolition of *class privileges* was put forward, alongside it appeared the *proletarian demand for the abolition of the classes themselves* — at first in religious form, leaning towards primitive Christianity, and later drawing support from the bourgeois equalitarian theories themselves. *The proletarians took the bourgeoisie at their word*: equality must not be merely apparent, must not apply merely to the sphere of the state, but must also be real, must also be extended to the social, economic sphere. [...]
> The demand for equality in the mouth of the proletariat has therefore a *double meaning*. It is either — as was the case especially at the very start, for example in the Peasant War — the *spontaneous reaction* against the crying social inequalities, against the contrast between rich and poor, lords and serfs, the surfeiters and the starving; as such it is simply an expression of the *revolutionary instinct*, and finds its justification in that, and in that only. Or, on the other hand, this demand has arisen out of the reaction against the bourgeois demand for equality, drawing from the bourgeois demand more or less correct, *more far-reaching demands* and serving as an agitational means for stirring up the workers *against* the capitalists with the aid of the capitalists' *own* assertions; and in this case it stands and falls with bourgeois equality itself. In *both* cases the *real content* of the proletarian demand for equality is the demand for the *abolition of classes*" (Engels, 1878, pp. 127–8).

The similarity to the article of 1886 is striking. Here too a complete 'historical tableau' of the 'logic of development' of the ideological class struggle centres on the question of legal demands. The same themes, the same words and yet: a *quite different* text. Since however it is *this* text and not that of 1886 which stuck in the theoretical memory of the labour movement and stands as one of the starting points of 'Marxist theory of law', it will be useful to look at the matter rather more closely.

As Engels himself says expressly, he is distinguishing here two forms of demand for equality:

(1) an instinctive, spontaneous demand (especially under precapitalist conditions) and

(2) the intentional taking of the bourgeoisie at their word. Of this second demand he also says that it 'stands and falls with bourgeois equality itself'.

Both demands, taken strictly, follow a model of *inversion*, only with the difference that the second emerges under historical conditions in which the class struggle itself already tends toward the definitive abolition of classes (if Marx's thesis is correct, that the proletariat can abolish its own exploitation only by abolishing every form of exploitation and class domination). This second demand for equality derives its '*real content*' from this *goal* of the classless society. This means however that its 'content' is not given materially in the class struggle itself — in which case the legal demand for social equality would necessarily appear as the 'form' of the class struggle — but solely in its *future*, which is already being *added on*. The philosophical schema that underlies this whole train of thought is none other than that of *negation of negation*, according to which real struggles and tendencies are always only the forms of appearance of an inner essence which forces its way inexorably toward a goal that from the start it always–already contains. The text's jumping-off point, to which all theoretical (and political) conclusions are oriented, is thus the figure of 'taking at word', which suggests, or contains, the inference that it is *sufficient* to take the bourgeois legal demands, or claims, 'at their word' and *turn them the right way up*, so as to take up a position that is 'more far-reaching', i.e. not only opposed to the bourgeoisie but revolutionary [34].

Our reading of 'Legal Socialism' has made it clear, on the other hand, that Engels has later differentiated and corrected his position, in that he distinguishes between such legal demands, which were only an inversion of bourgeois demands, *and* genuinely revolutionary demands, namely those grounded in proletarian ideology and 'actually existing relations'. The philosophical three-part schema, position/negation/negation of negation, is thus perforated (though, as we know, this by itself did nothing to render it *ad acta* ...). What in 1878 appears as a mysterious 'real (*wirklicher*) content', which in the last analysis is grounded only in the idea of historical development according to plan, in 1886 is concretely fastened to a complex process in which each legal demand raised is referred back to the existence of a new, *proletarian* 'world outlook'/ ideology (on which, incidentally, there is not a word in 1878!), which for its part first emerges under the combined influence of class struggle and Marxist science. And Engels and Kautsky then go yet another step further, in maintaining that *every* political class struggle must necessarily be conducted with legal demands. Even if they give no explanation of how these *different* legal demands, formulated under the determination of the bourgeoisie's legal ideology, have *different* effects from those that 'reinforce' the bourgeoisie's domination, they do say nevertheless that they *must* have a different character, if the proletariat is to struggle in a revolutionary way and with success. And they say expressly that it is *not sufficient* here to take the bourgeoisie 'at their word' and leave it at that. They thus shatter the idealistic belief, which is still present in the *Anti-Dühring* (or at least not expressly excluded) that it might be sufficient to adopt a position *symmetrically* opposed to that of the bourgeoisie, in order 'more or less' to ensure the revolutionary character of legal demands (with the consequence that in this direction an ideological struggle for the *right* demands is superfluous, since it is then just one more question of 'logic'). Rather, they stress that *counteridentifications* of this sort lead to 'irresolvable contradictions' that leave 'the heart of the matter' finally 'untouched' and which the modern, i.e. the Marxist labour movement must outgrow — even if the struggle between the 'free-thinking workers and those still dominated by old tradition' will go on for a very long time.

The comparison between the *Anti-Dühring* and 'Legal Socialism' thus brings to light two quite different conceptions of political and ideological class struggle:

— *On one side* the figure of *taking at word* predominates. It supposes that the capitalist present bears the socialist future in already finished form within itself as its 'real content'; the labour movement's 'mission' still consists here only in assisting this latent future to break through, by 'drawing conclusions'. Such a conception is continuous with the young Marx, for whom 'Reason has always existed, but not in a reasonable form'; the 'social truth' is then nothing other than the development of the contradiction between bad reality and 'ideal function' (Marx, 1843, p. 143).

— *On the other side* there predominates the sometimes explicit, sometimes implicit figure of *asymmetry*: the proletariat must indeed develop their demands within the capitalist system and accordingly also take its forms and claims entirely 'at word'. But this *per se* hardly predetermines the 'abolition of classes'. Quite the contrary: a socialist revolution, which does not simply change over the signs symmetrically but radically transforms relations, is then possible only if the proletariat succeeds, ever in new ways, in *actually* developing 'more far-reaching' forms of struggle and of demand appropriate to their struggle. While a 'logic of inversion' always remains reformist on the terrain of the existing state of affairs, a revolution in that state of affairs, which will not be guaranteed by any 'cunning of reason', depends on the permanent unfolding of 'autonomous' forms of practice.

Unlike a famous remark by the young Marx (Marx, 1844, p. 178), to revolutionise a society it is not sufficient to play its *own* tune to it and in the mean time (as at Jericho) wait for a miracle. Rather, as the same Marx said a few years later: revolutions are decided not by the *weakness of the strong* but by the *strength of the weak* (Marx, 1848, p. 281).

Notes

1 I have used the second edition (Menger, 1886*a*, *b*).

2 Many readers will be familiar with Menger's name at least from Engels' Preface to the second German edition of *The Poverty of Philosophy* in 1892. Here, therefore, are a few dates: born in Galicia in 1841 as A. Menger von Wolfensgrün; studied at Cracow and Vienna; doctorate 1865; higher doctorate (*Habilitation*) 1872; Chair in the Law of Civil Procedure at the University of Vienna 1877; Rector of the University 1895–6; early retirement 1899; died in Rome 1906. Menger, who, like his brother the economist Carl Menger, renounced his title at the beginning of the 1870s, was throughout his life an anticlerical democrat; his commitment to 'social–scientific' legal education and his political sympathies for the liberal left brought him again and again into difficulties with the university administration, until finally he pulled right out of his teaching functions; in 1894 he declined an invitation from the Democratic Party to be nominated as a candidate for the Imperial Council. Both in the realm of 'scientific socialism' and, incidentally, in mathematics, Menger counted himself a discoverer of genius, although unrecognised. His most important later works are: *Civil Law and the Nation's Propertyless Classes (Das bürgerliche Recht und die besitzlosen Volksklassen)* (1889); *On the Social Tasks of Legal Science (Über die socialen Aufgaben der Rechtswissenschaft)* (1895); *New Theory of the State (Neue Staatslehre)* (1903); *New Moral Theory (Neue Sittenlehre)* (1905); *National Politics (Volkspolitik)* (1906). For biographical and bibliographical data see, further, Kästner (1974).

3 Already on 16 November 1886, the Austrian social democrat Victor Adler informed Kautsky: 'The book is being accorded enormous importance here' (Adler, 1886*a*, p. 22).

4 Reprinted as a supplement (!) in vol. 21 of Marx and Engels, *Werke* (Engels & Kautsky, 1887*b*). To my knowledge, this text is not to be found in any of the numerous official Marx–Engels anthologies; only the first few pages — without reference to the whole text and to the co-author Kautsky — were included (significantly) in the collection *Über die Religion* (Berlin (East), 1958), which has also been translated into numerous languages [see Marx & Engels, 1975, pp. 269–72 (translator)]. In the Federal Republic there is so far only an abridged version in Reich (1972*b*).

5 Neither the original manuscript of 'Legal Socialism' nor work notes relating to it have apparently been preserved (information from Dr Götz Langkau, International Institute for Social History, Amsterdam); see also *MEW*, **21**, 617. A definitive clarification of the authorship of particular sections is therefore no longer possible. Ramm's suggestion that Engels wrote the article's beginning and conclusion (Ramm, 1975) is pure speculation. It must not be forgotten, either, that in this period Engels said of Kautsky: 'I rely on K. as on myself' (Engels, 1887, p. 635).

6 The first announcement of the real authorship was a footnote at the beginning of

the French translation, where it is said: 'The critique published here is the result of a passing collaboration between Engels and Kautsky. Engels had begun working on it but then suddenly fell ill and was not able to complete it. He asked Kautsky to carry it through' [(1904) *Le Mouvement Socialiste*, **6** (no. 132), p. 97]. Shortly afterwards, Kautsky himself came to speak of the origins of 'Legal Socialism', in a review of Menger's *New Moral Theory* (Kautsky, 1905, p. 77).

7 Informative hints on the circumstances and motivation of the article's birth lie in the correspondence between Engels and the Lafargues: see especially the letters of 30 October 1886, 2 November 1886 and 24 November 1886 in Engels, Lafargue & Lafargue, 1956–9.

8 Already, a few years earlier (1882), Engels had planned to write a pamphlet against legalistic and state–socialistic illusions within the labour movement, but the project was not carried out (cf. *MEW*, **35**, 359 and 427ff.). Menger's attacks now offered him a chance to do something in this direction.

9 Cf., on France, Arnaud & Arnaud (1975). On the resonance of Menger's writings in pre- and post-revolutionary Russia, see Reich (1972*c*, pp. 73ff.). On Italy, see the relevant essays in (1974–5) *Quaderni Fiorentini per la Storia della Pensiero Giuridico Moderno*, **1**.

10 Stuchka, who as the first Bolshevik People's Commissar for Justice worked closely with Lenin, reports in his memoirs that the article 'was probably also unknown to Lenin' (Stuchka, 1970, p. 555). Menger, on the contrary, seems to have been known to Lenin, since in *Materialism and Empirio-criticism* he reproaches Mach for speaking up for 'the bureaucratic socialism of (Josef) Popper and (Anton) Menger' (Lenin, 1909, p. 321 n.).

11 Although this was, incidentally, exactly the position of another 'legal socialist', Georges Sorel, who welcomed the October Revolution because there 'a new legal spirit' was breaking through (Sorel, 1920). But Sorel always rejected Menger's ideas (Sorel, 1908).

12 In his first 'self-criticism' (he was compelled to repeat this procedure several more times before finally being shot as an 'enemy of the people') Pashukanis once more clearly and impressively summarised his position: 'One cannot characterise the transitional period, in which the dictatorship of the proletariat effects the revolutionary transition from capitalism to communism, as a specific, completed socio-economic formation. For this reason, neither can one create a specific legal system for it on the model: feudal law, bourgeois law, proletarian law. In this lies a dangerous tendency to restrain the current movement toward socialism. [...] In this remnant 'proletarian law', despite all the revolutionary phraseology, lies a conservative core, namely the attempt to pause at the given stage, to systematise it and to transform the transitional period into a specific formation. [...] The creation of a specific system of proletarian law [...] also means turning one's back on both economics and politics. We jurists must, precisely, invert this — turning ourselves toward economics, politics, and classes' (quoted in Reich, 1972*c*, p. 229).

13 'Only in socialist society does law obtain a solid basis for its development. The epoch of socialism, not that of imperialism, is the most advantageous for the development of law, for the development of legality — for the triumph of law and the triumph of legality' (quoted in Klenner, 1953, p. 50).

14 As when Sellnow says of the Engels and Kautsky claim that a 'socialist philosophy of law' is impossible: 'Were the assertion that Engels makes to be presented in the

28 *Engels, Kautsky and 'Legal Socialism'*

same spirit today, it could not remain uncontradicted' (Sellnow, 1968, p. 70).

15 This is so e.g. in the intervention by Hase (1975), as also, despite its careful formulations, in the fine essay by Geil & Günther (1978). There has been a positive (if also highly debatable) assimilation of 'Legal Socialism' by the Projekt Klassenanalyse (1976).

16 This judgment rests on a check through the relevant literature. It is indisputable however that most jurists with Marxist interests have read 'Legal Socialism' at 'some time or other' and indeed, on occasion, have referred to it. But this is not the issue. The crucial matter is firstly that its theoretical–political elements are hardly ever discussed in print and secondly that, in contrast with other 'classic texts', the minimal interest that it has aroused has plainly been only within a single academic discipline — and that the discipline against which it is mainly directed — although its theses are entirely relevant to general historical–materialist theoretical discussion.

17 In connection with the concept 'additional value' Thompson also uses the expression 'surplus value', which however expresses only the 'manufacturers' commonplace illusion' that 'the working hour of a worker producing with the help of machinery etc. produces greater value than the working hour of a simple worker by hand before machinery was invented' (JS, p. 503). Menger throws all *three* concepts into the same pot.

18 Cf. in particular Engels' Preface to the second volume of *Capital* in 1885 (Engels, 1885, pp. 97ff.). See also, on this, Althusser's commentary in Althusser and Balibar (1968, pp. 152ff.).

19 In the *Communist Manifesto* the utopians are said to have furnished 'most valuable materials for the enlightenment of the working class' (Marx & Engels, 1848, p. 516).

20 On this interpretation of Marx's 'theory of law', see also Edelman (1973) — although, as will be seen later, I do not agree with Edelman's interpretation of the *Anti-Dühring* (Edelman, 1973, pp. 109–10).

21 I am thinking here principally of the famous final section of *The Poverty of Philosophy* (Marx, 1847), which for many still stands as 'the' explanation of the development of 'class consciousness'. It might be shown, I suspect, that, mainly under the impact of the Paris Commune, Marx had arrived at quite different images of the real dialectic of the proletarian class struggle. See e.g. Marx (1871).

22 'Ideology of lack of illusion': I use this expression to indicate the new mode of recognising reality which is characteristic of proletarian ideology. This however is not meant in any way to imply a 'supersession' of the difference between science and ideology or a transparency of proletarian ideology to itself.

23 The use of the expression 'Marxist science' looks suspicious nowadays. Readers for whom it at once has 'positivist' or even 'Stalinist' associations may be invited to consider that here I am only repeating Marx's claim to be founding a theory of the capitalist mode of production that is not philosophical but scientific and revolutionary.

24 Here of course one needs to avoid misunderstanding the 'materialist conception of history' as if it had already existed beforehand *for itself*, i.e. as having been developed by Marx *outside* the labour movement. Faced with writing a brief text, Engels and Kautsky abstract from this process of emergence of Marxist theory, which for its part was quite impossible without experience of and participation in

the proletarian class struggle. The 'assistance' that Marx gave to the labour movement is thus to be conceived not as external, but as *internal* assistance.

25 The expression *learning process* throws up problems that this is not the place to discuss in detail. In historical–theoretical debate, it has been introduced principally by M. Vester's book *The Emergence of the Proletariat as Learning Process* (Vester, 1970), where it is used both on the plane of philosophy of history (development of the proletariat from object to subject) and on that of psychology (learning process from child to adult). If however one detaches it from any teleological and/or psychological–educational model of development ('learning goal'), it can be useful as referring to the self-acting and self-critical character of the proletarian struggle for emancipation.

26 As is well known, this is not the only tàbleau in the work of Engels and Marx. It may be compared, e.g. with that in *The Poverty of Philosophy* (Marx, 1847, pp. 177–8), in order to measure the distance covered in between.

27 On evolution in Engels, see his pseudo-thesis: 'Everything that happens strikes in our favour. The most cunning measures to check the onward march of the proletariat merely accelerate its march to victory. The Enemy himself fights, and is thus condemned to fight for us.' (Engels, 1886, p. 258) — which, taken strictly, leaves, for analysis of class struggle, nothing more to be done. In a private letter, he is just as fatalistic: 'In Germany we have now got so far that we can put our hands in our laps and let our enemies work for us.' (Engels, 1884, p. 123). On the aged Engels' problematic of historical analysis, see Stedman Jones (1973).

28 The 'lack of illusion' of which Engels & Kautsky speak is also plainly distinct — despite the feuerbachian terminology — from earlier formulations, according to which the proletarian class struggle leads *directly* to 'laying bare the true state of things' and the ideological positions of the proletariat are '*only* the *open, undisguised* expression of that which the bourgeoisie perpetrates, *secretly* and *treacherously*, against the workers" (Engels, 1845, p. 502). In 1886 just this mechanistic principle of simple inversion ('only ...') is identified as the mark of spontaneous revolt and *not* of proletarian ideology.

29 Brecht named this effect of the *adequacy and difference* of proletarian politics when he said: 'Lenin did not just say different things from Bismarck, he said them in a different way' (Brecht, 1938).

30 For Engels and Kautsky, the expression 'legal demands' (*Rechtsforderungen*) evidently is not understood merely in the narrow sense of legally formulated proposals concerning the state, the courts and so on, but also denotes the programmatic demands and slogans that are put forward in the context, e.g. of demonstrations, press campaigns, strikes and so on, and to begin with have *no* legal form. If nonetheless they aim at being accepted 'in the form of laws' (JS, p. 509) and not merely at an unmasking rôle — though that can also be important — they must be 'concrete' and can afford to acquire a legal 'finish'. From this ensues the relativity of legal demands, whose form is closely bound up with the contemporary historical context: they can be 'taken over', i.e. taken from the opponent and turned around — depending on which power relations predominate in the society. With this 'broad' concept of legal demands, however, is bound up similarly the possibility of developing non-legally grounded demands and figures of argument within the bourgeois 'legal horizon'. Finally it must be mentioned that the political functionality of legal demands is valid only in, so to speak, the normal case of state

executive power; hence the present discussion abstracts from political forms in which the class struggle is conducted wholly or partly *without* legal demands — war, civil war, and so on.

31 Cf. Althusser, 1969–70, pp. 149ff; 1973, pp. 94ff; 1976. (For a short and very schematic introduction to Althusser's positions on theory of ideology, see Kammler, Plumpe & Schöttler, 1978. See also Pêcheux, 1975; 1984).

32 Engels: 'It is said that every political act means an acceptance of the existing state of affairs. But, if this state of affairs gives us the tools to protest against it, the application of these tools is *not* an acceptance of it' (Engels, 1871).

33 One desideratum would be a critical history of legal discourse within the labour movement. Apart from analysis of programmatic texts, this would require above all empirical studies of legalism in practice in the workplace, in the life of trade union and political organisations, in socio-political institutions and so on. I am currently researching in this field.

34 There is still another terminological variant of this figure of 'taking at word'. In the preparatory writings for the *Anti–Dühring*, Engels speaks in the same connection of 'proletarian *drawing of conclusions*' (*Konsequenzzieherei*). He argues: 'As with all demands by the bourgeoisie, here too the proletariat stands to one side of it as fatal shadow and draws its own conclusions (Babeuf)' (Engels, 1878, p. 407). This is to say almost more plainly that the question is of a teleological model of history, in which the proletariat functions as *personification* of progress.

References

Adler, V. (1886*a*) Brief an Kautsky, 16. November 1886. In *Briefwechsel mit August Bebel und Karl Kautsky* (1954). V. der Wiener Volksbuchhandlung: Vienna.

Adler, V. (1886*b*) Brief an Kautsky, 30 Dezember 1886. In *Briefwechsel mit August Bebel und Karl Kautsky* (1954). V. der Wiener Volksbuchhandlung: Vienna.

Althusser, L. (1965) *For Marx* (1969). New Left Books: London.

Althusser, L. (1969–70) ideology and ideological state apparatuses. In *Lenin and Philosophy and Other Essays* (1971). New Left Books: London.

Althusser, L. (1973) Reply to John Lewis. In *Essays in Self-criticism* (1976). New Left Books: London.

Althusser, L. (1975) Soutenance d'Amiens. In *Positions* (1976). Éditions Sociales: Paris.

Althusser, L. (1976) Anmerkung über die ideologischen Staatsapparate (ISA). In *Ideologie und ideologische Staatsapparate: Aufsätze zur marxistischen Theorie* (Schöttler, P., Ed.) (1977). V. für das Studium der Arbeiterbewegung: Hamburg.

Althusser, L. & Balibar, É. (1968) *Reading Capital* (1970). New Left Books: London.

Arnaud, N. & Arnaud, A.–J. (1975) Le socialisme juridique à la 'Belle Époque': visages d'une aberration. *Quaderni Fiorentini per la Storia del Pensiero Giuridico Moderno*, **1**, 25–54.

Bernstein, E. (1899) *Evolutionary Socialism* (1961). Schocken: New York.

Brecht, B. (1938) Die Expressionismusdebatte. In *Gesammelte Werke* (1976), **9**, 290–2.

Edelman, B. (1973) *Ownership of the Image. Elements for a Marxist Theory of Law* (1979). Routledge & Kegan Paul: London.

Engelberg, E. (1959) *Revolutionäre Politik und Rote Feldpost 1878–1890*. Akademie V.: Berlin (East).

Engels, F. (1845) *The Condition of the Working-Class in England* (1975). *MECW*, **4**, 295–583.
Engels, F. (1871) Apropos of working-class political action. In Marx & Engels, *Selected Works* (1968). Lawrence & Wishart: London.
Engels, F. (1878) *Anti-Dühring. Herr Eugen Dühring's Revolution in Science* (1975). Lawrence & Wishart: London.
Engels, F. (1881) A fair day's wage for a fair day's work. In *The British Labour Movement. Articles from The Labour Standard* (1936). Lawrence & Wishart: London.
Engels, F. (1884) Brief an Sorge, 7. März 1884 (1967). *MEW*, **36**, 122–4.
Engels, F. (1885) Preface. In Marx, *Capital*, vol. 2 (1978). Penguin: Harmondsworth.
Engels, F. (1886) Zum 15. Jahrestag der Pariser Kommune (1962). *MEW*, **21**, 257–8.
Engels, F. (1887) Brief an Sorge, 6. April 1887 (1967). *MEW*, **36**, 635–6.
Engels, F. (1888) Ludwig Feuerbach and the end of classical German philosophy. In Marx & Engels, *Selected Works* (1968). Lawrence & Wishart: London.
Engels, F. & Kautsky, K. (1887*a*) Juristen-Sozialismus. *Die Neue Zeit*, **2**, 49–62.
Engels, F. & Kautsky, K. (1887*b*) Juristen-Sozialismus (1962). *MEW*, **21**, 491-509.
Engels, F., Lafargue, P. & Lafargue, L. (1956–9) *Correspondance*, 3 Vols. Éditions Sociales: Paris.
Geil, H. & Günther, U. (1978) Wie und wozu soll das Recht auf Arbeit verfassungsrechtlich abgesichert werden? *Marxistische Blätter*, **16**, 77–84.
Hase, F. (1975) Antikapitalistische Gewerkschaftspolitik als Rechtsprogramm. *Kritische Justiz*, **8**, 64–9.
Kammler, C., Plumpe, G. & Schöttler, P. (1978) Philosophie der Ideologie oder Theorie des ideologischen Klassenkampfes? *Alternative*, **118**, 2–17.
Kästner, K.-H. (1974) *Anton Menger (1841–1906). Leben und Werk.* Mohr: Tübingen.
Kautsky, K. (1905) Mengers Neue Sittenlehre. (1905-6) *Die Neue Zeit*, **24**, 76–85.
Klenner, H. (1953) *Form und Bedeutung der Gesetzlichkeit als einer Methode in der Führung des Klassenkampfs*. Deutscher Zentralverlag: Berlin (East).
Lecourt, D. (1976) *Proletarian Science? The Case of Lysenko* (1977). New Left Books: London.
Lenin, V. I. (1909) *Materialism and Empirio-criticism*. In *Collected Works* (1962) **14**, 17–361.
Lidtke, V. L. (1966) *The Outlawed Party. Social Democracy in Germany, 1878-1890.* Princeton University Press: Princeton.
Luxemburg, R. (1898–9) *Social Reform or Revolution* (n.d.). Merlin: London.
Martiny, M. (1977) Das Recht auf Arbeit in historischer Sicht. In *Gewerkschaftliche Politik: Reform aus Solidarität. Zum 60. Geburtstag von H.O. Vetter* (Borsdorf, U., et al., Eds.). Bund: Cologne.
Marx K. (1843) *Letter to Ruge, September 1843* (1975). *MECW*, **3**, 141–5.
Marx, K. (1844) *Contribution to the Critique of Hegel's Philosophy of Law. Introduction* (1975). *MECW*, **3**, 175–87.
Marx, K. (1847) *The Poverty of Philosophy* (1976). *MECW*, **6**, 105–212.
Marx, K. (1848) *The Protectionists, the Free Traders and the Working Class* (1976). *MECW*, **6**, 279–81.
Marx, K. (1850) *The Class Struggles in France 1848 to 1850* (1978). *MECW*, **10**, 45–145.
Marx, K. (1859) *A Contribution to the Critique of Political Economy* (1971). Lawrence & Wishart: London.

32 *Engels, Kautsky and 'Legal Socialism'*

Marx, K. (1871) Letter to Bolte, 23 November 1871. In Marx & Engels, *Selected Correspondence*, 3rd Edit. (1975). Progress: Moscow.

Marx, K. (1875) Critique of the Gotha programme. In *Marx, The First International and After* (Fernbach, D., Ed.) (1974). Penguin: Harmondsworth.

Marx, K. (1883) *Capital*, Vol. 3 (1981). Penguin: Harmondsworth.

Marx, K. & Engels, F. (1848) Manifesto of the Communist Party (1976). *MECW*, **6**, 477–519.

Marx, K. & Engels, F. (1975) *On Religion*. Lawrence & Wishart: London.

Menger, A. (1886a) *Das Recht auf den vollen Arbeitsertrag*, 2nd Edit. (1891). Cotta: Stuttgart.

Menger, A. (1886*b*) *The Right to the Whole Produce of Labour* (1899). Macmillan: London and New York.

Mollnau, K. A. (1974) *Vom Aberglauben der juristischen Weltanschauung*. Akademie V.: Berlin (East).

Müller, E. (1975) *Anton Mengers Rechts — und Gesellschaftssystem*. Schweitzer: Berlin.

Negt, O. (1973) 10 Thesen zur marxistischen Rechtstheorie. In *Probleme der marxistischen Rechtstheorie* (Rottleuthner, H., Ed.). Suhrkamp: Frankfurt.

Pashukanis, E. B. (1929) Preface to the German Edition. In *Law and Marxism: a General Theory* (1978). Ink Links: London.

Pêcheux, M. (1975) *Language, Semantics and Ideology* (1982). Macmillan: London.

Pêcheux, M. (1984) Zu rebellierien und zu denken wagen! *Kulturrevolution* **5**, 61–4: **6**, 63–6.

Projekt Klassenanalyse (1976) Thesen zum Verhältnis von bürgerlicher Gesellschaft und Staat. *Beiträge zum wissenschaftlichen Sozialismus*, **1**, 81–101.

Ramm, T. (1975) Juristensozialismus in Deutschland. *Quaderni Fiorentini per la Storia del Pensiero Giuridico Moderno*, **1**, 7–23.

Reich, N. (1972a) Anton Menger und die demokratische Rechtstheorie. *Recht und Politik*, **8**, 93-101.

Reich, N. (Ed.) (1972*b*) *Marxistische und sozialistische Rechtstheorie*. Fischer Anthenäum: Frankfurt.

Reich, N. (1972*c*) *Sozialismus und Zivilrecht*. Fischer Athenäum: Frankfurt.

Sellnow, W. (1968) Zum Problem der Rechtsgeschichte im System von Marx und Engels. In *Marxistische Beiträge zur Rechtsgeschichte*. Wissenchaftliche Schriftenreihe der Humboldt-Universität zu Berlin: Berlin (East).

Sorel, G. (1920) Aperçu sur les Utopies, les Soviets et le Droit Nouveau. *Cahiers de l'ISEA* (1962), series S, **5**, 88–112.

Sorel, G. (1908) The Decomposition of Marxism. In *Radicalism and the Revolt Against Reason* (Horowitz, J. L., Ed.) (1961). Routledge & Kegan Paul: London.

Stedman Jones, G. (1973) Engels and the End of Classical German Philosophy. *New Left Review*, **79**, 17–36.

[Stuchka] Stutschka, P. (1970) Lenin und das revolutionäre Dekret. *Staat und Recht*, **19**, 553–60.

Tumanov, V. A. (1974) *Contemporary Bourgeois Legal Thought*. Progress: Moscow.

Vester, M. (1970) *Die Entstehung des Proletariats als Lernprozess*. Europäische V.-A.: Frankfurt.

Wagner-Beck, J. (1976) Review of Mollnau, 1974. *Sozialistische Politik*, **8**, 34–5, 242–5.

Date received: April 1985

[3]

The Concept of Justice in Marx, Engels, and Others

William Leon McBride

Purdue University

I

The concept of justice has always been among the foremost concepts of concern to political theorists. So it was at the beginning with Plato, whose *Republic* is a ten-book-long effort at defining justice in the state and in the individual. So it is as Western civilization, at least in the narrowly geographical sense of the term, enters into its period of decline, as John Rawls's *A Theory of Justice* and the many articles parasitic upon that flawed but monumental work dominate the attention of American political theorists.

For those of us who find Plato compelling but fundamentally wrong, and Rawls charming and admirable but anachronistic and abstract, Karl Marx is the most obvious theorist to whom to look for clarification. Surely, one is moved to suspect, there must be much wisdom about the concept of justice in those obsessively voluminous writings, published and unpublished, that Marx bequeathed to the twentieth century. Marx was thoroughly versed in the writings of classical politics, and was thus aware of the place that justice occupied in them; he knew his Hobbes, at least to some extent, and he was therefore aware of what we today would call the extreme legal positivist position on the subject. He also had some familiarity, at least second-hand, with Immanuel Kant's legal philosophy, in which justice is again the key term.

Unfortunately for us, a perusal of Marx's writings yields practically nothing that might satisfy these expectations. Perhaps a sophisticated scanning device might some day be employed to ferret out all the instances in which the word *Gerechtigkeit* appears in his works. I am confident that the yield would be amazingly impoverished—much smaller than the results of a similar analysis of practically any popular journalistic columnist of whom one could think. Marx wrote extensively about innumerable topics of interest to political theorists, even though he does, it is true, regard the whole domain of politics as somehow dependent upon that of economics and upon historical, material conditions. Therefore, it seems reasonable to speculate, it must have involved a considerable *effort* to keep his references to justice so sparse.

205 *The Concept of Justice*

Such speculation turns out to be well founded. In a brief note to Engels concerning a then recent criticism of volume 1 of *Capital* by an economist named Hildebrand, Marx says that he was moved to laughter at the thought that "now even political economy is to be dissolved into twaddle about 'conceptions of justice!' "[1] Both in this note and in a few other places in his works, Marx seems to agree with Engels in the total condemnation of justice-talk as mere ideology, and consequently in a totally relativistic analysis of the concept. 'Justice,' for both of them, seems never to mean anything more than "justice within a particular socioeconomic system." There was feudal justice, and there is bourgeois justice. Within the framework of the latter, it cannot be said to be unjust to extract surplus value from workers, though it might well be unjust to refuse to pay them agreed-upon wages. The thoroughgoing Marxist critique of the entire capitalist system and of the ideology of political economy that supports it cannot, therefore, rely to the slightest extent on the claim that that system is unjust. As Engels says by way of clarifying his attack on Proudhon's moralism in the supplement to his essay *The Housing Question:*

> And always this [ideal of justice, *eternal* justice] is but the ideologised, glorified expression of the existing economic relations, now from their conservative, and now from their revolutionary angle. The justice of the Greeks and Romans held slavery to be just; the justice of the bourgeois of 1789 demanded the abolition of feudalism on the ground that it was unjust. . . . The conception of eternal justice, therefore, varies not only with time and place, but also with the persons concerned, and belongs among those things of which Mülberger correctly says, 'everyone understands something different.'[2]

It is this passage more than any other, I think, that has inspired two recent American treatments of the subject of Marx on justice, namely, an article by Allen Wood in *Philosophy and Public Affairs*, and a chapter in Robert Tucker's *The Marxian Revolutionary Idea.*[3] Both are in substantial agreement that Marx did not take the bourgeois order or the capitalist system as such to be unjust, although Wood, whose article was the later of the two to appear, finds Tucker guilty of reading too much into Marx's motives for taking this position. In particular, Wood does not believe, as Tucker does, that Marx was highly fearful of workers' becoming trapped, by sloganizing about justice, into accepting measures of mere reform within the existing system (although Wood acknowledges that perhaps Marx *ought* to have feared this greatly); and Wood thinks that some of the linkage claimed by Tucker between the concept of justice and that of equality in Marx's mind is sheer interpolation on Tucker's part. At any rate, the important point is the agree-

1. Marx to Engels, July 20, 1870, in *Correspondence, 1846–1895*, by Karl Marx and Friedrich Engels (New York: International Publishers, n.d), p. 293.

2. Karl Marx and Friedrich Engels, *Selected Works*, vol. 1. (Moscow: Foreign Languages Publishing House, 1962), p. 624.

3. Allen Wood, "The Marxian Critique of Justice," *Philosophy and Public Affairs* 1, no. 3 (Spring 1972): 244–82; Robert Tucker, *The Marxian Revolutionary Idea* (New York: W. W. Norton & Co., 1969), chap. 3, pp. 37–53, reprinted from *Nomos VI: Justice* (1963).

ment between the two writers and their consequent dismissal of the idea around which Ralf Dahrendorf, for instance, constructed an entire monograph, *Die Idee des Gerechten im Denken von Karl Marx.* The point common to Wood and Tucker has caught on: I find a writer in a more recent issue of *Philosophy and Public Affairs,* for instance, using their joint authority to exclude Marxism from consideration under the rubric of "socialism" as he attempts to juxtapose an ideal-typical socialist conception of justice, which would distribute rewards on the basis of *effort,* with an ideal-typical capitalist conception of it, which would distribute them on the basis of success.[4] And John Rawls himself adverts to *The Marxian Revolutionary Idea* when he makes a very rare reference to Marxism by name; on Tucker's authority, Rawls tentatively labels Marxism as one of those systems of thought which holds as its ideal a form of social order *beyond* justice.[5]

On the other hand, it remains indisputably true that Marx's *Critique of the Gotha Programme* contains a sketch of possible future stages on the road to a fully socialistic society, the last of which is to be characterized by the slogan, "From each according to his ability, to each according to his needs!" Tucker is quick to point out that this is the only occasion on which Marx uses this borrowed slogan and that it occurs in the context of a vehement criticism of the Lassalleans, who had drawn up the Gotha Programme, for overemphasizing the theme of *distribution,* as opposed to production.[6] Marx never wavered from the conviction that arrangements in the latter sphere determined those in other spheres of the economy and determined other social institutional arrangements as well; consequently, a radical change in the sphere of production would automatically bring about a similar alteration in distribution. Moreover, it seems clear that the mention of this slogan was not intended by Marx to constitute a general blueprint for the society of the future; blueprinting was a utopian occupation that Marx scorned. So perhaps the famous slogan should not be taken so seriously. It is, unquestionably, the one sentence in all of Marx that can most readily be stamped "Marx's concept of justice" and then placed in a show window along with all the other formulas that have been proposed over the centuries.

I am inclined to think that Engels was quite serious in his ultra-relativistic approach to the concept of justice. I am also convinced that "to each according to his needs" is not intended by Marx as a directive for a distribution formula; he does not, for instance, expect us to quantify relative needs along a 100-point scale as a prelude to understanding how society ideally might be organized, or anything of the sort. However, I am struck by the continued existence of large numbers of unasked questions about the concept of justice in Marx and, since there is not much of a concept of justice in him, about the concept of justice in Engels. Raising these questions will, I

4. Michael Slote, "Desert, Consent, and Justice," *Philosophy and Public Affairs* 2, no. 4 (Summer 1973): 324.

5. John Rawls, *A Theory of Justice* (Cambridge, Harvard University Press, 1972), p. 281.

6. Tucker, p. 48.

hope, contribute to placing the concept of justice elsewhere in a somewhat new perspective, in light of Marx's critique.

II

To begin with, I feel somewhat uneasy about the failure of the two commentators whom I have mentioned to explore the bare *possibility*, at least, that there may exist some implicit diversity of views between Marx and his colleague, Engels, on the subject. This is a familiar general problem in Marxist scholarship, and a good deal has been written about it with respect to certain other topics, such as Engels's idea of a "dialectics of nature." It is a difficult matter to deal with, since the collaboration and mutual expressions of approval between the two were so total and frequent, and since Marx never explicitly contradicted Engels, to my knowledge, on any important theoretical issue. Nevertheless, everyone admits that there is a considerable difference in style and emphasis between them, and I think it would be surprising, on the face of it, if this difference were based on no differences whatever in their respective patterns of thought. Thus Wood is following a very commonplace custom when, immediately after citing a strong statement by Engels alone to the effect that capitalism cannot be considered "unjust," he refers to this view as being that of "Marx and Engels."[7] But perhaps this identification of the two is a bit too hasty. At least, as I have said, the possibility may be worth exploring.

Let us consider two passages written by Marx himself (and intended, unlike his letters, for publication) in which the concept of justice seems to arise. The first, cited by both Wood and Tucker, occurs in volume 1 of *Capital*. Apropos of the capitalist's extraction of surplus value from the worker by virtue of obtaining a full day's labor from him while paying him wages, in the example being used, that are equivalent to the productivity of only a half-day's labor, Marx says:

> The circumstance, that on the one hand the daily sustenance of labour-power costs only half a day's labour, while on the other hand the very same labour-power can work during a whole day, that consequently the value which its use during one day creates, is double what he pays for that use, this circumstance is, without doubt, a piece of good luck for the buyer, but by no means an injury to the seller.[8]

In the old, standard translation that I am using, the key word, as it will have been noticed, is 'injury.' In German, the word is *Unrecht*. Tucker, conscious of the demands of good scholarship, translates it as 'injustice' but places *Unrecht* in parentheses immediately following it. Wood simply translates it as 'injustice.' Germanists would be much better equipped than I to decide which of the two translations is better. It is clear, at any rate, that this passage brings us into confrontation once again with one of those primitive linguistic facts that hold innumerable theoretical implications for students of

7. Wood, p. 246.

8. *Capital*, vol. 1, trans. Samuel Moore and Edward Aveling (Moscow: Foreign Languages Publishing House, 1961), chap. 7, sec. 2, p. 194.

politics, namely, the well-known fact that the stem, *recht*, from which the German words for both wrong or harm or injury (*Unrecht*) and for justice (*Gerechtigkeit*) arise also serves as a word in itself, to convey the meanings of the English words 'right' and 'law.' It is clear that this fact was very much on Engels's mind when, in leading up to the passage that I cited earlier from *The Housing Question*, he wrote of the close historical connection between successively dominant legal systems and the successive and mutually contradictory ideologies of justice that have been used to support them. But this whole series of considerations leaves somewhat ambiguous, it seems to me, the question of whether Marx really intended to make a decisive pronouncement about the concept of 'justice' in this passage in *Capital*. In fact, the broader context of the passage, and especially the following paragraph, make it obvious that Marx is delineating the inherent ambiguity of the worker-capitalist relationship itself. Of course, no injury has been done the worker in terms of the legal definitions of 'right' and 'wrong' within the capitalist system. But the chapter in which the passage occurs is the very one that Marx introduces with his famous depiction of the descent from the sphere of circulation, where all has appeared to be "Freedom, Equality, Property, and Bentham," to the sphere of production, where the worker walks behind the capitalist with an air of expecting nothing but "a hiding." And immediately after the sentence concerning the lack of *Unrecht* in this disproportionate, unequal bargain between worker and capitalist, Marx says: "Our capitalist foresaw this state of things, and that was the cause of his laughter"; a few sentences later he concludes: "The trick has at last succeeded; money has been converted into capital." The use of the word 'trick' here is significant; it should not be forgotten.

Now let me turn to the second of my passages from Marx. It occurs in volume 3 of *Capital* in a discussion of *interest*. In a footnote, Marx refers to a book, *The History and Principles of Banking*, by William James Gilbart, in which it is claimed that it is "a self-evident principle of natural justice" that some portion of money that has been borrowed for the purpose of making a profit for the borrower should be given to the lender. Apropos of this, Marx says:

> To speak here of natural justice, as Gilbart does . . . is nonsense. The justice of the transactions between agents of production rests on the fact that these arise as natural consequences out of the production relationships. The juristic forms in which these economic transactions appear as wilful acts of the parties concerned, as expressions of their common will and as contracts that may be enforced by law against some individual party, cannot, being mere forms, determine this content. They merely express it. This content is just whenever it corresponds, is appropriate, to the mode of production. It is unjust whenever it contradicts that mode. Slavery on the basis of capitalist production is unjust; likewise fraud in the quality of commodities.[9]

In this passage Marx can be seen to adhere much more unambiguously than

9. *Capital*, vol. 3 (Moscow: Foreign Languages Publishing House, 1962), pp. 333–34.

in the first to the extreme Engelsian relativism concerning the concept of 'justice.' I would merely like to point out that the perspective from which Marx, in this passage, treats of 'fraud' as an example of an unjust action under capitalism seems quite different from the perspective from which he designated 'trickery,' a synonym of 'fraud,' as being a basic characteristic of the worker-employer contractual relationship under capitalism in the passage cited previously.

Enough, and probably more than enough, of exegesis. What are we to conclude about the concept of justice in Marx? At the very least, I think, we should conclude that Allen Wood is misleading us and others who have read his article when he uses such language as the following: (*a*) "the fact that Marx does not regard capitalism as unjust,"[10] or (*b*) "Marx's insistence on the justice of capitalism."[11] Of course, to take these phrases out of context is not to do justice, if I may be permitted the expression, to Wood's generally thoughtful and well-reasoned argument, but I am much more concerned at the moment with talking about justice than with doing it. And I am afraid that these phrases do misrepresent Marx's position, and probably even that of Engels.

III

We ought to begin our reformulation of that position (or those positions, if they are not totally identical) by recalling an elementary distinction, that between justice within a given ethico-legal system and justice from a perspective external to that system. Clearly, neither Marx nor Engels had any difficulties about admitting the meaningfulness of speaking of justice within the limits of a given system; it was for this very reason that they were so highly skeptical of talk about *justice éternelle*. Aristotle, after all, whom Marx greatly admired in certain respects, had thought that slavery in his slave society was eminently just, as long as the appropriate individuals served as the slaves. So the issue resolves itself into one of whether Marx and Engels, or perhaps Marx alone, would have been willing to concede that there was any meaning whatever to talking about the 'justice' or 'injustice' of a system from a perspective external to it. In one sense, of course, we have our answer already: in the passage from volume 3 of *Capital* that I cited, Marx says that slavery is unjust from the point of view of capitalist production. Similarly, Engels pointed out that feudalism appeared unjust to the bourgeoisie of 1789. But it is easy to report about what others have said; any would-be historian, for example, could quickly collate a great many statements that were once made about phlogiston, a term that Engels actually analogizes to 'justice' in *The Housing Question*, without thereby committing himself to any personal theories about phlogiston.

What is the perspective of Marx and/or Engels themselves on the concept of 'justice'? For Engels, clearly, it is that that concept is "social phlogis-

10. Wood, p. 245.
11. Ibid., p. 272.

ton," as he expresses it.[12] It is illusory, not a reality at all. But can the analogy really hold? 'Just' and 'unjust,' after all, were admitted by Engels and Marx to be meaningful words when applied from within the capitalist system to certain kinds of practices; therefore, the terms 'just' and 'unjust' must have real referents within that actual historical system. 'Phlogiston,' on the other hand, served a function within a certain early chemical *theory*, but Engels is too much of a realist to want to say that phlogiston ever actually existed. Eventually, he points out, most of the properties of oxygen came to be ascribed to this illusory element, but even after that the fight to acknowledge its illusoriness was a long and bitter one. Is there any exact or nearly exact parallel to be drawn in the case of the possible future of the concept of justice? In other words, phlogiston:justice::oxygen:*X*. Perhaps some sort of answer could be worked out, but I think that my point has been made: the two sorts of concepts are sufficiently dissimilar to put into question the value of the analogy.

Moreover, Engels is certainly contradicting himself, at least when we attempt to take him very literally, in conceding the correctness of his opponent Mülberger's claim that "everyone understands something different" about justice. If the basic Marxist point about the ideological function of the concept of justice in all past and present societies is to be taken seriously, as I think it should be, then there must have been a considerable core of *agreement* about its meaning in various places and at various times in the past.

In short, Engels cannot carry his ethical, historical relativism too far with respect to the concept of 'justice' without undermining the entire Marxist theoretical program. If that concept has had as powerful a function in shoring up both ideological and practical conformity to existing social structures as he rightly claims it to have had in the past and in his own era, then it is only at his peril that he can dismiss it as *mere* "illusion." Most especially, he cannot shift from treating justice as a class-bound concept to treating it as a totally equivocal term, a mere *flatus vocis*—perhaps an utterance of emotional approval, like 'hurrah!' as the ethical noncognitivists would have it—without depriving the Marxist account of ideology of its explantatory power. I think that there are several passages, not only in *The Housing Question*, but also in the so-called *Anti-Dühring*, in which Engels's zeal to eliminate all talk of "eternal truths," after the fashions of Plato and Dühring and Proudhon, brings him dangerously close to the brink of total dissolution of the truth-claims of Marxist theory.

Marx himself was much more cautious than his colleague in such matters; I like to think of Marx as the greater genius of the two, and to ascribe his caution to a greater awareness of some of the fundamental theoretical problems. Of course, Marx steered away from justice-talk because he thought of it as ideological twaddle, certain to detract from his rigorous critical analysis of the capitalist system if he should once introduce it in any explanatory role, however minor; as we have already seen, he was far more thoroughgoing

12. Engels, in Marx and Engels, *Selected Works*, p. 625.

than was Engels in abiding by this self-imposed prohibition. Marx wrote *Capital* from a radically critical perspective external to that of capitalism; from the fact that he regards, for example, wage labor as just within the premises of the capitalist mode of production, does it follow that he considers that mode of production *as such* to be a *just* one? He certainly never says so explicitly, *pace* some recent commentators. And I suppose that, if asked the question, Marx would have said that it was a poorly formulated question, unanswerable without considerable prior clarification of the terms in which it had been asked.

IV

One way in which we might consider beginning to undertake such a clarification is to consider certain other terms, similar to justice in the sense of being abstractions that have frequently been thought to embody major social values. I shall now propose three such terms and proceed to discuss very briefly how Marx's and/or Engels's treatments of each, in turn, might shed some light on the problem of what we ought finally to say about the concept of justice. The three terms are equality, freedom, and rationality.

1. The question of equality is a particularly interesting one for those seeking clues as to what Marx and Engels really thought about the concept of justice. Equality is important because it has so frequently been linked with justice: in the influential and magisterial treatment of the subject by Aristotle, for example, the idea of justice as "proportional equality" looms very large. The metaphor of the balanced scales is just one particularly graphic instance of the very close historical linkage between justice and equality. Marx and Engels never posed as complete egalitarians. In his *1844 Manuscripts*, for instance, Marx sketches a conceptual outline of a state of affairs that he calls "crude, egalitarian communism," which he sees as characterized by leveling, envy of all special talent, and, in effect, the universalization of the notion of private property rather than its abolition. In his *Anti-Dühring*, Engels includes an entire chapter on equality; its most revealing paragraph reads as follows:

> The demand for equality in the mouth of the proletariat has therefore a double meaning. It is either . . . the spontaneous reaction against the crying social inequalities, against the contrast of rich and poor, the feudal lords and their serfs, surfeit and starvation; as such it is the simple expression of the revolutionary instinct, and finds its justification in that, and indeed only in that. Or, on the other hand, the proletarian demand for equality has arisen as the reaction against the bourgeois demand for equality, drawing more or less correct and more far-reaching demands from this bourgeois demand, and serving as an agitational means in order to rouse the workers against the capitalists on the basis of the capitalists' own assertions; and in this case it stands and falls with bourgeois equality itself. In both cases the real content of the proletarian demand for equality is the demand for the *abolition of classes*. Any demand for equality which goes beyond that, of necessity passes into absurdity.[13]

13. Friedrich Engels, *Herr Eugen Dühring's Revolution in Science*, trans. E. Burns (New York: International Publishers, 1939), pp. 117–18.

Engels is claiming, first, that the call for equality sometimes has a positive value for revolutionary activity; second, that it may be useful to stress the contradictions between bourgeois ideas about equality and inegalitarian bourgeois practices; third, that the demand that all individuals have "equality" of class status can be translated and clarified into the demand for the abolition of class differences and hence of classes; and fourth, that the demand that all individuals in a possible future classless society be made equal in every way is an unjustifiable and senseless demand. He is also implying, quite obviously, that 'equality' is not a very useful conceptual tool with which to undertake a rigorous, and in that sense scientific, analysis of existing social structures. In this respect, there is a great deal of similarity between Marx's and Engels's treatments of equality and what we have seen concerning their treatments of justice; but there is no equivalent, in the case of justice, to Engels's more positive remarks concerning the potential strategic usefulness of the demands for equality. Could this fact perhaps be due more to circumstance—that is, to the far greater abuses traceable to the ideological cant about justice among other nineteenth-century writers—than to any difference in principle of a radical and ineluctable sort, between the two concepts considered as social values? Could it also be due in part to the fact that 'equality' has an unquestionably legitimate use as a key concept in mathematics and logic, whereas 'justice' can boast no similar legitimacy?

2. 'Freedom' is a term found frequently throughout the writings of both Marx and Engels. The latter, at least, finds no difficulty in referring to it as a principal characteristic of postcapitalist society; he speaks of the ascent to the reign of freedom. Marx, once again, is somewhat more cautious. In the *Critique of the Gotha Programme*, for example, he is highly critical of the Lassalleans' call for a "free state," because this implies perpetual retention of political structures that Marx considers eliminable. And in his description of the wage contract, he emphasizes that the worker is indeed a "*free* laborer," by comparison both with the ancient slave and with the feudal serf. At the same time, however, he readily admits that the worker is radically subservient to the economic structures within which he operates, and hence highly unfree, from his (Marx's) own critical perspective. In the case of the term 'freedom,' then, we find a pattern of dual meanings—meanings the relationship of which to one another can be spelled out, and yet meanings that are substantially different from one another. The worker, in short, is, according to Marx, truly free within the legal conceptions of the capitalist system, and yet truly unfree from the vantage point of critical, proletarian consciousness.

3. 'Rationality' is another interesting abstract value-term to compare with 'justice' in the present context. It may seem to us a trifle less emotive and value-laden than the first two. At any rate, it is a characteristic that is frequently said to be supremely present in the modern state and legal system, and the practice of so ascribing it owes much, historically speaking, to an intellectual tradition traceable from Max Weber through Marx back to Hegel. Both Hegel and Marx were fascinated by the achievements of the

science of political economy in discovering the intricate inner rationality of capitalism, and Marx's mature work consists primarily, of course, in working within that intellectual tradition in order to undermine both it and the system that it analyzed. The more we read what Marx has to say about rationality, the more we are struck by the duality—or perhaps plurality—of meanings that he considers the concept to contain. He finds no difficulty in accommodating the two meanings even within the same sentence, as when he says the following about the evolution of agriculture under capitalism: "The rationalizing of agriculture, on the one hand, which makes it for the first time capable of operating on a social scale, and the reduction *ad absurdum* of property in land, on the other, are the great achievements of the capitalist mode of production."[14] Marx's meaning is clear enough, I think. He is claiming that modern developments, bringing agriculture increasingly within the capitalist orbit, are resulting in more efficient farm production, but that at the same time the irrationality, or absurdity, of private ownership of land is being made increasingly evident. A system may well be simultaneously a rationalizing one, from an internal point of view, and supremely irrational, from an external standpoint.[15]

What are the implications of Marx's discussion of these three abstract concepts, rationality, freedom, and equality, for his theory of justice? Rationality from the standpoint of a "higher form of society" might well be called, without great distortion, a "higher rationality"; the freedom of Engels's "reign of freedom" might quite legitimately be called, in the Hegelian terminology, a "fuller realization of freedom"; a classless society might be said to be a state of greater equality than any in the past, though only in a very specific, delimited sense. (It would be senseless to speak of a "higher equality," and it would be misleading to speak of anticipating the achievement of greater equality *in every way*.) Justice, in the thought of Marx, is different from all these in some significant respects, because it is totally epiphenomenal and dependent on the existing order, whereas none of the others is quite as completely so. And yet, and yet . . . I do not see how Marx and Engels could, if pressed on the matter, logically avoid recognizing that justice, too, can meaningfully be referred to from a standpoint at least partially external to any particular past or present socioeconomic system. It, too, must, I am convinced, be said to be dualistic or pluralistic in meaning, so that at least at the present stage of society it cannot be understood strictly in terms of the standards of capitalism.[16]

14. *Capital*, 3:604.

15. As Marx expresses it near the end of his treatment of agriculture: "From the standpoint of a higher economic form of society, private ownership of the globe by single individuals will appear quite as absurd as private ownership of one man by another" (ibid., p. 757).

16. I thus seem to have come, by a very different route, to share some of Herbert Marcuse's insights concerning the function of abstract terms in both classical philosophy and modern dialectical thought. While there are serious deficiencies, I think, in his critical analyses of both operationalism in the social sciences and linguistic analysis in philosophy, as he expounds them in *One-dimensional Man* (Boston: Beacon Press, 1964), he is correct in seeing the importance of

Engels and Marx never pretended to be legal positivists in the simple fashion of Hobbes: justice, for them, is not simply action in conformity with the existing legal system, itself taken as a logically consistent whole. For the domain of ideology, of which justice-talk is a part, is a complex one in both a vertical and a horizontal sense. It is vertically complex with respect to justice, in the sense that it consists of several levels: the implicit and occasionally explicit statements concerning what is and is not just within the statutes themselves; the glosses on the statutes, especially within a common law system, by jurists and other officials of the system; the idealizations of the justice of the system, often involving reformist suggestions for its modification, by theoreticians; and the rough-and-ready, commonsense conceptions of that same justice that are held by the subjects of the system, or at least by that segment of its subjects who either belong to the dominant class or, not belonging, nevertheless accept its dominance. The meaning of 'justice' is certainly not univocal across all these levels. Moreover, as I have said, there is a horizontal complexity about justice that goes to the heart of the Marxian conception of dialectic: practical contradictions are constantly developing within the capitalist mode of production in its unfolding through time, through history. Consequently, it is totally inadequate for Marx to say that justice consists in the correspondence between a given concrete transaction and the mode of production dominant at the time, because this seems to imply that the mode of production is a rigid, inflexible structure within which certain practices either fit or do not fit; it is obviously not so simple as that. Rather, if dialectical processes are at work in *every* sector of a society, we would expect dissonances to develop among the various ideological formulations of the dominant conception of 'justice,' reflecting the dissonances in the socioeconomic structure itself. This, of course, is in fact what happens constantly.

At this point, Engels's remarks concerning the senses in which the demand for equality may be legitimate, from a proletarian standpoint, should be recalled. He spoke of the proletariat's "drawing more or less correct and more far-reaching demands" out of the *bourgeois* demand for equality. I see no reason for not extending this pattern to the area of justice. Conflicts among different conceptions of justice within a capitalist framework might well be utilized to demonstrate the limitations of that framework itself. One possible way of expressing the results of such an approach would be to say that

---

retaining a two-dimensionality in our understanding of such abstract terms if we wish to be genuinely critical thinkers. As he says: "The Socratic discourse is political discourse inasmuch as it contradicts the established political institutions. The search for the correct definition, for the 'concept' of virtue, justice, piety, and knowledge becomes a subversive undertaking, for the concept intends a new *polis*" (p. 134). The situation of Marx is more complicated, of course, inasmuch as he is "intending" a postpolitical society, rather than a new *polis*. And I have found, in rereading *One-dimensional Man*, that Marcuse feels much more at home with discussing such concepts as 'equality' and 'freedom' than with discussing justice. Nevertheless, he has performed an important service in showing that Marx's thought lies within the old tradition of Socratic-Platonic dialectic in some very important respects.

injustices, in terms of capitalist conceptions of justice, are bound to occur within even a perfectly functioning capitalist system, or that such a system can in principle never satisfy its self-generated "demands" for justice. If this can indeed be shown, then it might well be sensible to follow Marx's and Engels's advice and Marx's *nearly* exceptionless personal example, in his writings,[17] and to retire the very term 'justice' from our vocabularies. But in the meantime it would have served one last, useful function in abetting its own self-destruction, and it could not have been used in this way if it had had a purely univocal meaning that was purely internal to the capitalist system.

Realistically speaking, of course, there is little chance indeed that justice-talk will disappear from the discourse either of ordinary individuals or of political philosophers (better expressed, perhaps, "either of political philosophers or of other ordinary individuals") in the foreseeable future. Certainly not in this country, in the eras of Watergate and Rawls. Certainly not in the Soviet Union, where the expression, 'Soviet justice,' is used with as little hesitation as is the expression, 'Communist ideology,' despite all the pejorative connotations that Marx and Engels attached to the term 'ideology.' Moreover, Marx and Engels were not interested in posing as mere language reformers; they anticipated the withering away of justice-talk as only one by-product of a possible future fundamental social change from capitalism to socialism. (Coincident with this change would be both an increase in abundance, resulting in a diminution in the importance of those problems of distribution that have traditionally been linked so closely with justice, and the famous withering away of the state and its legal system, for which the invocation of 'justice' has always been one of the strongest ideological defenses. But it is impossible to discuss in detail in this paper the full range of factors supporting the Marxist belief that the transition to socialism would obviate references to justice in a future society.)

Such a fundamental change would have to be a collective one, not the result of a decision by just a few individuals. On the other hand, the fact remains that Marx and Engels, especially Marx, *did* provide what I have called personal examples of how to undertake extensive discussions in the area of social and political theory while making scarcely a single reference to 'justice.' It is an interesting specific and concrete illustration of attempting to cope with the revolutionary's dilemma: the need simultaneously to live somehow in the anticipated future, with its new patterns of life and even speech, and to function within the structures, including the linguistic structures, of the present social system. Some of the puzzlements with which I have been grappling concerning possible uses of the term 'justice' within a Marxian context can better be understood in the light of that dilemma.

17. References to 'justice' must be clearly and carefully distinguished from talk of historical "justification" of certain actions and practices. The legitimacy or illegitimacy of such talk is a rather different issue, though there are points at which it touches on the present one. Marx did not, on the whole, place much stock in the metaphorical personification of History as the Supreme Judge, the Final Arbiter of justice. But he did, of course, see the passage of events as clarifying the comparative worth of acts.

V

I would like to conclude this paper by referring very briefly to two individuals who are very much alive at present in the general area of American political theory; one of them shares the Marxian conviction concerning the ultimate eliminability of justice-talk, though he shares relatively little else with Marx, whereas the other has repopularized justice-talk with smashing success. The latter, of course, is John Rawls, to whom I have already referred on several occasions, and the former is the philosopher and Nietzsche translator Walter Kaufmann, in his recently published book, *Without Guilt and Justice*.

The Rawlsian world view is thoroughly permeated with a species of mitigated Platonism. What else is one to think of a writer whose first sentence in section 1, chapter 1, reads: "Justice is the first virtue of social institutions, as truth is of systems of thought," and who concludes the paragraph in which this occurs by saying: "Being first virtues of human activities, truth and justice are uncompromising"?[18] Or who concludes, nearly 600 pages later, with a reference to the perspective of eternity, followed by the moving words: "Purity of heart, if one could attain it, would be to see clearly and to act with grace and self-command from this point of view"?[19] In between, of course, there are many meanderings, and Rawls has absorbed and incorporated all the standard objections to classical Platonism. For detailed criticisms of some of the most salient of these meanderings, I can only refer to my review of *A Theory of Justice* in *The Yale Law Journal*;[20] it would be impossible for me to repeat them here. There is an implicit, rudimentary sense of historical relativity in Rawls's thought, in the sense that he sanctions a suspension of the normal "lexical ordering" of his two basic principles, according to which equal liberty for all is to be secured first and an equitable distribution in conformity with his so-called difference principle second, in early stages of civilization in which it may seem reasonable to restrict liberties to some extent. But, he says, "Eventually there comes a time in the history of a well-ordered society beyond which the special form of the two principles takes over and holds from then on."[21] The very fact that present-tense language is employed here to describe a development that, from the point of view of actual history as we know it, is a pure idealization shows how little Rawls's thinking has been influenced by the sorts of considerations —considerations, for example, about the uses to which ideologies of justice have been put and even about the etymological histories of the word and of its equivalents in other languages—that have been most influential in thinking about justice within the Marxian tradition. For Rawls, there will always be a justice; any suggestion to the contrary is unthinkable.

18. Rawls, pp. 3–4.
19. Ibid., p. 587.
20. "Social Theory *Sub Specie Aeternitatis:* A New Perspective," *Yale Law Journal* 81, no. 5 (April 1972): 980–1003.
21. Rawls, p. 542.

The situation is quite different in the case of Walter Kaufmann. He has absorbed, while retaining a critical stance toward, some of Nietzsche's theories about the origins of justice, and he is impressed by the impossibility—in small, apparently manageable situations as well as on a society-wide scale—of making exact determinations concerning distributions of goods according to any criterion of merit or need. Thus, he attacks the concept of distributive justice as the last bastion of the historical concept of justice as such, and he looks forward, as Marx and Engels did, to a world in which ideological talk about justice will have ended. Unfortunately, however, Kaufmann sees no inconsistency in expounding such a vision and at the same time preaching the gospel of what he calls "the New Integrity," in which four virtues—love, "humbition" (his neologism for a combination of humility and ambition), courage, and honesty—reign supreme.[22] In doing this, he shows that he has not absorbed the spirit either of the Marxian critique of ideological thinking or of Nietzsche's vision of a culture "beyond good and evil"—two intellectual achievements of the nineteenth century that, as increasing numbers of scholars are coming to recognize, have a great deal in common in their critical aspects (which are the more important aspects for both). There is nothing particularly radical about Kaufmann's vision of the future; there cannot be, since his principal concern remains, in the spirit of much of early existentialism, individual moral conduct, and the political dimension enters into his thinking only incidentally, in large measure because of the felt need to undertake a critique of justice. His example is an interesting one for us to have taken note of, however, because it illustrates how difficult it is to walk the tightrope between absurdity and banality when one attempts to reexamine in depth a concept so deeply ingrained in our thought and language as justice is—particularly when one goes about it with the passionate attitude of the moral reformer.

Most difficult of all, perhaps, is to try to imagine a world in which justice-talk would no longer be heard, not even among political theorists—except, perhaps, among historians of the discipline. No compulsion would be felt to place a verbal halo around positive, socially beneficial actions or rules that we might now tend to label "just." The hypocrisy level would have been considerably lowered; the famous sentence, "But it would be wrong!" would be regarded as a quaint anachronism. It is all simply too much to try to imagine. Still, our mind-bending efforts may receive some encouragement from one brief reflection on Plato's *Republic*, the most formidable of all writings on justice, with a reference to which this paper began. Plato, it will be recalled, analogizes justice in the state to justice in the individual. In fact, ostensibly at least, Socrates makes his detour through the territory of the *Republic* in order to gain a clearer vision of what might be meant by justice in the individual. It is often forgotten, because Plato is so familiar to most Western political theorists, that there is a serious difficulty in trying to render

22. Walter Kaufmann, *Without Guilt and Justice* (New York: Peter H. Wyden, 1973), p. 184.

Plato's basic schema contemporary. For the expression 'a just man' or 'a just woman' is an archaism, and there is no other phrase in our language (or, to the best of my knowledge, in the other major modern Western languages) that fully translates Plato's intended meaning, when he speaks of justice in the individual, that does not itself strike one as somewhat quaint or old-fashioned. In this one respect, then, we may be slightly less ideological in our thought and speech than our ancestors were. Is it not barely possible to conceive of a future in which the same state of affairs would obtain on the level of *social* 'justice,' as well?

Part II
Boundaries

[4]

MARXISM AND NATURAL LAW

William Leon McBride

1. To BRING into temporary conjunction, for purposes of comparison and contrast, two traditions of social philosophy that are putatively as disparate as those of Marxism and natural law might appear to be an interesting exercise in intellectual history, but little else. My own purpose in broaching the subject, however, is not that of contributing another footnote or two to the body of intellectual history, except, as it may happen, incidentally. Rather, it seems to me that a reconsideration of certain fundamental logical relationships between Marxism and natural law theory is desirable for its own sake and, to the extent to which both continue to retain some degree of philosophical acceptability, might prove useful for advancing current discussion.

A few prefatory cultural observations, by way of suggesting some special motivation for the enterprise at hand, are in order. In the postwar Western revival of interest in Marxism as a philosophical respectable theory, the roles of certain members of the Catholic intelligentsia — Calvez, Wetter, and Bochenski are three individuals whose quite varied contributions come immediately to mind as examples — were noteworthy. At first, this phenomenon might readily have been explained as an instance of the naturally great curiosity that one takes in one's most mortal ideological enemy; in addition, the identification of Marxism with a political movement (Communism) and state (the U.S.S.R.) whose dealings with the Catholic Church and Catholic political parties were generally very hostile gave an existential immediacy to the sense of ideological struggle. But a number of developments in more recent years have made it evident, it seems to me, that the simple explanation of interest based on total hostility is inadequate, at least for the *present* cultural situation. It may readily be conceded that the various efforts at Marxist-Christian (no longer just "Marxist-Catholic") dialogue have by no means been uniformly successful; in fact, the intellectual content of a book such as Roger Garaudy's *From Anathema to Dialogue*[1] (the title of which certainly captures the reality of an important historical development) seems to me to be, on the whole, disappointingly meager. But this judgment does not detract from the fact that efforts at "dialogue," that so greatly overworked word, have a real basis not merely in a vaguely felt need for attempting to have some communication, which constitutes a very minimal motivation, but also,

[1] Transl. by Luke O'Neil (New York: Herder & Herder, 1966).

and more importantly, in the recognition that some real intellectual community uniting the two sides already exists and now requires some more rigorous and sustained exploration and explicitation.

But what does all this have to do with the alleged relationship between Marxism and natural law theory? Natural law theory, after all, however strong its historical links may at one time have been with Christian theology, cannot logically present itself as a theological doctrine, and some of its best contemporary exponents have few or no religious commitments. This is true, but it is precisely the acknowledged historical links that are relevant to my present cultural observations. It would, I think, be quite safe to assume that most of the theologians and other religiously oriented individuals — Protestants to a lesser extent, on the whole, than Catholics, but still to a significant degree — who have been engaged in the dialoguing enterprise with Marxist thinkers are far more familiar than the average contemporary Western intellectual with the natural law tradition. (This would hold true, of course, whether or not the individuals in question still regarded that tradition, in any of its traditional formulations, as viable.) Now, this fact by itself proves nothing philosophically, but it may well indicate a philosophical direction in which to look in order to supplement the superficial historical account which would treat all the contemporary intellectual ferment concerning Marxism and Christianity as a mere *ad hoc* response to postwar political conditions. And since, as I take it, this ferment is one of potentially major historical significance, with importance for many more persons besides those who at present consider themselves to be either Marxists or Christians or both at once, the impetus to explore possible commonalities between Marxism and natural law is a strong one.

So much, then, for one particular — and, as I think, especially cogent — line of argumentation on behalf of the *prima facie* contemporary cultural relevance of my topic. Up to this point, the bulk of my remarks might have been made by any detached observer, without regard to his own evaluation either of Marxism or of the natural law tradition or of any contemporary developments. In fact, however, it would seem difficult for such an observer to refrain from framing at least some tentative initial evaluations of his own. Logically speaking, it would be perfectly conceivable for these evaluations to be negative. And they frequently are. More than once, I have heard intelligent commentators give utterance, informally, to a crude sequence of negative evaluations, the general form of which was as follows: It is no surprise to find many clergymen and others who once believed in the natural law and then became disillusioned with it now flocking to the study of Marxism; they have remained dogmatists, mystifiers, and generally non-positive thinkers, and have simply switched their allegiances from one dangerous metaphysical system to another. There is just a sufficient degree of plausibility to this crude caricature to warrant my having stated it here by way of indicating an initial bias from which I emphatically dissent. I, on the contrary, find considerable positive value in *certain* interpretations of both Marxism and natural law theory, and I do not believe that these acceptable versions can correctly be characterized by the pejorative epithets of the caricature.

In support of this judgment, I propose in this essay to consider some similarities of origin and doctrine between Marxism and natural law and then to try to determine the type of natural law theory, if any is to be found, which would be most compatible with a Marxist approach to social ideals. First, however, I intend to put into question, in a preliminary way, a few of the standard objections with which my endeavor will be met from the standpoint of the established wisdom of historical scholarship.

2. A. P. d'Entrèves, whose defense of natural law constituted the initial essay in the first issue of the present journal's predecessor, the *Natural Law Forum*,[2] strongly supports the view that the historical tradition of natural law, metamorphosed in the seventeenth and eighteenth centuries into the various theories of natural right, was most radically rejected by Marx's greatest immediate intellectual forebear, Hegel.[3] That this view has considerable plausibility is undeniable, most especially if one considers the unwontedly simple and unqualified admonition against the stipulation of societal "ought's" that is to be found near the end of the famous Preface to the *Philosophy of Right*.[4] Moreover, further confirmation of d'Entrèves' position can easily be adduced from the absolutely pervasive fact that Hegel introduces a very large degree of historical relativity into all his normative considerations about politics;[5] this orientation, too, certainly constitutes a radical break with the intellectual past, particularly if one substitutes the label, "relativism," for the more neutral description, "relativity," and if, as does d'Entrèves, one considers the purely atemporal moral philosophy of Hegel's

[2] "The Case for Natural Law Re-Examined," I *Natural Law Forum* (1956), pp. 5-52.

[3] "It is with Hegel that the final break with natural law occurs in legal as well as in political theory."— d'Entrèves, *Natural Law* (London: Hutchinson University Library, 1951), p. 72.

[4] "It is just as absurd to fancy that a philosophy can transcend its contemporary world as it is to fancy that an individual can overleap his own age. . . . If [the philosopher's] theory really goes beyond the world as it is and builds an ideal one as it ought to be, that world exists indeed, but only in his opinions, an unsubstantial element where anything you please may, in fancy, be built." — Knox ed. (Oxford: At the Clarendon Press, 1942), p. 11.

[5] As an exception to this, one might point to Hegel's much-disputed claim that history has reached some sort of culmination in his own civilization and time. To discuss this claim, which I do not believe Hegel to have taken in quite so absolute a sense as do some of his critics, would take us too far afield.

own immediate predecessor, Kant, to be a kind of culmination of the development of natural law thinking.[6]

Since it has been and continues to be a useful commonplace, though one that has recently begun to come under stronger attack from antihumanist Marxist scholars, to regard Marx as simply revising Hegelian thinking about law and right (*Recht*) in a more extreme (whether better or worse) direction, the acceptance of d'Entrèves' historical judgment about Hegel's relationship to the natural law tradition may logically be thought also to apply to Marx, with nothing more than the addition of a simple "*a fortiori*." In order, then, to overcome an initial predisposition against lending any credence to my fundamental thesis, I must try to cast some doubt on the chain of reasoning that begins with d'Entrèves' historical dictum. More specifically, I wish, first, to emphasize the sense in which both Hegel and Marx (the latter during the early period in his life when he was still interested in such matters) defended a normative approach to law against the school of one of the founders of legal positivism, thus aligning themselves with the natural law tradition at least for this purpose; and, second, to point out the obvious dissimilarity between Hegel and Marx on precisely the issue of philosophy's "transcending its contemporary world" which I have taken to be one of the main indices of Hegel's departure from earlier forms of natural law theory.

Professor d'Entrèves himself points out[7] the significant facts that the first half of the full title of Hegel's *Philosophy of Right* is *Naturrecht und Staatswissenschaft im Grundrisse*, and that one of Hegel's earliest published essays concerned *The Scientific Treatment of Natural Law*, its role in practical philosophy, and its relationship to positive legal science.[8] Now, it might be maintained, as it is by d'Entrèves, that Hegel's references to natural law are merely useful devices for subverting the entire concept.[9] But the charge of using, or abusing, a traditional concept such as natural law for an entirely new purpose must always be treated with caution. Cannot a strong case be

---

[6] "Kant was indeed the most forceful exponent of natural law theory in modern days." — d'Entrèves, *Natural Law*, p. 115.

[7] *Ibid.*, p. 72.

[8] "Ueber die wissenschaftlichen Behandlungsarten des Naturrechts, seine Stelle in der praktischen Philosophie, und sein Verhältnis zu den positiven Rechtswissenschaften," in *Werke*, Erster Band (Berlin: Duncker & Humblot, 1845), pp. 313-412. ("Zuerst erschienen im *Kritischen Journal der Philosophie*, B. II, St. 2 u. 3, 1802-1803.")

[9] The same could easily be said, it seems to me, about Rousseau's *Discourse on the Origin of Inequality*, which was supposed to answer, *inter alia*, the Dijon Academy's question whether inequality was contrary to the natural law, and which is constructed in such a way as to suggest that this question, with which Rousseau never deals explicitly, is badly posed and thus unanswerable. The debts of both Hegel and Marx to Rousseau's social philosophy are indeed very great. But they can hardly be considered greater than that of d'Entrèves' preferred natural law theorist, Kant himself, who uses the Rousseauan formula of "obedience to a law that one has prescribed to oneself" as central in his moral philosophy.

made, for example, for the contention that the medieval theorists of natural law were actually subverting its pristine, classical sense when they incorporated it within a Christian theological context? On the other hand, it seems equally plausible to say that the Christianization of natural law, at least in its more rationalistic forms such as that of St. Thomas, was an interesting development, rather than a perversion, of the original concept. So, too, I think it can be said, Hegel's historicizing of social norms constitutes as much of a new development within a broad ancient tradition as it does a radical break.

My proposed shift in historical emphasis from the position of d'Entrèves gains additional support, it seems to me, when we consider the virulence of Hegel's attack on his influential near-contemporary in the philosophy of law, Gustav Hugo. I have already alluded to this quarrel in a review article written several years ago for the *Natural Law Forum*.[10] The main point, for present purposes, is that Hugo's positivistic[11] approach to Roman legal history, which entailed the justification of even the most morally outrageous statutory provisions discussed, draws nothing but scorn from Hegel in the *Philosophy of Right*.[12] If the most diametrical opposition to the theses of natural law theory is that of legal positivism, with its insistence on the absolute validity, from the point of view of legal science, of whatever law may be in force at a given time and in a given place, then Hegel's thoroughgoing attack on one of the earliest formulators of this position should not be forgotten when an assessment is made of Hegel's relation to the earlier theory. This same evidence is useful in refuting the cliché that Hegel had retreated to a position of simple political conservatism by the time he wrote his major political treatise. If this overly simplistic view of him had prevailed in the period immediately following his death, it would be difficult to understand how the Hegelian Left could have regarded itself as Hegelian even at the *beginning*.

And it is at this point that Marx enters the historical stage. For it should be recalled that, during Marx's highly formative first year in Berlin, two rival instructors in legal philosophy appear to have had particularly important influences on him. The two were Gans and Savigny. The former was a disciple of Hegel's, incisive, liberal by the standards of the day. The latter was

---

10 Review of Norberto Bobbio's *Giusnaturalismo e positivismo giuridico*, 11 *Natural Law Forum* (1966), pp. 110-125.

11 As Professor Bobbio has shown (*Il Positivismo Giuridico*, ed. N. Morra, Turin, undated course notes), Hugo and the whole German historical school of law are rightly to be considered the forerunners of legal positivism.

12 Introduction, Paragraph 3 (Knox ed., pp. 16-20). The attack on Hugo comes in the context of a severe general criticism of those who would "obscure the difference between the historical and the philosophical study of law" (p. 17). It is as the latter type of study, "law from the philosophical point of view," that Hegel characterizes (p. 16) natural law.

a follower of Hugo's, who, by comparison with his colleague, made a most unfavorable impression on the young Marx. An early essay by Marx contains an expression of his negative attitude towards Hugo and the historical school which is quite similar to the critical stance of Hegel himself.[13] Though Marx had by this time already abandoned the study of law to strike out in new directions, there is no reason to suppose that his comparative judgments of these two teachers and of the doctrines that they upheld were ever reversed.

With the background of these historical and theoretical relationships in mind, one can more readily understand why, a year later, Marx devoted so much effort and energy to the internal criticism, paragraph by paragraph, of the *Philosophy of Right*; such an effort betokens, at the very least, enormous respect for the system that one is criticizing. In this *opus*, unfinished and fragmentary as it is in its surviving form, many of Marx's most important later ideas are already foreshadowed. These ideas are, in my opinion, often genuinely novel and constitute genuine advances beyond Hegel rather than, for the most part, returns to earlier formulations; nevertheless, as I shall shortly attempt to show in more detail, they take their inspiration from a very broad historical tradition of social philosophy, in which the theory (or, more exactly, theories) of natural law played a very prominent role. Moreover, there is at least one important sense in which Marx reverts, in this and other writings of the same period, to a world view that is more congenial to the heirs of a certain natural law tradition than is the philosophy of Hegel: in the fact that Marx constantly upholds what he calls his "naturalism" against the immanent Hegelian *Geist*, we can discern something more significant, for my present thesis, than the mere fortuitous identity of words.

There is another sense, too, in which Marx departs from Hegel, in his fundamental orientation, in such a way as to cast doubt on the standard identification of Hegel and Marx as being equally alien to the natural law tradition for essentially the same historicist reasons. D'Entrèves, in arguing for his historical thesis concerning Hegel's utter rejection of that tradition, places greatest emphasis on Hegel's defense of "the ethical State."[14] Despite the previously discussed attack on Hugo's historical positivism, there obviously remains, in Hegel, that complicated, ambivalent (or dialectical, if one prefers)

---

[13] This article, entitled "Das philosophische Manifest der historischen Rechtsschule," was written for the *Rheinische Zeitung* of August 9, 1842. Although Marx carelessly calls Hugo's book his "Lehrbuch des *Naturrechts*" (its full title was *"Lehrbuch eines civilistischen Cursus, Zweyter Band, welcher das Naturrecht, als eine Philosophie des positiven Rechts, besonders des Privatrechts, enthält"*), the text emphasizes, and ridicules, Hugo's employment of the word, "positive." See Marx-Engels *Werke*, Band I (Berlin: Dietz Verlag, 1961), pp. 78-85.

[14] *Natural Law*, p. 73.

justification of the allegedly rational core of the existing order of social institutions that has led to all the familiar political charges against him. Hegel fortifies this position with his methodological dictum (the mere existence of which, whether or not one agrees with its wisdom, helps in large measure to explain his theoretical stance *vis-à-vis* the *status quo* and thus partially to absolve him of some of the charges) that philosophy cannot and therefore should not try to transcend its own world and construct social ideals. But it is precisely with respect to this fundamental attitude that the whole Marxian theoretical endeavor, more than any single text or group of texts, exhibits its most complete opposition to Hegelianism!

Here, the basic point hardly requires any further defense. Far from being a theorist of "the ethical State," Marx looks beyond all state forms to the possibility of a post-political society; the most interesting issue concerning this is that of the exact degree of Marx's antinomianism. Far from agreeing with Hegel that philosophy (or rational thought, if one takes very seriously the Marxist thesis concerning the "end of philosophy" in its traditional sense) can only reflect its own time and is incapable of applying itself to the future, Marx orients his entire theoretical effort primarily in the latter time direction. Although it may be objected, and it is obviously true, that the overwhelming bulk of Marx's writings consists of critical analyses of past and present social structures and historical events, this does not in any way negate the fact that these analyses make complete sense only in the light of the Marxist presupposition that the existence of radically different social structures is a real future possibility. Although it is also true that Marx took very much to heart the Hegelian aversion to merely stipulative, *a priori* moralizing, so that the caricatural textbook approach to "systems of ethics" which presents them as if they were all alternative choices on the same level, like pies in a store window, is at least as absurd when applied to Marxism as it is when applied to the Hegelian philosophy, nevertheless there is a very prominent and important ethical vision of a possible future in Marx that is expressly omitted from the writings of his predecessor.

We may thus conclude this preliminary attempt to put into question certain familiar historical views concerning the allegedly negative relationship prevailing between Hegelianism and natural law theory and the alleged coincidence of Marxism with Hegelianism in this specific respect. Hegel's historically oriented social philosophy is, indeed, an important turning point in the history of thought, but it can be seen to have retained something fundamental from the natural law tradition when measured against the nascent legal positivism that was one of its contemporary rivals. And Marx most clearly repudiated Hegelianism on just that doctrine of "the ethical State" for which d'Entrèves, writing as one noteworthy contemporary defender of natural law theory, finds Hegel least congenial. It will now be appropriate to consider some of the positive evidence for my central thesis within Marx's own early thought.

3. It will be worthwhile to turn first to Aristotle in order to clarify my contention that important points of similarity prevail between Marxism and natural law theory. I am aware that many scholars are reluctant to count Aristotle as a natural law theorist in any very strict sense,[15] and I share this reluctance. Nevertheless, there is no doubt that the early, more universally-accepted formulations of natural law doctrine to be found in Cicero and in the Stoics have their basis in a certain pervasive conception of nature, of which human nature is a part, and that this conception itself had already received detailed and perhaps paradigmatic expression in Aristotle's philosophy. The suggestion that we return to Aristotle in this matter receives some initial sustenance from some kind words that Marx has to say about the Stagyrite in Chapter I, Part I, Volume I of *Capital*, in the course of discussing the crucial distinction between use value and exchange value:

> The . . . peculiarities of the equivalent form will become more intelligible if we go back to the great thinker who was the first to analyse so many forms, whether of thought, society, or Nature, and amongst them also the form of value. I mean Aristotle.[16]

Elsewhere, Marx calls Aristotle, simply, "the greatest thinker of antiquity."[17] The intellectual and even, as they might be called, temperamental affinities between Marx and Aristotle are very extensive indeed, and I think that they are of considerable importance for the present inquiry.

Both Aristotle and Marx tempered their tremendous underlying concerns for social ideals by laying great stress on the importance of what would today be called "empirical studies." Marx's diligent research into economic theories and data reminds one, in some ways, of the early efforts of Aristotle and his school with respect to the collection of constitutions. Just as the number of references made by Marx to an ideal society is quite small by

---

[15] "Aristotle passed for centuries as the 'father of natural law.' St. Thomas, in that section of his *Summa theologica* which deals with law, repeatedly appeals to him as the Philosopher par excellence. Aristotle, however, as should now be clear, was not the father of natural law. Nevertheless his theory of knowledge and his metaphysics have provided ethics, and consequently the doctrine of natural law, with so excellent a foundation that the honorific title, 'father of natural law,' is readily understandable." — H. A. Rommen, *The Natural Law,* transl. by Thos. R. Hanley (St. Louis & London: B. Herder, 1949), p. 16.

[16] Moscow ed., 1961, p. 59.

[17] *Ibid.*, p. 408.

comparison with the total quantity of his literary productions,[18] so only Book VII and the abbreviated Book VIII of Aristotle's *Politics* are devoted to the delineation of an ideal *polis*. Aristotle himself provides the rationale for his relative inattention, by comparison with, for example, Plato, to the construction of an ideal state when he lists four different kinds of political studies that should, according to him, be undertaken: the consideration of the ideally best constitution, he mentions, is only one of these. "Most of the writers who treat of politics — good as they may be in other respects," he says, "fail when they come to matters of practical *utility*."[19] Marx was similarly concerned to avoid the charge of "building an ideal [world] as it ought to be . . ., an unsubstantial element . . ."[20] which, moreover, never *could* come to be, and that is why he and Engels were always so anxious to establish a distance between their socialism and the varieties that they labelled "utopian." And yet, in the cases of both Marx and Aristotle, there never exists any doubt that their thinking about society is ultimately ideal-oriented. Aristotle's language, at any rate, contains constant references to the good life and the best life, and it is just because of this orientation that he was taken, by medieval writers such as St. Thomas, to furnish the basis for a political theory of natural law. These references, it is important to note, frequently include the qualifying adjective, "possible."

The concept of nature, *physis*, is, of course, one of the most prominent in Aristotle's system. There is, in that system, a close relationship between this concept and the category of possibility or potentiality: a natural entity contains within itself, at its inception, the potentialities for realizing its own highest perfection, its nature in the *fullest* sense of the word. Men, too, are considered in this fashion, and it is the same conception of self-realization of inherent natural possibilities that lies at the base of the Aristotelian ethics and politics. It is in this respect, I think, that the structural similarities between the Aristotelian and Marxist conceptions of social ideality are strongest. In his early writings, Marx sometimes equates the now much-disputed "humanism" of his thought[21] with "naturalism," and a glance at these writings shows his rationale, which is in some ways so strikingly Aristotelian, for using the

[18] In this and the following section, I shall allude to several of the relatively small number of texts that usually serve as the basis for commentaries on Marx's social vision. At least two of the most ringing and frequently cited phrases descriptive of this vision actually come from the pen of Engels; they are the metaphor of the ascent from the kingdom of necessity to the kingdom of freedom and the conception of replacing the government of persons by the administration of things, both of which occur in his essay, *Socialism: Utopian and Scientific*.

[19] *Politics* IV, 1, 1288b; Barker ed. (Oxford: At the Clarendon Press, 1946), p. 155.

[20] Hegel, *Philosophy of Right*, p. 11.

[21] For the disputation that has already become almost classical, see Louis Althusser, "Marxisme et Humanisme," in *Pour Marx* (Paris: François Maspero, 1966), pp. 225-258.

latter term. "Immediately," he writes at one point after making this equation,

> *man is a natural being.* As a living natural being he is, in one aspect, endowed with the *natural capacities* and *vital powers* of an *active* natural being. These capacities exist in him as tendencies and capabilities, as *drives.*[22]

Marx's insistence that man is, or at least can be, a *natural* and *objective* being also serves simultaneously as part of a polemic against Hegel's relegation, which Marx takes as demonstrating the fundamental alienation of Hegel's entire philosophical standpoint, of nature to the status of a mere necessary negative moment in the process of Spirit's self-realization.[23] But what is more important for our present purposes is to note the very clear sense in which nature is a normative concept with reference to human activity just as much for Marx in 1844 as it was for Aristotle and always has been for the mainstream of the natural law tradition.[24]

Marx, though the Aristotelian word, "possibility" or "potentiality," is not itself particularly central to his writings, in fact extends the *concept* of possibility far beyond its Aristotelian limits and thus effects a radical reorientation of the view of human nature as a norm. It may at first have seemed misleading to speak of human nature at all in reference to Marxism, for is it not possible to make a good case for the truth of Antonio Gramsci's claim that "the fundamental innovation introduced by Marxism into the science of politics and history is the proof that there does not exist an abstract, fixed and immutable 'human nature' "?[25] Surely, but this proposition does not refute previous contentions. For Marx's conception of normative human nature, as it emerges in his early writings, can be expressed by saying that *human nature does not yet exist, though it will be able to exist in the future.* Marxian "human nature," then, is a future possibility.[26]

---

[22] "Critique of Hegel's Dialectic and Philosophy in General," in Easton & Guddat, eds., *Writings of the Young Marx on Philosophy and Society* (Garden City: Doubleday & Co., 1967), p. 325. (It should be noted that the paragraph in which this particular formulation appears is among those which Marx later crossed out. But his reasons for this seem to have been more editorial than theoretical, since the thoughts expressed are so closely in keeping with the rest of the manuscript.)

[23] This point is clearly made, for example, by Louis Dupré, *The Philosophical Foundations of Marxism* (New York: Harcourt, Brace & World, 1966), pp. 122-133.

[24] I have added the qualification, "the mainstream," in deference to the fact that "nature" and the "natural" have been contrasted with and compared unfavorably to "reason" and the "rational" by some thinkers who, once the verbal difficulties of these usages have been surmounted, are seen clearly to qualify as natural law theorists.

[25] *The Modern Prince and Other Writings,* transl. by L. Marks (New York: International Publishers, 1957), p. 140.

[26] I find myself in initial agreement, therefore, with Georges M. M. Cottier, when he says: "Even when he did battle against the notion of human nature or against the notion of moral norms, Marx was inspired by [an] implicit norm of the truly human." — "Marx's

It is precisely this insight that serves as the basis of Marx's famous extended critique of alienation in these same early manuscripts. The objectionable forms of alienation of which he speaks are not conceived of as alienations from some primitive state of harmony and innocence ascribed to an enormously distant past,[27] or from some state of complete virtue which is held always to have been attainable by men of good will, if they happened to be living in virtuous societies and were endowed with a certain modicum of good luck, but are rather thought of by reference to an overcoming of them that, it is maintained, *could* take place in the future. It is only with this historical development that, according to Marx, human society would for the first time be truly humane. And although, as we shall see, it would be inappropriate to attempt conceptually to capture this society, in advance, within a determined set of fixed categories, it still seems to me correct to regard this vision as a logical extension of some very old themes in the Aristotelian and natural law traditions. Marx extends these themes even to the lyrical point of a discussion of the new possibilities for the human *senses* that would come about with the fundamental social change that is envisioned.[28]

Among contemporary Marxists, Ernst Bloch, the author of *Das Prinzip Hoffnung,* has shown special *finesse* in developing this conception of Marxism as a philosophy of human possibilities, though he is by no means alone.[29] It is interesting that Bloch is also the author of a treatise on natural law, a rarity among Marxist writers. Though Bloch shows comparatively little sympathy for natural law theory, particularly since he places great stress on the links between certain comparatively recent versions of it and a bourgeois individualism that denies human worth, even he rather grudgingly con-

Conception of Man," 8 *Natural Law Forum,* p. 97. However, I think that my present account of the framework within which Marx's attack on abstract conceptualizations of "human nature," to which Cottier refers, is to be understood is more satisfactory (i.e., less vague and fairer to Marx) than Cottier's conclusion that "this result [complete relativism, dissolution of the unity of human nature, a nominalist view of history] which seems to follow from Marx's historicism is compensated for, and even neutralized, by the affirmation that history is reason." — *Ibid.,* p. 101.

[27] Though one *can,* perhaps, detect a certain greater affinity with this romantic type of thinking in the writings of Engels, who was greatly influenced by Morgan's anthropological discoveries about primitive communities.

[28] "The overcoming of private property means therefore the complete *emancipation* of all human senses and aptitudes. . . ." (There is a significant word-play here on *Eigentum* and *Eigenschaften.*) "It is obvious that the *human* eye appreciates differently from the crude, inhuman eye, the human *ear* differently from the crude ear, etc." — Manuscript on "Private Property and Communism," in Easton & Guddat, eds., *op. cit.,* note 22, p. 308. It can be seen that the double meaning of the Greek root, *αἰσθ* —, has a philosophical significance for Marx, as for many other thinkers.

[29] The French sociologist, Henri Lefebvre, and the Yugoslavian philosopher, Mihailo Marković, are two others whom I would single out as also having made important contributions along these lines.

cludes, at the end of his chapter on "Marxist Distance from Law and also from Natural Law . . . ," that natural law "belongs to the noble power of anticipation of something better than what has happened up to now," and that it therefore has its source, like the utopian tradition with which he contrasts that of natural law and for which his preference is clear, in "the kingdom of hope."[30] But if this is so, then the alleged "distance" is not so great, after all.

All the various and often widely diverse versions of natural law theory can at least be said to have the common function of providing a rational basis for legal and political obligation. Such obligation does not always mean, of course, the obligation to observe every existing statute in a given locality at a given time; far from it, if we consider, for example, the implications of Aquinas' famous dictum that a positive statute which is in violation of the natural law is no law at all.[31] Marx, in his endeavor to achieve that union of theory and *praxis* (another noteworthy example of his employment of fundamental Aristotelian categories) that is most succinctly epitomized in the final clause of his *Theses on Feuerbach* ("the point is, to *change* it"), is also establishing, *eo ipso*, a basis of obligation to act — though the obligation in question would most correctly be called "social," rather than "political" or "legal." Moreover, like the traditional natural law theorists, Marx has a normative standard of human nature by which to measure or set a direction for such obligatory action; this standard, however, is of the very untraditional sort that I have noted.

Of course, this characterization does Marx something of an injustice by speaking of his thought in terms, notably that of obligation, of which he himself would not have approved. (No such compunctions were felt by Lenin or later Soviet writers, to be sure, but I have no hesitation in asserting that their simplistic moralizing constitutes a clear distortion of Marx's views on ethics.) Marx refrained from such language in order to stress the great difference in approach between his vision of future historical possibilities, based on a critical analysis of the structure of contemporary society, with all its internal contradictions, and the stipulative moralizing for which neither he nor

---

[30] *Naturrecht und menschliche Würde* (Gesamtausgabe, Band 6) (Frankfurt/Main: Suhrkamp Verlag, 1961), p. 237. Just prior to this conclusion, Bloch cites the famous passage in Marx's "Introduction to the Critique of Hegel's *Philosophy of Right*" in which Marx first clearly identifies the proletariat as the "universal class" — a sphere which "claims no *particular right* because no particular wrong [*Unrecht*], but *unqualified wrong*, is committed against it." Bloch comments: "But an unqualified wrong can as such neither be shown nor measured nor rectified if no unqualified right [*Recht*], no utopia of right [*Rechtsutopie*] is seen." The implication is that natural law theory (*Naturrecht*) at least served the function of making meaningful the notion of "unqualified right." (Translations mine.)

[31] *Summa Theologica*, Prima Secundae, 95, 2.

Hegel had any use. Nevertheless, it seems to me logically unavoidable, even if Marx considered it rhetorically inadvisable, to discern a certain theory of obligation in the remarks that Marx has left us concerning what Bloch calls the *Noch-Nicht-Gewordenen,* the human society or humane existence that is not yet. And this greatly facilitates the desired comparison between Marxism and natural law theory.

In summary, then, we find in both the natural law position traceable to Aristotle and in Marxism a view of human nature as a normative concept and at the same time as a descriptive one, in the special sense in which it is meaningful to speak of describing possibilities. For Aristotelianism, however, since it considers species, including the human one, to be fixed, this normative human nature is fully *given* at the present time; for Marx, men will only be able to become fully human after the achievement of certain preconditions (notably, the overcoming of scarcity by means of technological advances) will render fundamental social change possible in the future. Since such change is inconceivable apart from human agency, Marxism must be said to contain an implicit theory of social obligation to bring it about. This set of obligations, even if prudential considerations have usually prevented Marxists from employing such language, constitutes the Marxist equivalent of natural law.

What remains to be explored is the precise kind of natural law theory that would be most consonant with the structure of the Marxian approach to obligation as I have outlined it. But first, it is important to try briefly to meet the now-familiar objection that the approach on which I have concentrated, while it may be Marx*ian,* in the sense of being the product of the youthful Marx's pen, is not Marx*ist,* in the sense of representing the final formulation of Marx's ideas. Although this contention, based as it is on the historical claim that there is a sharp discontinuity between the thought of the earlier and of the later Marx, could conceivably be dismissed as philosophically irrelevant (for there is no good reason, other than a built-in, rather unphilosophical prejudice in favor of old age over youth, for regarding a writer's final works as necessarily his best or "most definitive"), it is of sufficient significance for the contemporary cultural situation to which I alluded at the beginning in order to merit at least a few comments.

4. Out of considerations of space, I shall have to be somewhat dogmatic in asserting my agreements with scholars, such as Shlomo Avineri, who find greater continuity than discontinuity of insight and systematic thought running through the entirety of Marx's writings.[32] The thesis of discontinuity

[32] See Avineri, *The Social and Political Thought of Karl Marx* (Cambridge: Cambridge University Press, 1968) and my review in *The Journal of Value Inquiry* III, 3 (fall 1969), pp. 228-233.

("*coupure*," to use the now-consecrated word), which has able defenders in Cornu,[33] Althusser, and a number of other contemporaries, usually takes Marx's *Theses on Feuerbach* and *The German Ideology* (a joint production of Marx and Engels) as the most crucial, though not necessarily the final, turning points towards an allegedly new theory that finds full expression in *Capital*. Though important differences in terminology and principal subject-matters clearly do exist, these by themselves are insufficient to establish the stronger thesis concerning basic theoretical divergences. The rejection of Feuerbach, previously so highly regarded by Marx, undoubtedly does carry with it a certain theoretical shift. But I do not believe, though I cannot here provide anything close to an adequate proof, that this shift is nearly so radical as some would maintain.

The rejection of Feuerbach, whatever its exact implications may have been, has an important bearing on the main theme of this essay. Some commentators see Marx as beginning, in this critique, to leave behind the humanism and naturalism of his early period. I would distinguish between the two concepts, admitting the abandonment of the first but not of the second. In Feuerbach, as in so many writers since his time, "humanism" becomes a sort of substitute for religion; man is the object of worship. Marx, at first attracted to this approach, came to see its shallowness and impotency as an intellectual tool for dealing practically with the inhumanity of existing social structures.[34] But this change did not, I think, radically affect the conceptual affinities between Marx's thought and those earlier philosophical considerations about nature as normative that I have just discussed.

It is in *The German Ideology* itself that one finds that most lyrical of all passages about a future society in which it will be

> possible for me to do one thing today and another tomorrow, to hunt in the morning, fish in the afternoon, rear cattle in the evening, criticize after dinner, just as I have a mind, without ever becoming a hunter, fisherman, shepherd, or critic.[35]

Here, the not uncommon Marxian combination of seriousness and satire

[33] Auguste Cornu, *La Jeunesse de Karl Marx* (Paris: Librairie Alcan, 1934).

[34] Engels' account is revealing in this regard. After dealing in some detail with the effect that Feuerbach's *Essence of Christianity* had had on the Young Hegelians, including Marx, at the time of its publication (Engels was writing about it more than forty years later), he says: "The real idealism of Feuerbach becomes evident as soon as we come to his philosophy of religion and ethics. . . . The chief thing for him is not that these purely human relationships [sex love, friendship, compassion, self-sacrifice, etc.] exist, but that they shall be conceived of as the new, true religion." — "Ludwig Feuerbach and the End of Classical German Philosophy," in Lewis Feuer, ed., *Marx and Engels: Basic Writings on Politics and Philosophy* (Garden City: Doubleday & Co., 1959), pp. 216-217.

[35] In *ibid.*, p. 254.

relies on the basic "natural" occupations of men in the first stages of civilization and on the contrast between them and the typical occupation of the modern German ideologist for its effect. Some commentators, however, would maintain that this passage is *also* typical of what Marx later rejected.[36] If *The German Ideology* will not do, then we might have recourse to one of Marx's very late (1875) writings, his brief *Critique of the Gotha Program*, in which the final stage of communist society is said to be characterizable by the famous slogan, "From each according to his ability, to each according to his needs."[37] This emphasis on *needs* is of considerable relevance to our present concerns; I shall return to it in the following section. At the very least, it can be said to show that Marx never entirely abandoned the future vision to which his earlier writings point. Finally, we might reconsider *Capital* itself, for I do not believe that the theory contained therein will be found seriously to contravene any of the strands of Marxist thought on which I have chosen to concentrate.

It is from Volume I of *Capital* that I have already cited Marx's eulogies of Aristotle. The intellectual admiration to which they bear evidence goes deep indeed, far deeper even than the structural similarities concerning normative human nature with which we were concerned in the previous section. In Chapter 5, for instance, Marx discusses the peculiar phenomenon of money-lending, in which the usual form of circulation, M—C—M', "is reduced to the two extremes without a mean, money exchanged for more money" (i.e., without the intermediary of a commodity), and goes on to cite, without further comment, the core of Aristotle's bitter denunciation of usury. This invective, which causes even Hilaire Belloc at his most antiusurious to pale by comparison, ends with the comment, "But interest is money [begotten] of money, so that of all modes of making a living, this is the most contrary to Nature."[38] Later on, in the passage in which Marx calls Aristotle "the greatest thinker of antiquity," Marx reports that Aristotle dreamed of a possible world in which what we call automation would take over the work of production, so that there would be no more need either for apprentices or for slaves. With his usual very heavy sarcasm, Marx upbraids the "heathens" of antiquity for failing to see that the introduction of machinery "is the surest means of lengthening the working-day," a fact that constitutes one of the great "discoveries" of those political economists (Marx here mentions MacCulloch and Bastiat, two of his special *bêtes noires*) who have at-

[36] Feuer himself holds this, as his introductory editorial note in *ibid.*, p. 246, indicates.

[37] In *ibid.*, p. 119.

[38] Moscow ed., pp. 164-165. The reference is to Book I, Chapter 10 of the *Politics*, 1258 a and b (Barker ed., pp. 28-29).

tempted to give rational justifications for the most inhuman excesses of the industrial revolution.[39]

These passages reflect something much more significant than Marx's personal admiration for Aristotle, though they also reflect this, of course. Fundamental to the entire purpose of *Capital* is the insight that the existing (capitalist) economic system is not the only possible advanced economic system — that its so-called "iron laws" are not, in fact, eternal, and that it does not represent the highest possible development of economic man. The bulk of the evidence in support of this insight is developed by a method of internal criticism, beginning with some of the concepts (e.g., the labor theory of value) of the bourgeois political economists themselves; but this evidence is constantly being complemented by normative considerations, since the insight itself concerns an issue of norms (namely, what man's highest possible development might be). Among the most basic of these considerations are the two that are implied in the Marxian references to Aristotle that I have just cited: first, the "unnaturalness" of the dominance of the medium of exchange, whereby, in the capitalist system especially, it is enabled to reproduce itself and accumulate without limit in disregard of human needs, and second, the desirability of ending all forms of human slavery and subordination through a rational use of the productive forces that technological progress has placed at the disposal of modern society. Marx's economic analysis culminates in a demonstration that the unlimited accumulation of capital, for which he clearly shows a repugnance that has its roots in (though it is not reducible to) the Aristotelian and medieval view of unlimited individual self-aggrandizement ("acquisitiveness") as unjustifiable,[40] tends to be ultimately self-destructive for the capitalist system. With respect to the norm of ending human slavery and subordination, Marx the economist tries to show that Aristotle's "dream" has in our time begun to become really, technically feasible. And both these instances of complementarity between normative considerations and economic analyses illustrate important continuities between insights in Marx's 1844 writings and his later thought.

[39] "They [the heathens] perhaps excused the slavery of one [person] on the ground that it was a means to the full development of another. But to preach slavery of the masses, in order that a few crude and half-educated parvenus, might become 'eminent spinners,' 'extensive sausage-makers,' and 'influential shoe-black dealers,' to do this, they lacked the bump of Christianity." — Moscow ed., pp. 408-409 (Chapter 15, Section 3b).

[40] One of the clearest breaks between classical and bourgeois political theory occurs, it seems to me, in Chapter 5 ("Of Property") of Locke's *Second Treatise of Civil Government,* in which, precisely, unlimited acquisition is sanctioned on the ground that the institution of money obviated the previous moral prohibition against hoarding more perishable goods than one could consume. The historical links between Locke and the later political economists, as well as the ideological implications of their justifications of unlimited accumulation, are very suggestive for our present theme.

It is also true that, in the so frequently-cited Preface to *Capital* and elsewhere in that tome, Marx speaks of his having discovered the "natural laws" of a society.[41] This particular verbal affinity with the central theme of the present essay, however, conceals a tendency in Marx's later thinking that constitutes, in fact, one of the strongest pieces of evidence in favor of the contrary thesis of *dis*continuity between the earlier and the later Marx. For the type of "natural law" to which he is here alluding carries deep resonances of a certain model of the natural sciences, transferred to the social sciences, which was extremely popular in nineteenth-century thought and which, in my opinion, dominates the thinking of Marx's colleague, Engels. It implies a strong determinism, historical inevitability — a theme of which Marx's earliest writings are comparatively free. It can be shown, I believe, that the prominence of this theme is not nearly so great even in Marx's later writings as the majority of critics maintain, or simply assume, and that its systematic elimination from the conceptual framework of *Capital* would not seriously damage the Marxist structural analysis that that work presents; for Marx himself speaks often enough of "tendencies" and "countervailing influences," and a conceptual framework sufficiently rigorous to perform the desired analytic task, though not to make those absolute predictions about future history which are so frequently attributed to Marx and so rarely to be found in his writings, can be constructed on this basis alone, without reference to allegedly absolute "natural laws." To prove this controversial point in detail would, of course, be beyond the scope of our present concern. However, it is important to note that *this* variety of "natural laws," based on nineteenth-century conceptions of the natural sciences, is of little or no use for our present purposes. It is either irrelevant or else actually opposed (it would be beside the point here to examine which formulation is more correct) to the meaning of that sort of "natural law" with which I have been attempting to show some Marxist affinities.

In the popularized versions of Marxism that were promulgated by Engels and, after him, by such diverse and mutually antagonistic "authoritative" turn-of-the-century theorists as Kautsky, Bernstein, and Lenin, the atmosphere is not particularly conducive to drawing the types of comparisons with which I have been concerned in this essay. Though this is not equally the case with all four of these writers (Lenin's work, in particular, encompasses a number of diverse theoretical tendencies that he never had the time completely to sort out and that make him potentially more amenable to such comparisons than most of his contemporaries), it can be shown, I think, that the natural

[41] Moscow ed., p. 10.

scientific model of "natural laws" to which I have alluded in Marx's later work is one of the major reasons, if not the single most important, for this less congenial atmosphere. Curiously enough, the emphasis on such "laws," even though it coexists with an insistence that each specific historical form of society has its own set, tends to diminish the sense of the possibility of radical historical change that one encounters so strongly in those elements of Marx's thinking to which I have been paying the greatest attention here.

The reason why this is the case can be epitomized by considering the fate of a short passage in Engels' posthumously published *Dialectics of Nature*. In this passage, he lists three most general dialectical laws which he takes to be applicable both to nature and to human history at all times;[42] as innocent as Engels' intentions might have been in scribbling down this particular formula, it came to be used as one of the keystones in a dogma known as "dialectical materialism" which still passes for Marxism in the Soviet Union and many other places. Precisely by presenting Marxism as a cosmological system capable of treating all of human history and in particular the era of capitalist society as increasingly specialized cases *sub specie aeterni*, "diamat" certainly *does* constitute an important shift in direction away from the sort of Marxism that we have been considering. But this shift is neither *primarily* the responsibility of Marx himself — even of the "later" Marx — nor has it proved, since Marxist scholarship ceased to be considered the private property of writers sanctioned by the C.P.U.S.S.R., to be irreversible.

5. We may now turn our attention more directly to natural law theory itself. My comparison between the "naturalism" of Marx and the proto-natural law theory of Aristotle has already indicated a direction in which to look in order to discover the variety of natural law that would be most compatible with Marxism. Marx, as Antonio Gramsci pointed out, denied the existence of "an abstract, fixed and immutable 'human nature.'" It seems most natural to ask, therefore, whether the notion of a historically *changeable* natural law is a tenable one. If it *is*, as I would contend, then this would seem clearly to be the variety of natural law theory upon which we ought to fasten.

Against the contention that historically changeable natural law is a tenable

[42] "It is, therefore, from the history of nature and human society that the laws of dialectics are abstracted. For they are nothing but the most general laws of these two aspects of historical development, as well as of thought itself. And indeed they can be reduced in the main to three:

"The law of the transformation of quantity into quality and *vice versa;*

"The law of the interpenetration of opposites;

"The law of the negation of the negation." — Engels, *Dialectics of Nature,* transl. and ed. by C. Butt (New York: International Publishers, 1940), p. 26.

and meaningful concept there stands a large body of historical evidence. Cicero, in the famous passage in the *Republic* which is so often cited as one of the earliest and most concise statements of the dominant natural law tradition, ringingly proclaims that "there will not be different laws at Rome and at Athens, or different laws now and in the future, but one eternal and unchangeable law will be valid for all nations and for all times. . . . "[43] In a fashion not untypical of contemporary writers, Guido Fasso, even while advocating the adoption of a "critical, non-dogmatic" version of natural law that would be historically oriented, acknowledges that "the characteristic of immutability was one of the few, '*per non dire il solo*,' that all the natural law doctrine of the past agreed in affirming."[44] He would find considerable agreement among both friends and critics of the natural law tradition.

The historical evidence itself, however, is not one-sided. Even Thomas Aquinas, for instance, occasionally indited the statement, "*Natura humana mutabilis est*."[45] Rudolf Stammler, the German Kantian philosopher of law, employed the formula, "natural law with changing content"; this formula arouses considerable uneasiness in the modern Thomist writer, Rommen, who nevertheless finds no difficulty in admitting the possibility of a change in content "with respect to the more remote conclusions."[46] Leo Strauss, interestingly enough, contrasts St. Thomas with Aristotle precisely on the ground that the latter, but not the former, accepts without qualification the changeableness of "all right — hence also all natural right."[47] Thus, contrary to what is perhaps the prevailing academic folk wisdom, the opinions of those who have considered it more carefully do not convey an impression of absolute uniformity within the tradition on this issue.

Beyond the pro's and contra's of historical debates, it seems to me, it is at least *logically* arguable that important strands in the traditional conception of natural law would remain if the phenomenon were to be regarded as historically changeable, and that this fact legitimizes the retention of the old

[43] *De Republica* III, xxii, 33; translation in d'Entrèves, *Natural Law*, p. 21.

[44] *La Legge della Ragione* (Bologna: Il Mulino, 1964), pp. 232 and 202. The full citation is from my review of this book in 10 *Natural Law Forum* (1965), p. 252.

[45] For a discussion of these texts, see Rev. M. D. Crowe, "Human Nature — Immutable or Mutable?" in *Irish Theological Quarterly* 30 (July 1963), pp. 204-231. Father Crowe stresses the importance of considering their contexts and of weighing them against the great number of comments by St. Thomas which carry opposite implications. One recent writer who cites these texts as evidence in support of his own theses, and to whom Father Crowe therefore pays considerable attention, is Charles Fay. His "Human Evolution: A Challenge to Thomistic Ethics" (*International Philosophical Quarterly* II, 1, Feb. 1962) develops an argument for natural law with changing content largely on the basis of anthropological considerations; he has apparently been influenced in his thinking by the writings of Père Teilhard de Chardin.

[46] *Op. cit.*, note 15, pp. 229 ff.

[47] *Natural Right and History* (Chicago: The University of Chicago Press, 1953), pp. 157-158.

label. To express it in the most general terms, what would remain is the view that, on the basis of an analysis of men in society and of the nature of man as it *could* be, characteristics are discoverable which indicate the desirability — or, to put it more strongly, the obligation in principle — for men to follow certain sets of rules rather than others with relation to their life in common in society. Once warning has been given that the expression, "the nature of man," is potentially misleading because it may connote an invalid reification, the qualified statement stands, I believe, as defensible. Accordingly, I shall now proceed, very sketchily, to outline one possible theory of a mutable natural law.

The preferred procedure is a detailed analysis of men in society as agents — as being characterized by, to use the Aristotelian-Marxist term, "*praxis*." Such beings, it can be shown, must always act in accordance with *rules* felt to be binding;[48] this would hold true even in a possible ("*antinomian*") future society that lacked legal and political institutions in any of the forms in which we know them today. (Such beings are also, of course, potentially criminal and potentially revolutionary; that is, they are capable both of deliberately violating certain of these rules and of putting the obligatoriness of the rules themselves into question.) Finally, these beings are characterized by the fact that they have *needs* that require satisfaction. The satisfaction of these needs leads to the development of *new* needs. Any widening of the range of satisfiable needs, which can come about through changes in men's material conditions, is equivalent to extending the field of human possibilities.

For the theorist, the most difficult problem is to decide just which features of the needs and possibilities of any given human society to treat as being relatively important and which as less important. This decision must be founded as completely as possible on an objective description of the structure and future possibilities of the particular society under investigation. The natural law theorist must thus be intensely aware of the historical conditions of his time, but he must not allow the results of his analysis to be dictated by any of the would-be authorities of that time — whether governments, or political parties or movements, or churches, or the findings of public opinion polls, or the tugs of his own subjective preferences and prejudices. The important thing for him to bear in mind is that such an analysis, however well executed at a given time, will not necessarily be valid for a future time; from this point of view, the task of analyzing men's social structures is unending, and it will

[48] For some important reflections on this, see, *inter alia*, Peter Winch, *The Idea of a Social Science and Its Relation to Philosophy* (London and New York: Routledge & Kegan Paul and The Humanities Press, 1958). The same point is also a fundamental presupposition of many modern philosophies of law.

always need to be done over again, because those structures are always capable of undergoing significant changes.

The results of such an analysis will be twofold: first, an enunciation of those social actions for carrying out which there exist the greatest human needs, and secondly, a working out of the set of rules that will have to be followed if these actions are to be carried out and the needs thus satisfied. Such rules can then be designated, after some further refinements, as the *natural laws* — natural because derived from a concrete analysis of real men in society and a projection of what "human nature," regarded as a social norm, would be like if their needs were met; laws because binding on all if this result is ever actually to be achieved. In this particular theory of natural law, it should be pointed out, there is a reconciliation between two senses of the word, "natural," that have often led to antagonistic theories in the past. For to act in conformity with the natural law, as I have defined it here, is at once to be most fully cognizant of the fact that men are parts of the world of *nature* (since they are creatures of need) and to pay the fullest possible attention to the demands of *reason*.

In the further elaboration of this type of concretely based theory of historically changeable natural law, additional complexities will inevitably arise, since the satisfaction of some of the needs enunciated will be seen to inhibit the satisfaction of others, so that the definitive set of natural laws for a given time cannot be completely worked out until preferences have been established among them. These preferences, as I have already indicated, cannot be the subjective preferences of the theorist himself. Here, the category of *possibility* — human society's possibilities, expanding with changing material conditions, for future development of the range of satisfiable needs — can furnish him with a basic criterion. For a rational decision as to which social actions to prefer in the present must take into account above all the question of which courses of action would lead to the fullest possible satisfaction of needs in the future. Courses of action that would restrict the future extension of human possibilities are to be rejected in favor of those that would promote it.

When our theorist considers the present world, in particular, he will find that it is an inhuman one in which many human needs are not met. His knowledge of future possibilities, given the concrete historical situation in which he finds himself, will indicate that these needs do not have to *continue* to remain unmet to nearly the same extent. Moreover, it is conceivable (and not incompatible with this procedure) that he may find the present historical situation to be unique, in the sense that the possibilities for overcoming, in some definable sense, the material scarcity that is at the basis of at least some of the most important kinds of human need may now exist for the first time.

What I have tried to do here is briefly to indicate a certain *framework* in terms of which the rules of a historically changeable natural law could be conceived. Serious problems arise at two decisive points in the analytic procedure that I have indicated. The first is in the process of considering alternative possible future social developments in order to determine which are *in fact* likely best to satisfy human needs and extend the field of human possibilities, and the second has to do with the choice of rules, when more than one set of rules appears feasible, for achieving this desired goal. The latter may frequently be treated as a question about "tactics"; only in certain cases does its resolution raise serious issues for a theory of rational action and social obligation. In these cases, it is crucial to recognize that the opening up of human possibilities in the course of history is an ongoing process, and that the discovery of the appropriate rules of action, of natural laws in my sense, should therefore be made in the light not only of a more distant future time but also of intervening periods. Thus, if two or more alternative sets of "laws" seem equally appropriate at first, there is an obligation to select that set which seems, upon closer scrutiny, less likely than others to sacrifice the possible satisfaction of human needs in the present and of further developed needs in the more immediate future.[49] The first-mentioned problem, however, that concerning alternative possible future social developments, is far more difficult to deal with. Its resolution ultimately depends, it seems to me, on the exact details of the initial concrete analysis of men in society.

And it is here that Marxism may be reintroduced as a complement to the theoretical procedure, based on the conception of a historically changeable natural law, that I have sketched. There is nothing in that sketch that runs counter, in my opinion, to any basic aspect of Marxist theory, and yet its language is somehow not that of Marxism. Why? My sketch, though it contemplated the concrete analysis of men in their particular social and historical settings, referred to this intellectual operation in highly formal, abstract terms, which would presumably be applicable to any and all times and places. (Only in my one-paragraph allusion to the possible uniqueness of the *present* historical situation did I make any more time-bound reference.) Much of the best natural law theory of the past has been elaborated on a similarly high level of abstraction; St. Thomas' fundamental precept, "Good is to be done and evil is to be avoided," and Kant's categorical imperative (if we follow d'Entrèves, as I agree that we should, in placing Kant within the tradition

[49] Leszek Kolakowski is a contemporary writer who, in his battle against Stalinism, has advanced some particularly cogent considerations along these lines within a Marxist context. See *Toward a Marxist Humanism* (New York: Grove Press, 1968), esp. the section on "Responsibility and History," pp. 85-157.

in question) are examples of this. Marxism, on the other hand, emphasizes the analysis of the particular historical situation and, consequently, particular content rather than abstract form. A conception of natural law which regarded it as historically changeable would be able to combine these two different emphases.

Near the beginning of my theoretical sketch, I pointed out the difficulty that the theorist would face in deciding which features of the needs and possibilities of any given society to treat as being relatively important and which as less important. Karl Marx, in his analysis of advanced industrial social structures of the mid- to late-nineteenth century, made a number of such decisions. Presumably, our own society is still sufficiently like his to give his conclusions considerable relevance. He pointed out, for instance, the dominance of economic factors, broadly defined, in the social structures that he examined. He demonstrated some of the ways in which the legal and political institutions that he saw as contributing in many instances to the denial of satisfaction of human needs in his society were themselves tributary to the requirements of the market system. And so there was and is a relatively determinate content to the concrete, "phenomenological" analysis[50] upon which the theory of social obligation that can be constructed from Marxism is based.

To the extent to which this particular analysis is considered acceptable, the serious problem, faced by the theorist of a historically changeable natural law, of deciding which of several alternative, logically possible future social developments is likely best to satisfy human needs receives, at least to a considerable degree, its resolution. For, first of all, the most desirable future society can be partly described negatively, that is, in terms of those features that it would *not* have, and such features are, precisely, those that the analysis has shown to alienate and restrict human individuals in the present. A clear *direction* in which society ought to develop is indicated, therefore, by a consideration of repressive features that it will be possible to eliminate. Secondly, one can legitimately make a series of *positive* projections of desirable and possible future developments, starting with whatever phenomena analysis has revealed to be of positive value in the present. Such phenomena may be

[50] I am using the adjective "phenomenological," in a broad sense, without necessarily implying any very close connection between Marx's method and the phenomenological movement in philosophy. It is important, however, to realize that a procedure to which this adjective may appropriately be applied lies at the basis of Marx's analysis. In one passage in *Capital* (in the very rich Afterword to the Second German Edition), Marx refers as follows to such a "method of inquiry" which, he says, must precede the finished presentation:

"Of course the method of presentation must differ in form from that of inquiry. The latter has to appropriate the material in detail, to analyse its different forms of development, to trace out their inner connexion. Only after this work is done, can the actual movement be adequately described." — Moscow ed., p. 19.

defined as those realities that are playing some role in efforts to abolish existing restrictions on human possibilities in the present state of affairs — "negations of negations," to use the formal Hegelian terminology of the early Marx. If, for example, the analysis has shown certain sociopolitical movements, such as the "communism" of which Marx speaks in one of his early manuscripts, to be playing such a role, then one can go on to conceive, in the detailed fashion in which Marx does in this manuscript, of decreasingly restrictive forms of such movements.[51] And so, by means of such a series of projections, a certain conception of the desirable future society, and hence of a normative standard of "human nature" by which to establish a direction for obligatory action in accordance with the historically changeable natural law of which I have been speaking, begins to emerge. Its basis, it should be clear, is the outcome of the initial concrete historical analysis.

It must be recognized, however, that any such positive projections will be at best only partial, subject to the potential bias inherent in any act of judgment, limited by the poverties of our own imaginations, and characterized by the tendency to become increasingly vague as they are carried out even further. (It is no mere coincidence that Marx's description of the highest form of communism is so vague.) The quantity of such possible projections of present possibilities is indefinite, as are human possibilities themselves. And so there can be innumerable positive descriptions of increasingly humane ways of acting in an increasingly human future; the very opennness of the vision permits the greatest possible amount of creative thought about future society. But it would be a mistake either to regard any particular set of such descriptions as definitive, or to think that any particular structure can be imposed upon, or final parameter placed around, the vision. (To speak of "the vision," as if it did, in principle, have parameters, is really just a concession to the limitations of language.)

In the final analysis, therefore, it should be recognized that the "ideal" that is the outcome of the sort of analysis that Marx conducted, and that I have

[51] In the manuscript in question, "Private Property and Communism," Marx distinguishes among three forms of communism, the second of which contains two subcategories. It is not clear whether he intends his division to be a necessary genetic one or simply a listing of alternative possibilities. At any rate, he regards the first, which he calls "crude, egalitarian communism," as levelling, filled with envy, contemptuous of talent, and yet dimly grappling towards a society of free individuals by virtue of its recognition that the alienating, restrictive phenomenon of private property must be abolished. The successive categories of his enumeration ("(2) Communism (a) still of political nature, democratic or despotic; (b) with the overcoming of the state, but still incomplete and influenced by private property, that is, by the alienation of man. . . . (3) Communism as *positive* overcoming of *private property* as *human self-alienation,* and thus as the *actual appropriation of the human* essence through and for man; . . . as completed naturalism [and] humanism") are increasingly positive projections of those possibilities for abolishing alienations which can be discerned even in the generally repulsive egalitarian form — *op. cit.*, note 22, pp. 303-304.

proposed for consideration as part of the procedure to be followed in elaborating a theory of a historically changeable natural law, has no *fixed* "nature" at all. Marx himself was very much afraid of abstractions — in particular, of the abstraction of "society" regarded as if it existed in independence of the individuals who constitute it. To delineate in detail the content of an envisioned ideal future "state of affairs" would be, precisely, to engage in an exercise of hypostatization, reification, abstraction.[52] By contrast with any such abstract ideal, the individual is real and concrete, and progressive social movements are real and concrete. The purpose of such movements — the "ideal," if one still wishes to express it in this way — is to abolish all those abstractions, such as state and law and fixed moral and economic systems, which have, through a process of mystification born of the past relationship between material conditions and human needs, become existing realities of a derivative kind ("superstructures," to use the familiar term that has unfortunately engendered many mystifications of its own), preventing the satisfaction of certain human needs and thus limiting the development of individual human possibilities. It would be highly illogical to work for this abolition only for the sake of a new, proposed, future abstraction. Consequently, for Marx and for any theorist who follows a similar path, the ideal is an open one — not specifiable in any bounded, definitive, once-for-all way.

If, nevertheless, as I maintain, this ideal can be made to serve as the basis of obligatory rules based on an analysis of the nature of man, then it fulfills the same essential function as that intended by earlier theorists within the broad natural law tradition. The consensus of that tradition may well have been that human nature, together with the "laws" of conduct which were discernible from the elaboration of a normative conception of that nature, was fixed; the insight that Marxism contributes with special cogency is that this is not the case. On the other hand, the contributions that can be made to Marxism by the revised theory of natural law which I have so briefly sketched are by no means negligible, either. In particular, the questions that can be asked of Marxism from the standpoint of a theory of historically changeable natural law point to possible formulations of a Marxist philosophical anthropology (the need for which has been much discussed by con-

[52] As the previously mentioned manuscript on "Private Property and Communism" concludes, "*Communism* is the necessary form and dynamic principle of the immediate future but not as such the goal of human development — the form of human society." — *Ibid.*, p. 314. Interpretations of this final sentence vary, but it seems to me clearly to imply Marx's unwillingness to reify human nature, even as a future social norm, in any *fixed* "state of affairs." This is confirmed by the following passage in *The German Ideology:* "Communism is for us not a *state of affairs* still to be established, not an *ideal* to which reality [will] have to adjust. We call communism the *real* movement which abolishes the present state of affairs." — *Ibid.*, p. 426.

temporary "Marxist humanists"), a doctrine of social obligation, and a conception of human behavior as "lawful," in the sense of "rule-governed."

But may it not be true that such a formulation reduces Marxism, after all (and very much against the wishes of most Marxists), to just an extension of the "*philosophia perennis*"? Since there is no suggestion, in the theory as outlined, that a time may come at which the questions to which I have referred will no longer be capable of being asked, it would seem that the older natural law tradition of immutability may implicitly have been vindicated, after all. For both Marxism and the theory of changeable natural law that I have sketched make use of several related characteristics, such as *praxis* and need and rule-governance, that are assumed to be transhistorical and attributable to man as such. "The revolution," if it ever took place, might bring about many fundamental changes, but it could not conceivably do so in *these* respects.

In response to this concern, assurance can be given that no "reduction" of Marxism is contemplated. The structural characteristics in question cannot be used as the basis for any system of norms of specifiable conduct that would necessarily be applicable across all time, since they are defined primarily in terms of capacities, potentialities, possibilities, and not substantively. Man considered purely in the abstract, as a being of *praxis*, of need, and of rule-following, is capable of engaging in an indefinite number of activities and assuming an indefinite number of social forms.[53] My point, in keeping with the theories of Marx, has been that this correct but abstract conception of man, when taken by itself, is one-sided, inadequate, and contentless. By contrast, the views that I have been attempting to bring into conjunction, when they *are*, in fact, joined, confer a sense of direction on the parade of human possibilities and thus make it possible to regard some of them as privileged.

6. In this essay, I have (1) advanced some considerations from contemporary culture for inquiring into possible common points between Marxism and natural law theory; (2) put into question a few assumptions of historical scholarship surrounding the allegedly high degree of incompatibility between the two traditions; (3) exhibited, with the aid of references to Aristotle, certain features in the doctrines of Marx's early writings which lend themselves to an interpretation favorable to a comparison with natural law theory; (4) denied the contention that these features were totally rejected by Marx in his

[53] When conceptions of an alterable "human nature" are advanced, it is usually the case that only men's socially relevant characteristics, and not their purely biological ones, are at issue. This does not, however, preclude either the possible social relevance of some biological characteristics or the chance that the latter, too, may change significantly over time.

later works; and (5) defended, by outlining one possible version, the conceivability of a historically changeable natural law that could have as its complement a concrete Marxist social analysis. Combined in a single social philosophy, I showed, these two strands of thought would lead to a very open vision of a possible future.

Underlying all the considerations and arguments that I have advanced has been the presupposition that neither natural law theory nor Marxism has come down to us bearing a single, canonical interpretation. In the case of natural law, this general point is usually accepted without dispute — except, perhaps, with respect to the one traditional feature that I have been concerned to challenge, namely, its alleged immutability. In the case of Marxism, my presupposition is more likely to meet with resistance, in part because the theory bears the name of a single individual, but in greater part, I suspect, because certain past and present political leaders *have* in fact pretended to be its canonical interpreters, and these pretensions have too often been accepted at face value even by their opponents. Marx's own writings, however, are at best suggestive rather than definitive concerning the topics of this essay, and the pretensions of the political leaders in question are, of course, mere mystifications. Once the mental barriers created by such mystifications have been surmounted, the resulting interchange between these two putatively antagonistic systems of social thought will prove more valuable, both intellectually and culturally, I think, than any "dialogue" in which the participants remain primarily at the level of their respective political and religious institutions.

[5]

Zdravko GREBO (Sarajevo)

»KELSENISM« AND MARXISM[1]

We will begin with the paraphrase of a statement by Kelsen, which I consider for a great part true: the most obvious feature of the Marxist classics' law theory is its »un-obviousness«. This indicates exactly to what Kelsen terms an »intolerable neglect« of this phenomenon within the whole teaching. In the »pure theory of law« this social set — state and law, and their unity — is situated on the normative plane exclusively; thus its most obvious flaw, in the above-said context, is its »over-obviousness«. In the writings by Marx and Engels, on the other hand, these categories are attributed to the sociological plane; or, to be more precise, political (state — law) theory is exhausted in the state. In this sense, what is said of the state, applies mutatis mutandis »also to the law«. Kelsen's teaching is a juristic theory of state and Marx-Engels' theory is a state - teching on law. In spite of the shared postulate about the necessity of an uniform methodological approach (to state and law), these are not two same things. I believe that it is this very feature that is the source of disagreements, both among the Marxists and no less among the non-Marxists, Hans Kelsen being one of them.

---

1. The decision to give this title to the contribution for the discussion upon the relation of the Marxist and classic methodology of law is supported by at least two reasons.

The first and more important one is the atempt to prove the applicability and value of the classic normative method of law cognition as a whole. Here I have in mind that there may be slight disagreements upon the statement that completendness demonstrated by H. Kelsen in the 2nd edition of »Reine Rechtslehre«, Wien, 1960, became the paradigm for the considerations of normative method in general. The purpose would be formulated with a greater accuracy if we said that the following pages try to prove that within the Marxist conception of law there is, among other manners, a legitimate space for the application of the normative method, since the polyvalency of the law's being shows, for a significant part, its normative face. In the same time it implies that we will not deal with normativism in particular, which in a very definite sense is not a methodology but a philosophical doctrine, and can on no cognitive level be joined with Marxism, as being — in one of its aspects — the same.

The second reason is of completely personal nature. The whole deduction will be checked using Kelsen's well-known challenge of the theoretical and methodological validity of Marxist approach to law, to the material we dealt with in more detail on another occasion (see »Marx and Kelsen«, Svjetlost, Sarajevo, 1979). The paper thus represents a synthesis adjusted to the subject we will discuss on this occasion.

Let us consider one thing at a time. H. Kelsen stresses that he agrees with the Marxist view on the uniform approach to state and law in basis (structure) — superstructure relation. This, however, in a specific sense: for him, this relation — »sociological dualism«, as he used to say — is analagous with the nature — society relation, since particular rules, different from the causal laws of natural reality, also apply to the whole social sphere — both to basis and to superstructure, spoken in Marxist terms. According to our critic, all social creations would make the ideology, »superstructure« (ideality), economic structure of the society being one of them; and the »real basis« would consist of the causally determined system of nature. Immediately a question arises, as to whether this parallelism (not accordance) in the conception of »sociological dualism« is the adequate ground for the »immanent criticism«. The answer must be a definite 'no'. Since, the actual reason of the critical failure is in that Kelsen attempts to stuff his neo-Kantian moulds with the »Marxist scheme«.[2]) As if pronouncing immanently Marxian postulates, he keeps using his own categories of »reality« and »idea«. Nature — society and basis — superstructure models, however, are not so easily compared. To criticise the latter from the viewpoint of the former — (i. e. »his own« (critic's) meaning) which is not his own — in the same time leads to an inevitable stumbling upon the discrepancies, if not even absurdities.

For Kelsen, the law is a (legal) norm. A norm is the »content of acts of will«. Nothing beyond this content, which is spiritual in character, is law. »An external fact, the objective meaning of which represents a legal or illegal act is... a part of nature and hence determined by causality. However this event as such, as the elements of the nature is not an object of legal cognition and hence are not legal at all.«[3]) According to Marxian teaching, on the other hand — (the interpretation is only a brief outline and thus inaccurate) — political, juristic, etc. relations and institutions, their origin, genesis and outcome, the nature of their function and aim, rest upon the economic structure of the society. It means that all the things mentioner are essentially determined by the economic »manner«, although the state-law phenomenon is not denied any independence and, consequently, a »feedback« impact on the economic structure. This »gradation«, however, and the reciprocal influence undergo various »Marxian« interpretations. According to ne version, state and law manifest in army, police, jails, property, rule, ... and thus are not the »forms of consciousness« (ideology), but actual — real social institutions and real social relations; »reality«, hence »nature«. Ideology in the proper sense is shaped only upon the political and legal superstructure.

2. Cf. I. Sabo, Gans Kel'zen i marksistkaja teorija prava. Sbornik statej: Protiv sovremenoj pravovoj ideologii imperializma. Izd. Inostrannoj literatury, Moskva, 1962, pp. 301 and 304/305; Bogdanov O. V., Tumanov A. A., Fal'sifikacija marksistskoj teoriji prava, Sovetskoe gosudarstvo i pravo, no. 3 1957, p. 146. See also, M. Adler, Die Staatsauffassung des Marxismus, Verlag der Wiener Volksbuchhandlung, Wien, 1922, pp. 86—89.

3. Reine Rechtslehre, p. 3.

According to this explanation,[4]) political and legal superstructure, together with production forces and production relations, constitute the social being. It is only this being that determines the consciousness (conception, »theory«) and it is only the consciousness that can be tinged with ideology. Our critic seems to agree at least with a part of such a teaching, since for him the ideology »in its true sense« can only be such a »law philosophy« or a »state theory« which justifies or attacks the »real« state or the »real« law.

Another possible interpretation, that can also be built upon the classic writings, is the one which consider the state and the law as the ideology. Whether their determinig factor is seen in the »basis« or in the »civil society«, the outcome is that these are derived (dependent) phenomena belonging to the ideological superstructure. This variant — like the first one (?!) — is also founded upon the too-much-known Marx' preface to »A Contribution to the Critique of Political Economy«. It is the statement starting with: »In social production of their life people enter the given, necessary relations . . .«, continuing with the sentence (that served as an argument to H. Kelsen also): »Human consciousness is not determined by their being. . .« and ending with »Together with the changes in the economic basis the whole vast superstructure is also, more or less quickly, being revolutionarised . . . (and) . . . a distinction must always be made between the material revolution in the economic production conditions . . . and juristic, political, artistic or philosophical, briefly i d e o l o g i c a l (spac. Z. G.) forms, in which people become conscious of the conflict and are solving it with a struggle«.[5]) Engels has similar, but much clearer descriptions in this respect: »The state appears before us like the first i d e o l o g i c a l force over a man. The society creates, for itself, organs for the protection of its shared interests . . . This organ is the state. Once it is created, the organ becomes independent in its relation towards the society . . . Having become an independent force, however, the state soon c r e a t e s a further ideology . . . Since in this case economic f a c t s must take the shape of legal motives . . ., legal form should be everything and economic content nothing . . .«[6]); or, elsewhere: »The reflection of economic relations in the shape of legal principles is also inevitably turned upside down . . . And this distortion which, unless it is descovered, constitutes what we call the i d e o l o g i c a l c o n c e p t i o n . . .«[7]) etc. According to all the things mentioned — less the quotations and much more the essential

4. V. Tumanov V. A., Buržuaznaja pravovaja ideologia, Izd. Nauka, Moskva, 1971, pp. 239/240; Similar in I. Sabo, op. cit. pp. 302/303.

5. Prilog kritici političke ekonomije (A Contribution to the Critique of the Political Economy), Izabrana dela (Selected Works), tom I, Kultura, Beograd, 1950, pp. 337/338.

6. Ludvig Fojerbah i kraj klasične nemačke filozofije (Ludwig Föerbach and the End of the Classic German Philosophy), Izabrana dela (Selected Works), II, pp. 384/385.

7. Pisma o istorijskom materijalizmu (Letters on the Historic Materialism), Kultura, Beograd, 1960, Engels to C. Schmidt, p. 41.

polarisation in the theory of law (and state) under the Marxist insignia — it indeed seems that there exist, in this domain, a m b i g u i t i e s, at least in the interpretation. The ultimate attitude, if possible at all, can be justly taken only after the repeated considerations of state and juristic issues of ontological nature and of methodological approaches to the phenomenon of state and law. Kelsen's criticism should by no means be ignored in this procedure.

»Inquiries« would, I think, again lead to the results showing — according to Marx — that »neither legal relations nor state forms can be understood within themselves or within the so-called general development of human mind. On the contrary, they are rooted in the material living relations the integrity of which was expressed, by Hegel, by the term »bürgerliche Gesellschaft«.[8]) Hence the »outflow of law« in the »material living conditions« and thus determined and shaped cultural development of the society. In its most profound preconditions it is an expression of »methajuristic facts«. This should underline, to a still greater extent, the Marxist »juristic« postulate: the law h a s n o h i s t o r y of its own, but springs from the material living conditions; or to put it simpler, from civil society built upon the private property and class relations, or from the »modern production relation«.[9]) Real social relations — even those regulated by law and being only its »real« manifestation — are not created by state (with law) but vice versa, they themselves create its power and »its« law.[10]) To use Gurvitsch' phrase from »Kelson-criticism« — they

8. K. Marx — Predgovor za »Prilog kritici...« (Preface to »A Contribution to the Critique...«), Izabrana dela (Selected Works), I, p. 337.

9. This approach is especially insisted upon by U. Cerroni. See »Diritto ed economia-Rilevanza del concetto marxiano di lavoro per una teoria positiva del diritto« Rivista internazionale di filosofia del diritto XXXV, 1958 and »Kelsen e Marx« Rivista internazionale di filosofia del diritto XXXVII, 1960. Continuing the thesis of the »non-existence of the autonomous history of law« Ceronni says that the »understanding of ideal (legal and all the ideological) relations is possible only within the given social (material) relations that find, in them, their »historical function« ... »The history of thought and ideal relations is included within the real history and represents an expression of social typology of the latter«. See also Ceroni's work »Marx e ill diritto moderno«, pp. 71, 76. Here we read that »the ideal world of law functions with the world materially determined by the contemporary law ... is an expression of a real social relation of production« ... It is, in fact, a »methodologic reduction of norm-making towards a sort of social material relation ...« Quotation according to Ž. Anzulović, Klasici marksizma i pravo, Zbornik radova, Pravnog fakulteta u Splitu, LV, 1966, p. 31.

Similar theses were pointedly advocated by Stuchka and Pashukanis — see Pashukanis' »General Theory of Law...« — and in Yugoslavia by Lj. Tadić, who was directly inspired by the »Soviet revolutionary law school«.

10. Cf., in this respect, Marx-Engels' »Werke«, 3. Bd. p. 331, Quotation according to »Philosophical grounds ...«, p. 143. It is interesting that H. Kelsen has — lexically — almost the identical statement. Cf. the review of the book by F. Lenz, »Staat und Marxismus« Archive für die Geschichte des Sozialismus und der Arbeiterbewegung 10 Jhg 1922, p. 447, »The reduction of the overall social process to »economic« determinants like primary or even exclusive is as mistaken and onesided as Lenz' ascribing to »force« or ... »state« the same role that the Marxists, he fights against, ascribe to the »economy«.

are »sources of law's sources«. If real relations determine the state and the so-called state law, they no less determine the so-called private law, »which essentially only sanction, in given conditions, normal economic relations between individuals«, Engels wrote. This sort of preconditions during the »juristic development« becomes more and more immediate; hence also more manifest and can be recognised with more exactness. Capitalistic legal forms — as is said by G. Lukács.[11]) as distinguished from the forms existing in the previous social and economic conditions where they made a constituent part of economic relations — has the function of f i x i n g links and relations functioning in a p u r e l y economic manner. It does not, however, lessen the truth of the statement that the ruling class, in the shape of general »public« (i. e. legally shaped) will expresses its own side of the social relation; its own »will«, since both itself and its will are determined by the character of these (material) links and relations. This is the meaning of the Marxist »social necessity«. Indeed, ruling class »must« want these and such — legal — relations. One could perhaps conclude that to follow Marx »juristically« primarily means to search for the real content of the »ought« of which then cannot consist of a mere higher »Sollen« as the answer to »why ought?« but exactly in the recognising if the »w h y«. It therefore implies the beginning at where Kelsen »finishes«; on the margins of the »order-created set of norms« that must be overstepped, on the destroyed limitations of the closed Sollen — system, in the moment when even the »pure theory of law« — truly or by a logical procedure (speculation), does not matter — must turn ideality, normativity, meanings to reality, facts, efficiency; or presume logically all this in the hypothetic »Grundnorm«.[12])

The first degree of law — law as a r e a l s o c i a l r e l a t i o n — is the »legal t r u t h«.

Law is, therefore — (for the time being, for easy reference we deal with »pure«, homogeneous notions) — reality, »nature«. H. Kelsen says: »... law ... with at least one part of its being, stands in the sphere of nature and seems to have quite a natural existence«.[13]) Does this quantita-

---

11. For more detailed reference see G. Lukács, Povijest i klasna svijest (History and Class Consciousness), Naprijed, Zagreb, 1970, pp. 119 and futher.

12. In »Der soziologische und der juristische Staatsbegriff«, Verlag von J. C. B. Mohr (Paul Siebeck) Tübingen, on p. 98 and further, Kelsen says: »On the other hand, we must establish the irrevocable fact that a triumphant revolution leads to f a c t u a l changes in state ideology, that it makes juristic considerations begin from a new basic norm, different from the previous one... F o r c e h a s b e c o m e t h e l a w« ... »Still« — and again the famous Kelsen's methodological 'still' (—Z. G.) — »The whole observation directed towards the shaping of the original norm (Ursprungnorm) content and the relation between the content of state or 12 (ctd.). legal order and the corresponding being (Sein) is completely beyond the cognition aiming at the state or law ideology as a spcific intellectual content (Sinngehalt). Only the latter cognition allows the u n i t y considered as the state (or legal order). Naturally, this should not cause any doubt in the importance of the first kind of observation; only establish its methodological difference«.

13. Reine Rechtslehre, p. 2.

tive measure (difference) — »at least with one part« — authorise the claim on the Marxist »natural law manner«?[14]) The point is somewhere else. Kelsen actually believes that each consideration of law beyond the limits of the positive law — relating and inquiring the relationship between law and other social phenomena, is illegitimate, from the viewpoint of the law theory.[15]) In the beginning of »Reine Rechtslehre« he writes: »In a completely uncritical manner, jurisprudence has been confused with psychology and sociology, with ethics and political theory. This confusion might be explained by the fact that all these sciences deal with subject matters doubtlessly closely tied with the law. When the pure theory of law undertakes to delimit the cognition of law against these disciplines, it does so not because it ignores or denies the connection, but because it tends to avoid the method syncretism which obscures the essence of the science of law . . .«[16]) Why is then the Marxist approch to law of natural law character; especially when having in mind the qualitative connotation that the »critic« ties with everything bearing a mark of the natural law. Marx only says that the fundamental legal principles are determined by the production and the corresponding class relations. They are not a priori derived (required) by a natural law's procedure, though they p r e c e e d the positive law. The basic principles spring from the essential, »distinctive« features of the social and historical moment; these are the p r i n c i p l e s of a given society, and »juristically« they grow out of the general rules applied to the law and the state. But, as is correctly observed by I. Sabo, »it is precisely because they rest upon the production relations, which determine the character of the society, that they do not have the character of the natural law, they do not preceed the society, do not spring from the mind or from the nature. . .[17]) Marxists do not recognise the classic dualism

14. Yugoslav professor Lukić almost agrees with Kelsen in maintaining that point. Cf. Lukić's review of Kelsen's book »The Communist Theory of Law«. Anali Pravnog fakulteta u Beogradu III, 1955, p. 231—236. Other writers from socialist countries are also willing to agree, conditionally, with the qualification of »natural law«, V. A. Tumanov, op. cit., p. 344. Also I. Sabo, op. cit., pp. 330/331.

15. In order to substitute for what Marx clearly terms as »material living conditions« — and what our critic regards as the metaphysical »natural law« postulate in Marxist juristic teaching — Kelsen uses the »basic norm«. As the most critics of the »pure teaching« observed, it is only the »latent natural law«. Is it not suggested by the author himlef: »If the n a t u r a l l a w can be seen in the basic norm which is here, in spite of its rejecting all the moments of material justice, defined as a necessary presumption of any positive law cognition, the statement can be as hardly denied as the designation of the categories of transcendental philosophy, since they are not given in the experience but establish it themselves, like m e t a p h y s i c s. It is simply a matter of the m i n i m u m, of metaphysics and natural law respectively, for the ability to conceive both nature and law... Hence the theory of the basic norm can best be described as the t r a n s c e n d e n t a l — l o g i c a l n a t u r a l l a w.« »Die philosophischen Grundlagen, der Naturrechtsichre und Rechtspositivismus, Pan-Verlag Rolf Heise, Charlottenburg, 1928, pp. 66, 68.

16. Reine Rechtslehre, p. 1.

17. More detailed in I. Sabo, op. cit., pp. 329—333.

in law — there are not two normative systems that could be in conflict with each other, since both »natural« and »positive« law have one and the same basis.[18])

We should now test the only remaining possibility. Marxist law theory, due to its (»materialistic«) constituent elements mentioned, could perhaps — in a Kelsenian sense — satisfy »at least« as the sociology of law? Since, the »Critic« points out, triumphantly and ironically at the same time: Anyway, if the »characteristic contribution of Marxism« should lie in the conception of state as »a part of society« one cannot help asking whatever theory does not consider the state as a part of society. The notion of society, in the broadest sense of the word — within which state and »society« in its more narrow sense may become »opposed« — is generally recognised. Nobody has ever maintained that state is not a social phenomenon.[19]) Or, as far as the law is concerned: The actual, history-made law order is by no means an accidental thing but an inevitable one, since it was created in a causally determined manner.[20]) Finally, — Hans Kelsen was forced by the polemic urge to express himself in the most explicit way possible: »According to my teaching, there is a normative and a »sociological« jurisprudence, which describes law in Seins-statements and is thus an empirical science ... In »Reine Rechtlehre« I also speak of the juristic sociology as a legitimate science ... «[21]) It is not clear then, why has the attempt to create a Marxist juristic science completely failed — and the reason for this is in that Marxism is »only one of the sociologies«, of sociological theories.[22]) It was now up to »the one« who utters contradictions, to decide: either Marxian social theory is not the

18. Cf., in this respect, in V. A. Tumanov, op. cit., pp. 343—344: See in detail in S. K. Vračar — »Socijalna sadržina funkcije državnopravnog poretka«, Beograd, 1965. (Social Content of the Function...), especially The Second Part: The notion of the function of state and juristic order.

19. Sozialismus und Staat, Archiv für die Geschichte des Sozialismus und der Arbeiterbewegung, 9. Jhr. 1921, p. 22.

20. Logisches und metaphysisches Rechtsverstandnis, östereichische Zeitchrift für öffentliches Recht, XVIII, 1968, p. 5.

21. General Theory of Law and State, Harvard Universiy Press, Cambridge-Massachussets, 1949, pp. V, XV, 164 etc. 21 (ctd.) The line mentioned is found in »Logisches und metaphysisches ...«, p. 23, and the attitude in Reine Rechtslehre, that Kelsen reminds of, is expressed as follows: »Legal sociology ... asks ... which were the causes that made the legislator create the norms the way they are and what were the effects of his orders. It asks in what manner the economic facts... factually influence the activities of the legislator and the court, what motives drive people to adjust themselves or not their behaviour to the legal order«.

22. See »Conclusion« in »The Communist Theory of Law«, Stevens & Sons Ltd. London, 1955, p. 193: »The attempt to develop a theory of law on the basis of Marx' economic interpretation of society has completely failed; and the reason for this failure is in the first place the tendency to substitute for-instead of adding to-a normative interpretation of the law, ..., a sociological inquiry of the conditions under which such a normative system comes into existence and is effective«.

»right sociology«[23]) or else, in spite of the declaration, an authoritative sociological statement about state and law is not possible at all. The latter answer seems more probable. Since, although wrapping it in the veil of methodology, Kelsen is quite clear when saying: (Only) having distinguished law from nature, and science of law as a normative one from all the other sciences aiming at causal cognition ... the safe criterion can be obtained for the unambigous separation of society from nature and social science from natural science.[24]) Nowhere does he speak of »normative« as distinguished from another science of law but of the science of law »as a normative one . . .«. He does not speak of two sciences of law, but of the »natural and social science . . .« After all, Kelsen was very clear and straight in rejecting the relevance of the sociological aproach, which »tends to treat the law as a mere fact«: — »a naturally given part of reality« — in his introductory writing already.[25]) If Marx maintains that the objective content of law is determined by production and class relations, and Kelsen says that »the norms of positive law spring from the voluntary act (Willkür) of the legislative authority«,[26]) and that: »Daher kann jeder beliebige Inhalt Recht sein. Es gibt kein menschliches Verhalten, das als solches, kraft seines Gehalts, ausgeschlossen wäre, Inhalt einer Rechtsnorm za sein;[27], then the leaving over the »contents« of legal notions to sociology, as M. Adler rightly says, »seems to be an »act precario modo«. Even polemics — an attack on the Marx—Engels' conception of law (and state) then shown itself as determined by and »antisociological« disposisition. It implies that the limitation of the Marxist state and law theory is actually

23. There is an interesting Adler's observation of a Kelsen's »oversight« which indirectly (directly?!) points to his evaluation of »Marxist sociology« and its scientific qualities. Adler observes that Kelsen in »Der soziologische und juristische Staatsbegriff«, — with a view to settling accounts with the sociological notion of state — deals with numerous sociopsychological attempts, such as Wundtom, Durckheim, Jerusalem, even Freud, while the Marxist attitude — »the only one«, as Adler put it, »that truly cuts the way to sociology instead of sociopsychology or sociometaphysics« — is not mentioned at all. »Naturally, if this conception of state is regarded only as a p o l i t i c a l theory of the Marxism . . .«, is what Max Adler concludes, not without an irony, Cf. op. cit... p. 70, Note 1.

24. Reine Rechtslehre, p. 78.

25. Cf. »Vorrede« for Hauptprobleme der Staatsrechtslehre, Verlag von J. C. B. Mohr (Paul Siebeck) Tübingen, 1923; also prefaces for Rechtslehre and Das Problem der Souverenität More detailed in H. Aufrioht, The Theory of Pure Law in Historical Perspective, Law, State and International Legal Order, University of Thenessee Press, Knoxville, 1964, pp. 30 etc.

26. Aufsätze zur Ideologiekritik, Luchterhand, Neuwied am Rhein-Berlin, 1964, p. 78. In this respect cf. remarks by R. Hofmann, Logisches und metaphysisches Rechtsverständnis, München, 1967, p. 20 and Kelsen's reply in Logisches . . ., p. 22.
The »relativisation of the law's content« in Kelsen's is also described by Lj. Tadić, Filozofske osnove pravne teorije Hansa Kelsena (Philosophical bases of Hans Kelsen's law theory), Veselin Masleša, Sarajevo, 1962, p. 120.

27. Reine Rechtslehre, p. 201.
See also Die Problematik der Reinen Rechtslehre, Öster. Zeitschrift für öffen. Recht XVIII, 1968, pp. 178/179.

a »sociological limitation«.[28]) But its broader aim — in M. Adler's opinion, is to point out once again, »in spite of the verbal persuasions« in the opposite, »that there cannot exist the sociological observation of the state«, especially of the law. The accurate formulation of Kelsen's programme[29]) goes on as follows: Recht ist Norm, Rechtswissenschaft ist Normwissenschaft. In spite of its wittiness, the phrase »methodological syncretism« is not quite convincing: »The essential significance (unerlässlich) of the knowledge of economy and its history for understanding the legal order does not imply that national economy and jurisprudence are m e t h o d o l o g i c a l l y the same sciences; are the two not often studied, in spite of their mutual relevance, even at different faculties.«[30])

Kelsen, thus, wants to study »law as law«. He has right to do so; »right of the subject choice« in the sense that this subject »has always been the central part of the observations in the legal science«. Does it, however, as Verdross believes,[31]) authorise the pure juristic teaching to quality all the other approaches as »Missverständnisse«? Kelsen frankly says: »The statement, understandable by itself, that law is the object of the juristic science, comprises the statement — a less understandable by itself — that legal norms are the subject of the legal science but human behavior only insomuch as it is defined, by a legal norm, as its condition or the consequence or, to put it another way — if it is the content of a legal norm. If human relations enter the discussion as a object of the legal science, they do so only as . . . relations constituted by the legal norm. Legal science inquires its subject »legally« i. e.: conceive it from the viewpoint of law. However, to conceive a thing legally can only mean to conceive it as the law, i. e. as a legal norm, or the content of a legal norm, as determined by a legal norm«. In the note under the text we read: »It is the attitude of the pure juristic teaching . . . as opposed to the Marxist theory which regards law as the aggregate of economic relations«.[32])

---

28. Adler believes that Kelsen's references to the sociology are only apparent, that what he terms as such at a closer inquiry shows to be partly the history of state and law and partly a sociopsychological treatment of legal and state relations. Cf., for more details, the quoted Adler's work, pp. 71/72.

29. H. Kimmel, Die Aktualität Kelsens,' Archiv für Rechts und Sozialphilosophie, XLVII, p. 291: »What is congruent from the first to the last version of the »pure theory of law« is the conception of juristic science as a n o n - c a u s a l — empirical, spiritual science a b o u t t h e s o c i e t y . . . Law is a norm, juristic science is a science of norms«. Simply, »R e c h t q u a R e c h t«.

30. H. Kelsen — »Rechtsgeschichte gegen Rechtsphilosophie?« pp. 3—4.

31. See A. Verdress — »Abendländische Rechtsphilosophie«, 2. Auft. 1963, pp. 190, 282 etc.

About the subject choice, in this sense, see also R. Walter — »Reine Rechtslehre und »Wertbetrachtung in Recht«, Festschrift für H. Kelsen zum 90. Geburstag, Wien, 1971, pp. 318/319, and »Kelsens Rechtslehre im Spiegel . . .« Öst. Zeitscrift für öffen. Recht, XVIII, 1968, pp. 331—352.

32. Reine Rechtslehre, p. 72. In the second edition of »Reine Rechtslehre«, which in its comprehensiveness and definiteness represents a Corpus Iuris Kelsenicus, the writer included only the statement of the rejection of the normative

*
* *

If there ever has been a juristic objection to Marx—Engels, it most certainly refered to the statement in »Communist Manifesto« about the law which is »the will of the ruling class turned into law«. »Will turned into the law«... by no means equals the »aggregate of economic relations«. In spite of all the »Marxian« juristic imprecisions mentioned in the beginning it is clear that law — (or to avoid misunderstandings: »legal form«) — is not a mere reflection of the economic basis. Law is a system; its structure is distinct, as it must be, in order to be able to perform the function imposed on it and »required« by the material »basis«. The distinctiveness mentioned is twofold: first, law is an expression of the class will, is established, according to Marx, like the public government — i. e. »like a necessary self-abnegation in legislation or law, and self-establishing the interests in the middle typical case«. As the state as the »official representative« includes the whole civil society of the age, the legislation (law) comprises all the individual (»ruling«) wills, that are inevitably egotistical in their individual existences, while in the legal, juristic form, they receive their average, objective, »ideal« expression.[33]) Needless though may be, I point out that this is the true meaning of the »Manifesto« words. Such a »systematic juristic necessity« is nicely illustrated in an Engels' letter: »... that a legislation represents a resolute, unsmoothed, true expression of the rule of a single class: only these words would be opposed to the »notion of law«.[34]) Thus the law starts on its long journey away from its real basis and source. The farther this field (each new — further step) is from its material pedestal and the closer to the »abstract ideology«, the more arbitrary it becomes — in the sense that it is determined only indirectly and adequate only approximately — and hence, as Engels says, can manifest its real substratum »according to circumstances, sometimes well and sometimes poorly«.[35]) The law itself — in itself — is, consequently, established as the ideology — »juristic principles are turned upside down« — and a new, independent field is

approach to law as an »ideological deceit« (although he has a very rich analysis of Marxist juristic speculations). Cf. the sub-chapter 26. »Die Leugnung des Sollens; das Recht als »Ideologie«, pp. 107—113. We read, for example: »The possibility of the normative juristic science, i. e. the science which describes the law as a system of norms becomes uncertain... after the argument that the legal obligation (Sollen), the expression of which is a norm, is senseless or is an ideological deceit... It is a typical element of the Marxian social teaching«.

33. This aspect of Marxian conception of law is in Yugoslav theory most radically and repeatedly pointed out by Lj. Tadić. See »Predmet pravnih nauka« (The Subject of Law Sciences) IDN Beograd, 1966; also »Filozofske osnove...« (Philosophical grounds...) and »Odnos bitka i trebanja« (The Relation between Being and Ought...) Godišnjak Pravnog fakulteta u Sarajevu (Annual of Sarajevo Law Faculty VII/1959.

34. »Letters...« Engels to K. Smit, p. 41.

35. Ludvig Fojerbah i kraj... (Ludwig Föerbach and the End...), Selected Works, II, p. 384.

being created still having, in spite of its general production — dependence, a separate potency of (independent) responding to its »basis«. It is exactly the »feedback impact« category, pointed out by the Critic also, that shows that the law — normative system, as a real occurence, is not the »ideology«; or to be more accurate: it is not the ideology in the usual sense of the word. It is not the ideology for it does not »lie« about the reality. Law as a norm is the ideology, but only as the idea, and it conceals and distorts nothing; it »reflects« accurately the reality. The fact that the reality is distorted and false is not a juristic sin. Normative system as an objectivised, formal one can only shape the content. Things change, however, if the contingency and history-dependence of the content are not taken into consideration and when its appearance in law is considered as absolute.[36]) Law as the ideality, like any ideology, is a distorted notion of the world, »false consciousness«, insofar as it offers an o n e s i d e d image of the world. (»In this sense«, the author goes on, »even Kelsen's law theory greatly consists of halftruths . . .«). »A halftruth«, (in the sense it has in the text quoted) is not a truth, but not a lie either; it is precisely — etymologically speaking — a half of the truth, a partial truth. . . Law as a norm — idea is a true as it can be, as the »consciousness« in general.

In the modern state, Engels writes, not only must the law be in accordance with the economic circumstances, but it must be harmonious itself, a h a r m o n i s e d entirety, »which by its inward contradictions« — that may be brought about by the immediate reflections of the economic relations in legal principles — »is not opposed to itself«. »In order to achieve all this it gradually looses the fidelity in reflection of economic conditions«.[37]) Law assumes an (seemingly) objective existence.[38]) On the

36. The ideological nature of law, in the true sense of the word, consists in overseeing the r e l a t i v e relation between (juristic) form and (juristic) content. Hence Kelsen's logical formalism« is not an essential obstacle for the understanding of »Marxist teaching on form-content relation«, as believed by I. Sabo; and particularly not of »Lenin's attitudes ... that form has the content and the content — the form«. It is no fundamental law of dialectics but a notorious fact known even by people with »poorer« mental capacities than those of H. Kelsen. The things are exactly the opposite. (For more details see I. Sabo, op. cit., pp. 306—308). About the form and content »n o t b e i n g t h e s a m e«, Marx says the following, in his treatise on rent: it is on this form of expression, which conceals the true relation and creates exactly the opposite image that all the juristic notions are established, both among the workers and among the capitalists, all the mystifications of the capitalist ways of production, all the illusions of freedom created by them, all the appologetic excuses of the vulgar political economy...« And all this is possible only because the legal relations are the f o r m of e x p r e s s i o n of the production relations.

L. Basso, la teoria communista del diritto, Mondo operaio, 1956, pp. 396/397, rightly observes the source of the »ideologisation of law«, but derives too strict, »anti-Kelsenian« conclusions.

37. Engels in his letter to C. Smit, p. 41; or in »Ludwig Föerbach...« p. 383: »law sanctions economic relations »but the f o r m of doing so may differ greatly«.

38. It is recognised even by the authors otherwise insisting upon the law as a »social relation«. Cf. J. B. Pašukanis, Opšta teorija prava i marksizam (General Theory of Law and Marxism), V. Masleša, Sarajevo, 1958, p. 579.

other hand, the distinctive shaping of law is influenced, as is the case with all the other spiritual phenomena, by a particular »history« of the discipline. In this respect, law does have »the history of its own«. This statement is true for law more than for anything else: its »Roman foundations« are another proof that the »transfer of values« is, in the ideality sphere, immanent to its notion. Law is thus shaped like a relative independent, distinctively structure whole, funcioning according to distincitve rules. If Kelsen's term [39]) »Rechtswirklichkeit« did not remind so much of the idealism, it could almost wholly be applied to what we here want to designate as the second degree of law and/or the first degree of law ideology. Speaking in M. Stockhammer's words, Kelsen »has indeed discovered a new world«, establishing that the juristic pattern is not a causal one — and the discovery should be made use of. It is there — in the »constructive Kelsenism« — that the lasting value of the »pure theory of law«[40] lies. It allows the juristic idea (ideology) to be considered properly: keeping in mind, doubtlessly, its »imperfection«. No »dialectic notion of the normative« can be of any use in this sphere.[41]) Law as a system is structured according to principles of the formal »uncontradictory« logic and therefore may, in this respect, be consider only in this — »uncontradictory« — manner. This does not, however, answer the question whether such a consideration is a science, or only a skill, or perhaps not even that much. The answer depends on the solution of very complex methodological questions — one of the most important being: do the spiritual sciences exist at all?

It is, however, certain that as long as we deal with the law there must exist a »formal«, »uncontradictory« discipline (we did not say 'science') about the law. And Kelsen does belong to it.

»Sein des Sollens« is a distinctive existence within the law, is what H. Kelsen says. »Sollen« is here a copula, i. e. a »distinctive sense« linking, in any normative system, the cause and the consequence. »Sein«, in turn, is a »general term« (Inbegriff) for all the empirically given facts. The cause and the consequence are not established by thinking, considerations. »Sollen« category must not be abstracted and purified of any reality.[42]) But, as Kelsen repeats, »I maintain that 'Sein' must not be under-

39. Kelsen introduced the notion of »Rechtswirklichkeit« in his theory in 1919, using it in the treatise »Zur Theorie der juristischen Fiktionen«, Annalen der Philosophie, I. Bd., pp. 630 etc. See in this respect in Lj. Tadić, op. cit., pp. 52—55 and P. L. Zampettia, Metafisica e scienza del diritto nel Kelsen, A. Giuffre Ed., Milano 1956, pp. 9—11.

40. In the sense described by Helen Silving. See her treatise »The Lasting Value of Kelsenism«, Law State and International Legal Order, pp. 297—306.

41. As is believed by Lj. Tadić, Cf. »Povodom kritike...« (On the occasion of criticism...), APDN 3/1963, pp. 438/439: »...However, the dialectical notion of the normative is not identical with the juristic dogmatic normativism, where the norm (...) is the only form of legal reality...« By the way, Tadić has nowhere said what the dialectic notion of the normative »looks like«.

42. Cf. Reine Rechtslehre, p. 81: »Aufsätze zur Ideologiekritik«, p. 245; »Logisches und Metaphysisches...«, p. 25; »Die Problematik...« p. 161.

stood only as the real, i. e. »Natur-Sein«, but also as the 'Sein' in the sense of »gedanklichen Gesetztseins«.[43]) It is, however, a »Sein« different from the natural one. »Sollen« is the »ideal Sein«: »Sollen« representing a norm is the »Sein« but not »Sein« of the fact. »Das Sollen, nicht das Sein«.[44])

»Our« purpose does not require Kelsen's opinion about it: whether the »ought« is conceivable: whether it is a term or a category; can it be defined or not.[45]) Since, we can use Kelsenian »language« (apparatus, instruments) even without answering these questions. The fundametal question about the nature of law is answered marxistically. Therefore, when in »Reine Rechtlehre« Kelsen vrites that: »The term Sollen may be described in the same way in which G. E. Moore describes the term 'good': 'good' is a simple notion just as 'yellow' is a simple notion . . . definitions which describe the real nature of the object or notion denoted by a world, and which do not merely tell us what the world is used to mean, are only possible when object or notion in question is something complex«[46]) — it is more than true. Law as a complex phenomenon can (and should) be described in one of its aspects — law as a norm: idea, ideology — without saying, in this way, »what it means«. Such a knowledge shall remain partial, but it does not make it less needed or necessary.

The second degree of law, or the first degre of law ideology is the »legal halftruth«.

One could say that law in the degree described — as a norm, an idea — »inclines« to ideology in the proper sense, but is not the ideology itself. It becomes such in a still higher sphere, in jurisprudence, — where the law is »interpreted« in one way or other — and it is only then that the well-known Marxian »turning upside down« is finally shaped. It is only then that the real relations are expressed in abtractions, categories and notions that »are going to mean something«; they become »meta-

43. »Der soziologische und der juristische Staatsbegriff«, p. 76.

44. See »Der soziologische . . .«, p. 76: Das Naturrecht in der politischen Theorie«, pp. 122, 124; »Logisches und Metaphysisches . . .«, p. 24; Also: Allgemeine Rechtslehre im Lichte materialistischer Geschichtsunffassung, Demokratie und Sozialismus, Wien, 1967, p. 81: »Here the ought remains a comparatively a priori category for the comprehension of the empirical material in law. This category of law is — . . . — of a purely formal character. It remains unchanged . . .«.

Reine Rechtslehre, p. 5: »The norm as a specific sense of an intentional act aimed at someone else's behaviour differs from the act of will it constitutes the meaning of. Since norm is »Sollen« and the voluntary act it constitutes the meaning of is »Sein«; p. 10: »Validity is the specific existence of the norm. It makes the norm particularly different from the natural being. The »specific« existence of norms consists in the difference of this kind of »Existence« from the existence of natural facts . . .«, etc. Cf. the register in Reine Rechtslehre where the term »Form« has 57, and »Sollen' 20 entries.

See also »Die Problematik . . .«, pp. 150—153.

45. Leimninger, pp. 63 etc, e. g. maintains that Kelsen gave »eighteen definitions of ought (Sollen)«.

See Kelsen's answer in »Die Problematik . . .«, pp. 165—170. Cf., about the possible definitions of »Sollen« Hauptprobleme and Reine Rechtslehre.

46. Reine Rechtslehre, p. 5.

physical or juristic illusions«.[47]) Science jurists do not surpass these relations, »the notions freeze in their heads into fixed abtractions . . .« The respect of their own profession — the independent Idea of law. It is only when the partiality of the second law's degree is claimed to be absolute, the »Value«, that we are faced with the ideology in the most literal sense of the word. The abstract extensions of the existing situations are then completely torn off, and the »history of dreams«[48]) is ended.[49])

The third degree of law, or the second degree of law ideology is the »legal lie«.

This manner of deduction, which is believed to correspond to the authentic Marxian »purpose«, does not contain, as Kelsen would put it »at least an ambiguity«. Legal relations are real ones, since they are social relations, insomuch as the »legal traffic« functions in »the only« possible — since being material determinant defined — manner. The conclusion: law is a reality. But legal norms, which give a legal accent to social relations, constitute a normative system, knowing the region of spirit as its habitus, and thus having specific patterns of creating (structuring) and applications (functioning). It is precisely for this reason that the legal order can be different is similar (»same«) social circumstances, and similar (»same«) — in different social circumstances. Besides, law in this sense. as the consciousness, is the »reflection« and thus, as far as adequancy is concerned, is not a »lie«; it is true as much as the reality it reflects. Conclusion: law as a normative system is the ideal (conceptual) expression

---

47. »Letters« Marx to Anenkev, pp. 13—14.

48. K. Marx — »Prilog kritici Hegelove filozofije prava« (A Contribution to the Critique of Hegel's philosophy of law), Rani radovi (Early works), 3. ed., Naprijed, Zagreb, 1967, p. 96.

49. Engels draws the whole itinerary — going away from the reality — of the »ideological journey« of law as follows: »On a certain, very low level of social development a need arises to include the acts of production, distribution and product exchange, into a single general rule... This rule, originally a habit, soon becomes law. Law inevitably brings about organs in charge for its maintenance — and the public authority, the state is being created. During further social development the law develops into the legislation of smaller or greater extent. The more perfect the legislation grows, the farther its way of expression is from the ways of expression of ordinary economic conditions of the social life. It appears as an independent element which does not draw the justification of its existence and the explanation of its further development from economic conditions, but from its own, inward reasons... People forget that their law springs from the economic conditions of their life... The development of legislation... (into) a completed, extensive whole, leads to the necessity of a new social distribution of work; a class of professional jurists 49 (ctd.) is created and, with them, the science of law. In its further development it compares legal systems of different nations and different ages... not as the reflections of given economic relations, but as systems finding their bases in themselves. The comparison presupposes something shared... under the term natural law the jurists pool what is... shared by all these legal systems. But the criterion which measures what the natural law is and what is not can be only the most abstract expression of the law itself: the justice... And the justice is always an ideological, heavently — high expression of the existing economic relations, both of their conservative, and from their revolutionary side... Cf. »O stambenom pitanju« (on lodging issue), Selected works, I., pp. 601—602.

of social reality, which is not its equivalent and therefore possesses a distinct reality »of its own«.[50]) Law finally occurs also as the object of jurisprudence (in the broadest sense of the word), which describes the law only as a system of norms and is therefore established as an ideal (conceptual) expression of the ideal expression of reality, thus having all the features of the ideology in the true sense of the word. There is no particular need to point out that the three described moments unite dialectically and are »in actu« always given together. The distinction is required only for the analysis' sake.

One should nevertheless — for exactness' sake — consider the accuracy; or to put it better: the completeness of the deduction. It reveals an obvious hypertrophy of the factual (as primary) at the expense of the normative (as secondary, derived, »ideological« . . .). There is a certain truth in Kelsen's remark that — ortodoxly understood and interpreted — the basis-superstructure scheme »splits« the sociality (»men's social being«) into two essentially different entities and that such a proposition (assumption) — of their varied substantiality — creates problems regarding the »possibilities« for interinfluence; of transformation of one into the other; or the problems of »determination« and »feedback effect«. Engels' »exculpatory« commentary (given in the plural form) may perhaps serve as the explanation: »In other words, we first attached, and had to attach, the greatest importance to the deduction of political, juristic and other ideological conceptions — and the activities caused by them — from the basic economic facts. In doing so the content part made us neglect the formal part: in what manner these conceptions are being formed«.[51])

Following to the letter« made the Marxist theory of law neglect the normative at the expense of factual element in law; it was believed that their reversed or »equal« relation would be a betrayal of Marxian thought. I regard this 'raison' at least incorrect. Kelsen indeed is mistaken in his strict separation of the sphere of ought (norms) from the sphere of being relations), of law from nature, where no mutual mediation is possible. He is mistaken in making a hiatus between the logically existence and the being,[52]) hence in his criticism of the Marxist conceptions of the »legal

50. We think of the difference observed by U. Cerron. - »Kelsen Marx«, p 666, »Thus Marx — it seems to us — in the polemics with Hegel and the apriorism earlier and with the natural positivism later on, considered the twofold figure of the law as Anordnung (or the ordered totality of the society) and as Ordnung (or a part of the positive structure, without interfering with the norm) although the polemics conditioned the stress on the latter.

51. »Letters«, Engels to Mering, p. 46.

52. Though Kelsen in Hauptprobleme..., p. 8, speaks of »Wechselbeziehung zwischen Sein und Sollen«, from the beginning to the end he believed that the viewpoint according to which Sollen may be deduced from Sein rests upon the »fundamental logical mistake«, Cf., e. g., Reine Rechtslehre *RR*, pp. 5—7. Upon this issue see also a valuable study by Ulrich Klug- »Die Reine Rechtslehre von Hans Kelsen und die formallogische Rechtfertigung der Kritik an dem Pseudoschluss vom Sein auf Sollen«. Law State and... On p. 154 Klug says the following: »... Isn't it a curiosity of spiritual history, under these circumstances, that in spite of the

reflection« — where the »Critic« maintains that it is the »life« that reflects the norms, and not vice versa. The theory of »reflecting« the reversed direction and sign, however, is no less mistaken. Not because »the facts also exist in the superstructure« (Ž. Anzulović) nor because »there are ideological element in law, as a part of »reality« (R. Lukić) — and the law thus belongs »here and there at the same time«. As U. Cerroni rightly says, the solution is not in tracing the way of fact and value unification in order to assing the functioning of the former to the latter but — essentially — in allowing the way out of the fact — value alternative as an undefining and purely ideal one.[53]) The determining quality of the fact. the author goes on to say, is not... u t s i c, as to intercede at its own will, nor does the functioning which does not surpass the immediate identity of fact and law... The consideration should assume the fact not as an orientation for human behaviour nor as a mere natural fact. This course of thinking — as it seems to us — leads to the instance of the cognition of social reality, which can, in the same time, be distinguished both from the mere h u m a n b e h a v i o u r and from the n a t u r a l o c c u r e n c e s o r h a p p e n i n g s. Still it is clear enough that the problem remains closed between two terms — socitey and nature: t e r t i u m non d a t u r.[54]) This model was realised in our inquiry because it clearly indicates — directs towards the necessary diagnosis of the reciprocity between normativeness and factualness, between the ideology (»juristic ideology« also) and the reality, where the two planes do not interfere in their own individualities but the distinguishing between them does not dissolve into an unmediated unity. Such is the right course of the dialectic »juristic« thinking.

When we turn back, after this quite a large digression, to our subject (then) the statements about the Kelsen's »misunderstanding of Marxian notion of ideology« (Lj. Tadić) and about the »absolutely mistaken interpretation of Marxian thought« (L. Basso) are only conditionally true. Kelsen obviously did not comprehend the full complexity (nor completedness) of the problem — one could even say its essence and his »Criticism« is therefore deficient. Insisting upon the clearest cognition of law

---

world success of Kelsen and his purely theory of law the juristic wished-for dream (Wunschtraum) about the deduction of the »ought« (Sollen) from the »is« being (Sein) is still being dreamed...«

53. U. Cerroni — »Kelsen e Marx«, p. 665.

54. More detailed in this respect, U. Cerroni, op. cit., p. 665. Cf., by the same author, »Marx e il diritto moderno«: »One should recognise the r e a l twofoldness of the law: as norm — making which determines the type of the society organised for the exchange — mediated production and as norm-making which is d e t e r m i n e d by the objective material social structure; then the ideally natural polarity of the law (...); human — naural unity of the social relations themselves (The relations between man-specie-nature). The recognition of the r e a l mediation of the society and the nature seems to allow scientific mediation between the idea and the reality, between value and fact, between legal meaning and efficiency,...«.

possible, and upon the ideologically critical attempts in this respect, he by no means »abolished the deceit and indicated to reality« nor did he »correct the 'false consciousness' of the ideology«, as believed by N. Leser.[55]) What Kelsen »wants« in science of law is not reality but the ideology; or at least the »reality of the ideology«. But it should be admitted that his criticism did direct the attention towards the other (normative) pole of law phenomen, which in the Marxist theory is not considered, at least not enough; — towards what Kelsen himself — though the question remains as to how adequately — terms the »consequences of (law) ideology«. Only the integration of the both aspects of the phenomenon (that we are interested in) alows the overall cognition, and the cognition, in turn, implies the consideration (not construction) the relation between norm and reality; the Marxist (legal) meditation beween them« — is the right term. It is only then that »critical« objections of the contradictory views on law »now as the ideology« (superstructure), »now as the reality« (basis). After all, such a comprehensive approach is required by the dialectics as a method.

*

* *

It is therefore by no means true that Kelsen »understood nothing« of the Marxism. Although it is certain that Marx' thought has its depths and heights where the »Critic« could not descend or climb, it must be said that there is a level where he understood everything (or at least the major part) and criticised. The »criticism« is relevant where it is correct. And it is correct in Kelsen's 'fach'-field. Kelsen's »familiar ground« — a »special spirit« — is the structural analysis of the positive law, the normative and logical foundations of juristic doctrine, general teaching on the legal form: the »phenomenology« of the law. Such an approach by no means exhausts the whole phenomenon of law. Lukács is right when maintaining that »for Marxism, after all, there is no independent science of law, national economy . . . etc., but a single, unique — historical and dialectical science of the development of the society in whole«. Kelsen cannot understand this wholeness totality. Neither does he understand the wholeness of the law. He is hopelessly lost in his partiality — in the »specialisation« imposed on him by the postulate of the »pure« science. The science simply is not true since it is one-dimensional, »one-factorial« in its nature. But it is true in a part. »A part« is a part of the whole, and the whole is true.

»Kelsen's part« is the normativeness of law »in itself«. It is also one of law's qualities. Hence Kelsen here — while »spelling out« the other issues — speaks meritoriously and thus indicates to the still unsystematic foundations of the Marxist theory of law.

55. N. Leser — »Reine Rechtslehre und Sozialismus«, Begegnung und Auftrag, p. 162.

»The pure theory of law«, therefore, »with the good reason (of its own)« observes the »... permanent tension between the two poles of all the approaches to science...«, between »Sein« and »Sollen«. From its viewpoint — whether it admits it or not — the distinction is a pragmatic request allowing the cognition of phenomena the basic quality of which is the Koerzibilität. In this case, Kelsen's position cannot be passed over by any science comprising, as U. Klug says, the notion of »ought« or an equivalent one. »There will always be the discussion... about the »resolute« (schroffen) separation of Sollen from Sein. It is basically the same thing as the discussion about the »resolute« separation of a triangle from a quadrilateral«. Always? — limited!

It is, in other words, obvious that Kelsen's doctrine is a »fictio iuris«; not only a Grundnorm Als-Ob construction; the whole theory is the Als-Ob thinking: »what would (perhaps should) happen if?« It is perhaps a teaching on the »moglichen Recht«, but not a general juristic teaching. When Kelsen begins his most important work with the sentence: Die Reine Rechtslehre its eine Theorie des positiven Recth; das positiven Rechts schlechthin, nicht einer speziellen Rechtsordnung. Sie ist Allgemeine Rechtslehre..«, it should be noted that the general juristic teaching means a teaching on the general law, and it is not only a form. The content, the function, and so on and so forth..., may also be general.

Therefore, Kelsen must be rejected as a whole in order to be agreed with partially. »Kelsenism« (a term which according to H. Silving should designate the technical applicability of juristic considerations in the »pure theory of law«) as a methodology is a (constructive) Denkbehelf, allowing us to understand the »specificity« of law. It is essentially a »practical instrument« of juristic analysis. »Fixed, context — independent concepts« are the »code« compatible, though, by the relation of a purely formal compatibility, with all and »any« legal order. This is the technical validity of the Kelsenism.

The theoretical validity is found somewhere else. Though indirectly, Kelsen pointed to the, completely unjustified, »masohism« of Marxist »jurists: They deal with what they despise from the bottom of their hearts. When Stuchka says that there should be more »good communists« than »proleterian jurists«, it sounds excluding — one or the other. The essential mistake lies in the opinion that the law is a phenomenom of the bourgeoise society and that the science on law must be bourgeois. But as long as the law exists, and »Gotha programme« telles us how long it will be, it should be dealt with.The »juristic ground« is, in this respect, also the »Marxist ground«. Marxism seeks for the actual, thus also of juristic, totality. And does it adequately: and it means, partly, in the Kelsenian way. Otherwise a fault recurs that a Yugoslav critic reproached Kelsen for: »the law« (contradictions expressed in law) is being abolished only mentally; — Marxists do it omissively: they abolishe the law by not dealing with it. The »amnesia« in the Marxian attitude is partial: »the second part of the statement« is ignored. It is true that a theory »cannot be realised without abolishing it«, but it is also true that it »cannot (even) be abolished without being realised«.

If the universal law is, in the way shown in this paper, dual in character, the two elements not having the same force but possesing the equal ammounts of necessity, it should be considered in the same. dualistic, manner. A space must be found for Kelsen's contributions in this respect.

It is not our purpose to complement or complete Kelsen, in order to become a »Marxist Kelsenian«. Kelsen himself does not believe in complementing. And he is quite right in doing so. It is not the task of the Marxist theory of law to complement Kelsen, but Kelsen may serve as doubtlessly important (even decisive, regarding the part missing) — complementation »to a certain percentage« in composing the completed knowledge of law.

Kelsen starts from the World's dualism (the ontological one) and seeks for the methodological monism: a united science of law. One should, however, start from the unitedness of the World, for it indeed is a unity, and require (conditionally) a dualistic science of law, for its subject is dual. Kelsen's postulates has a more correct (formal) logic. I would not say that the latter is the »image« of dialectical contradiction, for it is not true. It is only a way of the overall cognition of the law. »The latter« approach is a constituent part of the overall Marxist method. This, though, with a note: Pleading for »the second also« — »Kelsenian« — approach implies the »materialistic turnabout of Kelsen«. With is, in Kelsen, »turned upside down« should be placed on firm »Marxist feet«. Since being a »materialistic friend of Hegel's« is not a sin, why should being »a friend of Kelsen's« of the same sort be this dangerous? By this, of course, I do not maintain that Kelsen is a »Hegel«. I only want to say that the »rejectors« of Kelsen seem to have learned nothing of the trough, the child and the dirty water.

[6]

The Historical Concept in the Science of Law of the XXth Century

by

K. Kulcsár

Institute of Legal and Administrative Sciences of the Hungarian Academy of Sciences

In its introduction the paper dealing with the relations between historicism and jurisprudence points out that the notion of historicism has assumed different meanings in conformity with various ages and societies and this is particularly important in its impact on the science of law. In its first part, the paper starting from the social contents of the historicism in the historical jurisprudence of Savigny tries to define what this historicism means for the science of law of today, respectively how from the viewpoint of our days this historical way of looking at things is assessed. In the second part those forms are treated in which historicism appears in the jurisprudence of today, namely in the Anglo-Saxon doctrine (historical theory of law and pragmatic sociology of law), in the natural law doctrines brought into harmony with historical ages and in conjunction with the latter in the European science of comparative law. It also touches shortly upon the changes occurred in the social and ideological contents of legal history. In its final part the paper when analysing the historicism of Marxist jurisprudence it is concluded that this manifests itself especially in three aspects: 1. Legal phenomena and the concepts expressing them developed in the course of historical evolution, consequently their cognition cannot be but of a historical character. 2. It follows that this cognition is conditional, dependent on the state of existing society in the science of law, too; but this fact does not mean that this cognition would not have resulted for the totality of the science of law in true and useful conclusions or methodological traits, though reflecting the given social conditions, too, and eventually considering as absolutely prevailing importance of the element originating therein. The history of ideas, therefore, has come particularly into prominence also in jurisprudence. 3. Historicism comprises the concrete knowledge of the present time, too, thus these two elements constitute together the sociological view of Marxist science of law.

The main point, the principal gist of the critique of historicism may be characterized even now by the motto of Nietzsche: »... *gegen die Geschichte*, das heißt gegen die blinde Macht des Wirklichen ...«[1] This motto, however, by Nietzsche meant the claim to an emancipation from the historical constraint of the action, to a release from the traditions, in a wider sense, from culture, and even more from science, the claim to escape from rational thought, a stand for free human action, and, as the second part of his chain of thought emphasizes, the courageous observance of the "must" (Sollen). The word "must" is used in this context as a matter of course, not a "must" determined by the laws of history, but a subjective "must", the social-historical content of which

[1] F. Nietzsche, *Vom Nutzen und Nachteil der Historie für das Leben. — Unzeitgemäßige Betrachtungen*, Werke I. Leipzig, 1903, p. 357.

was borne out by the right-wing demand for action which ultimately materialized as a concrete reality in the practice of fascism. Contemporary criticism aimed at historicism, however, has been by now directed against historically determined activity, it is based on the knowledge of the laws of history, it is directed against the kind of "must", which reflects evolving reality. This results particularly clearly from the analysis of Karl R. Popper according to whom historicism is characterized by the belief in the laws of historical determinism and this, respectively the scientifically conducted moulding of the society relying on their knowledge served only the tyrants and the Utopists.[2] But we could also mention Ludwig von Mises, who maintains that the political content of historicism, which at the beginning expressed conservative thought, has already changed in the twentieth century and has become radical.[3] All that goes to show unequivocally that the modern *critics of historicism assess it by generalizing it on the ground of a certain form of its manifestation,* namely on the ground of that form which recognizes that the laws prevailing in history are a reality and their cognizance and application are also within our power. We cannot now discuss the social grounds underlying this thought but the explicit views of the two authors quoted above show that such a hostility against history is connected with a certain general claim to get rid of the facts and laws of history and envisages to be operative against progressive actions in society based on the knowledge of the laws of history.

Historicism, however, does not mean at all in all forms of its manifestation such a standpoint which would recognize the determination of the historical process by laws. Consequently, the critique of historicism departing from such a starting point puts on the same level the various forms of its manifestation, despite their differring substance. The conception emphasizing historical individuality, for instance, which may be traced back to Ranke and which characterized, with some alterations, even the philosophy of history of Dilthey, eliminated from the history not only the concept of progress ("All ages are alike near to God") but also the determination by laws of the historical process. It is very important to stress this point when the historical concept is discussed in relation to the science of law. In effect, the historicism of Ranke is not identical with that of Savigny (although the historical individuality of the epoch plays a certain role in the doctrine of Savigny, too) and the historicism of the jurisprudence of today is more closely connected with the Ranke–Dilthey-line than with the line of Savigny, respectively the historical conception of Savigny forms a part, with a specific interpretation of *today*, of the historical views in the XXth century.

[2] K. R. Popper, *The Poverty of Historicism*, Boston, 1957, pp. VII., IX–X.
[3] L. v. Mises, *Theory and History*, New Haven, 1957, p. 198.

Consequently, speaking of historicism it should be pointed out at the outset that the *concepts* and so the concept of historicism, too, *may only be understood historically, in conjunction with the social phenomena in their background which are reflected in them.* The assessment of historicism in jurisprudence becomes particularly distorted if we look at it from the angle of identical levels, not marking the inherent differences. As a consequence, one side of the historical assessment of the historical view is the differentiation resulting from its interdependence with the social-historical conditions. There is no doubt, naturally, that in the evolution, in the formation of jurisprudence the most decisive factor is the evolution of the law itself but taken in a wider sense, that is to say, including its contents, the social conditions. The problems and claims of this evolution manifest themselves in the science of law. The mode of posing the problem and the way of its discussion, however, and particularly the attempts aimed at its solution *reflect the mental and in the first place philosophical aspect of the epoch of the society.* These traits express on the whole and essentially identical social trends, consequently, do not show substantial divergencies; but as the evolution during several thousands of years of the law and of the science of law has accumulated certain characteristics, which attribute specific character to legal phenomena and constitute specific elements in jurisprudence, the metajuristic, in the first place philosophical trends, categories and concepts which had had an impact upon the conception of the science of law carried with them the dead weight of their history, the assertion of which in many instances in many respects involves specific features in the methods of discussing and solving problems in jurisprudence. That is the reason why the jurisprudence of the same epoch and of the same society, although reflecting evidently essentially identical problems, has shown varied aspects.

Consequently, the historical view in jurisprudence is, on the one hand, historicism of a special kind, evolved in compliance with the requirements of the legal problems, and is on the other hand, in itself a varied concept, which is tied to the philosophical appearance of historicism which reflects, however, to a certain degree, also the history of this concept.

I.

In analysing the historical view in the jurisprudence of the XXth century, a remark made by Saleilles at the turn of the century may be taken as a starting point according to which the application of the history on social sciences is a creative force, but the historical school has stopped half-way.[4] The science of law was

[4] R. Saleilles, *L'Ecole Historique et Droit Naturel,* Revue Trimestrielle de Droit Civil, 1902, p. 80.

indeed dominated in many respects, especially in Germany, by the historical legal school, starting with Savigny, but historicism invaded jurisprudence elsewhere and in other ways, too. Let us remember e.g. the historicism of Maine which had been interwoven with sociological elements the effect of which remained important also in subsequent periods; furthermore the ethnological and comparative legal theories developed from the Hegelian ideology, etc.. As far as the particular historical school of Savigny is concerned, this lost effectively its dominating role at the turn of the century, but the historical view itself has come to stay, though in a different form and often under the surface, as one of the constituents of the modern science of law. It is true that the far-reaching trend developed at the turn of the century which is used to be summed up under the term of the *New-Kantian* philosophy, disregarded this very historical element. It is also true that various trends of the New-Kantian legal philosophy practically embraced the science of law in the first half of the century, especially on the European continent, although other trends of the philosophy of law too had come under its considerable influence. It may be stated, however, that *the temporary domination of the New-Kantian philosophy* is coming to an end, and — among others — more and more such trends, too, are coming into prominence, which, although they could not be unequivocally termed historical, nevertheless contain historicism in addition to others, as a major constituent. Thus, if the science of law of our century may in many respects be characterized by the "renascence" of things past, we have every right to state that the *novelty of old ideologies consists in many instances in their ties with the historical view.*

The time of the independent, specific historical school is a thing of the science of law because it had been the offspring of a distinct historical-social situation, historicism, which at those times had a certain social substance, is really coupled exclusively with the historical school? The development of jurisprudence is characterized by the fact that concepts which had become essential constituents of the science have originated in a certain historical-social situation and have appeared frequently with a claim to absolute exclusiveness. That happened also in respect of the historical school, the sociological jurisprudence or the New-Kantian philosophy of law, etc., which all have contributed something to the universal development and method of jurisprudence. Consequently, if we want to analyze the present role of the historical view in the science of law, we should attempt to assess the absolute manifestation of the historical view, i.e. the historical legal school, in a way, by pointing out, on the one hand, the social-historical substance of its historical concept and, on the other hand, its limits originating therein, but also by revealing its characteristics which have proved to be lasting without placing on identical levels the substantive differences inherent in the nature of historicism mentioned previously.

This analysis, however, cannot be carried out by assessing the historical school in the light and in the interest of the aims and concepts of today, consequently in a *retrospective* way. Though there are instances for this type of treatment. Some western critics of our days, for instance, try to eliminate the national features from Savigny's doctrine in a rather interesting way. Koschaker, for example, emphasizing the European character of Savigny's work, points out that his idea of the German Empire was more a cultural than a political notion and thus through his German nationalist concept he strengthened the position of the Roman Law, i.e. the uniform basis of German law, adopting Natural Law features, too, which were closely related to the European evolution of law.[5] Wieacker, on the other hand, after having explained at great length the relationship of the historical legal school with the intellectual trends of his epoch, states that in Savigny's work his European self has triumphed in the conflict between the spontaneous historical experience and the European tradition when he made his decision — like Goethe, — he was led by the sense of responsibility for the common culture of Europe and its ancient basis.[6] And who was on the other side, who represented particular nationalism? That was Thibaut, the great adversary of Savigny, who urged that codification should be started. In effect, in the relationship between Thibaut and Savigny, according to Wieacker, the positions of culture and policy, the European tradition and the nation, or if you like better, the man of cognizance and man of action were opposed to one another approximately in the same way as Goethe's and Schiller's attitude was with regard to the French revolution or the modern nation. We cannot discuss in this context the relations between Goethe and Schiller, and between both and the French revolution. But it is absolutely certain that Goethe has never represented the medieval European unity, which is identified by many commentators of today of Savigny with the intellectual, cultural imperial idea, and which had been nothing else even in the epoch of Savigny but the Christian-German ideology professed and attempted to be put into practice by Frederic William IV, King of Prussia, the ideology in which the national and power substance of Prussian imperial strivings were necessarily wrapped up. We must, however, agree with Wieacker that this kind of nationalism could not be identified with progressive bourgeois nationalism (Thibaut was nearer to the latter); and it was precisely this feature which has determined the attitude of the great thinkers of the epoch and of the following years in respect of his doctrine. Consequently, if Goethe dealt severely with German nationalism, that is to say more properly, if he did not support it, it did not involve that he had stood on an identical basis of principle with

[5] See P. Koschaker, *Europa und das römische Recht*, 3. Aufl. München und Berlin, 1958, pp. 261–263., 275.

[6] F. Wieacker, *Privatrechtsgeschichte der Neuzeit*, Göttingen, 1853, pp. 237–238.

Savigny, who discovered an all-European culture in the reactionary national-imperial idea of the Middle Ages.[7]

The gist of the exposition of Wieacker may be found in a note. In effect, he writes: "The historical legal school has not broken up the basis of the all-European civil law, but, on the contrary, it has strengthened and deepened them."[8]

It is clear that the present forms and contents of the appearance of the historical view, its connection with the historical legal school cannot be judged on the basis of a retrospective valuation. Only the *historical substance* of the concept of the school of Savigny can direct us in this question. This historical substance, however, was moulded without any doubt by the historical-social conditions. These conditions determined clearly the *content* of the historicism of the historical school as a traditional, retrospective ideological trend, explicitly as the ideological trend of the Restoration following the Revolution, the characteristics of which may be deduced especially from the fact that it reflected the efforts of restoration, where there had been no revolution, but which had been affected by the results of the revolution, namely in consequence of a foreign domination, the French occupation. The national aspirations flaming up against the foreign domination, therefore, necessarily, repercussions in the *German* history, were not accompanied by the ideas of social progress, but as a consequence they could provide a basis for those Prussian power ambitions the purpose of which was the creation of the great German empire. Things being as they were the amalgamation with this ideology, in the form of Roman law, of the legal system required by the bourgeois economic conditions had been facilitated. Nowadays, however, it affords an opportunity to appraise, by referring to the adoption of the Roman law, the whole political imperial idea through existence of the historical legal school, as a "cultural" and "spiritual" notion. Although — as it is well-known — even within the historical legal school the influence of another trend — of the Germanists — who had been demanding the rejection of the Roman, was not negligible.[9]

Space prevents us to expound in detail what the role of the Roman law in the doctrine of Savigny was and to what extent this role was determined by the social conditions of his epoch.[10] It is, however, certain that the efforts aimed at representing the historical legal school, which had been embedded in an organic way in the romantic range of ideas as independent precisely of this context and determination, are not well-founded.

[7] Cf. K. Kulcsár, *Marxizmus és a történeti jogi iskola* [Marxism and the Historical School of Law], Jogtudományi Közlöny, 1955, No. 2. pp. 78—79 and Kulcsár, *A népi jog és a nemzeti jog* [People's Law and National Law], Az Állam- és Jogtudományi Intézet Értesítője, vol. IV. 1961, No. 1—2. pp. 154—156.

[8] Wieacker, *op. cit.* p. 228.

[9] Cf. Kulcsár, *A népi jog és a nemzeti jog* [People's Law and National Law], pp. 160. and seq.

[10] *Ibidem* p. 158.

What is more, only the dogmatic aspect of Savigny's work has been stressed even at the cost of sacrificing Savigny's actual historicism, based on his work and views connected with the Roman law (in this context, too, relying in the first place on the "System des heutigen römischen Rechts" as against his work on the history of medieval Roman law), with the explicit allegation that he and his followers had been enriching, developing rationalist Natural Law connected with the Roman law which had formed a part of the European culture. Such a one-sided appraisal of the historical legal school (what goes hand in hand with detaching the Germanist branch of the school, which, otherwise, had been similarly built on Savigny's views on jurisprudence) can only be considered as a way of retrospective assessment, which forms part — as it very clearly appears in respect of the endeavours of Koschaker and Wieacker — of the effort to lay the historical foundations of the legal unity of Europe.

Koschaker, Wieacker and other consider as the greatest merit of the historical legal school and personally of Savigny the furthering of the systematic legal thinking and of the dogmatic science of law as well. No doubt, these virtues are obvious especially in the systematizing work of Savigny and it is equally clear that Savigny himself in the "System des heutigen römischen Rechts" has not considered the historical method to be of *exclusive* importance and had indicated its content in a clear-cut way. In this work he protested against opinions which by distorting the historical view of jurisprudence considered the legal institutions originating in the past to be of a higher order, the prevalence of which should be maintained over the present and the future. The main point is, he goes on to say, that the independence and the value of every epoch should be emphasized and the "living connection" between present and past should come into prominence because without being aware of this connection the legal phenomena of the present can only be realized as external phenomena without comprehending their inherent essence. By applying the historical view at things to the Roman law a ground is provided to ascertain and to define in a given system of law the elements of really Roman origin and among these those, which had already withered away and had survived only through a misunderstanding in their misleading pseudo-existence. It is this way that the development and the beneficial effect of the still living part of the Roman elements may be assured.[11]

We think that the views of Savigny now mentioned are important for two reasons in respect of his own legal doctrine. Because these reflect to a certain degree his historical view in a more settled form, which, however, does not differ essentially of his views expounded in the "Beruf" or his programmatic

[11] F. C. v. Savigny, *System des heutigen römischen Rechts*. Vol. I. Berlin, 1840, pp. XIII–XV.

statement: "history is the only way to get real knowledge of our own situation". We may be convinced of the practical application of this view by reading the works of Savigny and, last but not least, by the "System" itself. From this follows the second important aspect, namely, that Savigny, who had laid down the theoretical foundations not only in jurisprudence but also in respect of the application and interpretation of law, *created* with this activity of his and with the new branch of law developed as a result of the historical method, i.e. with the formation of scientific legal history, *something that will last over and beyond the limits of his own theory*. And at this stage we have come to the next point of our problem: what has survived up to now from the historical conception of Savigny?

In defining more precisely the historical viewpoint, several elements of Savigny's doctrine may be turned to good use not only in modern jurisprudence but in Marxist jurisprudence proper, too. Among others the following theses of Savigny are valid even today: the substance of the science of law is not "arbitrary", but the whole legal material has to be considered in its history and as a consequence: the "historical" comprises *everything that has belonged to the past and that is still present*, because the past has had an influence also upon the present. And even if we cannot agree with his wording, with the emphasis on the epithet "organic" in the expression "organic state" constituted by the past and the present, it is certain that in Savigny's doctrine — apart from its social contents — that *element of reality* is apparent which with its historical-social content defines the limits of human action, consequently of legislation and in a wider sense of the law, too. This historical element of reality which — as has been seen — in whatever form it had appeared, had always evoked the criticism of people aspiring to a Nietzsche-type, that is freedom, barbarism, is a valuable trait, also from the humanitarian aspect, in jurisprudence and, as it has been proved by innumerable examples, *legislation and judicial practice cannot in the long run disregard it*. This is an interesting but not isolated example of the fact that even from historically and politically retrospective, consequently negative historical situations valuable recognitions may arise, enduring elements may be discovered; that perhaps might be explained by the fact that the truth value of a certain idea, especially in the science, is not determined in an absolute way by its social genesis even if for the revealing of its truth value the latter is absolutely necessary. We may add to what has been said that the *historical method* in law application and the *legal history* as a science have been born from the social-historical situation in Savigny's epoch but have been closely connected with the role Roman law had at that time played in Germany.

There cannot be any doubt that Roman law in the first half of the XIXth century in Germany was a historical structure. The first reception of the Roman law, its evolution since the period of the medieval Roman law required in a peremptory way the *historical* interpretation of the legal material. Historicism as a method engendered a new science, legal history. Legal history, however, was not only the history of Roman law, as some bourgeois lawyers allege today, but under the aegis of the legal history in conjunction with the reviving Germanic philology, German legal history emerged, too, which was striving to present the old German, Teutonic law with a certain *legal-political* objective. The important representatives of German legal history from Grimm and Baseler to Otto Gierke and right to national socialism, even to some legal historiographers of today, have been opposing German law to Roman law which was "alien for the people."[12]

The historical view in the jurisprudence of the XIXth century had relationship, as a matter of course, not only with Savigny's historical legal school. In Germany itself a new science of a historical character was born which was based rather on the Hegelian historical concept. We have here not only Eduard Gans, the direct disciple of Hegel, in mind and perhaps not even in the first place, but also the ethnological and comparative jurisprudence bearing the stamp of the works of Post and Kohler. This jurisprudence — especially in the case of Post — has drawn much from the ideas of the historical legal school (the spirit of the people) and although Post has separated ethnological jurisprudence from the historical legal school, more precisely he preferred the former to the latter, this jurisprudence developed more and more in a comparative-sociological direction and as a theory of law accomplished itself in the New-Hegelian theory of law. The English historical line, too, ranging from Maine to Vinogradoff, which will be treated later in connection with the historicism of Anglo-Saxon legal thought, was similarly of a comparative-sociological character.

II.

The fact that at the beginning of the XXth century Karl Wieland could still state the anti-historical view of the German science of law,[13] and that he could with reason refer to examples which, as e.g. a conclusion reached by Kantorowicz, separate entirely the historical and dogmatic view from one another and thus at the same time legal history from the systematical jurisprudence,[14] may be attributed to many circumstances. It is well-known that at the beginning of our century the struggle between the Germanistic and Romanistic trends fought about the German codification of the civil law was closed and the elaboration of the BGB has thrust dogmatics for a certain time

[12] See Kulcsár, *A népi jog és a nemzeti jog* [People's Law and National Law], pp. 161–162.

[13] K. Wieland, *Die historische und die kritische Methode in der Rechtswissenschaft*, Leipzig, 1910, p. 6.

[14] *Ibidem* p. 15.

into prominence. And although about the same time an evolution could be observed even in the law which essentially changed capitalist social conditions and thus in the territory of German law laid stress upon the *dissolution* of the legal view attached to the rigid statute, and moreover beyond this upon the dissolution of the rule of law itself, this process could not be carried out under the domination of the historical legal school. It has already been attempted in another paper to analyze the effect of the German social and legal evolution at the turn of the century upon the development of the science of law.[15] In this context it will suffice to point out that the various forms of the New-Kantian philosophy of law lent the ideological frame for the process of change mentioned to such an extent that the sociology of law which came elsewhere to a certain extent into prominence could not occupy — even in the form of "Free Law" — a "distinguished" place in jurisprudence. On the contrary, this sociology of law — in opposition e.g. to its American counterpart — started by criticizing Savigny. The historical legal school was condemned by Ehrlich and Kantorowicz, too,[16] who were blaming it for its mistake, which was considered as fundamental by Wieland, namely that it could not get rid of the doctrine of Natural Law according to which the judge *comes to know and applies the law and does not create it.*[17] This problem emerged already as the *central* question of jurisprudence by the beginning of the XXth century since the rules of law and the legal principles reflecting the state and conditions of capitalism based on free competition had to be moulded by judicial practice and substituted by legal rules corresponding to the new conditions.[18] The historical view was not susceptible of solving this problem in Germany, and thus dogmatics and legal history or theory of law and legal history were separated from one another for a long time. The emergence of closer relations between these branches of jurisprudence — in the first place due to natural law or relativistic efforts — may be observed in our days under the influence, as we shall see, of specific historical conditions.

The connection between Anglo-Saxon legal thinking and historical concept — in the first place because of the peculiar Anglo-Saxon legal evolution— pursued a different course. In this sphere too, the separation took place in the first half of the XIXth century, prompted namely by the legal theory of Austin.

[15] KULCSÁR, *A jogszociológia problémái* [Some Problems of the Sociology of Law], Budapest, 1960, pp. 19. and seq. Its summary by the author (in English) in Acta Juridica, 1961, pp. 227 and seq.

[16] E. EHRLICH, *Grundlegung der Soziologie des Rechts*, München und Leipzig, 1913, p. 12. — Further he accuses the historical school and legal history of having carried on research work only for rules of law independent of life and of not having been interested in the real law asserted in life, e. g. not having inquired into the historical development of legal relations (pp. 258—259).

[17] WIELAND, *op. cit.* p. 12.

[18] See in detail KULCSÁR, *A jogszociológia problémái* [Some Problems of the Sociology of Law], Chap. I.

It is interesting, however, to note that the same forces which had separated in Germany the historical concept from the theory of law, that is to say, the social conditions of monopoly capitalism, in the Anglo-Saxon world operated in the direction to bring them closer. Thus, if we now — in a rather antihistorical way — want to effect a juxtaposition of trends in which the historical view may again be observed in our century, then we may discern the following outlines.

1. Anglo-Saxon jurisprudence, in America the pragmatic sociology of law.

2. Natural Law made to conform historically relying on some doctrines of the philosophy of history.

3. The trends of the science of comparative law envisaging after a uniform European law and relying on legal history as a special branch of the science of law.

1. Discussing some new appearances of the English theory of law, Barna Horváth suggests: "they spring forth from historicism like all intellectual trends which have their roots in the culture of the *common law*".[19] If this statement is perhaps not absolutely correct in respect of all intellectual trends, it is nevertheless noteworthy and should be considered. The culture of the common law cannot be explained of course, by itself. The elements from which it has been built up and among which only one should be mentioned now, namely *historical continuity* emphasized nearly by all English and not English jurists, are in close connection with the evolution of the English society. The analysis of the connections of the English social evolution would lead us too far; it should be pointed out that those social-historical conditions which find expression in the continuity of the common law, have carried traditionalism also into the edifice and into the culture of the common law. Thus, the historicism of the common law is in many respects a historicism bound also by the past. From this often mentioned continuity follows the empiricism of the English lawyer, his "hostility against all theories", for it is clear, that the continuity, the compromise, which is so characteristic for the English social evolution, comprises many contradictory features in the accumulated legal material which can only be understood and outdone by a considerably empirical and critical historicism. It results from this that Anglo-Saxon legal thinking is rather characterized by the view of "is", more precisely this empirical "is" is more an Anglo-Saxon characteristic opposite to the German "Sollen". German empiricism is also historical in jurisprudence (it cannot be other), as far as the historical legal school is concerned, however, this empiricism turned rather with the characteristic of the "must" towards the past, considering in it not only the reality of the past but also a value bearing on the present. The theories aiming

[19] B. Horváth, *Angol jogelmélet* [English Theory of Law], Budapest, 1943, p. 528

at the logical solution of the contradictions, which otherwise were always resulting from some social changes already more or less closed, e.g. the legal theory of Bentham or Austin, and the efforts envisaging the rationalization of the English law tried as a rule to settle the question in a way contrary to the historical concept and by reminding of Nietzsche's well-known statement, they meant to discover the way of evolution in throwing away the dead weight of history. The legal repercussions of the theories moulded in that way by the social conditions, however, became parts of historical continuity and their understanding requires again the aid of the historical concept. Hence the hostility to a certain degree of the Anglo-Saxon and particularly English jurisprudence against logic[20] and its constant reference, in opposition to logic, to experience which was expressed in the following almost classical words of O. W. Holmes: "the life of the law has not been logic, it has been experience". This experience is, however, always historical even in respect of those jurists who refrain from adopting the historical view. Holdsworth, the great English historiographer of the law expresses the almost general English opinion by seeing in the legal history the guarantee with the aid of which one can master the English law and which assures the critical intelligence in appraising the theories of the philosophy of law.[21] Legal history as a means of criticism is recognized also in the present Anglo-Saxon jurisprudence. It may be read in a paper of Edwin Patterson that the legal history may be used for the correction of the erroneous hypotheses bearing on the present law, especially case law. The substance of his opinion appears from the fact as he quotes John H. Wigmore's famous paper on the law of evidence: One remedial method consists in showing that a contemporaneous legal norm or concept was established in response to a situation, a legal or social institution or some phase of one, which has since disappeared or been greatly modified.[22]

However, the original historicism of the English legal view as a tenet of principle which has influenced the philosophy of law, too, was conceived for the first time in a peculiar social-historical situation which had been particularly favourable for historicism. We have in mind Edmund Burke's time and work. Burke is considered perhaps by many people as the greatest and most typical English political and legal thinker, and as Goodhart says, he is at any rate typically English in his respect for the past.[23] This respect for the past, however, had a peculiar content, it meant rather the defence of the pre-

[20] Kulcsár, *A jogszociológia problémái* [Some Problems of the Sociology of Law], pp. 233 et seq.

[21] See B. Horváth, *A Common Law ideológiája és a jogismeret ideológiája* [The Ideology of the Common Law and the Ideology of Legal Knowledge], Társadalomtudomány, 1930, No 1–3. p. 91.

[22] E. W. Patterson, *Historical and Evolutionary Theories of Law*, Columbia Law Review, Vol. 51. No. 6. p. 683.

[23] A. I. Goodhart, *English Contribution to the Philosophy of Law*, New York, 1948, p. 24.

sent and even more the fear of the future. It is well known that Burke had been the first representative of the historicism of that type which took shape in the doctrine of Savigny and the legal historical school. The essential social substance of this historicism, as far as Burke is concerned, like in the case of Savigny was the fear of the revolution. His famous pamphlet[24] written against the French revolution contains that conservative historical concept which ranked him among the romantic philosophers of history and which manifested itself so strongly that it banished Meinecke as the representative of traditionalism from the circle of the essential figures of the "genuine" historical conception. There are, of course, who see precisely in that a genuine historicism. "We assess correctly the importance of Burke in the theory of law — writes e.g. Barna Horváth — if we see in him with Laski the precursor of that romantic and conservative trend which was represented a generation later by Hegel and Savigny in Germany, de Maistre and Bonald in France, Coleridge and Holdsworth in England. Burke's thought is inspired by that noble conservatism, that variable historical spirit which is the source of the theory of law with a historical tendency, of the historicism of the theory of law. Burke is the apostle of philosophical conservatism."[25] The identification of the "noble conservativism" with the historicism of the theory of law is characteristic for Barna Horváth, but is by no means a historical reality, not even in respect of all representatives of the historicism of English legal concept. It is true, of course, as far as the theory of Burke is concerned, because the content of his doctrine is in the first place determined by the social-historical situation and it is this situation which explains the historicism of a conservative character of the English legal concept emphasized by him, which — so to say — by the means of Burke's aid realized the social substance of the historicism of its own legal evolution.

It remains to be seen how this historicism as a method and an attitude could detach itself from this conservatism which had been determined by its historical content. There is no doubt that the historicism of the English legal evolution required a constant retrospection into the past and this fact has been contributing to the conservative character of the historical concept which is coupled with the irrational empiricism of English legal technics. The new period of the evolution of the social conditions, however, lends another content also to the bourgeois historical concept within the capitalist society. This period is that of the emergence of the monopoly capitalist society when the historical element appears to a certain extent with another purport in the Anglo-Saxon legal view and in the Anglo-Saxon legal thinking as well.

The more rational form of the Anglo-Saxon thinking of historical character, which in the first place meant an effort to understand certain general

[24] E. BURKE, *Reflections on the Revolution in France,* 1790.
[25] HORVÁTH, *Angol jogelmélet* [English Theory of Law], p. 243.

trends of the evolution of law, began to try its wings already prior to the monopoly capitalist evolution. As in Germany beside the legal historical school there was another type of historicism to be found, the historical concept going back to Hegel which tried to express the evolution in a rational way, so in England, more precisely in English jurisprudence a similar historical legal view of rational character was to be observed. The efforts at rationalist thinking later got shifted on the path of speculation and so the work of H. S. Maine produced, to a certain degree, the well-justified critical remark that it was not historical enough. The historicism of Maine is characterized otherwise, too, by the retrospective judgment, mainly by the historical generalization of the characteristic features of the English law in respect of the evolution of law. Evidently, English legal development is reflected, for instance, with a legal theoretical general character, in the assertion of Maine to the effect that substantive law takes its origin from procedural law or in his claim that the themis or themistes, as the primitive "judge-made" law occupied a central place in the formation of law. And after all, the same applies to the historically conceived apotheosis of the law of the capitalist society based on free competition, as well as to his concept of the legal development ranging from status to contract, which gained in Spencer's doctrine a sociological general character.[26] The historical concept departing from Maine and exerting efforts at generalizations, and characterized already by sociological attempts, too, grew later to full proportions and beside its inherent historicism connected with the English legal evolution and beyond that, at the beginning of the XXth century, created independent trends, although — as we could see it in Maine's example — this historicism was not devoid of the particular features of historicism originating in the peculiarities of the English legal evolution. This English historicism of the XXth century — beside the great English legal historiographs — reached a legal theoretical level in two trends. Of these two only one trend is an explicit historical theory of law, but historicism is present in the other one, too. The first one is the historical theory of law reflected in the works of Vinogradoff, the second is the pragmatic legal sociology.

Although the work of Vinogradoff is characterized in the first place by historicism (namely by a *comparative* historical concept which appeared for the first time in the doctrine of Maine), the sociological element, too, assumed in it a very great importance indeed to such an extent that many people include it already among the sociological doctrines.[27] The historical and the sociological concept — if it is indeed historical and really sociological, conse-

[26] The sound foundations of the well-known theory of Maine are criticized by several scholars in present bourgeois jurisprudence. See e. g. E. A. HOEBEL, *The Law of the Primitive Man*, A Study in Comparative Legal Dynamics, Cambridge, 1954, p. 329.

[27] See for instance J. STONE, *The Province and Function of Law*, Sydney, 1946, p. 463. et seq.

quently makes an effort to discover the laws of movement of history and of society — represent essentially identical concepts. Thus it can be understood in this way that in the bourgeois *sociology those theories have come near to reality in which the historicism was not wanting. As a consequence, history which neglected the sociological aspects was bound to remain from a scientific point of view sterile.* The legal theory of Paul Vinogradoff strove to have both the historical and the sociological viewpoints asserted. Thus, it became from the side of the historicism a counterpart of the pragmatic legal sociology which was attempting to apply the historical method in the sociology of law. The English legal and philosophical evolution is among others characterized by the fact that in England rather the *historical* whereas in America the *sociological* viewpoint was emphasized.

Vinogradoff considers historicism to be such an important element of the legal method that he disapproves of all contrasting of history with the theoretical study of the law and emphasizes that it is historicism which creates an atmosphere of scientific character also in respect of philosophy.[28] For this reason the starting point of historical jurisprudence may not be the chronological' viewpoint, this is the viewpoint of the legal history, the viewpoint of jurisprudence should be of an "ideological" character.[29] What does the ideological viewpoint mean in the doctrine of Vinogradoff? It essentially means that the historical method has to discover the characteristic features of the human evolution and it has to utilize them in its efforts aimed at ascertaining its types. All critics and analysts of Vinogradoff and to a certain extent Vinogradoff himself, too, state that in this essential point of his doctrine he relies on the theory of ideal type of Max Weber. It is by the aid of this method that he creates the various types of the legal development[30] which — as maintained by him — form the foundation of jurisprudence.

Such an "ideological" concept of the types of the legal evolution reminds us much of the theoretical construction of Hegel in which the idea materializes its essence in history and in the reality. Vinogradoff himself refers, however, to the correction of this concept by pointing out that the assessment of facts and theories in an ideological order does not mean the rejection or neglect of those geographical, ethnological, political, cultural and other conditions which determine the course of events. The ideas are embodied in facts — he says — and these are influenced by the material needs and forces. Consequently, the fact that the direct atmosphere is given by a shepherds', agrarian or industrial environment is not unimportant from the aspect of the development of legal principles.[31]

[28] P. VINOGRADOFF, *Outlines of Historical Jurisprudence*, Vol. I. London, 1920, p. 4.
[29] *Ibidem*, p. 155.
[30] *Ibidem*, p. 158.
[31] *Ibidem*, p. 159.

On this point, however, Vinogradoff's theory is obscure and his critics call upon him to substantiate the precision of the formation of the types. Julius Stone, for example, stresses that because of the ambiguity of the statements of Vinogradoff nobody can know whether he started in creating his types from the ideas or the social conditions. And as Vinogradoff explicitly rejects the doctrine of historical materialism on the socially determined character of ideas — writes Stone — remains the half-Hegelian concept and the hypothesis that history is determined by the materialization of the idea. It is true that in both cases it is about the abstraction of the concrete historical process, but it is decisive whether we consider the *idea* or the *social conditions* as the force determining the course of history. Stone criticizes not only the doctrine of legal development elaborated by Vinogradoff but also the similar doctrine of Pound,[32] starting from the fact that these doctrines are refuted by the facts of the evolution. In effect, the law is much rather the product of social conditions than the materialization of ideas.[33]

The contradiction seen among others also by Stone between the materialization of ideas and their determination by the facts inherent in society, cannot be solved entirely on the basis of the bourgeois theory of law. In effect Vinogradoff observed, as already Dicey did, who may be considered as his predecessor that in the legislation certain trends of ideas and political concepts are embodied. On the other hand, it was also observed that these legal institutions and legal rules change directly, too, as required by the facts of life. And also this observation was the consequence of the actual effects of the conditions of the monopoly capitalism which were directly reflected, as a rule, through the judicial practice, in the formation of the rules of law and legal institutions. Now, it is clear that Vinogradoff precisely because he has rejected historical materialism, and possibly also under the influence of Max Weber's doctrine, could not get as far as adopting the socially determined character of ideas. Thus, he only started from the fact that the ideas influence society and the ideas materialized in facts are subject to the moulding, formative effect of social factors. Consequently, the contradiction is only apparent and in truth it reflects the partial recognition of the reality, but not in the abstraction corresponding to the reality. This may be particularly well observed in his dispute with historical materialism. He maintains, for instance, that law does not express the interests of the ruling class because in the slave society the law is not only the outcome of economic factors and the prevailing political, moral views.[34] From this example not only the non-recognition of the socially determined

[32] On the theory of Pound on the development of law and jurisprudence see KULCSÁR, *A jogszociológia problémái* [Some Problems of the Sociology of Law], p. 48 et seq.

[33] STONE, *op. cit.* pp. 465–467.

[34] VINOGRADOFF, *op. cit.* p. 81.

character of ideas and theories appears clearly, but also a misinterpretation of historical materialism, which is common in the bourgeois sociology, and the erroneous concept appears, too, as if historical materialism did not allow for the activity of ideas fundamentally determined by society and as if historical materialism stood exclusively on the ground of mechanical determinism.

With the well-known hostility against all theories of the English legal concept is coupled that wide-spread concept, too, that the also historically valuable legal theoretical elements become constituents of the common law. Indeed, in some judicial decisions of principle quite lengthy legal theoretical explanations, the gist of which assumes a positive form in the given case have been suggested. Consequently, it is not by chance that in the English legal concept, especially in English legal historicism, the history of doctrines plays a very important role. H. T. Hazeltine, therefore, could assert with good reason in the introduction to one of Pound's books that the history of the meditations of the English jurists constitutes an integral part of the history of English law.[35] And this statement in the introduction to a book of Pound is particularly in its proper place as it is well-known that Pound has developed precisely in the history of doctrines that historical view which has become an essential part of his sociology of law. Pound, however, is in the first place a legal sociologist,[36] and therefore it is intended in this context only to evoke the historical foundations of his sociology of law. His doctrine concerning the development of law and in this development the role of jurisprudence, the satisfaction of the claim to stability and change in law is based on the assessment of legal history and legal thinking. He gives a very interesting analysis on the role of the historical school in this process. Pound connects the historical legal school with the need for the stability of the law, and it is on these grounds that he accounts for its hostility against all actions, its passivity and pessimism as well. His valuation in respect of the decline of the historical school is very characteristic: "...His break-up of the historical school coincides with a general abandonment of the nineteenth-century historical-philosophical thinking in every field and the revival of faith in the efficacy of human effort with an accompanying call for philosophies of action and creation in place of the political fatalism and juristic pessimism of the immediate past."[37]

It is striking in this valuation of Pound that ultimately he defines the substance of historicism like Nietzsche, as he sees in it passivity, non-acting, in his peculiar opinion an ideology connected with legal stability. So he opposes the historicism to the requirements of the XXth century which call for action and development in the law. Pound, however, precisely

[35] R. POUND, *Interpretations of Legal History*, Cambridge, 1923, p. X.

[36] See KULCSÁR, *A jogszociológia problémái* [Some Problems of the Sociology of Law], Chapters II, V and VI.

[37] POUND, *op. cit.* p. 11.

because his work is grounded beside the pragmatic philosophy and history of doctrines upon the roots of the Anglo-Saxon legal development, was well qualified to express the needs of his proper time from the aspect of jurisprudence *without abandoning the historical concept*. The force of his historical concept is shown otherwise by the fact, too, that he tries to appraise the characteristics of the historical school of Savigny in connection with the epoch, with the legal problems of the epoch, as the sociological understanding and the building up of jurisprudence of his own time is consciously connected with the contemporary social and legal problems, with the legal postulates originating in the needs of the epoch, with the so-called relative Natural Law. The epoch of Pound is, of course, the reality of the monopoly-capitalist society, with its accompanying social-economic trends, philosophical and legal traditions. This social characteristic determines the historical concept of Pound in respect of the past and the present which he includes into his sociological theory. In effect, it is clear that when the conditions of monopoly capitalism required a change also in the field of law, *action* was called for. Action, however, even in the opinion of Pound has an unhistorical character; his historicism, therefore, is rooted in the Anglo-Saxon legal and philosophical traditions, in a kind of restricted sphere of ideas which is the consequence of the fact that the social factors had become important for the first time in the doctrine of the historical school. The direct social tendencies of the epoch of Pound have an unhistorical appeal as in the United States the pattern of the new society, which can be moulded by rationalistic means was striven for and embodied at the turn of the century in sociology. It is very interesting, therefore, that the historical concept appears precisely in jurisprudence built on unhistorical philosophical and sociological theories after the turn of the century. And in this fact, the characteristics of Anglo-Saxon legal evolution are reflected, the traditions based on the ideology of continuity, consequently the influence of *elements which have a secondary importance as compared to social tendencies*. In England, where the ideological demand for the conscious forming of the society, consequently the demand to form the structure and traditions of society has not come to prominence to this extent, legal thinking is disposed, to abstract, if at all, the demands of law complying with the radical turn of the capitalist society at best, as the highest degree of the evolution amalgamated with the traditional historical concept — as is shown e.g. in the works of Vinogradoff. That is the reason why the historical element prevails in the doctrine of Vinogradoff and the sociological element is relegated to the background, whereas in the doctrine of Pound and in the pragmatic sociology of law the sociological element gained a primary importance.

Consequently, the historical concept of the pragmatic sociology of law, in compliance with the demand for a conscious formation of society embodied in the sociology, lent rational grounds for the historical concept of the historical legal school, more properly it detached from it the inappropriate elements which were concomitant with the epoch. That's why Pound explains the characteristics of the historical school by describing the conditions of the epoch — and correctly at that — and that is why we find such efforts in the great work of Julius Stone, too, when he appraises the historical concept as a part of the sociology. "In the writer's view — he says referring to Pound — insofar as historical jurisprudence inquires into "the historical origin and development" of law, its institutions and doctrines, it is of necessity but a part of sociological jurisprudence . . . The separate identity of historical jurisprudence up to the present seems to be due to the fact that it appeared on the Continent early in the nineteenth century as a part of the romanticist revival and in reaction from the universalist and creative juristic thought of the preceding Natural Law period: whereas sociological jurisprudence only emerged clearly with the rise of the social sciences in the second half of the century as a reaction against the formalistic juristic thought of the analysis and against the determinist whether ethical, idealist, political, biological or economic which captured the historical school. This order of appearance is no reason for keeping separate what functionally should be unified."[38]

2. "The historical consciousness of the finiteness of all historical phenomena, of all human or social situations, of the relativity of all belief is the last step towards the liberation of men. So we may attain the sovereignty of obtaining the content of every personal experience, of abandoning ourselves entirely to it, unbiassed as if philosophy or faith had no system by which we could be bound. Life will be exempt from the cognizance by the means of concepts, the spirit will be sovereign in respect to all cobwebs of dogmatic thinking . . . life is only present in the experience, understanding and historical conception."[39] (Dilthey)

If we follow step by step with attention this train of thought, it becomes clear that Dilthey offers in this context the same result with his historicism as had been done by Nietzsche with his unhistoric concept. Both expect the liberation of the human spirit, both attach the cognition to the irrational,

[38] STONE, *op. cit.* p. 35. — The sociology of law otherwise — in the opinion of nearly all sociologists — comprises in a form or another the historical element, too. Ehrlich does not reject it either, he rather criticized the insufficiency of the historical research carried out by the historical school. According to Timasheff, for instance, historical jurisprudence has, from the aspect of the sociology of law, in the first place an importance in respect of rectifying it (N. S. TIMASHEFF, American Journal of Sociology, 1937, p. 223.). B. HORVÁTH considers historical researches indispensable for the sociology of law in addition to the social aspect because law can be approached only in its historical individuality. But by generalizing he passes beyond legal history (HORVÁTH, *Rechtssoziologie*, Berlin—Grünewald, 1934, pp. 3—5.). However, while, for instance, Timasheff sees in the history the critique in the direction of the theories of sociology of law, in Horváth's work the view is reversed, the sociology of law serves as the criticism of the legal historical experience *(Ibidem*, p. 84.).

[39] W. DILTHEY, *Der Aufbau der geschichtlichen Welt in den Geisteswissenschaften*, Gesammelte Schriften, vol. VII. Stuttgart—Göttingen, 2. ed. 1958, pp. 290—291.

but while Nietzsche considers the history as a dead weight and bond of action, Dilthey, on the contrary, tries to prove by means of the history that all ties are relative, consequently they may be disregarded.

However, the ideas of Dilthey quoted above are to a certain extent characteristic of the historical concept of a certain circle of western jurisprudence of today, namely of the concepts of the historically relative Natural Law-doctrine relying on some historical-philosophical theories the representatives of which adopt the irrationalisti cmethod of cognition of Dilthey's philosophy, the requirement of intuition. It is, however, a very interesting question to what extent these trends of jurisprudence which utilize many elements characteristic of Dilthey and other philosophers of history, e.g. the idea of historical relativity, the requirement of irrational cognition, the idea of intuition, etc., to what extent they are characterized by the substantive features of this thinking which in the doctrine of Nietzsche and Dilthey, in spite of all appearances, may be discerned as identical, namely the rejection of restrictions with regard to action. If there are certain differences, which may be discovered already at the outset, their reasons may be given for the time being, in the following. One reason may be looked for in the expression of philosophies in the form of jurisprudence, because no matter how loose it is conceived, whatever incidental character is attributed to it, law means nevertheless a kind of restriction, consequently the rejection of the restriction may have only a certain relative importance. The second reason consists in that historical situation in which these legal theoretical trends had been taking shape, in the historical-social conditions developed after World War II. At any rate, it is very characteristic that this new historicism which appeared in the most varied forms but was always connected with certain representatives of the irrational philosophy of history had in jurisprudence always been inseparable from the idea of *Natural Law*. Stone wrote that an independent historical theory of law, besides the sociology of law, can only have, at best, a place and a reason if its aim is to interpret legal development in accordance with a category of the philosophy of history.[40] It seems that this was accomplished after World War II in the development of historical jurisprudence, with that difference that the independence of this jurisprudence has been made questionable not only by its fundamental historical-philosophical starting point but by its connection with the idea of Natural Law as well. Some authors hold that the development of the historical concept is directly connected with the revival in our days of the doctrines of Natural Law as historicism can thank Natural Law for its first historical appearance.[41] One thing is certain, namely, that the

[40] STONE, *op. cit.* p. 26.

[41] See the review by TH. WÜRTENBERGER of the book of G. AMBROSETTI, *Razionalita e Storicita del diritto*, Roma—Milano, Archiv für Rechts- und Sozialphilosophie, 1953, vol. XLIV. p. 276.

resurrection in our days of Natural Law resurrected indeed historicism, too, *not in opposition, but within the idea of Natural Law.*

It does not follow, however, from this that Natural Law would have given up the struggle in all its forms against historicism. Leo Strauss e.g. directly blames historicism for its revolutionary spirit, although with different arguments as compared to some other opponents of historicism. Strauss considers the concept of the "this world", of the "is" as the precursor of the revolution, opposite to Nietzsche who saw precisely in that the obstacle of action. This example shows in a very interesting way the change which ensued, on the one hand, in historicism itself, on the other hand, in the appraisal of the concept of transcendental idealism the content of which is social but is connected with the change taking place in the position of classes in society. The fact should not be disregarded that the present bourgeois adversaries of historicism see in it the *common* ideological basis of communism and fascism, and are of opinion that the "is" viewpoint of the historical concept which means the determinism of the laws as revealed in history (according to the critics the imaginary laws) results of necessity in the communist or fascist dictatorship, placed by the bourgeois ideology incorrectly on the same level. It results in a dictatorship which does not take into consideration the eternal values, is the adherent of positivism in law independent of its substance, which does not let a valuation surpassing the viewpoints of the given historical "is" and, thus, historicism reaches its highest point in the nihilism.[42]

Some of the bourgeois critics of the historical concept consider this nihilism, which — it is claimed — takes its origin in historicism (by historicism they mean the *non*-recognition of the objective norms binding everybody), as characteristic of those legal systems which do not correspond to the tenets of the bourgeois ideology. On this ground of principle they reject the legal system of the socialist society and the law of the fascist state. The great historical experience of the bourgeois society, the proletarian revolution and in consequence of this the formation of the socialist society, the creation of the socialist state and legal system, as well as the practice of the fascist states within the monopoly capitalist society, the wars started by them, which all appear in the eyes of the average citizen of the bourgeois society as being on the same level, and which are reflected in the bourgeois ideology as identical things, brought about after World War II the revival of the idea of Natural Law, respectively a certain effort to conceive a concept of values. One form of this endeavour, the relativism has proved susceptible of contributing, in connection with the historical concept under the banner of some trends of the philosophy of history, to the formation of the historical-natural law-ideology better suited to the bourgeois needs of the epoch. And in this

[42] L. Strauss, *Naturrecht und Geschichte*, Stuttgart, 1953, pp. 14—16.

context the profound identity of the apparent antagonism between Nietzsche and Dilthey comes to the fore. In effect, the role of the historical-philosophical viewpoint of Dilthey consists in the historical relativization of Natural Law, in the historical disintegration of the bonds of Natural Law which came necessarily into prominence after World War II in consequence of the disappointment on the part of the bourgeois society in positivism. That is to say, this historicism is not the historicism of the binding force of the reality, but of the disappointment, consequently no wonder that it is closely related to the idea of the eternal return expounded by Nietzsche.[43]

The historicism of this kind, which could best be characterized perhaps by the expression of Helmut Coing, according to whom: historicism is one of the latest nuances of relativism,[44] consequently historicism taken in a "relative" sense, when it turns against positivism, not only creates a basis for the disintegration of the positive legal bonds but, like American realism, dissolves as far as to the validity in individual cases Natural Law, too, which becomes finally nothing else but the positive law formed by the judge who takes his decision freely, not bound by any bonds expressing the given situation, the positive law in its *individuality* taken in an absolute sense. The ideological requirements created by history concur in this was with the concrete requirements of the social conditions, the reflection of which may be expressed in jurisprudence most properly with the words of Coing: to free the science of law from positivism, to seek a way towards Natural Law, to examine positive law itself in the light of Natural Law but not in the way of the enlightened rationalism of the XVIIIth century because (as borne out by history) there are no eternal basic principles in law.[45]

Consequently, in the relation between Natural Law and historicism it is not the rational historical concept which, with its theory of evolution, with the recognition of the objective laws of history mitigates the rigidity of the eternal principles as held in Natural Law, and not the sound relativism which may be drawn from the line of development of history, but irrational Natural

[43] The element of eternal return — appears in Nietzsche's work — in many formbut always with a pessimistic and reactionary tinge — directly as the central means os understanding history. "The doctrine of return — he says in the Zarathustra — is a turning-point of history." (NIETZSCHE, *Also sprach Zarathustra*, Leipzig, 1922, p. 487). The idea is correctly criticized by György LUKÁCS, this forming part of the critique of the whole doctrine of Nietzsche (*Az ész trónfosztása* [The Dethronement of Reason], Budapest, 1954, pp. 304 et seq.) and, therefore, it will not be dealt with in this place. It should only be pointed out to state that this element means the essence, for instance, of the "historical character" of the legal philosophy of Existentialism. (The philosophy of Existentialism itself is dealt with in detail by Vilmos PESCHKA, *The Legal Philosophy of Existentialism*, Acta Juridica, 1961, pp. 17. et seq.). So it appears in Maihofer's work (W. MAIHOFER, *Recht und Sein*, Frankfurt am Main, 1954, p. 105 and even more explicitly: *Die Natur der Sache*, Archiv für Rechts- und Sozialphilosophie, 1958, XLIV/2. p. 171.)

[44] H. COING, *Grundzüge der Rechtsphilosophie*, Berlin, 1950, p. 105.

[45] H. COING, *Die obersten Grundsätze des Rechts*. — Ein Versuch zur Neugründung des Naturrechts, Heidelberg, 1947, pp. 7—8.

Law is connected in this tenet with a reactionary historicism. This is not to be doubted if those philosophers are examined who appear in this context in the philosophy of history. The names of Wilhelm Dilthey, Arnold Toynbee, Spengler and Colingwood, may be encountered for whom historicism in the first place means irrationalism, intuition, as the method of cognition, but as philosophers reject the laws of historical evolution and — as György Lukács put it with regard to the philosophy of life — their relativism effectively "undermined the belief in historical progress . . ."[46]

The experience, we were speaking of, means, of course, only one source of the bourgeois efforts in the philosophy of law directed against positivism and not even the main source. The fundamental determining forces the legal principles and legal rules of classical capitalism, that development which even today keeps permanently in motion legal evolution, and the political situation which requires from the bourgeois state a less restricted enforcement of the rules of law, which for this very reason prefers to an increasing extent nowadays already from a theoretical aspect direct political action. This fundamental trend in the bourgeois legal evolution, as a matter of course, was aggravated by the experience of World War II in the bourgeois ideology, too, and this is reflected in its turn towards the values. These values, however, may only be, precisely on account of their fundamental trend, relative, only "hic et nunc" historical. Consequently, they require precisely that theoretical reflection which the historically relative Natural Law-theories relying on Dilthey and others may provide.

The development of this legal ideology since the times directly following the war up to our days is particularly interesting. It will be attempted to prove this trend through Coing's work. We can discover in the work of Coing published immediately after the war and in which he proclaimed his turn towards Natural Law, the core of the historical relativity relying on Dilthey's philosophy. Law — Coing writes — has to be conceived as the creation of the human mind and, therefore, it has to be studied by the method of the *Geisteswissenschaft*, consequently those intellectual forces must be revealed out of which law has been developing. The method is: to fulfil Dilthey's demands in the course of discovering these intellectual forces.[47] Positive law, too, may only be known by revealing the spirit of the legal order, since positive law is nothing else but the summing up of the solution of the conflicts of social interests, as a consequence, an intellectual, individual achievement accomplished by certain men in a certain epoch. Hence he deduces the necessity of the historical inquiries, namely, in compliance with Dilthey's philosophy, with an explicitly individualist view. By criticizing the legal historical inquiries

[46] Gy. Lukács, *Az ész trónfosztása* [The Dethronement of Reason], p. 332.
[47] H. Coing, *Die obersten Grundsätze des Rechts*, p. 6.

of the legal historical school, which were as a rule studies of sources (and which are even now prevailing in the German legal history) he comes to the conclusion that "the legal history built on the method of *Geisteswissenschaften* has to set as an aim the understanding of the historically determined legal order in its individuality as a special solution of justice, as the individual, specific accomplishment of the supporting legal value."[48]

The concept of historicism, however, means to a certain extent in Coing's work a certain social content. In effect, in his work published some years later he points out that the moral idea of man depends on a given epoch and culture. All laws are, therefore, relative, namely because — be they positive laws or certain legal concepts — they are determined by historical, political, social and economic constituents. Starting from this concept, he draws the attention to the necessity of a cultural synthesis emphasized already by Troeltsch, the individuality of which, as a matter of course, is only relative, it comprises, namely, the values of the corresponding epoch. In this sense "all epochs are indeed near to God". The subject of jurisprudence is the main question of the law in force in a certain legal community and in a certain epoch: what is lawful?[49] Positive law is an intellectual product and, as a result of the foregoing, a *historical phenomenon*. Its content is lent by the decisions taken in cases under dispute in society as required by the aspects of value. Jurisprudence, therefore, has to start from the cases. It is not by chance — he points out — that this was the most important point in the work of the Roman jurists.[50] According to the opinion held firmly by Coing, however, although the content of the law is furnished by the cases, nevertheless it may not be considered as shapeless conglomerate, since law has a natural unity constituted of two elements. These two elements are: *a)* all positive laws are based on certain concepts of value which form also by themselves a historical unity and constitute as the spirit of a certain people or of a certain epoch, as the comprehension of the idea of law, a historical-individual totality;[51] *b)* law is effective in certain relations of life, in the natural arrangement corresponding to the scope of life and to the phenomenon concerned.[52]

The departure of the doctrine of Coing from the exclusivity of Natural Law and its advance towards positive law is obvious. This positive law, however, assumes such a positivism which is furnished by its being determined

[48] *Ibidem*, pp. 138—139.

[49] H. Coing, *Grundzüge der Rechtsphilosophie*, pp. 105 and 260.

[50] *Ibidem*, p. 268.

[51] *Ibidem*, p. 276. Coing mentions here some instance. Relying on a book by Schulz (Prinzipien des römischen Rechts) he writes, for instance, that classic Roman Law was based on the "Cosmos" of the tradition, humanity, authority, freedom, fidelity and legal security. On the contrary, the law of the XIXth century was determined by the ideas of 1789.

[52] *Ibidem*, p. 277.

by the spirit of the epoch. That is the reason why case law acquires a central place in the doctrine of Coing what is rather unusual in the German science of law. Cases provide the real contents of law, the cases, in the decision on which the judge directly reveals the basis of value of the legal rule and the historical intent of the legislator; thus Coing starts from the direct inquiry into metajuridical factors. For this very reason in this doctrine of Coing the permanent element according to which *jurisprudence carries out a historical geisteswissenschaftlichen task* occupies a central position. In effect, a legal rule as a determined historical, intellectual product is rooted in a *historical situation,* from which certain problems given at that time, certain factors of value and objectives have followed. It is these phenomena and the assessment providing the ground for the legal rule concerned which should be comprehended by jurisprudence. Jurisprudence has to grasp in the individual case connected with a conflict what was in the mind of the legislator, by what considerations was the solution determined and what positive decision was adopted. Like every historical and *geisteswissenschaftlicher* analysis, jurisprudence in order to solve correctly and in historical proportions its task should start from the general fundamental trend of human intellect and from the basic structure of social life, it should conceive these things as an individual solution of a general task.[53] It can be seen from what has been said that the central position of the cases in the doctrine of Coing does not stem from the rational recognition of the relation between a legal rule and a case of law as in the relation between the general and the individual,[54] but from the effort to raise the individual case to the level of the general. This is borne out by his repeated assertion that the law-applying organ has to reveal the basis of value of the legal rule, the historical will of the legislator. In effect, the actual discovery of the original basis of value of the legal rule renders possible the evasion of the law should the latter be at variance with the appraisal professed by the law-enforcing organ. In effect, it follows clearly from the concept of Coing concerning positive law, the positivism of which is provided by its character of being determined by the spirit of the age, that between the two assessments, that of the law-applying organ, consequently the appraisal closely attached to the given epoch becomes decisive; and this is the result of the physiological processes taking place in the judge's mind which consist in the intellectual experience of the situation and are determined by the set of facts emerging in the case at law.

This *geisteswissenschaftlicher* constituent in the doctrine of Coing (otherwise which is related by him, too, with the doctrines of Dilthey and Spranger)

[53] *Ibidem,* pp. 265–266.

[54] In respect of the relation between a legal rule and the case see in detail KULCSÁR, *A jog nevelő szerepe a szocialista társadalomban* [The Educational Role of the Law in the Socialist Society], Budapest, 1961, Közgazdasági és Jogi Kiadó, pp. 87. et seq. Summary by the author in English: Acta Juridica, 1962. No. 3–4.

has taken in his further intellectual development an even more central position. In order to understand his recent — as to its bases, of course, old — concept, the essential role which Coing in the course of his whole scientifc activity has defined for legal history and the science of comparative law in the cognition of the law in force should be pointed out.[55] These two auxiliary sciences of the law which serve at the same time as means of interpretation too, in the doctrine of Coing have been completed recently by sociology, that is to say, through exposing that historical interpretation is tied with the respective epoch;[56] he came to the conclusion that historical interpretation has been today essentially replaced by the comparative legal and sociological method, and the historical concept is considered neither in the science nor in the practice of legal interpretation as an essential constituent of the method to be applied. As a result there is a gap between jurisprudence dealing with the law in force and the history of law.[57] This gap, according to Coing, is not only prejudicial but not even necessary since e.g. in the sociological method the research of those social forces which determine the contents of the legal norms requires also the study of history. And the comparative law researches cannot be successful without applying the historical aspect as it would be impossible to understand the peculiarities of the law of the various countries without studying their historical development. What is then this gap accounted for? The reply to this question is determined by the philosophy of history adopted by Coing, especially with regard to sociology. In effect, as far as comparative law is considered, he regards the view as acceptable that the productive effect of the historical concept is hampered by the, in many respects defective, historical knowledge but insofar as sociology is concerned it is no more the lack of historical experiences which is the hampering moment but the various axioms adopted by the sociologists and the sociologists of law. Coing chains the major hampering factor to be the hypothesis that society develops in conformity with certain determined laws, that there are various historical periods (he evokes Comte and Marxism) or that legal rules have their origin in the conflict between the forces of society in a chaotic state.

It may perhaps appear a little ludicrous that Coing attempts to lay aside precisely the historical concept as an obstacle out of the way of the "matrimony" between sociology and historicism. Coing was led by this train of thoughts to the *new pattern* of the constituent described as permanent of his theory. Such a concept of history should be sought for — Coing claims — which would render possible the bridging of the gap, would bring about a mutually productive effect between theory and history, legal interpretation

[55] H. Coing, *Grundzüge der Rechtsphilosophie*, p. 280.

[56] H. Coing, *Savigny et Collingwood : Histoire et Interprétation du Droit*, Archives de Philosophie du Droit, Droit et Histoire, Paris, 1959.

[57] *Ibidem*, p. 3.

and legal history, and at the same time would assure the possibility of reaching beyond the out of date theory of Savigny. He found such a concept of history in the philosophy of history of R. G. Collingwood.[58] It may be stated, however, that Collingwood respectively his theory has not contributed many new ideas to the results of the irrational philosophy of history attained till then. His essential conclusions are: there is a fundamental difference between history and natural science. For the first there are no facts we could observe, the facts must be reconstructed from the past, the subjects are human action or human thought and the materialization of the latter. Consequently, it would be incorrect to surmise the existence of laws in history and its science. Its fundamental category is the category of freedom. The compulsion which may be observed in the course of history is not the compulsion deriving from the situation — as man forms his resolution shaped by the situation. The study of the situation, therefore, leads to the ideas of the man who was acting.[59] Coing deduces the following conclusions from the philosophy of history of Collingwood in respect of jurisprudence.

Law is also the result of human activity displayed in the past and expresses much more human resolution than direct social forces. In fact, social factors do not appear automatically in a legal norm but through human resolution. True, this resolution depends more or less on a determined situation which is as far as the judge is concerned more individual. These, however, are not directly effective but in the form of ideas related to them. For instance, the activity of the French revolutionaries of the XVIIIth century as well as that of modern legislators has been attached to a certain doctrine concerning the society and the historiograph of law should discover how consistently these doctrines had been observed in the course of the legislative process. And as far as the position of the jurist is concerned who interprets the legal rules, Coing stresses that also the latter finds himself in a situation completely similar to that of the historiograph of Collingwood. The jurist, too, has to comprehend human actions displayed in the past, and for this end he has to reconstruct in his own mind the factors which had prompted the legislator or the judge in the past to activity, consequently, historical interpretation of the legal rules is unavoidable.[60] His final conclusion: Savigny's conclusion

[58] *Ibidem*, pp. 5—7.

[59] For the doctrine of Collingwood see R. C. COLLINGWOOD, *The Idea of History*, Oxford, 1946.

[60] H. COING, *Savigny et Collingwood*, p. 7. It is, however, quite clear that Coing tries only to support his former doctrine by relying on the philosophy of Collingwood. He emphasizes again that the research worker should re-create the same situation with which, for instance, the legislation had been confronted, he should discover the categories by the help of which the legislator had formed an opinion of the situation, and he should ascertain the social theories resorted to by him for reaching a solution, or those traditions which had shaped it. So, for instance, it is well known — he points out — that the German legislation on industrial combinations had been influenced by the *Genossenschaften*, etc. (*op. cit.* p. 9).

still holds true: history of law is the basis of all scientific doctrines of modern law.[61]

The elements of the philosophy of history of Dilthey, Spranger and Collingwood, which are on the whole identical — the irrational concept of history, the experience gained from the situation as the source of knowledge and following from that the central place occupied by psychological process of the individual — are essentially borne out in Coing's whole work. A certain change in the juristic ideas emerging in the wake of this historical-philosophical core is not incidental either. By placing into a fixed historical concept the manifold elements of bourgeois jurisprudence after World War II it has created a new variety of a psychological type of the historically relative Natural Law, which indeed meets the ideological requirements of its age and of its society.

The formulation of the problem by Coing in which he opposes to one another *the theoretical study of law and the history of law* is characteristic not only of the starting point adopted by Coing. And although several bourgeois authors recognize the merits of the German science in respect of the efforts aiming at the solution of the problem, this question was contested not only in German jurisprudence. Bruno Paradisi, for example, proceeds almost on the theoretical line of Coing. In effect, Paradisi similarly attempts to solve the antagonism between theory and history, which he conceives to be of a logical nature, by recognizing the historicism of law, namely in the way that he regards law as the complex product of history. And as the legal norm is the expression of a *historical situation*, he maintains that those bonds should be studied in the first place by which the norm is bound to its epoch.[62] The same problem appears in the construction of Giovanni Ambrosetti who evoking the present revival of the Natural Law opposes rationalism to historicism and endeavours to unite the two modes of thinking by maintaining that the "social" and "historical" are similarly integrated in the human personality. Such a central place of the human personality — as one of his critics has correctly stated — proves the Tomist concept of the author, which means indeed an extreme subjectivism.[62a]

Subjectivism, however, arises of necessity and not only in Ambrosetti's doctrine. All efforts which are inherent in the historical concept of the philosophers several times mentioned or which are related to it attempt by blending "rationalism" or the theory with historicism to create some sort of historical Natural Law, necessarily become subjective. This subjectivism emerges in spite of the fact that it recognizes in a certain sense and to a certain degree,

[61] *Ibidem*, p. 9.

[62] B. Paradisi, *Le Dogme et l'Histoire vis-à-vis de l'Historiographie juridique*. Archives de Philosophie de Droit, Droit et Histoire, Paris, 1959.

[62a] Cf. Würtenberger, *op. cit.* p. 279.

the authors vary in this respect, the historically determined character of the legal principles and legal norms because the philosophers in question characterize with irrationalism the recognition of the law and of the factors determining the law (the historical situation is expressed in some way, through intuition etc., in the individual), respectively reject the determined character of the historical process itself.

The almost exclusive domination of the irrational philosophy of history in western, in the first line German legal philosophy with a historical conception, its domination in the Natural Law connected so or otherwise with the concept of value of the historical epoch,[63] which essentially means the elimination of the historical progress in the field of the law, too, does not give cause for the optimism with regard to the so-called revival of the historical concept. In effect, this revival is the survival of the irrational historicism, of the "unhistorical" historical concept. Thus, if we pose the question of M. Villey in this sense: does a crisis of historicism exist now, we cannot accept his answer. In effect, Villey is not anxious about the future of historicism, provided that it does not attempt — as the historicism of the XIXth century had done — to give scientific explanations, but contents itself with understanding the phenomena.[64] And this concept is characteristic of the historicism in the philosophy of law of today. This concept, in compliance with the doctrine of the irrational philosophy of history detaches the natural, social and historical sciences from one another reserving for the former the scientific cognition and explanation, and for the latter the *understanding on the basis of intuition*. This, however, may transform the science of history and together with it jurisprudence resorting to such a concept into an arbitrary flight of wit.

3. In discussing Coing's doctrine it has already been mentioned what central importance Coing attributed to the inquiries of historical character in comparative law and to the history of law. This importance as an organic part of his theoretical conception is in a certain sense in a concrete way connected with the concrete requirements of western society and political endeavours.

As a matter of fact the science of comparative law has been assuming an increasing legal political importance. We have not only those movements in mind which have been started with this explicit purpose, but also the science itself in which, at least in Europe, just in our days those elements are augmenting which aim, with a well-defined ideology, at creating a *uniform European law*. And these very efforts are connected with the historical concept, inasmuch it is attempted to establish this uniform law by means

[63] K. Larenz, *Methodenlehre der Rechtswissenschaft*, Berlin—Göttingen—Heidelberg, 1960, p. 127.

[64] Villey, *op. cit.* p. 437.

of the *historical* method, namely relying on the Roman Law and in connection with it the Natural Law. The assessment of Savigny's work by Koschaker or Wieacker is coupled with this concept in these frames. The same applies to the work of Eugen Ulmer, too, only completed with another element. In fact, Ulmer maintains in respect of the common elements of the European law that these elements have been given in the course of historical development and have been due to the reception of the Roman and Canon Laws, to the process as the Roman and Canon Laws have been amalgamated with the institutions of the medieval Germanic Law. These common elements were reinforced by the ideas of Natural Law in the XVIIth and XVIIIth centuries which were *common European ideas* and lent a vigorous impetus to modern codification.[65] Ulmer points out that the European evolution towards a uniform European law based on the common elements enumerated above is in close connection with the idea of the European integration. This European integration must assure the "defense of the European culture" against the "powerful Soviet block".[66] Consequently, the three common elements mentioned by Ulmer would have the function, at least in the doctrine of some representatives of the comparative law, to justify the "European" culture of law by discovering its historical foundations, a "European" culture which may be opposed to the Socialist law. It would lead us too far and it is not our task to discuss the question how much the Socialist law owes, although it is in its content radically new and has assumed also many new elements of form to the tradition of the *European evolution*, the Roman Law, some ideas of the Natural Law, how its present existence may be conceived without the historical antecedents of the whole legal evolution or, and that is the most important thing, *to what extent it forms a part of the European culture and how far it shows the future path of the European legal culture*. It will suffice for us to conclude that the assertion of Ulmer relieves us from justifying why the science of comparative law is attached, especially in respect of its historical foundations, to certain political endeavours.

Erich Genzmer, a well-known figure of the western science of comparative law posed the question whether comparative law should be regarded as a method or as a science.[67] For us the question means the historical connection of both, namely, what otherwise is common in comparative law and legal history, it has *developed from a method to a science* as required by certain social conditions. Like the historical method necessarily gave rise to the history of law, and like legal history in conformity with the development of national states, more precisely with a certain nationalist ideology, has

[65] E. Ulmer, *Wege zu europäischer Rechtseinheit*, München, 1959, p. 4.

[66] Ulmer, *op. cit.* p. 7.

[67] E. Genzmer, *Zum Verhältnis von Rechtsgeschichte und Rechtsvergleichung*, Archiv für Rechts- und Sozialphilosophie, vol. XII/3, 1955, p. 326.

become an independent science especially in those countries where nationalism had a particular, retrospective character,[68] so the method of comparative law, too, which started at the outset with a certain historical character, as a new method of the science of law (e.g. in the doctrine of Mainz and Kohler) has become an independent branch of jurisprudence in the course of its development. This development is accounted for by the unheard of, unprecedented expansions of trade or in general the economic and other international intercourse, the increasing number of the phenomena of economic and political integration, the close relations evolving between states. (Although the law-unifying function of the comparative law had already been apparent, e.g. in the doctrine of Lambert, and with a much stronger emphasis under the aegis of Natural Law in the work of Saleilles, its outspoken political and legal political content have appeared only in our days. When discussing Ulmer's work the function of historicism as an important element of these efforts has already been shown. For this reason we want to discuss this problem because the historical concept is reflected in the science of comparative law with a specific content. This particular character, not only on account of its historicism, is connected in many respects with the concept of the historically relative Natural Law.

When at the beginning of the century Lambert has divided the comparative law into two parts, namely into comparative history and comparative legislation,[69] the historical element, which strictly speaking produced comparison as a method, was still alive but already meant a departure from the exclusively historical concept (Kohler, attacked the opinions of Lambert for this reason[70]). In the course of subsequent development this has to a certain extent, been obscured but in the years following World War II always an increasing number of bourgeois authors have been standing for the historical view in comparative law researches and this view is very often connected with a certain demand for normativism, too. *The "European Natural law" based on a historical comparison is the appearance in our days of the interdependence of the historical and normative concepts.* This concept is opposed by Genzmer to the rather abstract "droit ideal relatif" of Saleilles,[71] this is in the background of the European science of law of Koschaker based on the comparison of ideas; it was to serve this purpose that the historical elements have been detached by Koschaker and Wieacker from Savigny's

[68] The representatives of today of the national trend of legal history generally emphasize the German elements as opposed to the Roman elements, for instance, in German legal history. So, for instance, Fehr attributes to the reception of the Roman law the oppression of the genuine German law springing up from "the mind of the German people". (Cf. H. Fehr, *Deutsche Rechtsgeschichte*, 5th ed. Berlin, 1952, p. 197.)

[69] E. Lambert, *La fonction du droit civil comparé*, vol. I. Paris, 1903.

[70] J. Kohler, *Rechtsphilosophie und Universalrechtsgeschichte*, — Holtzendorff—Kohler, *Enzyklopädie der Rechtswissenschaft*, I. 1915, pp. 16. et seq.

[71] Genzmer, *op. cit.* p. 331.

work, with the view that the latter might remain a European, the dogmatist of the Roman law, the custodian of the uniform European legal culture, and this is the concept which connects — again according to Genzmer — in the empirical comparison of the European legal systems the historical and dogmatic methods.[72]

Otherwise, we meet precisely in the doctrine of Genzmer the historical concept which elucidates in the most characteristic way the historicism of the comparative jurisprudence. This concept is the theory of the "historical continuity" of the past-present-future. According to Genzmer the tripartite category of the past, present and future characterizes only our thinking since Parmenides and does not express reality at all. The connection between the past and the present was recognized among others in jurisprudence, too. Genzmer evokes, for instance, Mitteis, according to whom legal history is the past conjured up,[73] i.e. represented by the present. If, however, it is claimed that the present is determined by the past, we are thinking in a rather one-sided way — Genzmer maintains — and this is due to the fact that we conceive the running of time only in one direction, looking forward, because our mind had been accustomed to it. While the past is determined to the same degree by the future and this is difficult to understand only for those who are used to see in the time only a chronologically arranged measurable process. Of the numerous instances cited from the literature in order to support his views, only one as being characteristic should be singled out. Among others he quotes a well-known play of Thornton Wilder: The Skin of Our Teeth. In the play Antrobus and his family, who, according to the author's intention, personify at the same time the first human couple and the modern American petty bourgeois and represent both the present and historical mankind, and both the present every day and the every day of all times. Finally he also evokes the fact that this view follows from the doctrine of Einstein on the continuity in four dimensions of space and time.[74] Genzmer's concept of history, however, is after all unhistorical and this is shown precisely by the form of his reference to the play of Wilder. In effect, Genzmer does not stress in the play the idea according to which the man in a momentary situation of his own loses sight of the development of the whole of mankind, albeit history proves that humanity survives all catastrophes and continues to develop, but on the contrary, he emphasizes the circumstance that Wilder describes the every-day and the historical man in identical historical situations with the same strokes of the brush. There is no doubt that this concept, if we see a philosophy in it, means the negation of the historical evolution which in the historical view of Genzmer looks like if the future and the present

[72] *Ibidem*, p. 332.
[73] Mitteis, *op. cit.* p. 69.
[74] Genzmer, *op. cit.* pp. 336–342.

posed essentially identical problems among others in jurisprudence, too. Consequently, he essentially comes to the same conclusion, like Strauss, namely that history teaches that human mind is always dealing with identical problems. This, however, may hardly be called historicism. The example given by Genzmer in the field of law by which he tries to give a positive form to his theory, apart from being formalistic and meaningless, points to the same thing. In effect, he affirms that the European integration after some decades or perhaps in a century lead to the unity of the continental, European law of obligations. This fact, the present being determined by the future, obliges us to begin the comparative preparatory inquiries, namely in respect of the pattern of legislation. He believes to discover the most appropriate pattern in the Justinian codification, the basis of which is the expression of the old concept stemming from the East and penetrating into medieval Europe, that the legislator shows to the people the way towards law or teaches the people the law, namely the law which is not created but revealed and promulgated by the legislator.[75] Thus Genzmer's grandiose philosophy of history transferred into the field of law gave birth to a rather grey mouse.

What is the position from an ideological viewpoint in modern jurisprudence of the most historical research, legal history? It is not intended in this place to treat the problems of legal history, the relationships existing between legal history and sciences of history,[76] or the theoretical constructions suggested in respect of the connection between history of law and the theory of law.[77] It is, however, not by chance that the question of the history of law is posed in its ideological context precisely at the juncture of discussing the concept of European jurisprudence and of the European Natural Law. Schönfeld, who deals in his undoubtedly well documented work with the problems of the history of law, writes that the historical present is not the absolute present but the unity of the past and future. It results from this fact that legal history serves legal political aims, too, because scientific legal

[75] Genzmer, *op. cit.* pp. 343–347.

[76] See e.g. H. Mitteis, *Vom Lebenswert der Rechtsgeschichte*, Weimar, 1947. Mitteis sees the specific dilemma of legal history in the fact that it constitutes on the one hand a part of the science of history, on the other hand of the science of law.

[77] See e.g. W. Schönfeld, *Vom Problem der Rechtsgeschichte*, Halle, 1927. Schönfeld sees the bridge between theory and history, on the one hand, in the dogmatics of a historical content (p. 327), on the other hand in the fact that the theory of law as the critique of legal experience, of the legal cognizance is at the same time the critique of legal history, too (p. 338). The historical character of the theory of law or of the sociology of law shows a peculiar bifurcation insomuch as it separates rigidly the normative and factual aspects of law. Our impression is that he does not stress so much the historical character of the theory and sociology as rather the nussion of legal history beside both. The rigid separation appears also in the works of Gyula Moór. The historical character is in his opinion characteristic of the sociology of law dealing with problems of causality as it generalizes the experiences gained from legal history. Gy. Moór, *A jogtörténet és a jogszociológia módszertana* [Methodology of Legal History and of Sociology of Law], Budapest, 1942, pp. 9–11.

policy consists in the doctrine of right law, and policy can only be a historical policy.[78] Schönfeld's conclusion does not contain many new things for a Marxist lawyer as it is clear that legal history as a science, as a part of the legal ideology is determined by social and ideological conditions and objectives. Nevertheless his conclusion is not without interest and it is important because it hints at the theoretical recognition of the role and place of legal history in the bourgeois legal concept.[79] If the development of legal history as a part of jurisprudence most connected with the national ideology is appraised from this aspect, interesting phenomena may be observed.

The connection between legal history and national development and, in Germany, the romantic popular-national ideology is well-known.

Legal history as an ideologically important constituent, of the period of national development, as a matter of course, is connected not only with the romantic and reactionary nationalism. In the bourgeois revolution and in the course of its preparation, e.g. in the progressive Hungarian national movement, it played certain role and so it is not without reason that László Németh in his play "The Two Bólyais" speaks of jurisprudence as a science "which recently took under its wings history too, and with that it provides an excellent opportunity for encouraging the enthusiasm among youth." The retrograde character of the nationalist legal history as determined by social conditions appeared at the first time in publications about the turn of the century and in the XXth century, thus at a time when bourgeois evolution had in general already passed beyond nationalism itself. It is therefore natural that this national legal history at this time was coupled with other endeavours, too. The most characteristic instance for that is the ideological role played by German legal history with a Germanist tendency at the turn of the century and in the XXth century particularly after the short "intermezzo of Weimar" following World War I. Of the concept of both periods the views contained in the work of the German scholar Erik Wolf published in 1939 are characteristic. As a matter of fact Wolf when dealing with Gierke points out that legal history at the turn of the century became a collection of facts; people and law developed independently of each other, law and the Empire did not constitute an organic unity. In Gierke, however, the immutable conviction was alive that only a truly German law can express the national idea realized in the Empire of Bismarck, and only a popular and social law based on the unity of the people and the Empire may secure

[78] SCHÖNFELD, *op. cit.* p. 345.

[79] It seems that this was realized by the movement started for the researches connected with Hungarian popular law — although as a matter of course, in conformity with the historical-social situation with a different ideological character — what is proved by the fact that this movement stresses the legal political importance of the legal history made familiar on the basis of popular law.

its long-lasting character.[80] Gierke's legal history served this purpose — says Wolf — and we may add to this that Wolf in his work on the history of ideas in his epoch tried to reveal the "historical antecedents" of the national-socialist variety of the "national and social law" and attempted to present the great German lawyers as adherents of the same idea, respectively to make a selection among them as dictated by this idea. The national character of the legal evolution was in the historical situation preceding World War II accepted to such an extent in Europe that Gyula Moór, who otherwise was keeping aloof from the popular-national new romanticism, stated similarly that legal evolution was national and that there cannot be any question of a "European" legal evolution as a uniform process.[81]

The national ideological character of legal history (whether in a progressive or retrograde sense), which we characterized only rather briefly by way of illustration, too, has ceased as a rule to prevail in our days or is on the way of decline. As a result of changes in the historical situation, in conformity with the western economic-political conditions developed after World War II, legal history as a means of the legal policy — excepting a few representatives thereof — has come in its main line to serve the emphasis upon and the proof of the European legal evolution. Thus the European history of the Roman Law and the comparative method based on these historical foundations have come to play an increasingly important role. The values of the European historical-natural law developed as a result of the historical comparison became slowly the exclusive characteristics of the "civilized" law or of the "civilized" science of law. As Thomas Mann wrote about Nietzsche: ". . . er hat Moral überhaupt mit bürgerlicher Moral verwechselt";[82] thus by and large the values of European legal development corresponding to the conditions of today are becoming the characteristic features of law. This is not a question in the first place of the legal institutions because they might be found from a merely formal aspect in many cases in the socialist law, too (although not in the sense as Friedmann alleges, that socialist law did not produce anything new)[83] but the points in question in this context are the values and the way of thinking. "We have acquired in this way through the innumerable national boundaries such a community of thoughts which render possible for each lawyer who is well-informed in the field of law to find his way in the legal world of any other state. This uniform expansion of the modern legal evolution is continuing. The new labour law and the new economic law is getting a place everywhere in the legal systems of the European peoples to such an

[80] E. Wolf, *Grosse Rechtsdenker der deutschen Geistesgeschichte*, Tübingen, 1939, pp. 544—545.

[81] Moór, *op. cit.* p. 5.

[82] Th. Mann, *Nietzsches Philosophie im Lichte unserer Erfahrung*, Gesammelte Werke, vol. 10. Berlin, 1956, p. 663.

[83] W. Friedmann, *Law in a Changing Society*, London, 1959, p. 9.

extent that none of them may keep aloof from the manifestations of the European law and European jurisprudence."[84] The words of Carl Schmitt (who characterizes in his person the change mentioned) well illustrate in our opinion that has been said above.

III.

Being familiar with the historical concept as it appears in bourgeois jurisprudence, it may now be compared with the historicism of Marxist jurisprudence. The difference may be stated almost in one sentence. In fact, the historical materialism of Marxism sees in history a continuous, in its fundamental trend forward moving, consequently *progressive movement*, a movement which, through contradictions and leaps is directed by determined laws. György Lukács, writing about the changes after 1848 of the bourgeois historical concept, considers with good reason as the central problem of the historical concept the problem of progress. He concludes in this context that "the most distinguished poets and thinkers of the epoch preceding 1848 made the most important step forward by historically drafting the idea of progress: they got as far as the — although only relatively correct and never complete — concept of the contradictory character of human progress."[85] As the problems of progress were relegated into the background after 1848 in the bourgeois concept of history, as this concept rejects the idea of progress accomplished through contradictions, as the collapse of the Hegelian philosophy in Germany meant the disappearance of the knowledge concerning the contradictory character of progress,[86] as it was conserved in the ideology of the liberal bourgeoisie — as a certain survival of its old historical position — at the very most in its smooth, rectilinear form yielding afterwards its place to the idea of the eternal return, to the idea of the movement without any direction, later to the most various forms of the pessimist philosophy of history, so the Marxist concept of history has unfolded, disentangled this very element, the highest result achieved in the bourgeois historical concept[87] and defined its contents. The Marxist thesis of the progress through contradictions and leaps, however, is related to the concept of the laws prevailing in society. "The recognition of the historical progress means the adoption of the standpoint that in the course of historical development certain social phenomena and certain determined features thereof respectively, develop as

[84] C. Schmitt, *Az európai jogtudomány helyzete* [The Situation in the European Legal Science], Revista de la Universidad Nacional de Cordoba, 1953, No. 2. pp. 283—295.
[85] Gy. Lukács, *A történelmi regény* [The Historical Novel], Budapest, p. 145.
[86] *Ibidem, p.* 146.
[87] Cf. Lenin, *Works*, vol. 21. Budapest (in Hungarian).

required by the laws of society, in the same direction and to an increasing extent".[88] The regular process, however, produces of necessity in society side by side with progress also phenomena of decline. Erik Molnár quoting Lenin concludes with good reason that "it is not dialectical, not scientific, from a theoretical viewpoint incorrect, to conceive that universal history is progressing evenly and consistently without making huge jumps backwards."[89] "From the social progress its contrary: social decline is inseparable."[90]

The determination of history by laws is very interesting but it cannot be dealt with in detail in this place. All in all, we should like to cite as against the determination conceived by Genzmer a conclusion of the classics of Marxism from which, among others, it appears that Genzmer's view is not quite new. In effect, the classics of Marxism attacked already in the "German Ideology" a false interpretation of the historical determination by writing the following: "History is nothing else as the succession of the various generations of which all exploit those materials, capitals, productive forces, which all their predecessors bequeathed to them, but in a way, that on the one hand each generation continues the activity bequeathed to it in quite different conditions, on the other hand, it alters the old conditions by a quite different activity; and this may be distorted in a speculative way by making later history the purpose of the earlier . . . by which then history obtains its own particular objectives and becomes a person beside other persons . . . although what is meant by "destination", "purpose", "germ", "idea" of former history is nothing else but an abstraction from later history, an abstraction from the active influence exercised by the earlier history upon the later one."[91] This latter concept we have now criticized appears in the theory of Genzmer on the continuity of space and time conceived in a vulgar enough way. The transforming into the present reflected by mirror and the alleged determination of the conditions of the present by this supposed image appears in the rather inadequate application of his historical concept upon the law.

From the concept of history of Marxism result of necessity the often quoted but even in the Marxist social sciences not sufficiently observed conclusions of Marx and Engels according to which "we know only one science, the science of history".[92] This sentence, the methodical expression of the historical view of historical materialism, appeared already also in another form in Marxist scientific thinking. The opinion of Marxism in respect of the historicism of justice or the methodical requirement meaning the unity of the historical and logical viewpoint is, for instance, well-known. It is not

[88] E. Molnár, *Dialektikus materializmus és társadalomtudomány* [Dialectical Materialism and Social Sciences], Budapest, 1962, p. 347.

[89] Lenin, *Works*, vol. 22, Budapest, p. 322. (in Hungarian).

[90] E. Molnár, *op. cit.* p. 349.

[91] Marx–Engels, *Works*, vol. 3, Budapest, 1960, p. 37. (in Hungarian).

[92] Marx–Engels, *op. cit.* p. 20.

envisaged in this place to treat here the philosophical problems of historicism as a method; we should like only to suggest some conclusions with regard to jurisprudence which follow from the above-mentioned philosophical concept and which, perhaps will aid us in understanding the problem what historicism means in Marxist jurisprudence.

It has already been suggested that although the emphasis on the historical concept necessarily followed from the development of the bourgeois society, the element thus developed has in present bourgeois jurisprudence — in the first place on account of the direct political consequence of the development of the social conditions — an occasional, pragmatic character and a secondary importance. As it follows from the Marxist concept of history, however, it is the necessary methodical element of Marxist jurisprudence, which might be incidentally conceived in a vulgar way, and might also be applied superficially, — such a concept, however, becomes manifest in the negative nature of the result — but it cannot be denied. As a methodical element, historicism is for Marxist jurisprudence particularly important from two aspects: beyond its fundamental philosophical foundations, but following from them. The two aspects are interrelated and in this place they were separated for the sake of an easier understanding. 1. From the historicism of the phenomenon and of the concept containing it follows that their cognitions are possible only in a historical way. 2. From the historicism of the way leading to justice results the importance of the history of ideas in which the historical development of the knowledge relating to the legal phenomena and to the concepts reflecting them is expressed. It will be attempted to outline the contents of the two aspects in more detail.

1. On account of the fact that legal phenomena and the concepts containing them are based on social and historical conditions, their social content evolves as required by the social conditions. It follows from the fact that law has a character of form,[93] that the historical alteration of the social content is reflected in the legal content, too, thus it is, in spite of the incidental stability of the form, subject to changes. The legal content expressing the social content, on the contrary, has an influence on the legal form, thus the various elements of it are dependent on the historically changing content even then if in the course of the development the fact that it is bound as to its substance has already been obscured. It results from this that the knowledge of all features of the legal categories, concepts, institutions, etc. becomes possible only through historical inquiries. This forms also in a practical sense a bridge between the laws reflecting the various periods of the social development as well as in respect of the effectiveness of cognition. The surmise of Coing according to

[93] See Kulcsár, *A ténykutatások jelentősége a jogi jelenségek megismerésében* [The Importance of the Inquiry into Facts in the Cognition of Legal Phenomena], Állam- és Jogtudományi Intézet Értesítője, vol. IV, No. 4, pp. 500 et seq.

which the recognition of the evolution of the society in conformity with determined laws renders impossible the historical study of the law is thereby refuted. As a matter of fact it is clear that the historical study of a concept or institution does not only give a key to a certain extent for the understanding of the present functioning of the concept, institution, etc. in question,[94] but it also determines the "historical dead weight" resulting from the limited independent development, and reveals the historical determination of some elements, incidentally in connection with those elements which would appear without historical inquiries as necessarily accompanying the respective concept, institution, etc. though in fact they are not doing so.

2. It follows from the historicism of cognition that the cognizance of the legal phenomena is a historical process, too. From this two consequences may be deduced, on the one hand, it is clear that the cognition of legal phenomena is determined by history and society, there are expressed in it the social conditions and through them the social position, the subjective — but as a rule socially determined — views, the ideology, etc. of the person endeavouring at knowing them. On the other hand, from the social historical situation may follow the temporary coming into prominence of certain aspects or features of law and, in consequence, their scientific elucidation, too. The recognition and emphasis on the historical element of law is a characteristic example for that. As a consequence of a determined social situation the attention was drawn to the historicism of law, its appraisal and solution followed from a determined situation, yet it contributed with that characteristic to the success of efforts resulting in a more profound cognition of the law. Of course, we could adduce many other examples, too. Such are e.g. the stress on the problem of the change of the law in the legal sociology of the XXth century[95] and on a, to a certain extent, lower level the problem of the role of subjective factors in the judgments of the courts in the American realist jurisprudence,[96] etc.; all these being the products of a determined social situation which directs the attention to certain features, and the failure of the attempt at their solution is indicated, too, as a rule, by making absolute the importance of a specific aspect. However, in spite of the unsuccessful attempts at its solution, the problem discovered remains and so does the correct crux of the solution, or in many cases only the piece of it, which has not been entirely annulled by the fact that it has been supposed to be absolute. Consequently, the historicism of the study of the history of ideas means in Marxist jurisprudence that by this means it reveals

[94] J. GAUDEMET, *Etudes juridiques et culture historique*, Archives de Philosophie du Droit, Droit et Histoire, Paris, 1900. p. 18. draws the attention to the historical character of legal concepts.

[95] See KULCSÁR, *A jogszociológia problémái* [The Problems of the Sociology of Law], p. 7. et seq.

[96] *Ibidem*, pp. 81. et seq. 220 et seq.

the historical determination of one or another theory, doctrine, etc. relating to legal phenomena, it discovers their social roots and with its aid it concludes what the determination by time and society means, which has influenced the discovery or solution of the problem, furthermore what was the thing which gave expression to the given, in the first place class limits and what was significant, or even lasting in *the historical process of cognition*.

In addition to the views now discussed briefly, there is a third one which is also connected with the historical method of Marxist jurisprudence. This method may perhaps be so defined that historicism is at the same time the claim to comprehend actually the present, that is to say, that Marxist historicism deduces its conclusions not only from the regularities and trends which may be revealed in the course of investigating the past, but *observes the past in conjunction with the regularities and trends asserted in the present and attempts to reach as far as the concrete form of the social phenomena prevailing in the present. It is in this view that the historicism of Marxist jurisprudence is reflected in its sociological concept.*[97]

In conclusion an additional observation should be made and this observation is involved in the sentence stressed above. As a matter of fact the expression of historicism of Marxist jurisprudence in its sociological concept poses the problem of the relationship between the historical and logical methods in jurisprudence. It is well-known that Engels in his review on the work of Marx "To the Critique of the Political Economy" observes concerning the method of analysis chosen by Marx that "it is indeed nothing else than the historical discussion only disregarding the historical form and the interfering contingencies".[98] This observation which may be considered as the characteristic expression of the organic unity between the historical and logical methods, is very important not only from the aspect of the methodological problem of Marxist sociology, of the unity of the Micro- and Macro sociology reflected among others, in the course of the inquiries[99] but, by bearing out in essence the same methodological contents, it indicates the necessity of the logical generalization of the concrete nature of historicism, and expresses, in respect of the historical view of Marxist jurisprudence the requirement that over and above the contingencies of the historical material it grasps on a logical level the essence of reality.

[97] Cf. Kulcsár, *A ténykutatások jelentősége a jogi jelenségek megismerésében* [The Importance of the Inquiry into Facts in the Cognition of Legal Phenomena], p. 504. et seq.

[98] See the review of Engels in the *appendix* of the Work of K. Marx on the *Critique of the Political Economy*, Budapest, 1953, p. 976. (in Hungarian).

[99] See Kulcsár, *A marxista szociológia és az empirikus társadalomkutatás* [Marxist Sociology and Empirical Social Research], Magyar Filozófiai Szemle, vol. V, No. 3, 1961, pp. 347–348.

Part III
Trends

[7]

A Marxist Theory of Law?

Eugene Kamenka

I

The great German jurist, Rudolf von Ihering (whose direct descendants include the pop-singer Olivia Newton-John),[1] in the late nineteenth century poured scorn on the Platonic heaven of juristic concepts (Ihering, 1885) and proclaimed the jurisprudence of interests (Ihering, 1913). Ever since there has been a growing trend in Western societies towards so-called legal realism. The 'modern' tendency is to discount the internal coherence and historical integrity of law, its claim to mould society and to represent specifically legal traditions, procedures and ideals. Court decisions have been studied to bring out the extent to which they allegedly are not and cannot be derived from legal maxims, so-called principles of law, statutes or precedents, but reflect wider social conflicts and interests. The operation of law has rightly been recognized to extend far beyond the courtroom dramas recorded in law reports and casebooks – positively in the operation of that 'living law' internalized in a community's customs, expectations and ways of behaving, negatively in the uses and abuses of threat, negotiation and extra-legal power that precede or replace the courtroom appearance. The trend has been to de-intellectualize law, to pit life against what is written in the law books, to demolish the fences that an earlier generation had put up to distinguish law from custom, morality, politics and the legally irrelevant. We now insist that law stands neither above nor outside society, but within it, and that it does not simply make its own history. All this, of course, is true. It is not true, however, that legal history is simply social, or political or economic history – it *does* have its own traditions, concepts, nodal points, lines of development. When we go even further to argue that law is or should be a neutral, flexible and totally characterless *instrument* responsive to or serving uncritically elevated goals and needs alleged to have logical priority over law, that is also another matter.

More recently, anthropology and sociology have combined to

1. I draw heavily, in the first two and the last sections of this article, on my review of recent literature in this area published in *The Times Literary Supplement*, (Kamenka, 1981).

Law in Context Volume 1 1983

strengthen this reductive trend, or confusion. If law is a method of settling disputes in a regularized, predictable way, then what past Western theorists called 'law' is only one possible method among the many practised by different societies. Anarchic and violent self-help, or utter lawlessness, are not the only alternatives to a centralized, state-sanctioned codified legal system. Hobbes's social defence theory of law is clearly wrong, both logically and historically. Societies have rules, and quite sophisticated rules and procedures, without having a sovereign, codes, courts and constables (see Krygier, 1980). It may be, indeed, that the elevation of state-centred law, of the will of the sovereign and of a complex machinery devoted to producing stability and justice, is in inverse proportion to the authority of other norms: religion, custom and sheer fellow-feeling and neighbourliness (see Ziegert, 1980). Some theorists make this point by saying that law is only one form of domination or social control and not necessarily the most important or the most admirable; others reject altogether the claim that law is produced by or controlled on behalf of society, or that it has independent values. They insist that law stands not above but within class conflict or other social conflict — that law is the will of the ruling class, of notables or elites, and seeks to organize social life in the interest of one group at the expense of another. What the eighteenth and nineteenth centuries did to religion — showing that there were *many* religions, and that they were all made by men, reflecting different climates, periods, values and aspirations and much dastardliness and cynicism — the twentieth century is doing to law.

The rejection of traditional, external authority, of an authority of origins, was an important theme of Protestantism and then, more nakedly, of the French Enlightenment and the French Revolution. It has been followed more recently by a further rejection of the so-called 'liberal' conception of the rule of law, of the authority, that is, of abstract and impersonal laws, elevated by nineteenth-century thinkers and societies. The call now is to 'humanize' and 'demythologize' law and legal relations, to make law a servant and not a master, to set up over it and against it the values and demands of 'man', 'society', 'the people', or the 'rational' pursuit of 'rational' goals. The popular catch-phrases of today are not 'law and order', but 'steering society', 'promoting equality and community', planning for the future, providing scope for creativity, 'self-expression' and the natural life, protecting the environment and averting ecological disaster. They represent and bear witness to a remarkable strengthening and increasing popularity of socialist and sociological critiques of law. These, of course, have a long pre-history. Today, they have so much gained in strength and public appeal as to constitute what Professor A.E.-S. Tay and I have called a crisis in law and legal ideals (Kamenka and Tay, 1975).

Law in Context

The crisis is furthered by an unjustified current contempt for the Western tradition and Western achievements. At the same time, an active concern for concrete social equality, for the rights and benefits of the 'underprivileged', is leading to a constant demand for more and more law-making activity directed to specific ills on a frankly discriminatory basis. We do now believe that there should be one law for the poor and another for the rich — substituting benevolent discrimination in law for the hard extra-legal inequalities of concrete social life.

Without question, the new critical attitudes to law and legal ideals have done much to alleviate particular injustices and something to raise the critical standard of legal thinking and legal discussion. Law, in English-speaking countries, is no longer universally seen as an art, or more accurately as a craft or technique that makes no wider intellectual demands on its practitioners. In these countries it is now much more generally recognized, as it has long been on the continent of Europe, that law is a central field in social science, social administration and social thinking. The newer disciplines of anthropology and sociology have immeasurably deepened our understanding of the nature and functions of law through studying it in a wide range of social settings. Our increasing awareness of the problems and concerns of communist, socialist and developing societies has had the same effect. The proliferation of new legal areas, in the common law world and outside it, has perforce produced new legal attitudes and new views of the function and appropriate procedures of law, as well as a new sense of its limitations. But the current emphasis on seeing law in context is to put all the weight on the context and pay very little attention, if any, to the internal coherence and values of a legal system, of legal institutions, concepts and techniques or to the judiciary and the profession so closely associated with them, except to 'expose' them.

Both Marxism and radicalism, at least in England, eschew serious consideration of law as a system or as a social institution. They are more at home with a catalogue of injustices than with a theory of justice, with bias and distortions of the legal process than with the nature and function of law, with the politics of the judiciary than with the role of legal traditions, techniques and values. Thus one of the better Marxist books published in England in recent years, E.P. Thompson's study of the origins of the 1723 Black Act against poaching (Thompson, 1977), begins with a fundamental mistake — the belief that that Act is important in eighteeth-century legal history. It has no such importance whatever; it is illuminating for eighteenth-century *social* and *political* history. Its repeal in 1827 perhaps reflected a shift in eighteenth-century English class attitudes; it certainly involved no significant change in the structure of English law. An important item in eighteenth-century legal history, by contrast, is the development of genuine or at least better security of title, and of a sophisticated separation of interests in land and the consequent extension and abstraction of mortgageability which helped to revolutionize both law and the economy. One could give an interesting Marxist account of that; so far as I know, the economic historian R.S. Neale is the only one who has sought to do so (Neale, 1975:92–102). If we take such really central items in legal history as the thirteenth-century development of possessory assizes, of *novel disseisin* and *mort d'ancestor*, they stand in the most interesting and fundamental conflict with the feudal authority of the baronial courts and with feudal emphasis on status and title in the competing writ of right, which they ousted in importance. Consideration of this development and of the role of possession in the common law generally, creates a strong presumption against the Marxist view of law. Here is an opportunity for Marxist legal historians to do some real thinking. It has not been taken up.

II

Collectivism, A.V. Dicey wrote three-quarters of a century ago, did not come into the world with a theory of law and still has not attained to one (Dicey, 1914:67–68). Karl Marx was the son of a lawyer. He began his career as a law student and later made some highly successful appearances on his own behalf in court in Cologne, defending himself against charges of slandering officials and inciting insurrection during the 1848 revolution. Nevertheless, he wrote almost nothing extended or systematic about law, if we except a few early newspaper articles in which he proclaimed the indissolubility of marriage (at least according to its 'principle', if not quite in fact), the impropriety of new laws robbing the poor of old customary rights, and the need for the law-giver to reject the alien intrusions of religion and the demand of sectional interests.

Most of his life from then on Marx spent under the self-imposed duty of wading through 'economic filth', seeking to prove that the 'secret' of law, of politics, ideology and the State lay, in each case, in something else — in productive forces and relations of production, in the class struggle, in the 'material' life of society. In the truly human, self-managed society he worked for and predicted, there would be no law and no State. The conflict of rights and duties, the narrow horizons of bourgeois law and the abstraction and alienation of legal systems would have been totally overcome. Before that happy state, there was no law in general, but slave-owning, feudal, capitalist law. Of socialist law or a specific socialist legal system he did not conceive.

On all sorts of grounds, then, Marx and Engels refused to take law seriously as a specific or comparatively independent social institution,

Law in Context

having some character and history of its own. It reflected, for them, the mode of production, the economic organization of society, the class struggle, the will of the State and through it the will of the ruling class. It sanctified and protected social arrangements. It did not create them and it was not a fundamental social arrangement itself.

For those interested in the specific contribution of law to society, in a theory of law as a coherent system of concepts, norms and rules, and as the carrier of an abiding concern with justice, fairness and legitimacy, even the predigested 'Marx and Engels on Law' collections make dispiriting reading. Their interest lies in what they can tell us about Marxism, not in the insights they can give us about law. The Soviet collections, now slanted to make Marx stress the importance of law, make dull reading. Two new English attempts to present Marx and Engels on law will do little more to excite the unconverted. Paul Phillips's (1980) offers an earnest exposition of Marx's early philosophical treatment of law and of comments by Marx and Engels on the English Reform Bill, the Poor Law Amendment Act, 1834, the Ten Hours Bill and French legislation in the time of Louis Napoleon, followed by chapters on crime and criminal justice, regulation of economic institutions and 'law and society'. The book is described by its promoters as clear, simple and useful — a reasonably careful and honest choice of words. Phillips shares Thompson's view of 'legal' history — laws, not law. He ignores completely the Marxist belief in the 'withering away' of law. Cain and Hunt (1979) arrange substantial selections from Marx and Engels on law (rather than laws) thematically, according to the Althusserian belief that law is to be understood in relation to the three principal 'structures' in societies — the economic, the ideological and the political. The result is neither clear nor simple, and the commitment to an Althusserian Marxism is painfully obtrusive. But Cain and Hunt have sifted Marx and Engels carefully, arranged the extracts intelligently and done a much less sloppy job than is customary among many of their English Marxist confrères. The incapacity to distinguish laws that are part of a legal system and a legal tradition from those that are mere regulations that could be changed tomorrow without affecting the character of the legal system is common to both books and, as we shall see, to most Marxists.

Cain and Hunt are part of the growing interest in elaborating and promoting Marxist views of law that has followed the remarkable revival of intellectual Marxism in continental Europe, England, North America and Australia in the past decade. That revival has moved through the Marxian humanism and earnest rationality and moralism of the Frankfurt School into Althusserian structuralism, with its sophisticated mixture of idealist mystification and ruthless concentration on the class struggle —

Leninism masquerading as 'deep' philosophy — and with all culture treated as ideology.

The new trend has produced a whole series of journals, and of books, parading as 'critical' (but not of Marxism) and as relating law, State and society. They are at their best — which is usually not very good — in socio-legal studies (micro-sociology of law as opposed to macro-sociology), in drawing attention to specific malevolence or injustice and in studying, as F P. Thompson does, the social and political history that surrounds legal enactment and sentencing or punishment. When this work pretends to be conceptual, to deal with legal concepts, with theory of law, with law as itself a 'structure', it is pompous, confused and devoid of insight or bite. Sumner (1979) gives a reasonably clear presentation of structuralism, semiology and neo-structuralism, with its emphasis on symptomatic reading. The book will be of some interest to those concerned with the extent to which we cannot escape reading anything through the prism of our own 'ideologies'. Only 80 of its 300 pages even pretend to be devoted to law and they are the weakest part of the book, contrasting various Marxist trends but being critically perceptive about none of them. Still, this book is a great deal more readable than Edelman (1979), a work hailed by British Marxists as pathbreaking. This book, close, in its analysis, to the views of one of the only two significant Marxist legal theorists ever, E.B. Pashukanis — to be discussed below — turns Pashukanis's commodity exchange theory of law into jargon and converts a problem about copyright that is partly infrajural and partly a specific problem of French law into a 'contradiction' of bourgeois conceptions of ownership. A typical quotation (Edelman, 1979:97) should suffice to put most readers off this book and to remind us of the high level of infelicity in most English translations from the French:

> I can therefore reply to the question opened up by Althusser. If it is true that all bourgeois ideology interpellates individuals as subjects, the concrete/ideological content of the bourgeois interpellation is that the individual is interpellated as the embodiment of the determinations of exchange-value. And I can add that the subject in law constitutes the privileged form of this interpellation to the exact extent that the law assures and assumes the effectivity of circulation.

More critical of Althusserian structuralism, but sharing its epistemological premises, Hirst (1979) rejects the concept of totality and puts great emphasis on that side of Marx which sees men as making their own history. He gives an account of the analyses of property to be found in Marx, Pashukanis and Renner and himself prefers political struggle rather than economic production as the 'key' to law, while recognizing that law can, in principle, have a desirable social function.

Law in Context

Hugh Collins, whose recent study of Marxism and law is philosophically more serious and yet often both amateurish and obtuse, indeed takes the view that for a Marxist to have a general theory of law would be to subscribe to that fetishism of law which Marxists reject: Collins (1982:10). If Marxist radicals are making some impact on law teachers and students it is not because they have a theory of law or deal freshly and significantly with the history of legal thought and the foundations of legal philosophy. It is not even because they take law seriously in its own right. It is rather because they are impatient with law. An Australian radical law teacher, Andrew Fraser, put this point strongly in the Australian Marxist journal *Arena* (Fraser, 1976:123) and has been largely ignored. He says:

> Any serious examination of the few attempts which have been made in recent years to develop a radical theory of the legal process reveals a disturbingly high level of intellectual poverty and theoretical sterility. How else could one evaluate a theoretical project which seems to devote a major portion of its energy to measuring and emphasizing the political distance between itself and its object? Because radical legal theorists seem concerned above all else to establish their own authenticity as militant opponents of the legal system and a mainstream legal theory which is regarded as the servile hand-maiden of a repressive state apparatus, the task of actually comprehending the legal process as an important dimension of everyday social experience tends to be relegated to a second level priority, if it is not overlooked altogether. The most obvious manifestation of this tendency to reduce radical legal theory to the level of an elaborate war-cry is the prevalent radical image of the law as an external, repressive force which plays no essential part in our nature as social beings. As an external force imposed on the individual from without, the law need not be incorporated into any theory by which radicals seek to understand their personal needs and the relationship of those needs to the socio-historical process of which they are a product.

III

The thought of Karl Marx, like that of the founder of Christianity, has many conflicting and competing strains. It has made possible many Marxisms and given rise to an enormous literature of conflicting exegesis, interpretation and commentary. Nevertheless, a central traditional intellectual weakness of Marxism, separate from its past dogmatism, has remained. Marxists have overwhelmingly believed that they hold a special key, and a comparatively simple key at that, which will unlock and lay bare the secret of all significant social phenomena. Marxists as Marxists are never interested in the integrity, specificity and comparative independence of social phenomena, traditions and institutions or in the resultant complexity of problems. 'In the final analysis', they believe, the process of production or a mode of production and the class struggles arising out of it explain everything else. Their characterizations of the key — whether it lies in productive forces, relations of production, or the mode of production, in the process of production, in the process of exchange or in the class struggle of society — vary. They all agree, of course, that these factors are intimately related, only to be understood in connection with each other. Nevertheless, there are significant, indeed important, differences between those who put primacy on the process of production, those who put primacy on the market, and those who put primacy on the struggle between exploiters and exploited. But all of them see society as a functional monolithic whole; all of them think that the law, like literature, morality, and other superstructural or ideological features, 'in the last instance' has to be understood in terms of something else. It is in this sense that all Marxists have remained intellectually reductionist — in the law perhaps even more than in other areas. The fact that this is no longer true of the USSR, the People's Republic of China, and East European states may be a strong ground for saying that an unalloyed Marxism is no longer their official ideology.

The consideration of law and of problems of legal theory, as we have seen, does not form any significant part of Marx's work. He was significantly influenced, at various stages, not only by Hegel, but by Kant and the rather Kantian-Fichtean philosophy of law of the Young Hegelians, such as Eduard Gans, and perhaps by Savigny, the great figure in the historical school of law who taught Marx as an undergraduate. Nevertheless, attempts to ascribe to Marx a complex and coherent theory of law never derive from his own pronouncements on law. They rest, rather; on interpretations of his more general remarks on the relation between productive forces and relations of production (the economic base) and the superstructure, especially ideology, and his remarks on the forms and role of property in various periods of social life.

In Marx's work, in chronological sequence but without any earlier stage every being repudiated, we find three fundamental approaches to law:

a) Law is either coercion and therefore treats man as an animal, to be determined from without and not by the inner universal and universalizable rules of his being (his human and species essence); *or* it is the systematization of freedom, of the inner rules of human life and human activities, losing any independent or external character or force, but recognized as an internal necessity.

b) Law is a form of human alienation, which tears the juridical subject out of its human and social context, which abstracts and mystifies and rests on illusions made possible by such abstraction — the illusion of equality, the illusion of reciprocity.

Law in Context

c) Law is the reflection and the protector of specific modes of production, forms of economic organization and of class domination. Law, in the crudest version to be found in the works of Marx and Engels, is simply the will of the ruling class — though, especially in Marx, that will itself is the product of forms and modes of production.

It is now 100 years since Marx's death. Nevertheless, there are still only two Marxist legal theorists who have attempted seriously and with originality to come to grips with what I have called the specificity of law — with that which distinguishes law from other social arrangements or ideologies, which makes it express (if we use Austinian terms) a particular type of command, a particular sort of will, or, (in non-Austinian terms) a particular form of rule-consciousness and rationality. These two theorists are Karl Renner, twice President of the Austrian Republic, and E.B. Pashukanis, the foremost Soviet legal theoretician of the 1920's, disgraced, imprisoned and murdered by Stalin in the 1930's. Both men, though they hold very different views, reject completely the view that law is simply the will of the ruling class or that it is an arbitrary system of commands. Both also reject the view that law is an ideology, a passive element in the superstructure, and hold, as Pashukanis puts its, that law is a material force.

In the 1920's — the only period of genuine 'creative Marxism' that the Soviet Union has ever known — Yevgeni Bronislavovich Pashukanis was the foremost and ablest expositor of Marxist jurisprudence, though his treatment of intellectual opponents was quite as vicious as any Stalinist's, if less obtuse. His *General Theory of Law and Marxism*, first published in Moscow in 1924, went through three Russian editions in five years, and the German translation of the third edition, issued in Berlin and Vienna in 1929, attracted international attention. One finds in the book a freshness of style and of thought that was soon to disappear from Soviet intellectual life. Pashukanis combines a genuine and scholarly involvement in jurisprudence and legal history with an equally genuine feeling for Marx's method and concerns. Not only is he sensitive to the achievements of other scholars — of Laband, Jellinek, Duguit, Maine and Maitland — but he rejects the theoretically crude simplification of Engels and Lenin to focus on the subtleties of a Marx that most of his contemporaries had not yet fully appreciated.

A careful study of the Marxist classics leaves us with two competing tendencies. One, represented by Engels, takes an Austinian view of the law as a body of commands, and hence as primarily punitive in nature, enforcing the will of the state, or whatever will the state represents. The other, represented by Marx in his subtler mood, thinks of law as a system of adjudication and judgment in terms of abstract concepts linked to conflicts in civil society, and therefore takes civil law and its categories as the model in terms of which law is to be understood.

Lenin, though himself a lawyer by training and early profession, was interested in law only as a vehicle and expression of political power; for him, it represented the will of the ruling class backed by physical sanctions. After the 1917 revolution and the creation of the dictatorship of the proletariat, the law became the will of the working class, to be used both as an instrument of coercion against the enemies of the working class and as a form of propaganda within its own ranks, defining the aims of the revolutionary movement rather than binding its actions. Once the proletariat had completely triumphed and all men had become workers, law would disappear because there would be no particular class to impose its will on other classes. Men would live as a co-operative community, settling disputes informally and on the spot. This was the line followed in the more popular forms of Communist propaganda and ideological writing even in the 1920's. In sum, the law was seen as the instrument by which a section of society imposed its will on the rest, and the law of each historical stage of society simply represented the will of its ruling class.

In line with this view, the People's Commissariat of Justice in 1919 defined law as 'a system (set of rules) for social relationships which corresponds to the interests of the dominant class and is safeguarded by the organized force of that class'.[2] The serious Marxist academic lawyers in Russia, trained in the tradition of nineteenth-century continental jurisprudence with its emphasis on the categories of Roman private law, were in the main not Austinians and tended to see law not merely as a set of commands or decrees but rather as a system. On the whole, however, they stressed its normative and ideological character. Reisner (1951), drawing on the famous psychological view of law espoused by the non-Marxist Russian-Polish legal theorist L.I. Petrazhitsky, argued that law was the expression of predominantly internalized norms varying from class to class, so that Russia after the Revolution had competing systems of proletarian and bourgeois law along with remnants of feudal law, each expressing the interests and attitudes of the appropriate class. The new Soviet state, according to Reisner and a number of other legal writers, was sanctioning and enforcing a particular system of class-law — i.e. proletarian law — against other systems. When classes disappeared, the need for a formal system of sanctions would disappear, and law could dissolve into morality.

Pashukanis (1951) went farther and deeper in his analysis. His *General*

2. *Sobranie uzakonenii* RSFSR (Collected Laws of the RSFSR), 1919, No.66, p.590 (also cited in Stuckha, 1964:58).

Law in Context

Theory of Law and Marxism is essentially a radical and thoroughgoing critique of any attempt to treat law as mere class ideology or to speak of a proletarian system of law replacing a bourgeois system. The point on which any analysis of *law* must concentrate, he argues, is that not all rules or norms are *legal* relationships. Although most Marxists before him had taken the element of state compulsion to be the characteristic or defining element of law, Pashukanis rejects this view. Army regulations, rules binding the members of an order or priesthood, or the authoritarian prescriptions of a family head or elder, for example, do not constitute or become *law* if or because they are sanctioned by authority — be it even the authority of the state. They are not law and do not have the form of law because they are based on relations of domination and submission, because they involve obedience to rules rather than the determination of rights (Pashukanis, 1951:154).

What is characteristic of *law* and constitutes the essence or formal quality of law, according to Pashukanis, is the conception of a juridical subject confronting other juridical subjects on the basis of equality and 'equivalence'. 'The specific fact distinguishing the legal order from every other social order . . . is that it is based upon private, isolated subjects. A norm of law acquires its *differentia specifica* . . . by the fact that it presupposes a person endowed with a right and moreover actively asserting a claim' (Pashukanis, 1951:153). Law is thus characteristically adjudicative and is thereby distinguished from administration; its essence, as he puts it, is involved and revealed in the conception of *contract* rather than of decree (Pashukanis, 1951:170). The categories and principles characteristic of law presuppose the legal subject as an individual acting 'freely' in his relations with other 'free' individuals and having rights as well as duties. Such legal subjects must, in law, be abstracted from their social context and reduced to legal individuality and abstract equality, so that even the state can appear in litigation only as another individual subject having rights and duties *vis-à-vis* the citizen in the same way as the citizen has rights and duties *vis-à-vis* it.

In line with this, Pashukanis attempts to show how the contractual model in fact dominates all areas of law — public law, with its conception of the social contract and the rights of the citizen (1951:190–92); criminal law, which makes the wrongdoer 'pay' for his crime according to a scale of fixed penalties (1951:206–214); matrimonial and family law, which dissolves familial relationships into a system of reciprocal rights and duties. Here Pashukanis is much closer than Lenin or Reisner — or Vyshinsky and the contemporary Soviet legal theorists — to Marx's fundamental critique of 'abstract' law and 'abstract' bourgeois justice as proclaiming a formal equality which, in the concrete social situation of class societies, amounts to real *in*equality. 'The Republic of the Market', Pashukanis writes in the preface to the second Russian edition of his *General Theory of Law and Marxism*, 'conceals the Despotism of the Factory.'

Pashukanis further contends that many Marxist writers, in treating law as ideology and emphasizing the elements of state compulsion and hypocritically-concealed class interest, fail to notice the much more direct connection between law and the economic structure of society. The fundamental presupposition of law, i.e. the principle of the juridical subject (involving the formal principle of freedom and equality, autonomy of the person, etc.), is not, he argues, merely a hypocritical tool used by the bourgeoisie to enslave the proletariat; it is a real, active principle embodied in bourgeois society once it breaks free from the feudal-patriarchal order. Further, the victory of law is not merely an ideological process, but a real, material one — a 'judicializing' of human relationships which accompanies the development of a commodity and money economy (in Europe, of capitalism), and which involves the overthrow of serfdom and the separation of political power from society as a particular, *partial* power. Thus, law is not just the 'ideology' of the bourgeoisie, but a reflection of the assumptions of commodity exchange: it reflects and secures the conditions necessary for the barter and exchange of products on which all commodity production (i.e. production for a market) is built (Pashukanis, 1951:164–67). The possessor of commodities confronts other commodity-possessors in a market on the basis of autonomy and equality. His other pursuits and concerns are irrelevant.

Legal categories, Pashukanis goes on to argue, are a precise parallel to the similarly 'abstract' economic categories of commodity-producing societies — value, capital, labour, rent — which are fundamental to bourgeois economics and economies (and to all commodity-producing economies), but which lose their medium of existence in societies not oriented to exchange, where, for example, production is for use. Just as the bourgeois economy is the most highly-developed and most abstract form of commodity production, so bourgeois law is the most highly developed and abstract form of law and legal relations. The juridical subject is the abstract commodity-possessor elevated to the heavens (Pashukanis, 1951:169); the legal relations he enters into correspond to his commercial relations in the market place, express them, and safeguard the conditions of their existence. Thus, according to Pashukanis, law in the proper sense develops around the activities of barter and trade, finds its initial strongholds in cities, comes into conflict with patriarchal relations and all other relations of formal domination and submission, and finally reaches its apogee in bourgeois society. Pashukanis accepted the Marxist view of the state as a form of class domination, but regarded the state in this aspect as not capable of legal interpretation. The distinction between 'public' and 'private' law was a 'contradiction' inherent in bourgeois society — 'public' law is *not* law, but class-domination which fits ill into the bourgeois conception of law.

In socialist society, where production is no longer for exchange, Pashukanis believes that the categories of law will become as irrelevant, and are as fatally undermined, as the categories of market economics. Policy, economic planning, and administration replace law. The concept of the juridical subject will become as inapposite as it would be in a primitive commune, an army, or a work-team. It will give way to the socio-economic norm (Pashukanis, 1951:178–79).

On the basis of this analysis, Pashukanis took the position that the Soviet codes of the 1920s were in no sense 'socialist law' — in itself a contradiction in terms — but bourgeois law necessitated by the fact that exchange relations had not yet been eliminated in the Soviet Union. Even in criminal law, he argued, these codes were still bourgeois in that they were permeated through and through with the principle of equivalence of retribution. The systematic development of a genuine socialist principle based on the protection of society, he declared, 'would require not a tabulation of the separate constituents of crime (with which the measure of punishment ... is logically associated) but an exact description of the symptoms characterizing a condition which is socially dangerous, and an elaboration of the methods which must be applied in each given case in order to make society secure' (Pashukanis, 1951:223).

With the abolition of the New Economic Policy and the introduction of the first Five-Year-Plan, Pashukanis saw the elimination of the juridical element in human affairs beginning in earnest. In line with his theories, the institute he headed was named the Institute of Socialist Construction and Law — soon, he thought, the word 'law' could be dropped. Courses in civil law, under Pashukanis's influence, were replaced by courses in 'economic-administrative policy and law' dealing with the regulation of relations between the state and enterprises, which were seen as becoming increasingly non-juridical. Individual rights were relegated to a few hours at the end of these courses, and their status was regarded as merely temporary and linked with the hangovers of bourgeois relations.

By the mid-1930s, Pashukanis had become the acknowledged leader of a school of jurists who were developing and applying his theories in various specific areas of law. (Pashukanis himself did a good deal of work in international law, where he began by denying that there could be a concept of proletarian international law to be distinguished from bourgeois international law). Nevertheless, even in the 1920s there were critics of his views. The subtlety of his analysis of bourgeois law did not much appeal to Communist propagandists, who preferred to see that law as simply a hypocritical cloak for bourgeois interests; and his insistence that the new Soviet codes, because they still embodied bourgeois attitudes and provisions, did not constitute a creative 'socialist' contribution to law conflicted sharply with the growing Soviet penchant for vainglory. Many of his critics felt, more sincerely, that he minimized the normative element in law and ignored the ideological interests enshrined in specific legislation, which — they contended — were precisely what distinguished socialist from bourgeois law. P.I. Stuchka, for instance, argued that law reflected not only the categories of the market, but also the organizational needs of production.

E.B. Pashukanis was concerned with a problem not tackled by Marx or Engels, or by Marxists: what are the *differentia specifica* of law, what *distinguishes* law from other social manifestations, particularly from *other* bodies of rules and commands. The difference, according to Pashukanis, does not lie in the source or function of law, but in its *form*, its formal presupposition of an underlying juridical subject as the bearer of rights and asserter of claims, seen for the purposes of the legal form as autonomous and free, equal and equivalent to all other juridical subjects. Pashukanis sees law not as a command, but as a system of norms and concepts determining claims. In elaborating this view of the 'formal quality' or presuppositions and implied structure and values of law, Pashukanis had captured an important and central moment in the Western legal tradition that might be said to characterize it. I would not want to say that Pashukanis had correctly grasped the 'essence' of law — though he himself uses such terminology — or that his account exhausted everything that was important or fundamental about law. I do not believe that there are 'essences', 'true' definitions or exhaustive descriptions. Institutions are complex, torn by competing trends and traditions, inconsistent, changeable, and part of many histories. There is no central character of an historical institution from which all its other characteristics can be derived or explained. It is for these reasons that I interpret Pashukanis as grasping an important legal 'moment' — a systematic logical tendency built into the structure of law, working itself out over time. This I call the *Gesellschaft* moment — adjudicative, individualist, contractual — and I contrast it, as Pashukanis to some extent does, with other 'moments' that can be or have been called part of law — the *Gemeinschaft* moment and the bureaucratic-administrative moment. Any actual legal system will be a mixture of all these: but they pull in different directions, elevate different presuppositions, conflict with each other — especially sharply and self-consciously in modern societies, whether socialist or non-socialist, though the character of the mix varies and changes even within one system. (See Kamenka and Tay, 1980; Kamenka and Tay, 1982.)

Nor do I wish to claim that the *Gemeinschaft-Gesellschaft*-bureaucratic-administrative trichotomy and the relation of domination-submission to authority that lies behind it exhaust the important general things that can be said about law. One important — many would say central — aspect of sophisticated legal systems which this trichotomy does not single out at all, but which it rather takes for granted as part of the *systematic* character of systems of rules, is the existence of power-conferring rules, 'rules of recognition' (Hart, 1961:97–107). These define when power and decision are legitimate, *intra vires*, and when they are not — though I would argue that precise and specific separation of powers is a *Gesellschaft* phenomenon. But the concept of legitimacy is not.

The second great Marxist theoretician of law, the Austrian Social Democrat Karl Renner, devoted himself to a totally different question about law. He was trying to explain not the *differentia specifica* of law — what distinguished legal rules from other state-, society- or group-sanctioned rules — but the remarkable persistence of certain basic legal norms and institutions over time through fundamental social and economic change. How was it that the categories of Roman private law, developed in what Marxists considered a slave-owning mode of production, could persist, with so little change in their basic character, through feudal and capitalist society? And would they also persist into a socialist mode of production? Renner's concern is frankly sociological and based on a sharp distinction between law and its social function, between legal analysis and sociological analysis. But his treatment of his topic has important implications for the philosophy as well as for the sociology of law, and certainly for what I prefer to call the theory of law, a theory that relates the philosophical and the historical, sociological features of law, that draws its philosophy from legal realities.

Karl Renner was a distinguished Austrian Social Democrat. Born in 1870, he became a Social Democratic member of Parliament in 1907 and was Chancellor of the Austrian Republic from 1918–20, President of the *Nationalrat* from 1931–33 and then an inmate of various gaols under Chancellor Dolfuss. In 1945, after the defeat of Germany, Renner formed the first post-war Austrian Government; he served as President of the Austrian Republic until his death in 1950. A member of the Austro-Marxist School, he wrote on many Marxist and socialist questions — on labour and capital, on the economy, on fundamental principles of sociology, on current problems of socialism and Marxism. But the work that earned him a deserved place as one of the only two significantly original Marxist theoreticians of law is *The Institutions of Private Law and their Social Functions.* It was first published in 1904 under the title *The Social Function of Legal Institutions, Especially of Property* in a collection entitled *Marx-Studien* together with essays by Rudolf Hilferding and Max Adler. Renner, then 34, was working as a librarian in the Austrian Parliament; since he was a public servant he used the pseudonym Dr I. Karner. A new independent edition under the present title, substantially revised and issued under his own name, was published in 1929. Karl Mannheim and Otto Kahn-Freund, by then émigrés living in London, arranged for its translation into English and publication in London in 1949.

Renner's *Institutions of Private Law and their Social Functions* is primarily a study in the sociology rather than the philosophy of law; its central concern is with the relationship between economic life and economic change on the one hand and legal norms and institutions and their functioning on the other. It is thus a specific contribution to working out, in the legal sphere, the truth or falsity, or the most plausible interpretation, of Marx's materialist conception of history. Renner's method is to examine, over time, the character and the legal, economic and social function of certain central institutions of private law — ownership in land and chattels, contracts of various types, mortgage and lease, marriage and succession. He leaves public law outside the purview of his analysis. He argues (Renner, 1949:53) that:

> Every legal institution is to a conceptual approach a composite of norms, a total of imperatives. In the case of property, the most important imperatives convey that no-one shall withdraw from A's factual power of disposition a thing which belongs to A, and no-one shall disturb his quiet possession of the thing, etc. The lawyer sees the same institution of property wherever the same composite of norms applies. It does not matter to him whether the object is land, a retriever, a loaf of bread or a family portrait without intrinsic value. Legal analysis confines itself to collating the totality of norms, the systematic understanding, logical exposition and practical application thereof. Legal analysis is of necessity determined by history like its arsenal of concepts, its terminology. It is of necessity empirical; by the same token the *corpus juris civilis*, the '*Sachsenspiegel*' and the German Civil Code are all empirical.

Unlike Pashukanis, Renner is not concerned to give an economic or sociological or social account of the *origin* of legal norms and institutions. As Kahn-Freund puts it (1949:1–2), Renner assumes 'the stability and relative immutability of central legal institutions such as property and contract, and he asks: how is it possible that, given unchanged norms, unchanged conceptions of ownership and sale, contract and debt, mortgage and inheritance, their social function can nevertheless undergo a profound transformation?' How is it possible that the legal institutions can *remain* the same imperatives, be defined in the same way in 1750 and 1900, and yet produce in the latter period effects diametrically opposed to those they produced in the former? The stability and comparative abstraction of private law norms — their compatibility with different types of social organization (denied by Pashukanis) — has nevertheless struck most theoreticians of law, who see the legal genius of the Romans as lying in the ability to create a system of norms that has so long survived them. As Geoffrey Sawer has put it, the three great original characteristics of Roman law as a living system up to the time of Justinian, were firstly, a complexity which enabled it to cover the main social relationships of human life; secondly, a degree of abstraction enabling many of its principles to apply to a wide range of social relationships and over long periods of time without major change; thirdly, an autonomy of structure and development which gave law an independent role in the development of society as a whole. (See Sawer, 1965:112–13.)

Renner belongs, as I to some extent do, to the conceptual school of jurisprudence in the sense that he sees legal concepts as having their own character and implications and life in the law. He is, of course, a positivist in the sense that he sees such concepts as arising within human history and society, as I also do. He is not at all interested, in the work under discussion, in precisely how such concepts arise. He takes their existence — i.e. the existence of a conceptually structured legal system — for granted. He argues indeed that any society must allocate labour tasks, allocate goods or things and have a command structure to organize the hierarchical exercise of power or even to organize co-operation. These three general administrative imperatives Renner calls the order of labour, the order of goods and the order of power (Kahn-Freund, 1949:6–7; Renner, 1949: 70–72, 110–18). But such central legal institutions as property, contract and succession by inheritance in themselves are for Renner 'neutral' (1949:112), 'colourless', 'empty frames' (1949:92, 148, 217), 'blanks' (1949:271), as in themselves they are not feudal, nor capitalist, nor socialist, but legal. They do not 'reflect' an order of labour, power or goods, but help to create it and they have a conceptual integrity independent of such orders. A simple example is the Soviet law of inheritance, which is different from continental law only in *what* can be inherited, not how it can be. The aim of Renner's work, indeed, is to show that the central institutions of private law do not change but that they undergo a functional transformation, i.e. come to play a different social and economic role. Here Renner elaborates a theory — and largely I would think a correct theory — of the role of legal norms and institutions in social life. If we take a complex economy like the 'modern' (i.e. late nineteenth-century) capitalist one, it is not true that the organization of modern industry can be effected simply through the itself neutral norm of property. The legal concept of property can only serve as a basis for organizing a fundamental economic process of capitalism — industrial production — by being combined with a number of 'complementary institutions' — company law and patent law, the contract of sale and the contract of employment (Renner, 1949:196–97, 270–71). An apparently simple economic process thus requires not one legal category but a whole group of them, brought together by the requirements of the economic process. This is what Renner calls the economic function of legal institutions. When such complex sets of legal norms become dysfunctional, lose real connection with the character and needs of the economic substratum, they are rearranged or fall into disuse, though usually with a time-lag.

Economic processes are themselves part and parcel of the social process that Marx called production and reproduction, concerned with the maintenance of the human species at a given level of material activity. Legal institutions can and must be understood as tools used by society in achieving this ultimate aim. They are cogs in the whole mechanism of the production, consumption and distribution of social products — they are part of a total, though for Renner dialectical, social process. As Kahn-Freund puts it (1949:6), legal institutions and norms, for Renner, are bricks which may be used to build a manor house in one age, a factory in another, a railway station in a third. But the number of bricks is limited — we may have to pull down the manor house to have the bricks for the factory. The brick, the legal institution, 'is a rigid abstract, a congeries of crystallised imperatives', in the Marxist sense a 'fetish' as a 'commodity' is in economics. The lawyer as a lawyer is concerned with the internal structure and actual and possible logical relationships of these legal bricks. Their function, including the way they are brought together in the law at various times for various purposes, has to be understood through wider economic and social processes.

Although, or perhaps because, Renner insisted that legal norms were abstract and neutral, he did not see the norms themselves as epiphenomenal, as reflections of economic or social demands and requirements, as having no independent history or logic of their own. He rejected, in its crude form, the conception of an active, independent economic base and of a passive, dependent legal superstructure, though he saw the dialectic of legal development as lying in the correspondence or lack of correspondence of infra-jural economic facts and the laws that regulate them. The norms of law were part of the fundamental organization and description of economic and social processes, not something to be derived from them. In contrast with Pashukanis, Renner does not see law as carrying an ideology, or view of the world: he has rather a tradesman's view of law as being necessary for any complex social organization and as being capable of a great variety of uses. He has also a sense, to which I shall

Law in Context

return, of the inescapability of certain fundamental legal conceptions. Even in a society that has abolished private property in the means of production, distribution and exchange, the property norm will remain (Renner, 1949:260), for it is necessary to establish some nexus between man and things that will make someone responsible for dealing with them, that will thus determine the basis of responsibility for the thing (or process) and the harm it causes. For property in law is not only an advantage; it is also a disadvantage, the basis of a duty of care and control, the basis of responsibility. There are norms, however, in the past and there will be in the future, that fall into desuetude, disuse (Renner, 1949:257–58).

Renner is often accused by contemporary Marxists of sharing in the vulgar economic reductionism of the Second International. It is true that like many of the leading and sensible figures of the Second International, he put primacy on the cumulative effect of gradual economic change and not on dialectical breaks, class struggles and the directly political. But he did not reduce law to economics. On the contrary, he saw the description and reality of economic processes as involving legal concepts and legal powers. He was interested in the relation between a legal norm and its substratum — the empirical economic and social reality, the process, to which it refers. But Renner's substratum was not a *cause* of the legal norm. (See Renner, 1949:252; Sawer, 1961:154–56.) It was rather what Kocourek (1927) refers to as an infra-jural fact, without the existence of which the norm would have no empirical reference. Renner did take over from Marx and develop very strongly the notion that the development of law, or rather the lack of development of law, could be out of step with material and social changes in the substratum to which legal norms refer. Thus the definition of property does not change, at least in continental law (where it has a rigid formal definition, unlike that of Common Law) between 1600 and 1900 or even between 40 and 1900. Yet the nature of things owned, the kind of control exercised over them, changes and the law can and does lag behind in recognizing these changes. But in the end, as part of economic or social processes and as a social tool making them possible, it changes its character not by changing its norms but by rearranging their connections within the legal system, bringing subsidiary norms into play. It is the legal order — the complex of legal norms, concepts and institutions — that changes, not the fundamental legal norms or institutions themselves.

Law, for Renner, I have said, is a system of imperatives, a relationship of wills. Law therefore never deals with the relationships of persons to things in themselves. It is a relationship between a person and other persons. Property, legally, is the power to exclude *others* from control over a thing or process.

In tracing the development of the character and function of property and ownership as a legal norm and social fact, Renner does, in fact, follow Marx and agree with Pashukanis in making a fundamental distinction between feudal or rather simple commodity-producing society, and bourgeois society, or as I would put it more generally, between *Gemeinschaft* and *Gesellschaft* organization of property. The property of pre-bourgeois society is the household which represents the union of all economic and social processes affecting that household: the owner of the household is its head, with responsibility for everything that goes on in the social life of the estate – the order of labour, the order of power and the order of goods, the allocation of resources and things, which are still consumables or barterable for consumables rather than abstract commodities. The legal conception of property as the power to dispose according to your will and to exclude others, and the Roman law insistence that what is owned must be a tangible thing, is still near to economic reality. The property norm and the substratum have not parted company, and property is thus still the central institution of private law capable by itself of providing an order of goods, in part an order of power and initially an order of labour. The household organizes production and reproduction, allocates labour and resources, educates, maintains discipline, cares for the sick and the old – all as a unified activity resting on the (Germanic) *potestas* of the property owner as head of the household. The household is a microcosm of society; property functions, in law and in reality, are both private and public, serving as an organising concept in social life (Renner, 1949:83–87).

The fundamental change from pre-bourgeois to bourgeois society is that property becomes more abstract and that bourgeois society has no legally-sanctioned order of goods and no order of labour. Anyone may own and work freely, so far as law is concerned. It is the difficulty of providing a continuing and stable order of labour which led to the downfall of feudal society, which came to depend increasingly on independent artisans not regulated by the law of property itself, but by complementary norms, first derived from public guild law and then from the revolutionary law of free employment.

Renner's description of capitalist production and its social, political and legal consequences follows Marx's fairly closely and to that extent coincides with aspects of Pashukanis's analysis of bourgeois society. The capitalist order frees property from feudal restraints and especially from being seen as a continuing fund, as a real and tangible basis of social production and social role, which must pass to appropriate people, etc. Property becomes capital, an intangible thing, a mere exchange value or bundle of exchange values, and all social activities are separated from each other, become formally and legally separable and distinct. Property becomes fragmented and no longer holds a social process of production together through being a corporeal object, an item of nature. The abstraction of property, its becoming an aggregate of values, results in the fact that the object, property in the economic sense, acquires many functions while the subject, the *persona* of law who is the property owner, is deprived of all functions. The share has specific economic functions — the owner of the share has none, except as an appendage of the share. (See Renner, 1949:104–118, 195–209).

The result of all this for the legal order is that the legal property norm loses its centrality in the law, though it does not change its definition, much as the tangible object, the household, farm, or later the factory building and the machine, loses its centrality in the economic process. Economic property has become divorced from the owner and its economic function split up into partial functions. To assure capitalism of a legal order capable of carrying on as a framework for its social and economic activities, the property norm has to be supplemented by an unforeseen evolution of the contract of sale and purchase, the contract of employment and the loan, without which the property norm cannot perform its economic and social functions in a capitalist system of production. (See Renner, 1949:124–29, 104–122, 139–149.) What were formerly stop-gaps in a legal system become institutions as important as property, and without which its capitalist social function cannot be understood.

The internal dynamic of capitalism, however, is leading to a certain socialization from within, to a weakening of the central premise of capitalism as a society of 'private property'. The 'complementary institutions' of private law necessary to make the property norm perform its social function in capitalism have deprived the owners of their technical disposal of their property — the subject has become powerless. Secondly, the ever increasing ramifications of private property, their effect on society and the contradictions they produce, have led to an increasing recognition that economic property is not a private but a social function. 'The common will has subjected property to its direct control, at least from the point of view of the law. Elements of a new order have been developed within the framework of an old society', Renner writes (1949:298). The state plays a greater and greater role since the mid-nineteenth century, abandoning the mace and scales for much more active intervention in economic life. Public law comes to supplement and displace much of private law. Contemporary property, though *de jure* private, has in fact ceased to be private; the tenement house serves a number of strangers and the railway serves all and sundry. The legal concept of property no longer reflects its social function; 'it is the social working order which determines the real activities and gives a concrete content to the blanks which the law has provided' (Renner, 1949:271). The legal concept of property includes freedom of alienation. 'But is there any individual disposition of his property on the part of the bank customer . . ., of the share-holder or of the member of an association? Is it not the market which rules the most independent factory owner as well as the isolated peasant . . . on his solitary farm?' The legal concept of property includes an absolute right of exclusion of others. 'But the house-owner exercises his absolute right by taking in strangers from the street . . .; the landlord, by surrendering his possession completely to a tenant . . . for ten or even for 99 years . . . The owners of a railway even invite all and sundry to roam over their property, the more the merrier' (Renner, 1949:289). The legal concept of property establishes a specific relationship between an owner and his aggregated possessions:

> but an economic object, the substratum of the right, is not an aggregate of objects, not an independent microcosm, it is merely a particle of the whole of society's working order, admitting of one special manner of disposal only. Even the number of revolutions performed by a spinning wheel is prescribed by the requirements of industrial technique. The universal power of disposal given by the law is confronted, in economic reality, by a most limited scope for the exercise of this power. Property is universal with regard to subject and object, any individual may own any kind of object, and this was actually so in the period of simple commodity production, when every individual of full age had disposal of a microcosm which was made up of objects of every description. Now one part of the population, the great majority, owns nothing but a week's provisions, another part nothing but houses, another part nothing but machines and the raw materials to feed them, and still others nothing but printed paper. Modern possessions no longer form a cosmos, large or small, they are neither microcosm nor macrocosm. They are an amorphous agglomeration of possessions for the purposes of consumption and production, and in part they are mere 'paper-possessions' . . . These possessions represented by documents are in no way connected with the individuality of the owner, they can be increased as convenient . . . Such unity as modern possessions have, is a mere consequence of the legal abstraction which does not require a unitary substratum; their unity is artificial . . . (1949:289–90).

With diversification of 'possessions' goes a diversification in the 'character masks' which the property-owner may wear. 'Each actor wears the economic character mask suited to the scene in which he appears' (Renner, 1949:94; see Kahn-Freund, 1949:29, 36, and Sawer, 1961:137) and the same individual may switch 'character masks' from one context to another.

> The legal character mask of a monarch is compatible with the economic mask of a distiller of spirits, the legal mask of a state minister is compatible with the economic mask of a gambler on the stock exchange, the ecclesiastic mask of an Archbishop is compatible with the economic mask of an employer of sweated labour (Renner, 1949:290).

Law in Context

And so Renner brings his sociological analysis of legal change to a triumphant conclusion. 'Norm and substratum have become so dissimilar, so incommensurable, that the working of property, the way in which it functions, is no longer explained and made intelligible by the property-norm'. Instead we must look to its 'complementary institutions': the law of landlord and tenant, the law of the market, and the law of wages.

> Property remains only in the background as a general legal presupposition for the special law that comes into operation, an institution of which we are dimly aware as the necessary consequence of the regrettable fact that there must be someone who is in the last resort responsible for the disposal of any object. But primarily disposal rests with the labourer in the case of the machine, the tool or the plough, with the tenant in the case of the house, and in general with the non-owner. The subjective, absolute, and all-embracing power of disposal seems to the casual observer to be completely eliminated; yet it is perpetuated as the subjective, absolute, and all-embracing power of the capitalist class to dispose of the whole of society, of man and matter and their annual surplus product.
>
> But this fact is hidden from a merely legal interpretation, it is not intended, not expressed nor reflected, by the norm. Norm and substratum can scarcely be said to correspond, they are no longer similar, and the present function of the norm is the result of a process in the course of which the relations of production and the relations of the law entered on a disparate development. The conflict between a growing (and partly completed) social working order which is conscious of its own unity, and a law which is still in existence although adapted to a previous system of private enterprise based upon economic microcosms, results in property assuming the function of capital. As the conflict increases, the functions of modern property become more and more distinct and differentiated. An increasing number of complementary institutions is developed, and it becomes more and more obvious that property itself has withdrawn into a position where it is solely concerned with disposal over, and acquisition of, values (Renner, 1949:290–91).

Renner, like Pashukanis, though on the basis of different concerns and examples, sees the conception of private law and the social function of private law reaching their apogee in bourgeois society. But Renner is much more interesting and fruitful in pointing the way to the future — in seeing the law of the future as implicit in the changing law of the present and as resting on the internal contradictions of capitalist production. This contradiction for the purposes of law is the breaking of the nexus between private property and individual will, the growing strength of impersonal forces and arrangements, the conversion of the private into the public, the socialization of capitalism from within — a truth uncongenial to revolutionary Marxists but nevertheless a truth. That aspect of the matter was to be explored, soon after Renner's 1929 edition, by Berle and Means (1932) with their distinction between consumption property (where the private property legal norm still has some bite or empirical reality) and property for production and investment (which has become increasingly public and divested from individual ownership and control). It is in Berle and Means that the seeds of the theoretical conception of the managerial society and of non-property-owning ruling classes were developed (see Berle, 1959). Renner, among others, pointed the way. He and Berle and Means have all been proved right in essential respects, in their recognition of the decline in economic importance and legal centrality of private property as truly private — as the reification of individual will and individual control, as self-sufficient and easily definable.

Renner's view of law, in its emphasis on internal rearrangement of the legal order through the 'complementary institutions', is much more pluralistic than Pashukanis's. He sees law much more broadly as a systematic and orderly application of norms governing relations between people and in respect of things. He puts no weight on one very important aspect of law — the one emphasized by Pashukanis — the resolution of disputes in terms of formal legal presuppositions, rights and duties, bound up with a formal conception of the legal subject. Renner's law is much more a system of social administration, though he and Pashukanis agree in seeing law of the bourgeois period as not successfully doing, and not seeking to do, the job of administration through the principal categories of private law and both see property as being converted, by the logic of the productive process of advanced capitalism, from a private to a public function.

Both Pashukanis and Renner, in my view, draw attention to important features of law and legal development. Both recognize a certain integrity and internal logic of legal norms and concepts; both see that they are not passive reflections but ways of shaping the world. But they are not all-powerful; they break down or lose their relevance before economic or social developments they cannot restrain. Law has to be seen socially and historically, but not as though it were a passive reflection of forces outside itself, as though there were no legal norms or concepts but only disguised non-legal interests and demands.

We do not, however, have to choose between Pashukanis and Renner in the way we have to choose between those who say all A are B and those who say some A are not B. Pashukanis, and even the more pluralistic Renner, present us with paradigms of law in the one case and legal development in the other — both ignore or minimize countervailing tendencies, developments that do not fit, aspects of law not easily related to the economic process. For law as a social institution is never a coherent totality; it has neither a determining essence from which all its features can be derived nor a single function, purpose or coherent plan. There are therefore many things to be said about law. Some will be more central, more important; others less. Nothing will be central and important for all purposes, for explaining all features of law.

One important merit of Renner's analysis, which Pashukanis's does not share, is that it enables us to recognize both continuity and change in law and to explain conceptually how this is possible. Revolutionary Marxists like the doctrine of the clean break; they have always been uncomfortable with Renner's belief in an evolutionary path to socialism, in the gradual socialization of capitalism from within. But the recognition of legal continuity and even of a certain convergence between law in Marxist-socialist and contemporary non-socialist societies becomes inescapable when we examine the legal systems and legal theories of both groups.

All this suggests that a theory of law — i.e. an appreciation of the historical development, internal specificities and competing trends of legal systems — is a much more complex matter than Marxists have so far been able to see. It requires both logical analysis and a sense of historical context and development. It cannot proceed far without recognizing that the word 'law' can be and is used in different senses and that these must be distinguished for the purpose of a theory of law. But even within the one sense of the word, and within one legal system, there will be competing functions, concepts, traditions and ideologies. It is to the understanding of these that both Pashukanis and Renner, unlike Marx and contemporary Western radicals, have something to contribute.

IV

There is, perhaps, no better indication of the enormous gulf between contemporary 'Marxist' ideology in the USSR, Eastern Europe, and the People's Republic of China since the fall of the Gang of Four on the one hand and both classical Marxism and contemporary Western radical ideology on the other, than the enthusiasm with which Soviet bloc and Chinese Communist legal theorists now elevate the social function of law in socialist countries. Law there represents the common interest, it safeguards and protects the citizens, it guarantees stability and the proper working of social institutions, it educates and elevates. Nor, according to the latest view, does it do this only in socialist societies. There are legal precepts and legal techniques which, even in past societies, serve the interests of all. They reflect objective social and human requirements and are heritable from one social system to another.[3] Methodologically,

3. See Nenovski (1977). The Chinese law journal *Faxue Yanjiu* (Legal Studies) in 1979 and 1980 opened its pages to an extensive discussion of the heritability of law, stressing that both Chinese Communist and Soviet and East European laws contain provisions, concepts and procedures and actual sections and paragraphs taken over from laws of previous or foreign non-socialist regimes.

theorists in Communist countries are still crude. They write under conditions of censorship and repression of criticism which makes Western radical talk of ruling class ideological hegemony and repressive tolerance in the West seem merely ludicrous. They *have* to say that Renner is a 'Social Democratic opportunist', but they know that Pashukanis's vision of a socialist society in which Plan replaced Law and in which the concepts of 'social danger' and 'social harm' replace the 'bourgeois' conceptions of guilt and fault can lead to and justify the unbearable horror of Stalinism. Precisely because, unlike their Western rivals, they have seen real and pervasive social change, real class struggle and real class dictatorship, as well as the ruthless subversion and politicization of law, they are now much more confident supporters of concern for the future and development of law as a social institution which brings some conception of justice, equality, universality and predictability into social life. They understand what most Western Marxists do not — that a legal system may be a social product, used by many interests, and yet have a conception of itself as a form of public rationality and seek to extend that rationality through specifically legal conceptions, principles and institutions that both guide and take into account wider social sentiments. Are today's 'critical' Marxists really advocating a society without law, spontaneously self-managed, or are they merely seeking to destroy law to replace it with an all-powerful, uncriticized and unreflective system of social administration, emphasizing the subordination central to public law as opposed to the equality and equivalence central to private law?

REFERENCES

Berle, A.A., and G.C. Means (1932) *The Modern Corporation and Private Property*. New York: Macmillan.

Berle, A.A. (1959) *Power without Property*. New York: Harcourt Brace.

Cain, M., and A. Hunt (1979) *Marx and Engels on Law*. London: Academic Press.

Collins, Hugh (1982) *Marxism and Law*. Oxford: Clarendon Press.

Dicey, A.V. (1914) *Law and Public Opinion in England During the Nineteenth Century* (2nd ed.). London: Macmillan.

Edelman, B. (1979) *Ownership of the Image: Elements for a Marxist Theory of Law*. Translated by E. Kingdom. London: Routledge and Kegan Paul.

Fraser, A. (1976) 'Legal Theory and Legal Practice' 45 *Arena*. 123–156.

Hart, H.L.A. (1961) *The Concept of Law*. Oxford: Clarendon Press.

Hirst, P. (1979) *On Law and Ideology*. London: Macmillan.

Ihering, R. von (1885) *Scherz und Ernst in der Jurisprudenz* (3rd ed.). Leipzig: Breitkopf und Haertel.

—, (1913) *Law as a Means to an End* (*Der Zweck im Recht*). Translated by I. Husik. Boston: Boston Book Co.

Kahn-Freund, O. (1949) Introduction to K. Renner, *The Institutions of Private Law and their Social Functions*. Edited by O. Kahn-Freund and translated by A. Schwarzschild. London: Routledge and Kegan Paul (reprinted 1976).

Law in Context

Kamenka, E. (1981) 'Demythologizing the Law', *The Times Literary Supplement*, 1 May, pp.475–76.
—, (1982) 'The Sociology of Justice', in A.R. Blackshield (ed.), *Legal Change: Essays in Honour of Julius Stone*. Sydney: Butterworths.
Kamenka, E., and A.E.-S. Tay (1975) 'Beyond Bourgeois Individualism: The Contemporary Crisis in Law and Legal Ideology', in E. Kamenka and R.S. Neale (eds.), *Feudalism, Capitalism, and Beyond*. Canberra: Australian National University Press; London: Edward Arnold.
—, (1980) 'Social Traditions, Legal Traditions', in E. Kamenka and A.E.-S. Tay (eds.), *Law and Social Control*. London: Edward Arnold.
Kocourek, A. (1927) *Jural Relations*. Indianapolis: Bobbs-Merrill.
Krygier, M. (1980) 'Anthropological Approaches', in E. Kamenka and A.E.-S. Tay (eds.), *Law and Social Control*. London: Edward Arnold.
Neale, R.S. (1975) 'The Bourgeoisie, Historically, has played a Most Revolutionary Part', in E. Kamenka and A.E.-S. Tay (eds.), *Feudalism, Capitalism and Beyond*. Canberra: Australian National University Press.
Nenovski, N. (1977) *Preemstvennost' v prave* (Heritability in Law). Translated from the Bulgarian. Moscow: Yuridicheskaya literatura.
Pashukanis, E.B. (1951) 'The General Theory of Law and Marxism' (*Obshchaia teoriia prava i Marksizm*, first published 1924), in J.B. Hazard (ed.), *Soviet Legal Philosophy*. Translated by H.W. Babb. Cambridge, Massachusetts: Harvard University Press.
Phillips, P. (1980) *Marx and Engels on Law and Laws*. Oxford: Martin Robertson.
Reisner, M.A. (1951) 'The Theory of Petrazhitskii: Marxism and Social Ideology', in J.N. Hazard (ed.), *Soviet Legal Philosophy*. Translated by H.W. Babb. Cambridge, Massachusetts: Harvard University Press.
Renner, K. (1949) *The Institutions of Private Law and their Social Functions*. Edited by O. Kahn-Freund and translated by A. Schwarzschild. London: Routledge and Kegan Paul (reprinted 1976).
Sawer, G. (1961) 'Law as Socially Neutral: Karl Renner', in G. Sawer (ed.), *Studies in the Sociology of Law*. Canberra: Australian University Press (mimeograph).
Sawer, G. (1965) *Law in Society*. Oxford: Clarendon Press.
Stuchka, P.I. (1964) *Izbrannye proizvedeniia po marksistskoleninskoi teorii prava* (Selected Works on the Marxist-Leninist Theory of Law). Riga: Latvian State Publishing House.
Sumner, C. (1979) *Reading Ideologies: an Investigation into the Marxist Theory of Ideology and Law*. London: Academic Press.
Thompson, E.P. (1977) *Whigs and Hunters*. Harmondsworth: Penguin.
Ziegert, K.A. (1980) 'A Sociologist's View', in E. Kamenka and A.E.-S. Tay (eds.) *Law and Social Control*. London: Edward Arnold.

[8]

International Journal of the Sociology of Law 1981, **9,** 1–22

Pashukanis and the Commodity Form Theory

R. WARRINGTON
Part-time lecturer, City of London Polytechnic, U.K.

Introduction

Surprising though it now seems, just prior to the worst years of Stalinism, a startling success was achieved by a Bolshevik jurist who argued, quite literally, that law was about to be made superfluous. E. B. Pashukanis was the undisputed leader of the Soviet legal theorists of the 1920s and early 1930s and though little progress was actually made in transforming the legal practice of the period up to 1930 and beyond, Pashukanis, Krylenko and their colleagues worked ceaselessly towards the goal of a future society not dependent on legal control. They annually produced draft criminal codes consistent with the aim of the withering away of law, though none was taken up (Sharlet, 1978, p. 181). But the effect in the law schools of the Pashukanis movement was more than theoretical. The law schools were purged of bourgeois influences and the disarray in legal studies was remarkable.

Students were instructed to write essays on the pointlessness of their own studies, and in the somewhat rarified atmosphere of those law schools that existed, a real prospect of the imminent end to legal studies overwhelmed both student and teacher. Nowhere was the "theory/practice distinction" more marked, and it is therefore necessary to distinguish between "the salient characteristics of the real or actual legal process in place in Soviet Society at a given time and those characteristics associated with the Marxian ideal of 'withering away' of law" (Sharlet, 1977, pp. 157, 158).

The "paens of praise" (Sharlet, 1974, p. 111) with which Pashukanis's *General Theory* was received in the 1920s in Russia, when each new edition seemed, "to call forth a more positive response" (ibid., p. 110) have been matched by the ecstatic rediscovery in the West of this powerful, but enigmatic work. This rediscovery was fuelled by the publication of readable translations of his work (Pashukanis, 1978; 1980) [1]. This paper is a further contribution to the debate on Pashukanis. It attempts to restate the important facets of Pashukanis's theory, and outline some evaluations. The four sections of the

0194-6595/81/010001+22 $02.00/0

paper examine Pashukanis's object and method, his commodity form theory, some criticisms of the theory, and finally Pashukanis's commitment to the withering away of law.

It is sometimes forgotten that the *General Theory* always remained a preliminary draft. The turmoil of the period in which it was written, Pashukanis's own prodigious output of other work, and ultimately the political repression which destroyed him, all prevented Pashukanis preparing the more definitive text to which the *General Theory* was supposed to be a mere prelude. But the limitations of Pashukanis's work do not vitiate his whole enterprise. The problems of the theory do not destroy some interesting insights.

Section 1: The Object of the Theory and Pashukanis's Method

(a) *History and object*

Pashukanis saw legal theory as an historical enquiry, historical in at least two important senses. It was historical in that an understanding of bourgeois forms of law required an historical approach to the question of law because law was a result of a specific stage of social development only. Much of Pashukanis's work was based on this historical premise, though unfortunately, Pashukanis's historical assumptions often turn out to be untenable. But Pashukanis's theory is also historical in a second, perhaps more fundamental sense. Pashukanis saw the function of the jurisprudence of his day as more than mere development of legal concepts. For Pashukanis, the task of Marxist theory of law was to demonstrate that law was only to exist for a limited time and that it would shortly begin its final process of withering away. The legal form, writes Pashukanis,

> . . . only encompasses us within its narrow horizon for the time being. It exists for the sole purpose of being utterly spent. The task of Marxist theory consists of verifying this general conclusion and of following up the concrete historical material (Pashukanis, 1978, p. 133).

Pashukanis's enquiry was then in no sense an attempt at an "objective" theory of law; it was very definitely overlaid with the political demands of orthodox Bolshevism. It was designed to meet a purely political end, the speeding of the revolution which he saw as being in process, the revolution to end property relations entirely.

Pashukanis based his view of the revolution on the two stages outlined by Marx (1971 especially) as developed by Lenin (1975). This view of the proletarian revolution specifies first the introduction of a transitional society broadly characterized by the slogan "from each according to his ability, to each according to his work": the "dictatorship of the proletariat". It would only be in the second stage of the revolutionary process that the narrow confines of bourgeois right could be transcended and the slogan "from each according to his ability, to each according to his need", become social practice. As an orthodox "Old Bolshevik" (Sharlet, 1978, p. 170) Pashukanis assumed that 1917 had commenced the process of the revolution by introducing the first stage. The arguments were really as to the length of time this stage would take, and the correct method of theorizing the political and economic forms appropriate to this stage.

According to the orthodoxy of his day (to which Pashukanis adhered with unhealthy rigidity) there were at least two reasons for the revolution proceeding in two phases. One was in order to bring the productive forces to the required stage where it would be unnecessary to restrict access to wealth in society by the restraints of bourgeois or quasi-bourgeois legality. The second reason was to enable the traces of bourgeois mentality to be eradicated. The second stage of the revolution, introducing a harmonious co-operative society, would only be possible when bourgeois attitudes (not just to property) had been overcome. As an academic jurist, Pashukanis's function was to overthrow bourgeois attitudes in general, and the hegemony of the bourgeois jurists in particular. As late as 1929 Pashukanis wrote: "Even now, the struggle against the bourgeois legal view of the world represents a task of pressing importance for the jurists of the Soviet Republic today" (Pashukanis, 1978, p. 33).

It is on this latest point that Pashukanis faced a contradiction which he never resolved and which resulted in his liquidation. Pashukanis argued that the form of law in the Soviet Union after 1917 was still bourgeois. All juridical thought, he argued, was characterized by abstract general definitions, and it was his belief that the law of the transition was no different. Thus he said: "The fundamental, or formal juridical concepts have a continued existence in our statute books and the corresponding commentaries. Also still with us is the method of juridical thought with the procedures peculiar to it" (pp. 48, 49). Thus for Pashukanis, Russia in the 1920s was still dominated by a recognizable bourgeois legal system.

In 1930, Pashukanis wrote a paper which can be seen as a landmark in the development of both Russian legal theory and of Pashukanis himself. In this paper Pashukanis struggled to make his theory fit the new facts of the increasing power of a dictatorial state. The paper in no way succeeds, and for the next 6 years, Pashukanis tried to resolve the contradictions in his own position by sticking to his theory, and protesting his adherence to the new regime. Amongst the arguments in this paper is an assertion that socialized production had not been achieved (Pashukanis, 1951, pp. 270, 271). Three years earlier, Stuchka had also written that Russian society was still class divided (Stuchka, 1970, p. 213) and that therefore a bourgeois legal system was still needed if only to deal with the problems of distribution. Pashukanis never overcame the problem of categorizing the new regime in a form acceptable to the post-1930 Russian state. In so far as Pashukanis's theory was not changed by the pressure of outside political events that left him far behind, he saw the law of the transition period as thoroughly permeated by bourgeois concepts. Paradoxically, this

4 *R. Warrington*

gave Pashukanis his own "legitimacy", his own justification for working on and teaching legal theory. The desire finally to overcome the bourgeois world view was sufficient justification for his work.

(b) *Theory and reality*

Despite the apparent political naiveté of Pashukanis and his abject failure to perceive the tide of events, his theory is obsessed with "facts". Contemporaries, Stuchka included, accused Pashukanis of being too abstract yet Pashukanis prided himself on his theory's sound link with reality. "Scientific, that is theoretical study can reckon only with facts" (Pashukanis, 1978, p. 88). The argument he continually employed against the bourgeois theorists of his time (especially Kelsen) was that his own theory matched up to reality, whilst theirs did not. Thus Pashukanis saw his theory as being "sociological" rather than purely "juridical". "My aim was this: to present a sociological interpretation of the legal form and of the specific categories which express it" (ibid., p. 107).

Thus, not surprisingly, normative theories of law were totally unacceptable:

> To assert the objective existence of law, it is not enough to know its normative content, rather one must know too whether this normative content materializes in life, that is in social relations . . . When the legal dogmatist has to decide whether or not a particular legal form is valid, most often he makes no attempt at all to ascertain whether a certain objective social phenomenon is present or absent, but only whether or not there is a logical connection between the given normative proposition and the more general normative premise (Pashukanis, 1978, p. 87).

Natural law theory, state and will theory are similarly condemned because the picture they paint "in no way corresponds to reality" (ibid., p. 145). Even Renner, whom Pashukanis attacks in scathing terms, is unable "to comprehend the concept of law in its actual workings . . . " (ibid., p. 56). For Pashukanis legal theory has to discover what exists in the same way that political economy studies something which actually exists (ibid., p. 59).

Pashukanis's concern with "facts" appears far more problematic now than it must have done to his contemporaries. To Marxists working in the 1920s theories of law must have seemed completely out of touch with the everyday workings of bourgeois law. Yet Pashukanis's insistence on facts solves very few problems, if only because Pashukanis's downfall itself can be seen as a triumph of fact over theory. Whilst Pashukanis was trying to overplan the non-legal future, the ground was being cut from under his feet; a greater awareness of fact would not have come amiss. More important, Pashukanis himself treats facts as totally unquestionable, forgetting that what is fact for Pashukanis may be loaded interpretation, for example, for Kelsen. Othello actually thought he saw the handkerchief he gave Desdemona in Cassio's hand. He thought he "saw" a "fact". The problem was how to interpret it. Whilst the contract of employment is, for a Marxist, concerned with the "fact" of exploitation, the sale of labour power for an equivalent which is precisely not an equivalent, for bourgeois theorists a contract of employment is the "fact" of the free meeting of minds of equally uncoerced parties. These two "factual" positions cannot be reconciled, and they may be equally valid from the position they occupy within their own theoretical systems. What is at stake for Pashukanis is the validity of his own theoretical structure. Thus merely because "Kelsen had to admit that some part of real life, that is to say of people's actual behaviour, must in some way be injected into the ideal normative system" (p. 86) tells us nothing about the validity of the theories of Kelsen or Pashukanis.

(c) *Form and substance*

Nonetheless, Pashukanis's method did represent at least one major breakthrough for Marxist analysis of law; it emphasized the need to examine form as well as substance. There was, and still is, an almost inevitable tendency for Marxist theory, whether of law, economics, politics, or history, to concentrate on the substantive inequality that capitalism produces, to highlight the gross differences between different historical epochs. This is clearly a valid part of any Marxist analysis. But what Pashukanis attempted in his theory was to show that the form of law as well as its substantive workings, was inherently bourgeois. Thus for Pashukanis, unlike many quasi-Marxist theorists, there was no possibility of retaining the existing form of law, whilst revolutionizing its substantive content. The form of law itself demanded that the new society had to transcend law in its entirety, a point to which I return in the final section of this paper.

Section 2: The Commodity Form Theory and the Legal Subject

Pashukanis considered his most important contribution to jurisprudence to be the development of a commodity form theory. Both at the time the theory was published and since, this has been taken to be the centre of his critique. Some writers, such as Balbus (1977) have even argued that the commodity form theory has been the only worthwhile product of Marxist legal theory, and it is on the basis of the commodity form theory that Edelman (1979, p. 24) proclaims the necessity at last, of recognizing the genius of Pashukanis. Put simply, the theory argues that the legal form is the parallel ("homology" according to Balbus) of the commodity form. Law arises out of the needs of the commodity form of production. The commodity is the cell form of legal relations because capitalist society is basically a society of producers of commodities.

These commodities when produced are exchanged. All law is concerned with the process of the exchanging of commodities between subjects who act as the "guardians" of commodities and are created by law in order to enable the commodity production form of society to function. Law is thus the "philosophy of the subject". In order to appreciate this categorization of law, the theory can be explained as based on two premises, i.e. logical and historical.

(a) *The logical premise*

"Every legal relation" proclaims Pashukanis, "is a relation between subjects" (Pashukanis, 1978, p. 109). Therefore, he says the logical starting point for analysis is the subject. Property, says Pashukanis, is the basis of the legal form, but only property that can be disposed of in the market, that is, capitalist property. The subject in law is the expression of the freedom of property, that is, the freedom to alienate property. Thus the key to understanding law is the contradiction between things (commodities) and subjects. Commodities according to Marx relate to each other as values, that is exchange (buying and selling) takes place on the basis of equivalent amounts of labour-time embodied in commodities passing between buyers and sellers. (Unfortunately, here as elsewhere Pashukanis's failure to follow Marx's arguments beyond the "simple" beginnings of volume 1 of *Capital* causes problems; I discuss this further in section 3 (f) below.) For this to operate commodity owners must recognize that they stand towards each other in a relation of equals, where each is entering into a process of uncoerced exchange. "Exchange or the circulation of commodities is predicated on the mutal recognition of one another as owner by those engaged in exchange" (Pashukanis, 1978, p. 161). The exchange is uncoerced in the double sense that neither party is forced to exchange and that when the transaction is completed, both parties are satisfied. Exchange then operates on the principle that the parties to the exchange are gaining mutual advantages in an uncoerced harmonious process.

> For the products of human labour to be able to relate to each other as values, it is necessary for people to relate to each other as autonomous and equal personalities . . . Man as a moral subject, that is as a personality of equal worth, is indeed no more than a necessary condition for exchange according to the law of value. Man as a legal subject, or as a property owner, is a further necessary condition . . . The economics of value relations provides the key to an understanding of the juridical and ethical structure, not in the sense of the concrete content of legal or moral norms, but in the true sense of the form itself (Pashukanis, 1978, pp. 151, 152).

It follows that for Pashukanis contract is logically both the central legal premise on which all other aspects of law are based, and also the highest form of expression of the commodity owning subject. This is because it is the relations of contract that are crucial for commodity producing societies since the contract is the necessary legal expression of commodity owners' ability to use their commodities in the market, i.e. to trade with them. For Pashukanis, all other forms of legal relations in capitalism flow from this, since without the exchange of commodities persuant to legal contracts, society itself would not continue in its capitalist form. The commodity owners' legal relation is presented in two "absurd" forms, that is the form of the value of commodities and the form of the capacity to be the subject of rights. The former is the inherent "right" of the commodity expressing itself through the market "independently" of the individual. The latter is the "legal" proprietor, the personification of the abstract notion of a bearer of rights. As such they dominate commodities since legally they are the commodities' "guardians". The absurdity (contradiction) for Pashukanis lies in the paradox that economically the commodity dominates; the individual subject, glorified in the capacity to exercise rights, is no more than the necessary appendage of the cell form of the unit of wealth in capitalist society.

(b) *The historical premise*

Pashukanis's historical premise for his theory is even more fundamental than his logical premise. In his overwhelming desire to produce a theory based on history rather than on abstract notions of justice, equality etc., Pashukanis is determined to prove that the commodity form theory is almost the necessary outcome of an historical development from petty commodity production to capitalist production proper.

For Pashukanis, the fully developed form of exchange society, which Marx analysed, grew out of prior modes of petty commodity production. The commodity form of exchange historically precedes the legal system which emerges from it. It is this which expands and becomes the universal form as commodity production takes over. But it is not merely that the commodity form produces the legal form; it is that the commodity form exists prior to the legal form and that only with the full development of the commodity form is there the possibility of a fully developed abstract legal form at all. "Only when bourgeois relations are fully developed does law become abstract in character" (Pashukanis, 1978, p. 120). This potential for abstraction (in terms of rights, subjects etc.,) arises out of the logic of the commodity form as that form extends.

> Historically, however, it was precisely the exchange transaction which generated the idea of the subject as the bearer of every imaginable legal claim. Only in commodity production does the abstract form see the light; in other words, only there does the general capacity to possess a right become distinguished from concrete legal claims (ibid., p. 118).

The legal subject becomes an "abstract owner of the commodities raised to the heavens" (ibid., p. 121). Commodity production is developed through trade. Trade helps break the barriers of pre-capitalist production, and the law itself develops out of the increasing importance of trade. Trading nations required laws because they dealt in commodities (although within a society where commodity exchange was the exception). As trade expanded, the development of the particular legal form associated with the commodity expanded with it.

Pashukanis also examines the development of law in relation to contractual disputes. In summary, what Pashukanis argues, is that commodity owners, on the basis of the "recognized" reciprocity of equals, almost exchange without laws. The law steps in when disputes arise between parties to transactions which require a legal system capable of arranging settlements on a basis that does not violate the principles of equivalent exchange. Thus as exchange develops, so disputes increase and the necessity arises of a developed legal system to cope with disputes. "It is disputes, conflicts of interest, which create the legal form, the legal superstructure" (ibid., p. 93). But the implications of this development are that commodity exchange historically (and logically) is prior to law and, in some pure theoretical sense (but here not in any actual historical instance), exists independently of a legal system.

> Thus the economic relation of exchange must be present for the legal relation of contracts of purchase and sale to arise . . . the existence of a commodity and money economy is the basic precondition without which . . . concrete norms would have no meaning (ibid., p. 93).

(c) *Fetishism as summary*

One method of summarizing Pashukanis's commodity form theory is to point to its relationship with Marx's theory of fetishism, an approach recently adopted by Balbus. Marx argued that the commodity was a fetishized form because the formal equality that the commodity form postulated was only an apparent equality. Balbus has argued that what is at stake is the distinction between equality in law and inequality in fact (Balbus, 1977). He argues all citizens are formally equal before the law and find no overt discrimination in the law.

Balbus says the commodity form encompasses two aspects, i.e. the use value of the commodity and its exchange value. But when the commodity appears on the market, the "memory", as Balbus calls it, of the use value is extinguished, and instead all that concerns people is the equivalent amounts of labour-time which are exchanged. The commodity therefore, says Balbus, appears as a fetishized form because the commodity's connection with human origins is masked. This "gives rise to the appearance, the ideological inversion, that commodities have living human powers" (Balbus, 1977, p. 574). Balbus says it is possible to construct a similar theory of law from Marx's writings. Thus, he says, citizens also take on a two-fold form; that is, substantially they are unequal but they enter into formal relations of equals, which is the concern of the law. The "blindness" of the legal form to substantive human differences is the parallel of the blindness of the commodity form to the substantive differences in use value. Ultimately, Balbus argues, the legal form (as commodity form) exists independently of the will of the individual. The illusion is produced "that the law – as the universal political equivalent – has a life of its own" (ibid., p. 584).

Section 3: Some Criticisms of the Commodity Form Theory [2]

Pashukanis has probably had more vilification and abuse heaped on his head than any other twentieth century legal theorist (see Fuller, 1949). But one thing that has united both hostile and sympathetic critics is that the commodity form theory was Pashukanis's central insight. However, despite the merits of the theory, the neat parallel it presents with aspects of Marx's analysis, and its powerful commitment to attacking bourgeois notions of the hegemony of legal systems, the *General Theory* has several major flaws which mar its appeal. Ultimately these flaws may be so strong as to make the theory unusable. What follows is necessarily only a brief and outline account of some of the problems raised by Pashukanis's theory.

(a) *The priority of commodity exchange*

Pashukanis's argument that the commodity exchange form of social relations exists both historically and logically prior to law is extremely suspect. Although Pashukanis is consistent here in that he applies his notion to all forms of property, holding in effect that property itself only takes on a juridic form after the development of capitalism, the consistency does nothing to strengthen the argument. The problem is that Pashukanis has ignored the difficulty of conceptualizing and defining any form of developed property relations without using law. Although the legal form does not exhaust the concept of property, the property form itself is inchoate without the legal form. Whilst Pashukanis is right to criticize Renner's somewhat simplistic notion of property as a relation between people and things, Pashukanis's concept of property existing prior to law is unacceptable.

In discussing violations of the law, Pashukanis traces the problem of criminal law back to blood vengeance. Developing the theme of law arising out of disputes between already existing (factual) relations, he says: "Historically, the specific traits of legal intercourse were acquired primarily as a result of actual violations of the law. The concept of theft arose before the concept of property" (1978, p. 167). This argument is again the logical product of Pashukanis's commitment to the historical development of the laws of capitalism but it is no less problematic for that and left Pashukanis open to some fairly penetrating attacks from the bourgeois theorists he so despised, such as Kelsen (1955, p. 93) [and see also Lapenna, (1964, p. 26) and Schlesinger (1945, p. 151)]. The problem is to articulate the concept of theft without having a developed concept of property. Theft must involve the appropriation of property, since if an object or person is not regarded as property there is no way it, or he or she, can be appropriated wrongfully. Thus the problem with the Robinson Crusoe analogy of the classical economists, was not that Crusoe did not appropriate objects, but that mere appropriation does not turn objects into property. Property is a social concept, incorporating in part at least, the concept of the exclusion of others. It has nothing to do with, say, a primitive people (and Pashukanis is trying to trace his concept from primitive tribes) using or improving natural resources etc., where the tribe or community or whatever holds those resources communally. Where property develops, it does so on the basis of certain sections of the community being able to exclude other sections from what would otherwise be enjoyment of the particular object/person in question. Pashukanis argues that in contrast to other theories "Marxist theory considers every social form historically" (1978, p. 111). It can be argued that Pashukanis produced a most unhistorical work.

One possible defence of Pashukanis is that despite concentrating on history, Pashukanis's thesis is definitely not historical. Pashukanis focuses on an explanation of commodity production society only and makes no genuine attempt to be historical. Whilst Pashukanis assumed that laws were only necessary for particular forms of society, and thus quite unjustifiably tried to argue that feudal or slave societies were not legal, it can be suggested that this is not fundamental to his argument. If Pashukanis really had set out to write an historical analysis, then he failed. But Pashukanis's theory should be judged on its applicability to developed capitalism; in effect, it is this only which is analysed.

(b) *The dominance of exchange*

Pashukanis's theory concentrates on the exchange of commodities. That is, it focuses on the law's concern to see that the requirements of the free exchange of commodities are guaranteed. Law develops for this purpose and overcomes the practical problems that will arise where the free exchange of commodities is violated. Ultimately it serves to guarantee to the capitalist the ability to enter into that most important of "free" contracts, the purchase of labour-power. In this contract, according to Marx's analysis, the worker both receives a "fair" exchange, in that equivalents of value are passed between the contracting parties, and at the same time the capitalist is able to receive a surplus by the exploitation of the worker. This surplus is the source of all profits, and the source of funds for accumulation which serve to reproduce the conditions under which this process is repeated.

However, the process of exchange is not all that is involved. Capitalism is a process of production, and exchange is merely a part of that process. Legal theory must be as concerned with production as with exchange. Yet Pashukanis appears to have written production out of the law. This is unacceptable for Pashukanis. Historically the commodity form system is based on the development of the forces and relations of production to a particular stage where the commodity form becomes the dominant form. But this is the result of a specific process of technical and social development which encompasses a complete transformation of the production process. Legal theories which attempt to be historical cannot just bypass this process. Pashukanis has failed to make the logical allowances necessary for the importance of the production process itself in the development of a social system. Legal theories which attempt to base themselves on "social reality", as Pashukanis claimed, must incorporate the production process into their legal analysis or make sufficient allowances for its importance in relation to the legal system as a whole. Pashukanis's theory is based on a society of commodity production, yet almost eliminates the process of production from history.

(c) *The generality of commodity form*

Not only does Pashukanis apparently ignore the central influence of production on law, his legal theory is not based on capitalist commodity production at all. Pashukanis assumes that the commodity form itself produced legal relations but that this form did not so do at any specific stage in social development. He assumes that the legal form of pre-capitalist commodity production merely expands and develops as the commodity form of production becomes, in time, the dominant world form. What he ignores is the transformation commodity production undergoes in the process of development into the modern world system. Thus the theory can be criticized for being applicable to petty commodity production only, though even here Pashukanis's concepts are of doubtful historical validity.

(d) *The absence of coercion*

The historical period in which Pashukanis was writing makes the absence of coercion in the theory a puzzle, something contemporaries such as Stuchka (1970, p. 230) commented on. The dominant Leninist view of the time included the conception that all law is but the expression of the will of the ruling class to crush other classes and that in the revolutionary period of the dictatorship of the proletariat the role of law was to help crush the bourgeoisie. Krylenko wrote that revolutionary law was ultimately concerned with the forceful crushing of the class opponents of the dictatorship of the proletariat. "Thus revolutionary law is one of the weapons and one of the manifestations of the dictatorship of the proletariat" (Krylenko, 1933, p. 6). The extent to which Marxist theories of law should incorporate coercion is the subject of much debate. But some notion of law as a forceful action, as a weapon which despite enormous and sometimes quite unexpected contradictions, is part of the means for ruling class control, ought to be incorporated into Marxist legal theory. Yet Pashukanis excludes coercion almost by definition. As legal relations are but the expression of commodity exchange, and as by definition commodity exchange for Pashukanis takes place on the basis of the free meeting of minds, coercion must be relegated to a very minor role if not eliminated entirely. Indeed, Pashukanis writes of coercion actually contradicting the conditions necessary for the free and equal exchange of commodities and of exchange value ceasing to be such if its ratios are determined by an authority situated outside of the market (Pashukanis, 1978, p. 143).

Although Pashukanis does not totally ignore the role of force (the chapter on the state in particular brings in aspects of the coercive nature of the state), and although he can be seen as reacting against classic Marxist theories which overemphasised the role of force in legal theory, he has failed to incorporate an important element. It is possible that some of Pashukanis's recantations in this area represent a genuine desire to reject untenable positions. In 1932 Pashukanis wrote of his error in identifying law solely with exchange as this did not bring in the coercion and personal subordination which were essential elements of all legal system (Pashukanis, 1970, p. 235). Whether or not this and similar recantations are genuine, the lack of coercion in the theory can be linked to the question of class. Very broadly, Pashukanis ignores class relations in his concentration on bourgeois notions of equivalents. Whilst Pashukanis criticizes capitalist society, his legal theory ignores the division of that society into classes.

(e) *The use value/exchange value distinction*

Pashukanis's theory in part relies on Marx's distinction between the two aspects of a commodity, i.e., use value and exchange value. He argues that just as the market almost ignores use values and concentrates on the socially embodied labour-time in a commodity, where equivalent amounts of labour-time are exchanged, so law operates in a similar manner. The law, he said, deals only with the formal equality of citizens (i.e., the analogue of the exchange value) and ignores the substantive inequalities between citizens (i.e., the analogue of the use value).

The problem with this analysis is that it might be quite misleading. In one sense law can be seen as essentially concerned with substantive differences (i.e., for the purpose of the analogy, use values). As Pashukanis regards contract as the most important legal category and as he regards contract as the highest expression of the commodity owning subject (Pashukanis, 1978, p. 121) the best method of explanation here is to use contract. From Pashukanis's analysis it would be argued that when a dispute arises over the exchange of commodities (contracts) then the court merely looks to the form of the transaction and ignores substantive elements. The fact that one party is rich, the other poor, one employer, the other employee, are all, it is said, irrelevant.

This may be incorrect. First, in many areas (landlord–tenant, mortgagor–mortgagee, supplier–consumer, etc.) statute has intervened in most common law countries to try to redress the substantive imbalance, at least to an extent. In landlord and tenant cases, for example, a vast amount of legislation since before 1914 has altered the purely common law balance between the parties. Though the parties are clearly very differently placed prior to the contract being made, where in many cases (though perhaps not all) the power and wealth of the landlord overwhelms the tenant, in terms of bargaining strength, thus making a mockery of classic contract theory, once the contract is actually made, the law attempts to impose substantive contractual inhibitions on the landlord in favour of the tenant. The law then does not actually disregard substantive differences in many areas. Even in the most important and sensitive arena of employer–employee contracts, the law is by no means always the formal, impartial, but therefore hopelessly loaded creature Pashukanis claims.

Second, and more important, given Pashukanis's nineteenth century assumptions as to classic freedom of contract, assumptions which may be doubtful (see Atiyah, 1979, part 2 especially), there is an argument for saying that the analysis is inapplicable. In contract cases the one aspect with which the court is actually most definitely concerned is use value, i.e. the substantive subject matter of the contract. In English law especially on the breakdown of a contract, the court specifically excludes enquiry into the exchange value of the commodity, assuming that the parties, if of full age etc., have made a bargain knowing what they were doing. The rule that the court (subject obviously to exceptions) does not enquire into the adequacy of the consideration, means that in the average contract case the court is very much concerned with the use value of the contract, i.e. the substantive different items that are exchanged.

If this were not the position, the courts' function in contract disputes would be almost superfluous. In strict contract theory, the court looks to the substantive different objects that are being exchanged (i.e. usually commodities for money). In that sense, then, Pashukanis's argument breaks down completely. The actual object of contracts is not the exchange of equivalent exchange values, i.e. equal sums of money (a pointless exercise), but the passing between the parties of different use values. The court is and must be concerned with this substantive aspect of contract if legal mediation is to be of relevance.

Even with employment contracts, where the analogy and argument of Pashukanis are at their strongest, there are problems. It can be argued that the court, in classic contract terms, ignores the fact that one party is employer, with all the substantive advantages that entails, and that the other is employee with the corresponding disadvantages. Here the argument is that the law does "fetishize" the unequal relations and produce an inherently "biased" or "unfair" system under the guise of equality. However, what Pashukanis and his adherents ignore, is that substantively the law *does* recognize employer and employee as such. That is, it takes into account the fact that the two parties only appear before it because they are in the substantive and legal relation of employer and employee and therefore the law inevitably accommodates their true position. Pashukanis is perhaps only saying that the court itself does not change the substantive inequality of capitalist society. The intricacies of the commodity form theory are hardly necessary for such a result.

Ultimately, one of the difficulties here, is that Pashukanis is confusing the specific realm of the legal with the different realm of the economic. By taking a fairly unsophisticated approach to the base–superstructure metaphor, Pashukanis, in effect, ignores the potential of law for shaping economy and reduces law to the mere reflex response of the given economic. Law should be seen as having its own specificity, albeit that specificity is not to be seen as in any way purely independent of the "economic". Whilst arguments over the relative autonomy of law seem relatively endless, one theoretical advance that has been made since Pashukanis, arguably a point that both Marx and Engels anticipated, is the recognition of the effects of law on the economic. Pashukanis's theory elides the two, thereby seriously misjudging the importance of law in bourgeois society, whereas, "the work of Marx and Engels as a whole does not subscribe to essentialism, that is, to the view that all social phenomena can be reduced to or derived from the economic" (Sugarman, 1981).

(f) *The misreading of Marx*

Arguments as to "correct" readings of Marx must almost inevitably be sterile. Marx is open to an infinite variety of readings and even if a "correct" reading could be shown this does not of itself in any way guarantee the validity of the argument. On the other hand, if a writer justifies a theory by the claim in some way to "apply" Marx, then if the writer completely misunderstands Marx, the conclusion might be drawn that this indicates defects in the thesis.

Pashukanis regarded his object as the mere applying of Marx's economic analysis in the field of law. "The material pre-conditions for the community of law or for transactions between legal subjects are specified by Marx himself in Volume 1 of *Capital,* albeit only in passing, in the form of fairly general allusions" (Pashukanis, 1978, p. 111).

Pashukanis's task is impossible. Analysis designed for one field of enquiry cannot merely be appropriated and "applied" to a different field. "What is legitimate for a study of political economy is not legitimate for a study of legality . . . . " (Fine, 1979, p. 36). The form and substance of law have to be analysed from concepts which may be linked to the economy, and to a particular economic analysis, but cannot merely be the economic analysis as such.

In fact, Pashukanis has seriously misread Marx's economics. That is, given Pashukanis's own theoretical premises he has failed in the task he set himself. In summary, Pashukanis's error is similar to the problems of concentrating on the process of exchange noted above. He takes up Marx's opening remarks in *Capital* and treats these as the totality of Marx's economic theory. The beginning of *Capital* presents an examination of the individual producer and above all the individual exchanger of commodities. In some detail, Marx examines the process of individuals exchanging commodities to show that, on the face of it, equivalents of labour time are exchanged. Therefore, the source of wealth (profit) for the capitalist is not to be found in the sphere of individualistic exchange. The source of wealth, Marx argues, is in the production process itself. Labour-power is shown to be that unique commodity which (fortunately for capital) is capable, whilst being productively consumed, of reproducing its own value and an all-important surplus. Volumes 2 and 3 of *Capital* are concerned with circulation and distribution of this surplus. Marx's economics is an analysis of the production, circulation, and distribution of this surplus in a particular form of class society.

But it is just the aspect of socially produced surplus that is missing from Pashukanis's work. Pashukanis centres his analysis on isolated individuals who might have been valid subjects for analysis of pre-capitalist commodity production, but who are much less important (except possibly for the purposes of preliminary explanations as in *Capital*) when it comes to the laws of the social production of surpluses in the developed capitalist form. So when Pashukanis writes, "commodity exchange presupposes an atomized economy" (1978, p. 85) he is incorrect. Commodity exchange in its world dominant stage presupposes a highly developed socially intertwined state and eventually world economy. Dobrin pointed out that Pashukanis, having taken up theories of German jurisprudence, worked on the basis that: "All law is conditioned by relations between individuals" (Dobrin, 1936, p. 413). Pashukanis summarized this analysis when he wrote, "The legal system differs from every other form of social system precisely in that it deals with private isolated subjects" (1978, p. 100). But this is not the way capitalist society functions, it does not "represent" Marx's analysis of it, nor is it a suitable starting point for approaching the complexities of legal relations; the atomization of capitalism and its laws, at the best, can only be a part of any jurisprudential analysis.

Fine has pointed out that Pashukanis's work only applies to simple commodity production, and in effect to the exchange of commodities in simple commodity production (Fine, 1979, p. 41). For Marxists, Fine argues, it is necessary to take the analysis into production, which Pashukanis fails to do. However, even this criticism does not go far enough since it is not merely the need to follow Marx into production that is missing from Pashukanis, but the recognition that exchange is merely a moment in the (socialized) production cycle itself, that the commodity form that Pashukanis analysed is only one particular aspect the commodity passes through in its cycle of production, circulation, and distribution as a whole. Picciotto comes nearer to the fundamental critique of Pashukanis that needs to be articulated here. He points out that one problem with Pashukanis, is that he fails to appreciate the development that takes place when labour power itself becomes a commodity, i.e. capitalist production becomes dominant (Picciotto, 1979, p. 170). In a sense, this is correct, in that the domination of capital, its establishment as a world system, ultimately requires legal theory to go beyond the simple exchange of commodities.

Section 4: The Withering Away of Law

In 1927, Stuchka wrote that "Communism means not the victory of socialist law, but the victory of socialism over any law, since with the abolition of classes with their antagonistic interests, law will die out altogether" (quoted in Berman, 1963, p. 26). In essence this summarizes Pashukanis's view. It can be argued it is his most important contribution to legal theory, and therefore his commitment to the withering of law is more important than his commodity form theory. If this is correct, the flaws which mar his commodity form theory, although not unimportant, do not totally detract from Pashukanis's overall importance as a Marxist jurist. However, a theory which argues that the object of legal study is to work towards the annihilation of law is almost bound to contain contradictions. I wish to outline in this final section both Pashukanis's commitment to the withering of law and some of the contradictions in his position. In 1929, Pashukanis reaffirmed this fundamental precept: "The problem of the withering away of law is the cornerstone by which we measure the degree of proximity of a jurist to Marxism" (Pashukanis, 1980, p. 268).

(a) *No law prior to capitalism*

Pashukanis held that law was a peculiarly capitalist problem. This is a result of his commodity form theory. As Pashukanis defined all law as merely the outgrowth of the exchange of commodities, it follows that to be consistent social arrangements prior to the commodity form of society were not legal. Thus he wrote of the middle ages having "no abstract concept of the legal subject" (1978, p. 170) and of slavery not being a legal relation and thus requiring no specifically legal formulation (1978, p. 110).

Pashukanis acknowledged the gross over-simplification of this argument soon after the *General Theory* was first published, and continued to acknowledge it in later works. Untenable though the position is, its theoretical force is that it enhances his commitment to the abolition of all forms of law as means of social organization. Pashukanis's argument is, in effect, presenting bourgeois theory with an example of forms that are non-legal in the bourgeois sense. Pashukanis argues from this the inevitable conclusion that non-legal forms are both a possibility and something to be immediately worked towards.

(b) *No proletarian law*

The most heated legal debate in the 1920s in Russia related to the characterization of the legal system of the transition period. The view that eventually prevailed was that just as previous forms of society had their own specific forms of law, so too did the dictatorship of the proletariat. On the other hand, Pashukanis's view was that the transition period, because of its flexible character, did not have a form of law appropriate to it, and that the form of law in the transition period was still inevitably stamped with its inherent bourgeois characteristics. There was therefore no such thing as proletarian law. In 1930 Pashukanis wrote of the theoretical bedevilment of proletarian law and expressed his "deep regret that even Stuchka employs this term . . . " (1951, p. 269).

Pashukanis's objection to proletarian law was that it completely misled Marxist theories of law. Pashukanis explained that on the face of it, the call for concepts specific to proletarian law would appear to be "revolutionary *par excellence*" since it seemed to develop further Marxist theory in the field of law by use of an appropriate new theoretical tool. "In reality, however, this tendency proclaims the immortality of the legal form, in that it strives to wrench this form from the particular historical conditions which had helped to bring it to full fruition, and to present it as capable of permanent renewal" (Pashukanis, 1978, p. 61). Thus the call for proletarian law was inherently reactionary. The mere fact that bourgeois forms were still in use in Russia was not, for Pashukanis, a reason to change that form. "The proletariat", he explained, "may well have to utilize these forms, but that in no way implies that they could be developed further or be permeated by socialist content. These forms are incapable of absorbing this content and must wither away in an inverse ratio with the extent to which this content becomes reality" (ibid., p. 160). "The withering away of certain categories of bourgeois law (the categories as such, not this or that precept) in no way implies their replacement by new categories of proletarian law . . . The withering away of the categories of bourgeois law will, under these conditions, mean the withering away of law altogether, that is to say the disappearance of the juridical factor from social relations" (ibid., p. 61).

The move towards developing concepts of proletarian law was, for Pashukanis, inherently backward looking. Such developments sought to solidify the existing relations of society, whereas Pashukanis's position was that in a transitional society, by definition, no forms were immutable. He therefore argued that Soviet jurists must not hold back development with "any system that has been frozen into immobility even though it be dubbed proletarian law" (Pashukanis, 1951, p. 280).

(c) *The abolition of property*

Ultimately for Pashukanis, revolutions concerned property. He was of the view that the distinction between previous forms of revolution and the form of revolution he thought he was helping to build was the different relation of property. Thus for Pashukanis, previous revolutions merely replaced one form of property society with another.

> (They) did not shake the foundations of private property, the economic framework linking economic units through exchange. The same people who had rebelled against property had no choice but to approve it next day when they met in the market as independent producers. That is the way of all non-proletarian revolutions (Pashukanis, 1978, p. 124).

But future revolutions, revolutions that were to establish full communism, would be about the replacement of property entirely. The object of the revolution was the abolition of property relations, the abolition of commodity exchange social relations. Pashukanis thought that with the revolution, relations of property would "be historically absolutely done for . . . " (ibid., p. 130) property being abolished (ibid., p. 98). Thus property can be seen as the key to Pashukanis's understanding of his own and future society and the crucial barrier that had to be surmounted for full communism to be achieved. In as much as he saw the commodity form of property as the highest form, he also saw it as a final form. And as he saw the commodity form of property as the "creator" of laws, the transcendence of property meant the transcendence of laws.

(d) *Morality state and crime*

It is not possible to present a full discussion of Pashukanis's views on this area, but in summary Pashukanis linked morality, state and crime to commodity production society. It therefore follows that for Pashukanis, all three concepts are historically limited in that the completion of the revolutionary process would make these concepts redundant. "One must, therefore, bear in mind that morality, law and the state are forms of bourgeois society" (Pashukanis, 1978, p. 160).

However, Pashukanis is not totally consistent in his argument that the full development of law meant the complete disappearance of crime, state, and morality. His discussion of criminal law exposed the ambiguity. On one level Pashukanis is clear. Criminal law is a requirement of capitalist society only. It is related to the fundamental principle of equivalence of bourgeois society, in that the requirements of punishment are calculated by means of a trade off, severity of crime being equalled by the severity of punishment. However, the equivalent relation itself is only an aspect of bourgeois society. The categorizations of crime and criminal punishment are derived from the overwhelming requirements of the law of exchange of equivalents. "Conversely, the characterization 'criminal law' becomes utterly meaningless if the principle of the equivalent relation disappears from it" (ibid., p. 176).

This argument then points to a future society where relations are not dominated by the threat of the criminal process. Yet as Korsch (1978) and others have pointed out, Pashukanis contradicts himself. Thus Pashukanis writes: "Only the complete disappearance of classes will make possible the creation of a system of penal policy which lacks any element of antagonism" (p.

175). Pashukanis is calling for a society that has transcended the requirements of criminal law and yet talks of criminal punishment in that new society. The sentence following the one just cited states that it is doubtful whether there will be any necessity for a penal system in the new society. But Pashukanis does not explain how he contemplates penal systems, the results of commodity societies, in the future society of which he speaks.

The only possible excuse for Pashukanis here, is that criminal law, even more than history, fits uncomfortably into Pashukanis's project. Pashukanis's theory is really concerned with private civil law and the chapter on criminal law is only added to attempt a spurious theoretical consistency. Pashukanis merely tries to apply his commodity form theory which had a certain logical force for private civil law, to criminal law, where in the formulation of Pashukanis at least, it clearly has no place. The theory of equivalent punishment is faintly comic, and is very different from insights given elsewhere in the *General Theory* and in other works, in which Pashukanis displays a far more sophisticated approach to criminal policy. It is of course the result of trying to apply his theory (or as he thinks Marx's theory) mechanistically. It is consistent only in so far as Pashukanis pushes the equivalent principle to its illogical conclusion; but Pashukanis from time to time draws back from the full implication of his own argument.

(e) *Law versus plan*

Ultimately, Pashukanis argues that law is not something that can be seen as socially useful and that is why it is necessary to call for its complete abolition. Pashukanis fulminates against the view that law can be socially beneficical or used in the revolutionary process.

> But there is absolutely no formula, be it even drawn from the writings of the most progressive Western European jurists imaginable, which can transform the legal transactions arising out of our Civil Code into socially useful transactions, and can transform every property-owner into a person performing social (*sic*) functions. Such an abolition of private economy and private law on paper can only serve to obscure the perspective of its real abolition (1978., p. 98).

But if for Pashukanis law was now socially a restraint, "planning" was the basis of the future society which would enable the transcendence of the "narrow horizons of bouregois right" [see Kamenka and Tay (1971) on the importance of the plan for Pashukanis]. Indeed he berated legal theorists to the extent of suggesting all their work is unnecessary. "Only when the individualistic economic system has been superseded by planned social production and distribution will this unproductive expenditure of man's intellectual energies cease" (ibid., p. 80). The inevitability of legal intercourse is a product of the relations of commercial exchange. "The ultimate victory of planned economy will transform their relationship into an exclusively technical expedient, thereby doing away with their 'legal personality'" (ibid., p. 134, 135) Legal relations are characterized by Pashukanis as the opposite of the planned rational economy of the new society he worked for, but which never arrived. Whilst Pashukanis's concept of the plan is full of problems [see Binns (1980) for a discussion of the difficulties here] the commitment to the abolition of law which it entails is beyond question.

Conclusion: the Ultimate Commitment to Withering Away

The thesis that law would wither away was obviously unacceptable to the authoritarian Soviet state. Though the evidence as to Pashukanis's recantation is somewhat confusing, different writers suggesting different conclusions and citing inconsistent texts, Pashukanis did abandon his thesis.

However, Pashukanis's overwhelming theoretical commitment to the ultimate evanescene of law, and the importance of that thesis to his theory cannot be overstated. The withering away of law is the logical conclusion of the commodity form theory. If the commodity form theory is to be coherent, it must postulate that only commodity production society has legal systems. If, therefore, the object of 1917 was to go beyond the requirements of commodity production, and the straight-jacket of bourgeois relations and bourgeois thought, as Pashukanis and the 1917 Bolsheviks assumed, then the conclusion must follow that legal relations were to be overtaken. The moves by Pashukanis to abandon this thesis represented the ultimate defeat, the withering of his life's work.

By 1936 the critique of Pashukanis was universal, though most of the criticisms were restatements of the new orthodoxy rather than genuine attempts to discuss the failings of his works. The following rejection of the *General Theory* is probably fairly typical.

> Law, state and even morality are declared there to be bourgeois forms that cannot be filled with any socialist content and that must die away during the realization of socialism. In addition to this erroneous view, which has nothing in common with Marxism-Leninism, the meaning of the proletarian state, proletarian communist morality and finally the meaning of Soviet Law (which is the law of the proletarian state and serves as an instrument for the construction of socialism) became completely distorted. The concrete, true history of Soviet law as an instrument of the proletariat's policy . . . was replaced with abstract and erroneous arguments about the withering away of law, about the disappearance of the juridical superstructure etc. . . . The relationship between the owners of commodities was declared to be the true, specific content of all law . . . Naturally the principle class content, namely the ownership of the means of the production, was thereby neglected . . . The theory which asserted that all law is 'bourgeois' was

> based on the confusion of many distinct things . . . [The writer was Pashukanis (Pashukanis 1967, pp. 321, 322 and see also the final extracts in Pashukanis 1980)].

These and other abject obeisances were of no avail. On 20 January 1937 *Pravda* declared Pashukanis an enemy of the people (the most serious criminal category). Pashukanis disappeared without trace, trial or confession (see Sharlet, 1977, p. 169), but his own withering away represented more than another personal tragedy. It started the period when legal theory was no longer allowed to pursue wild flights of fancy, when legal academics became tied to the formality and professionalism of the new soviet legal order. The fact that the very same legal order that Pashukanis asserted was withering away became what Sharlet has called the "jurisprudence of terror" (Sharlet, 1977) is another story.

Notes

1 For reasons explained in the review of Pashukanis (1980) in this journal (1980, p. 325) I have used the 1978 translation of the *General Theory* throughout this paper.

2 For the fullest discussion of Pashukanis's contemporary Russian critics, see Sharlet (1968). For further criticisms, see Redhead (1978), Kinsey (1978) and some of the essays in Fine *et al.* (1979). Arthur (1976, 1978) presents some of the most fullsome praise of Pashukanis. As some of the materials published in the Beirne and Sharlet anthology (Pashukanis, 1980) show, Pashukanis recanted on many aspects of his work, at times abandoning parts of his thesis in necessary but unseemly haste. Whilst many, if not most, of the recantations were the result of other than theoretical pressures, some might represent genuine attempts to develop the theory.

References

Arthur, C. (1976) Towards a materialist theory of law. *Critique* **7.**

Arthur, C. (1978) "Editor's Introduction". In *Law and Marxism: a General Theory.* (E. B. Pashukanis). Ink Links: London.

Atiyah, P. (1979) *The Rise and Fall of Freedom of Contract.* Clarendon Press: Oxford.

Balbus, I. (1977) Commodity form and legal form: an essay on the relative autonomy of the law. *Law and Society Review* **11,** 3. Reprinted in *The Sociology of Law.* (Reasons, C. E. & Rich, R. M., Eds). Butterworths: Toronto.

Berman, H. (1963) *Justice in the USSR: An Interpretation of Soviet Law.* Harvard University Press: Cambridge Mass.

Binns, P. (1980) Law and marxism. *Capital and Class* **10.**

Dobrin, S. (1936) Soviet jurisprudence and socialism. *Law Quarterly Review* **52.**

Edelman, B. (1979) *Ownership of the Image: Elements for a Marxist Theory of Law.* RKP: London.

Fine, B. (1979) Law and class. In *Capitalism and the Rule of Law: From Deviancy Theory to Marxism*, Chapter 2. (Fine *et al.*, Eds). Hutchinson: London.

Fuller, L. (1949) Pashukanis and Vyshinski: a study in the development of Marxist legal theory. *Michigan Law Review* **47.**

Kamenka, E. & Tay, A. (1971) Beyond the French revolution: communist socialism and the concept of law. *University of Toronto Law Journal* **21.**

Kelsen, H. (1955) *The Communist Theory of Law*. Stephens & Son: London.

Kinsey, R. (1978) Marxism and the law: preliminary analysis. *British Journal of Law and Society* **5.**

Korsch, K. (1978) An Assessment. In *Law and Marxism: A General Theory*. (E. B. Pashukanis). Ink Links: London.

Krylenko, N. (1933) *Revolutionary Law*. Co-operative Publishing Society of Foreign workers in the USSR: Moscow.

Lapenna, I. (1964) *State and Law: Soviet and Yugoslav Theory*. The Athlone Press: London.

Lenin, V. I. (1975) The state and revolution. In *Selected Works*. Progress Publishers: Moscow.

Marx, K. (1971) *Critique of the Gotha Programme*. Progress Publishers: Moscow.

Pashukanis, E. B. (1951) The Soviet state and the revolution in law. In *Soviet Legal Philosophy*. (Babb, H. & Hazard, J. N. Eds). Cambridge: Mass.

Pashukanis, E. B. (1967) State and law under socialism. In *Soviet Political Thought*. (Jaworski, M., Ed.). John Hopkins Press: Baltimore.

Pashukanis, E. B. (1970) Exchange and law. In *Ideas and Forces in Soviet Legal History*. (Zile, Z., Ed.). College Printing and Publishing Inc.: Madison Wisconsin.

Pashukanis, E. B. (1978) *Law and Marxism: A General Theory*. Inks Link: London.

Pashukanis, E. B. (1980) *Selected Writings on Marxism and Law*. (Beirne, P. & Sharlet, R., Eds). Academic Press: London.

Picciotto, S. (1979) The theory of the state, class struggle, and the rule of law. In *Capitalism and the Rule of Law: From Deviancy Theory to Marxism* Chapter 11. (Fine, B. *et al.*, Eds). Hutchinson: London.

Redhead, S. (1978) The discrete charm of bourgeois law: a note on Pashukanis. *Critique* **9.**

Sharlet, R. (1968) *Pashukanis and the Commodity Exchange Theory of Law 1924–1930*. PhD Thesis Indiana University.

Sharlet, R. (1974) Pashukanis and the rise of Soviet Marxist jurisprudence. *Soviet Union* **1,** 2.

Sharlet, R. (1977) Stalinism and Soviet legal culture. In *Stalinism: Essays in Historical Interpretation*. (Tucker, R. C., Ed.). W. W. Norton & Co. Inc.: New York.

Sharlet, R. (1978) Pashukanis and the withering away of law in the USSR. In *Cultural Revolution in Russia 1928–1931*. (Fitzpatrick, S. Ed.). Indiana. University Press: Bloomington, Indiana.

Schlesinger, R. (1945) *Soviet Legal Theory: Its Social Background and Development*. Kegan Paul Trench Trubner: London.

Stuchka, P. (1970) My journey and my errors. In *Ideas and Forces in Soviet Legal History*. (Zile, Z. Ed.). College Printing and Publishing Inc.: Madison, Wisconsin.

Sugarman, D. (1981) Theory and practice in law and history: a prologue to the study of the relationship between law and economy from a socio-historical perspective. In *Law State and Society*. (Fryer, R. H. *et al.* Eds). Croom Helm: London, Forthcoming.

Date received: October 1980

RECHTSTHEORIE 18 (1987), S. 516 - 523
Duncker & Humblot, Berlin 41

LUKÁCS AND LAW

By Eugene Kamenka, Canberra

I.

The place of the Hungarian philosopher György (Georg) Lukács (1885 - 1971) in the history of Western, intellectual Marxism is assured. For many, the very concept of 'Western' marxism, with its rejection of simple economic determinism and its elevation of totality, dialectic and the work of the spirit (or at least of culture) takes its departure from his first major Marxist work, *History and Class Consciousness*, published in Berlin in 1923. That coincided with the publication of Karl Korsch's *Marxism and Philosophy*, also in Berlin. Both men, by then, had identified with revolutionary, communist Marxism against social democracy and the economism and reformism of its trade unions; both elevated, with Lenin, the role of consciousness against mechanistic causality and deterministic formulae for calculating the incremental growth of social forces. 'It is not the primacy of economic motives in historical explanation that constitutes the decisive difference between Marxism and bourgeois thought,' Lukács then wrote, 'but the point of view of totality.' In the language of a Hegelian philosopher steeped in Kantianism and neo-Kantianism as well, Lukács insisted that 'the totality of an object can only be posited if the positing subject is itself a totality.'[1] Subject and object must become unified through the socio-historical process and the social totality must be understood dialectically as a complex of complexes – themes that Lukács was to explore for the rest of his life, first in literature and aesthetics and finally in ontology. *History and Class Consciousness* was condemned by leaders of the Communist International – Béla Kun dubbed it a 'Marxist theology.' It was based on enthusiasm and idealist ethical preoccupations and sincerely repudiated by Lukács himself at subsequent stages of his life. It nevertheless exercised an enormous influence on some of the ablest European Marxists and neo-Marxists of the inter-War period (until the Nazi and the Stalinist darknesses fell upon them) and again on the radical student movement of the late 1960s. The essays that constituted *History and Class Consciousness* emphasised the dialectic against mechanical causal determinism, developed a theory of alienation and reification some years before the publication of Marx's early work on these themes and helped to create the sociology of knowledge and the Frankfurt School of Critical Theory. Though Lukács' view of philosophy was fundamentally at variance with Lenin's elevation of materialism and the copy theory of knowledge,

---

[1] *G. Lukács*, History and Class Consciousness (Geschichte und Klassenbewußtsein), new ed., transl. R. Livingstone, London 1971, 'The Marxism of Rosa Luxemburg', pp. 27 - 28.

Lukács' conception of the role of revolutionary consciousness in history closely parallelled Lenin's conception of making history through the conscious revolutionary vanguard, the Party. Lukács, of course, ascribed that revolutionary consciousness to the standpoint of the working class, but his view, like Lenin's, led readily to the recognition that the actual, empirical working class fell far short of understanding or actualising its mission. The emancipation of mankind, the exposure and shattering of bourgeois reification and fragmentation, was best done by the revolutionary intellectual, by a cultural elite understanding the significance of the proletariat as a concept and as a force in history.

In continuing to focus primarily on *History and Class Consciousness*, Western radicals and critical theorists do Lukács less than justice – finding it easier, perhaps, to elevate the importance of (their own) spirit than to follow Lukács into his extraordinarily rich and subtle acquaintance with the whole range of modern European culture and with the vicissitudes and tragedies of Germany, Eastern Europe and the communist world after 1918. By the time Lukács, a Hungarian Jew born in Budapest, was thirty, he had studied in two Hungarian universities (one of them now in Romania) and in Heidelberg, had formed personal contacts with Max Weber, Georg Simmel, Ernst Bloch, Gustav Radbruch and Hans Kelsen, had passed from neo-Kantian idealism to Marxism as a revolutionary commitment, had dropped his pretensions to nobility and returned to Hungary to take part in Béla Kun's Hungarian Soviet Republic. With the downfall of that Republic, he returned to exile in Germany, writing both theoretical studies and political and agitational pamphlets. Condemned after 1929 to abandon active communist politics by the growing Party disapproval of his *History and Class Consciousness* and the rejection of his 1929 *Blum Theses* advocating a popular front seven years before the Communist International was ready to do so, Lukács spent the 1930s and half the 1940s in the Soviet Union. Here, he worked on *The Historical Novel* (1937) and *The Young Hegel* (1938) and on literary studies later collected into the three volumes published as *Studies in European Realism, Goethe and His Age* and *Essays on Thomas Mann*. Returning to Hungary in 1945, he was heavily involved in cultural and political activities in the communist interest, but compelled to withdraw to philosophical studies after 1949 when cultural life became totally Stalinised. Under new conditions, he became Minister of Culture in Imre Nagy's shortlived government in 1956: with the Soviet invasion 'to restore order' he was briefly deported with other members of the deposed government to Romania. He returned to Budapest in the summer of 1957 and resumed his place as the country's ablest Marxist philosopher – capable of tough and uncompromising identification with communism in some respects and always politically suspect in others. Before 1956, he had already completed *The Destruction of Reason* and *Particularity as an Aesthetic Category;* in the latter year he wrote *The Meaning of Contemporary Realism*. The last fifteen years of his life were devoted to the volumes that became his two major syntheses, his *Aesthetics* and his *Toward the Ontology of Social Being*. The most important disciples of his later years in Hungary, many of them now in exile (some in Australia), bear witness, in their own work, to the power and fertility of his thought and the mixture of cultural sensibility and critical logic that he could inspire. They have tended toward a form of Marxist humanism that describes itself as the Budapest School of Marxism and that seems to me, at least, much sharper logically and more tough-minded than the Marxist humanism of an Erich Fromm and the Yugoslav *Praxis* group.

Like Karl Marx, and perhaps for the same reason – that an intelligent Jew in a hostile and uncertain society had to secure his status and his livelihood – Lukács began his intellectual career with the study of law, enrolling in the Faculty of Law and Political Sciences of the Royal Hungarian Péter Pázmány University of Sciences in Budapest in 1902, but transferring to the Royal Hungarian Franz Joseph University of Sciences at Kolozsvár (now Cluj-Napoca in Romania). There he received his doctorate in political sciences in 1906 before going to study philosophy in Germany. A study of Lukács' thought on the place and problems of law[2] seems at first sight a remarkably unprofitable enterprise. But Dr. Csaba Varga, of the Institute of State and Law of the Hungarian Academy of Sciences who worked in the History of Ideas Unit of the A. N. U. in the first half of 1987, has given it both distiction and point.

Even more so than Karl Marx, Lukacs paid only occasional and passing attention to law. His concern is usually with law as an illustration of something else. Thus, the chapter on 'Reification and the Consciousness of the Proletariat' in *History and Class Consciousness* set forth its central (rather Weberian) message on the basis of legal structure, but it deals with reification and with the proletariat. In his politically activist periods, Varga reminds us, Lukács writes about particular laws and tactics and strategies in opposing them, but these, too, are passing and limited interests. Apart from a few works of almost universal interest, such as those of Max Weber or Hans Kelsen, and other volumes acquired on the basis of early friendships, Lukács, an indefatiguable collector, collected no books on law. Law is not mentioned in the fifty-five manuscript pages of Lukács' last work, *The Fragments of an Intellectual Autobiography,* intended to be a summary of his lifetime experiences. It was not discussed when his students gathered round their dying mentor to glean, in final exchanges, as much as they could of his own view of his life work and experiences. Yet, though for Lukács law remained always an instrument of politics, an example of abstraction and reification and a component of more comprehensive units, in his final published work, *The Ontology,* it no longer appears in simple functional subordination to the social whole, to politics, the economy, etc. Here, Dr. Varga argues, law is seen in its specificity, influenced on the one hand by the formal enactment of a system of norms and on the other hand by the dialectical contradictions that keep breaking through the logic of internal legal development and force it toward practical compromise solutions. In the *Ontology,* according to Varga, Lukács was making considerable efforts to work out a genuinely Marxist theory of law on a comparative basis, distinguishing his own views from Marxist orthodoxies of the 1920s

[2] *Csaba Varga,* The Place of Law in Lukács' World Concept, Akadémiai Kiadó, Budapest 1985 (Price: £ 10.50).

and of the 1960s. Drawing on an 'extraordinary sensitivity towards legal issues' displayed throughout his work but never put to extended theoretical use, Lukács in this final work outlined his approach to law generally.

Dr. Varga sets this, most ably and seriously, in the context of Lukács' intellectual biography and, even more importantly, in the context of Lukács' wider philosophy. In the process, we learn a great deal not only about Lukács but about the dissolution of the naive social utopianism and aggressive legal nihilism which communists proclaimed in the hour of revolution during and after the First World War and in some countries since. That utopianism and legal nihilism Dr. Varga has effectively criticised and set in historical perspective on his own account.[3]

Following Lukács' own criticism of his early Marxist writings, Varga notes – as other Hungarian communist writers have done – that they were based in enthusiasm, issuing in 'the messianic expectation that the dictatorship of the proletariat, as the practical embodiment of the last judgment, would, at one stroke, dissolve all contradictions through revolutionary practice' (p. 41). Revolutionary practice, as then seen by Lukács and other determined Marxist theorists, was 'in the last resort and to no small extent inspired by a merciless revolutionary intention and a missionary consciousness' (p. 42). Decisions and resolutions were to be the master and not the slave of facts. The circle within which Lukács himself operated in 1918 and 1919 strove to propagate these aspirations 'by working out the most radical methods, and by proclaiming a total break with every institution and mode of life stemming from the bourgeois world.'[4] Lukács, indeed, in such lectures and pamphlets as 'Terror as a Source of Law', *Legal Order and Violence, Tactics and Ethics* and 'The Changing Function of Historical Materialism', emphasised sharply that law was organised violence. As an institution, it was only an institutionalisation of means subordinate to external ends. Concepts of order possessed at most a relative validity; they were based on violence and its acceptance. Therefore, communists should be fearless in the face of the law: 'the risk of breaking the law should not be regarded any differently,' he was to write in *History and Class Consciousness,* 'from the risk of missing a train connection when on an important journey.'[5]

In *History and Class Consciousness,* Lukács draws on the neo-Kantian formal analysis of law and on Weber's concept of a calculating, technical rationality as characterising the developing capitalist order to make rationality and the advancing division of labour a universal scapegoat identified with all the dehumanising and negative features of capitalism and responsible for them. G. S. Jones[6] sees this as representing 'the first major irruption

---

[3] Cf. e.g., *Varga,* Utopias of Rationality in the Development of the Idea of Codification, in: F. C. Hutley / E. Kamenka / A. E. S. Tay (eds.), Law and the Future of Society, Archiv für Rechts- und Sozialphilosophie, Beiheft N. F. nr. 11, Wiesbaden 1979, p. 27 and *Varga,* Rationality and the Objectification of Law, LVI (1979) Rivista Internazionale di Filosofia del Diritto, p. 4.

[4] *N. Tertulian,* L'evoluzione del pensiero di György Lukács, in: G. Oldrini (ed.), Lukács, Milan 1979, p. 52, cited by Varga, on p. 42.

[5] *G. Lukács,* History and Class Consciousness, (vol. cit.), p. 263.

of the romantic anti-scientific tradition of bourgeois thought into Marxist theory' – a useful reminder that Marxists can use the term 'bourgeois' for anything from the seventeenth century onward that they dislike. Varga reminds us that such romanticism was not Marx's, since Marx always saw industrialism and industrialisation as necessary and potentially liberating elements in human progress. Thus, Lukács at the period elaborated an idealised version of Hellenism as a real alternative to 'bourgeois' fragmentation, objectification, alienation and reification – to a calculating rationality that produced only a synthesis of 'rationalised' systems and made man a mechanical part incorporated into mechanical sub-systems. (Compare Agnes Heller's idealisation of *Renaissance Man*.) For Varga, all this is utopian – as Lukács himself began to recognise in an unworked-out way in *The Destruction of Reason*, though his view of the sciences in that work even further radicalises the far from moderate views of *History and Class Consciousness*. In *The Destruction of Reason*, Lukács, as Varga argues, treats the legal theoretician Carl Schmitt as an example of the way in which German sociology is attracted to Nazism. Yet Lukács identifies with Schmitt's attack on the neo-Kantian emphasis on formal relations as constituting the essence of state and law. He objects to the neo-Kantian use of dogmatism masquerading as exact epistemology to turn law into an autonomous sphere of values, with rules of its own, and pays no attention to any connection between this legal nihilism and Schmitt's support of the Nazis. By 1948, writing on the tasks of Marxist philosophy in the Hungarian 'New Democracy', Lukács still insisted: '*Nothing* that a democracy can formally give is valuable in *itself* . . . This means that actually and practically, the political and social content is prior at any time to the legal form.'[7] But he proclaimed that 'this priority of content should not deteriorate into an abolition of all forms.' That was the line of fascism; that would lead to the chaos and anarchy that the New Democracy is established to overcome.

Here, then, lies the fundamental tensions or 'contradiction' – no doubt to be resolved 'dialectically' – that stands at the centre of Lukács' earlier view of law and at the centre of many contemporary radical views. The second, and more substantial part of Dr. Varga's book seeks to show that Lukács' *Ontology* constitutes a Copernican revolution that points the way to such resolution.

II.

The difference between the older Lukács and Dr. Varga on the one hand, and contemporary Western radicals, the Frankfurt School of Critical Marxism, the students of the 60s and their offshoot, the Critical Legal Studies movement on the other – not to speak of the Red Army Fraction and other 'Red' terrorists – is that the former have to live in and accept some degree of responsibility for and commitment to what Dr. Varga calls 'the institutional set-up of socialism.' Varga attacks sharply in the second part of his book

[6] *G. S. Jones*, 'The Marxism of the Early Lukács', in: Editorial Board of the New Left Review (eds.), Western Marxism, London 1977, p. 33.

[7] Cited from the Hungarian by *Varga*, p. 65, fn. 109.

Pashukanis' emphasis on the direct contradiction between socialism and law and his direct reduction of law to bourgeois economic categories. He writes equally sharply of Western radicalism:

> In our days it is the New Left which regards *History and Class Consciousness* as the only intellectual food fit for consumption from the array of Lukács' Marxist work; the New Left would limit interest in socialist legal theory exclusively to the experiments of the first decade of the Russian revolution. One of the characteristic features of the legal theories in the West is that they see the question of the withering away of law as the most original contribution of Marxism to theorizing on law and also as one of its most acute theoretical problems. (p. 81).

Against this, Varga believes, we can find a less simplistic and more responsible understanding of law by following the general theme and the specific references to law to be found in Lukács' *Ontology* and in some passages of *The Destruction of Reason* and of *The Aesthetic*. The fundamental theme of the *Ontology*, for Varga – who leaves aside as a matter for philosophical rather than legal discussion whether the *Ontology* really contains two inconsistent ontologies, as Feher, Heller, Markus and Vajda suggest – is the contrast between the epistemological approach (condemned as simplistic and leading to unmediated antinomies) and the ontological approach. The *epistemological* approach contents itself with conceptual analysis, presenting as true or false the results of reflections about social processes and their components treated analytically. The *ontological* approach concentrates on the effects of social processes and their components in a given social context and their relation to the totality. On this basis, Varga elevates what is in effect a historical and sociological approach to law – none the worse for that. He distinguishes between Marxist theory of law, which attempts to become a general social scientific theory of law, and socialist theory of law, which has to lay the theoretical foundations for a socialist system of law in harmony with the legal-political and social requirements of the society in which it arises. Even the general Marxist theory of law as a social phenomenon has to be based on an historical outlook, appreciating that the present is a transitory product of development. It has to be comparative, appreciating that contemporary socialist legal systems with their roots in the Civil Law tradition constitute only one of several possible historical alternatives, even if each is, in a given context, historically inevitable. It has to describe the actual workings, regularities and effects of the legal system and not its preferred or projected principles.

Linked with all this is Varga's recognition, also ascribed to the later Lukács, of the 'relative autonomy' of law. Lukács' totality in the *Ontology*, Varga rightly insists, is complex and heterogeneous; sub-structures are determined both by their place and function in the totality and by their consequent internal requirements and characteristics and their internal history. The connection between relatively autonomous complexes is dealt with by Lukács' theory of 'mediation' – a role that is both complex and the source of historically inevitable contradictions that make complexes historical, not eternal.

All this, as in Engels, leads to a more 'differentiated', 'complex', i.e., unclear and problematic, treatment of the three important categories of objectification, reification and alienation. Even the two latter come to be tendencies to be watched and combated, especially in law, rather than simply *aufgehoben*.

Dr. Varga approaches all this very seriously, though it is one major weakness of his book that its historical mode of presentation brings Lukács to life at the expense of sustained and systematic examination of his views. The only reference to justice in the book is in the Index, where it says 'See law as *dikaion*', which leads us not to a concept of justice, but to the problem of adapting rules and principles to concrete cases. On validity as a central legal concept, Dr. Varga has a little more to say, but what his book cries out for is missing – the specificity of law, or of particular legal systems, as social traditions. Before a social institution can have an effect, it must *be something*. Marxists now recognise the social value of law as such, but they are still not at home with discussing in what that social value might lie. In the end, there is – one feels – no real progress, except in scholarship, from Engels' belief that law serves ruling economic classes but does so by appealing to a sense of justice and order that gains wider social response and mitigates the harshness of oppression. Has Lukács made any of this clearer or more convincing by reformulating it all in the language of Hegelian philosophy, substituting ontological for 'socio-historical', 'mediation' for functional interconnection, 'objectification' for the recognition that things work independently of our will? To discover the 'dialectic' of law, or one of them, in the difference between 'the immanence' and closed nature of the legal system and its incessant correction through the facts and demands of social life is not to make a great discovery or, indeed, any discovery at all. To call that a 'contradiction' is to place a Hegelian gloss on facts, on social and historical complexes that carry an anti-Hegelian message. This is the message that conflict and 'contradiction' are neither unnatural nor ultimately resolvable; the tensions of life and of social systems are not like the contradictions of logic. They exist and will continue to exist, much as their forms may change. Without this basic assumption being clearly brought to the fore, the 'ontological' (i. e., socio-historical) approach to law cannot do its work. Nor can we write about historical systems of law, or even 'law generally' (if there is such a thing) without more complex tools than 'state', 'economy' and 'classes', 'feudal', 'bourgeois' and 'socialist', without substituting complex institutions, traditions, social activities and social longings for formal categories and logical concepts. Nowhere is that approach more necessary, or less welcome, than in the countries of 'actually existing socialism.'

The movement of Lukács' thought, it is often implied, is from an early idealism to a thoroughgoing Marxist 'materialism'. Yet Lukács' conception of reality remains, like Marx's, in a crucial sense idealist through its continued elevation of the concepts of the dialectic, of contradiction, of the totality, of coherence and mediation. All of these terms, in the use made of them by Lukács, and Marx, are not features of reality, of processes in space and time, but of theories, of explanations, of mental constructions. They arise from the problematic of Kant's antinomies and those antinomies *are not* antinomies found in reality, but antinomies that arise from misdescription of reality, from the false belief that there is a finite totality to be called 'the world' or that time itself, as opposed to events, has a duration. 'Contradiction', 'partiality of view', 'mediation' are characteristics of or relations between theories and statements, not events. For the idealist, this distinction is annihilated by a fundamental assumption that what exists is a theory or an idea in the mind of God. When the true reality is treated as an Idea in nobody's mind, both the concept of an idea and the concept of reality become incoherent. But incoherence, contradiction, inadequacies are all terms that apply to statements, ideas, theories, not to events, processes, to what actually is.

[10]

MICHAEL JAWORSKYJ

SOVIET CRITIQUE OF THE "BOURGEOIS" PHILOSOPHY OF LAW

Contents

Criticism of Methodological Approaches of the "Bourgeois" Science of Law

The critique of "bourgeois" theories of law is one of the tasks of a Soviet social discipline called the "Marxist-Leninist theory of state and law". The scope of study of this theory embraces what is known in the non-Soviet world as philosophy of law, history of state and law, sociology of law, general theory of law, methodology, and in a great measure political theory. Soviet theorists claim that their theory of state and law is diametrically opposed to all the aforementioned disciplines of the "bourgeois" social science. Its uniqueness consists presumably in that it alone employs a "truly scientific method", and that because of this it offers scientifically correct answers to all problems concerning the state and law[1]).

The assumption that the "Marxist-Leninist theory of state and law" is the only one capable of offering scientific interpretation of law been entertained since the very beginning of its existence. It should be noted, however, that while advancing the claim contemporary Soviet theorists discard the fact that theories of law advanced by individual Soviet writers at different times frequently have been at variance with one another. This will be seen more clearly in the following pages. At this point it may suffice to indicate a few, but nevertheless crucial, changes in Soviet interpretations of law. For example, initially Soviet theorists conceived of law as a "bourgeois" and thus inherently "evil" phenomenon. Following Marx and Engels, they argued that law is an instrument of exploitation, of injustice, and of inequality. Though they admitted the need of using the law in the "transition period" preceding communism, they were in agreement that the law employed by Soviets preserved its "bourgeois" character. But this interpretation was gradually given up after Stalin's proclamation of the doctrines of "capitalist encirclement" and "strengthening of Soviet state". Henceforth they no longer claimed that law is inherently a "bourgeois" phenomenon. On the contrary, they argued that Soviet law has acquired a "socialist" character and that in comparison to "bourgeois" law it constitutes a "new" and "higher" type of law. In contrast to earlier interpretations, contemporary Soviet theorists contend that Soviet law is a "true law", meaning thereby that it is presumably the incarnation of justice and equality.

The basic assumption of the Soviet theory of state and law is that a science of law and a scientific critique of "bourgeois" theories of law are attainable only through employment of the "Marxist dialectic method", which is also known as the "Marxist Leninist method", "revolutionary dialectic method", or simply as the method of "historical" or "dialectic" materialism. The method is acclaimed by Soviet political and legal theorists to be the only scientific method for the study of social phenomena in general and of state and law in

[1]) *Карева, М. П., Кечекъян, С. Ф., Федосеев, А. С., Федькин, Г. И.*, Теория государства и права (*Kareva, M. P., Kechek'ian, S. F., Fedoseev, A. S., Fed'kin, G. I.*, Theory of state and law) (Moscow, 1955), p. 7.

An Index of Authors mentioned in this article can be found on pp. 33—34.

particular. An elucidation of this method is beyond the scope of this paper. It may suffice here to state that the critique of "bourgeois" theories of law, or, in M. Rezunov's words, the "socialist and sociological critique of the bourgeois legal order and its theoretical expression in juridical categories", is a constituent part of "Marxist dialectic method"[2]).

By employing this method the early Soviet writers expected to accomplish a number of things. First, it was hoped that the critique of "bourgeois" theories of law, by means of the Marxist method, would reveal their "unscientific" character. Second, that it would help to ferret out "progressive" elements from "bourgeois" theories of law that were adaptable to Marx's economic theory of society. Third, the hope was entertained that the study of law through this method would eliminate the diversity of antagonistic interpretations of law that were so characteristic of non-Soviet theories of law. Finally, it was optimistically predicted that ultimately a "true science of law" would be created, namely, a "Marxist science of law"[3]).

But study of the Soviet theory of law reveals unequivocally that the hopes attached to the "Marxist dialectic method" have not materialized. In the relatively short period of its existence Soviet theory of law experienced a split into antagonistic schools of law corresponding to those of "bourgeois" natural law, psychological, sociological, and normative theories of law. Even more revealing is the fact that while claiming to be employing only the "Marxist" method in studying law and in criticizing "bourgeois" theories of law, Soviet theorists are in disagreement as to its contents, meaning, and manner of application[4]).

The failure to bring about a "Marxist" and thus "solely scientific theory of law" became evident to Soviet legal theorists of the late 1920's. However, instead of questioning the suitability of the "Marxist dialectic method" in the study of law, the First All-Union Conference of Marxists-Jurists of 1930 attributed the responsibility for the failure to the "influence of bourgeois methods" upon the thinking of Soviet legal theorists[5]). This line of reasoning became especially pronounced after the "First Conference of Learned Workers-Jurists" in 1938, under the leadership of Andrei Vyshinskii. The failure to produce a "Marxist science of law" was explained as political sabotage on the part of legal theorists

---

[2]) *Резунов, М.*, К вопросу о методе изучения права (*Rezunov, M.*, On problems of method in the study of law), "Советское право" (Soviet law) (Moscow, Leningrad), 1928, No. 3 (33), p. 52.

[3]) *Ibid.*

[4]) On the conflicting interpretations of the "Marxist dialectic method" see *Д. Магеровский* (*D. Magerovskii*) — the first Soviet writer to have offered a rather systematic formulation of dialectical method —, Советское право и методы его изучения (Soviet law and methods of its study), "Советское право," 1922, No. 1; *Корнилов, Ф. Д.*, Юридический догматизм и диалектический материализм (*Kornilov, F. D.*, Juridical dogmatism and dialectic materialism) (Saratov, 1925); *Ксенофонтов, Ф.*, Государство и право (*Ksenofontov, F.*, State and law) (Moscow, 1924); *Резунов, op. cit.* (note 2); *Аскназий, С. И.*, Некоторые вопросы методологии советского гражданского права (*Asknazii, S. I.*, Some methodological problems of the Soviet civil law), "Советское государство и право" (Soviet state and law) (Moscow), 1940, No. 8—9; "Советское государство и право" — a principal Soviet journal dealing with problems of theory of state and law — will hereafter be cited as "Сов. гос. и право"; *Денисов, А. И.*, Диалектико-материалистический метод теории государства и права (*Denisov, A. I.*, Dialectical materialistic method in the theory of state and law), "Труды научной сессии Всесоюзного Института Юридических Наук" (Works of a scientific session of the All-Union Institute of Legal Science) (Moscow, 1948); *Федосеев, П.*, Значение марксистко-ленинской теории познания для общественных наук (*Fedoseev, P.*, The significance of Marxist-Leninist theory of cognition for social sciences), "Коммунист" (Kommunist) (Moscow), 1955, No. 8.

[5]) *Пашуканис, Е.*, За Марксо-Ленинскую теорию государства и права (*Pashukanis, E.*, For a Marxist-Leninist theory of state and law) (Moscow-Leningrad, 1931), p. 12.

who had not succeeded in "divorcing" themselves from "bourgeois methodology", especially from "juridical" and "sociological formalism", but who, on the contrary, had attempted to adapt some aspects of the latter to the "Marxist method" [6]). During the conference A. Vyshinskii delivered a criticism of the methodology of "bourgeois" theories that in years following became a stereotype in the Soviet theory of state and law. He proceeded by stating that "Marxism, and in particular historical materialism, is the greatest achievement of scientific thought" and that "no other scientific system exists that would as correctly and completely define . . . the laws of development of human society, as truly and infallibly explain the past of this society, and as penetratingly show its future" [7]). Marxism, in his opinion, "has answered the most complicated questions of history, philosophy, political economy, law, and morality, which seemed to be unanswerable" [8]). In comparison to Marxism, he argued, the "pre-Marxist sociology and historiography" may "at best" be deemed to constitute "accumulated raw facts, collected chaotically and merely reflecting separate aspects of historical process" [9]). In fact, he thought, "neither a science of law nor a scientific theory of state existed prior to Marx" [10]), and the same applies to contemporary "bourgeois" theories:

> As a matter of fact the bourgeois science of law does not exist unless, obviously, one considers the collection of arbitrary constructions covered with scientific phraseology to be a science. Indeed, such a science exists in the capitalist world. But a science that could be called such in the true meaning of this term does not exist [11]).

Vyshinskii placed the responsibility for this upon the multiplicity of competing schools of law, the fact that individual writers "define the law each in his own way", but primarily upon the "perversity and impotence of the method used by this science, namely, the juridical method of study that separates itself from the concrete peculiarities of the studied phenomena" [12]). In his opinion,

> The innumerable schools and trends in the bourgeois science of law (the school of natural law, historical psychological, normativist, positivist, sociological, etc., schools) constitute a variety of the same phenomenon — the juridical ideologism, which attempts to cognize legal phenomena in themselves, without any connection with the economic and production relations in society, and without any connection with the struggle taking place in a class society [13]).

Such an approach to the law, or, in Vyshinskii's words, "passing social relations through the prism of formal-juridical and idealistic interpretation", renders it possible for the bourgeoisie to "utilize the science of law . . . for its exploitative interests", for the "purpose of distorting reality, for presentation of social relations not as they are in reality

---

6) Академия наук СССР, Институт права. Основные задачи науки советского социалистического права (Academy of Sciences of the USSR, Law Institute. Basic tasks of the science of Soviet socialist law) (Moscow, 1938), pp. 7 ff.; English translation (without last part — discussion on the various branches of the law): *Soviet Legal Philosophy*, Translated by Hugh W. Babb, with an introduction by John N. Hazard (20th Century Legal Philosophy Series, Vol. 5, Cambridge, Mass., 1951), pp. 303—341; German translation: *Sowjetische Beiträge zur Staats- und Rechtstheorie* (36. Beiheft zur "Sowjetwissenschaft," Berlin, 1953), pp. 50—108.

7) *Вышинский, А.*, Марксисткое учение о праве и государстве (*Vyshinskii, A.*, Marxist teaching on law and state), "Большевик" (Bolshevik) (Moscow), 1938, No. 12, p. 12.

8) *Ibid.*

9) *Ibid.*

10) *Ibid.*, p. 13.

11) Основные задачи, *op. cit.* (note 6), p. 22.

12) *Ibid.*

13) *Ibid.*, p. 182.

but as they are portrayed by the bourgeoisie in the interest of its class domination"[14]). Consequently, he argued, in the "bourgeois" theory there "prevails the juridical art of abstracting the 'foreign', i. e., the so-called metajuridical phenomena from the law", which makes legal theory "one-sided and deprives it of content"[15]). Furthermore, it is the reason why the "dogmatic-juridical method by means of which bourgeois scientists intend to discover secrets of social phenomena is as unsuitable for this purpose as is the medieval theory . . . for cognition of natural phenomena"[16]).

> Juridical method means logical operation with concepts and ideas instead of operation with phenomena which are concealed under the cover of these concepts and ideas. It is purely a logical method, investigating phenomena as such, as existing for and by themselves . . .
>
> Juridical method is a method abstracted from the real world of phenomena, a method of cognition of these phenomena . . . by means of pure theoretical speculation and by means of pure theoretical analysis of these phenomena[17]).

Vyshinskii's objections to the "juridical method" stem from his assumption (which he accepted as a "self-evident truth") that the "Marxist method" or, more accurately, "dialectical laws"[18]) as the content of this method, are not a conceptual device of science but that they have a "natural" existence. That is to say, he assumed that they are an organic part of natural and social reality, i. e., a part of the object under cognition, and that as such they do not "conceal real phenomena" but, on the contrary, being part of the phenomena they help to bring about knowledge of this phenomena from "within". Indeed, the assumptions on which Vyshinskii's criticism was based are not uniquely "Marxist" as he claimed. They were advanced prior to Marx by proponents of naturalistic philosophy who, like Vyshinskii, have never cared to explain how it is possible to describe a natural or social phenomena without "logical operation with concepts", i. e., without conceptual devices that are the product of the human mind and not part of the phenomena under study.

A more systematic presentation of views on methodology advanced by Vyshinskii in

---

14) *Ibid.*

15) *Ibid.*, p. 23.

16) *Ibid.*

17) *Ibid.*

18) It should be noted that the problem of dialectic laws and especially of their number and meaning has never been settled either in Soviet philosophy or Soviet theory of state and law despite the crucial significance attributed to it by these disciplines. The interference of Soviet political authorities in order to settle the problem brought about an even greater confusion. Thus, for example, in 1938 Stalin asserted the universal validity of four dialectic laws; (1) the organic connection of everything in the world; (2) the continuous mutability of things; (3) transition of quantity into quality (also known as the "law of precipitated development"); (4) the struggle of opposites (known also as the "law of contradiction").

In 1950, however, Stalin denied the universal validity of the third and fourth laws. He claimed that only the first two laws were universally valid, whereas the third and fourth were applicable only to "bourgeois social orders" but not to the Soviet Union. The reasons for rejecting the universal validity of the latter laws were obviously political. The fourth law, the "law of contradictions," was at one time considered by Marxists to be the most significant dialective law: it was interpreted as the source of natural and social development. The third law, the "law of precipitated development," asserted that at a certain "stage of social development" revolution is inevitable. Indeed, the recognition of the universal validity of the latter law implied that at a certain "stage of social development" revolution would take place in the Soviet Union. It was primarily to eradicate this implication that Stalin declared the "law of precipitated development" to be inapplicable to Soviet social conditions.

On the changing status of "dialectic laws" in the Soviet Union, see Philipov, A., *Logic and Dialectic in the Soviet Union* (Research Program on the U.S.S.R., New York 1952).

1939 was undertaken in the late 'forties by M. A. Arzhanov. He contended that "methodological pluralism" is responsible for the "inability" of "bourgeois" theories to produce a science of law. His criticism of "methodological pluralism" stemmed from his belief that there is only one method, namely, the "Marxist method", which alone is capable of offering a scientific explanation of law, but this method is "inaccessible to be bourgeois theory of state and law"[19]). He argued that the "Soviet theory of state and law" consistently follows the "solely scientific philosophy, dialectical materialism", and hence its assertions on state and law are based on "authentic, verified, and exact knowledge, having the meaning of objective truth"[20]). This theory "portrays the state and law exactly as they are in reality", and hence it is "in complete conformity with reality"[21]).

In Arzhanov's opinion, the "highest methodological level of bourgeois jurisprudence" was attained with the introduction of Hegel's dialectic and his philosophy of law. But precisely in Hegel's philosophy of law dialectic became "mutilated, crippled, and distorted with extreme idealism and mysticism", and was "replaced by artificial and false sophisms"[22]). Another positive landmark in the "bourgeois" theory were the views of the French materialists, Diderot, Helvetius, Holbach, and La Mettrie. However, according to Arzhanov, their materialistic interpretation of nature was "metaphysical and mechanistic" and the conceptions of state and law were idealistic. Henceforth "bourgeois" theory declined and divided itself into numerous competing trends, all of which had in common an "idealistic and metaphysical basis", which in contemporary legal theory is to be found under the names of neo-Kantianism, empiricism, and pragmatism[23]). The theory of O. Gierke rested on such a basis. Gierke insisted that the method of study should correspond to the peculiarities of the object under study. The theory of G. Jellinek, who advocated that the method of studying the state should be distinct from that employed in the study of law, was also based on this ground[24]). Finally, and primarily, the methods of Rickert and Hans Kelsen are grounded on "metaphysical" and "idealistic" foundations. In conformity with "Kantianism" they draw a distinction between natural and social phenomena and "maintain that the former deal with causality, determinism, regularity, and 'is'", whereas the latter deal with "indeterminism, 'oughtness', and the world of chance"[25]).

In Arzhanov's opinion "idealism" and "metaphysics" as the "basic feature of the bourgeois world outlook" find their expression in:

(a) *Agnosticism* that "denies, directly or in a concealed form, the possibility of an exact scientific knowledge" and that maintains that "cognition in general has a relative, approximate, conditional, and subjective character"[26]). In Anglo-American countries agnosticism manifests itself in *pragmatism* which, in opposition to materialism, "conceives practice and experience not as a means for verification of the conformity of a given theory with objective reality, but merely as a measure of the 'usefulness' and 'utility' of

---

19) *Аржанов, М. А., Кечекъян, С. Ф., Манъковский, Б. С., Строгович, М. С.*, Теория государства и права *(Arzhanov, M. A., Kechek'ian, S. F., Man'kovskii, B. S., Strogovich, M. S.*, Theory of state and law) (Moscow, 1949), p. 43.

20) *Ibid.*, p. 12.

21) *Ibid.*

22) *Аржанов, М.*, О классическом философском труде товарища Сталина (*Arzhanov, M.*, On classical philosophical work of comrade Stalin), "Сов. гос. и право," 1939, No. 6, p. 44.

23) Теория государства и права (1949), *op. cit.* (note 19), pp. 42—43.

24) *Ibid.*, p. 41.

25) *Ibid.*, p. 45.

26) *Ibid.*, p. 44.

this theory"[27]). Otherwise agnosticism appears in the neo-Kantian philosophy which opposes "content" as an "uncognizable thing in itself" against the "form" as a "cognizable" but only "relatively cognizable external manifestation of the thing"[28]).

(b) *Formalism,* which has its origin in the "agnosticism of Kantians" and which "asserts that only forms and manifestations of the state and law are susceptible to scientific cognition, but not their nature"[29]). The "vice" of formalism consists in that legal theorists "operate . . . with 'pure', juridical concepts derived from the 'idea of law'", that they employ "logical categories divorced from economic, political, and moral contents", that they "conceive of law as a certain form . . . independent of concrete social relationships", and that they "separate legal and political forms from their economic content"[30]).

(c) *Dogmatism,* which is but a "variety of the formalist method", and which limits itself merely to a description of law without taking into consideration the "social, economic, ideological, and class causes of law"[31]).

(d) *Relativism,* by "means of which bourgeois jurists aim to justify agnosticism, irrationalism, scepticism, formalism, and psychologism in jurisprudence"[32]). Furthermore, in "opposition to scientific, i. e., dialectic materialist historicism", relativism denies the possibility of an "objective scientific analysis of nature of values", and insists upon the "impossibility of a scientific proof", i. e., upon the "impossibility of determining objective correctness", of a social value and especially of "justice"[33]).

In general, according to Arzhanov, "no 'methods' used by bourgeois science can satisfy the requirements of scientific cognition". He contended that "Marxist analysis of the contemporary bourgeois philosophy has unequivocally proved that 'new methods' . . . are even more reactionary and anti-scientific than 'old' methods"[34]). Hence, in his opinion, the attempts of some "bourgeois" theorists, especially Kelsen, to create a "politically indifferent, non-partisan, and objective" theory of law have no scientific validity. The "so-called bourgeois 'objectivity' as an ideology of 'supra-partisanship' is merely a mask under which bourgeois partisanship is concealed, which is contrary to science and to

---

27) *Ibid.*

28) *Ibid.*, p. 45.

29) *Ibid.*

30) *Ibid.*, pp. 46—47. Whereas Arzhanov attributed "formalism" primarily to H. Kelsen's theory of law, he contended that it is an essential characteristic of Western "decaying culture." Hence he argued that sociological schools of law, especially that of Roscoe Pound, merely claim to be anti-formalistic but are not so in fact. Sociological notions like "control, function and behavior" are, in his opinion, "merely formal concepts" as long as they "do not reveal the real, i. e., class content and material conditioning of these concepts." (*loc. cit.*, p. 48). It should be noted that the critique of "formalism" is a permanent feature of Soviet theories of law. On the one hand, this critique is directed against "formalism of bourgeois science," and on the other hand, against "formalism" of Soviet theorists in interpreting social phenomena. As will be seen in later pages, the main political argument against "bourgeois formalism" is that it "serves to conceal the exploitative character of a class society." As concerns formalism in theories of Soviet writers, Arzhanov contends that it is "one of the survivals of capitalism in social consciousness." See his Об очередных задачах в области теории государства и права (Recurrent tasks in the field of theory of state and law), "Сов. гос. и право," 1948, No. 8, pp. 10—12.

31) Теория государства и права (1949), *op. cit.* (note 19), p. 48.

32) *Аржанов, М.*, Реакционная пошлость и эклектика (*Arzhanov, M.*, Reactionary vulgarity and eclectic), "Сов. гос. и право," 1948, No. 5, p. 33. (This is an article directed against W. Friedman's *Legal Theory* [1946]).

33) *Ibid.*, p. 34.

34) Теория государства и права (1949), *op. cit.* (note 19), p. 41.

objective truth"[35]). An "impartial" science of law, a science that is "independent from a definite class ideology" is, in Arzhanov's opinion, unattainable in a "bourgeois" society with "antagonistic classes". A truly "objective" and thus a "real science" is possible only under conditions of a "classless" society which, he claims, exists in the Soviet Union[36]). But paradoxically, according to Arzhanov, this "real science" is not bound by the prerequisite of impartiality. The lack of impartiality is a deficiency of "bourgeois" theories but not of the "real science". The "real science", that is to say theories of law advanced by Soviet writers, is admittedly partisan: it is "permeated with the spirit of militant partisanship"[37]). The "Marxist-Leninist theory of state and law", argues Arzhanov in conformity with other Soviet theorists, "defends openly the principle of partisanship in science" because the "interests of truth, of science, and the interest of the working classes do not contradict one another but, to the contrary, coincide completely"[38]). Or, as stated in recent years by S. F. Kechek'ian, the "partisanship of the Marxist theory of state and law . . . secures a truly scientific approach toward the study of state and law", and helps to develop a "true science which serves for the progressive development of society"[39]).

In short, the measure employed by Soviet theorists in determining the scientific character of a theory of law is its political usefulness; the very usefulness which, if employed by "bourgeois" pragmatists, is interpreted by Soviet theorists to be anti-scientific. If a theory of law serves what Kechek'ian called the "progressive development of society", that is, if it helps to promote Soviet political objectives, then it is a science; if not, then it is not science.

Soviet Interpretation of Natural Law

The attitudes of the Soviet theorists toward natural law vary, depending upon what they call "reactionary" and "progressive" contents of natural law. The natural-law ideas of St. Augustine and of Thomas Aquinas are characterized as "reactionary". The seventeenth and eighteenth centuries' ideas of natural law, especially in J. J. Rousseau's inter-

---

35) *Ibid.*, p. 24.

36) *Ibid.*, pp. 22—23. The assumption behind Arzhanov's opinion that a science of law is unattainable in a "bourgeois class society" stems from his belief that in a "class" society the views of the social theorist are determined by his "class" membership regardless of his intentions to the contrary. This opinion is essentially in conformity with Marx's view that social views of a theorist are merely "reflections" of his "class" position, and as such they constitute a "distorted picture" of society, i. e., an ideology, a justification of existing social conditions. Indeed, Marx exempted from this rule the views of the "proletariat" and those like himself and Engels who wanted to change existing social conditions in conformity with the "interests of the proletariat," who interpreted social phenomena accordingly, and whose views, because of this, were considered to be scientific. This was the meaning of the so-called "scientific socialism" advanced by Marx and Engels. It was also the assumption on which Stalin based his view that "Marxism is a scientific expression of the fundamental interest of the working class." Arzhanov, however, goes further in his reasoning. He argues that science is unattainable under conditions of a society "divided into classes," and that only under conditions of a "classless" society, i. e., presumably under Soviet conditions, is science atainable. This implies that political and economic theories of Marx and Engels (who wrote in Germany and England, i. e., in countries recognized by Marx, Engels, and Soviet theorists as "class" countries *par excellence*) are not "science" in Arzhanov's meaning of the term which he, paradoxically, advances as the "Marxist" meaning. Furthermore, this implication throws a definite light upon the Soviet claim of offering the "solely scientific" interpretation of law because their theorists are employing methods used by Marx and Engels.

37) *Ibid.* (note 34), p. 25.

38) *Ibid.*, p. 23.

39) Теория государства и права (1955), *op. cit.* (note 1), pp. 14—15.

pretation, are considered to be "progressive" regardless of their "unscientific and idealistic character". The "progressive" doctrines of natural law are interpreted as being essentially an "ideology of bourgeois revolutions" (i. e., French and American revolutions) but nevertheless are recognized as "positive historical phenomena" in that by replacing the ideology of feudalism with doctrines of "bourgeois democracy" they opened the way for the next "historical stage", namely, socialism [40]).

The Soviet critique revolves primarily around the "revival of natural law" in the twentieth century, which they associate with the appearance of J. Charmont's *La renaissance du droit naturel* (Paris, 1911), but mainly with writings of European and American natural-law theorists that appeared after the second World War, such as O. Bachof, Clark, H. Coing, A. Coste-Floret, A. d'Entreve, G. del Vecchio, G. L. Gressay, J. Haesaert, Y. Haves, H. Hubman, V. B. Kennedy, M. Labord-Lacoste, M. Laserson, F. Lebuff, J. Maritain, H. Mitteis, G. Radbruch, H. Rommen, P. Roubier, L. Strauss, Truvot, S. A. Truyol, and B. F. Wright.

Soviet writers denounce the tendency of the abovementioned theorists to revive the "reactionary" instead of the "progressive" doctrines of natural law. Thus, for example, V. A. Tumanov maintained that the revival of natural law in Europe and America is "very closely related with the reactionary teaching of contemporary catholicism", and that it is "neo-Thomist" in outlook despite the fact that some of its proponents are protestants [41]). In his opinion, behind the phrases of "eternal justice, ethical ideas, supra-legal values", the "reactionary consciousness of law of the imperialist bourgeoisie is to be found [42]). This "consciousness of law" is expressed in that in the "transition period" from "bourgeois democracy" to "political reaction" the bourgeoisie strove to "free itself from the bondage of its own legality" [43]). The characterization of natural law as "eternal" and "immutable" and thus "superior" to the positive law aims at justifying the "violations of the rules of the existing positive law" [44]). In fact, according to Tumanov, the doctrines of the "revived" natural law proved to be a "successful means" for a "theoretical justification of violations of bourgeois legality and for adaptation of a legal system to the needs of monopolistic capitalism" [45]).

On the other hand, in Tumanov's opinion, the aim of the revival of natural law is to identify as "eternal" and "immutable" the norms of the positive law that "secure political domination of the bourgeoisie"; to "mask the exploitative character of bourgeois law", and to "persuade . . . the masses that the capitalist system is eternal" [46]). On the international level the revival of natural law aims at justifying a "cosmopolitan idea of abolition of boundaries between the states, of the dying away of national sovereignty, and the creation of a 'world' state under the guide of American imperialism" [47]). This tendency, in Tumanov's opinion, is especially apparent in del Vecchio's views of natural law as a "world law", in

[40]) *Туманов, В. А.*, Критика современной буржуазной теории права (*Tumanov, V. A.*, Critique of contemporary bourgeois theory of law) (Moscow, 1957), pp. 62—63. Hereafter cited as *Туманов*, Критика (Reviewed in: "Сов. гос. и право," 1958, No. 11, pp. 134—137 and *Osteuropa-Recht*, 1959, No. 1, pp. 54—55).

[41]) *Ibid.*, p. 72.

[42]) *Ibid.*

[43]) *Туманов, В. А.*, Что скрывается за "возрождением" естественного права (*Tumanov, V. A.*, What is hidden behind the "revival" of natural law), "Сов. гос. и право," 1954, No. 5, p. 89.

[44]) *Ibid.*, p. 92.

[45]) *Ibid.*, p. 89.

[46]) *Ibid.*

[47]) *Ibid.*, p. 92.

J. Maritain's idea of a "supra-national consultative council" whose aim would be to "materialize . . . the divine idea of natural law", and, finally, in the views of A. d'Entreve and A. Coste-Floret, who maintain that natural law is "the only available recourse to suppress the dangerous doctrine of absolute state sovereignty" [48]).

Tumanov is in agreement with an East-German theorist, A. Baumgarten, that the revived doctrines of natural law are reactionary in character and are directed against socialism [49]). Behind the facade of "eternal justice" which proponents of revived natural law advance as a "norm of norms", i. e., as the basic source of positive law, is "hidden bourgeois 'justice'", and that means, in Tumanov's opinion, the desire of the "bourgeoisie" not to be bound by the rules of positive law [50]). However, he thought, in this respect the "revived natural law" is not essentially different from other schools of legal thought: "in its very nature the 'theory of revived natural law' is not different from the advocacy of lawlessness and arbitrariness that are hidden under the facade of the 'sociological' and 'realist' trends of contemporary bourgeois jurisprudence" [51]).

The character of the criticism advanced against natural law by Soviet writers suggests unequivocally that it is grounded on political considerations. It is not the concept of natural law itself but the political ends it presumably helps to bring about that are objected to by Soviet writers. They object to these ends because, from their point of view, they are reactionary. They offer, however, no objections to the natural-law idea if it is conducive to what they call the "interest of the proletariat". In fact, the "Marxist-Leninist theory of state and law" is continuously making use of this concept, though under a different nomenclature. The idea of natural law is to be found in Soviet theory under the name of "dialectic law". As distinct from "bourgeois" natural law, which Soviet writers interpret to be merely a political ideology, they claim that the dialectic law is the "true" natural law. Following this line of reasoning, some Soviet writers, for example I. Il'inskii, contended that Soviet positive law is but "one of the forms of natural law" [52]), and that probably means that it is a social manifestation of presumably universally valid "dialectic law". Without going into a discussion of the validity of the Soviet claim, it may reasonably be argued that employment of the concept of "dialectic law" in Soviet theory served purposes in principle similar to those attributed to "bourgeois" natural law by V. Tumanov. Soviet writers take special pains to emphasize that their theories are scientific because they interpret "bourgeois" and Soviet positive law from the viewpoint of dialectic law, meaning that they describe it as being or not being in conformity with natural, i. e., dialectic, law. But, as noted earlier, the content and meaning of "dialectic laws" are determined by political authority. Hence, by subjecting the positive law to such an interpretation they describe it, in effect, as being or not being in conformity with views of political leaders. In part this explains why, by employing this method of interpretation, Soviet theorists define "bourgeois" positive law as being contradictory to, and Soviet positive law as being in conformity with "justice". Assuming that Soviet objections to the political ends brought about by the concept of "bourgeois" natural law are correct, the same objections could be advanced against the concept of dialectic law. If it is true, as

48) *Ibid.*
49) *Туманов*, Критика, *op. cit.* (note 40), p. 63. Tumanov refers to Arthur Baumgarten's article published in "Deutsche Zeitschrift für Philosophie" (Berlin), 1953, No. 2.
50) *Ibid.*
51) *Ibid.*
52) *Ильинский, И.*, Право и быт (*Il'inskii, I.*, Law and social life) (Moscow, Leningrad, 1925), p. 17.

Soviet writers claim, that the concept of "bourgeois" natural law serves as a justification of "bourgeois" legal order, it could hardly be disputed that the concept of dialectic law aims at justifying the existence of Soviet positive law by identifying it with "justice".

Soviet Attitudes Toward Psychological Theories of Law

The first systematic formulation of the psychological conception of law, or, in M. Rezunov's words, "one of the first attempts to create a science of law comparable to that of the natural sciences", is associated by Soviet writers with L. Feuerbach and especially with his student, Ludwig Knapp [53]). The psychological theories of F. Iodl, M. Hess, L. Green, Sturm, Adler, L. I. Petrazhitskii, and M. Reisner, as well as the theories of contemporary "psycho-physiologists" and "reflexologists", are interpreted as constituting merely "modified historical stages" of assumptions postulated by Feuerbach and Knapp.

From the political point of view the psychological school of law is interpreted as a "classical school of a society founded on principles of individualism and private property" [54]). However, Soviet writers acknowledge that while they are "essentially utopian", psychological theories of law "historically have played a positive role", and only with the "popularization of Marxism" and the "growth of class consciousness of the working class" have they lost "their previous revolutionary significance and been transformed into a reactionary ideology" [55]).

Paradoxically, despite the "popularization of Marxism" in the Soviet Union, the psychological approach to law is still apparent. It was especially pronounced in the decade following the revolution. The main proponent of this approach was M. Reisner, who, prior to the revolution, attempted to adapt the psychological conception of law to the Marxist interpretation of society. He argued that "legal life is split into two antagonistic worlds of intuitive and positive law, each of them having its own life", and that the "primacy and primogeniture of the former is beyond doubt" because it constituted the "factual basis of the social legal order" independently and prior to the enactment of positive law [56]). After the revolution Reisner developed a so-called "class-theory of intuitive law" which he considered to be a synthesis of Marxism and the psychological theory of law, and argued that "intuitive" law "should become the basis of the future state and law of the revolutionary masses", i. e., of the future communist society [57]).

Apart from Reisner, the psychological conception of law found its expression in the writings of such Soviet theorists as I. Il'inskii [58]), D. Dembskii [59]), and, especially in the

[53]) *Резунов, М.*, Марксизм и психологическая школа права (*Rezunov, M.*, Marxism and the psychological school of law) (1931), p. 31.

[54]) *Стучка, П.*, Материалистическое или идеалистическое понимание права (*Stuchka, P.*, Materialist or idealist conception of law), "Под знаменем Марксизма" (Under the banner of Marxism) (Moscow), 1923, No. 1, p. 167.

[55]) *Резунов, op. cit.* (note 53), p. 35.

[56]) *Рейснер, М.*, Теория Л. И. Петражицкого, марксизм и социальная идеология (*Reisner, M.*, Theory of L. I. Petrazhitskii, Marxism, and social ideology) (Petrograd, 1908), p. 87; English translation: *Soviet Legal Philosophy, op. cit.* (note 6), pp. 71—82.

[57]) *Рейснер, М.*, Право, наше право, чужое право, общее право (*Reisner, M.*, Law, our law, foreign law, general law) (Leningrad, Moscow, 1925), p. 22; English translation: *Soviet Legal Philosophy, op. cit.* (note 6), pp. 83—109.

[58]) *Ильинский, И.*, Введение в изучение советского права (*Il'inskii, I.*, Introduction to the study of Soviet law) (Leningrad, 1925).

[59]) *Дембский, Д.*, Нравственность и право с точки зрения исторического материализма (*Dembskii, D.*, Morality and law from the viewpoint of historical materialism) (Proletarii, 1925).

Ukranian SSR, in the "reflexological" theory of law of M. Chel'tsov-Bebutov[60]). In the late 1920's the theories of the writers mentioned above were stigmatized by some Soviet writers, (e. g., A. K. Stal'gevich) as an outgrowth of Freudianism which asserted itself as a "distinctly anti-Marxist trend" in the Soviet philosophy of the early 1920's[61]). Again L. Uspenskii, following the views of a "bourgeois" theorist, A. Meinong, argued that the psychological method of studying law is "psychology in the wrong place"[62]). In his opinion the "psychic process of perceiving law is hardly different from perceiving any other object, be it a thing of the external world, an object of mathematics, or a logical axiom... The task of science is to explain what the law is and not how it is perceived"[63]). Another writer, I. Razumovskii, thought that attempts to fuse the psychological concept of law with Marxism were grounded on a misinterpretation of Marx's concept of law. Razumovskii admitted that Marx and Engels spoke of law as an "ideological form", which implied that they conceived law to be a psychological phenomenon. He argued, however, that Marx conceived the law as an "ideological form" dependent upon an "economic basis", which made it "diametrically opposed" to the views of "Freudians" in Soviet legal science who conceive the law merely as a "psychological phenomenon", as a "phantasma", or as an "imperative-attributive experience" presumably "perceived variously by different classes"[64]).

Additional reasons for the incompatability of the psychological conception of law with the Soviet theory were offered by V. Raikher. He thought that from the "philosophical point of view" the basic assumptions of psychological theories of law are identical with those of Berkley's "subjective idealism", and with the "naive" and "sham realism" of Mach, Avenarius, and Bogdanov[65]). The "confinement of law to the narrow scope of an individual human psyche" leads, according to Raikher, toward "extreme individualism" and in the final analysis toward "legal solipsism", and, as a result of the latter, to a "legal relativism" which manifests itself in the view that "positive law is what takes place in the mind of a 'law-perceiving' individual"[66]). In short, in his opinion, the psychological theory of law is a "projection of empirio-criticism into the sphere of law". Instead of interpreting law as a "social class phenomenon" and thus as a "historical category", psychologists describe law by means of "biological concepts" as an "unconscious process of socio-psychological adaptation"[67]).

---

[60]) *Чельцов-Бебутов, М.*, Социалистическое правосознание и уголовное право революции (*Chel'tsov-Bebutov, M.*, Socialist legal consciousness and the revolutionary criminal law) (Kharkov, 1924).

[61]) *Стальгевич, А. К.*, Пути развития советской правовой мысли (*Stal'gevich, A. K.*, Ways of development of Soviet legal thought) (Moscow, 1928), p. 12.

[62]) *Успенский, Л.*, О задачах марксисткого метода в юриспруденци (*Uspenskii, L.*, The tasks of the Marxist method in jurisprudence), "Вестник юстиции Узбекистана" (Journal of Justice of Usbekistan) (Tashkent), 1925, No. 1, p. 40.

[63]) *Ibid.*

[64]) *Разумовский, И.*, Октябрская революция и методология права (*Razumovskii, I.*, October revolution and methodology of law), "Под знаменем Марксизма," 1927, No. 10—11, p. 103.

[65]) *Райхер, В.*, Психологическая теория права в свете Ленинской критики эмпириокритицизма (*Raikher, V.*, Psychological theory of law and Lenin's critique of empiriocriticism), "Сов. гос. и права," 1940, No. 7, pp. 17 ff.

[66]) *Ibid.*, pp. 20, 22.

[67]) *Ibid.*, pp. 21, 22. Cf. from a non-communist viewpoint: *Гинс, Г. К.*, Советское правоведение и психологическая теория права Л. И. Петражицкого (*Guins, G. K.*, The Soviet legal science and the psychological theory of law of L. I. Petrazhitskii), "Вестник Института по изучению СССР" (Journal of the Institute for the Study of the USSR) (München), No. 2 (27), May—August 1958, pp. 64—79. Guins criticizes A. A. Vyshinskii and A. I. Denisov who also attacked Petrazhitskii's school of thought.

According to V. A. Tumanov the abovementioned characteristics refer also to contemporary psychological theories. To be sure, in his opinion contemporary "bourgeois" psychological theories are such in name only, not in fact. In general they are "eclectic" in character. R. Pound's[68]) and J. Stone's[69]) theories of law are especially so. Pound, a proponent of sociological jurisprudence, argues that the "most significant change in bourgeois juridical science of the last decade was the return . . . of 'juridical thought' to 'contemporary psychology'" [70]). However, according to Tumanov, Pound had in view "not the true materialist science of psychology" but a "reactionary idealistic psychology whose aim is to belittle man's consciousness" by claiming that "instincts, unconscious inclinations, and race factors are motive forces of human behavior" [71]).

Among contemporary "bourgeois" theories of law Tumanov found the American "realist school of law", represented by T. Arnold, V. Cook, L. Green, J. Frank, K. Llewellyn, and H. Oliphant, to be principally psychological in character. The realist school of law is, in his opinion, the "most reactionary, vulgar, and anti-scientific trend in the bourgeois 'philosophy of law' . . . which aims at theoretical justification of repudiation of the principle of legality . . ." [72]). The "discreditation" and "repudiation" of legality, i. e., of the rule of law, is accomplished by several means. First, it is brought about by "applying to the study of legal phenomena Freudianism and neo-Freudianism", on the basis of which realists assert, as did Justice Holmes, that law is "what the judge does"; that judicial decision is but a "psychological act"; that the source of this act is not law but "biological impulses, prejudices, and antipathies . . . which motivate the behavior of the judge"; that the "rule of law is a childish need"; and that "uncertainty of the law is preferable to certainty and stability of the law" [73]). All these lead, in Tumanov's opinion, to "the denial of the normative character of law", to "unlimited judicial discretion", and in effect constitute a "theoretical justification of lawlessness and arbitrariness" [74]). Second, it is achieved by subjecting "legal phenomena" to the interpretation of "behaviorism . . . that denies the consciousness of man" and conceives "man's psychic activity" and "judicial process . . . to be a complex of mechanical reactions", which means, in other words, that it denies the validity of the normative interpretation and insists upon causal interpretations of human and judicial behavior. Third, it results from applying to the study of law postulates of pragmatism asserting that "the criterion of truth of a scientific proposition is its usefulness" and that "science cannot and should not explain the true nature of law" but "should merely give 'working definitions'" [75]). In addition, in view of the fact that "'realists' declare factual conditions 'uncognizable' and consider logic to be 'medieval scholasticism', it is obvious" — concluded Tumanov — "that the manner of posing the question by 'realists', urging the judge not to take into consideration legal norms, facts, or logic, justifies the possibility for the most unlimited judicial discretion that could take care of the interests of governing authorities . . ." [76]).

---

68) *Туманов*, Критика, *op. cit.* (note 40), pp. 25 ff. (Reference to Pound's *Social Control through Law* [1942]).

69) *Ibid.*, p. 30 (Reference to Stone's *Province and Function of Law* [1950]).

70) *Туманов, В. А.*, О некоторых психологических теориях в новейшей буржуазной юриспруденции (*Tumanov, V. A.*, On some psychological theories in the recent bourgeois jurisprudence), "Сов. гос. и право," 1955, No. 5, p. 105.

71) *Ibid.*

72) *Ibid.*, pp. 105—106.

73) *Ibid.*, pp. 106—108.

74) *Ibid.*

75) *Туманов*, Критика, *op. cit.* (note 40), p. 34.

The theory of American realists is in Tumanov's opinion merely a variety of the continental "school of free law". In opposition to Western writers, who associate the latter school with R. Stammler, Tumanov argued that its founder was F. Geny, whose approach to law was based on "philosophical subjective-idealist intuitivism of Bergson" and who, consequently, reduced the problem of law to the "intuition of the judge" [77]). Tumanov considered the "Upsala school of jurisprudence" to be another example of the intuitive approach to law. With this school he associated A. Hagerstrom, A. Lundstead, and K. Olivecron, who contended that the "basis of legal concepts are certain 'mystic-magic' ideas", that "concrete rights and obligations of a person are exclusively the result of psychological factors", and that the "concepts 'right' and 'obligation' designate definite psychological and primarily irrational experiences" [78]). However, in Tumanov's opinion the psychological element is even more pronounced in the theory of Alf Ross, who views the science of law as a "branch of social psychology", and claims to be studying the "psycho-physical reality of law" which presumably helped him to avoid the dualism between "empirical facts and juridical norms" in which Kelsen's normative theory is involved [79]). This, and Ross' view that "law consists of psychological impulses of many persons", must be interpreted, according to Tumanov, as an "extreme idealism adorned with . . . the phraseology of realism", and, thus, antagonistic to the "solely correct materialist" conception of "class-will expressed in law" which A. Ross replaced with the "psychic of the undefinable abstract individual" [80]).

The abovementioned "idealistic" features are also characteristic of the theories of N. Timasheff, G. Gurvich, and P. Sorokin, who attempted to adapt Petrazhitskii's theory of law to "recent achievements of bourgeois ideology" [81]). What distinguishes them from other psychological trends, and especially from Ross' theory, is, in Tumanov's opinion, that Timasheff and Gurvich have fused Petrazhitskii's theory with the behaviorism of Durkheim's "collective and social psychology" and interpret law from the viewpoint of "group psychology" which is a "subjective idealist" concept opposed to the materialistic notion of "class will" [82]). In effect, in Tumanov's view, the theories of law advanced by Timasheff, Gurvich and E. N. Cahn constitute a "classical example of eclecticism", a "sort of socio-psychological jurisprudence" attempting to "replace laws of social development with psychological laws" [83]).

It is of interest to note that while they are critical of "bourgeois" psychological theories, Soviet writers do frequently resort to the employment of psychology in the Soviet theory of law. "Bourgeois" theories are stigmatized as unscientific because, as mentioned, they employ "reactionary idealistic psychology" in opposition to the presumably "true materialist science of psychology" employed by Soviet writers. Curiously, by means of the latter psychology Soviet writers have arrived at some conclusions closely resembling the *organismic* theories of state and law of the early nineteenth century. Organismic theories attributed to the state the essential elements of human personality, i. e., they conceived

---

76) *Ibid.*, p. 107.

77) *Туманов,* Критика, *op. cit.* (note 40), p. 35. Tumanov refers to Geny's *Science et Technique en droit privé positif* (Paris, 1925), p. 143.

78) *Ibid.*, p. 36.

79) *Ibid.*, p. 37.

80) *Ibid.*, pp. 37, 38.

81) *Ibid.*, pp. 38—39.

82) *Ibid.*, pp. 39—40.

83) *Ibid.*, pp. 40, 41.

the state as capable of acting, thinking, and willing like a human being. In addition to the state, Soviet writers attribute such characteristics to social "classes". Proceeding on such assumptions they developed notions of "class will", of "class consciousness of law", and of the "true will of the Soviet people", which presumably supercedes all individual wills, and finds its expression in the "form of law" [84]). The "true will" ensues from what M. P. Kareva called "Soviet consciousness of law", which in turn is presumably grounded on the "moral-political oneness of the Soviet people", and which U. Kudaibergenov described as a "living thing" existing only in Soviet society [85]).

M. P. Kareva and U. Kudaibergenov were aware that the "living thing", *i. e.* "consciousness of law" which they claimed is the source of the Soviet positive law, closely resembles the idea of *Volksgeist* once advanced by German historical romanticism. They contended, however, that "Marxism interprets consciousness of law not as a sort of blind feeling, as *Volksgeist*, or legal experience, but as a living thing verifiable by practice, and explainable by the intellect as a militantly active ideological category" [86]). This would suggest that the "Soviet consciousness of law" is an effective ideology of the positive law. But neither Kareva nor Kudaibergenov admitted it. They claimed that "moral-political oneness", "Soviet consciousness of law", and "true will" ensuing therefrom, which presumably manifests itself in the "form of law", have a "real", i. e., non-ideological existence. According to Kareva, the "true will" can be explained neither psychologically nor juridically.

It is, in part, for these reasons that Kareva denied the validity of H. Kelsen's differentiation of "oughtness" of legal norms from the "will" in the psychological sense. Such differentiation, she thought, aims at showing that assumptions of the Soviet theory of law, namely, that the "basic notion of law — the will of the definite social unit (class, state, people) — are fictitious and unscientific" [87]). More specifically, she argued, "the attempts to contrast the will 'in the juridical sense' to the will 'in the psychological sense' may lead to the conclusion of the relativity and even illusiveness of the concept of the class, state, and people's will . . ." [88]). Because of the above implication she also rejected Professor Marton's suggestion that the "science of law should renounce the concept of the class, state, and people's will because the science of psychology knows only the individual will" [89]). Marton's view, Kareva contended, is unscientific because it is contradictory to the Marxist concept of will expressing "oneness" of mind, purpose, and feeling of the Soviet people.

Soviet Theory and Sociological Conceptions of Law

The metamorphosis of Soviet attitudes toward the "bourgeois" sociology of law is indicative of at least two things. One, that a dictatorial regime of the Soviet type adapts and discards interpretations of social phenomena, and especially of state and law, in accordance with its political needs. Second, that the so-called "solely scientific dialectic

---

84) *Карева, М. П.*, Право и нравственность в социалистическом обществе (*Kareva, M. P.*, Law and morality in the socialist society) (Moscow, 1951), pp. 107—110; German translation: Karewa, M. P., *Recht und Moral in der sozialistischen Gesellschaft* (Berlin, 1954), pp. 108—111.

85) *Кудайбергенов, У.*, О социалистическом правосознании (*Kudaibergenov, U.*, On socialist consciousness of law), "Сов. гос. и право," 1952, No. 5, p. 29.

86) *Ibid.*

87) *Карева, op. cit.* (note 84), p. 109.

88) *Ibid.*, p. 107.

89) *Ibid.* Reference to Marton's *Les fondements de la responsabilité civile* (Paris, 1938), p. 126.

method" can "prove" two or more contradictory theories of law to be in conformity with Marx's interpretation of society.

In the decade following the revolution a majority of Soviet theorists believed that sociological conceptions of law were in agreement with Marx's and Engels' methods of looking at social phenomena. For example, writers like L. Uspenskii[90]), P. Stuchka[91]), I. Podvolotskii[92]), F. Ksenofontov[93]), N. V. Krylenko[94]), A. G. Goikhbarg[95]), V. Adoratskii[96]), N. Bukharin[97]), and I. P. Razumovskii[98]), argued that a materialistic interpretation of state and law is essentially a sociological one. A majority of the writers mentioned employed sociological methods without acknowledging their "bourgeois" origin. Some of them, *e.g.* L. Uspenskii, advocated openly the employment of sociological methods because they thought that the "Marxist theory of law is primarily a sociology of law"[99]). Uspenskii proposed that special attention be given to methods pursued by such "bourgeois" sociologists as Max Adler, G. Cunov, E. Ehrlich, Frenzel, L. Gumplovich, I. Kornfeld, Meinong, J. Schein, Sinzheimer, and Wurzel. The theories of some of the writers, however, offered a number of pitfalls to Soviet writers. The main difficulty was what Uspenskii called "sociological atomism", which he defined as a tendency toward understanding society as "consisting of solitary actions of man "instead of seeing it as "group behavior"[100]). Another writer, I. D. Il'inskii, defined it as an "idea of individualism" that finds its expression in the assumption that "out of the association of individuals in society a certain order arises recognized by them as obligatory and as delimiting their arbitrariness"[101]). The assumptions and their implications were incompatible with Marx's conception of "class society" and with his contention that law comes into being because of the "division of society into classes". Apart from these rather infrequent individualistic aspects, the traditional sociology tended to agree with the Marxist method of treating many of the principal questions of social phenomena. First, it denied the validity of the so-called "abstract" or "formal" study of law. Second, it refused to recognize the normative character of law and the methodological distinction between normative "ought" and descriptive "is", which resulted in confusion and in identification of legal norms with actual human behavior. It thus spoke of "legal relations" in society as distinct from other "social relations" without taking into account legal norms, notwithstanding the fact that

---

90) *Успенский, Л.*, Очерки по юридической технике (*Uspenskii, L.*, Essays on juridical technique) (Tashkent, 1927), pp. III ff.

91) *Стучка, П.*, Революционная роль права и государства (*Stuchka, P.*, Revolutionary role of state and law) (1921), p. 11; English translation: *Soviet Legal Philosophy*, *op. cit.* (note 6), pp. 17—69.

92) *Подволоцкий, И.*, Марксисткая теория права (*Podvolotskii, I.*, Marxist theory of law) (1923), p. 36.

93) *Ксенофонтов, op. cit.* (note 4), p. 13.

94) *Крыленко, Н. В.*, Беседы о праве и государстве (*Krylenko, N. V.*, Discussions on law and state) (1924), p. 13.

95) *Гойхбарг, А. Г.*, Основы частного и имущественного права (*Goikhbarg, A. G.*, Foundations of private and property law) (1924), p. 63.

96) *Адорацкий, В.*, О государстве (Adoratskii, V., On the state) (1923), p. 9.

97) *Бухарин, Н.*, Теория исторического материализма (*Bukharin, N.*, Theory of historical materialism) (Moscow, 1922), p. 170 (English translation: New York, 1925; German translation: Hamburg, 1922; French translation: Paris, 1927).

98) *Разумовский, И. П.*, Социология и право (*Razumovskii, I. P.*, Sociology and law) (1924), p. 3.

99) *Успенский, op. cit.* (note 62), p. 33.

100) *Ibid.*, p. 37.

101) *Ильинский, op. cit.* (note 58), Part I, p. 58.

only through presupposition of the latter is an interpretation of human behavior as a "legal" behavior conceivable. Third, it was primarily interested in discovering the "forces" responsible for human behavior in a given social environment. For the most part these "forces" turned out to be so-called "economic" or "historical" forces. Fourth, it tended to disregard individual man as a biological unit and spoke of social "groups" and "classes" as biological entities capable of thinking and acting like individuals. Finally, it interpreted social order as a constantly progressing "process" or "development" subject to certain natural law and thus beyond the control of man. Indeed, it may be quite reasonably argued that the sociology of the late nineteenth and early twentieth centuries was a version of Marx's economic and class theory of society. At any rate, it was the belief entertained by many Soviet theorists in the decade following the revolution. They therefore assumed that by subjecting "bourgeois" sociology of law to a "dialectic analysis", i. e., by introducing a stronger version of the "class struggle" theory and economic determinism to sociological interpretations of law, they would be able to produce a "genuine Marxist theory of law". P. Stuchka stated the opinion of a majority of Soviet writers of that time when he argued that "since the appearance of the sociological school at least one thing became settled in the science of law, namely, that law is a system of social relations" [102]). He considered the view that "law is not simply an aggregate of norms . . . but is precisely a system, an order of social relationships", to be the main contribution of the "sociological school of bourgeois jurists" [103]). He thought such a conception of law was in conformity with Marx's notion of "social relationship" under which Marx understood "human relationships ensuing from production and exchange" [104]). Hence, Stuchka expressed a hope that the "time is not far away when all revolutionary Marxists will acknowledge the system of social relationships and the *class interest* determining this system as an *objective* and *material law*" [105]).

Stuchka's hope has not materialized. The sociological conception of law as existing "social relationships" — and that means identification of law with actual human behavior, identification of "ought" with "is" — was based on deterministic premises asserting that social events, and that means human acts, take place according to certain "economic", "historical", or "dialectic" laws independently of man's intentions. This conception of law was in conformity with Marx's views as expressed in the preface to his *Critique of Political Economy*. But it was in conflict with the political aims of the early 1930's which were directed toward creating a political system grounded on Stalin's interpretation of socialism. The success or failure of these aims depended largely upon the planning of social action and, thus, upon purposive regulation of human behavior by means of law. The political re-orientation away from social determinism and toward social planning and execution of planning by means of legal regulations is known in Soviet political and legal theory as a doctrine of "maximal strengthening of the Soviet state and law" [106]). Its introduction

---

[102]) *Стучка, П.*, 13 лет борьбы за революционно-марксисткую теорию права (*Stuchka, P.*, 13 years of struggle for Revolutionary-Marxist theory of law) (1931), p. 44.

[103]) *Стучка, П.*, Марксисткое понимание права (*Stuchka, P.*, Marxist conception of law), "Коммунистическая революция" (Communist revolution) (Moscow), 1922, No. 13—14 (37—38), p. 71.

[104]) *Стучка, П.*, Учение о государстве пролетариата и крестьянства и его Конституции (*Stuchka, P.*, Theory of proletariat's and peasantry's state and its constitution) (Moscow, Leningrad), 5th ed. (1926), p. 4.

[105]) *Ibid.*, p. 5.

[106]) Основные задачи . . ., *op. cit.* (note 6), p. 33.

constitutes an end of the anti-normative period and the beginning of the period of excessive legalism.

To be sure, some Soviet writers maintained an antagonistic attitude toward the "bourgeois" sociology of law even prior to the introduction of the abovementioned doctrine. For example, D. Magerovskii — who claimed to have overcome the "artificial" dichotomy between the "cause" and "value" and between the "is" and "ought" — objected to sociology on the ground that because of its "mechanical mode of thinking" it confines the objects of its study solely to the "sphere of causality and power" without "noticing . . . its organizational-volitional nature" [107]). M. Rezunov argued that the association of "Marxist sociology" with its "bourgeois" counterpart was a result of an erroneous understanding of "Marxist sociological method" which "must be distinguished from the idealistic method of the so-called sociological school of law" represented by A. Comte and E. Ehrlich [108]). In 1937 A. Vyshinskii attributed political subversion to Soviet writers who found assumptions of "bourgeois" sociology to be in conformity with Marxism. He argued that "their 'scientific' activity was directed toward arresting . . . development of legal disciplines, toward discrediting and underminding the Soviet science of law" [109]), and toward "depriving Soviet law of its active, creative role" [110]). Voicing the new trend in theory, he urged legal theorists to describe Soviet law as a "mighty tool of the revolutionary struggle for socialism" and the "socialist state" as a "defender . . . of the revolutionary legal order" and of "revolutionary legality" in opposition to "bourgeois" and "fascist" states that promote the sociological interpretation of law in order to "justify violation of their own legality" [111]). A decade later, N. G. Aleksandrov, arguing against A. K. Stal'gevich's revival of the sociological conception in Soviet theory, asserted that "anti-normativism", *i. e.*, anti-normative interpretations of law by the sociological school, was "erroneously accepted . . . as the materialistic approach toward understanding of law". He thought that the "deleterious effect of survivals of the ideology of the bourgeois 'sociological' school consists primarily in that the 'sociological' definition of law implants into practical workers a nihilistic attitude toward laws and decisions of the government"; that "'sociological' definition of the law implies . . . that Soviet law can secure only relations already established, and that it does not serve as one of the most significant tools of communist reorganization of social relationships"; and that, finally, the "transfer of views of the bourgeois sociological school into Soviet law is especially harmful if one takes into account the special significance of the ideological superstructure of the socialist society organized according to the plan" [112]). In short, Aleksandrov thought that the sociological conception of law implied social determinism, political voluntarism, and legal nihilism both in theory and practice, which is contradictory to the Soviet positive law that aims at bringing about social conditions corresponding to the intentions of the Communist Party.

107) *Магеровский, Д.*, Социальное бытье и наука права (*Magerovskii, D.*, Social existence and the science of law), "Научные известия," Академический центр Наркомпроса, Сборник 1: Экономика, история, право (Scientific news, Academic Centre of the People's Commissariat of Education, Collected vol. 1: Economy, history, law) (Moscow, 1922), p. 6.

108) *Резунов, М.*, К вопросу . . ., *op. cit.* (note 2), p. 53.

109) *Вышинский, А.*, К положению на фронте правовой теории (*Vyshinskii, A.*, About the situation on the front of legal theory) (Moscow, 1937), p. 3.

110) Основные задачи . . ., *op. cit.* (note 6), p. 32.

111) *Вышинский*, К положению . . ., *op. cit.* (note 109), pp. 3 ff.

112) *Александров, Н. Г.*, К критике пережитков буржуазной идеологии в определении права (*Aleksandrov, N. G.*, On the critique of survivals of bourgeois ideology in definition of law), "Сов. гос. и право," 1948, No. 10, p. 49.

Alexandrov argued that legal nihilism is purposely promoted in "bourgeois" theory in order to justify "unlawful" activities of the bourgeoisie. He maintained that it was implicit in the writings of earlier sociologists such as L. Spiegel, Sinzheimer, and Murovtsev, and is pronounced even to a greater degree in contemporary sociological theories, especially in the writings of J. Dewey and L. Green, who are representatives of "American pragmatism, behaviorism and instrumentalism". The latter, in his opinion, "pursue the aim of justifying an increasing arbitrariness of judicial and administrative authorities in the period of imperialism" [113]).

A similar objection was made by V. A. Tumanov against R. Pound, H. Cairns, J. Stone, B. N. Cardozo, and J. H. Wigmore, but especially against Pound's concepts of "social control, social engineering, social compromise, legal process", and against the concept of "social interest", which, Tumanov claimed, American sociologists inherited from R. Ihering [114]). In his opinion, sociological concepts advanced by Pound and his followers essentially pursue two political goals. One, to "justify the rule of the bourgeoisie" by portraying "bourgeois" positive law as a "supra-class" phenomenon, and by identifying "bourgeois class interest" with the interest of the whole society. Second, to justify the "violation of its own legality" (*i. e.*, violation of legal rules that were created by the "bourgeoisie", but which in the course of time presumably became detrimental to its interests) by means of advancing the view that there is a conflict between "stability of law" and "social change" [115]).

As can be seen, the objections raised by Soviet writers against sociological theories of law are essentially of a political and not of a scientific character. Initially sociological interpretations of law were found to be in conformity with Marx's interpretation of society and thus they were acknowledged to be more "scientific" that other "bourgeois" theories. Later they were found to be contradictory to Stalin's interpretation of Marxism, and hence were stigmatized as having nothing in common with science. Some contemporary Soviet writers, e. g., M. A. Arzhanov, went so far as to assert that there is no distinction between sociological theory and other "bourgeois" theories, and that it is founded on methodological premises identical with those of Kelsen's theory, namely, on "formalism", which is conceived by Soviet writers to be anti-Marxist and thus an anti-scientific trend by definition [116]).

Soviet Critique of Normative Theories of Law

The normative, or what are frequently called positivist, theories of law are associated by Soviet writers with R. Stammler, J. Austin, G. Jellinek, H. Kelsen, J. Kunz, A. Verdross, J. Binder, E. Lask, F. Cohen, and F. S. C. Northrop. It is, however, Kelsen who is the primary object of Soviet criticism. In fact it may reasonably be argued that criticism of Kelsen's pure theory of law constitutes the backbone of the Soviet theory of state and law. For certain reasons Soviet writers have constantly expressed apprehension that Kelsen's concept of the science of law as distinguished from an ideology of law, *i. e.*, as opposed

113) *Ibid.*, pp. 44—45.

114) *Туманов*, Критика, *op. cit.* (note 40), pp. 25, 114.

115) *Ibid.*, pp. 114 ff. For recent Soviet criticism of sociological conceptions of law see *Пиголкин, А. С.*, Буржуазные теории права на службе реакции и произвола (*Pigolkin*, *A. S.*, Bourgeois Theories of Law in the Service of Reaction and Arbitrariness), "Правоведение" (Jurisprudence) (Leningrad), 1958, No. 3, pp. 48—58.

116) *Аржанов, М. А.*, Об очередных задачах в области теории государства и права (*Arzhanov*, *M. A.*, Recurrent tasks in the field of the theory of state and law), "Сов. гос. и права," 1948, No. 8, pp. 10—11.

to an interpretation of law in conformity with certain value preferences, is exerting a detrimental influence upon the Soviet theory of law and prevents it from becoming a "pure Marxist theory". Curiously, although Kelsen's theory is the most frequent object of criticism, Soviet writers have demonstrated a remarkable lack of familiarity with and understanding of the pure theory of law. Judging on the basis of references and comments, their knowledge of Kelsen's theory is derived in part from his early work, *Hauptprobleme der Staatsrechtslehre* (1911), and in an even greater measure from secondary sources, primarily from critical comments by German and Austrian sociologists [117]).

Apart from political considerations, the lack of familiarity with Kelsen's theory may be deemed partly responsible for the fact that criticisms advanced by Soviet writers against this theory run in two diametrically opposed directions. On the one hand, Soviet theorists are critical of the pure theory of law because they find it to be value-free, value-neutral, and thus non-ideological in character. Among other things, it is on this ground that they have refused to recognize it as a scientific theory. On the other hand, it became a stereotype in Soviet political and legal theories to consider Kelsen as an expounder of an official "bourgeois" ideology of law. Soviet writers argued that the "ideological strategy of the contemporary capitalist world is characterized by two trends: first, idealization of the capitalist system; second, a tendency to slander and distort scientific socialism . . ."[118]). Kelsen's theory is viewed to be a "striking example of the application of this strategy to bourgeois juridical science" [119]). Hence it is interpreted as a perfected ideology under the disguise of a science, or, in Arzhanov's words, a theory which "under the banner of political

---

117) There is neither a translation of, nor a reasonable commentary on Kelsen's theory available in the Soviet Union. The only available Soviet sources are: *A. Vacheshvili* [*Kelsen's Theory of Law and State*] (1929), written in the Georgian language; *N. I. Palienko* [Theories of the nature of the state and its unity in contemporary jurisprudence], published by the Commissariat of Education of the Ukrainian SSR, in "Под знаменем Марксизма," 1924, No. 8—9; *Разумовский, И.* (*Razumovskii, I.*) [Revival of the philosophy of law in German juridical literature], Сборник статей (Collection of articles) (1927); *Вольфсон, С.* (*Vol'fson, S.*) [Contemporary critics of Marxism], Революция права. Сборник первый (Revolution of the law. First collection) (1925), and a chapter on Kelsen's theory in *Туманов*, Критика, *op. cit.* (note 40).

It may be assumed that more recent publications by Kelsen in the English and German languages are available to Soviet writers. For one reason or another, however, they are not referred to. A. Vyshinskii pointed this out in his О некоторых вопросах теории государства и права (About some problems in the theory of state and law), "Сов. гос. и право," 1948, No. 6, p. 16—17 (German translation: *Sowjetische Beiträge zur Staats- und Rechtstheorie*, *op. cit.* [note 6], pp. 109—128, here p. 127). He stated that Soviet writers "do not go beyond materials other than those written at least 20 or 30 years ago. Consequently, for example, in discussing and criticizing normativism, they limit themselves, as a rule, to the repetition of things already known . . . Referring to Kelsen the writers ignore his latest works . . ."

There are reasons to believe that Soviet writers deliberately ignore Kelsen's recent publications, and other Western writers' as well, in order to throw a distorted light upon the "bourgeois" theory of law. Such distortions are not merely limited to theories of the various writers but to their personalities as well. For example, H. Kelsen is constantly referred to by Soviets writers as an "apologist" or a "servant of American imperialism." A classical distortion took place, however, in the case of a British semanticist, P. F. Philbrick, author of *Language and the Law* (New York, 1950). A Soviet writer, *А. Ф. Клейнман* (*A. F. Kleinman*), denounced him as an undercover F.B.I. agent. It was only two years later that another Soviet writer corrected Kleinman by pointing out that the British semanticist had been confused with an American, H. A. Philbrick, author of *I Led Three Lives* (1952). (Editorial, "For a closer study and criticism of bourgeois jurisprudence," "Сов. гос. и право," 1956, No. 4, pp. 5, 6).

118) *Туманов*, Критика, *op. cit.* (note 40), p. 56.

119) *Ibid.*

indifference propagates the reactionary ideas of the imperialist bourgeoisie"[120]). In Arzhanov's opinion, Kelsen's endeavor to attain a "politically indifferent, non-partisan, and objective" theory of law is grounded on the "false" assumptions that the "science of law . . . is an impartial search for truth, independent from political views and convictions, and that objective judgments on the state and law are independent from the class basis"[121]). The objectivity Kelsen strives for, that is, in Arzhanov's words, "the so-called bourgeois 'objectivity' as an ideology of 'supra-partisanship'", is "merely the mask under which is concealed bourgeois partisanship that is contradictory to science and to objective truth"[122]). Similarly, in Tumanov's opinion, "objectivity" in Kelsen's theory is purely "imaginary" because by separating the theory of law from its "economic, political, and moral contents" Kelsen "replaces analysis of legal reality with an analysis of the logical structure of juridical norms", and hence "introduces into the science of law a separation of the logical form from the objective world, which is characteristic of contemporary idealistic philosophy that conceives logical concepts as independent from reality"[123]).

The denial of objectivity in Kelsen's pure theory of law because of the "separation" of law and "logical form" from "objective reality" is to be found in practically all Soviet writings concerning problems of the general theory of law. Usually it appears in an abbreviated form, namely, under the name of "formalism". Whereas since the late 1930's "formalism" was attributed to all "bourgeois" theories, it has traditionally been reserved for Kelsen's theory. It is employed by Soviet writers in a derogatory sense, to designate a theory as subjective, idealistic, and thus unscientific. However, the stigma of formalism attached to the pure theory of law covers a number of more specific objections.

1. Soviet writers are critical of Kelsen's systematic employment of rules of logic which, being "formal", are conceived by them to be "inferior" to "laws" of dialectic method that are employed in Soviet theory, and which are claimed to be an inherent part of "objective reality", *i. e.*, which are conceived as "natural laws" in contradistinction to rules of logic that are merely an "artificial" creation of man's intellect[124]).

2. They deny the validity of Kelsen's view that the science of law should be descriptive and not prescriptive in character because it is opposed to the Soviet view of science based on the principle of "partisanship".

3. They object to the "purity" of Kelsen's theory in the sense that the object of its cognition is the positive law, because it is diametrically opposed to Soviet theory, which studies law as an indissoluble component part of justice, morality, ethics, psychology, economics, and nature[125]). Tumanov has argued, for example, that Kelsen's idea of describing law as it is without evaluating it from the point of view of "justice" as good or bad is unscientific because it is grounded on an "agnostic" premise asserting that "justice" is beyond the methodological scope of scientific cognition and, furthermore, because it is opposed to the principle of "partisanship", whose application to the Soviet theory of law makes it a "real science". By "opposing partisanship and truth" Kelsen is incapable of understanding, in Tumanov's opinion, that the "true nature of social phenomena like state and law can be discovered . . . only from the point of view of the

---

120) Теория государства и права (1949), *op. cit.* (note 19), p. 23.
121) *Ibid.*
122) *Ibid.*, p. 24.
123) *Туманов*, Критика, *op. cit.* (note 40), p. 47.
124) *Резунов*, К вопросу . . ., *op. cit.* (note 2), pp. 56—57.
125) *Карева*, *op. cit.* (note 84), pp. 107 ff.

proletariat as a class", that is, if interpreted in conformity with what the "proletariat" deems to be "just"[126]). This, Tumanov thought, Kelsen cannot do because interpretation of positive law as just or unjust would "reveal the exploitative character of bourgeois law"[127]). It is because of the latter, Tumanov thought, that Kelsen has developed a theory of "incognizability of justice and of truth" by means of which he "advances a reactionary view that acknowledgement of bourgeois law and legal order as unjust . . . lacks a rational basis"[128]).

4. Soviet writers are also opposed to Kelsen's differentiation of the social from the natural order, of positive law from "natural law", e. g., the "law" of causality, and to his methodological distinction between "is" and "ought". They claim, though without offering convincing proof, that by means of the "dialectic method" they succeeded in overcoming the "artificial" and thus "unscientific" dichotomy between "is" and "ought", between "cause" and "value", and blended them into one "dialectic" amalgam[129]).

In addition to being "formalist", the abovementioned distinctions are considered by them to be the main features of "normativism". The latter is interpreted by Soviet writers to be an "idealistic" trend in contemporary "bourgeois" social theory which is antithetical to materialism, and which was developed by Kelsen under the influence of Kantian philosophy. "Normativism" is especially to be found, in Tumanov's opinion, in Kelsen's notion of norm, which serves as a "disguise" for the "exploitative content of bourgeois law"; in the concept of "basic norm", which as a "certain primary spiritual source" of positive law comprises elements of "ecclesiasticism"; and in the normative interpretation of the state as a legal order, which presumably aims at "diverting attention from the class-exploitative role of the bourgeois state and its mechanism of coercion"[130]).

It should be noted, however, that "normativism" as an antithesis to the Soviet materialist interpretation of society (which draws no distinction between social and natural occurrences, and maintains that social occurrences take place in conformity with presumably universally valid "dialectic laws" regardless of man's intentions, and which thus denies the possibility of a purposive social action) has been employed in Soviet theory in two different senses. Prior to the "First Conference of Learned Workers-Jurists" (1938), Soviet theorists, a majority of whom then adhered to the sociological interpretation of law and society, denounced Kelsen in "anti-scientific normativism" because of his understanding of law as a normative, and that means prescriptive technique, for the regulation of human behavior. The view that the meaning of law is norm, i. e., prescription and not description, that law is not identical with "is", with the human behavior that it aims to regulate, was deemed to be "idealistic" and contradictory to Marx's conception of society. "Normativism" acquired an additional meaning after the conference of Workers-Jurists in 1938 adapted A. Vyshinskii's definition of law which, *inter alia,* defined Soviet law as a "system of norms" or "rules of conduct"[131]). The definition implied recognition of the normative character of law and, moreover, implicitly denied the validity of the Marxist theory of society heretofore adhered to by Soviet sociologists. The latter, and especially A. K. Stal'gevich, denounced it as "normativist", and thus unscientific, anti-Marxist and anti-Soviet[132]).

---

126) *Туманов,* Критика, *op. cit.* (note 40), p. 48.
127) *Ibid.,* p. 43.
128) *Ibid.,* Tumanov refers to Kelsen's *Was ist Gerechtigkeit?* (Wien, 1953).
129) *Магеровский,* Социальное бытье . . ., *op. cit.* (note 107), p. 7.
130) *Туманов,* Критика, *op. cit.* (note 40), pp. 42 ff.
131) Основные задачи . . ,. *op. cit.* (note 6), p. 183.
132) *A. K. Stal'gevich* is the only Soviet writer who, despite purges of some sociological theorists in the mid-'thirties, consistently followed the sociological conception of law and

In their defense, proponents of the definition (which has since acquired an official status in Soviet theory) have constantly been pointing out that it is in no way related to Kelsen's "normativism", that it merely "reflects the active ancillary role of the Soviet law", and that denial of its validity would be tantamount to a return to sociological legal nihilism [133]). Furthermore, they insisted that "normativism consists not in that it conceives the law as a system of norms, but in that it separates this system from real life, from real social relations, and attempts to study it from the position of neo-Kantian philosophy as a thing in itself" [134]). This would suggest that the positive law by itself is not a legitimate object of cognition, and that, to become such, it must be studied in connection with the "real social relationships". The latter are defined in Soviet theory as constituting "human relationships ensuing from production and exchange" [135]). Hence, it follows that the meaning of "normativism" consists in that Kelsen studies positive law apart from "human relationships ensuing from production and exchange". But, even assuming the validity of the objection, it can hardly be taken seriously. This objection can be made against any theory of law. For one, it can especially be made against the "Marxist-Leninist theory of law". The latter is primarily concerned with interpretation of Soviet law as being or not being in conformity with dialectic laws whose meaning is determined by political authority. The objections advanced by contemporary Soviet writers against normativism in Kelsen's theory are as unrealistic as is their criticism of "phenomenological school of law". They associate the latter with F. Kaufman, F. Schreir, A. Reinach, J. Haesaert, and J. Ph. de Azevado. In Tumanov's opinion, the phenomenological school of law is but a "variety of normativism" [136]). Its proponents are followers of Kelsen who "replaced the

---

rejected the normative interpretation as "anti-Marxist normativism." He elaborated his views in his Пути развития советской правовой мысли, *op. cit.* (note 61). Under the political pressure during the "First Conference of Learned Workers-Jurists" (1938), he declared himself to be in agreement with Vyshinskii's definition of Soviet law as a "system of norms," but in the years following he denounced it as "normativist" and thus anti-Marxist. In his "On the problem of conception of the law" (*Стальгевич, А. К.*, К проблеме понятия права, "Сов. гос. и право," 1948, Nr. 7, p. 59) he defined "normativism" as consisting in that "the law is reduced to legal norms (rules of conduct), the basic juridical concepts are formulated in a normative one-sided way, legal phenomena are examined formally-dogmatically, the socio-economic causes are not explained, the law is metaphysically separated from the state, the leading role of the Party in the Soviet state is not explained, and legal norms are converted into the means of juridical formalism."

To be more convincing that the "normativist" conception of law is antagonistic to Marx's interpretation of society, Stal'gevich pointed out that the "enemy of the people," Bukharin, defined law also as a "system of coercive social norms sanctioning and regulating social relationships in the interest of the ruling class" (*loc. cit.*, p. 61).

Stal'gevich's criticism was answered by Vyshinskii in О некоторых вопросах теории государства и права, *op. cit.* (note 117), and by *Aleksandrov* in К критике пережитков . . ., *op. cit.* (note 112).

They insisted that the definition of law as a "system of norms" that "express the will of the ruling class," that are "safeguarded by coercive force of the state against violation," and that "regulate social relations . . . in conformity with the interest of the ruling class" should not be interpreted as recognizing or implying a normative character of law in Kelsen's meaning of the term. "Normativism," asserted Aleksandrov, "consists not in that law is conceived as an aggregate of norms safeguarded by the state from violations, but in that norms are conceived not as an expression of the will of the politically dominant class but as something self-contained and independent from the real relations of a class society" (*loc. cit.*, p. 45).

133) *Александров*, *op. cit.* (note 112), p. 46 ff.

134) *Туманов*, Критика, *op. cit.* (note 40), pp. 45—46.

135) *Стучка*, Учение о государстве . . ., *op. cit.* (note 104), p. 5.

136) *Туманов*, Критика, *op. cit.* (note 40), p. 57.

neo-Kantian basis of the pure theory of law with the philosophical system of Husserl" [137]). As a "subjective idealist theory" phenomenology asserts that "along with the positive law there exists certain 'eidos', that behind each legal norm is hidden its *a priori* 'essence'" which constitutes the "ideal source" of positive law, that a "rational cognition of 'ideal sources' is impossible, that they can be known only by means of 'eidetic intuition', and that means through mystical intuitive guesses" [138]). Like Kelsen's theory, in Tumanov's opinion, so the phenomenological interpretation of law is "directed against the materialist explanation of law as a specific reflection of social reality in social (class) consciousness" [139]). For this reason, Tumanov contended, phenomenologists advocate the "pure science" which refutes the validity of "empirical facts and of the principle of causality", and introduce "irrationalism and mysticism" into the science of law in order to "mask economic and political conditioning of legal norms" [140]).

Criticism of "bourgeois" theories of law advanced by Soviet writers stems primarily from political and not scientific considerations. Regardless of the fact that "bourgeois" natural-law, psychological, sociological, and normative schools of law differ in their basic philosophical and methodological assumptions, and their political implications as well, they are all subsumed by contemporary Soviet writers under the category of "anti-Marxist formalism". It is hardly possible not to arrive at the conclusion that Soviet writers either misunderstand or intentionally misinterpret the contents and aims of these theories. The impression that Soviet criticism creates is that "bourgeois" theories without exception are politically motivated, and that they are but a part of an anti-Marxist and anti-Soviet political conspiracy. There are, indeed, other reasons for the Soviet critique, and those are the same reasons that cause the Soviet theorists to deny the ability of "bourgeois" theorists to bring about a scientific interpretation of society. It is the cult of Marxism-Leninism-Stalinism that claims to be the ultimate source of scientific knowledge. The great paradox of this claim consists in that, while presumably possessing the key to knowledge, the Soviet theorists failed in the creation of a consistent Marxist theory of law, and were forced to borrow the views of some "bourgeois" theories of law.

AUTHORS OF WORKS IN RUSSIAN

quoted in this article are listed below in Russian alphabetical order. Numbers refer to the footnote where the full title of the work appears.

137) *Ibid.*
138) *Ibid.*, pp. 56—59.
139) *Ibid.*, p. 58.
140) *Ibid.*, pp. 59—60. For recent Soviet criticism of normativism see *Пиголкин*, *op. cit.* (note 115), pp. 49—54.

34 *M. Jaworskyj — Soviet Critique of the "Bourgeois" Philosophy of Law*

INDEX OF PERSONS

Index of persons mentioned or quoted in this article are listed below for reference purposes. Numbers refer to pages (mention in a footnote is indicated by n). Authors of works in Russian are listed, in addition, on p. 33.

[11]

MARXISM AND THE LAW: PRELIMINARY ANALYSES

INTRODUCTION[1]

(i) Some general considerations

Lord Hailsham has said that "there is a sense in which all law is nothing more nor less than a gigantic confidence trick.[2] Statements such as this readily conjure up images of conspiracy and ideological deception to stand alongside the repressive legal apparatus of the strong state as twin mainstays of bourgeois oppression. The imagery misleads however, for the role of law is complex and not to be reduced to easy phrases and catchwords. Unfortunately it is necessary to labour this point at the outset since as E.P. Thompson has said, "some theorists today are unable to see the law except in terms of the 'fuzz' setting about inoffensive demonstrators or cannabis smokers".[3] Thompson is right. Matters are more complex than that. It is not possible to conceive of the complex division of labour of a capitalist order and the totality of its social relations without law. Law is embedded, inextricably, in the organisation and culture of our social existence. And just as that social existence presents a many-sided reality, so too does the law.

In this paper I shall begin to outline the extent to which the values and institutions of private law — the legal person, the contract and private property — are necessarily so buried in the socio-economic order of capitalism. Remote as these legal conceptions may be to immediate experience, I shall argue that they are absolutely central to the articulation of developed capitalist social formations, and that in consequence their analysis is fundamental to more general considerations of the capitalist mode of production. In doing so a whole series of important theoretical problems and debates, not only within Marxism, will be touched on but deliberately glossed over. My intention is not to deny the importance of such debates, but to put forward the elements of an analysis which ultimately must serve to give body to arguments which, at their present level of abstraction, require concretising if they are to be furthered.

The analysis presented here derives much from the work of the soviet theorist E.B. Pashukanis who first published his major work, *The General Theory of Law and Marxism* in 1924, of which a German translation

[1] The most part of this paper was written during the autumn term of the academic year 1977/78, during which time I was a guest of the Institüt für Rechts-und Sozialphilosophie, der Universität des Saarlandes. I would like to express my gratitude to the members of the Institute, and especially to Professor Alessandro Baratta and Dr. Gelinda Smauss, both for their helpful and instructive criticism and for their kindness and hospitality during my stay. I would also like to thank Professor D.N. MacCormick and Mr. Z.K. Bankowski for their comments on later drafts of the paper, for their patience and tolerance.

[2] Hailsham L.C., Speech to Devon Magistrates *The Time* 12 April 1972.

[3] E.P. Thompson, *Whigs and Hunters* (1975) 260.

appeared in 1929, and an English translation in 1951.[4] Both translations are inadequate however, and there have been in consequence considerable difficulties and disagreements as to the interpretation of the work. In part however problems relating to textual irregularities and the precise meaning of particular passages should be reduced by the publication of a new translation from the Russian which is currently in progress, and for these reasons I shall not engage here in a detailed critique of Pashukanis' work.[5] I will say however that the interpretation of the work given by Poulantzas and others as extreme economism seems to me to be exaggerated, and, although in this respect I do not think the work can be treated uncritically, it would be wrong to dismiss it on these grounds.[6] The major importance which I attribute to Pashukanis' work lies in his conception of law as the organisational form which facilitates capitalist commodity circulation, and his consistent and powerful rejection of analyses of law, put forward by contemporary revisionist-marxist theorists such as Karl Renner, in which law in its form is treated as neutral, so that the problem of law is reduced to one of the selection of ends.[7] In Pashukanis' work the form of law, and not merely its content, is subjected to rigorous critique, so that, for example, the very framework of rights and duties is shown to be premissed upon a particular and ultimately limiting ontology. As Karl Korsch has pointed out in this dimension Pashukanis' work represented a significant break with the dominant problems of the orthodox Marxism of his time, and therein lies both its strength and its rigour.[8]

On the other hand the major weakness in the work is a tendency to display a rather pedantic formalism and historical insensitivity which leads to a rather uncertain conflation of the legal and the economic and renders aspects of his work open to the criticism of being culture-bound.[9] For Pashukanis, in some ways rather reminiscent of Max Weber, bears to an extent the marks of much European theory. Thus the general and abstract normative structure of the historically particular 19th century civilian codes is treated implicitly as the form of bourgeois law in general. There is little

[4] E.B. Pashukanis, *Allgemeine Rechtslehre und Marxismus* (1960) and E.B. Pashukanis, "The General Theory of Law and Marxism" in *Soviet Legal Philosophy* (ed. Babb and Hazard, 1951).

[5] See the forthcoming E.B. Pashukanis, *The General Theory of Law and Marxism* to be published by Inklinks Ltd., translated by Barbara Einhorn with an Introduction by C.J. Arthur. Also, see the forthcoming work P. Beirne and R. Sharthet, *Pashukanis and Soviet Legal Theory: The Commodity Exchange Theory of Law* (Academic Press 1979).

[6] See Poulantzas, "A Propos de la Théorie Marxiste du Droit" (1967) 12 *Archiv de Philosophie du Droit* 145-6.

[7] See Karl Renner, *The Institutions of Private Law and their Social Function* (1949) *passim.*

[8] Korsch, "E. Pashukanis: Allgemeine Rechtslehre und Marxismus" (1930) 15 *Archiv für die Geschichte des Socialismus und der Arbeiterbewegung*, reprinted in E.B. Pashukanis, *op.cit.*, (1960) *passim.*

[9] See Tay, "Law, the Citizen and the State" in *Law and Society* (ed. Kamenka and Tay 1978) 8 and also E.B. Pashukanis *op.cit.*, (1960) xi.

concerted attempt to address the problem of the historical development and mediation of the law, which becomes particularly obvious if the analysis is extended, *simpliciter*, to the English common law. However, this does not vitiate the fundamental point of Pashukanis' argument as to the relationship between the form of law and the commodity form. To this end in the paper I try to develop a distinction, which I believe to be implicit in the work, between what I term the *juridical relation* and the *law*, the one being a determinate theoretical abstraction necessary to the critique of the capitalist mode of production in general, and the other being a specific, historically mediated expression of that relation in concrete historical social formations.

Bearing this particular qualification in mind, like Pashukanis I start from a conception of the individual in capitalist society as a *legal person*. The individual is given his social existence at law. Within the complex social division of labour of the capitalist mode of production the individual only has meaning, only exists as a social being in so far as he defined reciprocally — that is, in relation to others. In practical terms this means that in his social existence (that is, as a member of a particular capitalist social formation) the individual is defined in the bearing of legal rights and duties, powers and liabilities etc. Thus the individual is constituted as a (legal) person reciprocally, in relation to others similarly defined in terms of correlative, actual or potential, rights and duties etc. The individual *is* a legal person, or like the convicted criminal or the insane, deprived of his legal capacity, he is nothing. Living outside the law is an impossibility. Thus, in theoretical terms I shall refer to the individual subject as defined in the juridical relation. This terminology is employed to emphasise the relations of reciprocity which define the independent but interdependent individuals of the complex social division of labour in the capitalist mode of production. The analysis of the social division of labour I must however take as read, as in the paper I shall be concerned primarily to elaborate this notion of the juridical relation.[10]

In what follows it will be evident that I am led to reject certain positions which have been variously attributed to the Marxist theory of law. Firstly, I reject any reduction of law to the status of a mere superstructural force, whether of a voluntarist, economist, or structuralist tendency. Indeed I would reject the base-superstructure metaphor in its entirety. Secondly, I reject any analysis which reduces the problem of law to the problem of coercion and thus to the typification of law as a "repressive apparatus" or as "class rule". This is not of course to argue that coercion and class relations are in any sense epiphenomenal to capitalist social order, but simply that coercion is at best only a secondary element in the structure of bourgeois legal relations. This perhaps requires brief elucidation. Marx himself consistently argued that the exercise of coercion (discipline) obtained at the point of

[10] For that analysis see in particular Karl Marx, *Capital* (1970) Vol. I part IV, 296-473 and Karl Marx, *The Poverty of Philosophy* (1975) 118-133.

production, that is, within the particular conditions of the labour process, whilst:

> The sphere of circulation, or rather the exchange of commodities, within the limits of which moves the purchase and sale of labour power, is *in reality* a veritable garden of Eden of natural rights of man. There reigns only Liberty, Equality, Property and Bentham.[11]

Coercion is particular and concrete, whereas in the sphere of circulation freedom is universal, but abstract. In 20th century capitalist societies, as Melossi and Pavarini have argued, the exercise of the particular function of discipline has been rationalised and extended, and is operative through a series of additional "ancillary institutions" such as the family, the schools and increasingly the agencies of the Welfare State.[12] Although this undoubtedly makes the analysis of control more complex, nonetheless it in no way denies Marx's basic formulation of the inverse relationship between "liberty and equality" in the social division of labour (the sphere of circulation) and despotism in the manufacturing division of labour (the labour process). Thus Marx wrote that:

> It can even be laid down as a general rule that the less authority presides over the division of labour inside society the more the division of labour develops inside the workshop, and the more it is subjected there to the authority of a single person. Thus authority in the workshop and authority in society, in relation to the division of labour, are in *inverse ratio* to each other.[13]

Thus, in so far as law functions primarily in the sphere of circulation to facilitate commodity exchange, the logic of its form is to be found not in coercion, but elsewhere, namely as a fetishised expression of the value-form.

The third implication of the analysis put forward here is the rejection of any analysis which reduces law to the status of a "mere" ideology, a confidence-trick, the "civil liberties lie".[14] And, fourthly, to reiterate the point made earlier I reject the exaggerated formalism and the ahistorical dimension to the work of Pashukanis.

In this paper I am primarily concerned to argue that the analysis of the juridical relation be derived from the analysis of commodity exchange, and that law must be understood in terms of the facilitation and organisation of commodity circulation rather than as a technique of repression or coercion.

[11] Karl Marx, *Capital* (1970) Vol. 1, 280 (emphasis added).

[12] D. Melossi and M. Pavarini, *Carcere e Fabbrica* (1977) *passim; Prisons and Factories* (forthcoming, Macmillans (1979)); and Melossi, "Istituzioni di controllo sociale e organizzazione capitalistica del lavoro: alcune ipotesi di ricerca" (1976) 2 *La Questione Criminale*, 293-319. See also Kinsey *"Risocializzazione e Controllo nelle Carceri Inglesi"* (1976) 2 *La Questione Criminale* 571-595.

[13] Karl Marx, *The Poverty of Philosophy* (1975) 126; see also Marx *Capital* 1970 Vol. 1 357.

[14] I am thinking here of the populist anarchist/Marxist material that emerged especially in America during 1968 and its aftermath. See e.g., M. Kennedy, "The Civil liberties Lie" in *Law Against the People* (ed. Lefcourt 1971) 140-150.

In addition however I have chosen to encounter some of the fundamental problems of jurisprudence, and I include preliminary comments on the relation between law and morality, on the nature of legal equality, as well as a discussion in the last section of the general and abstract nature of legal norms. These are large areas of dispute, and I have made no attempt to locate what I have to say within the wider debates of jurisprudence. My intention is rather to develop an alternative theoretical language within which to encounter and reformulate those problems. It is sometimes argued that such problems should be rejected as the "pseudo-problems" of "bourgeois science", and more generally that the coming of "sociology of law" has somehow displaced the problem of jurisprudence altogether.

In answer to such criticisms, should they make themselves heard, I would quote the following passage from Pashukanis' criticism of Karl Renner's sociology of law:

> We may agree . . . that legal science begins where jurisprudence ends; but it by no means follows that legal science must simply cast overboard the fundamental abstractions expressing the essence of the principles underlying the legal form. For political economy, too, began its development from practical problems pre-eminently concerned with the circulation of money and of course it too originally set itself the task of pointing out "means of making governments and peoples wealthy". Nonetheless we already find in these technical counsels the foundations of the concepts which — in a form deepened and generalised — become integrated into the structure of the theoretical discipline: political economy.[15]

(ii) The base-superstructure metaphor

In the course of this paper I argue that legal relations are intrinsic to the social-economic order of contemporary capitalism. This entails abandoning the traditional Marxist conception of legal relations as superstructural phenomena. Indeed I shall assert a priority to the law which within the terms of Marxist orthodoxy requires elaboration.

In 1859 Marx wrote:

> At a certain stage of development, the material productive forces of society come into conflict with the existing relations of production, or — this merely expresses the same thing in legal terms — with the property relations *within the framework of which they have operated hitherto*.[16]

The implication is clear: any separation of the legal expression and the social-economic relation is wholly artificial. The legal expression provides the ideological boundaries, or the definitions of social economic practices; hence the difficulties experienced in Marxist theory of defining relations of the so-called "base" without reference to legal, and hence "ideological" conceptions of private property, ownership possession etc. The base-superstructure metaphor has resulted in the theoretical separation of the legal and the economic in a manner which presents a false object of enquiry.

[15] Babb and Hazard, *op.cit.*, p. 113.

[16] Karl Marx, *A Contribution to the Critique of Political Economy* (1971) 21. (emphasis added).

It is essential to my argument that the metaphor is rejected. Marx wrote as follows:

> In the social production of their existence men inevitably enter into definite relations which are independent of their will, namely relations of production appropriate to a given stage in the development of their material forces of production. The totality of these relations of production constitute the economic structure of society, the real foundation on which rises a legal and political superstructure and to which corresponds definite forms of social consciousness.[17]

In this passage Marx summarised his own complex method and theoretical development in a few innocent words which have lent to Marxism an armoury of metaphor and language of which the consequences and implications have been immeasurable. This language of construction and foundation has served to unite a plurality of diverse theories and practices, but more than this it has built into theory unnecessary preoccupations and assumptions.[18] Nowhere is this more clear than in the analysis of law.

In his theoretical studies of law Poulantzas has argued that the "deformations" of Marxist theory, and legal theory in particular, can be seen as variations upon the voluntarist-economist theme.[19] The economist interpretation puts forward the law as a simple and immediate reflection of economic relations. There is a direct correspondence between the needs of capital and the content of the law — law is merely "appended" to the economic order. The voluntarist tendency, on the other hand, treats law as norms issuing from the state, embodying the will of the dominant class. Both tendencies, Poulantzas argues, rest upon a misconception of the relation between base and superstructure, denying specific effectivity of, and the dialectic between, the various "levels" of this "decentred unity". In the one the study of law is reduced to the pure "science of the economic" and law is denied any status as "a theoretically constructed and specific object of scientific investigation" in its own right. In the second "the economic base, conceived in a mechanistic manner, consists in an inert field 'energised' by the will and human consciousness (*conscience*)". Thus in the second, law is theoretically constructed as an object of study only in so far as it is attached to a creative historical subject, that is, the ruling class. According to this perspective law is thus inextricably linked to the history of

[17] *Ibid.*, p. 20.

[18] For a general analysis, see L. Colletti, *From Rousseau to Lenin* (1972) 45-111.

[19] See Poulantzas, *op.cit.*, pp. 146-52, and also Poulantzas, "L'examen Marxiste de l'Etat et du Droit Actuel" 1964-5 20 *Les Temps Modernes* 281-321, and *Nature des Choses et Droit* (1965).

a class and can only be studied in relation to it, as a class instrument, a "tool of oppression".[20]

These objections are to the point; however Poulantzas' contention that law can be studied "as a scientific object in its own right" is itself a further "deformation" consequent upon the theoretical separation allowed by the base-superstructure metaphor. For, just as the economist and voluntarist interpretations in different ways move away from the idea of legal relations being intrinsically bound to economic through the value-relation (see *infra*) — in the one by stipulating law as a separate "effect" of the economic and, in the other by identifying law and class will — so too Poulantzas reproduces the separation by introducing a highly dubious and indeed Weberian conception of legal structure. Thus for example in *Nature des Choses et Droit*, although he is careful to emphasise the historical specificity of law and to deny the existence of "universal and eternal structures of law", Poulantzas works with an *ideal-typification* of occidental law and speaks of the characteristic qualities of this (relatively) autonomous object of science:

> La plupart des juristes tombent d'accord pour considérer comme tels leur abstraction, leur généralité, leur formalisme, et leur fixation en règles juridiques présentant un fort degré de systématisation. Or, ces traits fondamentaux des structures internes spécifiques — présentant une autonomie relative á l'égard de l'infrastructure — des droits occidentaux actuels sont engendrés en définitive eux-mêmes à partir de l'infrastructure, à partir des besoins et entérêts que l'activité practique des hommes revêt dans le structures sociales et économiques correspondentes.[21]

Again, in his criticism of the voluntarist position Poulantzas locates the problem in terms of the importation *into* the base-superstructure model of the Hegelian historical subject; rather than in the metaphor itself. It is more plausible to see the importation of this notion as consequent upon the metaphor itself: the language of construction inevitably leads to the problem of the "constructors".

[20] Thus, for example, Tumanov argued at the 1930 Georgian Conference on law.

> We Marxists assert that law is carried out in practice by means of coercion and violence, because all law is a class law, and the law of a class without coercion is not a law.

Tumanov continues with the chilling and historically pregnant words:

> . . . understand that in our country of proletarian dictatorship, in the epoch of an intensified class struggle . . . a calm academic presentation of the view of our enemies is unsuitable . . .

Cited in D. Lloyd *Introduction to Jurisprudence* (1972) 670.

[21] N. Poulantzas, *Nature des Choses et Droit* (1965) 256. It should be noted here that in later work Poulantzas has rejected aspects of this work as being "influenced by the humanist historicism of the young Marx". This perhaps makes it all the more remarkable that in the later "Althusserian" work his conception of legal science and the law remains the same. Thus in "A propos de la Theorie Marxiste du Droit", *op.cit.*, (1967), p. 160, Poulantzas writes.

> J'ai essayé de montrer ailleurs, et je ne reviendrai pas ici, à partir du concept du mode capitalist 'pur' de production, ou peut construire ainsi le concept théorique du droit moderne comme système à normes générales, abstraites, formelles et strictement réglementiarisées en ce sens qu'elles possèdent une réversibilite complète . . .

In his article "Base and Superstructure in Marxist Cultural Theory" Raymond Williams has pointed to the numerous qualifications which have had to be made to avoid some of the more ludicrous distortions consequent upon the rigid use of the metaphor.[22] Positivist and economist notions of "reflection" very soon were found to be unsupportable, thus:

> Since in many real cultural activities this relationship cannot be found, or cannot be found without effort or even violence to the material or practice being studied the notion was introduced of delays in time, the famous lags; of various technical complications, and of indirectness, in which certain kinds of activity in the cultural sphere — philosophy for example — were situated at a greater distance from the primary economic activities.[23]

In the area of law, as early as 1890 Engels was already invoking such qualifications, and indeed providing the cue for Poulantzas' later development of the idea of the relative autonomy of law:

> It would be difficult to prove for instance that the absolute liberty of the testator in England, and the severe limitations in every detail imposed upon him in France are due to economic causes alone. Both react back however upon the economic sphere to a very considerable extent because they influence the distribution of property.[24]

The problem in the use of the metaphor runs much more deeply than simply an empirical lack of fit, however. It lies in the very separation and differentiation between levels which are entailed in this "Marxist topography", which has tended in Marxist analysis of law especially to treat the legal and economic as empirically as well as analytically separable. Whether economist or voluntarist, structuralist or historicist, the language of base and superstructure requires its problems to be posed and thought in a specific manner. The language has "hegemonised" theory. Take for example the following passage from Althusser:

> [T]he great theoretical advantage of the Marxist topography *i.e.* of the spatial metaphor of edifice (base and superstructure) is simultaneously that it reveals that questions of determination . . . . are crucial; that it reveals that it is the base which in the last instance determines the whole edifice; and that, as a consequence, it obliges us to pose the theoretical problems of the types of "derivatory effectivity" peculiar to the superstructure, *i.e.* it obliges us to think what the Marxist tradition calls conjointly the relative autonomy of the superstructure, and the reciprocal action of the superstructure on the base.[25]

The power of this linguistic hegemony is such that any demand to collapse the distinction appears tantamount to an heretical rejection of theoretical tradition. Indeed the heresy seems to require the "scientifically" — because architecturally — impossible. Williams however presents us with a more limited objective:

[22] Williams "Base and Superstructure in Marxist Cultural Theory" (1973) 82 *New Left Review* 3-17.

[23] *Ibid.*, p. 5.

[24] Engels, Letter to C. Schmidt in Berlin 27 October 1890 in *Marx/Engels Selected Works in One Volume* (1968) 687.

[25] L. Althusser, *Lenin and Philosophy* (1971) 130.

> We have to revalue "determination" toward the setting of limits and the exertion of pressure, and away from a predicted, prefigured and controlled content. We have to revalue "superstructure" towards a related range of cultural practices, and away from a reflected, reproduced or specifically dependent content. And, crucially, we have to revalue "the base" away from the notion of a fixed economic or technological abstraction, and towards the specific activities of men in real social and economic relationships, containing fundamental contradictions and variations and therefore always in a state of dynamic process.[26]

The combination of the social and the economic, and the emphasis upon the dynamic of process is necessary and well placed. But even within this prescription, the analysis of law requires further revision, if not outright rejection, of the metaphor. Firstly, as we saw above, Engels quite rightly pointed out that laws amount to material social conditions which do actually limit the economic. Laws circumscribe and define the available means and forces of production so that, although at one level "ideal", laws must be counted amongst the concrete conditions of social existence. Secondly, and more importantly, laws and the principles of organisation they embody, actually make possible capitalist production for exchange, in that the relations of private property and contract, define the very act of capitalist exchange: the commodity, "free" wage labour, etc. Not simply however as Weber maintained, in providing a rational-calculable frame of reference within which to plan and effect exchange, but in providing the categories through which production in general and the relations between individuals in particular obtain. Thus Thompson argued in relation to 18th century:

> If we look closely into [the] agrarian context the distinction between law on the one hand . . . and the actualities of productive forces and relations on the other becomes more and more untenable. For law was often a definition of actual agrarian practice as it had been pursued "time out of mind". How can we distinguish between the activity of farming or of quarrying and the rights to this strip of land or that quarry? The farmer or forester in his daily occupation was moving within visible or invisible structures of law.[27]

How those structures of law are articulated or expressed in a particular social formation is largely a problem of historical analysis. The specific content of laws will vary as Engels correctly realised; and indeed, as we shall see later, a developed system of law is not even necessary to the capitalist mode of production. What however is invariable and necessary to the mode of production is that the juridical relation is expressed through abstract and general norms — such as those of the laws of contract and private property — which in turn are premissed upon the juridical relation being established as a concrete practice. These problems provide the subject matter of the remainder of this paper.

[26] Williams, *op.cit.*, p. 6.

[27] Thompson, *op.cit.*, p. 261.

LAW AND THE ALIENATION OF COMMODITIES

In this part of the paper I shall argue that Marx's analysis of capitalist commodity exchange presupposes an analytic distinction between exchange-value and the juridical relation, but that in the value-relation — through which the social order of the capitalist mode of production is expressed — these two dimensions of the exchange relation are mutually dependent.

(i) Exchange-value and the juridical relation

In the first chapter of *Capital* Marx makes the following fundamental comments:

> Exchange-value generally is only the mode of expression, the phenomenal form of something contained in it, yet distinguishable from it.[28]

That something is human labour in the abstract, the magnitude of that value being measured in terms of the quantity of socially necessary labour-time embodied in it, that is, the labour-time which would have to be consumed on the average, in the production of the commodity. Exchange-value is the *phenomenal form* of abstract labour.

We need not be delayed here with the problem of the derivation of price from value however, for the full implication of Marx's analysis of exchange-value is only to be grasped through the wider context of his analysis of the value-relation or "commodity-fetishism", which provides the basis to Marx's sociology of order.[29] Through the analysis of the exchange of the social product in the form of the commodity, Marx demonstrates the logic of social order within the capitalist mode of production, where commodities — the product of autonomous *private* labours — are produced *for exchange* within an anarchic social division of labour, and become the *objectified* medium of *social* connexion and interdependence within that anarchy. It is in this respect that Marx refers to social relations as taking on the "fantastic" but taken-for-granted *appearance* of relations between things.[30] This Marx terms "the fetishism of commodities".

In the analysis of the commodity form of the product Marx provides a sociology which is specific to capitalist social order. Colletti has written as follows:

> If this social division of labour were a conscious or planned distribution . . . the products of individual labour would not take the form of commodities . . . [I]n conditions of commodity production, the work of individual producers is not labour

[28] Marx *Capital* (1970) Vol. I 45.

[29] On Marxism as a sociology, see Colletti, *op.cit.*, pp. 3-45.

[30] Thus Marx writes:

> The labour of the individual asserts itself as part of the labour of society, only by means of the relations which the act of exchange establishes directly between the products, and indirectly, through them, between the producers. To the latter, therefore, the relations connecting the labour of one individual with that of the rest appear, not as direct social relations between individuals at work, but as what they really are, material relations between persons and social relations between things.

Capital (1970), Vol. I 78.

> carried out at the command or on behalf of society: rather it is private autonomous labour, carried out by each producer independently of the next. Hence lacking any conscious assignment or distribution on the part of society, individual labour is not *immediately* an articulation of social labour, it acquires its character as a part or *aliquot* of aggregate labour only through the medium of exchange relations or the market.[31]

In short, in so far as both the distribution of the social product and the articulation of social relations, occurs through the medium commodity-exchange, commodity production is specific to the capitalist order.[32]

However, in order that the many, materially diverse products of labour may be exchanged they must both be rendered commensurable and also be of utility (a use-value).[33] In that commodity production is production for exchange, the product does not have use-value for the producer except and in so far as it can be exchanged. To be exchanged the product must be useful for others, but this presupposes criteria of exchangeability. For, as Marx argued:

> All commodities are non-use-values for their owners and use-values for their non-owners. Consequently they must all change hands. But this change of hands is what constitutes their exchange, and the latter puts them in relation with each other as values and realises them as values. Hence commodities must be realised as values before they can be realised as use-values.[34]

Thus in exchange commodities must be realised as exchange-values, that is, rendered commensurable according to some common property. As we have seen, Marx argues that this common property is the (socially necessary) labour time embodied in commodities. In exchange, particular private labours are transformed into and have significance only as a quotient of aggregate socially necessary labour, so that particular private labours are treated solely in terms of average or "abstract" labour, thus negating the particular conditions of that labour. This I shall refer to as the appropriation of subjectivity in production through exchange.[35]

Thus it is that Marx argues that within the complex social division of labour of capitalist production the social interdependence of autonomous (independent), private labours is expressed in, or thought within, the fetishised idea of exchange value as the phenomenal form of abstract labour. The social order of the capitalist mode of production is articulated in the value-relation.

The process of the negation of the particular and the objectification of the abstract (or universal) form is the key to Marx's sociology. I shall return to this later in relation to the "fetishistic" appearance of law in the last part

[31] Colletti, *op.cit.*, p. 83.

[32] Of course commodity production and exchange may be present in non-capitalist social formations, for example in Roman slave society, but not as the articulation of social relations in general.

[33] *Cf.* Marx *Capital* (1970) Vol. I Chapter II *passim*.

[34] *Ibid.*, p. 34.

[35] This terminology is derived from Colletti, *op.cit.*, pp. 82-92.

of this paper. For the present however it is essential to the argument of the previous section to note that the phenomenal form exchange-value only represents one aspect of the value-relation as the total social-economic relation. For exchange-value is an incomplete expression of the value-relation, in that the value-relation entails not only the representation of private labour as abstract labour and thus the appropriation of subjectivity, it also entails the relation of interdependence obtaining in the exchange of that abstract labour.

In the capitalist mode of production, the act of alienation of the commodity must be an intentional and voluntary act, between "free and equal" parties.[36] As such, this requires the re-ascription of subjectivity in the exercise of autonomous will. The subjectivity thus ascribed, I shall argue presently, is to be conceived of as a juridical subjectivity of an equal and abstract personality. In the meantime let us note that exchange-value is incomplete in that, for its realisation as a concrete social relation, it requires the complementary *juridical relation* between "equalised" subjects — equalised that is in the act of alienation. Thus in the value-relation subjectivity is at once denied in the abstraction/equalisation of labour and ascribed, though transformed, in the abstraction/equalisation of subjects in exchange. Both exchange value and the juridical relation are thus intrinsic to the value-relation, and in this respect the juridical relation cannot be treated as epiphenomenal to the social-economic structure of the capitalist mode of production, that is as superstructure.

[36] This point is crucial to Marx's analysis of the appropriation of surplus labour in the capitalist mode of production. Under capitalism profit (or rather, all surplus value) is derived not from exploitation in the market, but as a function of the use-value of the commodity labour power. In the labour market the exchange value of labour power is determined according to socially necessary labour time embodied in it, that is in terms of the average labour necessary for its reproduction. On the labour market the owner of labour-power and the owner of money "meet . . . and deal with each other as on the basis of equal rights, with this difference alone that one is buyer and one is seller, therefore equal in the eyes of the law" (*Capital* (1970) Vol. 1 165.) What the buyer of labour power obtains is a unique commodity, in that unlike any other commodity, it has "the specific use-value . . . of being *a source not only of value, but of more value than it itself has*" (Capital (1970) Vol. 1 188.) The buyer of labour power thus pays the full price of a day's labour (*i.e.* the cost of its reproduction) but for that price obtains the capacity to produce a surplus-value, i.e. the value produced over and above the value of the products necessary for the reproduction of the labour power consumed. Thus "The seller of labour-power *like the seller of any other commodity*, relaises its exchange-value and parts with its use-value. He cannot take the one without giving the other. The use-value of labour-power, or in other words, labour, belongs just as little to its seller, as the use-value of oil after it has been sold belongs to the dealer who has sold it. The owner of money has paid the value of a day's labour-power; his therefore is the use of it for a day; a day's labour belongs to him. The circumstances that on the one hand the daily sustenance of labour-power costs (for example) only half a day's labour, while on the other hand the very same labour-power can work during a whole day, that consequently that the value which its use during one day creates, is double what he pays for that use, this circumstance is, without doubt a piece of good luck for the buyer, but by no means an injury to the seller." (*Capital* (1970) Vol. 1 188, emphasis added.) Exchange on the market is thus equal exchange, between parties who are "equal in the eyes of the law".

(ii) A methodological note: the abstract is determinate

At this point it is convenient and necessary to elaborate a distinction between what I have termed the juridical relation and the law. The law, or "legal relations" I propose to treat as the historically specific mediation or expression of the juridical relation, in a manner analogous to Marx's treatment of exchange-value as the phenomenal form of abstract labour. The juridical relation is thus an abstract but determinate theoretical construct appropriate to the analysis of the capitalist mode of production, whilst the law is one historically specific mode of expression of that relation. The mediation and realisation of the juridical relation as law occurs in the material practices of its administration — primarily through the courts, sometimes through administrative and executive agencies, QUANGOS etc., but also in customary, conventional and private legal systems such as, for example, Macaulay has pointed to in the practices of certain American business communities.[37] This implies that the study of law will take place through the study of the history of its conventions and of the apparatuses which administer it.

It is worth emphasising however that the distinction between the juridical relation and the law as social practice is not a replication of the idealist distinction between a universal and timeless form of law and its content. The conception of the juridical relation is derived from that series of culturally dominant conceptualisations and practices which serve to provide the frame of reference within which exchange actually occurs and indeed is made possible. For, as Marx and Engels said, a mode of production:

> must not be considered simply as being the reproduction of the physical existence of individuals. Rather it is a definite form of activity of these individuals, a definite form of expressing their life, a definite mode of life on their part.[38]

Thus, although the relation entailed in the act of alienation is theoretically expressed in the abstract as the juridical relation, the concreteness of this abstract relation must not be in doubt. This apparently paradoxical point can be clarified by further reference to Marx's analysis of abstract labour. For Marx, methodological use of the "concrete concept" abstract labour is not merely a methodological category or "ideal type" through which arbitrary sense can be read into social reality, but rather it both specifies and *is present in* the concrete act of alienation itself. As Colletti has argued, the equalisation/abstraction of human labour actually occurs in the determinate act of exchange, not merely in the mind of the theoretician. Thus Marx wrote:

> When we bring the products of our labour into relation with each other as values it is not because we see in these articles the material receptacles of homogenous human labour-power. Quite the contrary, whenever by exchange we equate as values our different products, by that very act we also equate as human labour the different kinds of labour we expend on them. We are not aware of this nevertheless we do it.[39]

[37] See S. Macaulay, *Law and the Balance of Power* (1966).

[38] Karl Marx and Frederick Engels, *The German Ideology* (1970) 42.

[39] Karl Marx, *Capital* (1970) Vol. I 78.

Precisely because the relation between private labours becomes in practice the abstraction "abstract labour" it can be posed theoretically as such. Nonetneless it is a lived relation. Equally, the juridical relation between men in alienation as abstract wills can be posed theoretically as such, precisely because it is a determinate relation of commodity exchange. Not only therefore is the juridical relation a methodological abstraction, it is also a determinate and necessary relation obtaining within the capitalist mode of production — hence it is a *determined abstraction*.[40] As such, for Marx, as is demonstrated in the passage quoted below, such an abstraction can never be treated as an abstract universal separable from the production process, that is, its history:

> [The] distinctive social character [of buyer and seller] are by no means due to individual human nature as such but to the exchange relations of persons who produce their goods in the specific form of commodities . . . It is . . . as absurd to regard buyer and seller, these bourgeois economic types, as eternal social forms of human individuality as it is preposterous to weep over them as signifying the abolition of individuality. They are an essential expression of individuality arising at a particular stage of the social process of production.[41]

In this passage Marx points to the abstraction/equalisation of individual wills in alienation — the *ascription of subjectivity* which he refers to as the "essential expression of individuality" — as necessary moments of commodity exchange, in which the social character of alienation is also realised. It is this relation which is expressed in the concrete concept of the juridical relation, and which as a theoretical concept is derived by abstraction from the determinate social relation.

Obviously the epistemology entailed here warrants detailed examination. For the present the following comments must suffice.[42] It would seem necessary that "determined abstraction" can claim the status of a scientific proposition only within the conditions of its historical production: to state this in another way, if the "is" is always in the process of "becoming", that is, of its negation, so science is always incomplete. The theoretical concept can never be treated as if it were unrelated to its history, that is, universally true, except in a very limited sense:

> The example of labour strikingly demonstrates how even the most abstract categories, despite their validity in all epochs — precisely because they are abstractions — are equally a product of historical conditions even in the specific form of abstractions and *retain their full validity only for and within the framework of these conditions.*[43]

Thus the determined abstraction is both derived from and retains its validity in terms of its present history; such "objective understanding" however, says Marx, can occur "only rarely and under quite special conditions", that

[40] For a more detailed discussion of this position and its significance for the theory of value see Colletti, *op.cit.*, pp. 76-92.

[41] Marx, *A Contribution to the Critique of Political Economy* (1971) 95.

[42] For criticism of the position held here see L. Althusser, *Reading Capital* (1975) 119-45.

[43] Karl Marx, *A Contribution* . . . 210. (emphasis added).

is only when "concrete development is most profuse, so that a *specific quality is seen to be common to many phenomena or common to all.* Then, it is no longer perceived in a particular form".[44] Thus for example Marx argues the theoretical development of the concept of value of classical economics was only possible once "the notion of human equality acquired the fixity of popular prejudice" which occurs only within commodity structure.[45] In the same way, the question "what is law?" is posed fully and for the first time in bourgeois "legal science". Obviously the question was asked in earlier epochs, but the answers necessarily remained incomplete — for example classical natural law — in so far as the grounds of the question remained invisible.

In summary of a complex position it can be said that the theoretical concept (determined abstraction) once derived can be of methodological use in the reconstruction of its present history, that it, its own genesis.[46] Such concepts "provide an insight into the structure and relation of production of all formerly existing social formations" in so far as the relations of pre-capitalist modes of production, "the rules and component elements of which were used in the creation of bourgeois society", are reproduced in their transformation in the historical present. Thus the juridical relation as a theoretical concept is appropriate to the analysis of pre-capitalist legal relations; however it is only present in its full development in bourgeois society only for which and within which it retains its full validity. It is this latter problem which is the present concern.

(iii) The juridical relation and alienation

I have argued that the juridical relation cannot be treated as merely epiphenomenal to the "economic", as a mere element of superstructure. Equally, legal relations must be regarded as intrinsic to any developed capitalist social formation.

Marx himself showed how the generic form of order under the capitalist mode of production — "the anatomy of bourgeois society" — lies within the commodity structure. Whereas under the feudal mode of production the extraction of surplus labour remains direct, coercive and consequently transparent, in so far as the producer still has actual possession of his means of production, under the capitalist mode of production the worker "freely" disposes of his own labour-power as an abstraction, as a commodity bearing exchange-value. At this point Pashukanis has quite rightly insisted that the necessary ideal (ideal in the same sense as Marx refers to "value" as an "ideal" relation) counterpart to the order inherent in commodity exchange is to be located in the legal expression of the juridical relation, that is, in the conception of the legal person, as bearer of abstract rights and

[44] *Id.* (emphasis added).

[45] Karl Marx, *Capital* (1970) Vol. 1 60-65.

[46] See for example Marx's brief note on the property relation *A Contribution* . . . 207-8.

[47] Karl Marx, *Capital* (1970) Vol. 1 88.

duties upon which rise the institutions of the contract and property. It is in this connexion that Pashukanis takes the following, very important passage from *Capital*:

> It is plain that commodities cannot go to market and make exchange of their own account. We must therefore have recourse to their guardians who are also their owners. Commodities are things and therefore without the power of resistance against men. If they are wanting in docility, he can use force. In other words he can take possession of them. In order that these objects may enter into relation with each other as commodities, their guardians must place themselves in relation to each other as persons whose will resides in those objects and must behave in such a way that each does not appropriate the commodity of the other, and part with his own except by means of an act done by mutual consent. They must therefore recognize in each other the rights of private proprietors. This juridical relation, which expresses itself in a contract, whether such a contract be part of a developed legal system or not, is a relation between two wills, and is but a reflex of the real economic relation between the two.[47]

In this passage there are three points crucial to the analysis of law. Firstly, as we have seen, commodity exchange in general requires *a relation between wills*, that is, a juridical relation, which by extrapolation is thus essential to the structure of capitalist production for exchange and the appropriation of surplus value. Secondly, for commodity exchange to occur the rights of private proprietors must *be at least recognized by consent*. Thirdly, the juridical relation thus established *need not be expressed through the institutions of a developed legal system* (although it seems reasonable to argue that in a developed capitalist social economic formation, with a high social division of labour it becomes functionally necessary to guarantee the rights of private proprietors through the mechanism of private law).

In short, the social-economic relation of commodity exchange can only obtain in so far as the juridical relation is expressed through "informal" means of "consent" or morality, *or* through the formal mechanism of private law. Either way, as Pashukanis said:

> At the very same time that the product of labour is taking on the quality of goods and becoming a bearer of value, man acquires the quality of a juridic subject and becomes the bearer of a right.[48]

These points, especially in relation to the legal person, will be developed further. In conclusion to this section I will only add that so far as the commodity structure "penetrates society in all its aspects and remoulds it in its own image" so the juridical relation obtaining between separate and abstract, right and duty bearing subjects, expresses that economic relation in all its aspects either through legal institutions such as property and contract, or through what may be termed positive morality.[49] In that sense, the civil society of a capitalist social formation is a juridical society; this is the full meaning of the rule of law (*cf.* Tonnies: "gesellschaft",

[48] Babb and Hazard, *op.cit.*, p. 162.

[49] The quotation is taken from Lukacs' analysis of the commodity structure in G. Lukacs, *History and Class Consciousness* (1971) 85.

Weber: "rational-legal", and so on). Bourgeois society is ruled by law. I shall return to this problem in the final section of the paper.

THE REALISATION OF THE JURIDICAL RELATION AS A CONCRETE HISTORICAL PROCESS

(i) Morality and Legality

In so far as the commodity structure (the value relation) provides the generic order of the capitalist mode of production, I shall assume that the juridical relation permeates every dimension of capitalist social relations. In the last section we saw that juridical relation is realised or expressed in two major cultural practices: in the dominant conceptions of morality on the one hand, in tacit notions of responsibility and self-control, and of legality, on the other hand, in formalised or institutionalised notions of reciprocity and equality. The two are typically intertwined in the idea of the "moral obligation to obey the law", but this is not a necessary combination. It may be that a "juridical morality" is a sufficient expression of the juridical relation to facilitate capitalist production. Where however legality operates to formalise, guarantee and thereby regulate capitalist production any disjuncture between morality and legality will only be momentary.

As all undergraduate law students are told, in everyday life individuals make and break contracts and enter all manner of legal relations without knowing or indeed having to know it. Thus Pashukanis pointed out:

> It must be noted that the legal [*juridische*] viewpoint is incomparably more remote from the consciousness of the ordinary man than is the economic viewpoint, for the reason that when the economic relationship is carried into effect simultaneously as a legal relationship too, it is nevertheless the economic side of that relationship which has reality for the participants therein in the vast majority of cases, whilst the legal element remains in the background, and emerges in all its definiteness only in special and exceptional cases (legal proceedings, a controversy concerning the law).[50]

Here we have what Thompson calls "the visible and invisible structures of the law". What is important here however is not so much the invisibility of the legal relation, but its possibility. That is, the possibility of the concretisation in legal relations of all social relations of commodity production and exchange, a possibility which is essential and specific to the commodity structure of the capitalist mode of production. It is this *potential* for the extension of legal relations to include and define all social relations which marks the full and mature development of law in the bourgeois epoch and displays the inherently bourgeois character of law as a lived relation, as a definition of subjectivity.

The structure of law, then, is such that legal norms and definitions can be infinitely extended to assimilate all social economic relations within its own terms. This however is not solely a property of the formal structure of the law, but speaks of the structure of the social economic relations to which the law applies. What this means is not simply that those social

[50] Babb and Hazard, *op.cit.*, p. 121.

economic relations are limited or constrained by the system of laws (Engels, *supra*), nor, in the least, that the system of laws generates those social-economic relations (Weber). Rather, it must be understood that those relations occur, and are thought and practised within a world view (a mode of production) which, by its very nature and genesis in commodity exchange and the social division of labour, is compatible and isomorphic with the structure of law. That is, within an ideology which is intrinsic to commodity production for exchange. There is thus a fit between the "intuitive knowledge" or "taken-for-granted morality" and the specific laws and institutions of the particular capitalist social formation. The "form" of morality and that of legality must be identical, and are precisely because each are different mediations or expressions of the juridical relation.[51]

As such it is necessary not to conflate morality and legality. As we have seen the individual, in practice, need have no knowledge of the specific legal norms which regulate his social activity. Indeed the "ordinary" man cannot know the law in all its detail, for then he would be no ordinary man at all but a "lawyer". On the other hand however the law must know the ordinary man and the conditions of his (moral) existence. The law constitutes the ordinary man in the abstract as "the reasonable man", the "man on the Clapham omnibus". It is in that sense that the law and juridical/positive morality together specify historically the mode in which the juridical relation is realised in a particular social formation.

It was, I think, precisely with this in mind that Gramsci wrote:

> the revolution that the bourgeois class has brought into the conception of law and hence into the function of the state consists especially in the will to conform (hence the ethicity of the law and the state).[52]

What Gramsci points to here is the logic of control in bourgeois society, whereby consent is secured to domination as a moral necessity rather than externally imposed in relations of superordination — subordination (a relation which would be a denial of the basis premise of the commodity structure, that is, equivalence in exchange).

This can be clarified through consideration of the "free" contract for the sale of labour-power. No *law* can enforce the sale of labour-power for to do so is not only impossible in practice, but more importantly would be

[51] It has been pointed out to me in criticism that I do not show how, sociologically, the process of mediation occurs. I argue in the body of the text that the juridical relation is particularised historically. To trace this out in any detail requires careful analysis of the particular constellation of the institutions and ideas and their so-called "uneven development" which constitute the particular social formation in question. Any analysis of English legality would of course have to account for what Thompson has described as the "peculiarly English" transformation of English society. Thus the non-revolutionary transformation of the "Property norm" the absence of Natural Law thinking as the *cri-de-coeur* of a revolutionary bourgeoisie and the impact of utilitarianism in the generation of 19th century moral economy and more, would have to be considered alongside the unique development of the common law and the legal profession in England.

[52] Antonio Gramsci, *Prison Notebooks* (1970) 260.

to deny the very ideological basis of free wage labour and commodity exchange between free and equal individuals. The worker must voluntarily and "freely" sell his labour-power; in so doing he controls himself, acts with responsibility and consents to his own domination. As we shall see, the free exchange of all commodities presupposes that in the social relation of exchange the actors be treated as formally equivalent — in the abstract as legal persons. This equivalence is expressed both in the broad generalities of bourgeois morality and in the specificity of legal relations.

Thus, it is, I think, possible to argue that a "juridical morality" must prefigure in its development — that is as particular mediation of the juridical relation — the articulation of the juridical relation as law. For law, just as Marx argued was the case with the idea of value, is in its fullest development only realised as a practice in a society in which formal equivalence and equality of its members has already "acquired the fixity of a popular prejudice". The quality of the infinite extension of norms is the mark of fully developed, bourgeois legality. As sucn it corresponds clearly to notions of individual autonomy and freedom; and serves to mark off the fully developed form from law in feudal or slave societies, where relations of domination and subordination, legal privilege and immunity serve to deny the universality of legal personality and hence negate the form of law in its fullest extension.

(ii) Law and history

If law is taken as one particular historical mediation or realisation of the juridical relation the problems of "simple reflection" and "super-politicisation" of the economist and voluntarist positions are avoided. I have said that a materialist analysis of law will emphasise a conception of law as a dynamic historical process, through which juridical freedom and equality — the necessary complement to equivalence in "free" exchange — is established and maintained. As such I am opposing in particular those voluntarist analyses of law in which coercion and class power dominate. To such analyses I would counterpose a conception of law which takes as its starting point the idea of legal personality — that is the "average" or abstract person who is constructed in the act of commodity exchange — on the basis of which I counterpose a further elaboration of the conception of law as a mode of organisation and facilitation of capitalist production and commodity circulation. For the command of capital is not established through simple political relations between classes, but in the structure and expansion of commodity production for exchange itself, that is, in the appropriation of subjectivity and the self-expropriation of the free wage labourer in the value relation.

In the *Critique of the Gotha Programme* Marx argued that equal rights at law are in effect no more than equal rights to economic inequality, and that freedom at law is no more than a formal or illusory freedom.[53] This

[53] Karl Marx, "Critique of the Gotha Programme" in *Marx Engels Selected Works in One Volume* (1970) 320.

is not to argue however that law is a simple "ideology" merely appended to the "real" workings of political economy. We have seen in principle at least that in so far as the capitalist mode of production requires the generalised "self-control" of the individual in free exchange as an autonomous commodity owner, the freedom and equivalence of the legal person is necessary to the circulation of commodities as a guarantee of that autonomy. This formal or "abstract" equality is nonetheless a concrete practice, and as such a *real* equality, but it is an equality which is contained within the limits of the value form and expansion of the commodity structure itself. Any negation of that equality — by reproducing in law relations of social or economic superordination/subordination — of course is a denial of equality in exchange.

In so far as this is so, it would seem at least plausible to argue that as the commodity structure of the capitalist mode of production permeates a particular social formation so the tendency in legal development will be towards established juridical equality and formal freedom at law. Historically this process can be identified in English law throughout the period of political and legal reform in the 19th century, and which stretches well into the 20th century.[54]

The significance of such developments should not be overlooked, for, as Engels in one of his brighter moments noted:

> In the industrial world . . . the specific character of economic oppression that weighs down the proletariat stands out in all its sharpness only after all the special legal privileges of the capitalist class have been set aside and the complete juridical equality of both classes is established.[55]

The realisation of juridical equality is thus necessary in so far as the functional requirements and expansion of commodity production and

[54] With the expansion of capitalist commodity production for exchange and the concurrent extension of the value relation as the articulation of social order, we can speak of the historical tendency toward juridical equality. However in so far as this must occur within the history of socially given institutions — the family, the workshop, the state *etc.* — the juridical relation may be expressed — and this is especially true of England — through extremely contradictory forms. Basically this means, to far as the English law is concerned, through the archaic and outmoded institutions of the absolutist state, which, together with its Hobbesian justifications, have hung over and distorted the contemporary history both of the practice and of theory of the English law. Hence the domination in English legal thought — especially in the 19th century — of notions of command, sanction, the absolute power of the sovereign *etc.* as typifying legality. If I had more time I would want to argue that the modern history of the development of English law, spanning the 19th century, bears witness to the struggle to rid law of the constraints of the political institutions of the old order, and to assert the new basis of legality: freedom, reciprocity and consent, *i.e.* the organisational structure of generalised commodity exchange. Thus we see the strictures of Austin on "judicial arbitrarium" and of Dicey on discretion, and on the other hand the emphasis in the work of J.S. Mill and Matthew Arnold upon education and culture, self-control, responsibility and "inner-morality". In so far as the ideas of an epoch speak to its history the movement is from Austin to Hart.

[55] F. Engels, "Origins of the Family, Private Property and the State" in *Marx-Engels Selected Works in One Volume* (1970) 501.

exchange — and the operation of the law of value — demand it. That this ultimately makes visible in the law the disparity between the universal juridical equality of the sphere of circulation, and the social economic inequality of the particular level of the labour process, is the condition which dictates, within the particular history of the institutional and political development of the legal system in question, the subsequent development of the law in response to crises in legitimacy. Thus Gramsci noted the singular vulnerability of the law at such moments, and pointed out:

> . . . how lapses in the administration of justice make an especially disastrous impression on the public: the hegemonic apparatus is more sensitive in this sector, to which arbitrary actions on the part of the police and political administration may also be referred.[56]

Arbitrary and particular acts thus negate the abstract and general form of the law, a negation which goes to the root of both bourgeois morality and legality. The crisis over the Industrial Relations Act might be a case in point.

(iii) Legal Authority

During periods of crisis the expansion of legality and morality through the ethical state is limited, so that:

> the conception of the state as pure force is returned to, the bourgeois class is saturated; it does not only expand, it starts to disintegrate; it does not only not assimilate new elements, it loses part of itself.[57]

At such moments the juridical order of bourgeois society is in crisis, in need of reconstruction; the "legal authority" of the state is questioned if not abandoned, in so far as the implementation of pure force (arbitrary coercion) is the denial of "legality". In this section we shall be concerned to untangle the theoretical determinations of the notion of "legal authority" or "legality" as external to the individual and which in England is particularised in the idea of "the rule of law". To that end this section will seek to establish the theoretical connections between, on the one hand, the forms of bourgeois law — as the concretisation of the juridical relation defining the abstract right and duty bearing juridical subject of civil society — and, on the other, "legal" or "public authority" for which Weber's terms "the legitimate monopoly of coercion" is quite appropriate for the developed capitalist mode of production. For just as the juridical relation in its fullest development is contingent upon the expansion of the commodity structure and in that contingency alone displays its full character, that is, as facilitating the inter-dependencies of independent individuals, so too it will be argued the notion of "legal authority" in its fullest extension rests upon a further mediation of that same juridical relation. To understand this it is necessary to work out some further implications of what has gone before.

[56] Gramsci, *op.cit.*, p. 246.

[57] Gramsci, *ibid.*, p. 260.

We have seen that the juridical relation is crucial to the realisation of generalised commodity exchange within a complex social division of labour. As such it is a relation of juridical subjects — between the "autonomous" individuals of civil society. Such juridical subjects however must be and can only be defined in relation to each other.

The juridical subject as bearer of rights expresses the autonomy of will of the "free" individual in the desire to "alienate as it acquires and acquire as it alienates". The juridical relation is a relation of wills, expressing the formal freedom of commodity exchange. *If this were not so the products of individual labour could not be exchanged as commodities* (see *supra*).

We therefore take the formal freedom of the legal person as the starting point for the analysis of the forms of bourgeois law (contract, property and so on). This however would seem to run against common sense which would be more likely to emphasise objective "duty" and "obligation" imposed by "external" coercion and constraint, rather than the exercise of subjective will and individual autonomy. Obviously it is the case that the law does constrain and in its application may involve the use of coercion, but to declare therefore that law is coercive, to equate law and political domination is to confuse the functions of law, which may be multiple, with its form, and is to be guilty of the empiricism of both vulgar Marxism and the more sophisticated revisionism of for example Karl Renner. Thus Renner, who derives his analysis of law from the labour process, sees domination in a political relation of superordination and subordination, and, by directing attention away from the social relation of the value-form as it is reproduced in and through the juridical relation, manages to "neutralise" the form of law and render it mere technique. It is on the contrary, however, precisely the "objectivity" and "externality" of the legal obligation which when unravelled displays the fetishism of the legal form, wherein the social relation of generalised commodity exchange appears in the "fantastic" form of an external obligation between legal persons.

That a legal duty is the correlative of a legal right is a jurisprudential truism. The real problem then lies in the transformation of the rights of the legal person to appear as the generalised imperative, "authoritative" and external to the individual. The explication of that transformation is to be found as a necessary condition of commodity exchange itself.

We have seen that the magnitude of exchange-value of the commodity is determined according to the quantity of socially necessary labour-time embodied in it, but that it is only in the actual act of exchange that labour is so averaged or equalised to become *abstract* labour. Equalisation of labour can however only occur where the subjects of the exchange appear equal; they must be *seen* to hold an equivalent position. If on the other hand a relation of domination and subordination is apparent in the exchange relation, the presupposition of equivalence, that is, the exchange relation as a relation of wills between free and equal autonomous subjects, is denied. In commodity exchange however, as that which is being exchanged is equated only as an average (that is, a quantity of abstract labour) the material conditions in which the actual production occurred and the particular inequalities in the magnitude of labour-time embodied in the commodity are irrelevant in establishing its exchange-value. By the same token the equivalence ascribed to subjects in the exchange is also merely an abstract equivalence which must equally deny any substantive inequality of the individuals concerned. Thus the appropriation of subjectivity equally requires for its realisation the abstraction/equalisation of the subjects in the act of exchange; this equalisation being expressed, in the abstract as the formal equality of abstract juridical subjects and in practice in the ascription of legal personality. Thus Pashukanis wrote:

> Only with the complete development of bourgeois relationships does the law acquire an abstract character. Each man becomes a man in general, labour of every sort is reduced to socially beneficial labour in general and every subject becomes an abstract juridic subject.[58]

The abstract form of the juridical subject is reproduced in the maxim, "equality before the law", in the representation of parties to disputes through depersonalised advocacy, in certain jurisdictions in the anonymity of the parties and so on.

We have seen that the act of exchange is at once a private and social act (see *supra*). It is through the dual character of the act of exchange that the social *function* of law is revealed, in relation to its form as the concrete expression of the juridical relation.

This twofold character of exchange reveals the double aspect of the legal person, who as an abstract autonomous subject exercises his "private" right of self-determination, but in order to do so however is constrained by the correlative duty — his private rights "being neither more nor less than the obligations of others made secure in his behalf".[59] The exercise of the legal right must be both private and "free" but also socially guaranteed. This requires that the juridical order is expressed as external legal authority, in that the exercise of will must be constrained precisely because commodity exchange is also a necessary social transaction of general character.

However as we have seen, constraint cannot take the form of domination/subordination:

> the more systematic the development of the principle of authoritarian regulation (which excludes any inkling of separate and autonomous will) the less ground there is for the application of the category law . . . [for] exchange value ceases to be exchange value, commodities cease to be commodities if the exchange-ratio is determined by authority situated outside the inherent laws of the market. Constraint as the command of one person addressed to another and confirmed by force contradicts the conditions precedent to the intercourse of commodity possessors.[60]

[58] Babb and Hazard, *op.cit.*, p. 169.

[59] Babb and Hazard, *op.cit.*, p. 155.

[60] *Ibid.*, p. 154.

In this case, in so far as constraint is a necessary aspect of commodity exchange itself, it cannot be expressed as a unilateral and *particular* power of command of either party to the exchange, for this would be to deny the presupposition of equivalence. Constraint is thus necessarily conceived of as the exercise of the abstract will (the general will) of the law making body which in turn appears as *universal* legal personality (the state) with rights *vis-à-vis* juridic subjects in general. Such rights are expressed as external obligations, and as imperatives in the general norms of private law. Further, in so far as that universal personality has rights made good in the obligations of others, it may have correlative duties in the norms of public law and limitations of its law-making powers. In that sense the democratic state in which the individual is transformed to become the abstract will is the natural complement to legal authority, the political form of "representation" being a further mediation of the juridical relation — hence the full significance of theories of the social contract. Thus Marx wrote in *The German Ideology* of the problems faced by theorists of law:

> In actual history, those theoreticians who regarded power as the basis of law were in direct contradiction to those who looked on will as the basis of law . . . If power is taken as the basis of law, as Hobbes *etc.* do, then law, statute *etc.* are merely the symptom, the expression of *other* relations upon which the state power rests. The material life of individuals, which by no means merely depends on their "will", their mode of production and form of intercourse, which mutually determine each other — this is the real basis of the state and remains so at all the stages at which division of labour and private property are still necessary, quite independently of the *will* of individuals. These actual relations are in no way created by the state power; on the contrary they are the power creating it. *The individuals who rule in these conditions, besides having to constitute their power in the form of the state, have to give their will which is determined by these definite conditions, a universal expression as the will of the state,* as statute — an expression whose content is always determined by the relation of this class, as the civil and criminal law demonstrate in the clearest possible way. Just as the weight of their bodies does not depend on their idealistic will or their arbitrary decision, so also the fact that they enforce their own will in the form of statute and at the same time make it independent of the personal arbitrariness of each individual among them, does not depend on their idealistic will. *Their personal rule must at the same time be constituted as average rule. Their personal power is based on conditions of life which as they develop are common to many individuals, and the continuance of which they, as ruling individuals, have to maintain against others, and at the same time, maintain that they hold good for all.* [61]

The universality of the general norm is but the reverse side of commodity fetishism. In Colletti's words, exchange value, the phenomenal form of abstract labour, presents "subjective human labour . . . in the form of a quality intrinsic in things; these things themselves, endowed with their own subjective social qualities, appear 'personified' or 'animated' as if they were independent subjects". It is in this "exchange of the subjective with the objective and *vice versa* in which the fetishism of commodities exists".[62]

[61] Marx and Engels, "The German Ideology III" in *Karl Marx, Economy, Class and Social Revolution* (1974) 270. (Emphasis added.)

[62] Colletti, *op.cit.*, p. 41.

Just so, in the juridical relation, in equalisation and abstraction, the juridical subject appears as the bearer independently of his will of rights and duties ascribed to him in the objective legal norm. He has become the predicate of a universal subject, which has the power of command over him — a government of laws, not of men". Thus it is that the mediation of commodity exchange requires the abstraction and generality of norms issued by "authority" outside and above bourgeois society, that is, the state as universal legal person.

Throughout I have emphasised that the extent and particular realisation of the juridical relation is dependent upon the historical development of the economic social formation in question. It is useful here to return to Poulantzas' typification of law mentioned earlier, in which Poulantzas emphasises not only generality and abstraction, but also formalism and systematisation of norms as witnessing the quality of law. It would seem indisputable in the light of the argument above that abstraction and generality are necessary dimensions of bourgeois law, in so far as abstract and general rules are to be applied to an infinite number of particular cases. Systematisation and formalism however are no more than an historically particular mode of expression of these two necessary elements of bourgeois legality, and not necessary elements in themselves. Indeed it would seem justifiable to argue that the greater the formalisation and systematisation of the law in technique and institutions, the greater will be the apparent contradiction between the formal freedom in the sphere of circulation and the subordination of the labour process. It is no surprise that Max Weber, writing of the highly formalised German law at the beginning of the 20th century, should have pinpointed this contradiction with crystal clarity:

> The democratic ethos, where it pervades the masses in connexion with a concrete question, based as it is upon the postulate of substantive justice in concrete cases for concrete individuals, inevitably comes into conflict with the formalism and rule-bound objectives of bureaucratic administration. For this reason it must emotionally reject what is rationally demanded. The propertyless classes in particular are not benefited in the way in which bourgeois are, by "formal" legal equality and calculable adjudication and administration.[63]

It was of course Weber's error to have identified civilian legal systems as the very apotheosis of bourgeois legality. On the contrary; in the sense that by its very systematisation and formalism law is prevented from fulfilling its social function — that is the facilitation of commodity exchange and production — codification and rational formalism in legal method represents a low point in the development of bourgeois legality. In that sense the English legal system represents a much more highly developed system of bourgeois legal administration precisely because it is not systematically limited in its application. It seems at least arguable that formal limitations placed upon the law-making body, which attribute to it its universality as abstract juridical subject, are displaced in the English system where the universality of the legislature and judiciary is created and recreated through that

[63] Max Weber in *Law in Economy and Society* (ed. Max Rheinstein, 1954) 355.

"peculiarly English" admixture of ritual symbolism which pervades our legislature and judicial practice. It is precisely the flexibility and pragmatism embodied in the common law of England, which, whilst providing the necessary frame of generality and abstraction, allows the maintenance of the appearance of justice and the belief that law holds good for all. To that extent it is true that "all law is nothing more nor less than a gigantic confidence trick".

RICHARD KINSEY*

*Department of Jurisprudence, University of Edinburgh.

Part IV
Contemporary Issues

[12]

Acta Juridica Academiae Scientiarum Hungaricae, Tomus 18, (3–4), pp. 263–272 (1976)

The Notion of Law

by

Prof. I. SZABÓ

Director

Institute for Legal and Administrative Sciences of the Hungarian Academy of Sciences

The author of the present study sets out from the thesis that the search for a notion of law is an unbroken, yet not uniform process. He then proceeds with the description and critique of some of the principal concepts of the theory of law in the historical sequence. He marshals his principal arguments against the Neo-Kantian school of the theory of law, challenges the tendencies following in the wake of Neo-Kantianism, in the first place the various manifestations of normativism and the doctrines of logic of law.

For that matter he argues with the normative school of socialist law, and in the first place with Vyshinsky. On dissociating himself from those considering the sociology of law the veritable theory of law he believes that law should be approached from the social aspect, and that the Marxist-Leninist theory of State and law should also be developed in this sense in order to bypass the normative doctrine. The Marxist-Leninist theory of law should rely on the fact as its basis that law is a social relation having definite ties with other social relations. It is built upon the production relations and is integrated into the social relations associated with the superstructure.

1. We are often apt to speak in jest of jurisprudence as a discipline time and again reverting to the search for a notion of law and to giving the definition of this notion. Yet there is nothing peculiar or extraordinary in all this: it is quite natural that all sciences should cast a light into the depth of their subject-matter, to explore its substance as good as it can, and in this course continually to enrich the notion of the subject under study with ever more and ever newer factors, to extend the scope of this subject and to improve its definition. On this understanding and viewed from this angle jurisprudence is but a round in the unbroken scientific struggle for the elucidation of the essence of law.

It is an unbroken, yet not uniform process. The path of deliberations directed at the definition of the notion of law is meandering and in the process itself a variety of often contradicting traits and trends may be discovered. The history of jurisprudence and of the theory of law is but an analysis of the path theory has so far covered in the study of the notion of law. This analysis is still going on. The analysis of the principal traits of this path, including its detours and error, from the other standpoint, is the analysis of the state in which this path continues its course together with its various trends.

2. A difference, in a certain sense a fundamental one, in the domain of theory exists in the approach to the notion of law in the sharp line drawn in the differentiation of the law between signs of contents and formal signs. When Kant described the law as the reconciliation of the freedom of one man with that of

another man, he offered a relatively notional definition of the law. Still this definition may be considered one of contents rather than a formal one, a definition which aimed at the essence of law and where Kant was, though by correlating human relations, in search for the notion of the contents of the essence of law.

Some of his followers took a different course. In any case in a point of vital importance they differed radically from Kant. The school giving itself the name of Neo-Kantians, by strongly emphasizing the anti-Marxist edge of the watchword "back to Kant", definitely abandoned even an attempt to offer a definition of the contents of law. The only Kantian element which they preserved was the distinction Kant made between form and substance, contents and form. The followers, the Neo-Kantian philosophers of law unambiguously placed the law on the side of form and so they contrasted the essence with the material contents.

3. The protagonist of the Neo-Kantian theory of law, Rudolf Stammler, in his work "*Wirtschaft und Recht in der materialistischen Auffassung*"[1] and also subsequently, made a definite distinction between the social contents and the legal form, and this in a way that he drew the line between "social economy" and "coexistence", i.e. briefly between economy and law by considering their true interrelations the other way round. There is no doubt that the relation between them is that of form and substance, and that in this interrelation law and legal rules stand for the notion of the form as contrasted to substance. So far there is nothing wrong with what Stammler brings forward. Still as regards the sequence, the defining and the defined element in this relation Stammler writes „... daß im logischen Rangverhältnisse die *Rechtsbegriffe* die notwendige Voraussetzung der *sozialwissenschaftlichen Vorstellungen* sind. Es gibt keinen *sozialwissenschaftlichen* Begriff, der sich nicht auf *rechtliche* Begriffe, als seine *logisch bedingenden* Elemente zurückführen ließe". He then continues: „Darum können Rechtsbegriffe, in denen wir diese bedingende Regelung fassen, von *wirtschaftlichen* Erwägungen nicht abhängig sein. Jene sind die logischen Bedingungen der letzteren, aber nicht umgekehrt."[2]

Hence the response of Neo-Kantianism to Marxism reads as follows: Economy is in fact connected to law, yet it is not economy that is the determining factor, the factor which, in the last resort, governs also law. Law is the factor determining economy, too, for it is also the form of economy, or in a more policy-making generalization it is not the form that is eventually defined by the content, but it is the content that is defined by the form. Finally the conclusion suggests itself that law is but a form and in its formalness it defines economy, digs a channel for the content, and keeps the content in bounds. Law on the other hand is but a rule or a norm, a norm keeping the content within precise bounds, or a system of these bounds.

[1] STAMMLER, R.: *Wirtschaft und Recht in der materialistischen Auffassung.*
[2] STAMMLER, R.: *Theorie der Rechtswissenschaft,* Halle, 1911. pp. 307—309

This latter idea has been adopted and made the focal point among others by what is called the normative school. This school has explicitly moved this factor to the focal point, conceived law exclusively as a norm, and laid the stress on this concept. „Denn das Recht, der einzige Gegenstand der Rechtserkenntnis, ist Norm;“ „... Vorstellung vom Recht, das man ja gemeinhin nur als ein System genereller Normen betrachtet.“[3]

This school of thought, i.e. the perception of the law as a norm, a perception which was concomitant of the perception as the essential, defining form, subsequently gained a fairly general currency in the theory of law, namely in the theory which mostly relied on law conceived as a norm and placed the norm before the social content. In the theory, law was normally conceived as a norm. Thus e.g. Nawiasky writes: „Die Wissenschaft vom Recht hat also näher qualifizierte Normen zum Gegenstand und gehört demgemäß wie andere Wissenschaften, die sich mit Normen irgendwelcher Art befassen, zu den sogenannten Normenwissenschaften.“[4] The theoretical concomitant of this thesis is the perception of the law as a form, yet a form providing a framework for the social content.

Following upon the classical theory of law as developed by Kant or Hegel jurisprudence in this way turned away from the analysis of the content of law and in the system of social relations conceived law simply as norm, or in other words, considered the external side of the law, its form of appearance, the essence of the law. At the same time it conceived law as a substantial form. Law had become a form-science, contrasted to other social phenomena; however, it was at the same time a determinant, a phenomenon lending a form, therefore logically primordial. In its entirety this concept threw open the path to formalistic jurisprudence, where the external side of law had become essential. Jurisprudence studied the structure of the norm and not its social content, which, it was alleged, was defined by it.

4. Exactly because of the perception of the law as a norm there are attempts to regard jurisprudence as a science of a peculiar, specific character as contrasted to the other social sciences, or at least differing from them. Jurisprudence deals with the external, the form of manifestation of the social phenomena, the guise of manifestation. If the law, too, were a social phenomenon, the statement could be made that various sciences corresponded to various social phenomena, so law could be understood as the form of phenomena, for that matter as a by itself normative form, and discussed accordingly. Nor is the sociological treatment of law wholly precluded, still in this case it is to be feared that the form might be ignored. In the light of these two contingent approaches Max Weber as the scholar of sociological jurisprudence is contrasted to Hans Kelsen as the scholar dealing with the law as "legal" jurisprudence and setting the legal form, viz. the norm in the focal point.[5]

[3] Kelsen, H.: *Reine Rechtslehre.* Wien, 1934. pp. 6, 108

[4] Nawiasky, H.: *Allgemeine Rechtslehre.* Köln, 1941. p. 2.

[5] See Rheinstein, M.: *Einführung in die Rechtsvergleichung.* München, 1974. p. 146

Yet has not a social phenomenon its single science through the agency of which we could have a grasp of the substance of the phenomenon? Is it merely a contingency of approach that we consider law in the first place a social phenomenon or a norm, and approach it from the one or the other aspect? As for its substance is not the law a social phenomenon whose existence can be grasped exactly by legal social science and not by a formalistic jurisprudence of a specific kind, departing from all other social sciences and analysing the norm and its structure only? Is normative jurisprudence as conceived by Kelsen, ignoring the content of law, showing an interest only in the logical structure of the norm and barring any other "metajuristic" elements from jurisprudence, capable of exploring the substance of law apart from its external appearance? Ought not the science exploring the substance of law to be in all cases a social science? (Not in all cases something today given the name of sociology of law, yet in any case a legal social science.) In our opinion the substance of law can be explored by a single science only, viz. the social theory of law. This is what this author has tried to demonstrate in his work "*Les fondements de la théorie du droit*".[6]

Therefore it is the function of the theory of law going into the depths of the substance (and a theory of this kind is the Marxist-Leninist) to break away from any formal approach to the law, an approach manifesting itself in the reduction of the law to the norm, the rule. The theory of law as conceived here has to return to the substance of law, i.e. to the recognition of the social character of the law, or in other words, it has to become in any case a theory of the content of law. Even if the law appears in the guise of norms of rules, it is the function of the theory of law to reach beyond these norms and explore their determinants and their content.

5. This is what the Marxist-Leninist theory of law has embarked on. Accordingly the substance of the legal relation (and this is the central element in law and not the norm) has to be sought outside the law, in the production relations. In reality law is a superstructure, i.e. governed by other social relations. What remains the truth is that the social substance, i.e. the production relations determine the substance of the form, namely of law, i.e. the superstructure of law and also its secondariness, and not what the Neo-Kantian school with its normativism proclaims, that it is the form, i.e. the superstructure which lends its form to the substance and therefore it is logically the primary. Now what remains is to get out of Neo-Kantian stocks which squeezes law into the narrow framework of the norms and identifies law exclusively with the norm.

It was with this intention that Marxist-Leninist jurisprudence embarked on this work in 1917, viz. the creation a Marxist-Leninist theory of law going into the very details. The Great October Revolution threw open the gates also to the elaboration of a new theory of law. This theory then tried to break away from the purely formal perception of law. In fact, law is by itself an autonomous social

[6] Szabó, I.: *Les fondaments de la théorie du droit*. Budapest, 1973

relationship, when at the same time it is the expression also of other social relationships. The new theory of law also tried to dissociate itself from the concept of law as a pure norm, and so also from the exclusive study of the legal structure.

These attempts in a number of directions (in fact the first tendencies could be considered but attempts) dragged on till 1938, and the disputes which flared up simultaneously with them were particularly lively in the first decade following upon the revolution.

6. In 1938, in the first all-union congress convened to discuss the problems of Soviet jurisprudence and political sciences A.Y. Vyshinsky laid down the foundations of the new socialist school of the theory of law, which he regarded as an exclusively socialist theory. At that time the attitude of Vyshinsky might have appeared as appropriate, still today it is useful to revise the teachings of the then new school. Although Vyshinsky himself emphatically protested against his doctrine's being regarded as normativism, nevertheless it was but a kind of a new-type, one may even say, socialist normativism. Any kind of normativism, however, is in the concept of law of necessity formal. It was in vain that Vyshinsky laid stress on the determining role of the production relations, these were left in the cold by the normativist-formalistic formulation: society did not penetrate it.

This normativist concept started by Vyshinsky came to be recognized throughout the Soviet Union. In 1945 it began to spread also in the popular democracies.[7] From the writings of this time it stood out clearly that in the opinion of their authors, law was substantially a norm, i.e. the fundamental nature of the law was its being a form. The normativist concept of law was dominant in the socialist world.

Vyshinsky conceived the theory of law as something wholly independent of the concrete content of the law or branches of law.[8] Yet can law be independent of its content, or still better, can it be independent at all unless we conceive law in its generality as a mere form? Vyshinsky wrote that his definition of the notion of law (which meant the totality of the rules or norms of conduct)[9] was based on the relations of dominion and subordination finding expression in the law.[10] Still is law this, or exactly only this? Undoubtedly, Vyshinsky frequently emphasized the social determinedness of the law, still the definition he offered was in the last resort a normativist one. He regarded law as a norm and this meant that law was merely

[7] So e.g. the works recently published in the *Soviet Union*: Марксистко-ленинская общая теория государства и права (The Marxist-Leninist general theory of state and law). Vol. I. Moscow, 1970. pp. 387 et seq.; in *Czechoslovakia*: Boguszek, J.: *Teoria státu a práva* (Theory of State and Law). Part I. Praha, 1967. p. 278; in *Hungary*: Anntalffy-Samu-Szabó-Szotáczky: *Állam- és jogelmélet* (Theory of state and law). Budapest, 1970. p. 349; in *Poland*: Opalek-Wroblewski: *Zagadnenia teorii prawa* (Questions of the theory of Law). Warszawa, 1969. p. 38, etc.

[8] Вопросы теории государства и права (Questions of the theory of state and law). 2nd ed., Moscow, 1949. p. 74

[9] Op.cit. p. 84

[10] Op.cit. p. 5

a form, void of any social substance. As has already been said, in this he was followed and is still being followed everywhere in the socialist countries.

7. Everyday legal thinking, even in the socialist countries, sets out from the thesis that for any legally regulated human behaviour the primary factor is the existence of some sort of legal regulation, i.e. a certain norm. This is therefore the starting point and at the same time the basis. This norm is then observed in practice by legal relations, i.e. by the relations and behaviours of particular persons. In reality, however, this is but one aspect of the social interrelations, notably the aspect which reaches from the norms to the behaviours. Still how do the norms come into being, i.e. what was there before the norms and what leads to them?

Lenin writes in *"State and Revolution"* that law is the regulator (determinant) of the distribution of products and work.[11] Therefore first come the relations of work and distribution (here Lenin resolves the relations in their totality called economic), which stand in the first place, and which call for regulation. These relations are followed by the system of norms, i.e. the definition of the manner of regulation. There are undoubtedly social relationships (such as ownership relations, employment, family relations, etc.) which invariably precede the norm. The norm is merely an intermediate link between certain in a general way viewed social relations and individual relations. It might even be said that the norm defines the manner of the individual manifestation of general relations.

8. The reduction of the law to a norm may amount to a peculiar kind of "jurisprudence", in any way to a certain type of "legal method". Still if jurisprudence is reduced to the method, it can never offer an answer to the question of the substance of law, i.e. of its social determinedness. An answer has, however, been given to the question of the structure of law, and mainly of the legal norm, yet not of the content of law. This question can be answered only by a theory which sets out from society and through the law returns to society, but now to its form atomized to individuals. In our opinion in this way the theory of law can be of a sociological character only. This follows from what has been set forth. Still here we cannot go into further details.

9. Vyshinsky by making normativism of general validity in the Marxist-Leninist theory of law returned in fact, to the Neo-Kantian trend in the theory of law, or more accurately he was unable to go beyond it, however often he repeated the watchword "socialist" by the side of the norm. A contemporary task for the Marxist-Leninist theory of law is to get beyond the normative concept of law, to find its way to the genuine, substantial and social theory of the law, and to define the place the law has to occupy in the system of social relationships.

The rather smooth approach to the normativist theory of law and its relative lucidity cannot be argued. This theory offers a simple interpretation of law when it approaches it from the formal-structural and not from the social aspect. Naturally

[11] Сочинения (Works). Vol. 25. Moscow, 1949. p. 439

the norm, and so behaviour in so far as it is general, are already certain features of society: the norm, too, is product of society. Still what is mere appearance in the normative concept is that law tells in beforehand what human behaviour should be adopted. Yet why should it be this way, and not the other, why so and not otherwise, why is the norm such a "standard", and why is not the standard something else?[12] In Samoshtchenko's view the form of law is, in the objective sense, the legal norm; this is again an indication of the correlation, respectively, identity of the normative and formal constituents. The statement that law is regulation is by itself far from telling the whole story. It stands to reason that in the search for the substance of the law we have to go further, and it does not suffice to approach this substance from the world of norms. On this normative path namely we shall in all cases come closer only to the form of law, but never to its substance.

The statement that in the latter decades the Marxist-Leninist theory of State and law has come to a standstill at Vyshinsky's normativism is by no means an exaggeration. This normativism of Vyshinsky is even in its socialist guise a kind of survival of Neo-Kantianism. Even when it will become harder to grasp the substance of the law, theory will at last have to get beyond this socialist version of Neo-Kantianism. Briefly, the rule of normativism must be put to an end in the socialist theory of law.

10. To bring about a turn of such an extent in a definite trend in the theory of law, in particular in a closed theory of law like what the Marxist-Leninist theory is, is by no means a task easy to tackle. Considerable resistance will have to be overcome because of the general reluctance to depart from a superficially simpler concept. Still progress cannot stop at a definite point.

Even bourgeois jurisprudence consistently adhering to the normativist standpoint has not come to a standstill at this concept: the extraordinary growth of legal logic during the latter decades is sufficiently known. Although there are tendencies which conceive legal logic as a formal science as contrasted to sciences dealing with the essence of things, authors writing on the logic of law stand up against these tendencies, when as far as the structure of law is concerned they discover in legal logic the means creating clarity and move deontology closer to the theory of law.[13] There are authors according to whom legal logic is equally useful for the normative and the sociological concept of law.[14] This is obviously an arbitrary assumption, since as for its substance legal logic is a logic of norms, whatever may be brought forward against this thesis.

[12] According to Samoshchenko in the objective sense the norm is the form of the law; this too, is an indication of the intertwining and assimilation of the normative and the formal. See: Братусь, С. Н. — Самощенко, И. С.: Теоретические вопросы систематизации советского законодательства (Theoretical problems of the systematization of Soviet legislation). Moscow, 1962. p. 32

[13] WEINBERGER, O.: *Rechtslogik.* Wien-New York, 1970; CORNIDES, TH.: *Ordinale Deontik.* Wien-New York, 1974.

[14] See e.g. WROBLEWSKI, J.: *Normativity of legal science* in: *Etudes de logique juridique.* Vol. I, Bruxelles, 1966. pp. 60 et seq.

Modern logic of law, in the first place deontology, is but the straight continuation of the legal doctrine of norms, a school carrying the legal doctrine of norms further, expanding it, and rendering it even more speculative. At the same time legal logic, in its present form, is the modern transcendence of the normativist concept. The centre of legal logic is the norm and the normative concept throughout. Rightly therefore logic of law may in a certain sense be considered the modern continuation of the normative concept.

11. The Marxist theory of law, as a matter of course, has to turn against this transmutation of the concept of law into logical speculations of the slipping of jurisprudence into the realm of logic. The unequivocal reply of the Marxist-Leninist theory as regards the substance of law makes it clear that since law is fundamentally a social phenomenon, therefore it has to turn to the social sciences and not to logic, jurisprudence being a social science.

It should be added that modern legal sociology is not a social science in the strict meaning of the term, for it does not get as far as society or a phenomenon of it, viz. the substance of law. It is not even in search for this substance, it stops on the surface of the legal phenomena. It is overwhelmingly pure empiricism and deals with the empirical study and description of legal phenomena. Modern sociology of law is not identical with the earlier, traditional sociology of law, the sociology of law as cultivated by Ehrlich in his times. Although this author disagrees with his views it should be left not unmentioned that he advanced on the path of sociology at all times in the search for the substance of law. His famous fundamental thesis which he has brought forward in the foreword of his work and which has become the cardinal truth of any sociology of law is well known: „Der Schwerpunkt der Rechtsentwicklung liege auch in unserer Zeit wie zu allen Zeiten weder in der Gesetzgebung, noch in der Jurisprudenz, oder in der Rechtsprechung, sondern in der Gesellschaft selbst.“[15]

As regards the putting of the fundamental question strictly speaking the Marxist-Leninist theory of law ought to return to the sociology of law in its genuine form, i. e. it should go on living as a discipline looking for the substance of law in its social determinedness and also finding it there. It is almost immaterial whether or not this branch of science is given the designation of legal sociology or theory of law. As has already been indicated, in this connexion we think and speak of the theory of law as the social theory of law. This decided turn towards sociology is in our opinion the next, overdue step of the Marxist-Leninist theory of law. In any case this is the direction in which the Marxist-Leninist theory of law will presumably advance. This is at the same time and mainly equal to the breaking away from formalism and the taking up of a definite stand against formalistic legal logic as the continuation of normativism, on the whole a radical departure from it.

12. If the Marxist theory of law finds it difficult to part with the so simple and attractive normativism (as a matter of fact, every law manifests itself externally in

[15] EHRLICH, E.: *Grundlegung der Soziologie des Rechts.* München-Leipzig, 1913. Vorrede.

norms), how more difficult this will be for statutory law. In statutory law its scope or its domain is from the outset defined by a single group of norms, to which the practice of applying these norms ensues. Eventually it may be assumed that as regards statutory law the situation is much the same as in the theory of law, moreover from a certain standpoint even one easier to handle.

Civil law, criminal law, constitutional law, family law, etc. deal namely unarguably and quite clearly with each a social relation of definite content and definite scope, and are the legal consequences and the expression of these relations. Anything which is before the norm will become in these relations quite clear and segregated by clear outlines from the generality of the law. Could not these relations be analysed in their social determinedness before there was a law? Is not this a function of jurisprudence, and then to explore the consequences exactly of the social determinedness in the treasure of norms built upon this analysis and relating to it in a way that this treasure of norms eventually finds expression in individual legal relations? Could not the particular branches of law create sociologies of their own, or at least in this direction try to obtain a reply to the fundamental problems of the respective branch of law?

In this way the breaking away from the normativist concept is the function not only of the theory of law, which discharges this function for the law as a whole. It is at the same time the function of every branch of law and therefore also of jurisprudence. As a matter of fact, theory of law and branches of jurisprudence are in the last resort homogeneous, they are equally social and legal sciences.

It appears as if we must advance further, in jurisprudence as a whole, in the general as well as special, and to return to the idea that this is a process which cannot be completed at a single stroke. In all likelihood all we can do at present is to begin the search in this direction in order that later we might appear on the scene with a new Marxist-Leninist concept of jurisprudence.

13. In any event already at present we may accept as fact that the fundamental error of Vyshinsky's normativism may be explained by the Neo-Kantian influence. Neo-Kantianism is in reality the substance of Vyshinsky's concept of law.

It remains also a fact that as regards the practical existence of law sociological research is overdue not only in jurisprudence, but also in research in the substance of the law, moreover of the particular branches of the law.

Finally, owing exactly to the substance of Marxism, a sociological character has to be given to the Marxist-Leninist theory of law, and this not in the modern fashionable empiric sense of sociology, but in its deepest sense, in the meaning it has in the social sciences.

In our opinion new pathways have been opened up before the development of the Marxist-Leninist theory of law. Still in order to make headway on these new pathways we have to subject to criticism the former, the old, unrelentingly and have to go out in search for the new pathways more courageously than before. This is the principal function of the Marxist-Leninist theory of law in our days.

[13]

LAW AND MORALITY FROM A MARXIST POINT OF VIEW

By Wiesław Lang, Toruń/Polen

There are three preliminary questions which should be made clear at the very beginning of the discussion: 1. What do I mean by a Marxist point of view, 2. what do I mean by law and morality? What problems will be discussed in this paper?

1. I mean by a Marxist point of view in legal and moral theory any theoretical insight into the nature of law and morality inspired by the Marxist philosophical tradition. There are, of course, actually different trends in Marxist philosophy. I should like to discuss my topic from the point of view of the contemporary Marxist-Leninist theory. I assume that the most fundamental concepts and ideas of this theory are well-known. I see no need to repeat the basic Marxist views on law and morality. I shall try to show in my paper how the Marxist approach to law and morality can elucidate the fundamental problems concerning the relations between these two basic forms of social control. I shall also try to prove that the acceptance of the basic views of the Marxist-Leninist theory leads to some very significant and not trivial consequences in legal and moral philosophy.

2. The second preliminary question I have to answer is the question of the definition of law and morality.

I do not intend to give any strict definitions. I think that for the purpose of this paper it will be enough to frame and delineate in a very rudimentary way the field and the object of my inquiry.

I mean by the law in a narrow sense (legal system), a body of general rules and patterns of conduct (both substantive and procedural) enacted, authorised and enforced by the state's agencies. That is what the lawyers usually have in mind, when they use the term "law" (if they are not sophisticated philosophers of law). I shall mean by the legal order a cultural phenomenon consisting of following elements:

a) Legal system as a body of rules of conduct.
b) Legal profession as a distinct social group.
c) Legal doctrine as a specific ideology produced by lawyers and legal scholars.
d) A system of legal education.
e) A set of social practices relevant to legal rules and legal doctrine.

All these elements are mutually interrelated in different ways within the structure of the social order.

I mean by morality a body of general rules, standards and directives of human conduct based upon the concepts of "right" and "good". These rules and standards are accepted in a society or a social group as the guidelines for choosing, evaluating and criticising the courses of action and social practices. They are also reasons for moral judgments and motives of conduct.

I shall also use, sometimes, the term "ethics". I shall mean by ethics a rational normative theory of justice, goodness or rightness, providing the reasons and guidelines for choosing or criticizing the rules of conduct, rules of preferences and standards of moral judgments.

The term "morality" is also used in a broader sense (as "morals"). It means a complex of the following elements:

1. the standards and rules of conduct (as featured above),
2. the relevant moral doctrine justifying and systematizing these rules and standards,
3. a set of relevant social practices.

These characteristics of law and morality are not very precise and they do not satisfy the requirements of a Marxist theory. But in order to concentrate our discussion on the important issues I propose as a starting point, such preliminary clarifications which seem to be the least controversial and the most consistent with common sense and the intuitive understanding of these terms. I am aware that the characterization presented above does not provide us with the criteria of a threshold and comprehensive classification of all possible norms of human conduct into the three categories: a) legal norms, b) moral norms, c) other norms.

The listed features of law and morality are also not sufficient for making a clear-cut distinction between a legal and a moral rule in every possible situation. But such a distinction is not necessary for my inquiry.

I shall not discuss in this paper the problem of the separation of law and morality on the level of theoretical analysis, or in moral or legal discourse. The proposed characterization makes possible a bare distinction of law and morality, when we are contrasting these two notions as two opposite forms of normative order. But such a distinction is not identical with the logical classification of the norms of conduct. This characterization seems to be helpful in distinguishing of legal and moral norms in most typical situations occurring in contemporary societies. And I think that it will be sufficient for the purpose of this inquiry.

3. The relations and interdependencies between law and morality are very complicated problems involving many controversial standpoints and

views. The least controversial point of different contemporary theories of Law and Morals is the view that legal Order is always linked with some kind of Morality. Almost all students of legal and moral philosophy agree that the law enforces and implements the basic values and standards of the so called public morality. A legal order implies also some essential values of public morality which are not enforced by law and some of them are even not enforceable by the law (the ideals of personal excellence such as generosity, courage, frankness and so on). Also such values (virtues) of a perfectionist ethics are not legally irrelevant if they are the elements of the public morality. They usually do not constitute the ground for legal responsibility, but they are relevant when motives are taken into account as they are on occasion in the administration of justice e. g. sentencing.

There is also a common opinion of the students of Law that the scope of possible human conducts which are relevant from a moral point of view is in almost all cultures much broader than is the scope of the conducts regulated by Law.

I do not intend to give a comprehensive survey of these problems nor to discuss from a Marxist point of view all important questions relevant to this topic.

I choose for my inquiry only one problem which seems to me very important for the Marxist theory. Namely, the controversial question of *the moral neutrality or moral content of the notion of law and legal order*. And I shall try to expose the possible ethical and metaethical consequences of a Marxist view.

The controversy concerning the moral neutrality of the notion of law can be formulated as the controversy between the two following sets of statements.

1. The notion of law has no moral content nor moral significance. It is a purely technical or instrumental concept of social control. This view does not deny that law can have some substantial connections with morality or it may be the object of a moral judgment. It contends only that, a) legal orders need have no moral content or b) a legal order may have any content, because the range of values enforceable by law is unlimited. In both cases the notion of law may be the explicated without any reference to moral notions[1].

2. The notion of law is an ethical and moral loaded notion. It has positive ethical significance and implies some moral values (such as goodness, rightness, fairness, justice). Law must be good enough from a moral point

[1] *H. Kelsen*, "General Theory of State and Law", Harvard 1949; *H. Kelsen*, "What is Justice?", Berkeley, California 1957; *L. A. Hart*, "Positivism and the separation of Law and Morals", Harvard Law Review 71/1957 - 58; *L. A. Hart*, "The Concept of Law", Oxford 1963, p. 195 - 207.

of view to be law at all. Every legal order must meet some moral requirements to be considered as legal order, because some moral values are intrinsic to law. The range of values which can be implied, implemented or enforced by law is substantially limited. The legal qualification of human conduct can have by itself a genuine moral significance[2].

These two sets of statements have been formulated as contradictory views concerning the nature of law and the controversy is considered as fundamental dispute between natural law theory and legal positivism[3]. I shall try to prove that this controversy formulated in such an abstract way is apparent or meaningless.

These two groups of statements are contradictory views only on the level of a specific kind of discourse, but in many instances of legal, moral or sociological discourse they are really not incompatible statements.

In order to discover the real nature of this alleged controversy we must realize clearly that the controversial statements about the moral content of the notion of law can have quite different meanings.

They can be understood as *ethical or as metaethical propositions.*

I. Ethical interpretation of the controversy

A. 1. Law implies or enforces some values which are good moral values.

2. Law does not imply or enforce any good moral values.
   a) The values enforced or implied by Law are morally bad.
   b) The values enforced by Law are morally irrelevant (neither good nor bad).

B. 1. Law enforces moral values which are good in reference to a definite system (P).

2. Law enforces moral values which are bad in reference to a definite system (P).

3. Law enforces moral value which are irrelevant in reference to a definite system (P).

C. 1. Law enforces moral values which are good moral values in reference to system P.

2. Law enforces moral values which are not good values in reference to System S. (The values which are morally good within the System P are morally bad or irrelevant values within the System S).

[2] *L. Fuller*, "The Morality of Law", New Haven, Yale University Press 1964.

[3] *L. A. Hart*, "Positivism ..." (see note 1), *Lon. L. Fuller*, "Positivism and Fidelity to Law — a Reply to Professor Hart", 71 Harvard Law Review 593 (1958).

II. Metaethical interpretation

A. 1. Law implies or enforces some values which in all or at least in some cultures are considered as moral values (as morally relevant values).

2. Law implies or enforces values which in no culture are considered as moral values. (Law enforces values which in all moralities are considered as morally irrelevant values — values which could be qualified neither as good nor as bad.).

B. 1. Law implies or enforces some moral values which in all moralities or cultures are considered as positive values.

2. Law does not imply or enforce any values, which in all cultures or moralities are considered as positive moral values.

a) Law implies or enforces the values which in no culture or morality are considered as positive moral values.

b) The values implied or enforced by Law are only in some cultures or moralities considered as positive moral values.

C. 1. Law enforces moral values which are considered as positive moral values according to ethical system P.

2. Law enforces values which are considered as negative moral values according to System P.

3. Law enforces moral values which are considered as neither good nor bad within the System P (values morally irrelevant within the System P).

D. 1. Law enforces values which are considered as good moral values according to System P.

2. Law enforces the values which are considered as not good according to System S (The values enforced by Law are considered as morally good within the System P and as morally negative or morally irrelevant values within the System S).

The view that Law implies or enforces some moral values does not mean that every single legal norm (within a definite legal system) is morally relevant or value loaded.

The ethical interpretation in version B and C makes the implicit assumption, that normative systems to which the propositions about the moral value of Law are referred (P or S), are morally good systems. This assumption provides good reason for the derivation of a deontological conclusion of the statement that Law is a positive value-loaded concept. The moral obligation to obey the Law is derived from the moral goodness of Law (within a definite ethical system). Metaethical statements are purely empirical propositions. Metaethical interpretation makes no assumption concerning moral goodness of the system to which the ethical propositions on moral value of Law are referred. No deontological consequences (concerning the duty of obedience to Law) can be drawn from these propositions.

The presented above analysis of the ethical and metaethical interpretation of the controversy on the moral content of Law proves, that the sphere of real controversies are rather limited.

The ethical controversies between normative propositions which are not referred to any system of values cannot be reasonably settled. The propositions which are related to the different systems of values are in fact not contradictory statements. The only ethical contradictory propositions are the controversial ethical judgements (on moral value of Law) referred to the same system of values. But this controversy concerns the interpretation of the referred system of values and can be also settled in the metaethical discourse.

It seems that there can be no real theoretical controversy as far as concerns ethical propositions on the moral content of Law. It will be reasonable to suppose that also between ethical and metaethical views there can be no theoretical controversy because they belong to different levels of discourse. The relations between ethical and metaethical statements is very complicated and disputable. The ethical propositions and doctrines are used as empirical material to prove or to falsify the metaethical theories. The content of the ethical propositions can be used as an argument for the verification, modification or falsification of a metaethical theory[4]. Metaethics provides some recommendations for normative ethics, which can be used as arguments or reasons in ethical discourse. They can have substantial impact on the formulation of ethical propositions. But it seems to me that it would be misleading to say, that it can be theoretical controversy between an ethical doctrine and a metaethical theory. And it does not make sense to say that ethical and metaethical propositions can be discussed as contradictory statements. It seems to me that a theoretical controversy in a proper sense may exist only on the metaethical level of discourse. Only some metaethical propositions concerning the moral significance on the notion of Law can be considered as controversial views (or as really contradictory statements). How two questions can be made clear:

1. The problem of the moral neutrality of Law is not identical with the question of the separation of Law and Morals neither in ethical nor in metaethical plane. The view that Law and Morals are two distinct forms of social control and should be conceptually separated in the process of the interpretation of Law or in the course of sociological investi-

---

[4] See *Alan Gewirth*, "Mind", 1960, vol. 69; *L. W. Summer*, "Ethics", 1967, no. 2, vol. 77, The University of Chicago Press.

gations of legal institutions — does not imply necessarily the view that the notion of Law is morally neutral. Also the view that Law is linked with Morality in the sociological plane does not entail the conclussion that there are some moral values intrinsic to Law.

The identification of these problems seems to be the main source of confusion in the discussion between Hart and Fuller on Law and Morality[5].

2. The view that Law is a morally neutral notion should not be confused with a morally indifferent approach to Law. Bentham and Austin advocated the moral neutrality of the concept of positive Law in order to justify their strong moral criticism of the existing English Law. They criticised this Law from the point of view of the utilitarian ethical theory[6].

The original Marxist theory conceives the law as a mere device of coercion and an oppressive instrument of force used by the dominant class against the oppressed classes of society. In the light of this definition, the notion of law has no intrinsic moral significance and legal order has no moral value. But in some writings of Marx, Engels and Lenin and in Marxist-Leninist literature dealing with the theory of state and law we can find also some statements about law and legality as moral values. Especially the intrinsic moral values of socialist Law have been emphasized. It seems to me that there is no genuine contradiction in these different views on the nature of law in Marxist theory.

The Marxist approach to Law and Morality has two different meanings in marxist theory, namely an ethical and a metaethical one. In the original Marxist-Leninist theory there has been no conscious distinction between ethical and metaethical discourse. Nevertheless it seems to me, that introducing this distinction into the analysis of the Marxist views on Law and Morality will dispell some traditional confusions and elucidate many problems of Marxist theory. From the ethical standpoint the Marxist original concept of Law contains plainly an ethical criticism of Law as a device of coercion used by the ruling class against the exploited and oppressed classes in all class structured societies. If we contend that according to this definition Law has no intrinsic moral value then we understand this basic Marxist view on Law as *an ethical judgement* about the very essence of Law in all societies based upon the private ownership of the means of production.

The "Communist Manifesto" and "Capital" exposed explicitly a radical moral criticism of bourgeois Law and Morality and denounced both as deprived of the true moral value from the standpoint of the revolutionary

---

[5] *Hart*, "Positivism . . .", *Fuller*, "Positivism . . .", note 1, 3.

[6] See *L. A. Hart*, "Positivism . . ." (see note 1).

communist ethics. But this criticism does not mean that Law is morally neutral (from a metaethical standpoint). It means only that Law has no intrinsic moral values from the point of view of the moral standards implied by the Marxist ideology and Marxist ethos (ethical proposition referred to a definite ethical system).

In a metaethical interpretation Marxist theory of Law and Morality has a very different meaning. Now, I shall try to develop this theory in a metaethical interpretation.

In an organized class structured society there is only one unique Legal Order as the device of coercion. This order is established and enforced by the state, which is the organization protecting the basic interests of the dominant classes. But there is no unique morality in a class structured society. There are many different inconsistent and colliding moralities and moral doctrines. They are the rationalizations of the interests, aspirations and objective social situations of different social groups and classes. Particularly one should distinguish in a class structured society two fundamentally opposed moralities and moral doctrines; the morality of the dominant class and the morality of the oppressed classes.

Nevertheless some basic values implied and enforced by the Law must be shared by the majority of those to whom the Law applies, otherwise Law enforcement will not achieve the minimum level of efficacy.

A set of socially shared values is a necessary condition of the existence of a Legal Order. According to the Marxist theory law can exist and operate only when the ruling class is able to control the consciousness of the society especially, in a class structured society, the consciousness of the working classes. And law itself is also a device of this control. But according to this theory, law used to operate in societies in which conflicting moral values and interests are the expressions of the objective antagonistic situations of different social groups and classes. If the control of the consciousness of the society by the ruling class is not total and fully effective (and such a situation of effective control is rather unusual) then the revolutionary ethos of the oppressed classes is going to be formulated. This new emerging ethos is substantially opposed to the dominant ethos, including Law and Public Morality. The values and standards of the ethos of the revolutionary social classes have been radically opposed to the values of the dominant class embodied in the Legal Order.

It may be argued that if the Law is compatible with every ruling class morality and can enforce any kind of a dominant morality — then on the ground of Marxist theory Law has no intrinsic moral values. A strong argument supporting this view may be also the Marxist theory of the withering away of the State and Law in a developed Communist society. But in the metaethical and metalegal political discourse Marx,

Engels and Lenin emphasized the significance and role of some moral values intrinsic to the bourgeois legality in the class struggle and in the revolutionary strategy of proletariat. The classical Marxists' examinations and accounts of the revolutionary situations and revolutionary strategies indicate clearly that Law can be used by the dominant class as an effective device of social control only if this class respects at least to some degree intrinsic values of Law. Only under these conditions can the dominant class impose upon the whole society its own moral values as the values of the society and can protect its interests by Law. The revolutionary class movement can also challenge the existing social and legal order by appealing to some intrinsic values of Law or to some specific values implied or enforced by a given Legal Order. This kind of a revolutionary strategy seems to be particularly successful in a political situation, in which the ruling class uses the Law as a device of coercion and oppression but abandons the Principles of the Rule of Law and ceases to respect in practice the moral values intrinsic to Legal Order. Then the existing Legal Order breaks down and only two alternatives are open the lawless dictatorship of the oppressive dominant class or the successful revolution of a new class, going to establish a new social and Legal Order.

It seems to me that these are essential views of the original Marxist metaethical and metalegal theory of Law and Morality. These views seem to provide good reasons for the hypothesis that Marxist-Leninist theory of Law in metaethical interpretation does not imply necessarily the idea of the axiological neutrality of the concept of Law (as the general idea of the notion of Law). Even the theory of the withering away of the Law is not sufficient argument to prove the contrary. The theory that the Law as a means of social control will be withered awy in the remote future is not logically incompatible with the view that the Law, being a historically transitional form of social control, has been linked with a set of lasting moral values. In a historical perspective these moral values intrinsic to Law can occur more lasting than the Law itself.

The Marxist standpoint on Law and Morality implies a much more developed and complicated theory than are the theories of modern positivism or Natural Law Theories.

I will now propose a conceptual framework of the analysis of the relations between Law and Morality which can be elaborated on the ground of the modern Marxist-Leninist philosophy.

In the plane of metaethical discourse following hypothesis on the moral content of Law seem to be plausible on the ground of the Marxist theory.

1. Every Legal Order proclaims, implements and enforces a minimum of substantial moral values which are indespensable for the existence

and functionning of any organized social group. These are some elementary values such as human life or certain minimum of safety and freedom of human being to which positive value is assigned on the ground of almost all ethical systems in all moralities. These elementary moral values are not specific for Law but without taking into consideration and protection of these values (to certain even minimal extent) — the Legal Order cannot work, i. e. it cannot reach the minimal degree of efficiency, being the essential feature of the Legal regulation[7].

2. The Legal Order implies or enforces a set of moral values and principles which are the formal features of legal regulation (for instance the the principle of formal justice).

3. Some legal systems imply or implement some specific moral values and principles developed and accumulated in the long run of history of legal institutions and legal doctrine (for instance the concept of inalienable human rights). This increasing moral potential of Law is the outcome of the cumulative historical process.

4. The Legal Order implies or enforces some moral (or non moral) values which are neither necessary nor specific substantive ingredients of a legal regulation but are specific moral values of a definite type of legal system (for instance capitalist or socialist Legal Order). These values must not be of cumulative character. They are historically transitional moral values of Law linked with a defined type of socioeconomic structure and determined exclusively by the public morality and interests of the ruling classes. (According to the Marxist theory the main function of Law consists in the expressing and protecting the fundamental values and vital interests of the dominant class.)

The first two ingredients of the moral potential of Law are constant elements of legal regulation. The next two elements (3. and 4.) are the variable moral elements of Law. There is a dynamic interdependences between these four elements. The ingredients 2. and 3. form together a set of moral values specific of Law, which is usually called the legalistic Ethos. The ingredients 1. and 2. are the original sources of the cumulative moral values (ingredient 3.). All four elements of the moral potential of Law are also the standards of moral estimation of the Legal Order. The constant moral ingredients of legal regulation (ingredients 1. and 2.) play a double role in the process of the social perception of Law e. g. cognitive and evaluative. These elements are determinative features of Legal Order but because of their gradualness they are also used as standards and criteria of the moral estimation of Law or a definite legal institution[8]. The variable elements of the moral potential of Law provide

[7] *L. A. Hart*, "The Concept of Law", Oxford at the Clarendon Press 1963, p. 189 - 208; *Lon. L. Fuller*, "The Morality of Law", New Haven 1964; *Graham Hughes*, "The existence of a Legal System", New York Law Review vol. 35, 1960, p. 1001 - 1029.

much more feasible but also more controversial criteria of the moral estimation of the Legal Order.

The distinguished above moral ingredients of Law are determined by the functions performed by Law as a means of social control. The constant and the cumulative elements of the moral potential of Law are determined by the integrative and stabilizing function of legal regulation. (From the standpoint of this function Law is conceived as a normative system integrating and stabilizing the society devided into conflicting social classes and strata.) The transitional variable elements of legal regulation are determined by the functions of Law as a device of the protection and preservation of the basic economics and political interests of the ruling class.

According to this metaethical theory the range of possible values which can be implied or enforced by Law is limited by the constant ingredients of the moral potential of Law. However the historical scope of values enforceable by Law is very broad. Within this scope the Legal Orders can imply and enforce different contradictory public moralities and values, reflecting ideologies of different social classes and groups. Despite its intrinsic moral source Law is compatible with a great deal of iniquities. And therefore, from the standpoint of a definite ethical system, one can always reasonably criticize a Legal Order as immoral or deprived of true moral values. Such a kind of strong moral criticism of the value of Law is sound especially on the ground of an ethical doctrine which rejects or does not consider as morally important the values of the Legalistic Ethos.

The Marxist ethical views on the relations between Law and Morality are determined by the fundamental axiological assumptions of Marxist ethical theory and by substantial features of this theory.

The supreme value of Marxist ethics is human being and his creative development. The fundamental ethical principle of Marxist ethical doctrine is the principle of selfrealisation of human being (the full development of all potential human capacities). The ideal of the classless Communist society is the ideal of a society in which this principle will be actually accomplished. The fundamental moral duty (a categorical imperative) derived from this principle is the duty of the strugle against all the social and economic conditions in which human beings are oppressed, helpless or alienated from their real selves.

The constant and the cumulative moral values of Law linked with the great humanistic tradition in moral philosophy have been accepted by the Marxist ethical doctrine. Especially the cumulative moral elements of contemporary Legal Orders have become also the values intrinsic to the Marxist conception of Justice. These moral principles and

[8] *Wiesław Lang*, "The Legal Phenomenon in the light of the controversies on the nature of Law", Acta Universitatis Nicolai Copernici No. 7, 70/1975.

values particularly the concepts of human rights are the historical achievements of the class struggle of the oppressed and exploited social classes in the long run of human history. They have been proclaimed and embodied in legal codes by the revolutionary social classes fighting for the establishment of new progressive social order.

But the Marxist revolutionnary ethos implying a radical criticism of all inhuman conditions of human existence is of course not a legalistic ethos. Moral values intrinsic to Law are not the superior or primary principles of Marxist ethical doctrine. Within the Marxist ethical conception they are considered as consequences or derivations of the mentioned above fundamental axiological principles of Marxist ethics or as the effective means of the accomplishment of these principles. In particular the formal moral principles and values intrinsic to the idea of Law such as principle of formal justice are on the ground of the Marxist Ethics fully subordinated to the principle of self-realisation and to the substantive requirements of the Marxist concept of social justice. (The priority of the substantive equality of the distribution of the primary goods over the principles of impartiality and formal justice.)

The Marxist-Leninist ethical theory is not a static deductive or quasi deductive system, like deontological systems of Spinoza or Kant, in which the positions of ethical principles (both formal and substantive) within the system are stable and unchangeable. Marxist ethical doctrine does not constitute a system in this sense. This doctrine has an open, historic and dynamic character. It presupposes its own historic development. Only the fundamental values and principles of Marxist ethical doctrine are completely immune for change (also their supreme position in the ethical doctrine is unchangeable). But in Marxist ethical theory the secondary values, rules and principles are not considered as logical derivations from the supreme moral principles. The position of secondary principles and the relations between these principles within the Marxist ethical doctrine are not stable. They are open to change and determined by historical, economic and sociological factors. In different historical situations and different economic conditions the significance and rank of the subordinated moral principles can be different on the ground of the Marxist ethical theory. The confrontation of the Marxist fundamental moral principles with new historical situations or new scientific theories can generate new secondary values and principles and challange the significance or rank of the old principles. This was the case with the historical evolution of the Marxist ethical views on the institution of marriage and family. Also the positions of the principles and values of the legalistic Ethos within the Marxist ethical theory have been changing in the course of historical development of this theory. The significance of the moral values intrinsic to Law has been increasing in the Marxist-Leninist theory and practice (however they cannot become the supreme or leading principles of Marxist ethics). The values of legalistic Ethos were realized by Lenin, when he emphasized, after the Revolution, the necessity of a new revolutionary Legal Order based upon the Rule of Law. The successful Socialist Revolution needs Law as an instrument of social and economic change and as a device of protection of new socialist order. But after a period of historical experiences it became obvious that the Socialist Law could operate affectively in the Socialist States not as a purely technical device of social control suitable for achieving every political goal, but as a normative order, which had some intrinsic moral values. It means the acceptance by the Marxist ethical doctrine of the internal ethical approach to the Socialist Legal Order (from the standpoint of the moral values inherent to this order).

The contemporary Marxist-Leninist political doctrines developed in the programs of the Communist Parties of Western Europe, United States of America and Canada accept the substantial elements of the Legalistic Ethos. It may seem that the content of these programs are substantially inconsistent. On the one hand the Communists criticize the bourgeois Law as the device of oppressive political power of capitalists and landowners used by them against the working classes of the society. The Communist political programs are the programs of Socialist Revolution (peaceful or violent) challenging the very foundations of the capitalist Legal Orders. On the other hand the Communists are stressing in their political programs the values of the bourgeois legality for the working classes in capitalist states and they defend in theory and in practical activity the Rule of Law in bourgeois governments. Nowadays, not the Communist Parties but the right wing and fascist movements are the real threat for the government of Law in most capitalist countries. The communist approach to bourgeois Law has been criticized as motivated by purely strategic, tactical or opportunistic reasons. It has been said, that the Communists have no moral deontological principles (concerning their political activities) their political programs contain only pure political strategies, which are deprived of any principled moral justification. This view, if considered seriously and not only as slogans of anticommunist propaganda, seems to be completely wrong. The contemporary Communist approach to the bourgeois Law is based upon solid ethical (as well as metaethical) foundations. Communist political doctrine is based upon the Marxist ethical theory. This theory accepts the ingredients 1. 2. and 3. of the moral potential of bourgeois Law as the subordinated (secondary) values of the Communist Ethos. The Communist use the values of Legalistic Ethos as the standards of moral criticism of the bourgeois Law. Using these standards they desguise in ethical, ideological and political discourse the oppresive functions of the bourgeois Law "in action" and the misuse of Law and of the legal system and the legal institutions by the ruling classes of the capitalists and landowners in protecting their own economic and political power[9]. The communist radical criticism of the bourgeois Legal Order reveals the striking discrepancies between the principle of the Rule of Law and the actual practices of the capitalist system. In the plane of metaethical sociological discourses the Marxist-Leninist theory explains this discrepancy as a contradiction inherent to the capitalist economic structure, based upon the private control of the basic means of production.

The Marxist ethical theory rejects the transitional elements (ingredients 4.) of the moral potential of capitalist Law (for instance the moral priority of the value of private ownership over the other values protected by Law)[10]. These moral values and principles are determined only by the oppressive functions of the bourgeois Legal Order and therefore are considered as deeply immoral from the Marxist point of view. So the Communist revolutionnary challange of the political and economic foundations of the bourgeois legal system is fully justified on moral grounds and consistent with the whole structure of the Communist ethical doctrine. In particular this challange is fully consistent with the acceptance of the moral values of Legalistic Ethos and the principles of the Rule of Law.

I am not arguing that tactical and strategic reasons have no impact upon the Communist approach to the problems of Law and Morality. Surely this impact is obvicus. I am trying only to prove that the emphasis of the moral values of Law in some political und social situations on the ground of Marxist theory is not only a problem of the revolutionary strategy or political prudence. It has its roots in the original Marxist ethical and metaethical philosophy. The Marxist concept of morality has never been fully relativistic neither in ethical nor in metaethical discourse. "The founding fathers of Communism" have expressed their moral beliefs implicitly in terms of politics und political economy, but their relativistic historical and sociological approach to the questions of moral values has been substantially limited by some fundamental ethical ideas. The historical dialectical development of societies has been conceived as the moral progress of mankind, being achieved in the historical process of the struggle of the antagonistic classes.

Lenin has emphasized the existence and role of some elementary basic rules and principles of human conduct, which are intrinsic to the cultures and moralities of almost all societies and are also common to the moralities of antagonistic social classes. These rules and patterns of conduct, developed in the long run of human history, Lenin considered as fundamental ingredients of the new Ethics of a communist society[11].

[9] *H. Lefcourt,* "Law against the People", New York 1971; *Kenneth Cloke,* "Law is illegal", "Radical Lawyers" . . ., see note 1, p. 27 - 43.

[10] See "*Howard Zinn*", "A Fallacy on Law and Order: that the Civil Diobedience must be absolutely nonviolent" in "Civil Disobedience and Violence", ed. by Jeffrie G. Murphy . . ., see note 1, p. 103 - 111.

From the standpoint of these views the genuine connections between the Law and the dominant moralities have for the Marxist theory a specific ethical as well as metaethical significance.

Many traditional controversies and disputes concerning the relations between Law and Morality seem to be pointless from a Marxist point of view. The question of these relations is substantially meaningless if put in abstract terms, without any historical, sociological or political context and without the methodological awareness of the character of the discourse. Let us take as an example the problem of the moral criticism of Law. From a Marxist point of view there can be two possible different types of criticism, namely the internal criticism from the point of view of the dominant Morality and the external ethical criticism from the standpoint of nondominant Ethos opposed to the Ethos of the dominant class.

On the ground of the internal ethical criticism Law is criticised from the standpoint of implied and enforced moral values. The legal institutions and settings are evaluated as consistent or inconsistent with these values, or as sufficient or insufficient to protect and enforce the values of the Public Morality. The conflicts between Law and Public Morality may be sometimes strong individual moral conflicts. They can evolve the conflict between different inconsistent moral values of the same (dominant) Ethos, but they have not a fundamental political or social character. This kind of criticism can suggest or stimulate some improvement of the existing Legal Order from the point of view of the values of this Order.

The conflict between Law and an external opposed Morality is in fact a collision of two different moralities. This conflict reflects the irreconciliable interests and values of the antagonistic social classes or groups. A moral criticism of Law from this standpoint is a criticism challenging the foundations of legal and social order.

Let us take another very controversial problem: the question of the moral obligation to obey the Law. Is there an absolute obligation to obey the Law? Or is there only a prima facie obligation? Or is there no such obligation at all[12]? These questions as ethical questions cannot be discussed meaningfully without previously answering a basic preliminary question. What kind of morality (or set of values) do we accept as the ethical ground of the moral obligation of obedience to Law? Such an obligation is obviously implied by a legalistic Ethos (at least a prima facie obligation). On the ground of this Ethos, Law itself is a positive moral value. Within this Ethos a legal qualification has always a positive moral

[11] *W. I. Lenin*, "State and Revolution", Moscow 1946.

[12] *Richard A. Wasserstrom*, "The obligation to obey the Law", U.C.L.A. Law Review 1963.

significance. The illegality has always, from this standpoint, a negative moral value. The strength and importance of a moral qualification based upon legal qualification can be different in different cases and situations. But we must also have in mind that the values of a Legalistic Ethos are not elementary nor universal human values. There have been cultures, philosophies and moralities which explicitly rejected the values of legalism[13].

From the standpoint of a dominant morality (which is enforced Law) there are, of course, good reasons to accept at least prima facie obligation to obey the Law. Law implies necessarily the concept of legitimacy of the Lawgiving authority as the moral justification of the state authority. But from the standpoint of an Ethos opposed to the dominant Morality (enforced by Law) there may be no ethical reasons for recognizing a priori even the prima facie obligation to obey the Law. Even the general acceptance of a legalistic Ethos may be not a sufficient reason for the acceptance of moral obligation to obey the Law within a Legal Order, which is considered as substantially immoral or unjust. Nevertheless there may be some prudential, theological or even moral reasons to obey the Law in particular situations. Especially there may be some moral reasons to comply with Law but only because of the positive coincidence of moral and legal qualifications of definite sets of conduct. Even if the illegality is morally irrelevant the violation of Law may be still morally wrong, if the conduct, which is illegal, is by coincidence, also immoral. Marxist moral philosophy has never morally justified the violations of the bourgeois laws forbidding murder or larceny, unless such violations have some specific moral or political reasons. Marxist moral doctrine has never approved or inspired the individual terrorism or violence as a proper method of the class struggle in a capitalist society.

For the Marxist ethical doctrine the discussion of the problem of the general moral obligation to obey the Law is pointless. On the ground of this doctrine there is *no general moral obligation either to obey nor to disobey the Law.*

Neither the obedience nor the disobedience to Law are considered as virtues or wickedness by themselves.

From a Marxist ethical standpoint the moral values intrinsic to Law are important but not sufficient reasons for the acceptance of the prima facie obligation to obey the Law within a given Legal Order. There may be good ethical reasons, in respect to different Legal Orders, to accept or to reject the moral obligation to obey the Law.

The Marxist issue in this question will always depend upon the substantive evaluation of the involved Legal Order.

[13] *Judith N. Shklar,* "Legalism — an essay on Law, Morals and Politics", Harvard University Press, Cambridge 1971.

[14]

Studies in the Theory
and Philosophy of Law
1985, vol. I
PL ISSN 0239-9997

JERZY KOWALSKI

Idea of Equality and the Law

1. Society is made up of various members. Differences among them have basis in genetics and social institutions. If any difference is valued negatively as inequality. which is to be abolished, we use the idea of equality. This idea is our measure of value and the aim which is to be reached. The situation of inequality is often defined as unjustice, slavery, oppression. Every kind of difference, independently of its basis is potentially nonacceptable and may be valued as inequality. Even such as health, intelligence, beauty. Hence it may be said that equality is an evolutionary notion. But as long as that difference is acceptable by the society, it affords no social trouble, and we do not name it "inequality". Approach to inequality may be various in the society. Some people want to abolish it, others – to strengthen it, or only to reform it. The law is a main instrument, which is to be used for these various social aims.

2. From our point of view, the idea of equality has (and ought to have) a principal position in philosophy of law. This notion plays such a role with reference to the main notions in jurisprudence such as justice, freedom, rule of law. Justice is one of central notions in the philosophy of law but many philosophers determine justice by means of such or other criteria of equality.[1] There are opinions that the notion of justice means nothing new in comparison with the notion of equality. In Pashukanis writings there are many good arguments for that point of view.[2]

There is also no sense to argue about freedom without reference to equality. Many arguments for this opinion can be found in papers of the World Congress of Philosophy of Law and Social Philosophy organized in St. Louis – August 1975.[3]

We find there a view that the idea of equality is a basis of the idea of justice and the idea of freedom.[4] The authors of the papers describe the tensions between

---

[1] We may call here such prominent authors as Aristotle, St. Thomas and contemporary – Ch. Perelman: see also W. L a n g, J. W r ó b l e w s k i, *Sprawiedliwość społeczna i nieposłuszeństwo obywatelskie w doktrynie politycznej USA* (*Social Justice and Civil Disobedience in the American Political Doctrine*), Warszawa 1984, p. 46–47 and citated there literature.

[2] E. B. P a s h u k a n i s, *Izbrannye proizwiedenija po obszczej tieorii prawa i gosudarstwa*, Moskwa 1980 p. 153.

[3] *Equality and Freedom*, ed. G. Dorsey, New York – Leiden 1977.

[4] Cf. V. K u b e s, *Bemerkungen zu den ideen der Gleichheit und Freiheit*, [in:] *Equality*..., p. 627.

freedom and equality and their dialectial connection.[5]

Although the idea of freedom was found in particular in the writings of liberals there is a very characteristic opinion of A. de Tocqueville that the idea of equality stimulates discovering of other ideas and transforms our all other notions.[6]

There is also a very important role of the idea of equality in the rule of law and law enforcement. The main problem here is to create the same decision in the same circumstances.[7]

These examples show us that idea of equality has come to hold a significant position in the philosophy of law and jurisprudence. From my point of view, it has to have a top position. A big equalitarian movement which we are now observing in the whole world creates a demand for researches in the light of this notion.

3. The idea of equality before the law is so old as the idea of the law itself, only its essence is changing in history. If we could use the Fuller's concept called "the internal morality of the law"[8] it would be true to say that idea of equality is a basis of its internal morality.

First of all, we have in mind this kind of equality, which we find already in ancient Greeks, especially in the writings of Plato and Aristotle. It is an idea that all men are to be obedient to the law. Common obedience to the law is a secular concept corresponding to the common obedience to the God. Plato in full consciousness creates this secular idea with reference to mythology.[9] It seems that this kind of equality in the law has softened the hard relation among people and especially between the ruler and people, because also rulers should display obedience to the law. In Sparta in the 5th century B.C. the king was obliged to swear obedience to the law.[10]

In this way law was an instrument of rationalisation of personal power. It means that the law governs and not the man.

4. Another kind of equality in the law is this which is determined by generality of its rules. This form of equality called "equality before the law" is immanent to the law independently if there is present consciousness of the principle that juristic valuation and juristic measure should be governed by

---

[5] Cf. O. Weinberger, *Gleichheit und Freiheit. Komplementäre oder Wiederstreitena ideale*, [in:] *Equality....* p. 641; Alejo de Cervera, *The Paradoxes of Equality*, [in:] *Equality....* ; 237.

[6] A. de Tocqueville, *Demokracja w Ameryce (Democracy in America)*, Warszawa 1974, 292.

[7] Cf. J. Wróblewski, *Sądowe stosowanie prawa (Judicial Application of Law)*, Warszaw 1972, p. 371–387.

[8] L. L. Fuller, *The Morality of the Law*, New Haven – London 1964, p. 96.

[9] Plato, *Prawa (Laws)*, Warszawa 1960, p. 154–158.

[10] Ksenofont, *Lukedaimonion politeja 15*.

general rules. But it is equality only in this frame. which is delimited in hypothesis of a rule. The classes of subjects of the rule may be various. How wide they are it depends on technical, sociological or ideological problems. Social conflict was very often articulated as a postulate for widening classes of subjects in legal regulation, for more equality.

Hence. if we meet legal rule that every human being has a legal ability (power) we may suppose that this legal system accepts some concept of equality of the human being.

Every legal system has some criteria of creating classes of legal subjects. which are equal.

These criteria are not only formal but also substantive. Therefore. the problem of equality before the law in any legal system as a whole cannot be described only with a concept of formal equality. Equality before the law in any legal system has some formal and some substantive aspects.

The principle that juristic valuation and juristic measure should be governed by general rules determines not only some formal aspect but also substantive aspects.[11]

Also substantive aspect is necessary because we must limit the class of subjects. and it cannot be done without substantive criteria. Our conception is adequate to constitutional practice of capitalist states.[12]

In some contemporary capitalist states. the only restrictive criterion in definition of the legal subject in its legal ability is age. This equality before the law. which is fully developed in the capitalist legal system is equality of legal chances. These legal chances in some social relations are attainable for an average citizen. in others not. In some social relations they are attainable only for a small part of citizens because realization of some legal abilities depends on ownership. we may say big ownership. Hence. for the capitalist class it is enough to have legal chances for attaining some aims. Everyone as a subject may gain. only some of them are winning. This is the problem of mystification of the equality before the law. which is interpreted as a real equality by some apologetics of the capitalist social system.[13]

We underline that it is only a question of mystification. We can see a dialectial function of the principle of equality before the law.

On the one hand. it brings (from the historical point of view) more equality in social relations and on the other hand it serves to enforce inequality in the social system and petrification of this inequality. This function of the equality before the law to the not equalitarian capitalist system is realized not directly but indirectly through the economic laws of this system. Hence. the law and its regulation

---

[11] In this sense I do not agree with O. W e i n b e r g e r. *op. cit.*

[12] Cf. J. V e t u a l n i. *Ogolna zasada rownosci w konstytuciach Weimarskiej i Bonskiej w świetle niemieckiej nauki i orzecznictwa (General Principle of Equality in the Weimar and Bonn Constitutions in the German Science and Judicial Decisions)*. Zesz. Nauk. UJ Prace prawnicze. 1962. 9.

[13] Cf. F. E n g e l s. K. M a r k s. *Dziela (Works)*. vol. II. Warszawa 1961. p. 679. Many

appear to be a neutral factor. In reality it is not a neutral factor but a very active factor. Therefore, if we wish to change this function of equality before the law we must change some regulations in the body of law.

Radical changes are brought about by the socialist revolution. But some symptoms of erosion of the capitalist legal system through pressure of public aims are remarked by many observers of this system.[14] Some authors see it as a strenghtening of the social equality and freedom, others as a danger for freedom.

5. So we may say that contemporarily the idea of equality before the law in its formal and substantive aspect has developed to its limit.

Therefore our attention is focussed on problems, which concern equality before the law, but they are new problems: our attention does not concentrate on equal legal chances but on equal real chances.[15]

It is quite understandable that these equal real chances may be realized also by means of legislation.

This problem is a main problem of the socialist and the communist movement and of plan and praxis of socialist states.

For instance in Poland we continue the idea of equality before the law in all branches of the legal system and in some regulations we develop this idea. This is done e.g. by abolishing discrimination on account of sex of parentage of a child, by abolishing privileges for some categories of officials in labour law and by improvement of standards of application of the law.[16]

But independently of this, in the law and in political programs we find ideas of equality of real chances. The main legal basis of it is nationalization of means of production and right to self-government of the members of a crew in a factory.[17]

This main fact makes possible such legal regulation, which creates guarantees for some egalitarian legal rights, the realization of which depends on economic means. The social control over economic means makes possible all equalitarian social politics.

Nationalization of means of production abolishes the main social division: owners and not owners. This division was a source of many inequalities in the entire history of the mankind. Institutionalization of this new social reality is not finished. It creates some new problems in the state enterprises.

But we may say with certainty that it brings a new kind of equality in social reality and also in the law.

---

interesting remarks we may find in E. B. Pashukanis. *op. cit.*, and F. Gerard. *Droit égalite et ideologie: Contribution a l'etude critic des principes generaux du droit*. Bruxelles 1981.

[14] Cf. P. Selznick. *Law, society and industrial justice*. New York 1969. p. 240. and V. Aubert. *Force and resources in the development of law*. [in:] *Equality...*

[15] Very characteristic on this is *The Alva Myrdal Report to the Swedish Social Democratic Party*. Towards Equality. Lund 1971.

[16] Cf. J. Wróblewski. *Sądowe stosowanie....* part III.

[17] Cf. A. Lopatka. *The prospects of man's equality and freedom*. and Mihailo Marković. *Basic institution of participatory democracy*. [in:] *Equality...*

Generally speaking, it is a problem of equality in decision-making (participation), in consumption (the so-called collective consumption), equal participation in culture and so on. It is not only a problem of legal ability but also such legal guarantee that every citizen may (if he wants) participate in all these social relations independently of his economic power. This kind of equality may be created through legal protection of the common interest in one or another area of the social life and not only through the market.

Perhaps to emphasize this new step in the developing of equality in the law it would be right to call it not "equality before the law" but "equality in the whole body of the law". No matter how we call it, it is a new kind of equality as compared with the equality before the law.

A legal system, which starts to develop on a principle of equality in the whole body of law, is creating not only legal chances for such or another behaviour but also such legal guarantees which make this behaviour really possible. It seems that this kind of equality overcomes this dialectic (equality that makes new inequality) we mentioned above.

This kind of equality which we call "equality before the law" is produced under the influence of a market equality that "has become equivalent to interchangeability and is the very negation of individuality". Equality, instead of being a condition for the development of each man's peculiarity, means the extinction of individuality, the "selfness" characteristic of the "market orientation".[18]

We agree with this remark of Fromm. We think that at this level of the developing of equality in the whole body of the law every human being has the best capabilities for his developement. In such way, this equality produces human beings which are not equal as individuals. And it is a new step of dialectical development of the human society, which will bring us new problems. As we noticed at the beginning of this paper, every kind of differences may be valued as inequality, which ought to be abolished in the name of the idea of equality.

Development of equality in the human society is progressive, because we do not observe restoration (for a longer period of time) of these inequalities, which have been abolished. But the limit of this progressive development will not be seen, if we do not catch the problem from the utopian point of view. In this case we can find help also in the philosophy of law, because legal ideas and legal practice create interesting inspirations.

---

[18] E. F r o m m, *Man for himself*, London – Henley 1982, p. 74. About dependence of idea of equality before the law and capitalistic market are interesting remarks in F. E n g e l s, *Anty-Duhring*. Cf. also the part: *Moral and Law*, [in:] *Equality*.... and E. B. P a s h u k a n i s, *op. cit.*

[15]

Problems of Legality in Marxist Theory*

BY JERZY WRÓBLEWSKI, ŁÓDZ

I. *Introduction*

1. There are many problems concerning any legality and the socialist legality is no exception. The scope of my paper is confined to the discussion of the concept of legality in socialist theory, and covers neither the institutions thought of as guarantees of this legality nor the vital aspect of the realization of the principle of legality. The level of research is, hence, that of general theoretical analysis. In my opinion many of the problems I shall present are not confined to the discussions within the framework of socialist legal philosophy, or as it is called of the theory of state and law.

The problems I analyse are controversial. I have singled them out to present the discussion and not to state opinions that are agreed upon and, therefore, are less interesting and more widely known as standard opinions of the marxist legal thought. A part of my exposition refers and critically analyzes the various viewpoints, based mostly on the Polish legal writings exceptionally abundant from 1956 on[1]. A larger

* One of several lectures delivered at Wayne State University in Detroit, Michigan, U.S.A. in the fall of 1975.

[1] Cf. the positions concerning legality in 1956–1959 period: S. Ehrlich, *Praworządność (Legality)*, Warszawa 1956; Z. Izdebski, "Rewizja pojecia praworządności" ("Revision of the Concept of Legality"), *PP (Państwo i prawo)* 3, 1967, and polemics by S. Zawadzki, "W sprawie pojecia praworządności" ("Polemics Concerning the Concept of Legality"), *PP* 4/5, 1957; W. Zakrzewski, "Pare uwag o zagadnieniu praworządności" ("Some Comments Concerning the Problem of Legality"), *PP* 7/8, 1957; K. Opałek and W. Zakrzewski, *Z zagadnień praworządności socjalistycznej (The Problems of Socialist Legality)*, Warszawa 1958; S. Ehrlich, "Uwagi o praworządności socjalistycznej" ("Comments on Socialist Legality"), *PP* 8/9, 1958; K. Opałek, "Spór o pojecie praworządności" ("A Controversy Concerning the Concept of Legality"), *PP* 10, 1959; id., "Praworządność" ("Legality"), *Zagadnienia prawa karnego i teorii prawa*, Warszawa 1959.

Among the items of the later period cf. K. Opałek, "Formalne i materialne pojęcie praworzadności" ("The Formal and Material Concept of Legality"), *Rozprawy prawnicze*, Krakow-Warszawa 1964; id., "The Rule of Law and Natural Law", *The Publication in Honour of K. Olivecrona*, Stockholm 1964; A. Burda, *Demokracja i praworządność (Democracy and Legality)*,

ARSP (Archiv für Rechts- und Sozialphilosophie), Bd. LXII/4 (1976)

part, however, contains my own propositions, which are thought of as a tool for clarifying the issue and to explain certain phenomena of the legal activities qualified from the point of view of their legality.

2. The common core of all concepts of legality is that of a behavior consistent with a legal norm. The elementary formula for this common core is a "relational statement" of the form "X is consistent with N" where the variable X stands for a behavior of the subject, the N for a valid legal norm[2]. Then stating that a behavior X is legal means that it is consistent with the valid legal norm.

Starting with the elementary formula of legality we can map out basic conceptual problems concerned with this notion. There are two sets of problems and in each of them there are two sub-problems to be dealt with.

The first set of problems concerns methodological questions. There are two of them: a) whether the concept of legality is a descriptive or an evaluative one or whether it is used descriptively or evaluatively[3];

Wrocław–Warszawa–Kraków 1965; id., *Praworządność w systemie demokracji socjalistycznej (Legality in the System of Socialist Democracy)*, Wrocław–Warszawa–Kraków 1968; id., "Instytucjonalne gwarancje praworządności i ich rola w państwie socjalistycznym" ("Institutional Guarantees of Legality and their Role in Socialist State"), *PP* 8/9, 1971; J. Nowacki, "Materialne i formalne pojecie praworządności" ("Material and Formal Concept of Legality"), *PP* 4/5, 1968; H. Suchocka, "Rodzaje konstytucyjnych gwarancji praworządności w europejskich państwach socjalistycznych" ("Types of the Constitutional Guarantees of Legality in European Socialist States"), *Ruch Prawniczy, Ekonomiczny i Socjologiczny* 4, 1974; J. Wróblewski, *Wartosci a decyzja sądowa (Values and Judicial Decision)*, Wrocław–Warszawa–Kraków–Gdańsk 1973, chapt. III; K. Opałek and J. Wróblewski, *Zagadnieńia teorii prawa (Problems of Legal Theory)*, Warszawa 1963, chapt. V (3); W. Lang and A. Mrózek, "Teoretyczne modele legalizmu" ("Theoretical Models of Legalism"), *Zeszyty Naukowe u. M. Kopernika w Toruniu, nauki humanistyczno-społeczne* 27, 1968.

The concepts of legality are also formulated in text-books, cf. e.g. A. Łopatka, *Wstep do prawoznawstwa (Introduction to Legal Science)*, Warszawa 1969, 1. ed., chapt. VIII; J. Kowalski, *Wstep do nauk o państwie i prawie (Introduction to the Sciences of State and Law)*, Warszawa 1971, 1. ed., chapt. XVII; S. Ehrlich, *Wstep do nauki o państwie i prawie (Introduction to the Science of State and Law)*, Warszawa 1971, chapt. XX.

[2] J. Wróblewski, "Statements on the Relation of Conduct and Norm", *Logique et Analyse* 49/50, 1970.

[3] In my essay I write about the use of the concept of legality. One can discuss, of course, how the concept in question should be used.

b) whether the concept of legality is to be applied to any norm belonging to any system or only to the norms to some specially qualified systems.

The second set of problems concerns the questions dealing with the content of the concept of legality. There are two such questions: c) whether the class of addressees of the legality (that is the class of subjects whose behavior X is given elementary formula of legality) contains only the organs of the state or is referred to all norm addressees, that is to say also to citizens as individuals; d) whether the content of the norms (or systems of norms) in respect to which one qualifies the behavior as legal or not-legal (that is the norms denotated by the variable N in the elementary formula of legality) is irrelevant or relevant for the use of the legality qualification.

In my essay I discuss the answers to these questions, but in a sequence that seems best for the purposes of a systematic exposition.

First I deal with the problem of the generality of the concept of legality, that is to say with the answer to the methodological question (b). Secondly I discuss the class of the subjects whose behavior is relevant for the use of the concept of legality, that is with the answer to the question (c) dealing with the content of the discussed concept. Thirdly I discuss the opposition of the material and formal concept of legality, which forms the answer to the second of the questions of content (d). Fourthly I analyze the evaluative and descriptive use of the legality concept, and this concerns the answer to the first of methodological problems (a). In the last part of my essay I present the use of the concept of legality in the ideology of the judicial application of law.

II. *The Generality of the Concept of Legality*

3. One of the methodological questions formulated above is whether the concept of legality is applied to a norm belonging to any system or only to the norm belonging to some specially qualified systems. This question is very close to that of content of the norms relevant for the use of the qualification of legality, that is to say with the opposition of the formal and material concept of legality (see section IV below). Here, however, we are concerned only with the generality of the use of the concept, and not with the material criteria, which determine the degree of this generality.

The problem of generality appears patently in the discussion whether there exists a concept of legality which can be used both in description of the socialist and the capitalist systems. The discussion of this problem has taken place in the early fifties coupled with the cold war period[4]. Making abstraction of the underlying political issues let us analyze here the methodological aspect of this issue. From this point of view there are two problems to solve: (a) the conditions of constructing a general concept of legality and its operational features, and (b) the conditions of constructing a non-general (or more concrete) concept of legality and its operational characteristics.

4. The condition for any construction of a general concept of legality is the comparability of the phenomena this concept is referred to. There were several arguments in East-West discussions on legality against this comparability.

Axiological arguments stress the fundamental opposition of the axiological basis of the two compared systems, which does influence the conceptual apparatus used in their description and determines the content of legal institutions belonging to the systems in question. Institutional incomparability is based on the different systems of the so-called guarantees of legality such as the systems of the control of administration of the state and of its legal responsibility. The persuasive political argument, which lurks in the other arguments, is that the formulation of a common concept implicitly tends to undermine the basic difference and to weaken the politically important dichotomies in treatment of highly politically relevant issues.

These arguments can and should be refuted. There is always a possibility of finding common features of the phenomena of legality in both of the compared legal cultures. Of course the common use of the term "legality" is not sufficient, because of the vagueness of the concept and the possibility of various meanings of the same term in different legal languages. There is, however, a common core of the concept of legality expressed in the elementary formula given above — legality at least means a behavior consistent with legal norm (comp. point 2).

There are various common features and common problems of legality. The use of a general concept is necessary for any comparative research,

[4] Comp. materials of the *Colloquium on the Rule of Law as Understood in the West*, September 1957, organized by the International Association of Legal Science. For a clear statement of a position negating the value of a general concept of legality see C. J. Hamson, "General Report", *The Vth International Congress of Comparative Law*, Bruxelles 1958. On the discussion of this argument cf. K. Opałek, "Spór . . .", *op. cit.*, p. 520–524.

stating both similarities and differences of the compared phenomena. Methodologically it is not possible to state either the former or the latter without using a common concept. A use of this concept does not hinder to assert the basic axiological differences, and is not related with any political consequences on the level of serious discussion. It seems that to argue the necessity of the general concept of legality is now breaking the open door — but the problem is worth mentioning, because it was thought of as vital in the very recent history of political sciences.

5. The construction and operational qualities of the general concept of legality is consistent with a construction of less general and more concrete concepts of legality designed for determined research purposes. There is constructed, as we know, a concept of socialist legality as well as that of Anglo-Saxon concept of the "rule of law". One can compare the various systems of controlling the activities of the state organs and make a typology adapted for the concrete purposes. The use of these typological concepts of legality is necessary, indeed, in any deep-going comparative research. But the condition of their use is the general concept of legality. Adequate methodology requires the whole set of the concepts of legality from the most general and, therefore, highly abstract concept to the less general concepts used in research.

It seems that these remarks are methodologically trivial, but are needed to be repeated always where the discussion concerns notions deeply involved in axiological and political oppositions.

III. *The Wide and Narrow Concept of Legality*

6. In socialist legal science there is a discussion of the scope of the concept of legality. The question is: whether the class of the addressees of the legality (that is the class the behavior of which is denoted by the variable X in the elementary formula of legality) contains only organs of the state or refers to all subjects whose behavior is regulated by legal norms, that is also to citizens as individuals. The preference of the former results in a construction of a narrow concept of legality, of the latter — in a construction of a wide one[5].

[5] The views proposing the wide concept of legality are dominant in Soviet legal theory. The partisans of this concept in Poland cf. the cited positions of S. Ehrlich and A. Burda. For the narrow concept cf. Opałek and Zakrzewski, *op. cit.*, chapt. II; Opałek and Wróblewski, *op. cit.*

The narrow concept of legality restricts the qualification of "legal behavior" only to a behavior of the state organs. If this behavior is consistent with the valid legal norm, then it is legal. The principle of legality is formulated as one of the basic principles for the activity of the socialist state. It is applied to all kinds of the activity of the state organs, and the spotlight is on the application of the law by the courts and by the administrative agencies. In this narrow meaning the behavior of citizens is not relevant for legality, although functionally this behavior of the population can influence the attitude of the state officials, and vice versa.

The wide concept of legality is referred to any person, which is the norm addressee, whether it is a "private" citizen or a state organ. The common feature of the behavior of the former and of the latter is the relation to the valid norm. And the common qualification of this behavior is that in terms of legality.

7. The discussion between these two concepts is still vital in socialist theory. There are three main arguments for the wide concept and they can be summarized as follows:

The legality is treated in the text of the Polish Constitution (and in other constitutions of the socialist states) in the wide meaning, as a principle of the activity of the state and of citizens. It is synonymous with the duty of the behavior consistent with valid norms by every norm-addressee. Further one stresses that for the functioning of the whole state (or in other words of a national community organized in the political form of the state) the behavior of all citizens according to law is of highest importance. Hence one even tends toward a definition of legality as an order or socio-political climate resulting from the due behavior of citizens and of the state. Lastly one stresses that the tendency of the socialist state, explicitly formulated in constitutional provisions and proclaimed in political programs, is the growing participation of citizens in the administration of the state. This is thought of as a general tendency of evolution, which in the long run prepares the way for the withering away of the state. Hence, the conceptual separation of the behavior of the state and the behavior of citizens, expressed in the narrow concept of legality is contrary to the letter and spirit of the constitutional provisions and does not fit with political tendencies of the evolution of the relation between the state and citizens, and hence is even politically wrong.

It seems that in spite of the suggestivity of these arguments one can argue, that they are not conclusive. Granting the role of the citizens' behavior and the importance of political participation on all levels of government, the question remains whether the wide concept of legality has the operational qualities important in theory and relevant for practical legal activity. In my opinion the answer is negative.

In theory the wide concept of legality has a very restricted use, because the number of relevant theses concerning a behavior of such different subjects is rather limited. But the more serious reason is, that the social impact of the legality of "official" and of "private" behavior is quite different. The impact of the state breaking the law and a citizen committing a crime has another social dimension and needs different measures of counteraction. Hence the institutional controls of the legality for both of them are quite different. The use of the narrow concept of legality is not inconsistent with the political objectives of the socialist state. Even if a citizen participates in a state-organ decision, he functions not as a "private" person and is not responsible for his action as an individual. Using the narrow concept one does not reject either the influence of the citizens' fidelity to law upon the operation of the state machinery, or the educational impact of the legality in the operation of the state on the attitudes of an average citizen.

IV. *The Formal and Material Concept of Legality*

8. The controversy between the adherents of the formal and material concept of legality has a deep ideological background. It is closely linked with the problem of the evaluative character of the concept of legality, which will be discussed later (section V).

Not going into historical and doctrinal details it is sufficient here to point out the main features of both concepts.

The easiest way is to present the concepts in question as models, which reconstruct the clusters of various doctrinal opinions[6]. Both of these models will be analyzed in detail when I analyse the problem of the descriptivity and the evaluative character of the concepts in question. Here I present only an outline without bettering the current constructions.

[6] For general presentation of the controversy see K. Opałek, "Spór . . .", *op. cit.*, p. 524–533; id., "Formalne . . .", *op. cit.*; id., "The Rule . . .", *op. cit.*; Opałek and Zakrzewski, *op. cit.*, chapt. I; Nowacki, *op. cit.*

The model of the formal concept of legality is described by the elementary formula of legality given above (point 2) as "X is legal" means "X is consistent with N". In this formula there is no explicit reference to any evaluative component. The matter is simply of comparing the behavior of X with the content of N and expressing this in a relational statement. It is assumed, that this statement can be true or false, that is that it is a sentence in the logical meaning of this term. But in practice the formal concept of legality is commonly connected with the positivist attitudes writ large. Not entering here into the large debates on the opposition of legal positivism and natural law it would be sufficient to stress that the analysis of positivist attitude demonstrates that it is not as axiologically neutral, as it claims[7]. Then the concept of formal validity expressed in the elementary formula is not wholly adequate because it does not make explicit the evaluative component (or "evaluative" or "emotional" meaning) it has in reality. To make this component explicit I propose a more complicated formula defining the term "X is formally legal". This formula is synonymous with "X is consistent with N and every Y consistent with N is f-valuable". This formula states, that the use of the concept of formal legality is linked with an ascription of an f-value to X. This ascription is based on the positive evaluation of any behavior consistent with a valid norm without taking into account the content of this norm or the qualities of the system this norm belongs to. Thus the "positivist attitude" or "positivist mentality" is reflected in the given formula.

The model of a concept of material legality qualifies a behavior X as materially legal only when this X is consistent with N which has a determined content or belongs to a system, which has certain properties. Take some examples to make clear this concept: For the content of the norm one can demand for example that this norm were consistent with some axiological system (of natural law, of morality, of policy). For the qualities of the system one demands that this is a system of the rule of a statute, or a system based on the (formal) equality of citizens before the law, or to contain some guarantees of democracy such as a division

[7] E. g. N. Bobbio, *Giusnaturalismo e positivismo giuridico*, Milano 1965, chapt. V, VI; U. Scarpelli, *Cos'è il positivismo giuridico*, Milano 1965, chapt. VI–IX; S. I. Shuman, *Legal Positivism. Its Scope and Limitations*, Detroit 1963, chapt. VIII; K. Opałek and J. Wróblewski, "Pozytywizm prawniczy" ("Legal Positivism"), *PP* 1, 1954, sec. V.

of powers etc.[8]. These requirements express patently a determined political (or ethical) ideology and can be linked with some ideas how to protect rights thought of as vital for an existence of the "lawful" or "just" state and law.

The concept of material legality can be also expressed in a standard formula. I think that the relatively adequate formula asserts the synonymity of "X is materially legal" with the expression "X is consistent with N and N has an m-value". The criteria for m-value are determined by the various ideological ideas as shown in the examples given above.

9. The critical analysis of the concept of material legality is relevant for the current doctrinal opposition of this concept and the concept of formal legality.

There are several arguments for the concept of material legality. These arguments can be summarized as follows: the concept of formal legality leads to conclusions, which are contrary to accepted political and ethical ideologies. Namely one cannot speak about legality if some basic rights, which are the result of historical progress, are not safeguarded. E.g., to speak about legality there should be a law equal for all (thus there is no legality for the system based on slavery or of feudal system). The most dramatic occurrence of the failure of the concept of formal legality was the experience of Nazi regime. The widely discussed changes in G. Radbruch's philosophy[9] coupled with the ascription of some responsibility of the positivist thinking, undermining the liberal natural faith, for the lack of opposition against the coming of this regime, are the arguments of some persuasive force.

[8] For socialist conceptions comp. e.g. S. Ehrlich, "Comments . . .", *op cit.*, p. 238; Burda, *Demokracja . . .*, op. cit., p. 53. For other conceptions see e.g. *The Rule of Law in the United States*, New York 1958, p. 28, 30; *The Rule of Law in a Free Society*, Genève 1959, p. 5, 196; *The Rule of Law in Italy*, Hague 1958, p. 18, 45; as a definition of the rule of law one can also interpret L. L. Fuller's postulates of the inner morality of law, cf. L. L. Fuller, *The Morality of Law*, New Haven – London 1964, 1. ed., chapt. II.

[9] Cf. Radbruchs papers: "Rechtsphilosophische Gesinnung" (1945); "Erneuerung des Rechts" (1946); "Gesetzliches Unrecht und übergesetzliches Recht" (1946), printed in the volume: G. Radbruch, *Der Mensch im Recht*, Göttingen 1957. About the change of the legal philosophy of Radbruch cf. J. Wróblewski, "Relatywistyczne teorie prawa" ("Relativist Theories of Law"), *PP* 8/9, 1963, p. 216 sq.

Against these arguments thought of as a justification of the concept of material legality by refutation of the concept of the formal legality one uses various counter-arguments. Besides the refutation of the *reductio ad Hitlerum*, which is the standard but spurious argument against any kind of positivism[10], one points out the lack of precise and not controversial criteria of the concept in question, the appearing from time to time bias of natural law, and, generally, the mixing of the descriptive and evaluative approach[11]. The last argument is based on the constatation, that a qualification of the norm N as fit for being the basis of material legality is of an evaluative nature, whereas the concept of formal legality does not pressupose any evaluation and is confined, therefore, to the area satisfying the scientific criteria of descriptivity.

10. It seems that the doctrinal opposition of the two discussed concepts is spurious in the sense that one does not exclude the other one. The reason for this assertion is, that both concepts deal with different problems or, in other words, each of them operates on a different level of discourse.

The concept of formal legality is confined to the internal point of view of the law. The concept refers to the relation of the regulated behavior X to the norm N. This relation is stated in a relational statement. If there is an evaluative component in the use of this concept then the evaluation is limited to the approval of the consistency of a behavior with norm as such, that is to say, it does not evaluate the law and does not depend on its content. Or one can also say, that this concept is based on the internal values of law, because each law assumes the value of a behavior which is consistent with it.

The concept of material legality expresses the external evaluation of law. Then content of law is evaluated according to assumed criteria. If the law satisfies the conditions for a positive value set forth by these criteria, then the law has such a value and the behavior consistent with law is evaluated positively. Such behavior is materially legal. If, however, the law is evaluated negatively, then this value is transferred on the behavior consistent with that law. Such behavior is materially illegal, in spite of its formal legality.

[10] Cf. G. Fassò, *Società, legge e ragione*, Milano 1974, p. 54.

[11] For a criticism of the concept of material legality cf. papers of K. Opałek cited in note 6 above.

Obviously it is possible to evaluate law both from an internal and external point of view [12], and these evaluations are independent. But the problem is, whether this or that evaluation is admitted within a given paradigm of legal or political science and, what criteria ought to be chosen for an external evaluation, if such evaluation is treated as admissible. Hence the opposition of both concepts of legality is relative and the solution of admissibility of each of these concepts is based on the more fundamental issues of descriptivity or evaluative character of legal or political science.

V. *The Descriptive and Evaluative Concept of Legality*

11. The opposition of description and evaluation is one of the fundamental problems of ontology, epistemology and methodology, and on the solution of this problem depends the fate of axiology. We cannot even touch here such kind of problems. It is sufficient to mention, that the axiological opposition between cognitivism and anticognitivism has an effect upon the legal methodology, as a methodology of one of the social sciences. The question is, whether evaluation can take place in the paradigm of social science, and if so, what kind of evaluations are accepted. The known controversy on the peculiarities of social sciences or humanities in comparison with the (strict) sciences of nature is the example of the basic methodological problems involved here.

On a somewhat lower level of the legal science the opposition of description and evaluation forms the background of the positivism and natural law controversy [13] and the issue of the so-called naturalist fallacy [14]. Roughly speaking positivism taken as an approach to law is the standard example of a descriptive attitude, whereas natural law is one of an evaluative attitude. But even a lawyer applying the law and

[12] The opposition of internal and external aspects of dealing with legal problems is due for H. L. A. Hart, *The Concept of Law*, Oxford 1961, 2. ed., p. 55, 86 sq., 99 sq., 108, 112, 118, 134, 197. The way the author uses this opposition is open for many interpretations, cf. my review in *Ruch Prawniczy, Ekonomiczny i Socjologiczny* 1, 1963.

[13] Cf. K. Opałek and J. Wróblewski, "Axiology: Dilemma between Legal Positivism and Natural Law", *Österreichische Zeitschrift für öffentliches Recht* 18, 1968.

[14] Cf. the basic monography by G. Carcaterra, *Il problema della fallacia naturalistica*, Milano 1969; J. Wróblewski, "Natura a reguły postepowania" ("Nature and the Rules of Behaviour"), *Etyka* 6, 1970 passim.

facing the issues of legal interpretation and of qualification of facts is aware of the differences between the fact determined descriptively and the fact determined evaluatively by the applied legal norms; and he sees that in some extreme cases the distinction is quite clear, whereas there are vague borderlines of penumbra, when the mixture of cognitive and evaluative elements is hard to deal with [15].

The difference between descriptive and evaluative concepts is, hence, dependent on very fundamental issues, but it can be also dealt with on a lower level assuming some fairly common intuitions and based on common legal experiences in legal science and in legal practice. Within this restricted framework I would like to discuss the descriptive and evaluative features of the concept of legality. It is one of the methodological questions put forth in the introduction to this essay (comp. point 2) and now we are prepared to face it. This means going further into the analysis of the concepts of formal and material legality as used in legal discourse and in ideology of the activity of the state organs. The preliminary question, however, is that of the value of legality.

12. It seems that there are two different manners of treating a value of legality, which can be ascribed to the concept of formal legality and of material legality.

Formal legality is treated either as axiologically neutral or as a statement of a relative value of any legal order, without taking into account the content of the law in question (comp. point 8 above).

If one uses the concept of formal legality in a purely descriptive manner then the issue of the legality as a value does not exist at all. Theoretically there remains a question of the conditions for the truth / falsity qualification of the relational statement constructed according to the elementary formula (comp. point 2), but this does not concern us here. If one uses the concept of formal legality in an evaluative manner then one treats the conformity of behavior with valid legal norms as "relatively valuable". This relativity means, that the order introduced by law has a relative value as an order, which is better than a disorder or a chaos in societal relations. Order means some kind of stability, of certainty in social relations. The relativity of this value

[15] Cf. J. Wróblewski, "Facts in Law", ARSP 2, 1973; id., *Sadowe stosowanie prawa (Judicial Application of Law)*, Warszawa 1972, chapt. VIII (2), X (4).

is obvious, since there are good and bad orders evaluated from an external point of view, from which one appraises the content of law.

The use of the concept of material validity seems to assume an "absolute value" of legality consisting in a conformity of a behavior with norms which have a positive value. The use of the term "absolute" in this context points out only the opposition to the relative value in the above presented conceptions of the formal legality, and nothing more pretentious. This means that a law, which fulfills the criteria put forth for material validity is "just", "right", "natural", "truly valid" etc. These criteria, sometimes fix the borderline between the "(true) law" and "no-law", between *gesetzliches Unrecht und übergesetzliches Recht*[16]. This concept implies qualification of the behavior consistent with the norm evaluated negatively as materially illegal, although it is formally legal. And in this sense it assumes the background of "absolute value", or value more absolute than the relative value of keeping law for preserving some order.

The reconstruction of the values of the two concepts of legality can not be reasonably challenged by pointing out doctrines, which do not fit in the dichotomy here presented. This is so because I deal with the simplified models, not with the analysis of concrete constructions, which can blurr the issues using rather vague notions.

13. The deeper analysis of the concept of formal legality leads to the conclusion, that the current constructions of this concept and ways of its use demand further clarification[17].

I single out the three modes of this concept expressed in corresponding formulas, namely one used in a weak sense and two used in strong sense.

One uses the concept of formal legality in a weak evaluative sense when one asserts that a formally legal behavior realizes the internal values of the law which is applied. This statement can be expressed in a formula "X is consistent with the norm N and X realizes the internal values of N". This expression does not involve in principle any evaluative attitude of the speaker, if he can state descriptively the legality of X (a relational statement) and if the internal values of the

[16] Cf. the title of G. Radbruch's paper cited in note 9 above.

[17] The following text is based on my analysis in: Wróblewski, *Wartości* . . ., op. cit., chapt. III.

norm can be stated descriptively. Then the expression is about values, but does not imply any evaluative attitude.

One uses the concept of formal legality in a strong evaluative sense, when one asserts that the behavior consistent with the norm is a behavior making a part of an order realized by the keeping of law, and one ascribes to that order a relative value in the meaning explained above (point 12).

This concept can be expressed in an evaluative relational expression of the form "X is consistent with the norm N, and every Y as consistent with N is f-valuable" (comp. point 8). Here the use of the concept in question implies an evaluative attitude. I call this kind of relational value judgement in a strong sense a judgement of general approval.

There is also a corresponding relational value-judgement in strong sense formulating a particular approval. It expresses the positive evaluation of the consistency of X with N because one approves of the N in question. The applied norm is evaluated as c-valuable, because it fulfills some accepted criteria of evaluation. The criteria in question are internal values of the legal system the norm belongs to or the values internal of the applied norm. The corresponding formula for such concept of formal legality is: "X is consistent with the norm N, and the norm N is c-valuable and then every Y consistent with N is c-valuable".

Characteristic for the use of the concept of formal legality in a strong evaluative sense is the approval of order (general approval) or approval of a particular norm (particular approval). This approval is granted by the use of the concept of formal legality, because it is founded in the internal values of the system or of the particular norm of this system.

This approval is an unconditional appreciation of any behavior consistent with the valid norm. And this expresses the attitude of an acceptance of an existing legal order and of the legal norms in force which is ascribed to the positivistic fidelity to law. As is shown by my analysis this attitude is nuanced according to the ways in which one asserts the validity in question, expressed in three kinds of relational evaluative statements.

14. The concept of material legality, as said above, is linked with the evaluation of the norm or of legal order when the criteria of this evaluation are based on the values in principle external to the law in

question. The formula expressing the material legality means that "X is consistent with N and N has an m-value" (comp. point 8). If these external values coincide with the internal values of the law in question, then there is no conflict between the two concepts of legality we are speaking about. On the contrary, the motivating pression of the law is in its highest. If these values, however, are opposite, we have a dramatical situation of the contradiction between the formal and the material legality and this situation gives rise to the conceptual controversies concerning these two concepts (comp. point 9).

The closer analysis of the content and the use of the concept of material legality leads to distinctions strictly analogous to those concerning the concept of formal legality. We can, therefore, present these concepts in a brief manner.

The concept of material legality used in a weak sense states the relation of the behavior X to the norm N, which is evaluated according to assumed criteria. One does not approve of those criteria and only states the consistency of the norm N in question with them. Hence the element of evaluation of the speaker can be excluded if the statement of the consistencies in question fulfills certain conditions. The formula expressing such kind of concept is "X is consistent with the norm N and X realizes the external values of N".

The concept of material legality can be used in a strong evaluative sense. *Ex hypothesi* there is the approval either of the legal order in general according to the external criteria (version of general approval) or the approval of the norm N in question according to these criteria (version of particular approval). The formula for a strong sense is: "X is consistent with the norm N, and if N is m-valuable, then every Y consistent with N is m-valuable".

VI. *The Concept of Legality and the Ideology of the Judicial Application of Law*

15. The concept of legality is one of the crucial concepts in any legal thinking. It is applied as a qualification of any behavior of the state organs (the narrow concept of legality) or one uses it sometimes to qualify even a behavior of private persons (the wider concept of legality) (point 6). Using this concept in a narrow manner we have to single out various activities of the state and, if only there is a legal regulation of these activities, can one apply to them the concept of legality.

The typical area of the use of the concept of legality is the judicial and administrative decision-making. In the latter case the whole operation of the state machinery is at stake and the known problems of the effectiveness of administration, of administrative discretion and of the protection of the rights of individuals is at stake. In the former case we are dealing with the administration of justice which is thought of as satisfying the highest standards of objectivity in solving the cases according to rules which can be realized in a society[18]. Owing to these standards one speaks rather about and decisions taken *praeter* or *contra legem*, but not about their illegality.

Legality as a qualification of the activities of the state is viewed as a principle and as reality. Dealing with the former case we are interested in the normative side of legality, that is in principles requiring the legal activities and in legal institutions thought of as factors controlling or guaranteeing the realization of legality; dealing with the latter we are interested in facts, that is to say in qualifying the behavior of officials in the terms of the determined conceptual framework of legality. This framework can be oriented descriptively or evaluatively depending on the concept of legality one uses.

In the final part of this essay I would like to refer briefly to the role of the concepts of legality in the ideologies of the judicial application of law and try to formulate a version of such ideology for a socialist system. I use the term "judicial application of law" in a loose manner to denotate judicial decision-making in solution of cases, without entering into the problem whether and to what extent this activity is a "pure" application of pre-existing rules (statutory rules or *rationes decidendi*) or is a more or less free creation of law[19].

16. The ideology of judicial application of law consists in a set of directives of judicial activity and/or goals set for it as values it should realize[20]. There are three types of such ideologies reconstructed for the civil law systems, namely the positivist ideology of the bound judicial decision, the ideology of the free judicial decision proper for *Freirechts-*

[18] On the objectivity comp. O. Brusiin, *Über die Objektivität der Rechtssprechung*, Helsinki 1949; J. Wróblewski, *Wartości* . . ., op. cit., chapt. VI.

[19] Cf. J. Wróblewski, "Décision judiciaire: l'application ou la création du droit", *Scientia* vol. CIII, N.DCLXXIX–DCLXXX, 1968.

[20] The concept and typology of the ideology of judicial decision: cf. J. Wróblewski, "Idéologie de l'application judiciaire du droit", *Österreichische Zeitschrift für öffentliches Recht* 25, 1974; id., *Sądowe* . . ., op. cit., chapt. XII.

bewegung, libre recherche scientifique or *giusliberismo*, and the ideology of the legal and rational judicial decision, which seems to dominate in contemporary legal culture. I have tried to apply these types for common law systems, and especially to seek some parallels between the styles of American appellate courts' decision-making singled out by LLEWELLYN and these types[21]. There is a close correspondence between the ideology of the bound judicial decision and the "Formal Style" and the ideology of legal and rational decision and the "Style of Reason", but the style of the "Grand Tradition" has no direct corollary in the trichotomy valid for statutory law systems.

In a very rough outline one can characterize the three types of ideologies in question in the following manner.

Ideology of the bound judicial decision treats the judicial decision-making as a purely mechanic or logical reasoning in which there should be no interference of the judge's evaluations. The decision is, in principle, determined by the applied legal rule.

Ideology of the free judicial decision in the extreme version postulates the freedom of the judge to decide according to his sense of justice or equity, even *contra legem*, when this law is not consistent with his evaluations. The moderate versions are not going so far, but stress the great freedom of judicial decision-making based on the lee-ways given for a judge by the features of the formulation of legal provisions and by the inconsistencies and gaps existing in legal system.

The ideology of a legal and rational judicial decision postulates the deciding according to law, but sees the lee-ways the judge has and postulates the rational choices as a guiding principle. The impact of the evaluative element in judicial activity depends on the nature of cases and of the features of law, but in principle is almost always present and, hence, the judicial cognitive and evaluative attitudes are highly relevant for decision-making.

17. Each type of ideology can be also characterized by its use of the concept of legality.

[21] The basic ideas of a trichotomy of styles: see K. N. Llewellyn, *The Common Law Tradition. Deciding Appeals*, Boston–Toronto 1960. Comp. J. Wróblewski, "Ideologia sądowego stosowania prawa w doktrynie amerykańskiej" ("Ideology of Judicial Application of Law in American Doctrine"), in: ed. W. Sokolewicz, *Instytucje i doktryny prawno-polityczne Stanów Zjednoczonych Ameryki*, Wrocław–Warszawa–Kraków–Gdańsk 1974.

The ideology of the bound judicial decision is connected with the concept of formal legality. In the classical formulation of the partisans of this ideology, legality appears as a top value. The exposition of the judicial activity tends to make an impression that the judge only compares the behavior X with the norm N in an axiologically neutral manner, and that the result of this comparison is a relational statement in the form of a true sentence stating the relation in question. Here is no place to criticize this view; it is important, however, to stress that this view obfuscates the properties of judicial decision-making by presenting it as non-evaluative activity. The criticism can demonstrate, that the positivist uses the concept of formal legality also in an evaluative manner. In fact in deciding he takes into account the internal values of law, e.g. in legal interpretation, using this concept in a weak evaluational sense. And as the critics point out, positivist ideology as a whole is based on the concept of formal legality used in strong sense with the general approval: the legal order is valuable as an order.

The ideology of the free judicial decision is evidently for a concept of material legality. In the most spectacular manner it is manifested in the extreme versions of this ideology, when it postulates to decide *contra legem* and materially right, if the decision formally legal does not satisfy the accepted axiological criteria. Hence the formal validity is either no value at all, or — in moderate versions — a rather second-rank value. The concept of material validity is used in a strong sense and in a particular version.

The ideology of legal and rational decision sets the value of formal legality at the top of its axiological system, but sees that the applied norms as a rule do not determine the decisions because of existing lee-ways. Therefore the choices within these lee-ways should correspond to the criteria determined by the axiology which is treated as relevant for the judicial decision-making within a determined socio-political context. What kind of axiology is chosen is not determined, provided that the rational decision should take into account the internal values of the system the applied norm belongs to.

18. As the example of determining a concrete ideology of the judicial decision-making I would like to reconstruct an ideology which seems to be accepted in the judicial activity in the socialist system[22]. This is an

[22] J. Wróblewski, *Wartości* . . ., op. cit., p. 88 sq.

attempt to formulate the strong version of this ideology, but it can be made weaker by changing certain elements of the proposed model. This model was presented and discussed during a conference organized by the Supreme Court of Poland and to my satisfaction received a generally approving opinion.

This ideology is expressed in four postulates: (a) the judge ought to observe strictly the valid legal norms and only decisions consistent with law should be made; (b) the judge should approve of the consistency of his decision with the law accepting the internal values of the applied legal norm; (c) the external evaluation of law is not excluded, but there is no possibility to decide *contra legem*; (d) the evaluations made in the decision-making process should be made according to the internal values of law if these are relevant for the issue, or, if these values give an evaluative lee-way, then the choices should be made according to the external values of the socialist axiology (or at least of an axiology not inconsistent with the socialist axiological system).

This ideology is formulated in a very strong form, because it demands from the judge the complete internalization of the internal values of law and of the socialist axiology. The postulate (a) is typical for all ideologies of the legal and rational judicial decision. The postulate (b) demands the internalization of the values inherent in the socialist legal system the applied norm belongs to; this means that the judge uses the concept of formal legality in both of the strong senses. The postulate (c) states the superiority of the value of formal legality over all external criticism of the law which is important in any *de lege ferenda* activities of the law-making, but this does not belong to the judicial decision-making. The postulate (d) expresses the evaluative attitude of the judge as a person who accepts the socialist axiological system (or at least a system not inconsistent with it). This postulate works for the evaluations, which are not determined by a reconstruction of the internal values of law.

The analysis of ideology of the judicial application of law only partially utilizes the conceptual framework dealing with legality elaborated in the present essay. This framework can be used also for analyzing various attitudes to the observance of the law and the reasons which are used for its justification.

[16]

Rationality and the objectification of law

by CSABA VARGA (*)

I. *Rationality and its place in social and legal development.*

« *Rationality* » and « *rationalization* » are relatively new categories. Both have been transmitted to our age in their contemporary interpretation by Max WEBER. He was the scholar who with a view of the age to come, gave the first comprehensive theoretical exposition of these concepts.

As it is known, WEBER's social reality was the one of the closing period of the 19th century. Unlike MARX, he could study *capitalism* in a *more advanced stage*, in its *clearly unfolded intrinsic administrative complexity* (1). WEBER's critics all agree that the categories in question have formed some sort of an organizing centre in his sociological concept. This will hold true both when he explains rationality as the *ethos* of the way of living characteristic of the West — offering an answer to the question: « what concatenation of circumstances accounts for that, exactly on the soil of the Occident, and only here, cultural phenomena have emerged which, at least in our wishful thinking, point to a direction of development of *universal* importance and validity? » (2) — and when he produces evidence for the causal role of the *ideological forms equivalent*, moreover superior, *to econo-*

(*) Ricercatore presso l'Istituto delle Scienze giuridiche e dell'Amministrazione dell'Accademia delle Scienze di Ungheria.

A paper presented at the international seminar on « Rationalitet och rationalisering i lagstiftning och rättstillämpning » organized by the Lund University Department of Sociology in May, 1977.

(1) MAYER, J.P., *Max Weber and German Politics: A Study in Political Sociology*, London, 1944, pp. 43-44.

(2) WEBER, Max, *Gesammelte Aufsätze zur Religionssoziologie*, 2nd ed., vol. I, Tübingen, Mohr, 1922, p. 1.

mic life so as to arrive at a series of conclusions in which even the *substance of capitalism* is but the rationalization of economic and social life, the *rational calculability of all phenomena* (3). In any event it remains a fact that the otherwise wholly different qualities such as *capitalistic mode of production, legal rule* / as distinguished from the charismatic and the traditional /, or *western development* in general, in WEBER's theory possess one and the same specifically common motive, i.e. a rational state of organization.

In the same way as for MARX the appearance of product as a power mastering and threatening the producer, i.e. the phenomenon of *alienation*, was the focal problem, with WEBER this role was acted by *rationalization*, i.e. by the circumstance that the structures purporting the extension of liberty became independent, and turned into a power restricting this verp liberty itself (4). The print of WEBER's age on his notion of rationality is to be found in the first place in the *absolutizing*, even hypertrophical, *significance* assigned to its notional sphere. « The experience of the genesis of bureaucratic machinery of capitalist soicety ... came to be reflected in WEBER by the image of the rule, móreover historical, of rationalism » (5). This, and « something of the Prussian enthusiasm for the military type of organization » (6), made WEBER discover the *bureaucratic organization* as the *basis of modern economic and social development*, which in universal development has gradually become the basis also of the *ecclesiastical, military, political* and *party* activities of organization.

This kind of the variety of the phenomena concerned forms suspicion about that rationality and rationalization are by far *not uniform, homogeneous notions* identical in meaning in WEBER's *oeuvre*. In one of his most challenging and perhaps most misunderstood writings / where he tried to throw light on certain correlations of the capitalistic mode of production and the devotional development

---

(3) LUKÁCS, Georg, *La destruction de la Raison*, vol. II, Paris, L'Arche, 1959, p. 186.

(4) LÖWITH, Karl, *Max Weber und Karl Marx*, in « Archiv für Sozialwissenschaft und Sozialpolitik », LXVII (1932), pp. 77-99.

(5) KULCSÁR, Kálmán, *A szociológiai gondolkodás fejlödése* (Development of sociological thinking), Budapest, Akadémiai Kiadó, 1956, p. 383.

(6) FRIEDRICH, Carl J., *Some Observations on Weber's Analysis in Bureaucracy*, in « Reader in Bureaucracy », ed. by Robert K. Merton - Ailsa P. Gray - Barbara Hockey - Hanan C. Selvin, New York, The Free Press, 1952, p. 31.

as well as the advancement of life-styles / he himself called attention to possible ambiguities. As he wrote, « life can be rationalized so as to suit a number of different ultimate ends and tendencies running widely apart. Also rationalism is a historical concept which embraces a whole world of contrasts » (7). At the same time, however, he did little to reconcile the notion of rationality as used in various contexts.

Now if we compare the elements concealed in the various uses of the category of rationality, we shall find that ultimately, as regards both the economic and the bureaucratic as well as the legal organization, WEBER draws a line between two senses, namely the *formal* and the *substantive*, of the word ' rationality '. As a matter of fact the *economic*, and the *bureaucratic-legal*, types of rationality bear common traits for being rooted in a common stem. These are but the application of one and the same substance on different fields. On the other hand, the *formal* and the *substantive* senses of rationality appear as homonyms devoid of any theoretical community. Their relationship often reminds the one of mutually independent trends which are on and off antinomically running counter each other. Nevertheless, historically they may appear both alternatingly, and even mutually reinforcing each other, too. Their occurrence together, however, is never an aprioristic, absolute necessity, but in all cases the product of a *concrete* historical situation.

Formal rationality of *economic action* stands for the « quantitative calculation or accounting », « in which the provision for need, which is essential to every rational economy, is capable of being expressed in numerical, calculable terms, and is so expressed ». On the other hand *substantive* rationality is something of a hardly delimitable content: its « concept ... is full of difficulties ». Here « it is not sufficient to consider only the purely formal fact that calculations are being made ... In addition, it is necessary to have account of the fact that economic activity is oriented to ultimate ends of some kind, whether they be ethical, political, utilitarian, hedonistic, the attainment of social distinction, of social equality, or of anything else. Substantive rationality cannot be measured in terms of formal calcul-

(7) WEBER, Max, *Die protestantische Ethik und der Geist des Kapitalismus*, in WEBER, Max, *Gesammelte Aufsätze zur Religionssoziologie*, vol. I, 2nd ed., Tübingen, Mohr, 1922, p. 62.

ation alone, but also involves a relation to the absolute values, or to the content of the particular ends to which it is oriented » ([8]). In both the *bureaucratic organization and the legal one, formal* rationality, too, means « a particularly high degree of the calculability of results » ([9]), which bureaucratic administration translates into reality by the establishment of « an impersonal order », by the « limits laid down by legal precepts » ([10]), whereas law does the same by the « formalization of itself » ([11]), i.e. by organizing abstract norms, previously objectivated in a statutory form, within the framework of a system, on the one hand, and by deciding upon concrete facts at issue through the strict logical application of abstract norms conceived of as a closed system, on the other. *Substantive* rationality qualifies here as rationality « in the meaning of the observance of constant fundamental principles », or « of the substantive principles of social order, whether they be the carriers of political, welfare-utilitarian, or ethical contents » ([12]). In this sense even law and administration, in the organization of which formal rationality is missing, may be rational, too.

If we set out to clarify the concept of rationality as developed by WEBER, we may agree on seeing the gist in calculability /*Berechenbarkeit* / ([13]). Formal rationality has been appraised in a similar manner by Karl MANNHEIM, adapting WEBER's categories to his own system of ideas. As he terms it, *functional* rationality consists of « a series of action ... organized in such a way that it leads to a previously defined goal, every element in this series of actions receiving a functional position and role ». Functional rationality will be of the lighest order when « it co-ordinates the means most efficiently ». At the same time it is necessary neither that it should attain its goal,

---

([8]) WEBER, Max, *The Theory of Social and Economic Organization*, translated by A.A. Henderson - Talcott Parsons, London, etc., Hodge, 1947, p. 170.

([9]) *Ibid.*, 309.

([10]) *Ibid.*, 302.

([11]) « Formally every formal law is at least relatively rational. Law is 'formal' in so far as externally unequivocal general signs of facts at issue are observed in substantive, as well as procedural, law ». WEBER, Max, *Rechtssoziologie*, ed. by Johannes Winckelmann, Neuwied, Luchterhand, 1960, p. 102.

([12]) *Ibid.*, 247.

([13]) DICKMANN, J., *Max Webers Begriff des « modenen okzidentalen Rationalismus »*, Düsseldorf, 1961.

nor that the goal itself should be rational. « ... we should call this behaviour rational because it is organized, since every action has a functional role to play in achieving the ultimate aim ». There is therefore a duality of criteria: « (*a*) Functional organization with reference to a definite goal, and (*b*) a consequent calculability when viewed from the standpoint of an observer or a third person seeking to adjust himself to it » ([14]).

The difference in the approaches indicate that WEBER has defined this kind of rationalization formally, i.e. as *a means for itself*, what is clearly contrasted to MANNHEIM's functional definition, i.e. as an organizational activity *bound for an end*. At the same time the difference is a merely ostensible one: in point of fact the functional approach does not convey anything more than WEBER's accentuated formalism. Their substance is common, i.e. both, the formal rationality and the functional one are in themselves *neutral media with optionally replaceable contents*. This kind of indifference was emphasized by both the WEBERian characterization of their quality as proved to be « formally capable of being applied to all kinds of administrative tasks » ([15]) and by the MANNHEIMian endeavour at segregating functional rationalization from the substantive one ([16]).

The present analysis brings us to the conclusion that in WEBER's theory *formal rationality* is but *pure instrumentality*. This explains the distinguished yet restricted presence of *substantive rationality*: all in all its role is to become the *antipole of formal rationality*. This is why the role it acts appears to WEBER as being of necessity, but of *no autonomous* existence. Indeed, it is necessary that the value-neutrality of formal rationality should be counterbalanced. At the same time, substantive rationality as a counterbalancing motif has no autonomous life to live in WEBER's *oeuvre*. It goes hardly beyond accentuating that formal rationality is devoid of any contents. Here we have come to a further conclusion, namely that according to WEBER substantive rationality is but the *carrier of the purposiveness of formal rationality*, i.e. of the social, etc. contents of its functioning. Our conclusion, however, is but partial.

([14]) MANNHEIM, Karl, *Man and Society in an Age of Reconstruction*, London, Kegan Paul - Trench - Trubner, 1940, p. 53.

([15]) WEBER, *The Theory of Social and Economic Organization*, p. 309.

([16]) MANNHEIM, pp. 58-59.

Formal rationality and substantive rationality are *not* necessarily *exclusively complementary* phenomena. As we have seen, both may occur independently of each other, moreover, they may appear in a way denying or even destroying each other as mutually antinomic antipodes. On the one hand, substantive rationality is not *only* to describe economic, legal, etc. organizatory activity, imbued with formal rationality. On the other hand, owing to the stress laid on the purely technical nature and universal applicability of formally rationalized structures, WEBER had to reckon also with cases of formal rationality which had no substantive rationality whatever as their equivalent ([17]).

At the same time we cannot conclude that formal rationality is devoid of contents in a historically general way.

Being a category focussed on the technical aspects of given organizatory processes, it is true that formal rationality with its direct notional contents is void indeed. However, in order that any formalization might turn rational, first *the intrinsic properties and regularities* of the processes in question have *to be explored.*

LUKÁCS writes: « For the essence of rational calculation is based ultimately upon the recognition and the inclusion in one's calculations of the inevitable chain of cause and effect in certain events — independently of individual caprice » ([18]). This is the reason why he created but a *single*, uniform, concept of rationality. For he presupposed a *preliminary cognition* at the very outset, still he did not project this as something necessarily inherent in the concept, into a separate category.

As a matter of fact it was the *monopoly capitalism* and its *bureaucratic machinery* growing *powerful* at the end of the 18th century, which acted an inspring role in WEBER's theoretical concept. Endeavouring to reflect capitalism and its bureaucracy as ideal types, how-

---

([17]) The question may be raised whether this is to be meant by the irrational-formal type in the webersque ideal typology of law as explained by FREUND, Julien, *Sociologie de Max Weber*, 2nd ed., Paris, Presses Universitaires de France, 1968, p. 223, this type being characterized by formalized irrationality, like an administration of justice relying on pure revelation or prophecies.

([18]) LUKÁCS, George, *Reification and the Consciousness of the Proletariat*, in LUKÁCS, George, *History and Class Consciousness: Studies in Marxist Dialectics*, translated by R. Livingstone, Cambridge (Mass.), The MIT Press, 1971, p. 98.

ever, WEBER absolutized these historically more or less particular tendencies. Under the guise of formal rationality he generalized the dominant trends of his age. At the same time he intended to provide *universally valid* definitions for his ideal types. In the framework of such an a-historical historicity we have to read his epistemologically sceptical lines: « The increasing intellectualization and rationalization do *not* ... indicate an increased and general knowledge of the conditions under which one lives. It means something else, namely the knowledge or belief that if one but wished one *could* learn it at any time. Hence, it means that principally there are no mysterious incalculable forces that come into play, but rather that one can, in principle, master all things by calculation. This means that the world is disenchanted » (19). It means that on the level of the totality of historical processes he recognized the *more conscious and effective appropriation of the world through formal rationalization.*

On the other hand LUKÁCS, who viewed *formal rationalization* from the aspect of the organization of economic and working processes, relying on *actual cognition* and having an *alienating effect*, treated cognition not only as a natural precondition, but discovered one of the roots of *alienation* exactly in the *specialization made possible* by cognition. « If we follow the path taken by labour in its development from the handicraft via cooperation and manufacture to machine industry, » he wrote, « we can see a continuous trend towards greater rationalization, the progressive elimination of the qualitative, human and individual attributes of the worker ». « Rationalization in the sense of being able to predict with ever greater precision all the results to be achieved is only to be acquired by the exact breakdown of every complex into its elements and by the study of the special laws governing production. Accordingly it must declare war on the organic manufacture of whole products based on the *traditional amalgam of empirical experiences of work*: rationalization is unthinkable without specialization ». « The formal standardization of justice, the state, the civil service, etc., signifies objectively and factually a comparable reduction of all social functions to their elements, a comparable search for the rational formal laws of these carefully segregated

---

(19) WEBER, Max, *Science as Vocation*, in WEBER, Max, *Essay in Sociology*, translated by H.H. Gerth - C. Wright Mills, London, Kegan Paul, etc., 1947, p. 139.

partial systems. Subjectively, the divorce between work and the individual capacities and needs of worker produces comparable effects upon consciousness. This results in an inhuman, standardized division of labour analogous to that which we have found in industry on the technological and mechanical plane » ([20]).

As far as the embeddedness of WEBER's types in his age is concerned, it manifested itself at two points which, for WEBER, meant a newly emerged, acute socio-political problem. Their timeliness, however, has not remained tied exclusively to that age: it has been preserved even to the present day.

The one point is the *universal applicability* of formally rationalized structures. This means that the structures in question, being *created and actuated in a formal way* ([21]), may operate in diverse *manners serving opposite functions.* Although formal definition is in all cases a definition of concrete contents, by concentrating on formal marks it incorporates them as they are given only at its birth. Considering its whole span of life, formal definition is therefore gradually gaining independence. *Its independence* is, of course, *not simply a burden* on it, *but one of its very basic functions.* Formal definition will be objectified merely in order that *by grasping* the phenomena, etc. *by their formal marks it might be turned against* its *original contents, and made to master them.*

The other point is to be found in the circumstance that, historically, with the mass utilization of these structures, a *practically indestructible form* has come into being, whose objective indispensability and impersonality have brought about that notwithstanding considerable *politico-economic changes* these structures *go on operating formally unscathed, continuously.* « A rationally ordered system of

---

([20]) LUKÁCS, *Reification and the Consciousness of the Proletariat*, pp. 88 and 98-99.

([21]) In this connection he writes: « the broad masses of those guided acquire merely the external, technical, for their interests practicable, issues to adapt themselves to them (in the same way as we ' learn ' the elements of arithmetic, or so many lawyers the technics of law), whereas the ' idea ' contents given to by the issuing factor remains irrelevant to them. This is what the thesis wants to emphasize: rationalization and rational ' order ' revolutionize ' from the outside ', whereas Charisma, the other way round, ' from the inside ' ». WEBER, Max, *Wirtschaft und Gesellschaft*, Studienausgabe herausgegeben von Johannes Winckelmann, zweiter Halbband, Köln-Berlin, Kiepenhauser und Witsch, 1964, p. 837.

officials ... merely need to change the top officials », writes WEBER. As precedents he merely had to think of the practice of the *coups d'État* in France, or of the bureaucracy Bismarck had created which, while eliminating Bismarck, survived him and went on living the life of its own (22).

Universal applicability as derived from formal definition is, of course, a polarized term: it refers to the *ambiguities of the merely formal, which follow from any indefiniteness in contents.* In any event universal applicability seems to be an inseparable property of formal rationality, capable of turning it into substantive irrationality.

In this manner formally rationalized structures are phenomena of many potentialities permitting their use as *continuous elements in the discontinuity of socio-economic development.* At the same time these are structures which, even if at a given moment historically adequate, are but static reflections of reality: they *petrify* reality, and *stunt* it in its development. Hence the static nature of these structures will thrust the *erstwhile adequacy*, too, into the abyss of sure inadequacy.

The startling fact that formally rationalized structures have started to grow beyond their original conditions and, by this, *instead of mediation*, they have begun *imposing* themselves upon reality in the teeth of the prevailing socio-economic needs and tendencies, caused WEBER to discover the ambivalence of rationality, i.e. the conclusion that processes of rationalization « combine at once the specific achievement of modern world and the whole questionability of this achievement » (23). This is why LUKÁCS considered the formal rationalization *artificial creation* of realities, whose *independence* as only *partially defined by socio-economic reality*, is its inherent quality. By the way this independence is to appear expressedly in exceptional situations only, when these structures are shattered. « This rationalization of the world ... is limited, however, by its own formalism. That is to say, the rationalization of isolated aspects of life results in the creation of — formal — laws. All these things do join together into what seems to the superficial observer to constitute a unified system of general laws. But the disregard of the concrete aspects of the subject matter of these laws, upon which disregard of their autho-

(22) WEBER, *Essays in Sociology*, p. 229.
(23) LÖWITH, p. 88.

rity as laws is based, makes itself felt in the incoherence of the system in fact. This incoherence becomes particularly egregious in periods of crisis. At such times we can see how the immediate continuity between two partial systems is disrupted and their independence, form and adventitious connection with each other is suddenly forced into the consciousness of everyone » ([24]). Simultaneously with the processes of rationalization, situations have come into being in which, as LUKÁCS writes, « men are constantily smashing, replacing and leaving behind them the natural, irrational and actually existing bonds, while, on the other hand, they erect around themselves in the reality they have created and made, a kind of second nature which evolves with exactly the same inexorable necessity as was the case earlier on with irrational forces of nature / more exactly: the social relations which appear in this form /. To them their own social action, says MARX, takes the form of the action of objects, which rule the produces instead of being ruled by them » ([25]).

Thus formal rationalization has been turned inside out. It becomes a two-edged tool: a paradoxical phenomenon. Formal rationalization has been completed in order to fill indispensable socio-economic functions. Its *practical functioning*, however, *leads* with inexorable regularity *to disfunctionality limiting the socio-economic need itself*.

WEBER emphasized that the formal rationalization of private economy, the bureacratic administration and the law, was the product of *feudal absolutism*. This was the age when the advance of *capitalist production* and *state bureaucracy* / i.e. the mutuality of interests among the feudal ruler, the armada of career civil servants and the rising bourgeois layers/made the rule of formally rationalized structures the *conditio sine qua non* of further development ([26]).

In whatever acute form the formal rationality problem emerged in WEBER's age, the novelty was not the mere appearance of formally rationalized structures, but their development to *exclusive dominance*, notably *the integration of the part systems of formally rationalized structures to the very foundations of the socio-economic system itself*.

As far as the appearance and pecularity of formal rationality in the field of law is concerned, in the first place it is to be noted that

---

([24]) LUKÁCS, *Reification and the Consciousness of the Proletariat*, p. 101,
([25]) *Ibid*., p. 128.
([26]) E.g, WEBER, *Rechtssoziologie*, p. 249.

the historically conditioned nature of the need for calculability has been denied by several tendencies. Tendencies namely which have had their origin in preconceived ideologies and philosophical standpoints.

This was the case above all with Nazi Germany, where the institutions of democracy, parliamentarianism, constitutionality, and legality, had been rejected, and in sake of a political leadership relying on the *Führerprinzip*, any *limitation* imposed *by the formal law* had been *liquidated.* For the National-Socialist German Workers' Party and the *Reichsführer* the *formally rationalized law, exactly because it kept power in bounds and refined even arbitrariness to systematic oppression, became simply unacceptable.* This explains why already in 1933 some definitively pseudo-historical ideological statements were formulated for annihilating the law: « substantially, law is conceived by liberalism as a set of legal norms ... for defining the freedom of action of the individual ... Individualism strives for clearly delineating the boundaries of the freedom of action ... For individualism, security in the law is not supposed to guarantee intrinsic justice; what matters to him is only the outer calculability of the series of one's own affairs ... For this security in the law, expressedly defined legal provisions and regulated fields of law are needed; indeed, the main aim of liberalism is codification, the regulation and consolidation of all extrinsic rights of a people » ([27]).

In a peculiar manner the theoretical roots of such and similar ideas drew their nourishment from a tendency, general all over Western Europe ever since the closing years of the 19th century. It is

---

([27]) LANGE, Heinrcih, *Liberalismus, Nationalsozialismus und bürgerliches Recht*, Tübingen, 1933, p. 5. It should be noted that although Lange's standpoint has practically never been denied, it must have been considered an exaggeration usual with neophytes. For officially the National-Socialist constitutional law formulated the same thesis on manipulating the question how to offer a resolution to the conflicts between the statute and the law. « In the 'völkisch' ... constitutional state ... the exercise of rights has to result from firm norms within the boundaries of the national living order, and legal regulation for the individual 'Volksgenosse' will become calculable therefrom ». However, any guarantee inherent in formal standardization will be dissolved by the fact that « [i]n a National-Socialist constitutional state the idea of law will be decisive instead of any form of law. The law comes first, and then the statute ». KOELLREUTTER, Otto, *Deutsches Verfassungsrecht: Ein Grundriss*, 2nd ed., Berlin, Junker und Dünnhaupt, 1936, pp. 14 and 15,

well known that *monopoly capitalistic development* made the gradual adaptation of the law, once codified in a liberal spirit, an urgent requirement. It was fulfilled through the liquidation of the exegetic way of law-application, closely adhering to the wording of the code while reducing the judge's function to the one of a deductive machine. This is the genesis of the *free law movement*, the counterpole of exegesis, whose historically limited character had not been recognized even by the sociologists of the age. Most of them valued the movement not only as a new achievement, but one acquired once for all. This was how Karl MANNHEIM looked at it: « the fundamental principle of formal law by which every case must be judged according to general rational precepts, which have as few exceptions as possible and are based on logical subsumption, obtains only for the liberal-competitive phase of capitalism and not, as MAX WEBER believed, for capitalism in general ». For « [t]he correlations between liberal-competitive capitalism and formal law, and between monopoly capitalism and increasing legal irrationalism are ... historically limited *principia media* » (28).

The development as demonstrated by the free law *judicature of monopoly capitalism* was however *irreversible only in relation to the exegesis as the kind of formal rationalization resulting in extremely disfunctional and substantially irrational issues.* Development temporarily denied formal rationality only in order to render possible the detachment from exegesis, and the continual adaptation of the law to the new needs. What appeared as the disintegration of legality was merely a *historically limited concept of legality*. It was the rule of law idea particular to bourgeois revolutions that was in a state of disintegration. After the free law movement was over, development led gradually to a relatively stabilized new, though looser, concept of rule of law, and not to an anarchistic nihil.

If we consider *legal development* in its whole complexity, it will become evident that one of its determining tendencies is the *more optimal and effective expansion of formal rationality.* Unlike the processes of reification, however, here the case is not of the self-development of form. We may, in general, make the statement that *in social commerce the formalities / manifesting themselves in the institutionalized functions of security, safety, unambiguity and con-*

---

(28) MANNHEIM, pp. 180, 181.

trollability / have their origin in the need for having an efficacious modelling and controlling of social conducts ([29]).

It will suffice to bear in mind that although the political power-enforcement organization and its law have come into being only with the splitting of society into classes of antagonistic interests, the regulative function itself which later has become institutionalized as the specific means of the class struggle considerably preceded the establishment of the law *as law*. When « somewhat more closely examining the complex which is supposed to perform the legal regulation of social activities », it becomes evident that « this need was to come about at a relatively low stage of development of the social division of labour. Even at a simple cooperation / e.g. hunting / the duties of each participant have got to be most precisely regulated on the basis of the concrete working process, and on that of the concrete division of labour evolving out of it / e.g. beaters and hunters at hunting /. But it must be remembered ... that the regulation consists of influencing the participants in such a manner that they shall perform, on their behalf, the teleological postulations that they have been allotted to perform in the overall plan of cooperation» ([30]). It is this *regulative function* which has soon achieved its *formally most rationalized expression in law*. In the process from the *cognition* of the effects of social action to their *formal prediction* through establishing a network of regulatory patterns of conduct, *law has got the farthest*. It was law that has projected as a formally enacted system of norms the patterns of conduct in which « the measured itself changes into the measure », i.e. « which sets instrumental activity as a target before man » ([31]).

Consequently on the one hand the *minimum of formal rationality*, i.e. *standardization*, appeared already in the *prototypes of law*. On the other there can be no doubt that this quasi-law in its formally rationalized structure will *survive* both the state and the law, taken

---

([29]) Cf. LÉVY-BRUHL, Henri, *Réflexions sur le formalisme social*, in « Cahiers internationaux de Sociologie », XV (1953), pp. 53 et seq.

([30]) LUKÁCS, György, *A társadalmi lét ontológiájáról* (Toward the ontology of social being), vol. II, Budapest, Magvetö, 1976, p. 208.

([31]) MAKAI, Mária, *Az erkölcsi tudat dialektikája* (The dialectics of moral consciousness), Budapest, Kossuth, 1966, pp. 136 and 153. Also cf. VARGA, Csaba, *The Preamble: A Question of Jurisprudence*, in « Acta Juridica Academiae Scientiarum Hungaricae », XIII (1971) 1-2, pp. 108 et seq.

in their class function. For it is beyond doubt that whatever an idea we may have of the *communist society* as foreseen by the classics of Marxism, we cannot even imagine this without some sort of an objectified system of social norms, i.e. without having structures of formal rationality in it.

Just in this connection it is worthwhile to note that the almost uniform positions which in the wake of the programme approved by the XXIInd Congress of the Communist Party of the Societ Union, tried to prognosticate the future society, and eventually declared moral norms the heirs of the legal organization of soceity ([32]), have been revised. The new position relies on the conviction that formal rationality is to be preserved, precisely on the ground of historical experiences. It has been recognized, namely, that the normatives of social co-existence cannot, in their majority, be restricted to moral norms. As has been pointed out, the « social organizational » as well as the « technical-organizational », norms have to control conduct with a normative force, binding all and everybody, as being formally objectified in a written from ([33]).

II. *Rationality as an Aim of the Objectification of Law.*

A change perhaps of the greatest moment took place in legal development, when *law* became *detached from social practice* un-

---

([32]) E.g. WILNYANSKY, S.I., *Pravovye normy i inye sotsialnye normy v period razvernutogo stroitelstva kommunizma* (Legal norms and other social norms in the period of the building development of Communism), in « Sovetskoe gosudarstvo i pravo v period razvernutogo stroitelstva kommunizma », Charkov, 1962, p. 16; ALEKSEEV, S.S., *O pererastanii sovetskogo prava va sisteme norm kommunistitcheskogo obshtchezhitiya* (Transition of Soviet law into the system of norms of the period of Communist coexistence), in « Sovetskoe gosudarstvo i pravo », 1962/5, p. 21; MITSKEVITCH, A.V., *Nekotorye tcherty vzaimodeystvia prava i nravstvennosti v period perekhoda k kommunizmu* (Some of the traits of the correlations of law and morals in the period of transition to Communism), in « Pravovedenie », 1962/3, pp. 21 et seq.

([33]) E.g. LEYST, O.E., *Normy prava i pravila kommunistitcheskogo obshtchezhitia* (Legal norms and the rules of communist coexistence), in « Razvitive marksistko-leninskoy teorii gosudarstva i prava XXII s'yezdom KPSS », ed. N.G. Aleksandrov - S.N. Bratus, Moscow, Gosizdat. Yuriditecheskoy Literatury, 1963, p. 136; KRASAVTHIKOV, O.A., *Yuriditcheskaya nauka i kommunizm* (Jurisprudence and Communism), in « Pravo i kommunizm », ed. D.A. Kerimov, Moskow, Yuriditcheskaya Literatura, 1965, pp. 178-179.

divided till then, *and changed over to a formal objectification, what meant its reduction to being formally enacted in a written form* (34). *The transition from custom to statute* (35) is the dividing line that separates *prehistory* of law from its *history proper*, whence a « peculiarly legal-formal process » starts, which with the expanding role of the State has brought about the ever more perfected normative form (36). Law is to veritably become the regulator of life only when it has come objectified with an autonomous « *ought* »-structure as a *category wedged between social objectives and actual social practice* (37). By spining of the everyday practice, law is to gain an independent existence. Thereby it ceases to be the pure reflection of the conditions of social life.

This has been given expression by the fact that causal relationship between social conduct and its outcome disappears in the process of objectification. *As the objective postulated by the norm, exclusively the action, normatively judged as an appropriate means of achieving the result, will appear, instead of the socially desired result itself.*

Consequently law is nothing else but the *congeries of instrumental conducts postulated as objectives.* Indeed here something is conceived as possessing existence, which is not yet reality (33). Exactly in order to translate it into reality, as *mediator* a structure has to be *extracted from reality*, which is at the same time but a *transformed reality*, not being given in it directly. The fact, on the other hand, that on the ground of a series of teleological postulations we make

---

(34) Cf. VARGA, Csaba, *Kodifikációs előformák az ókori jogfejlődésben* (Primitive forms of codification in the ancient development of law), in « Állam- és Jogtudomány », XVII (1974) 1, pp. 83-100.

(35) « At a given, very original stage of social development the need arises for subjecting the daily recurring acts of production, distribution and exchange to a common rule in order that the individual submits himself to the common production and exchange conditions. This rule, at first custom, soon develops to a law ». ENGELS, Friedrich, *Zur Wohnungsfrage*, in MARX, Karl - ENGELS, Friedrich, *Ausgewählte Schriften*, vol. I, Moskau, Verlag für fredmsprachige Literatur, 1951, p. 592.

(36) SZABÓ, Imre, *Les fondements de la théorie du droit*, Budapest, Akadémiai Kiadó, 1973, p. 109.

(37) PESCHKA, Vilmos, *Grundprobleme der modernen Rechtsphilosophie*, Budapest, Akadémiai Kiadó, 1974, pp. 45 et seq.

(38) HEGEL, Georg Wilhem Friedrich, *Die Phänomenologie des Geistes*, Leipzig, 1949, p. 426.

the *conducts*, having *instrumental* role only in the interrelations of reality, *independent normative ends*, betrays that by establishing the *norm-structures we have already brough about a formally rationalized structure*. For the construction of norm-structures brings things or relations, not patently interrelated, into a *normative relationship*, and makes them calculable. By exploring the regularities of reality a second reality is going to be built on it. This second reality will be built on reality as a *system of references*, which *by converting social conducts to a series of positive or negative fulfilments of the normative system, provides facilities for the calculation of the normative consequences of any conduct conforming (or non-conforming) to the conduct normatively judged as desirable.*

As far as the different kinds and possible manifestations of formal rationality in the development of law are concerned, we have to begin with WEBER's ideal typology (39). There are two *substantive types*: first, *the irrational-substantive* (which can hardly be discovered in the historical forms of law, being mostly closed to the despot's pure arbitrariness), and, secondly, the *rational-substantive* (which embraces the early practive of Hindu, Moslem, etc. sacred books; the traditional Chinese, Japanese, African, etc. procedures of conciliation; further the attempts at converting political will directly into law, e.g. the administration of jjustice relying on mere ' revolutionary legality '). At the same time there can be no doubt that even WEBER considered *formal law* the *law proper*, truly productive of development. Formal law has likewise two ideal types. First, there is the *irrational-formal* (which means formally bound irrationality as appearing in the administration of justice by revelation, prophecy, etc.), and, secondly, the *rational-formal* (represented by the French *Code civil* and its exegetic practice).

The logical equivalence of these ideal types is no more than an appearance projected into a notional classification covering realities which cannot by far be equated. Realities referred to by the ideal types have no direct correspondence to the very reality. There-

---

(39) The ideal types of law are enumerated here on the ground of FREUND's interpretation (p. 223). Naturally another typology might as well be read of Weber's work. See e.g. GROSCLAUDE, Jacques, *La sociologie du droit de Max Weber*: Introduction et traduction, Strasbourg, 1973, pp. 57-98. This seems to be, however, less convincing, not satisfying even some requirements of logic.

fore they betray only that beyond its rational-formal type, law also had *other* potentialities. It says a word neither of the true historical ratios of these potentialities, nor of the fact that among them there was one which, step by step, permeated all others until it did get hold of an optimum exclusiveness.

Indeed, already in the development of the Antiquity and the Middle Ages each step which tended towards the *objectification of law*, i.e. towards its *embodiment in statutory* written form, and thereby towards the reduction of the *ius* to the *lex*, eventually prepared the path for the *formally more and more rational structures of law*.

We may ponder on the ostensible lack of antecedents in the high cultures sprung up in the Near East. Nevertheless it remains a fact that the *first* formally rationalized structures of law were at the same time the *earliest surviving relics* of any written law, i.e. *reform codes*, which as the results of accelerated economic development, bear testimony to the law-centralizing tendencies of the early empires embarking on territorial expansion and translating into reality the conscious legal change through having enacted *written law by the side of customary law* ([40]). In the course of subsequent development the *objectification of law with rationalizing effects* took place primarily in a similar context, i.e. as successfully performed tasks of *strongly cenralized, consolidated, absolutistic regimes*. Naturally it should be remembered that these were the regimes where the need for *a uniform administration and judicature* had to be defined both politically and economically in the first place. These were also the regimes where for the performance of governmental tasks an *army of civil servants* had to be organized which, for its part, became a claimant for and at the same time the propagator of such rationalized structures.

At the same time, however, we have to bear in mind that the creation of the formally rationalized structures of law was in the development of neither the Antiquity nor the Middle Ages the exclusive privilege of absolutistic regimes. Where *economic, or political, need* for them emerged still there was *no power which would have advanced their establishment*, they were brought about as *oeuvres of doctrine*, while their practical enforcement came to be

---

([40]) Cf. note 34.

entrusted to the *self-assertion* of the economic-political need. This was the role proper of various private codifications of feudal particularism (i.e., among others, that of many unoficial draft-codes prepared to obey a royal command but never receiving its seal, or of the notion-analysing and notion-systematizing doctrinal works of jurisprudents), that is of all the quasi-code products which lacked both statutory form and formal validity ([41]). These were products which in practice, like the 19th century text-books and other kinds of theoretical codification of the Common law ([42]), filled the codification vacuum with the available *theoretical* objectifications most appropriate for operation as quasi-codifications.

The significance of the codificational work characteristic of the Antiquity and Middle Ages development was twofold. First, it was the offspring, and, at the same time, the parent, of the rise to domination of conscious legislation with a claim to creative power, advancing its victory by formal rationalization. Secondly, it meant a qualitative progress by itself. For it was characteristic even of its earliest occurrence that such codes had *organized the norm-structures within the framework of some sort of a mutually interrelated system.* Their system-character, maybe purely contingent, could manifest itself in a set of historically superimposed 'systems', in a casuistic sequence of casual provisions, or in a mere quantitative amalgam ostensibly void of any 'system', they still indicated a qualitative progress. Their 'system'-character manifested itself at least *in objectively synthetizing the norms which were hitherto atomized* by having nothing but mutual isolation from each other.

The rationalizing effect of the early codes, taken into account also by WEBER ([43]), is, however, not to be overrated. Amist their own conditions they performed *codificational functions* and prepared the path for modern codification, on the one hand, and explored the *element of formal rationality* in law as the *conditio sine qua non* of any conscious, planned, willed and controlled, social influencing, on

---

([41]) Cf. VARGA, Csaba, *Kodifikációs megnyilvánulások a középkori jogfejlődésben* (Manifestations of codification in the medieval development of law), in « Állam- és Jogtudomány », XVIII (1975) 1, pp. 135-158.

([42]) VARGA, Csaba, *Kodificáció az angolszász rendszerekben* (Codification in Common law), in « Állam- és Jogtudomány », XVI (1973) 4, pp. 611-634, in particular sections 3-4 and 7-8.

([43]) E.g. WEBER, *Rechtssoziologie*, p. 253.

the other. Formal rationality gained independent existence, concentrated on a calculability in a new type way, *only* in the course of bourgeois development.

The category of formal rationality has become predominant when history has made its core, *calculability*, the virually indispensable structural element of *economic development*. It may be therefore stated that development in the professional rationalization of law is but one of the consequences of « the economic rationalization resting on the soil of competitive market and the freedom of contract » ([44]).

Or, more precisely, in the same way as in the calculatory forms of economic oragnization not only the rising bourgeoisie were interested, but the *total of social motions* was *instrumental* well ahead of the coming into political power of the bourgeoisie, so neither the calculatory form of legal organization was the particular class interest of solely the bourgeoisie. First, « bourgeois interests demanded a law ... operating *in a calculable manner*, ... freed from irrational administrative arbitrariness and the irrationality of concrete privileges ». Secondly, since « the rise of both the formal equality of rights and positive formal norms met with the ruler's interests as opposed to feudal privileges », the « alliance of interest between the ruler and the bourgeois strata was the most potent driving force of formal law-rationalization ». As complementary motives there were, on the ruler's side, the need for uniform operation of *the army of civil servants*, and, on the side of these latter, the demand for the « manageability » of the law, as well as « the technical needs of administration ». Thus WEBER understood the impersonal system of norms, striving after completeness, of the bureaucratic *Herrschaft* in a rather generalized form ([45]).

Feudal absolutism came nevertheless to naught. This was the case because, notwithstanding the partial assistance absolute ruler extended to bourgeois interests, it remained the principal obstacle in the way of capitalist development, and brought to light its historical limitation in every form of rationalization dictated by its *own* interests. Thanks to monarchical benevolence and self-complacent enlightenment, such extreme rationalizations had been called to life which were symbolic of « the cosmos of legal obligations: the universality

---

([44]) *Ibid.*, p. 100.
([45]) *Ibid.*, pp. 249 and 250.

of damned duties and obligations », and turned the rationalism of calculability inside out ([46]).

That kind of alliance of interest was in fact the carrier of any preparatory work to codification. Modern codification as a new type in formal law-rationalization was brought about by *bourgeois revolution*, when the new political establishment permitted the formation of a superstructure reflecting the needs of the economic set-up.

As regards the *ideological and technical antecedents of modern codification*, they had their *roots, too, in the needs of the bourgeoisie. Modern codification* introduced something qualitatively new into the idea of codification by laying the stress on the *reorganization of legal norms within the framework of a by itself coherent and interrelated system*, instead of their merely quantitative consolidation. So the *antecedents* of modern codification were provided by the idea of *mathesis universalis*, the axiomatic tendencies of natural law, as well as the *notion-analysing work* done by the jurisprudents preparing the reception of the Roman law, i.e.. by the *theoretical anticipation of the system-idea* later to be embodied by the codes ([47]).

Hence, such forms of thought assisted at the preparation of modern codes, which, too, were calculatory structures, patterns of thought, or ideologies, underlying the economic-political struggle of the bourgeoisie. These forms of thought were themselves *defined by the same economic-social factors* which, within the overall process, invested them with the special function to bring about formally rationalized structures in law. In this way WEBER's thesis — according to which « [i]t is (material and ideal) interests and not ideas that directly control human activity. Still very often like pointsmen working the switches, the images of the world, created by ideas, define the tracks on which activities, motivated by the dynamics of interests, will go on » ([48]) — proves to be shortcircuited.

([46]) Here WEBER offers a description of the *Prussian Allgemeines Landrecht. Ibid.*, p. 259.

([47]) Cf. VARGA, Csaba, *A kodifikáció klasszikus tipusának születése Franciaországban* (The birth of the classical type of codification in France), in « Állam- és Jogtudomány », XVII (1974) 3, pp. 457-479, in particular section 2/a. As regards some preliminary questions cf. VARGA, Csaba, *Leibniz és a jogi rendszerképzés kérdése* (Leibniz and the question of the formation of systems in law), in « Jogtudományi Közlöny », XXVIII (1973) 11, pp. 600-608.

Determining images of the world, created by ideas, have been on their part defined by common roots.

« It is anything but a mere chance, » writes LUKÁCS, « that at the very beginning of the development of modern philosophy the ideal of knowledge took the form of universal mathematics: it was an attempt to establish a rational system of relations which comprehends the totality of the formal possibilities, proportion and relations of a rationalized existence with the aid of which every phenomenon — independently of its real and material distinctiveness — could be subjected to an exact calculus ». This explains why *mathematics*, as well as the axiomatic system-idea, within it, have become the methodological pattern of modern thinking. « For the way in which their axioms are related to the partial systems and results deduced from them corresponds exactly to the postulate that the systematic rationalism sets itself, the postulate, namely, that every given aspect of the system should be capable of being deduced from its basic principle, that it should be exactly predictable and calculable » (49).

The theoretical possibility that *law should be treated as the subject-matter of exact logical calculation*, and that *logical* operation with legal propositions and relevant conducts should constitute both the *framework and the stepping stone of all legal reasoning*, should be looked for in two directions equally referring to bourgeois tendencies. Historically the possibility of any logical view of law came about at a time when *Roman law* had *shed its* national *character* and, through the notion-analysing and notion-systematizing work by jurisprudents, gained a for its contents *renewed*, for its form *in itself consistent, structure* in order that it might be adapted and applied, as some sort of a European universal law, to the exchange relationships characteristic of bourgeois development (50). On the other hand *laws, too, came to be constructed as mental anticipations only*, laws whose background was provided by the methodological and ideological postulates of universal mathematism and natural law. Whole *systems of doctrinal law* were in this way built up *by axiomatic deduction* departing from general principles and arriving

(48) WEBER, *Gesammelte Aufsätze zur Religionssoziologie*, vol. I, p. 252.

(49) LUKÁCS, *Reification and the Consciousness of the Proletariat*, pp. 129 and 117.

(50) WEBER, *Rechtssoziologie*, pp. 101 and 256-257.

at particular provisions. As the prevailing doctrine considered *natural law* more original and universal in validity than positive law its *rationalist* variant tended to ideologically supporting the political struggle of the bourgeoisie, on deducing as the Law of Reason the social order desirable for the bourgeoisie, from a few artificially worked-up basic principles. In order that formally rationalized structures might afford a guaranteed basis for calculation, a formal-technical desire for and independent ideology of the *subjective rights* and the *equality of rights* developed with an edge pointed at feudalism and its privileges. And how strongly natural law was imbued by the way of thinking characteristic of universal mathematism, is indicated by the fact that even at the bursting of natural law as an ideology, its methological conclusion escaped unscathed. « Of the tents of natural law the only one to survive was the idea of the unbroken continuity [' lückenlosige Zusammenhang ', i.e. quite propertly, 'a connection without gaps' — a note by Cs. V.] of the formal system of law », as stated by LUKÁCS with reference to the age of bourgeois disillusionment with the prevalence of positivism abandoning natural law ([51]).

As far as the concrete social background and historical necessity of the rationalization of law, and codification as its means, are concerned, even WEBER came to the conclusion that « conditions of life, and also the bourgeois interests in a ' calculable ' law ...., might as well or often even better be guaranted by a formally empiric law tied to precedents » ([52]). Here WEBER was undoubtedly right. For the *English-American* and the *Continental* bourgeois transformations, even if taken place in different ways at different times, did not create a difference which would have altered the *fundamental bourgeois demand for calculability* in economic, etc. organization. And yet the historical continuity characteristic of Common law development must have harboured something in it, which hampered it from following the Continental path.

Consequently it seems as if all we have told of the economic and social need for *calculability*, of the *ideological forms* advancing its establishing, etc., were *by themselves too little for producing the veritably rational forms of rationalization* ([53]).

([51]) LUKÁCS, *Reification and the Consciousness of the Proletariat*, p. 108.

([52]) WEBER, *Rechtssoziologie*, pp. 257-258.

([53]) It should be noted that this need has been satisfied also in Common law, however, by paths defined by traditions, therefore circuitous, more

WEBER's reply, however, that for both reshaping law by logic and systematizing it by codification, the decisive incentive was « given by the intrinsic intellectual needs of the law theoretician and the literary 'erudition' prevailing in the domain of law » ([54]), can hardly be accepted as satisfactory. For the peculiarity which exclusively the *European* legal development concealed in itself, was above all the series of consequences of *feudal particularism* issuing at the *dismemberment of law*, i.e. at *the want of the unity of law*, more and more hampering the economic-social advancement of bourgeois civilization. This was the milieu which made possible and even necessary the *'de-nationalization' of the classical Roman Law*, i.e. the specific dogmatic legal work, in consequence of which law became, in a formal sense, a set of norms organized into a logical system, and, as for its contents, a common European law regulating barter conditions in a manner more appropriate and predictable than anything else before. It was this want of unity which as early as the age of feudal absolutism in Europe, led to experiments in the *codificational renovation of law*, and then, as a result of the French Revolution, to the creation of the ideal and basic type of formal law-rationalization.

The same act which had created formally rationalized structures, launched these on to the path of a *development gradually following the course of its own*. In order that formal rationality might become consolidated, there emerged a need for an ideology according to which « law is henceforth to be regarded as a formal calculus, with the aid of which the legal consequences of particular actions ... can be determined as exactly as possible ». The need for exact calculation involved a further ideological demand, namely that « the legal system should confront the individual events of social existence as something permanently established and exactly defined, i.e. as a rigid system » ([56]).

---

expensive, but in efficacy inferior. At the same time this solution has been at most the calculability of results, achieved by irrational structures and methods.

([54]) WEBER, *Rechtssoziologie*, p. 258.

([55]) VARGA, Csaba, *Kodifikációs megnyilvánulások a feudális abszolutizmus korában* (Manifestations of codification in the age of feudal absolutism), in « Jogtudományi Közlöny », XXXI (1976) 2, pp. 70-80.

([56]) LUKÁCS, *Reification and the Consciousness of the Proletariat*, pp. 108 and 97.

And here we have before us in a ready, evolved, completed form the classical law of the classical society of formal rationality, which exactly because of being a *formally rationalized* structure, detaches itself from the social-economic conditions giving birth to, and reflected in it as, a *second reality*, and lives a *life of its own*. For the formal, rigid structure underlying the exact calculation strives after *exclusiveness* and *completeness*. Calculability means universal applicability: it cannot have limits. To each conceivable relevant question it must get a definite reply. On the one hand it is obvious that the structure having to reflect the need of a complex reality dynamically moving and never identical with itself, cannot be merely formal and rigid, presenting both exclusiveness and completeness. On the other hand, however, for the sake of exact calculation the structure serving as a basis for calculation is *expected* to be regarded as such. And what is factually impossible, will nevertheless become normatively possible. Although jurists are aware of the fact that law does not dispose of these properties, *they act as if* the structure in question was *in reality* invested with. *Fictitiousness* will be apparent in both the practical application and the background ideology of these structures. As a by-product of their application a *separate reality* will appear, which above all puts on the form of postulates. According to WEBER « The present day juristic work attaining the highest degree of methodological-logical rationality sets out from the following postulates: (1) Any concrete legal decision can be but the 'application' of some abstract proposition of the law to a concrete 'issue of facts'. (2) From the abstract propositions of the law in force, decision has to be derived for each concrete issue of facts with the means of legal logic. (3) The positive law in force to incorporate such a system, or, at least for its application, it has to be considered as such. (4) Anything that cannot be 'constructed' rationally in a juristic way, cannot be legally relevant. And, in general, (5) the social activity of men has to be conceived of as either the 'application', 'enforcement' or, on the contrary, a 'violation' of the propositions of the law » ([57]).

What is of interest in these structures first of all is that their existence is not merely an ideological distortion. They are *not only*

([57]) WEBER, *Rechtssoziologie*, p. 103.

postulated as some sort of a *separate, second reality*, but *even applied as such* with more or less consistency. Their transplantation into social practice entails their becoming *social facts* themselves: they are to become veritably acting, as well as re-acting, moments of social processes. In this way even the social existence of the law gains a peculiar duality resulting in a duplication in the concept of law itself ([58]).

On summing up some of the results of the present paper I may advance the statement that the creation of *formally rationalized structures* as the means of social transmission and mediation is an indispensable condition of any *conscious, planned, willed and controlled, exercise of social influence*, an influence, namely, that was already formed in the early phases o fthe history of mankind, still acquired a decisive, determing, autonomous and typical significance only in the course of capitalist development. As the means of controlling social life, in most elementary forms some primitive kinds of such structures turned up already with the first relics of written law. Nevertheless the *strictly speaking* formal rationalization of the law has taken place at a time when in Europe the legislator had, as the heir of both the mathematical-axiomatic way of thinking and the experience of the system-creation in natural law, organized the positive law within the framework of a logical system.

It is a conclusion expressing world-wide experiments that « [l]egislaton is ... the characteristic mark of mature legal systems, the final stage in the development of law-making expedients » ([59]). Now codification seems to have brought about the technically most developed

---

([58]) For more details, see VARGA, Csaba, *Quelques questions méthodologiques de la formation des concepts en sciences juridiques*, in « Archives de Philosophie du Droit », vol. XVIII, Paris, Sirey, 1973, pp. 215-241, in particular pp. 224 et seq., and VARGA, Csaba, *Law and Its Approach as a System*, in « Acta Juridica Academiae Scientiarum Hungaricae », XXI (1979) 3-4, forthcoming. As to the re-formulation of the whole problematic on the basis of Lukács' posthumous work, see VARGA, Csaba, *The Concept of Law in Lukács' Ontology*, in « Rechtstheorie », X, (1979) 3, pp. 321-337; furthermore VARGA, Csaba, *Geltung des Rechts - Wirksamkeit des Rechts*, in « Die gesellschaftliche Wirksamkeit des sozialistischen Rechts », herausgegeben von Karl A. Mollnau, Berlin, Institut für Theorie des Staates und des Rechts der Akademie der Wissenschaften der DDR, 1978, pp. 138-145.

([59]) ALLEN, Sir Carleton Kemp, *Law in the Making*, 6th ed., Oxford, Clarendon Press, 1958, p. 410.

device of legislative law-making expedients. Codification in its modern sense has re-established law as the elements of a relatively autonomous system. It is the objectification of law through a system-structure, which is predictably mostly in line with the demand of calculability: hence it is the realization of formal rationalization of the highest order.

This is the recognition which, based decidedly on the practical demand for legality and the citizen's knowledge of law, has been implicitly attained also by the socialist theory of law considering codification the most appropriate form of law ([60]). On the scale of comparative history and by quoting the challenging expression of Gyula Eörsi ([61]), we may even add that the case of Judge-made law v. Code-law, 1970, reminds only in some of its structural marks of the case of Judge-made law v. Code-law, 1500. For since then many of its social, etc. components have *changed*, and to all appearance *Code-law has won the day.*

Yet none of these statements can be made *absolute*. For in point of principle the appraisal given in the present paper relies on the methodological postulate of formal rationality, so its *social validity* is but *limited*. Consequently its social validity is the function of the postulate of formal rationality ,as well as of its concrete social-historical adequateness to the consequences forthcoming from it ([62]).

(testo inglese dell'Autore)

([60]) Cf. above all Szabó, Imre, *Les problèmes de la codification à la lumière des expériences acquises dans les conditions actuelles*, in « Studies in Jurisprudence for the 6th International Congress of Comparative Law », Budapest, Akadémiai Kiadó, 1966, pp. 18 et seq.

([61]) Eörsi, Gyula, *Comparative Civil Law*, Budapest, Akadémiai Kiadó, 1979, ch. X.

([62]) Concerning some further questions of the conclusive illusions, as well as the socio-political contents of the core of formal rationalization, in codification cf. Varga, Csaba, *Utopias of Rationality in the Development of the Idea of Codification*, in « Rivista internazionale di Filosofia del diritto », LV (1978) 1, pp. 21-38, furthermore Varga, Csaba, *Types of Codification in Codificational Development*, in « Acta Juridica Academiae Scientiarum Hungaricae », XIX (1977) 1-2, pp. 31-34.

[17]

The Old Law Cannot Be Critically Inherited, It Can Only Be Used as a Mirror*[a]

Li Changdao

What Does Critical Inheritance Mean?

Can the old law be inherited? Though this question only takes up again an old discussion, it now is of great theoretical and practical importance. The "Little Discussion of the Heritability of Law" makes its points clearly; after reading it, one feels that here is something fresh and new. Its argument may be summed up in the main as saying that the old law, both in the rising period (of the then ruling class) and in the period of decline, may be inherited critically. What then is to be called "critical inheritance"? From a philosophical point of view, the author explains that "the new things, while negating the old things, confirm, adapt, and use part of the content of the old things, making them an integrated part of themselves". I think that such an explanation of critical inheritance is at least not concise enough. According to materialistic dialectics, new things do not simply annihilate old things in their entirety—there is annihilation, and there also is inheritance. The negative elements in the old things are annihilated, the positive elements in them are inherited. Adopting Hegel's technical term, Engels called this kind of negation *aufheben* (sublation). In sublation, the new things take up the positive elements of the old and adapt them, making them an organic part of their own body. The tree of life remains forever green; in taking up nourishment from the outside world, it extracts its essence and rejects its dregs, so that useful things are put to use and useless things are excreted. With regard to capitalism, the proletariat must annihilate the tools capitalism uses to exercise its dictatorship, it must annihilate the capitalist private ownership of means of production and the system of rotten capitalist thinking; but the production forces, the science and technology, the cultural heritage amassed during the historical periods of capitalism and of transition are not simply annihilated but critically inherited. In this way, the reactionary, rotten things of capitalism are annihilated and the positive things left by capitalism are conserved. Therefore, I consider that the object of critical inheritance is the "rational core", the "extractable essence" of the old things, and that there is no old thing that can be critically inherited in its entirety, that can in its entirety be made to "lose its original attributes". Though the author of the "Little Discussion of the Heritability of Law" points out that "the new things, while negating the old things,

* Originally published in *Faxue yanjiu* 1979 No. 3 (June), 45-47. Translated by Frank Münzel.

6 *Rev. Soc. Law* 1980 No. 3, pp. 287-291
0165-0300/80/03/0287-05$00.20/0

confirm, adapt, and use part of the content of the old things, making them an integral part of themselves", he does not clearly answer the question if this part is the positive element. Therefore, he only shows the form of critical inheritance but does not explain its substance. According to his view of critical inheritance, just anything in the world, regardless of whether it is revolutionary, reactionary, positive, negative, progressive, or backward, can be inherited critically, everything can be made to "lose its original attributes" and be put to our use. Critical inheritance is not the same thing as "treating somebody with his own medicine". Poisonous weeds, reactionary words and actions absolutely cannot be inherited critically, they can only be completely annihilated and destroyed. We cannot extend critical inheritance to include just about everything, or we shall disregard the meaning of critical inheritance in materialistic dialectics.

Why Can There Be No Critical Inheritance of the Old Law?

Understanding critical inheritance in the way described above, I consider that the old law cannot be inherited critically. The "old law" means the old legal rules (not including jurisprudence and legal thought; they are a cultural heritage, and the question of their inheritance can be discussed separately). For socialism, this old law has no "positive element", no "rational core", and even less can there be any "extractable essence" in it, for two reasons:

1. One is the class nature of the old law. As everybody knows, the old law is the will of the exploiting classes cast into the articles of statutes; Lenin taught again and again that the whole law of the capitalist classes must be smashed. On (14) January 1949, comrade Mao Zedong included the "abrogation of the sham constitution" and the "abrogation of the sham legal system" among the eight conditions for peace (with the Guomindang government); in February, 1949, the "Directive on the Abrogation of the 'Six Laws' of the Guomindang and the Determination of Judicial Principles for the Liberated Areas" was proclaimed, and on the eve of the establishment of the state (*i.e.* of the PRC), art. 17 of the "Common Program" determined the "abrogation of all the laws, ordinances, and judicial institutions with which the reactionary Guomindang government oppressed the people, and the determination of laws and ordinances protecting the people and the establishment of the people's judicial institutions". It can be seen that the "abrogation" of the old laws has been clearly determined not only once; if abrogated things can also be critically inherited, then the feudal land system and other reactionary things, all discarded long ago, can also be critically inherited. Is even that possible? Will the people of the whole country agree to that? Is that in conformance with upholding the four basic principes?[b]

2. The other reason is the practice of the old law. Throughout history, the old

law has been a tool used by the exploiting classes to rule and to suppress the people; *e.g.* the laws proclaimed by the Guomindang during the more than 20 years it opposed and betrayed the revolution were all intended to protect and strengthen the interests of imperialism, of the feudal class, of the bureaucratic-capitalist class, and their ruling position in old China; they all clearly reflected and served the reactionary policies of the Guomindang. Take the "Provisional Rules for the Suppression of Bandits", the "Law on the Urgent Suppression of Crimes Endangering the Republic", the "Method to Hinder Activities of Other Parties", the "Rules on the Urgent Suppression of Crimes Endangering the Republic During the Period of Disorder",[c] etc., etc.—thousands upon thousands of revolutionary heroes, countless numbers of the people have been cruelly tortured and killed under these laws; if that sort of thing also can be inherited critically, how can we propitiate the souls of the martyrs in heaven!

Some say: The old law of the rising period (of the then ruling class) can be critically inherited. The old law of the rising period has some progressive meaning; but while its methods were not the same as those of the period of decline, its class practice was that of the capitalist class, and for the working people, where basic questions were concerned, it was a fraud. *E.g.* Le Chapelier's Law, proclaimed in France in June 1791, not long after the Great French Revolution, prohibited workers from forming associations; actually, it was a law directed against the workers. Or take civil law: In 1922, Lenin pointed out to the people working on the draft of a civil code that reliable jurists should be appointed to form a committee to guarantee thoroughly the interests of the state of the proletariat and "not to model (the new law) slavishly on the civil law of the capitalist class".

Some say that the old law can be used in the opposite direction. That is sophistry. It means that we may take counterrevolutionary suppression of the revolutionary people, negate its nature, and adapt its substance, to become suppression of counterrevolution by the revolutionary people. If that, too, is regarded as critical inheritance, then we may basically copy any reactionary law proclaimed by the Guomindang; we only have to "use it in the opposite direction"; would that be acceptable?

Some say: The concepts and technical terms of the old law can be inherited critically. Concepts-and words, including some technical terms, are commonly agreed upon and used through history; they have no class nature and do not belong to the realm of critical inheritance. Some technical terms reflect legal thinking and legal principles—*e.g.* the embodiment of the capitalist form of equality in (the principle) that all are equal before the law; independence of jurisdiction; consultation (of the judges on a decision); juries; defense; publicity (of trials)—they all belong to the legal thinking of the old law; they can be treated in accordance with the principle of critical inheritance of the cultural heritage.

The Old Law Can Be Used as a Mirror (jian) [(a)]

Jian is the name of an ancient instrument, a kind of mirror made of copper. Therefore, to use as a *jian* means to use the things of others as a mirror, "borrowing clarity from the mirror to reflect it" (*i.e.* the thing reflected), as the (2nd century BC book) *Huai-nan-zi* (chapter "zhu shu xun") put it; it also means to probe, to use as a lesson. Nowadays it generally means to use as reference. Use as a mirror and inheritance are two different concepts. Comrade Mao Zedong said: "We absolutely cannot decline to inherit and to use as a mirror the things of ancient times and of the foreigners, even if they are things of the feudal class or of the capitalist class".[1] Inheritance and use as a mirror are listed together, they are connected, but there also is a difference between them.

The use of old law as a mirror includes: the form of laws, the substance of norms, legal principles, the construction (of rules), concepts and technical terms; they can all be used as a mirror. *E.g.* that, more than a hundred years ago, Germany's capitalist class treated everybody as a thief who picked up any dead twig in its forests may be used as a mirror when we determine a Forest Law and protect the property of the state.[(d)] The rules in Napoleon's criminal code, in the U.S. Federal Penal Code, or in the German criminal code, on crimes committed by officials in connection with their official activities can be used as a mirror when we determine our criminal and administrative law and protect the democratic rights of the people. The rules in the Tang code[(e)] on law officials losing their office and being punished when they do not treat cases in accordance with the law, and on limiting the time of procedure in judging cases may be used as a mirror when we determine our law of criminal procedure. Or, taking the form of law, we find, in the ancient law of our country, a whole set of forms—laws (*lü*), edicts (*chi*), ordinances (*ling*), rules (*ge*), and procedures (*shi*)[(f)]—that may be used as a mirror. Economic legislation is to be found both in our ancient and in foreign law; some of it belongs to the area of technology and can even better be used as a mirror and adapted. And finally, legal thought, such as (the saying) of our feudal period, that "the law does not curry favor with nobility", "the law does not curry favor with relatives" (of the judge or of the mighty), "punishment of faults does not evade high officials, nor does recompense for good deeds evade the low"; or the freedom, equality, democracy of the capitalist class, as advocated by jurisprudence—they all are very much worthy of our attention.

(ORIGINAL NOTE)

1. *Mao Zedong's Selected Works* (Chinese ed.), vol. 3, 817.

(TRANSLATOR'S NOTES)

a. The Chinese term *jie jian* that is used here usually is translated as "to use for reference". We have to translate it verbatim to make the explanation of its origin in the text of the article comprehensible.
b. The four principles now providing the frame for any permissible discussion: keeping to (1) the socialist road, (2) the dictatorship of the proletariat, (3) leadership by the party, (4) Marxism-Leninism and Mao Zedong thought.
c. All these statutes were directed against the communists.
d. Allusion to Marx's articles on the debates, in the Rhenanian provincial assembly, on the draft of a Forest Law, on one hand, and to the new Forest Law of the PRC of 23 February 1979, on the other.
e. The code of the Tang dynasty, of 653-654 AD, is the oldest Chinese code preserved in its entirety and was the model of all later Chinese imperial codes.
f. These were the different forms of Tang law. The main law or code (*lü*) was linked to penal sanctions. It was supplemented by the *ling* that treated the same subjects but generally did not contain penal sanctions. *Lü* and *ling* were promulgated by the emperor, who also gave *ad hoc* orders in the form of *chi*. *Ge* and *shi* were rules developed by the administration, though occasionally revised under the authority of the emperor. All the *lü*, *ling*, and *chi* were generally published, but only a part of the *ge* and *shi* was, another part being available only to the officials concerned.

Part V
Perspectives for Socio-Legal Analysis

[18]

Acta Juridica Academiae Scientiarum Hungaricae, Tomus 14 (3–4), pp. 231–244 (1972)

The Social Limits of Law

by

I. Szabó

Director of the Institute for Legal and Administrative Sciences
of the Hungarian Academy of Sciences

The study sets out from the thesis that actually the Marxist theory of law has as its task the enrichment of the social theory of law. In the course of his analysis the author comes to the conclusion that law is a social relationship which at the same time is the form of other social relationships. This explains the specific character of law. As a matter of fact law gives expression to social relationships occupying various levels in a hierarchical order, it so to say "translates" them to its own level, so e.g. the relationships associated with the economic foundations and superstructure of society. Still in this process law cannot attend sufficiently to the scale of values of the various social relationships. Therefore there may be doubts of the social indifference of law, or at least of its relative indifference. This peculiarity is not associated with the abstract character of law, but has its origin in the trait of law that in its system of norms it expresses the whole wealth of social relationships extending in three dimensions reduced to a two-dimensional plane.

The legal relationships themselves, as generalities, may be described as "enchanted" social relationships, i.e. social relationships enchanted to law. This enchantment is lifted by life partly in the application of the law, still even more in the observance of the law, and the practice of this observance. In fact in practice men so to say bring back the law expressing social relations imperfectly as if by magic into the many-colouredness of social practice.

Social practice compels the jurist to make his choice of two extremes, viz. he has to decide whether he will act ungenerously as jurist only, this would be the one extreme, or relax in sociology, this would be the other extreme. In this dilemma the jurist will have to find the place between the two extremes where he may synoptically view law equally in its social bearings and in its legal substance. As regards the socialist jurist, his theory, his relations to socialist society and his position in it will equally persuade him to study law as a social form in all cases in conjunction with the social relationships whose form is the law.

We are still in search for the notion of law

Non-jurists, if speaking of jurists, and even those learned in law among themselves, with a certain irony and even self-derision, often quote the devastating statement of Kant, that jurists are still in search for a definition of law. This was in fact the case, and it is still: jurists were in search for a notion of law in the days of Kant and are so today. Yet is this not the case with the notions of other phenomena, in the same way? Are physicists satisfied with the definition of matter? Is their present concept of matter identical with that of two hundred years before? It is the natural trait of the process of cognition, the endeavour to descend to yet greater depths of the cognition of the phenomena that their definitions continually change, expand and grow richer. We may say almost with the same justification that the physicists are still in search for a concept of matter, the biologists for one of life. The word is almost, because the form to which jurists had recourse, and are still having, in their search for a notion of law was not void of certain formal, we may say scholastic elements. The form of the disputes did not trigger off Kant's sarcastic remark without any reason, and does not elicit references of posterity to this remark without any reason either.

Well, here we are at the usual approach, at the comparison of law to one sort of form, so familiar when it comes to speak of law. In the given case the specific outward appearance of the dispute may have given rise to the Kantian statement, yet even the content of the dispute itself may be responsible, namely that the search for a notion of law usually came to a deadlock at the form, at the formal concept of law. Still speaking of law in a certain respect and in a certain connexion we are still apt to come to a standstill at the form, we so to say run against it. In point of fact in the last resort, and now we do not wish again to offer a new concept of law, law is but a form, more closely a social relationship which at the same time is the form of other social relationships. Here we may perhaps make a halt.

How far has modern Marxist theory of law got in its investigations with regard to law? Again and in general all that can be said is that it has not gone beyond certain tentative attempts at the intensification of the concept of law. Essentially these attempts are directed to a more intensive and detailed definition of the place and function of law in society, to the analysis of law in its relations to other social conditions embedded in the relation between foundation and superstructure, its determination by the conditions of society, and the determination and influencing of these conditions by law. Setting out from the Marxist dichotomy of the social conditions the Marxist theory goes on in its investigation of the social character of law, it is making efforts in order that the Marxist theory of law might become in the deeper meaning of the term a social theory of law based on Marxism.

We may even make the statement that at present the Marxist theory of law is in search for the sociological concept of law, still it is exactly this it was always in search for. Incidentally the term sociology, somewhat differently from its Leninist interpretation, is perhaps unreasonably reserved for denoting the concrete investigations from which beyond doubt certain general conclusions may be drawn as to law. The Marxist scholars of sociology are even eager to draw them. However, these investigations, have in their segregation, together with generalizations directly derived from them, penetrated to the threshold only of the theoretical conclusions, the Marxist theory of society and of law.

The theory of law, i.e. the Marxist theory of law, strives actually to become a theory on the level of the theory of society in a manner worthy of it, and a social theory of law, if this is not a pleonasm. In this sphere and on this level Marxist theory of law advances to the relations between law and other social conditions, to the study of these relations. In the course of this study it endeavours to analyse those in many respects not new, however, in their present form too general theses whose starting point is the statement already referred to, that viewed from a social aspect law is but a social relationship which is the form of other social relationships.

Law — the form of other social relationships

As a matter of course no rigid meaning taken by itself can be assigned to the form. Form too is a multiple relative notion. First of all in its generality, as known from materialist dialectics, form together with content constitutes a pair of antitheses between whose members a dialectic contradiction exists. The defining and the defined elements, i.e. the content as defining factor and the form as defined factor, this is the basic relationship between the two. Still in certain cases this relation may turn the other way round, and the defining factor, i.e. the form may itself be defining the content. Thus law, which is not simply only form, but the form of other social relationships, will influence the social conditions expressed, or cast into a form, by it.

Second, the relation of content and form are in different relationships conditioned on different levels. Law, which though in respect of other social relationships is merely a form, by itself too has its own content and formal side. Moreover even procedural law, which from a certain point of view is but the form not of extraneous, but directly of legal relationships, i.e. of legal relationships of content, otherwise called substantive, has its content and form. In this case, if the statement may be made, the form is the derivative of the third degree of the form which law as the form of other social conditions expresses in a most generalized manner.

There is nothing novel, or at least not much novel, in what has been set forth so far. Still we have to set out from this point, i.e. from the general approach to law, in order to define law in general as the form of other social relations. To this we have to add at the spot that this stands for the widest and richest sense of the notion of form. Consequently we have to approach to the essence of law from these two aspects, viz. the nature of law as a social relationship and its peculiarity lending a form to other social relationships, and to grasp the social character of law. Hence the question may as a matter of course be asked whether law in its generality is the adequate form, i.e. precise expression of other, i.e. economic, financial, family, political or labour relations? The reply to the question may be manifold. In its most general form any legal system may for its nature be the adequate expression of the economic and social relationships which constitute the essence of a social system. Thus, on a general level, law as a form is the adequate expression of the social content. However, this is still a rather vague approach, although on this level it is true at the same time.

As a matter of fact it is a peculiarity of the law of certain social systems, in the like way as of other superstructural elements of the social systems, that it gives expression to the social relationships by camouflaging their essence. In his "The Capital" Marx in many respects, and so among others also in connexion with law, draws a line between the essence of social phenomena and the form of their legal manifestation, by pointing not only at the difference of the two, but directly at their contradiction. Is the freedom of contract as a legal institution in fact the form of freedom-relations, or is socially ownership in fact as absolute as suggested by the legal form? In this connexion and by assuming the exploiting systems of society as underlying, the statement may be ventured that law will become the adequate formal expression of other social relationships when it expresses them by camouflaging their very nature, i.e. socially it will be adequate, when for its essence it is exactly an inadequate expression of the social relationships. This reality distorting adequate character is associated with the ideological nature of law, still in this case ideology will be the ideology characteristic of bourgeois society whose peculiarity is exactly a perverted, distorted method of expression.

Under socialist conditions the meaning and the social contents of ideology change also in the realm of law, the adequate expression changes also in the social sense. Here we will not speak of shortcomings of the adequate expression which are simply due to the fact that the competent governmental agencies "translate" the social conditions to the legal language in the wrong way, i.e. the legal or statutory solution is inaccurate or wrong owing to its failure to lend the corresponding form to the social content to be expressed. This is a phenomenon which does not rise to the theoretical level of being adequate. On the other hand there is no doubt that occurrences of this kind are all but rare even under socialist conditions.

Still although under the conditions of a socialist society it is not a social necessity to conceal the real contents by the legal form, nevertheless even as regards socialist law it holds true that law is by its very nature in a certain sense an imperfect form. In this we have to perceive one of the fundamental traits of law. We shall now examine more closely, how this trait manifests itself. Let us take a few examples from the different spheres of law.

In family relations socially the maintenance of the parents is not of the same character and weight as the social significance of the maintenance of the offspring, and neither is identical with the maintenance of relations beyond the grades of parents and children. Nevertheless family law classifies these socially different types of maintenance as a single category. The civil code essentially deals with a sales contract and a contract of deposit under the same heading, notwithstanding the quantitatively, and also qualitatively considerable differences between the many millions of sales contracts entered into daily, and the latter contract of deposit of little significance and concluded on rare occasions only. For criminal law wilful homicide and theft are equally criminal offences, although socially the two are not of uniform character, society "putting" them on different scales of value. It would be superfluous to continue the enumeration, because certain conclusions may be drawn even from so many.

Law as the expression of social relationships of different order

Essentially these conclusions are derived from the recognition that law owing to its social function is a social institution destined to give uniform expression to social relations of different significance and frequency rather than to uniform ones. At the same time it also stands to reason that as indicated by the examples law gives expression to the different social relationships serving as its content in an imperfect manner only when it casts them into a form on an essentially uniform level. This imperfection of legal expression, it should be made clear, is in principle not the fault of the formulation of legal provisions, it is not the specific feature of a single social order, but a characteristic trait of every legal system.

This imperfection may be designated as the social insensitiveness, or at least relative insensitiveness of law. As regards law it is the case of a specific social relationship or phenomenon which is incapable of giving an adequate idea of either the quantitative or the qualitative differences of other social relationships expressed by it. Law fails to express the differences of the various types of contracts as for their importance or significance. Criminal law independently of their frequency equally qualifies as criminal offences relations which otherwise for their social significance, i.e. character and weight differ from one another and so on.

Still within the same sphere of thought it is obvious that social relationships have a certain hierarchical order. Marxism defines two basic units of this hierarchical order; the one is formed by the relations which Marxism formulates as the economic foundations of society, the other is the offspring of relations which constitute the superstructure of society relying on these economic foundations. Now in its various branches law too is the synopsis of these relations differing in their character, it indifferently translates them into its own language, transforms them to its own autonomous system of concepts and norms, or system of sanctions. Within the further differentiation of the social relations by foundation and superstructure other sub-categories of social relationships will come to light which differ by their social weight and value and which will therefore themselves constitute a hirarchical scale of social values. Property relations differ from exchange or barter relations, from employment, the political relations from administrative or cultural relations to some extent also of weight not only of character. Law is incapable of reproducing these rich hues and shades of the social relationships. It is for this reason that we may speak of the social insensitiveness of law.

If these quantitative and qualitative differences of the social relationships are conceived as sited in space, i.e. as three-dimensional, then law may be represented as projecting this three-dimensional picture from space to the plane, i.e. expressing it in two dimensions. It can be perhaps said in an evaluative way but also regretfully that law reduces social relationships to two-dimensional phenomena. However, it should again be emphasized that this is the characteristic trait of law, of every law, rather than a deficiency of a given legal system. The evaluative remark, the representation of law as something flattening out or impoverishing social relationships will hold true only in a comparison of law to the social relationships as a whole. Law may be conceived as something poorer than the system of social relationships as a whole only in this connection. Therefore law may be considered something poorer in this respect, only because it is one of the social relationships, a part, a single aspect of social relationships as a whole. It is a social relationship the function of which consists in projecting the wide sphere of social relationships, or so to say all of them, to a single plane.

In this connection it should be noted incidentally, still not by the way, that this projection, the transformation of certain social relationships to other social relationships, viz. to legal relationships, has become the function of the State. This transformation is the business of definite governmental agencies, no matter whether of specifically legislative agencies, or agencies in charge of the application of law. In any way we cannot talk of law without speaking of the State at the same time, in the first place as of the agency of general or individual transformation.

Abstract law — socially insensitive law

One may advance against the arguments brought forward above that the statement on what may be called insensitiveness of the law betrays nothing that may be termed novel. It but expresses in a different manner that law abstracts from social relationships as they are, and the distortedness which has been pointed out corresponds to, and is the outcome of, this abstraction-caused withdrawal or alienation. However, we believe that the abstract form of law and its social insensitiveness are nevertheless two different things: the one cannot be explained by the other, or more precisely, from the point of view of society the abstract character of law is not only the less significant trait, nor is it this abstract character that is responsible for the social insensitiveness of law. E.g. it is generally known that Common Law is appreciably less abstract than Continental law with its system of rules distilled into codes. Still it cannot be maintained as if Common Law were more responsive to the social relationships serving as its content, and expressed them with greater precision and abundance than Continental law. Nor can the statement be made as if it would, if only partially, remove the trait which we have figuratively described as something comparable to a geometrical sphere of notion other than society itself with the whole system of its manifold relations. Common Law too translates social relationships into the language of its specific system of legal institutions, and by doing so in principle it abstracts them in the same way as Continental law.

Furthermore the fact that law gives expression to concrete social relationships in an abstract form is not identical with the social distortion of law. Legal relationships are in any case concrete, even when their expression in the form of a legal provision, though on various levels of abstraction, is equally abstract. Briefly, it is not abstraction that is responsible for the qualitative disagreement of the legal and social relationships which the former express or the forms of which they are. Law as a social institution is simply void of the means, it is not able (it is not even its task) to translate social relationships in their fullness, or give expression to them. If it did this, it would forfeit its legal peculiarity, and at the same time its social necessity. In fact in this case it would coincide with the social relationships it has been called to express, it would be identical with them.

Incidentally — and now we pay attention also to this circumstance — law is socially not wholly insensitive or callous. It is relatively insensitive only, it is void of the capacity to give expression to social relationships in a complete three-dimensional form. Still even within its two-dimensional potentialities it makes a certain quantitative, and even qualitative distinction, between the social relationships it gives expression to. Obviously this distinction is made in a most spectacular manner by means of sanctions which in the first place are the apparent means and signs of a qualitative distinction. In this respect the system of sanctions of criminal law is the most developed, for here the socially established types of sanctions are defined by the legislator himself in a specifically legal form, in a manner corresponding to the social valuation of the facts at issue. The civil law sanctions of a financial character are in general simpler, i.e. qualitatively less shaded, and distinction is drawn in the first place only in the course of application of the law, e.g. by the amount of damages.

For that matter legislation endeavours to draw a distinction between the types of relationships by principle and according to their weight not only when it comes to specify the sanctions, but also at the formulation of the facts at issue. This is again most apparent in criminal law, where some legal systems introduce the multi-level categories of criminal offences. It is an altogether different question whether criminalists have succeeded in finding socially sound criteria for this differentiation. Still other branches of law give birth to legal institutions by taking into consideration their social significance from the very outset, thus at the same time giving evidence of the active character of the transformatory operations of the State. To all this the very branches of law do not give expression exclusively in the sanctions, or perhaps exactly not there. In fact the distinction made by law between the legal institutions of *locatio conductio operis* and *locatio conduction operarum* may be quoted as an example of the indication of an endeavour directed to the translation of a social difference into the language of law.

We shall now return briefly to the problem of abstraction. From this point of view it is obvious that even if the abstract character of law is not identical with its social insensitiveness and not even the primary cause of it, abstraction cannot be independent of the correct or less correct expression of the social content. Although the exaggerated abstraction by itself does not lead to this result, it may surely intensify the social alienatedness of law. It is sufficient to refer here to criminal offences committed within the sphere of profession. In the manner as recognized by the Hungarian system of criminal law, the offence has been formulated in an abstract way to the extent that socially wholly different relationships are united by this legal rule. This does not, however, mean that if medical malpractice were defined by the criminal code as a special offence, this provision would not remain socially insensitive to some extent given the rich variety of different kinds of malpractice in everyday life. This imperfection may be relieved by legal practice, yet slightly only, namely within the framework resulting from the conditions provided by law and by the character of law, i.e. with the continuance of a certain kind of relative insensitiveness.

Legal relationships — enchanted social relationships

The perhaps fundamental problem or characteristic trait of law as a social phenomenon, and at the same time its so to say greatest difficulty, displays itself with a different intensity in the several aspects of legal life. It is clear that law being itself a sort of social relationship, is imperfect in its quality as the expression of different social relationships. It may be even said that the State on transforming the social relationships to legal relationships, "enchants" them. The characteristic manifestation of the enchanted form is the abstract legal provision. Undoubtedly when a legal rule is created in principle there exists the possibility to take into consideration the character, essence, manifoldedness of the social relationships which constitute the content of the legal relationships. Still, it should be emphasized, only within the potentialities offered by law, and the to some extent corrigible, yet in the last resort ineluctable limits of the biplanar quality of law.

On this understanding the diverse methods of approach to the law of social orders of conflicting nature will become particularly obvious. The generalization that the legal systems of capitalist societies abuse to some extent of the distortion inherent in legal transformation is by no means exaggerated. It is nearby the endeavour of bourgeois law to alienate law from the social relationships as they are or from the reality of social relationships, on the assumption of course that alienation is understood here in its vulgarized sense. Here we shall not speak of the what may be called trivial endeavour to bring about the estrangement of law from men by way of its unintelligibility achieved by creating a lawyers' law. In principle the socialist approach to law is different from this. It differs from capitalist law already in its material of legal provisions. In this respect socialist law is struggling for an expression of the social character of the legal relationships by an as adequate and complete as possible exploitation of the potentialities offered by the legal form. In addition socialist law is eager to eliminate the forensic formulation of law.

Besides the relative possibility of a legislative dimming of law the true field of enchantment, where law is so to say "conjured back" into its real social character, or at least where there is ample chance for this "conjuring back" is the application of law, or still better the observance of law, i.e. the aspect of legal life where law again displays itself as a concrete legal relationship. In these fields the individuals make attempts to add to the "legality" of the concrete legal relationships the appraising elements which cleave to the given social relationships. The concrete legal relationships will be completed with values resulting from the given social order and represented by the different groups of men. Through this completion the social relationships and together with it two-dimensional law will be conjured back to three-dimensional social relations.

What does this mean more explicitly? What is meant here is that in cases of concrete legal relationships men take into consideration the hierarchy of the social relationships to which law is insensitive or at least more or less insensitive. Men will make valuating social distinctions where law standardizes, they will classify in the to a certain extent drab monotony of law. In other words in the concrete legal relationships men try to complete the series of the components of social relations imperfectly expressed by the law.

In this respect further differences issue from the application of law and the law-abiding conduct of the citizens. In a simplified form one may say that in the application of law, i.e. in the course of application there is a certain struggle going on: even those in charge of applying the law, if they harbour some sort of social pretensions will be striving for an adjustment of the social content and the legal form in the one way or the other, or one may be tempted to say, for the resolution of the contradictions between social content and the legal form in the law-applying act. On the other hand the parties will contend against both the formality of the legal form and the tendency of those applying the law to trimming a social relationship to a legal one in all circumstances. Naturally the struggle of the parties for a disclosure of the social character of a legal relationship differs according to their quality in the litigation, i.e. according as they are the accused or the injured party.

The formula will become a by far simpler one in the observance of law; where men are bound by the legal form only by virtue of the consciousness of law and coercion of the State will loom up as a distant contingency only filtered through this consciousness of law. Here the citizen will be led in his conduct from the very outset by a more realistic hierarchical order of the social relationships in their natural foundations conceived in accordance with his social status. This hierarchical order will at most be mitigated by the consciousness of the legal form. Here exactly the social scale of values (its various species will be only indicated here) in respect of the type of the legal system more or less departing from the legal expression, however, to a certain extent, precisely owing to the "legality" of the law departing from it in all events, is if not of full validity, still of a higher degree, moreover fundamental in the conduct of the citizens. Finally we may sum up this series of ideas in the statement that in his life and in his conduct the citizen will more or less conjure back the social relations enchanted in the law as abstraction.

The jurist's dilemma

What is now the function of the jurist who manages law as a social form departing from the social relationships he is called to give an expression to? He will have to avoid the Scylla and Charybdis of the two extremes in any case and equally, the one extreme being the conception of law as form as omnipotent, the other the neglect of this form. The jurist who takes the position that he is solely and exclusively the representative of the legal form, follows the self-movement of the legal form, or keeps track of its movement irrespective of the content and social relationships expressed by law, and smoothes the path only of this form, will in the judgement of society become a jurist in the pejorative meaning of the term, somebody who does not perceive the "spirit" of the law, but only its "letter", who is "soulless", who "abuses" of the legal form, whose principle is . . .*pereat mundus*. This type of jurist is condemned by the judgement of society, and not wholly without reason. A jurist of this type is in a degenerated sense the technician of law, who for any argument wants to find a legal form, who simply flouts any demand for the cognition and recognition of the formal character of the form. He is the "poor" jurist, he who is too much of a jurist.

Still even if socially he may act more correctly, the jurist who now ignores the legal form, brings into relief a single kind of social expedience, tries to carry into effect the content of social relationships in their crudeness, by ignoring the exigencies of the form, which disguises the social relationships in the form of rights and duties, who is unaware of the advantage of legality i.e. the consistent enforcement of the legal form, who briefly is jurist in a way that he denies the specific social relationships whose keeper he is, i.e. law itself, also denies the nature of law in its substance. He too is a "poor" jurist, for he is too little of a jurist.

All in all, to avoid big words, we may say that the jurist's tragedy consists in the danger of these two extremes, and for that matter a danger is always present. Still we should be satisfied with the less dramatic formulation that it is the danger of this tragedy where the equivocal position of the jurist in society has its origin. Obviously essentially this position will be influenced by the character of the given social order on which the cause of the juristic deflection in the direction of the content or form as well as the social nature of the jurist's conduct as whole depend.

In other words the matter in question is that if as compared to the social relationships expressed by it the autonomy of law is merely relative, as a consequence and in this connexion also the autonomy of the jurist as such will be relative. The social relationships of which law is a form will not only limit, but at the same time even influence any movement within these spheres of activity.

Still only the autonomy of law, and in association with the law of juristic activity, will be relative in this meaning? Not at all. We do not intend to go beyond the boundaries of jurisprudence, still we may perhaps be allowed to indicate that the autonomy of all types of social relationships is more or less squeezed between barriers. In fact there are interrelations of extreme complexity of mutual determinedness and influencedness among the types of these relationships. It is the problem of society as a unit, still a unit disintegrating into parts and displaying itself in this state of disintegration, a problem which some try to solve in its reflection in the theory of science sometimes with the all-amalgamating generality of sociology, sometimes with the fiction of the self-enclosedness of social relationships contemplated as mutually independent. However, from the point of view of science obviously the solution does not lie here. In any solution the given social science, and evidently also the underlying social relationship, has to be conceived in its independence taken into consideration its influencedness by other sciences or other social relationships, i.e. exactly the relativity of autonomy has to be recognized and expressed.

Law and jurists amidst socialist conditions

The problem, namely the problem of the unity and differentiation of the social relationships and legal form serving as content of the legal relationships, displays itself in a new guise in socialist law and jurisprudence, or still better, emerges as novelty for the socialist jurist. We have said that the biplanar character as a form of expression is an "eternal" trait of law. In the exploiting types of society to this accedes the camouflaging-distorting character of the legal relationships, and in conjunction with it the trait of exploiting law to enable the ruling class of society to make use of this biplanar character of law, or in other words, in exploiting societies, owing to the exploiting nature of society, the reality of social relationships will of necessity manifest itself socially distorted in law, i.e. in a manner screening the true social content. This holds in particular true for capitalist society where law means everything and where the legal framework means an almost insurmountable barrier for the outlook of the jurist. The circumstance that the absoluteness of this juristic outlook tends to waver owing to the crisis of the last phase of the capitalist system, does not alter the truth of the statement, and may be attributed to the relative insufficiency of the legal form in its defence of the bourgeois conditions in jeopardy at least in the same way as to the break-through of the unfolding new forces of society in the camouflaging barrier of the law.

However, under socialist conditions this situation will change the other way round, and the turn in the situation is significant to the extent that it will render a similarity to exploiting law not merely a relative one, but directly place the socialist outlook to law in contradiction to the bourgeois outlook. Theory and practical application of socialist law equally and in all circumstances calls for the recognition and ideation of the unity of the legal relationships and other social relationships serving as their content and in the knowledge of this unity for a possible dimming of the social insensitiveness of law. The task is the exploration of the social content behind the legal form, still without neglecting this forme, on the plane of legal activity, the recognition of the unity of the two, and its contemplation in conjunction with reality. Therefore the socialist theory of law and legal practice cannot go without intensified social research.

Here we are at the ultimate conclusions of our discussion which also affect practice. In the world of socialist law there is need for a theory of socialist law which does not tear away the legal relationships from their social content, which makes the at the outset imperfect form of expression complete, or at least more complete, with a social content. To this a legal practice has to be added and in fact it has even been added, which breaks the spell disguising the essence.

This at the same time indicates the perspective path of development: the future has in store the union of the social content with the form of legal relation, a union where the segregation and insensitiveness of the form will become a thing of the past and with this eventually the social isolation of law, i.e. the legal form itself will wither away. The social approach and interpretation of law which displays itself in a fundamentally new manner under socialist conditions are components of the historically obviously long, yet in point of principle indispensable process which points in the direction of the cessation of the existence of law as law. In this way the jurists are not mere external onlookers of this process but also its promoters.

[19]

International Journal of the Sociology of Law 1981, **9,** 159–176

Towards a Sociological Concept of Law: An Analysis of Lukács' Ontology

CSABA VARGA
Institute for Legal and Administrative Sciences of the Hungarian Academy of Sciences, 1250 Budapest, Hungary

I. Lukács and Problems of Law

It is a little-known fact that Georg Lukács, one of the most influential Marxist thinkers of recent times and the man whose personal achievement was to promote the renaissance of Marxism, obtained his first degree in law and political sciences. After his studies in Budapest – and of these we know only that he was a student of Gyula Pikler, (known as Julius Pikler), who already enjoyed a considerable reputation for his work in philosophy of law, psychology, and ethnology – he took his doctorate in political sciences at the University of Kolozsvár in Transylvania; this was in 1906. His studies here led to his friendship with Bódog Somló, (known as Felix Somló), a friendship that was to last for more than 10 years. Their relationship came about because it was for Professor Somló, a philosopher of law and a committed bourgeois progressive, that Lukács wrote his thesis, the title and text of which remain unknown to this day. They met and corresponded frequently, the result being that Lukács was one of those who helped prepare the way for the publication in Germany of Somló's *Juristische Grundlehre*, the work which brought the latter immortality.

The years spent in Heidelberg before and during the First World War led to new friendships. Above all, we think of Max Weber who, of course, also produced great work in the sociology of law and was Lukács' chief supporter in the latter's ambitions to acquire a University chair in Heidelberg. Others come to mind, such as Emil Lask, Georg Jellinek, and Hans Kelsen, all of whom had an interest in jurisprudence and had already produced their great pioneering works in both constitutional law and in the philosophy and theory of law. His closest relationship, however, was with Gustav Radbruch, whose lectures he attended as a friend. Their discussions concerning the philosophical premises of

0194–6595/81/020159+18 $02.00/0

Radbruch's philosophy of law, which was then taking on more systematic shape, had such an impact on Radbruch that he dedicated his first work, *Grundzüge der Rechtsphilosphie,* to Lukács, the man who had encouraged him to publish it.

This list of names is in itself enough to suggest that Lukács, in the most sensitive stage of the formation of his intellectual ego, was able to acquire the neo-Kantian concept of modern formal law from a direct source, that is, through friendships and debates in Heidelberg. It is well known that these friendly contacts all ceased as a result of Lukács' intellectual change in 1918. But this in no way altered the fact that the base line of Lukács' theoretical ideas about law remained, to the end, this circle of Heidelberg intellectuals on whom the influence on Windelband and Rickert had been so marked. Whether we think of the early works, that is, the studies which were written about the time of *History and Class Consciousness,* of the *Dethronement of Reason,* or whether we think of the *Ontology* itself, the same names crop up, the same works, indeed, the same quotations, whenever law is being discussed. In fact, we could go so far as to say that in the course of time, Lukács' interest in law did not so much broaden as become clearer and more classical: Radbruch and Somló are gradually lost to oblivion, whilst he grasps Weber's and Kelsen's more recent works, in order to acquire a fuller and clearer picture of law in so far as it accorded with his own earlier stock of knowledge and experience. (The only significant exception perhaps being the *Dethronement of Reason,* where, for cogent political and ideological reasons, he simply had no alternative but to take cognizance of Carl Schmitt's expositions on the philosophy of law.) This, by and large, covers the sources, influences, and limits of Lukács' legal culture. We could note, by way of supplementation, that Lukács' otherwise unbelievably rich and varied personal library is strikingly bereft of other legal volumes. For the most part, it does not even contain contemporary Hungarian works, which he must certainly have received in his capacity as a member of the Academy.

Our remarks are slowly beginning to revolve around the question of what kind of relationship with problems of law Lukács actually had. Briefly, we can say that he did not espouse the discipline of law of his own volition. It appears that he chose to study law and political sciences for want of anything better, and it was, of course, in line with the general practice of the day. Even in his relationship with Somló it was presumably the attraction to the radical bourgeois thinker which was the dominant factor, just as with Radbruch it was not so much the lawyer which attracted him as the conscious pacifist in times of war, in whom social conscience was extraordinarily well-developed. And during the Heidelberg years the philosophers of law who have been mentioned were not isolated figures, but were rather situated in a circle of philosophers, sociologists, historians etc. who were of a similar grand stature. We could include amongst them such men as Gothein or Troeltsch.

To put it briefly, then, Lukács was not very interested in law *as law*. It is generally known that in his work in the field of literary criticism, too, what primarily interests him in the work in question is not so much the literary creation itself as its political-social environment (more precisely, the picture of this environment presented by the creative work). In the majority of Lukács' expositions, law really has a purely illustrative role. It is frequently just a case of returning, for example, to the neo-Kantian opposition of pure morality to pure legality, whereby he always points to the necessity of transcending the said opposition but, in the absence of any detailed analysis, hardly ever manages more than a merely verbal solution. However, when he found it useful for some other purpose he made copious use of law as a means of illustration.

The most classical example is to be found in the study *Reification and the Consciousness of the Proletariat,* published in *History and Class Consciousness.* After the collapse of the Hungarian Soviet Republic, which had held out the promise of being the Day of Judgment, he erected a monument to the movement, a monument that depicts the moribund present as a negative utopia. Here the moribund present is characterized by the aspiration to predictability, formal rationalization and, in order to achieve the latter, the alienation from human qualities and the disruption of natural processes. The basis and outcome of all this is reification in the *Hegelian* sense, a concept which, however, is distorted by Lukács into alienation understood in the *Marxian* sense. Thus, modern formal law is identified with capitalist law, the transcending of which was demanded by the socialist revolution. So the negative utopia leads to a positive one, that is, the dramatized legal perception of the present leads to the vision of a socialism which does not even know, does not even recognize, socialism in its specific, technically constructed and bureaucratically guided, institutional structure. This practical, legal nihilsim, which, setting out from ideological presuppositions, Lukács embraced even as late as the mid–1920s, tallies neither with the then Soviet reality nor with the Hungarian Soviet Republic's aim to build in 133 days a legal system, endeavours in which Lukács himself played an active part.

As far as the contrast between formal legal enactment and practical legal enforcement is concerned, extremely important statements of principle are to be found in the pages of the *Dethronement of Reason* as well. I mention this here since all this is occasioned for Lukács by the circumstance that the path taken by Carl Schmitt led from sociology to fascism. At the same time, it is characteristic of Lukács' primarily ideological-critical viewpoint that his conclusion was not dictated at all by a calculation based on principle and concept but by the political and ideological context of the attitudes treated. So the Lukácsian reaction was different when Schmitt formulated a theoretical thesis as a critique of neo-Kantianism in general, and different again when he used this same thesis in 1934 to justify the brutal liquidation of the S.A.

Thus, Lukács' attitude towards legal problems is, at root, determined by the fact that, for Lukács, the prevailing total context remains the decisive factor, i.e. in the field of social-political events, the question of the power that fundamentally directs these relations. When formulating policy, however, he does come up against the law, though, this does not go beyond the bounds of the occasional. Consequently, in these expositions, law always figures as the combination of more overall entities (as an instrument of politics), and Lukács is interested precisely in the context of these larger entities and not in the specific *inner* world and workings of the law.

As for his starting-point, not even the exposition on *The Ontology of Social Being* went beyond such a level of interest. Still, in it the sketch of legal problems assumes a radically different aspect. A decisive question in the *Ontology* concerns the character of social mediation: it presumes a specific functioning of relatively autonomous complexes of being and is constructed in an unprecedented fashion. Lukács could not have found a better example than law, for it is at one and the same time a formally independent structure and yet organically integrated into social activities. So now law does not appear simply in its functional subordination to the prevailing totality (politics, economy etc.), but precisely (i) in its enacted nature and in its specific inner working according to its normative postulates, and (ii) in the dialectical contradiction which breaks through the logic of its specific workings in the course of its practical implementation, and by means of a number of manipulations pushes towards practical solutions, which then result in compromise solutions.

II. On the *Ontology* in General

The final version of the *Ontology* has been passed down to us in typescript form, corrected in the author's hand. Although the text is complete, it is still a fragment. The three volumes are not constructed consecutively but rather express the author's ideas in parallel. Their edition in this form is not the outcome of Lukács' original conception but is rather the result of his death before completion of the work. Thus it is not simply the possibility of contradictions and changes of emphasis within it that is of interest, but chiefly the circumstance that the author's illness compelled him to complete the manuscript in such a hurry that he had insufficient time fully to marshal his arguments and organize the network of interrelationships into a well-proportioned, rounded system. So far, the full text of the German work has only appeared in Hungarian translation; however, Hungarian philosophers, apart from academic criticism bearing on the manuscript itself, have still not dealt with it with philological and critical rigour. They have merely taken appreciative cognizance of it.

In order to develop the *Ontology's* view of law in conjunction with a number of basic questions, I must sketch out some methodological reflections and category definitions which decisively determine the direction and character of Lukács' thoughts on law and their place in his system of thought. With this in mind I am here unable to aspire to completeness or logically sufficient consistency.

(a) According to Lukács, the relationship between the *ontological* and the *epistemological-logical* approach is basically determined by the fact that social existence is only acquired by a phenomenon if it actually exerts an influence on its environment and performs an actual function. Since social events take place with the prevailing consciousness of individuals active in society, in the medium of the objectivations of consciousness being reproduced in society and with the interacting of their organizing influence, the various structures, ideologies, etc. of consciousness play an active and actual role, independently of whether they turn out to be true or not. The assessment of phenomena as reflections, therefore, the evaluation of their reflective adequacy, does not lead to an understanding of the actual influence they exert. Indeed, the opposite is the case: the analysis of the reciprocal influences at work in social processes can lead us to a revelation of the role of factors of consciousness participating in these processes, their true or false content, indeed, the socially presumed facticity of their true or false content.

(b) The ontological approach thus does not simply comprise the search for connections, but the recognition that these connections can only be understood within the prevailing totality, as elements of the latter. Thus the world cannot be constructed from nothing but a stack of constituent components, for it is precisely the prevailing totality, the overall social-historical movement, that provides the inquiring intelligence with the basis for its separation into components and for the demonstration of their specificity. Lukács' adherents and critics agree on one point. It is that the methodological claim to the *totality approach* accompanies the whole Marxist phase of Lukács career. To quote the powerful formulation given in the *Ontology:*

> the total context of the complex in question takes precedence over its individual constituents. The latter can only be understood from their concrete interaction within the complex of being involved, whilst it would be futile for us to try theoretically to reconstruct the complex of being itself from its constituents (Lukács, 1973, pp. 63–64).

(c) By attempting to separate the individual components from the movement of the prevailing totality, from the reciprocal influences taking place within it, and to determine the position and function they occupy in the totality and further to determine the specific quality of their movement (the quality of whose parameters are also drawn by the function they fulfil in the total movement), the totality approach makes possible the historically concrete dialectical interpretation of the individual categories. This is, for Lukács, the often-voiced hope and possibility of the *tertium datur*, the third possibility of a good choice between two evils, which avoids forcing all social processes into the Procrustean bed of an abstract, *a priori,* conceptual-systematic hierarchy, and which avoids all the vulgar Marxist explanations which endeavour to replace dialectical philosophical analysis with a mechanical construction relying on some fundamental categories.

(d) One of the most important new categories in Lukács' work is that the *ontology of complexes* treats the prevailing reality (the total complex) as a complex consisting of complexes. Its application determines the method of his approach to such an extent that it appears simply to replace the Marx/Engels' category of the social relationship. But if we look more closely it transpires that it is not a question of recasting the latter. The total complex consists of complexes which are themselves complexes of part-complexes. Thus reality is made up of the reciprocal influence of various kinds of composite structures, a reciprocal influence in which the quality of the individual complexes is derived from their relative autonomy, but whose direction and parameters are fixed by the interplay of these structures as realized in the total complex. It can easily be seen that we are here dealing with the question of the ontological expression of the totality approach, an expression in which reality is none other than the concrete totality of the movement of the part-complexes as given at any time. True to his essayist's style of expression, Lukács did not provide a definition of the category "complex"; neither did he bother to separate it theoretically from social relationships. Without going into the analysis in any greater detail, we must nevertheless determine the following characteristics: the ontology of the complexes is based on the dialectic of interactions within the given totality; their existence is characterized by the irreversibly progressing continuity; they embrace all objectivations brought about in the course of man's social praxis, as well as all subjects that cannot be separated from these and that effect and reproduce the objectivations in question; that is, features and definitions which barely fit into the category of social relationship with convincing metaphorical power and conceptual rigour.

(e) Returning to Marx, Lukács asserts that *categories* are nothing but forms of defined existence, determinations of existence; and *existence* is identical with irreversible continuity. To quote Lukács' expression: "existence is composed of the endlessly reciprocal relations of continually progressing complexes, relations which both in their parts and (relative) totalities result in concrete, irreversible processes" (Lukács, 1976, Vol. II, p. 172).

(f) Just as existence essentially means *self-reproduction*, and just as this is increasingly accomplished under conditions which are absent from nature but brought about by men themselves in the course of their social praxis, Lukács attributes pivotal importance to the phenomenon of *socialization*. This chiefly means that in the reproduction of social existence purely social relations, mediations, and determinations come into the foreground more and more. Social complexes turn into increasingly complicated structures, a result being that their relative autonomy continues to grow, the specificity of their functioning becomes more marked, and their reciprocal interactions lead to syntheses creating interconnections of a more and more composite nature, which then not merely enhance the cohesive powers of the social but bring in their wake the growth of unforeseen consequences.

(g) It is clear from the category of *mediation* what kind of processes socialization accelerates. The former is an extraordinarily general category in Lukács' work. In general, it can be said that mediation is a continuous medium in which the interaction of the complexes is effected. When we talk of socialization and of reciprocal interactions growing more complicated, we must think of their network as being so intricate that that which is mediating itself becomes mediated. In a really highly socialized existence mediation is so mediated that not only do unidirectional and extreme determinations fall outside its dialectic, but a variety of intermediary forms mediate in such a way that in the process they themselves, in their reciprocal interactions with other complexes, will be mediated.

(h) Lukács saw the model of all human activity in the basic ontological structure of *labour*. In labour he formulated the possibility of the transfer from natural existence to social existence, precisely via the dialectical and mutually dependent relation of teleological and purely causal processes. "On the one hand, teleology is only possible under the dominance of causality, while on the other hand new objects, forms and connections arise in society only as a consequence of teleological projects." (Holz Rottler Abendroth, 1974, p. 77). As is elegantly shown by the example of the wheel, the *teleological proposition* is able to project new connections onto reality which are not given in reality and cannot be spontaneously developed from it, and which are then realized by bringing causal progressions into motion, in such a way however, that, in line with their specific workings, they tend to exceed the original proposition and, in the end, produce more than or something different from, what was the original intention. If we regard the act of labour from the point of view of mediation and socialization, it is immediately apparent what universally significant changes are brought by the development Lukács had in mind. For in the elementary act of labour, the ontological project is immediately related to labour activity. However, with socialization all further mediating projects are wedged in between them, all the more clearly with the formation of purely social (economic, political, religious, moral, legal, etc.) structures, the object of whose specific projects is another project which is itself only mediating in the series which stretches between the project of the act of labour and its actual implementation.

III. The Relevance of the *Ontology* for Marxist Legal Thought

The significance of the *Ontology's* view of law can only be truly evaluated if we see it together with the role it proves itself capable of performing in the *present* development of Marxist legal thinking.

Nowadays it is almost a banality to assert that the intellectual preparation of the socialist revolutions did not demand the elaboration of an independent legal theory of Marxism. The overriding point of a revolution is to seize power, and this, as we can see, for example, from Lenin's *The State and Revolution* and from his lecture on *The State*, only leads directly to raising problems concerning the state. At the same time, the ascendant stage of the victorious revolution was already fostering a flood of ideas and thereby a certain utopianism. The first

Soviet attempts at a theory of law (and we associate with this the names of Stuchka, Reisner, and Pashukanis) followed upon each other in such a way that at first, hoping for the imminent withering away of law, they annihilated law; they rated it as a transitional phenomenon, the bourgeois remnant *par excellence;* eventually they recognized the simultaneous existence of socialism and law, however, they only understood it as a kind of forced co-tenancy. With the consolidation of the socialist revolution it clearly became necessary to go beyond these concepts and to lay the theoretical foundation of socialism's specific constitutional and legal arrangements. However, as a result of the historical peculiarity of Soviet development, this task coincided with the coming to power of Stalin and the methods and structure known by the label of the "personality cult", and became the expression, composite and also theoretically heterogeneous, of these two tendencies. This is the trend which the literature calls *socialist normativism* (Szabó, 1976, pp. 267 ff.). As far as its essentials are concerned it does not go far beyond the theoretical formulation of prevailing legal policy, based on the requirement for a smoothly operating and centralized legal apparatus designed for the practical implementation of prevailing central decisions. Correspondingly, it made a strict distinction between law-making and law-application, and for the description of legal phenomena and their workings it paradoxically relied on the exclusive, formal enforcement of the rule of law attitude, not allowing the sociological point of view to be posed.

The first to attempt a critique of Vyshinsky's normativism was Stalgevitch (1948). Then, with the integration of legal relationships into the very concept of law around the time of the 20th Congress of the Soviet Communist Party, we had the work of Kechekyan and Piontkovsky. However, it took a long time before there was any progress in the theoretical field; this did not come until the acknowledgement of the sociological point of view on the one hand and the social-theoretical renewal of Marxist legal philosophy on the other (in Hungary, for example, Kulcsár, 1960, on the one hand; Szabó, 1973 and Peschka, 1974, on the other).

The least we can say, therefore, is that Lukács' *Ontology* came along at the very best time for the development of Marxist legal theory. It provides the philosophical-methodological basis and the opportunity to move forward for tendencies which were, from the very beginning, latent in the above-mentioned efforts at progress.

IV. The *Ontology's* Concept of Law

As can be seen from the tremendous variety of cross-references and interconnecting analyses, but most coherently from the chapter in the volume *The Most Important Problems* concerning *Reproduction*, the *Ontology's* approach to law points in the direction of an incredibly broad and ramified spectrum of problems. In the following I shall attempt to introduce the most important of these with reference to a number of fundamental questions.

(1) For Lukács it is the most general of conclusions that law is, above all else, a *practical category*, and, as such, must be evaluated primarily ontologically and not epistemologically. In the final analysis it is praxis itself that is its judge. So far as law is concerned, any question raised and any view held ultimately hinges on the answer to the question whether or not it proves capable of functioning. And if this does prove to be the case, for the ontological approach the criterion of whether a given phenomenon is to be qualified as law or not cannot be purely internal, defined by the law itself. That is to say that the question "what is law?" is, in the final analysis, not decided by its enactment as law but by its practical realization as such.

(2) The character of the practical realization of law and also of the significance of socialization is most eloquently highlighted by the dialectic of the use of force as one of the vehicles of the specificity of the *mediating role of law*. In other words, according to Lukács the legal organization of society represents the admission of a contradiction whereby the ultimate guarantee of the integrity of society is invariably naked force, although it is impossible for society to be based exclusively on it. To this extent law is the medium of the homogenization of divergent interests, which helps the "constant facticity" of force to turn into a "predominantly latent possibility" (Lukács, 1976, Vol. II, pp. 223, 247).

This social contradiction is expressed in the internal contradictoriness of the construction of law as well. The rules of law are formulated in such a way that in the event of their not being observed, formally, full sanctions *should* follow. In contrast to this formal project, in practice, the rules *can* still only be maintained for as long as the necessity arises of these sanctions actually being applied against a mere fragment of society. Thus force is necessary. But since it is impossible to rely on force alone, it only serves as an ultimate guarantee. At the same time, this ultimate guarantee can only be applied against an insignificant minority.

This has the paradoxical consequence that law can only exercise any influence at all if its rules are, at least in an external way, otherwise observed "voluntarily" and on a mass scale. Such a mass scale and "spontaneous observance" of the law, however, is only possible as long as a number of other institutional and ideological factors which move in the same direction as law also exercise an influence. This has two further consequences for theoretical generalization. First, the fulfilment of the mediating function of the legal complex is by no means independent: it depends on the ultimately identical stimulation of the total movement of the total complex. Secondly, what the strictly juridical viewpoint is inclined to regard as "law-observance", i.e. the practical effect and realization of the law, is, in the majority of cases, none other than a summation of the total movement of the total complex, including a great variety of non-legal influences (political, economic, religious, moral, etc.). This is a summation whose only legal feature is that externally it conforms with the law. Therefore, the numerical growth of patterns of behaviour evaluated as being positive from the point of view of the law can in itself in no way be equated with any growth in the influence of law.

(3) It follows from the methodological basis of the *Ontology* that in its social existence the legal complex must also be regarded as an *irreversibly progressing process*. However important, however much a vehicle of independent functions law-making becomes as an unavoidable sign of socialization, it cannot basically alter the position it occupies within the legal complex, that is to say, the relationship between the *making* and *application* of law is always historically and concretely determined; correspondingly, a changing yet definite balance between them must always evolve. Thus their relationship is based on the dialectic of a contradictory entity, which also includes, as its inevitable components, legal objectivation, its actual practical functioning. This is synonymous with the assertion that ontologically law-making cannot be isolated from the application of law, for it continues to be the actual practical influence which is the vehicle of the function of the legal complex as a whole. In the actual practical exertion of influence, however, law-making, as we shall see immediately, plays a mediating role, too, for its primary task is to ensure that the legal solution of social conflicts be effected, directed into the appropriate channels, and standardized to the highest degree possible and desirable.

Ontologically, a legal enactment can be assessed to the extent that it leads to practical influence. Whether we think of classical principles of the rule of law (*nullum crimen sine lege* in criminal law or the parliamentary mandate in the fixing of taxes), or whether we think of the question of human rights which is being raised with unprecedented urgency nowadays, it is obvious that we can hardly over-estimate the importance of the mere existence of written rules. And still less may we under-estimate the truth of the statement that they can be ontologically evaluated and fulfil an actual function only in the totality of the legal complex, that is to say, when its norm-structures are realized in practice.

It is also a consequence of this complexity of law that, when talking of the class character, elements, continuity, etc. of the law as a superstructure, it is an inadmissible simplification to relate the formulation of questions, not to the legal complex in its working, but merely to its individual forms of objectivation, for example to the individual norm-structures.

(4) The traditional Marxist literature treats law, the system of enacted norm-structures, mostly as the *reflection of social relationships*. Then, however, it often remains unclear whether it is a question of reflection in the epistemological sense.

Lukács related every element of goal-setting to the cognition of reality, although it did not follow, for him, that cognition was mixed up with the teleological project. Quite to the contrary: here it is a question, as he puts it, of "two heterogeneous types of approach to reality" (Lukács, 1973, p. 36). Heterogeneity means incongruence; and with incongruence, as in Marx's examples of the incongruence between property relationships and their legal conception, congruency is, in principle, impossible (Lukács, 1978, p. 125).

Lukács' resolute position does not in the least, of course, affect the truth of the fact that every activity of consciousness expressed a living reciprocity with reality. If we make reflection a general category which transcends epistemological meaning, then we are merely establishing the materialist *Weltanschauung* which, in connection with existence and consciousness, properly refers to the preponderant element but is not capable of specifying the peculiar nature and content of structures of consciousness. In this general sense we can also understand the teleological project, for example the legal norm-structure, as a reflection. Nevertheless, we must add that the ontological specificity of these types of reflection is precisely that they cannot be grasped epistemologically.

The creative character of the legal enactment is already revealed at the level of the *individual norm*. With its goal-project, the norm projects a connection into reality which was not given in it and could not spontaneously have been developed in it. Secondly, the goal-project is only present in the legal norm in a latent form: in the definition of the conduct which the legislator considers instrumental behaviour appropriate to the realization of the goal in question. Thirdly, in order that the legal norm should, in an exclusively relevant way, define this behaviour conceptually and, on this basis, make the qualification of real patterns of behaviour irrefutable, it describes the instrumental behaviour in its external features and in such a way as can be discerned from the formal assessment of the facts of the case. This one-sidedness leads to the opposition of legality and morality, to the possibility of legal correctness being associated with extreme hypocrisy (Lukács, 1976, Vol. II, p. 213). Fourthly, the description of instrumental behaviour becomes a legal norm when the legislator imposes a defined sanction in the event of its being proven or not proven.

Legal norms, however, do not exist independently of each other; they are established, *organized into a system* with each other. The creation of a coherent, consistent, and contradiction-free system assumes, at the time the individual norm is formulated, a further detachment which is heightened still more by its interpretation as a component of the system which shares its prevailing spirit. In the shaping of the legal system, legal institutions and sanctions, a role is played by purely practical considerations, coloured by professional traditions. It is "an abstract and conceptual homogenizing manipulation . . . of reality", the accomplishment of which at a given moment "is not anchored in social reality itself but only in the will of the ruling class to arrange social praxis according to its intentions" (Lukács, 1976, Vol. II. p. 218).

If we apply Lukács' analysis to the historical changes in the legal concept of things (Varga, 1980), then in the end we come to the following conclusion: the legal concept is a fiction of reality. In essence, the question of what content we attribute to what legal concept is a conventional one. We cannot treat it as a scientific concept which is in itself a reflection of reality. It should rather be treated as a conventional idea, for example, the axiom of an axiomatic system produced as a conceptual construction, which above all directly reflects itself and, through itself, the theoretical and practical considerations concealed behind its emergence: not as exterior reality. In other words, in the historical changes of the content of the legal concept it is not, in the final analysis and in the long term, the claim to an epistemologically adequate reflection that is decisive, but the fact that the concept (organized in a given way and in the context of a given system), as a sufficient practical instrument, is expected to contribute to the actual functioning of the legal complex.

(5) Every complex in the service of social regulation exhibits a specific internal contradiction in its functioning. As an instrument of mediation and in its relationship to other complexes it can obviously only play an instrumental and subordinate role. At the same time, its mediating task has to do enough formally to assert its own laws in the process. That is, "the social task requires for its fulfilment a system whose criteria, at least in a formal sense, can neither be derived from the task itself nor from its material foundation, but must be specific, internal and immanent." (Lukács, 1978, pp. 126–127). It is the technical-organizational consequence (which fundamentally affects the practical working of the law) of what a moment ago we characterized as an incongruence

The formally formulated requirement for a *specific system for fulfilment* receives a more heightened emphasis in the case of law than in the case of other devices for social regulation. And this, of course, is natural: society's most polarized conflicts of interest are, in the final analysis, settled by the law, by the use of institutionalized force, by means of a mediation which is accomplished by an extraordinarily widespread and ramified organizational apparatus set in motion as dictated by legal norms. Thus, when law is described ontologically, it is almost impossible to ignore the question of how its actual operation can be reconciled with satisfying its need for the specific system for its fulfilment: that is, with the principle of the rule of law.

The dilemma of *actual functioning* and/or *rule of law* is not an artificially extreme posing of the question: it springs from the quintessence of law itself. It is suggested by the ontological totality approach; that is to say, we have to recognize, at one and the same time, the ultimate determination by the total complex and the heterogeneity of legal complex within this determination. Translated into the language of law, this is a self-contradictory requirement which finds expression in the duality of legal enactment analysed above. Namely: law attempts to achieve the realization of the originally set social-political goal in such a way that in the process it realizes itself, *i.e.* through its own instrumental, teleological project. This, the observance of the rule of law, is an official and formal requirement made of the functioning of law.

But we should not forget that this is a principle that only operates within the legal complex: it is socially desirable on the one hand, and, on the other, of purely instrumental significance in the relationship between the total process and the legal complex. Ontologically, this means that the principle of the rule of law is itself mediatory and not of a determining effect. In the case of extreme situations the legal complex's specific system for fulfilment can in no way prevent the total process from eventually taking place. The realization of the rule of law (and with it, of individual norms) depends, therefore, on the extent to which it enjoys the general support of the total process. Within this basic definition, the question of what degree of socialization society has attained, or to what degree the relative independence of the legal complex is developed, can only be considered a subsidiary factor.

(6) The possibility of a confrontation between actual functioning and the rule of law principle also raises the possibility of a duality in their ideological reflection.

Lukács, retracing the steps of Max Weber, accepts the historical appearance of the claim to predictability and the fact that this created a formal rationality in all areas of social organization. Unlike in *History and Class Consciousness*, in the *Ontology* Lukács evaluates formal rationalization not as a specific sign of capitalist development; indeed, discussing all this in the context of socialization, he comes to the clearcut conclusion that it is a component of development, one that is universal and points even beyond socialism. *Formal rationalization* assumes a particular type of formation and implementation of the legal norm-system. It is, above all, necessary to regard law as a regulating power sufficient unto itself. Secondly, it is necessary to take the organization of the system of legal norms to its logical end. Thirdly, in order to satisfy its specific system for fulfilment, it is necessary to conceive of its implementation as a logically determined operation.

An ontological examination demonstrates that all this is an illusion. But it is an illusion that has its source in the ontological essence of the phenomenon since a real social claim stands behind it.

The ephemeral transition between illusion and reality can also be observed in the case of one of the most basic organizing concepts of law, *validity*. Validity is the concept with the aid of which we distinguish between what is to be considered as legal and as non-legal. Formal rationalization also formalized the concept of validity; as a result, the legal complex became formally differentiated from all other complexes. Validity determines what is to be considered as belonging to the legal system; its acceptance as an axiom is, therefore, a natural starting-point for any sort of preoccupation with the law, be it theoretical or practical. Validity, however, is only an organizing principle within the legal complex. Thus it shares all the illusory and conditional features which we have established concerning the logical organization and regular working of law. It is breached by the *de jure* invalid practice of state organs (which is nevertheless *de facto* enforced as permanent legal practise) in just the same way as it is breached by revolution. It can therefore only be evaluated ontologically to the extent it is associated with effectiveness, that is, becomes actual in the process of the mediation. To put it in a different way: effectiveness defines the circle within which validity can be at all intelligibly propounded (*cf.* Varga, 1978).

Earlier we suggested that law, as a specific object, presumes its own specific conserving-implementing reproducing subject: i.e. the qualified profession of lawyers. *Lawyers* also have an ontologically necessary dualistic relationship to law. On the one hand they operate and reproduce it as a system of norm-structures; on the other, they are the vehicle of, and, in their own professional praxis, realize optimally, the ideology which we call the juridical world concept.

To describe the essence of the process once again: as the natural concommitant of socialization, law has to emerge as a mediating complex of being; its relative autonomy has to be unravelled; the social goals it serves must be realized through the realization of its own instrumental projects; to this end its specific system must be formalized; and finally, the claim of the rule of law must be developed as an internal operative principle guaranteeing the possibility of formal control. Formally, therefore, law appears as a closed structure, feeding on itself, sufficient unto itself, and moving according to its own workings. For a while, there is no doubt for Lukács that this not only raises the problem of subsumption, but also generates specific discrepancies. For the ultimate determinant is the conflict of class interests and logical subsumption is only deposited on it as a phenomenal form (Lukács, 1976, Vol. II, p. 220). *Logic* is in this way exposed as an illusion, although this only affects it in the function of the determination. It is not the illogicality of reality that crops up behind the logical illusion. First, in law, systematic and logical consistency is not an uncovered requirement but is really an aspiration to optimal effectiveness. Secondly, if its self-assertion meets with obstacles then this merely means that the content contexts come to the foreground instead of the purely formal ones. Thirdly and finally, the specific logic of law is not eliminated here, since it exercises a controlling function to the very end (*cf.* Varga, 1980a).

Lukács' ontological rigour is startling for traditional ways of thinking because it retains law, in the final analysis, as an object of action rather than as its director: "The operation of positive law is based on the following method: to manipulate a maelstrom of contradictions in such a way that the result is not only a unified system but one that is capable of regulating contradictory social occurrences practically and with a tendency towards the optimal, and also of moving flexibly between . . . antinomic poles, in order to produce and influence the decisions of social praxis, most favourable for this society at any given time, in the course of the constant shifts of balance within a class rule that is changing more or less slowly. It is clear that this requires a very special manipulative technique, and this is sufficient explanation of the fact that this complex can only reproduce itself if society continually produces the requisite specialists (from judges and barristers to policemen and executioners)." (Lukács, 1976, Vol. II, pp. 225–226.)

According to traditional usage, *manipulation* means an unlawful operation performed within the law. With Lukács, however, it becomes a category lacking any such valuation: it signifies the practical medium which guarantees the social existence of the legal complex (and, within it, of the legal norm): its irreversibly progressing continuity. In his letter to Konrad Schmidt, written on

27 October 1980, Engels was already raising the possibility of an antagonism between the economy and law, the critical situation in which the economy and law confront each other and in which the question of which one of them will temporarily be subordinate is one of total determination. With Lukács, it is not the recognition of the possibility of this antagonism that is the new element, but rather that he pointed to the uninterrupted sequence of diverse intermediary paths as the basic ontological characteristic of the actual workings of law. Accordingly, the practical life of law is the continuous manipulation of the legal norm-system, which first recasts social conflicts and turns them into conflicts within the law and then, complying with the formal requirements of the principle of the rule of law, refines them into illusory conflicts. It is not in any way necessary for this to be spectacular in day-to-day legal routine. In individual cases it can be overlooked, indeed, it can even be unrecognizable. It assumes no more than what is desired by a mediation of the social movement via a static objectivation. The components of the process can still add up to significant changes in direction. As Lukács notes: "Naturally, at certain primitive stages the deviation might be quite minimal, but it is quite certain that the whole of human development depends on such minimal displacements." (Holz Rottler Abendroth, 1974, p. 18).

The withering critique by Marx and Engels of the *juridical world concept* in *The German Ideology* was directed at the alleged autonomy of the part complex and demonstrated the superiority of the total determination. As an ideological critique it therefore fulfilled its role, though it did not provide an ontological explanation. Yet the particularity of the problem is concealed in the fact that the legal complex not only develops its relative autonomy but, by virtue of its formalization, is expected to institutionalize operational principles and a corresponding professional ideology that allows the legal complex to be seen in precisely this autonomy. To put it another way: the task of the legal profession is to recognize and solve real social conflicts; at the same time, however, these must be brought to expression not in their dialectic diversity and constant flux, but in the closed conceptual stock of the valid legal enactments and in a rigid, homogenizing fashion. It is not the task of lawyers to reflect reality in its own multifariousness, but to assess it as the realization or non-realization of one of the predefined facts that constitute a case. Thus their *professional ideology* invites them to grasp reality through the filter of this specifically distinct system and to influence it by keeping to the internal operation principles of the system.

At the same time, the lawyer is clear about the ontological status of his own existence and knows that his ideology suggests illusions and requirements which cannot be verified epistemologically. A sort of dualistic consciousness comes about which could be called *double-talk*. It is not a glossing-over of this duality, but rather the awareness of it that makes the lawyer someone who has a conscious and active influence on social processes. The source of this recognition is that the duality in question is rooted not in the professional ideology but in the internal contradiction existing within the instrument at the disposal of the lawyer. This is the reason why the lawyer must be in the service of both society and the law: to serve law in such a way that he is simultaneously serving society.

V. Question-Marks and Lessons for Marxist Legal Theory

In Lukács' life-work the above analyses owe their specific colour to two circumstances. For one thing, Lukács was possessed of a decided legal erudition, which made him capable of displaying the appropriate sensitivity *vis-à-vis* the internal movement of law and its workings. Secondly, he obtained this erudition in such a way that he never came into direct touch with the legal profession. He was in no way influenced by the ideology of the legal profession, he was not affected by prevailing official legal policy requirements, he was able to analyze law rigorously and with the cool detachment and objectivity of the thinker who was on the outside and yet sensitive to its problems. Thus the totality approach of his *Ontology* came together with impulses which made him see law not through the embellishing filter of the normative Ought-element of legal enactments, but in its practical realization, in its actual functioning.

I should like to sum up the numerous issues and lessons Lukács' work raises for Marxist legal thinking in one single question: "is due distinction made between *Marxist* legal theory, which aims at being a general, social-scientific theory of law, and *socialist* theory of law, which is called upon, with the support of socialist law, to provide law in socialist societies with a theoretical foundation, in accordance with social requirements and principles of legal policy?" Lukács' lesson appears to be that Marxist legal theory can only become a general theory of law if it assesses the present as a transitional product of development (the *historical* view); if it sees the socialist legal arrangements on the European continent as one of many developmental alternatives, as being historically and concretely necessary for the respective countries (the *comparative* approach); and finally, if it describes the actual movement of the phenomenon serving as the object of analysis and its workings and not its desired and/or enacted principles (the *sociological* approach).

In the absence of any such differential thesis it is not guaranteed that the evaluation of law at the level of the total complex and the approach within the legal complex leads to an adequate theoretical synthesis. In consequence of its professional and ideological restrictions, it easily runs the risk of becoming not a theory of law so much as a theory of an ideal type of law, which views any divergence from what is accepted as desirable not as the objective characteristic of actual functioning but as a negligible defect which, it is believed, can be eliminated.

References

Holz, H. H., Kofler, L. & Abendroth, W. (1974) *Conversations with Lukács*. (Pinkus, T., Ed.). Translated by D. Fernbach. The Merlin Press: London.

Kulcsár, K. (1960) *A Jogszociológia Problémái* (Problems of the sociology of law). Közgazdasági és Jogi Kiadó: Budapest.

Lukács, G. (1973) *Zur Ontologie des Gesellschaftlichen Seins—Die Arbeit.* Luchterhand: Neuwied and Darmstadt.

Lukács, G. (1976) *A Társadalmi Lét Ontológiájáról* (Toward the ontology of social being). Volume I to III. Magvető: Budapest

Lukács, G. (1978) *Marx's basic Ontological Principles.* Translated by D. Fernbach. The Merlin Press: London.

Peschka, V. (1974) *Grundprobleme der Modernen Rechtsphilsosphie.* Akadémiai Kiadó: Budapest.

Szabó, I. (1973) *Les Fondements de la Théorie du Droit.* Akadémiai Kiadó: Budapest.

Szabó, I. (1976) The notion of law. *Acta Juridica Academiae Scientiarum Hungaricae* **18.**

Varga, Cs. (1978) Geltung des rechts – wirksamkeit des rechts. In *Die Gesellschaftliche Wirksamkeit des Sozialistichen Rechts.* (Mollnau, K. A., Ed.). Institut für Theorie des Staates und des Rechts der Akademie der Wissenschaften der DDR: Berlin.

Varga, Cs. (1980) Chose juridique et réification en droit. *Archives de Philosophie du Droit* **25.** Sirey: Paris.

Varga, Cs. (1980a) Law and its approach as a system. *Acta Juridica Academiae Scientiarum Hungaricae* **22.**

Select Bibliography of Georg Lukács' Books*

The works cited below appear in order of publication, not in order of writing.

Studies in European Realism: A Sociological Survey of the Writings of Balzac, Stendhal, Zola, Tolstoy, Gorki and Others (1950) Hillway: London. Reprinted Grosset and Dunlap: New York (1964).

Die Zerstörung der Vernunft (The dethronement of reason) 1962) Luchterhand: Neuwied.

The Historical Novel (1962) Merlin: London and Beacon: Boston. Reprinted Penguin: Harmondsworth (1969).

The Meaning of Contemporary Realism (1962) Merlin: London.

Die Eigenart des Ästhetischen (The peculiarity of the aesthetic) I-II (1963) Luchterhand: Neuwied.

Essays on Thomas Mann (1964) Merlin: London. Also Grosset and Dunlap: New York (1969).

Realism in our Time: Literature and the Class Struggle (1964) Harper and Row: New York—Evanston.

Der junge Hegel: Über die Beziehungen von Dialektik und Ökonomie (The young Hegel: On the connections of dialectics and economy) (1967) Luchterhand: Neuwied.

Goethe and his Age (1968) Merlin: London.

* For the most complete, although unfinished, bibliography, *cf.* Hartmann, J. (1966) Chronologische Bibliographie der Werke von Georg Lukács (A chronological bibliography of Georg Lukács' works) in *Festschrift zum achtzigsten Geburtstag von Georg Lukács* (Benseler, F., Ed.). Neuwied: Luchterhand pp. 625–696. For a comprehensive bibliography in English, *cf.* Murphy, P. (1976) *Writings by and about Georg Lukács: A Bibliography,* The American Institute for Marxist Studies: New York.

Probleme der Ästhetik (Problems of aesthetics) (1969) Luchterhand: Neuwied.
Lenin: A Study on the Unity of his Thought (1970) NLB: London and MIT: Cambridge, Mass.
Marxism and Human Liberation (1970) Dell: New York.
Solzhenitsyn (1970) Merlin: London and MIT: Cambridge, Mass.
Writer and Critic and Other Essays (1970) Merlin: London and Grosset and Dunlap: New York (1971).
History and Class Consciousness: Studies in Marxist Dialectics (1971) Merlin: London and MIT: Cambridge, Mass.
The History of the Novel (1971) MIT: Cambridge, Mass.
Tactics and Ethics: Political Writings 1919–1929 (1972) NLB: London.
Conversations with Lukács (1974). (Pinkus, T., Ed.) Merlin: London.
Frühe Schriften zur Ästhetik (Early writings in aesthetics) I-II (1974) Luchterhand: Neuwied.
Soul and Form (1974) Merlin: London and MIT: Cambridge, Massachusetts
A társadalmi lét ontológiájáról (Toward the ontology of social being) I-III (1976) Magvető: Budapest. Book I chapters 3 and 4 in English: *Hegel's False and Genuine Ontology* (1978) Merlin: London; *Marx's Basic Ontological Principles* (1978) Merlin: London. Book II chapter 1 in German: *Die Arbeit* (1973) Luchterhand: Neuwied.

Date received: October 1980

[20]

Ann. Rev. Sociol. 1983. 9:103–24

MARXIST PERSPECTIVES IN THE SOCIOLOGY OF LAW

Steven Spitzer

Department of Sociology, Suffolk University, Boston, Massachusetts 02108

Abstract

This review considers the problems and prospects associated with the development of Marxist perspectives in the sociology of law. Taking as its starting point the efforts to construct a Marxist understanding of law through the traditional approach of legal economism, a number of directions and themes in the development of a new Marxist vision of law are explored. Alternatives to "legal nihilism" are examined in conjunction with a survey of the movement of Marxist theory toward a "looser" and "flatter" conception of the relationship between law and society. The role of politics, ideology, and history in the reconstruction of Marxist legal theory are then considered with special attention to the virtues and limits of "imbricationist" and "constitutive" accounts. The analysis ends with a reexamination of the points of convergence and divergence among Marxism, sociology, law, and socialism.

INTRODUCTION: THE CRISES OF LAW AND MARXISM

The last decade has witnessed an explosion of interest in Marxist perspectives on law. Just over ten years ago, Elliot Currie (1971 : 137) could observe with confidence that there were "very few Marxian analyses in the academic sociology of law." Today, although Marxist insights have by no means revolutionized our understanding of law, the sociological questions that they have raised are no longer, as Currie charged, "unasked." To the contrary, Marxist theory in general and Marxist interpretations of law in particular have become more central to the sociological enterprise.

A number of explanations may be advanced for this noteworthy and surprisingly rapid shift. Most generally, there was what Hunt (1981 : 49) has

0360-0572/83/0815-0103$02.00

called a "deeply felt 'crisis' that enveloped law and legal institutions from the end of the 1960s" in Western Europe and the United States. This crisis was associated with a number of developments that breathed life into Marxist approaches to the law: (*a*) the exhaustion, if not total collapse, of the "normative integration" paradigm in sociology (Abel 1980; Hunt 1981) and the decay of "liberal legalism" within legal thought and jurisprudence (Unger 1975, 1976; Klare 1979); (*b*) the "opening out" (Sumner 1981) of theoretical perspectives on law and other "superstructural" elements within European Marxism (see Althusser 1971; Williams 1973; Thompson 1975; Cohen 1978; Hall et al 1978; Poulantzas 1978); (*c*) the growing interest in political and economic dimensions of law generated by the emergence of "radical criminology" (Taylor et al 1973; Quinney 1974; Greenberg 1980a; see Sparks 1980 for a critical review) and "radical legal practice" (Black 1971; Lefcourt 1971); (*d*) the broadening of interest in the relationship between law and social change through the study of punishment and its historical transformation (Hay 1975; Spitzer 1975, 1979; Foucault 1977; Ignatieff 1978, 1981; Lea 1979); and finally (*e*) the rediscovery in the English-speaking world of two "classical" Marxist interpretations of law: the work of the Austrian Marxist Karl Renner (1949) (for commentary see Kahn-Freund 1949; McManus 1978; Hirst 1979; Kinsey 1979) and the work of Evgeny Pashukanis (1978, 1980) (for commentary see Balbus 1977:fn. 5; Kinsey 1978; Sumner 1979: Ch. 8; Hirst 1979: App. I; Binns 1980; Mullin 1980; Greenberg & Anderson 1981; Beirne & Quinney 1982).

Taken together, these developments help us to identify the major stress points in the Marxist theory of law and to interpret the directions its development has followed. Some of the factors outlined above are the product of political struggles, others are tied to cultural and intellectual debates, and still others are the result of the pervasive discontent with modern forms of law in all its guises. To assess the shape and substance of this ferment accurately it will be helpful to look more carefully at both the deconstruction and reconstruction of Marxist perspectives on law that have taken place over the last decade.

The Problem

Although recent collections (Cain & Hunt 1979; Phillips 1980) have done much to dispel the myth that Marx and Engels were oblivious to legal issues, it is still fair to observe that they never identified law as a major theoretical problem (Campbell & Wiles 1980:x). In the absence of an adequate treatment of law in their original writings, the Marxist conception of law that first emerged in the 20th century reflected the weltanschauung of "orthodox" Marxism (Gouldner 1980; Jacoby 1981). Embracing what Hirst (1979) has called "essentialism," these accounts were wedded to the "view that all social phenomena can be reduced or derived from the economic" (Sugarman 1981:81). It is this tendency to trace all legal phenomena back to economic forces and structures that has created the greatest obstacle to the development of a Marxist sociology of law.

The purest form of legal economism is embodied in the identification of Law as a social form with Capitalism as an economic system. The earliest proponent of this position was Pashukanis (1978:61) who reasoned that "the withering away of the categories of bourgeois law will . . . mean the withering away of law altogether." Basing his theory of law on Marx's analysis of commodity exchange, Pashukanis consistently argued that there was an homology between the logic of the commodity form and the logic of the legal form (Beirne & Quinney 1982:21).

While this insight has proven valuable in demystifying the law as an ideological form in capitalist societies, it has also created a cul-de-sac for Marxist attempts to come to grips with law. To the extent that law can only be understood as a negative force and form peculiar to bourgeois society, its explanation begins with the critique of capitalism and ends with its eclipse. If this view is taken seriously, then as Marxism achieves its objectives the theory of law self-destructs: "Laws as a specific object of analysis disappear" (Hirst 1979:163). When it is tied to this logic Marxism does not so much offer a theory *of* law as a "theory *against* law" (Santos 1979; Cotterrell 1981a). Insofar as Marxism is forced to throw the legal "baby" out with the capitalist "bathwater," any systematic consideration of the law is stymied before it starts.

The mechanical equation of Law and Capitalism by "legal nihilism" (Sharlet 1978; Hunt 1981:35) has proven an embarrassment and a frustration for those who have sought to advance Marxist theories of law: an embarrassment because of the unmistakable and persistent presence of the legal form, legal ideologies, and repressive law in "socialist" and other noncapitalist societies; a frustration because as Law is disentangled from Capitalism, the entire edifice of Marxist theory threatens to collapse.

A number of strategies have been pursued by Marxists since Pashukanis in an effort to overcome the shortcomings of economism without sacrificing the basic structure of Marxian theory. The problem these strategies face is exactly how to disentangle Law from Capitalism and fashion a more sophisticated, flexible, and empirically defensible understanding of the nexus between the two. Before examining these strategies in greater detail it will be useful to outline the context within which they have emerged.

Functional Analysis and the "Loosening Project"

As early as 1906 an alternative to the emphasis on legal form in Marxist legal theory became apparent in the work of Karl Renner (1949). Renner located the roots of capitalist law in bourgeois property relations, but unlike Pashukanis he was "principally concerned with the *ends* to which law is put, rather than with the *form* of law itself" (Kinsey 1979 : 52). For Renner law is a "neutral framework of legality or the rule of law, upon which would evolve the social functions of a 'Socialist Commonwealth'" (Kinsey 1979 : 53). And since law can serve different ends under different economic regimes, it is possible not only to envision a socialist law but also to see how law can become a political as well as an economic tool. The connection between law and economy is thus preserved but the functional relationship between the two is "loosened" in an important respect.

The most obvious problem with this "solution," however, is that it fails to specify the connection between legal form and content. As a number of commentators have noted (Klare 1979 : 135; Kinsey 1979 : 52; Beirne & Quinney 1982 : 6), law cannot be treated as an "empty frame" into which new content is poured without forcing us to introduce other factors (e.g. power, mystification, etc) to explain *how* the law accomplishes its ends. In this sense, Renner's loosening and the elasticity (McManus 1978) it provides presage "instrumentalism" (see Miliband 1977), one of the other types of reductionism identified in revisionist debates.

When approached from the standpoint of the "needs" of an economic system, the essence of the loosening project (Greenberg 1976) is the denial of the functional necessity of law for that system. The question thus becomes: Is it possible to provide an explanation of law that ties it to economic organization without reproducing the circularity and teleology of functionalism? (See A. Horwitz 1977; Spitzer 1977.)

One of the most straightforward ways of distinguishing Marxist theory from traditional functionalism is to emphasize the fact that for the former elements of a class system are always *dysfunctional* as well as functional. More specifically, the central mechanism of social change in class society is, according to Marxist theory, a dialectical process through which the relations of production inevitably come into conflict with (are dysfunctional for) the developing forces of production. Thus, for example, as capitalism develops we should expect that legal arrangements functional under feudalism (e.g. the Elizabethan Poor Laws) would become dysfunctional for and have to be replaced by laws compatible with the emerging capitalist order [e.g. the Poor Law Reform of 1834 (see Polanyi 1957 : Ch. 6; Piven & Cloward 1971)]. Taking this a step further, we should also expect that "forms and principles of socialist legality [are] developing within capitalist societies" (Sumner 1981 : 88).

When systematically applied to the analysis of law these insights encourage us to view law as always at least somewhat at odds with the mode of production in which it is found. But while an inventory of the functions and dysfunctions of various laws for any mode of production establishes the contradictory character of law (Chambliss 1979; Grau 1982), the question of why these contradictions exist or how and when they are likely to be "resolved" remains unanswered. Moreover, since law can always be said to be ahead of, behind, or parallel with a given economic order, we have no way of establishing the precise functional significance of any given law.

Deconstructing Marxism: Structuralism, Culturalism, and the "Flattening Project"

Of the many "isms" identified in the debate over the revision of Marxist theory, "structuralism" and "culturalism" are two of the most important. Centering around the work of Louis Althusser in France and E. P. Thompson in Britain, respectively, these two tendencies have in many respects defined the terms and limits of the recent investigation into the role of law in Marxist theory. Beginning as efforts to refine traditional conceptions of the base-superstructure metaphor, they have in very different ways tried to respond to the challenge of economism in the Marxist perspective on law. The recurring issue facing both of these tendencies or "schools" (Laclau 1977: Ch. 2; Redhead 1982: 330) is, as I argue below, how to redefine the relationship between external structures, human subjects, and the law (Hirst 1980).

A major point of departure in the "structuralist" approach is the concept of the "relative autonomy" of the law. As a touchstone for many revisionist accounts (Balbus 1977; Edelman 1979), it offers an approach to rethinking the law/economy nexus in structuralist terms. Louis Althusser (1970: 99–100) suggests that the law, along with philosophy, aesthetic production, scientific formations, and other "superstructural" elements, have their "own history" and exist as "relatively autonomous and hence relatively independent" features of the "whole." Law is thus conceived as independent of the economic system but also dependent in some sense. This "some sense" is the rub since the movement and structure of all superstructural elements (including law) are ultimately traced back to the economic system.

Balibar (1970: 306), Althusser's collaborator, illustrates this logic in his argument that the interventions of the State, law, and political power, such as those that occurred in the transition from feudalism to capitalism (e.g. factory legislation and the enclosure acts in England), "*transform* and *fix* the limits of the mode of production." What he means by this is that at least in transitional periods "the forms of law and of State policy are not, as hitherto, adapted to the economic structure . . . but *dislocated* with respect to it" (Balibar 1970: 306–7). Thus law is somehow "broken loose" to do its dirty work. But this dislocation does not block the path between economy and law, it only serves to make that path more tangled and circuitous. In the final analysis, the path leads back to a version of the very economism that the theory is ostensibly designed to overcome. The knee-jerk relationship between law and the economy is abandoned (Beirne & Quinney 1982: 13), but law is still accounted for in the "last instance" by pulls on the visible or hidden economic strings.

Why then has structuralism been taken so seriously as a way out of the theoretical impasse facing the Marxist analysis of law? One answer may be found in extensions and refinements of the structuralist position by Nicos Poulantzas (1973, 1978). Poulantzas breaks with the Althusserian portrayal of law in an important respect. Specifically, he observes (1982: 190) that "Law does not only deceive and conceal . . . nor does it merely repress people by compelling or forbidding them to act." Thus law is not simply, as Althusser (1971) would have it, an "ideological state apparatus." "It also organizes and sanctions certain *real rights* of the dominated classes (even though, of course, these rights are invested in the dominant ideology and are far from corresponding in practice to their juridical form)" (Poulantzas 1982: 190). Even though Poulantzas is quick to add that the rights granted are in an important sense illusory, he has at least opened the door to a broader view of law as a partly positive (i.e. active and creative) as well as partly negative factor in the "political-social field" (cf. Edelman 1979).

The emphasis on law's active, shaping, embedded, and "lived" character in the work of Poulantzas and to some extent in that of Antonio Gramsci (see Hall et al 1978; Sugarman 1981) has helped structuralism move beyond a unidimensional conception of law. Recent commentators have drawn attention to these "functions" and tied them to the emergence of what has been called the "constitutive theory of law." According to Klare (1979: 128, 132), this theory of law shifts the emphasis from law as an abstract and objectified structure to the notion of law-making as praxis: the view that law represents "a form of expressive social practice in which the community participates in shaping the moral, allocative, and adjudicatory text of social life." The constitutive theory thus demands "recognition of the role played by all social actors, including even oppressed individuals and groups, in the constitution of the legal order" (Fraser 1978: 148). In opposition to the lockstep of legal nihilism and the system imperatives of classical structuralism, this approach seeks to "bring men (and women) back in" (cf. Homans 1964) to the explanatory system and to redefine history as a process driven by human subjects (Thompson 1978: 79).

This perspective is echoed, albeit from the vantage point of "culturalism," by E. P. Thompson. Thompson, whose position is described by several observers as "imbricationist" (Sugarman 1981; Beirne & Quinney 1982), assumes that law is "deeply imbricated within the very basis of productive relations" (Thompson 1975: 261). Law is, moreover, both within and without; there are "invisible" as well as "visible" structures of law (Thompson 1975:261). From the point of view of some structuralists, Thompson's position is one of "cultural reductionism" (Merritt 1980:210). But Thompson is not simply suggesting that the economic infrastructure is "absorbed" by the superstructure of legal, political, ideological, or cultural practice; he is arguing that the very distinction between infrastructure and superstructure is flawed. For Thompson law does not simply influence the material basis of society, it becomes part of that basis. The impulse to treat law in this way is part of what may be described as the "flattening project": the denial of the topographic metaphor of base and superstructure in Marxist theory.

Conventional Marxism has proceeded on the assumption that the architectural metaphor can and should be rehabilitated—as, for example, in Cohen's (1978:231) suggestion that the "roof" (superstructure) is not only supported by the "struts" (infrastructure) but also renders them more stable. But the flattening project involves a movement away from this sort of theorizing for both structuralism and culturalism. Whatever their continuing differences, both schools seem to be moving toward an obliteration of the distinction between the "upper" reaches of consciousness, culture, religion, art, politics, and law and the "lower" economic processes and structures.

Once it is redefined and flattened in this way, the theory of law can begin to take the interpenetration of the legal and extra-legal worlds seriously. It becomes possible, for instance, to ask questions about the law-making process in socialist as well as capitalist societies (Fraser 1978; Kinsey 1978). What remains crucial to this task, however, is the ability to distinguish *expressive* from *repressive* law and to demonstrate how particular social arrangements prove consistent or inconsistent with each. If law is social practice, then how do we decide whether that practice is expressive, repressive, or both? Moreover, since the theoretical center of gravity is shifted from the reified economic system to the flesh and blood people who create and live it, a new problem arises: How can we understand the nature and significance of law as a social institution as well as a social practice?

Law is never simply praxis. No matter how fluid, spontaneous, and revolutionary a society is, it must create institutions that at some point guide and define the limits of social practice. As a series of crystallized social practices within history, law becomes a condition as well as a form of social practice, a framework within which law-making itself takes place. Law is thus always structure as well as practice, if only because laws inevitably outlive their makers.

By downgrading the structural, constraining side of law the "imbricationists" have created another problem: They have dissipated the structural tension at the very heart of Marxist conceptions of social change. For Marxism the movement of class societies through history is premised on the tension between the forces and relations of production. If law is "reconstituted" (Fraser 1978:150), does its status change from a static relation of production to a dynamic productive force? To say that law is expressive under socialism and repressive under capitalism hardly solves the problem. An agenda is not a theory.

Thus the flattening project not only demands that Marxism reconceptualize the system at rest, it also entails a rethinking of the system in motion. If law is embedded in the very foundations of class societies the question becomes: How can law both support and inhibit the transformation of such societies? Are we to understand law as both a force and a relation of production, its precise status being determined in each empirical instance; or is it better to distinguish different kinds or levels of law? In either case, the reconstruction of Marxist legal theories requires that we take a closer look at the relationship between legal and other "noneconomic" social forms.

RECONSTRUCTING MARXIST LEGAL THEORY: THE ROLE OF POLITICS, IDEOLOGY, AND HISTORY

The deconstruction of Marxist legal theory has opened up an important breathing space for those who are pursuing emancipatory conceptions of law and society. For those interested in its reconstruction the greatest amount of attention has been focused on the significance of politics, ideology, and history.

Law and Politics

Once legal theory has been freed from the stranglehold of crude economism, it is hardly surprising that the links between law and politics become far more salient. Modern law is always in some sense a creation of the state just as the state is in some sense a creation of modern law (P. Beirne, personal communication). The connections between the institutionalization of power and the practice and structures of law are thus far too important to ignore. Nevertheless, the relationship between law and the state raises serious questions for any Marxist vision of law (Miliband 1977).

The major difficulty associated with the introduction of politics into the Marxist consideration of law grows out of the fact that Marxism is ill-equipped to treat it as an independent and relevant variable. Politics has typically been submerged in classical Marxist discussions of law because of the tendency to focus on the "private" (economic) functions of law and to treat "public" law as a "second-order" problem (Steinert 1977:438–39). But in those cases where public law is addressed, it is usually treated as an extension of the state and the will of the ruling class. In consequence, there is little incentive to distinguish public law and state policy, much less approach law as a factor in opposition to the state (Grau 1982). Neither politics nor law can be taken seriously when they are either dissolved into the economy (economism) or equated with the will of the dominant class (instrumentalism).

Marxism's analysis of the state as an historical form also weakens its explanatory force. The reason is that Marxist theory has traditionally comprehended capitalism "as the first mode of production in history in which the means whereby the surplus is pumped out of the direct producer is 'purely' economic in form—the wage contract" (Anderson 1974:403). In contrast to capitalism, "all other previous modes of exploitation operate through extra-economic sanctions—kin, customary, religious, legal or political" (Anderson 1974:403). Since Marx (1970a:689) emphasized the ways in which capitalist control was based on the "dull compulsion of economic relations," it may be argued that while the superstructural elements of kinship, religion, law, and the state become part of the "constitutive structure" of precapitalist modes of production, they remain "marginal" to the organization and regulation of capitalist life. Thus, at least traditionally, the same reasoning that leads Marxists to treat law as epiphenomenal under capitalism removes politics and the state from serious theoretical consideration. And insofar as Marxism limits itself to a critique of capitalism, the "political problem" fails to emerge as either a theoretical or practical issue.

At its core Marxist theory prefers to approach capitalism as if politics were an external rather than an internal precondition of its existence. The logic behind this reasoning becomes suspect, however, when we recognize that the "wage contract" of which Anderson speaks, capitalism's "glue," is itself a legal construct. In fact, the classic definition of capitalism—private ownership of the means of production—itself contains two important legal concepts: "private" and "ownership" (Tushnet 1982:10). There are many instances in Marx's analysis, as Cohen (1978:216–30) has revealed, where he defined economic structure in legal (and therefore political) terms. And while some purists, like Cohen (1978:224–5), may feel compelled to separate the economic "wheat" (e.g. production relations) from the legal "chaff" (e.g. property relations), the consistent interpenetration of the two illustrates the significance of the legal/political dimension in the reconstruction effort.

Two directions in the recasting of politics within Marxist legal theory appear promising. They may be roughly characterized as (*a*) Law against the State, and (*b*) the State against Capital. Beginning with E. P. Thompson's contributions and the ensuing "rule of law" debate (Fine et al 1979; Sumner 1981; Redhead 1982), a number of commentators within Marxism have begun to suggest not only that Law and State are empirically distinguishable, but also that they frequently stand in opposition. This opposition is typically rooted in the contradictions of legal development within class societies. Since the capitalist state must continually legitmate itself in terms of the values of individual rights, equality, freedom, and justice, it must develop a system of rules, procedures, and practices (Law) that actually serves these values, at least some of the time. By juxtaposing "arbitrary power" and "the rule of law" it may be argued that law can operate against the state as well as in its service (see Thompson 1975).

The notion of Law against the State captures the contradictory reality of capitalist arrangements. The nub of the problem for Marxist theory comes in specifying the conditions under which the rule of law and the "rights" it provides are in fact a barrier to power, an extension of power, or both. The theory must not only specify the ways in which "rights" such as habeas corpus, trial by jury, and the right to organize unions (Thompson 1979) are situated within history (Picciotto 1979), but also address the interplay between abstract rights and principles on the one hand and concrete procedures and practices on the other. In this endeavor the lines between the public and private spheres, although frequently blurred (Unger 1975, 1976; Fraser 1978; Klare 1979), must be distinguished as clearly as possible. Thus the freedoms granted *against* the State that Thompson and other imbricationists explore are not at all the same as those granted *through* the State [e.g. freedom of contract and property (see Neumann 1957)]. Certain kinds of individual rights help the State to grow while others hold it in check.

Yet to talk of "granting" these freedoms and rights is, of course, to miss part of Thompson's point. Because he and other imbricationists present law as an "arena for struggle" rather than as either a reflection of economic imperatives or a benefaction of the state, there is a strong emphasis on "winning" rather than granting rights. In fact, the rule-of-law analysis is largely defined in terms of the possibility and desirability of reconceiving law as a product of class struggle—the "missing link" in orthodox and structuralist accounts (Sumner 1981; Grau 1982; Redhead 1982). Hall (1980: 10) summarizes the position well: "We are arguing . . . that the civil rights and freedoms which make our society what it is are rights which were defined and won in struggle against the dominant interests in society, not bestowed on society by theory."

A second consideration of politics within Marxist legal theory focuses on how the state sometimes operates against rather than in the service of Capital. In challenging traditional Marxist concepts of the state, a number of observers have drawn attention to two important but neglected facts:

(*a*) The "capitalist state" may use law as a means of "disciplining" specific capitals in the interest of capitalism as a whole, and (*b*) power groups in capitalist societies may use the state and its laws against the interests of both specific capitals and capitalism in general.

In the first case specific laws (i.e. antitrust legislation, certain types of administrative law, environmental law, products-liability law, etc) become a brake on renegade capitalists and a coordinating, organizing, and regulating factor in the interest of capitalism. One variant of this position is developed by the "capital logic school" (Jessop 1980:340). Emphasizing the functions that must be performed to maintain the capitalist system as a whole (e.g. securing social order, providing necessary infrastructure, guaranteeing internal and external markets, reproducing labor power, long-range planning, and investment in human capital), this school argues that "since the state and state intervention developed exactly because these tasks could not be performed profitably by single capitals (otherwise they would have) and since the state has to step out of the competition between capitalists to fulfill those tasks it must (and does) have a certain amount of independence from capital and its factions" (Steinert 1977:439).

This independence explains how and why the law can work against "particular capitals" (e.g. "profiteers," "unethical" manufacturers, union-breaking companies, corporate polluters, etc) yet remain loyal to "capital in general." But because the "logic of capital" forces the state to pay for its independence by serving another and deeper set of "system needs," these theories never really release the state from capitalism's grasp. What they do provide is a more complex analysis of the articulations among the economy, politics, and the law.

The second way of interpreting the role of the state vis-à-vis capitalism is based on the recognition that in some circumstances the power of the state may be harnessed by groups that lie beyond the immediate boundaries of capitalism's "interests" and "needs." Two possibilities are relevant here: the seizure of power from "above" and from "below." On the one hand, it is clear that capitalism has taken a number of "exceptional" forms (e.g. fascism) wherein the power of the state was "captured" and used to diminish if not destroy the ability of the capitalist class to administer the economy and "make" the law (see Neumann 1944; Kirchheimer 1969; Gramsci 1971; Hall et al 1978). On the other hand, there is the obligation to explore the seizure of power as part of the process through which capitalism is transformed into socialism—keeping alive the possibility that history is always made, at least in part, by men and women and that neither Capitalism nor the State is an eternal social form. If Marxism is to be taken seriously as an analysis of capitalism and socialism, it must address both of these questions as part of any investigation into politics and the law.

Law and Ideology

The major obstacle to the investigation of the relationship between ideology and law has been the long-standing Marxist habit of defining the former as "false consciousness" and the latter as "repression." If ideology is, by definition, no more than a veil pulled over the eyes of the working class by its masters, then there is little point in studying its connection to the political/legal apparatus or assessing its role in promoting or inhibiting social change. By beginning and ending its consideration of ideology with the epigram "the ideas of the ruling class are in every epoch the ruling ideas" (Marx 1970b: 64), classical Marxism restricts the role of ideology to that of a "confidence trick" (cf. Kinsey 1978) by which capitalists rule.

But recent work on the theory of ideology in Marxism (Lichtman 1975; Kellner 1978; Hirst 1979; and Sumner 1979) has stimulated a reexamination of ideology's meaning, function, and role within Marxist theory. Several aspects of this process are relevant to the position of ideology in Marxist legal theory. The most general of these is the recognition that ideology must be distinguished from propaganda. As Arnold Hauser (cited in Muraskin 1976: 566) has suggested, "what most sharply distinguishes a propagandistic from an ideological presentation and interpretation of facts is . . . that [the former's] falsification and manipulation of truth is always conscious and intentional. Ideology, on the other hand, is mere deception—in essence self-deception—never simply lies and deceit." Insofar as ideology is embedded in the consciousness of both the deceivers and deceived, it can no longer be confused with direct manipulation. From this perspective, the ruling class never creates legal ideology out of thin air. Rather, it must be collected from a kind of "ideological pool" within the sea of beliefs, half-truths, cliches, and assumptions making up the culture and consciousness of any society. And to the extent that this pool is fed by the everyday experiences, traditions, aspirations, and frustrations of *all* classes within society, the relationships among ideology, law, and politics become interesting and complex.

Freed from the assumption that ideology is simply reality turned upside down, as in a *camera obscura* (Lichtman 1975), by a scheming ruling class, investigations of legal ideology become central to the reconstruction of Marxist legal theory. Not only can ideology itself be defined as an imbricated force (see the discussion of "flattening," above), but the ideological sources and implications of law can also be subject to more careful scrutiny. Two dimensions of law have recently been explored in this regard: law as magic and as doctrine.

Part of the significance of law in class societies resides in its ability to mystify social life. To the extent that Law as a way of reasoning, as doctrine, and as practice is couched in "professional secrecy, esoteric language, grand ceremony, special clothing, carefully structured courtrooms, the rituals of legislation and the occupational status of the judge" (Sumner 1979:275), and to the extent that it is embedded in commonplace rituals such as the pledge of allegiance, it becomes something special and mysterious: a reified social form (Gabel 1980).

As an ingredient in the glue used in the attempt to put the humpty-dumpty of culture back together after capitalism has pushed it off the wall, Law (like Science) performs an important set of ideological functions. The reified character of Law as both practice (reflected in its ritual, ceremonial, and totemic character) and consciousness (reflected most generally in bromides like "all men are equal before the law" and "a government of laws not men") provides an important ingredient in the foundation of class rule —an ingredient often taken as seriously by the rulers as by the ruled. In this respect Law is the opium of both the masses and the ruling class. The fact that the ruling class has a more strategic position and a greater interest in the manufacture of this opium (Sumner 1979:270) in no way exempts them from all its addictive effects.

The ideological functions of legal doctrine within capitalist societies have been demonstrated in a number of ways. Part of the critique concerns shortcomings in both liberal and conservative accounts of the patterning of legal decisions and discourse. The main targets here have been legal formalism (Kennedy 1973; M. Horwitz 1977: Ch. 8) and liberal legalism (Kennedy 1976; Unger 1976; Klare 1979) as efforts to construct coherent legitimating accounts of the nature of law. Thus, for example, legal formalism can be interpreted as a specific legitimating ideology corresponding to a particular stage in capitalist development. As such it formed "an intellectual system which gave common law rules the appearance of being self-contained, apolitical, and inexorable, and which, by making 'legal reasoning seem like mathematics,' conveyed 'an air . . . of . . . inevitability' about legal decisions" (M. Horwitz 1977:254).

Legal interpretation is the primary process of self-legitimation for the legal profession. When it is "decoded" (Klare 1981) in this way, the ideological functions of doctrine are both revealed and rendered less effective. The assumption here is that legal texts provide an important part of the ideology of law—an ideology that helps legitimate and mediate repression through a "logic of obfuscation" (Kennedy 1979:220). The task of critical inquiry is thus to "uncover the constellation of assumptions, values and sensibilities about law, politics and justice these texts evince, to reveal their latent patterns and structures of thought . . ." (Klare 1981:451).

At another level specific types of law and their interpretation are analyzed as they contribute to the ideological reproduction of capitalism. In this body of work, the ideological features of particular types of laws are delineated and tied directly to the fact that capitalist law, in spite of its claims to transcendence, must always reflect the underlying contradictions and grim realities of capitalist life. Thus the law, in spite of itself, becomes a prism through which the alienating, divisive, and exploitative features of capitalism are refracted.

Many examples of this type of analysis are beginning to appear in American law journals and other publications. The ideological dimensions of law have been explored in areas as diverse as private (Kennedy 1976) and public (Tushnet 1979) law, the law of contracts (Gabel 1977; Gabel & Feinman 1982), torts (Abel 1981), constitutional law (Tushnet 1981), labor law (Klare 1978, 1981, 1982; Stone 1981), criminal law (Kelman 1982), and law relating to race relations (Freeman 1978, 1982), health care (Rosenblatt 1981), the family (Olsen 1983), and gender roles (Rafter & Stanko 1982; Polan 1982; Taub & Schneider 1982).

In most cases, inquiries of this sort seek to establish a link between the legal principles reflected in the evolution of doctrine and specific imperatives of capitalist society. A few examples may be considered: In discussing the "assumption of risk" doctrine in workmen's injury cases, Morton Horwitz (1977:210) argues that it expressed "the triumph of contractarian ideology more completely than any other nineteenth century legal creation . . . the law had come simply to ratify those forms of inequality that the market system produced." Looking at the ideological significance of the legal contract, Cotterrell (1981b:63) suggests that the idea of "equivalence" and "universality" embodied in this genre of law "promotes the breakdown of all major status differentials unconnected with the needs of an economy based on market exchanges and confirms and defines the particular form of individualism in terms of which capitalist social relations are conceptualized." In a critique of American tort law, Abel (1981:206–7) indicates that tort doctrine is significant in the reproduction of bourgeois ideology because it reinforces individualism, offers symbolic support for inequality, and "responds to intangible injury by extending that fundamental concept of capitalism—the commodity form—from the sphere of production to the sphere of reproduction." Finally, Klare (1981:452) argues that "collective bargaining law articulates an ideology that aims to legitimate and justify unnecessary and destructive hierarchy and domination in the workplace."

As the legal profession and those who reproduce it (law professors) have become more self-conscious about the ideological sources and implications of their work, the notion that the law is simply a neutral instrument—a notion itself associated with the rise of capitalism (M. Horwitz 1977: Ch. 1)—has become ever more suspect. And this suspicion has grown *pari passu* with Marxism's increasing attention to the links among law, politics, and ideology.

The interpretation of the law as doctrine is a vital process in the demystification of law. Yet it is also clear that ideology is never fully formed, articulated, or internalized at the doctrinal level. There may be value in destroying the artificial coherence and legitimacy of legal thought, but it isn't clear what those beyond the legal establishment can build on the ruins. "Legalism" suffers from "an overemphasis upon judicial institutions and the relative neglect of the formulation and administration of law" (Abel 1980: 828). But to the extent that "critical legalism" (see Unger 1983) restricts its critique to the level of doctrine and ideology, it suffers the same fate.

Law always responds in some fashion to the voices and actions of those who are its subjects; in this sense ideology is as much emergent as it is imposed. The concrete struggles, disputes, and agreements that are transformed into law leave their imprint on both the form of legal institutions and the content of legal ideas. Hence, legal ideology not only reinforces, enshrines, and legitimates the victories of the capitalist order, it also registers and presages its defeats. Once again, the contradictory nature of law threatens to destroy the symmetry and closure of any Marxism that refuses to acknowledge its mediative and transitory character.

Perhaps more than anything else, the explanation of legal change forces Marxist theories of law out of their analytical straitjacket. It is this issue, as it invokes the role of history, to which we now turn.

Law and History

At the heart of any Marxist inquiry lies the question of social change. Whatever else it may claim to be, Marxist theory must measure itself by its ability to explain major transformations in the organization of economic, political, and social life. But like most of the 19th century attempts to understand the workings of Western societies (Bock 1952), Marxist theory is haunted by the "ghost of evolutionism" (Jacoby 1977: 78; Gouldner 1980: Ch. 2). The power of the ghost is evidenced in the willingness to reduce social change to "a developmental schema, registering a progression —difficult, halting, occasionally stopped and reversed—when there may be none" (Jacoby 1977: 74). Many of the excesses and distortions of orthodox Marxist legal theory may be traced to the insistence that law *must* follow society and society *must* change according to a preordained plan. The "withering away" thesis, based as it was on visions of inexorable progress toward "lawlessness," is only the most blatant of these themes.

But there is another side to the Marxist vision of history. Marx (cited in Jacoby 1981: 22) was careful to note that "human history differs from natural history in that we have made the former, but not the latter." As a product of human activity rather than nature, the history of law reflects all of the contingencies, uncertainties, human failings, and misunderstandings of social existence. If we study the movement of law within its own history, rather than forcing it to follow the movement of "historical laws," it becomes possible and desirable to examine the richness of law in the past as well as the present.

Two major advances are associated with the introduction of historical considerations into Marxist legal theory: (*a*) the historical specification of the functions of law; and (*b*) the reexamination of the major time frames within Marxist analysis: the modes of production. On the one hand, it has been recognized that the functions of law are historically contingent; that the same law can accomplish different tasks and serve different masters over time. On the other hand, it has become obvious that legal change does not correspond neatly to the life course of any given mode of production; nor do specific legal arrangements necessarily stay within the boundaries of the mode of production in which they are expected to appear.

Although Marxist legal theory has clearly suffered from an insistence that specific legal forms and contents must be linked with distinctive modes of economic organization, a few studies in the Marxist tradition have recognized that laws may serve different purposes under the same economic conditions and the same purposes under different economic conditions. Several examples may prove instructive on this point: (*a*) Vagrancy laws served two very different functions over several hundred years in precapitalist England (Chambliss 1964); (*b*) the writ of trespass under capitalism "derives originally from feudal ideologies of landowners, reflecting feudal relations of production where territoriality and battles for land were crucial features" (Sumner 1970:273); and (*c*) in general, "legal techniques may be created in the course of development of particular spheres of economic activity while legal systems . . . have no place for such techniques within their body of legal doctrine" (Cotterrell 1981b:57–58).

As these examples suggest, Marxist investigations of law may also benefit from a more careful look at the nature of law both between and within different modes of production. Comparing law across modes of production allows us to acknowledge the "slippage" between law and economy without denying the connections between the two. Comparisons of this sort may be made over the actual passage of time or by looking at the ways in which different modes of production (e.g. capitalist and precapitalist) confront each other in the modern era. In the first instance, the focus is on how specific laws operating under one mode of production (e.g. Roman civil law under slavery) are appropriated to fit the instrumental and ideological purposes of another, more modern, way of organizing economic life (e.g. capitalism) (see Cohen 1978:245–48). In the second case, the process of "modernization" is explored (Greenberg 1980b; Fitzpatrick 1980a; Cohen 1982) in order to understand how the varieties of economic, political, and cultural organization prevailing in precapitalist societies acquiesce, resist, or compromise with the legal imperatives of the capitalist world system (Fitzpatrick 1980b; Snyder 1980). Through this type of historical comparison it becomes possible to investigate simultaneously both diachronic and synchronic aspects of legal and economic life.

In addition to the value of studying law across modes of production, it is also useful to pay closer attention to historically specific legal variation within these economic forms. An interesting example of how this sort of periodization may advance Marxist understandings of legal relationships is found in the work of Richard Kinsey. In an investigation of despotism and legality, Kinsey (1979: 48–49) delineates three periods in the development of capitalist production "within which qualitative changes in the control of organization of the labor process are visible." Each of these three periods —manufacture, the early period of modern industry, and advanced capitalist production—constitutes, according to Kinsey, a peculiar form of despotism: the despotisms of property, the factory, and legality. Here Kinsey is suggesting that the nature of social control under capitalism adapts to and reflects the historically rooted problems associated with class rule. The despotism of legality is, as Kinsey (1979: 62) has observed, epitomized by the fact that "the content of the contract may be disputed but the form is never questioned." By distinguishing this type of social regulation from earlier varieties based on control over property [cf. Blackstone's 18th century emphasis on the security of private property (see Kennedy 1979)] and control over machines (as found, for example, in claims to commercial liberty), we can begin to refine our understanding of how phenomena as broad as capitalism and law are intertwined through time.

The recovery of history from the "genetic fallacy," like the recovery of politics from "instrumentalism" or "statism" and ideology from "false consciousness," offers the hope of a new life for a theory facing rigor mortis (Jacoby 1981: Ch. 1). But in breaking loose from the chains of orthodoxy, Marxist legal theory also faces centrifugal forces that threaten to "loosen the theory until it vanishes into a cloud of words and intentions" (R. M. Unger, unpublished). This dialectic of danger and hope must inform any attempt to move beyond what we have considered thus far.

SOCIALISM AND LAW: TOWARD A CONCLUSION

While Marxist theory has much to say about law and capitalism, on the subject of law and socialism it has been strangely silent. The historical and contemporary reasons for this silence are not so strange as to be belabored here. What is important, however, is whether in light of the deconstruction and reconstruction I have described a theory of law under socialism is likely to emerge.

Such a theory will have to explore the nature of law in two contexts: "actually existing" socialist states (Bahro 1978) and states (or collectivities within them) that are moving toward socialism. Despite the relative longevity of "actually existing socialism" in the Soviet Union, China, and Eastern Europe, relatively few accounts of law have been able to penetrate cold war ideology in the West and party science in the East. Since socialist law is rarely presented to the West in other than approved form, it has been extremely difficult for Western scholars to assess its deeper dimensions and implications. This may also be true in insurrectionary or revolutionary situations, although their very fluidity and confusion create greater opportunities for study (e.g. Santos 1977, 1982; Issacman & Issacman 1982; Spence 1982).

However, neither "Socialism" nor "Capitalism," at whatever stage of development, can be treated as a monolithic social formation or deformation. The growing gaps between the ideologies, self-conceptions, and realities of legal affairs in both types of systems provide a fertile ground for critical research.

A promising way of looking at these inconsistencies is the examination of what Santos (1979) has called "dual power." Under stable pre- and postrevolutionary situations as well as during periods of revolutionary ferment it is possible to identify embryonic, poorly organized, and more or less transitory and submerged systems of "people's law." These arrangements may exist alongside, within, or in explicit defiance of official law. Everything from neighborhood justice, worker's courts, tribunals, and local mediation systems on the one hand, to vigilantism, the hidden economy, and persistent forms of "crime" (Black 1983) on the other, can embody these structures and episodes of law. The relationship between political constellations of this sort and their more institutionalized counterparts can be studied within all types of economic systems as part of the dialectic between law as alienation and praxis. In this and certainly other ways, questions about law and socialism can be productively redefined.

The fundamental question framing this inquiry may now be restated: Which is likely to wither—law, sociology or Marxism? The answer will depend, of course, on whether Marxism can meet the challenge posed by its theoretical crisis. A blinkered Marxism will remain content to discount both law and sociology in the "revolutionary struggle": law because it will inevitably "wither away"; sociology because "socialism suppresses social science" (Cohen 1980: 302). The unification of theory and practice promises to end the sociology of law: "in the bright light of socialism the torch of the specialized investigator is invisible" (Cohen 1980: 302).

But the bright light of what has traditionally been promoted as socialism may blind as well as reveal; it may be Marxism, therefore, rather than law or sociology, that actually withers away. The decline of conventional Marxism as an explanatory system—only one aspect of which I have examined here—is even more striking when we consider that it has been accompanied by the unprecedented "success" (see Jacoby 1981) of Marxism as a political rallying point. Whatever we think of Marxism's theoretical strengths and weaknesses, it is important to keep in mind that "about one third of the world's population lives under the governance of states regarding themselves as Marxist, and all this has come about in little more than half a century" (Gouldner 1980:4).

In reflecting on the contradictions between Marxism's political and theoretical status it is clear that the Marxist analysis of law need not stand or fall on the basis of legal "successes" in actually existing socialist societies, or, as some ideologs would have it, on its ability to provide a logically impenetrable, appropriately pedigreed, and totally explanatory system. In those cases where Marxist theory gives up its search for "universal rationalizing principles" (Horwitz 1981) and its claims to being an all-encompassing cosmology—aspirations shared, ironically enough, by its archenemy positivism—it can get down to the business of studying law. At that point, Marxist perspectives on law can become part of the project that Marxism holds so dear—the harnessing of law to the purposes of society rather than the harnessing of society to the purposes of either capitalism or law.

Literature Cited

Abel, R. L. 1980. Redirecting social studies of law. *Law Society Rev.* 14:805–29

Abel, R. L. 1981. A critique of American tort law. *Br. J. Law & Society* 8:199–231

Abel, R. L. 1982. Torts. In *The Politics of Law,* ed. D. Kairys, pp. 172–84. NY: Pantheon. 321 pp.

Althusser, L. 1970. The object of *Capital.* In *Reading Capital,* ed. L. Althusser, E. Balibar, pp. 71–198. NY: Pantheon. 340 pp.

Althusser, L. 1971. *Lenin and Philosophy and Other Essays.* NY: Monthly Review Press. 253 pp.

Anderson, P. 1974. *Lineages of the Absolutist State.* London: New Left Books. 573 pp.

Bahro, R. 1978. *The Alternative in Eastern Europe.* London: New Left Books. 463 pp.

Balbus, I. 1977. Commodity form and legal form. *Law & Society Rev.* 11:871–88

Balibar, E. 1970. The basic concepts of historical materialism. See Althusser 1970, pp. 199–309

Beirne, P., Quinney, R., eds. 1982. *Marxism and Law.* NY: Wiley. 381 pp.

Binns, P. 1980. Law and Marxism. *Capital & Class* 10:100–13

Black, D. 1983. Crime as social control. *Am. Sociol. Rev.* 48:In press

Black, J., ed. 1971. *Radical Lawyers: Their Role in the Movement and in the Courts.* NY: Avon Books. 320 pp.

Bock, K. E. 1952. Evolution and historical process. *Am. Anthropol.* 54:486–96

Cain, M., Hunt, A., eds. 1979. *Marx and Engels on Law.* London: Academic. 281 pp.

Campbell, C., Wiles, P. 1980. Foreward. In *Marx and Engels on Law and Laws,* ed. P. Phillips, pp. ix-xi. Totowa, NJ: Barnes & Noble. 238 pp.

Chambliss, W. J. 1964. A sociological analysis of the law of vagrancy. *Soc. Probl.* 12:67–77

Chambliss, W. J. 1979. Contradictions and conflicts in law creation. In *Research in Law and Sociology,* ed. S. Spitzer, 2:3–27. Greenwich, CT: JAI Press. 274 pp.

Cohen, G. A. 1978. *Karl Marx's Theory of History: A Defense.* Oxford: Oxford Univ. Press. 369 pp.

Cohen, G. A. 1980. Karl Marx and the withering away of social science. In *Marx, Justice and History,* ed. M. Cohen, T. Nagel, T. Scanlon, pp. 288–309. Princeton: Princeton Univ. Press. 309 pp.

Cohen, S. 1982. Western crime control models in the third world: benign or malignant? In *Research in Law, Deviance and Social Control,* Vol. IV, ed. S. Spitzer,

R. J. Simon. Greenwich, CT: JAI Press. 238 pp.

Cotterrell, R. 1981a. Conceptualizing law: problems and prospects of contemporary legal theory. *Econ. & Society* 10: 348–66

Cotterrell, R. 1981b. The development of capitalism and the formalisation of contract law. In *Law, State and Society,* ed. B. Fryer, A. Hunt, D. McBarnet, B. Moorhouse, pp. 54–69. London: Croom Helm. 234 pp.

Currie, E. 1971. Sociology of law: the unasked questions. *Yale Law J.* 81: 134–47

Edelman, B. 1979. *Ownership of the Image: Elements for a Marxist Theory of Law.* Boston: Routledge & Kegan Paul. 217 pp.

Fine, B., Kinsey, R., Lea, J., Picciotto, S., Young, J., eds. 1979. *Capitalism and the Rule of Law.* London: Hutchinson. 200 pp.

Fitzpatrick, P. 1980a. Law, modernization and mystification. In *Research in Law and Sociology,* ed. S. Spitzer, 3:161–80. Greenwich, CT: JAI Press. 344 pp.

Fitzpatrick, P. 1980b. *Law and State in Papua New Guinea.* London: Academic. 290 pp.

Foucault, M. 1977. *Discipline & Punish.* NY: Pantheon. 333 pp.

Fraser, A. 1978. The legal theory we need now. *Socialist Rev.* 40–41:147–87

Freeman, A. 1978. Legitimizing racial discrimination through anti-discrimination law: a critical review of supreme court doctrine. *Minn. Law Rev.* 62:II 1049–1119

Freeman, A. 1982. Antidiscrimination law: a critical review. See Abel 1982, pp. 96–116

Gabel, P. 1977. Intention and structure in contractual conditions: outline of a method for critical legal theory. *Minn. Law Rev.* 61:601–43

Gabel, P. 1980. Reification in legal reasoning. In *Research in Law and Sociology,* ed. S. Spitzer, 3:25–52. Greenwich, CT: JAI Press. 344 pp.

Gabel, P., Feinman, J. M. 1982. Contract law as ideology. In *The Politics of Law,* ed. D. Kairys, pp. 172–84. NY: Pantheon. 321 pp.

Gouldner, A. W. 1980. *The Two Marxisms.* NY: Oxford Univ. Press. 397 pp.

Gramsci, A. 1971. *Selections From Prison Notebooks,* ed. Q. Hoare, G. N. Smith. NY: International. 483 pp.

Grau, C. W. 1982. What happened to politics? a critique of structuralist marxist accounts of state and law. See Beirne & Quinney, 1982, pp. 196–209

Greenberg, D. F. 1976. On one-dimensional marxist criminology. *Theory & Society* 3:610–21

Greenberg, D. F., ed. 1980a. *Crime and Capitalism: Readings in Marxian Criminology.* Palo Alto, CA: Mayfield. 506 pp.

Greenberg, D. F. 1980b. Law and economic development in light of dependency theory. See Gabel 1980, 3:129–60

Greenberg, D. F., Anderson, N. 1981. Recent marxisant books on law: a review essay. *Contemp. Crises* 5:293–322

Hall, S. 1980. *Drifting Into a Law and Order Society.* London: Cobden Trust

Hall, S., Critcher, C., Jefferson, T., Clarke, J., Roberts, B. 1978. *Policing the Crisis: Mugging, the State, and Law and Order.* London: MacMillan. 425 pp.

Hay, D. 1975. Property, authority and criminal law. In *Albion's Fatal Tree,* ed. D. Hay, P. Linebaugh, J. G. Rule, E. P. Thompson, C. Winslow, pp. 17–63. NY: Pantheon. 352 pp.

Hirst, P. Q. 1979. *On Law and Ideology.* Atlantic Highlands, NJ: Humanities. 181 pp.

Hirst, P. Q. 1980. Law, socialism and rights. In *Radical Issues in Criminology,* ed. P. Carlen, M. Collison, pp. 58–108. Totowa, NJ: Barnes & Noble. 212 pp.

Homans, G. 1964. Bringing men back in. *Am. Sociol. Rev.* 29:809–18

Horwitz, A. 1977. Marxist theories of deviance and teleology: a critique of Spitzer. *Soc. Probl.* 24:362–63

Horwitz, M. J. 1977. *The Transformation of American Law 1780–1860.* Cambridge, MA: Harvard Univ. Press. 356 pp.

Horwitz, M. J. 1981. The historical contingency of the role of history. *Yale Law J.* 90:II 1057–59

Hunt, A. 1981. The radical critique of law: an assessment. *Int. J. Sociol. Law* 8:33–46

Ignatieff, M. 1978. *A Just Measure of Pain.* NY: Pantheon. 257 pp.

Ignatieff, M. 1981. State, civil society and total institutions: a critique of recent social histories of punishment. In *Crime and Justice,* ed. N. Morris, M. Tonry, 3:153–92. Chicago: Univ. Chicago Press

Issacman, B., Issacman, A. 1982. A socialist legal system in the making: Mozambique before and after independence. In *The Politics of Informal Justice,* ed. R. L. Abel, 2:281–324. NY: Academic. 338 pp.

Jacoby, R. 1977–78. The politics of objectivity: notes on the U.S. left. *Telos* 34:74–88

Jacoby, R. 1981. *Dialectic of Defeat: Contours of Western Marxism.* Cambridge: Cambridge Univ. Press. 202 pp.

Jessop, B. 1980. On recent Marxist theories of law, the state, and juridico-political ideology. *Int. J. Sociol. Law* 8:339–68

Kahn-Freund, O. 1949. Introduction. See Renner 1949, pp. 1–43

Kellner, D. 1978. Ideology, marxism, and advanced capitalism. *Socialist Rev.* 43:37–66

Kelman, M. 1982. The origins of crime and criminal violence. In *The Politics of Law,* ed. D. Kairys, pp. 214–29. NY: Pantheon. 321 pp.

Kennedy, D. 1973. Legal formality. *J. Legal Stud.* 2:351–98

Kennedy, D. 1976. Form and substance in private law adjudication. *Harvard Law Rev.* 89:1685–1778

Kennedy, D. 1979. The structure of Blackstone's commentaries. *Buffalo Law Rev.* 28:205–382

Kinsey, R. 1978. Marxism and the law: preliminary analyses. *Br. J. Law & Society* 5:202–27

Kinsey, R. 1979. Despotism and legality. In *Capitalism and the Rule of Law,* ed. B. Fine, R. Kinsey, J. Lea, S. Picciotto, J. Young, pp. 46–64. London: Hutchinson. 200 pp.

Kirchheimer, O. 1969. The legal order of National Socialism. In *Politics, Law and Social Change,* ed. F. S. Burin, K. L. Shell, pp. 88–109. NY: Columbia. 483 pp.

Klare, K. 1978. Judicial deradicalization of the Wagner Act and the origin of modern legal consciousness, 1937–1949. *Minn. Law Rev.* 62:265–339

Klare, K. 1979. Law-making as praxis. *Telos* 40:123–35

Klare, K. 1981. Labor law as ideology: toward a new historiography of collective bargaining law. *Indust. Relat. Law J.* 4:450–82

Klare, K. 1982. Critical theory and labor relations law. See Abel 1982, pp. 65–88

Laclau, E. 1977. *Politics and Ideology in Marxist Theory.* Atlantic Highlands, NJ: Humanities. 203 pp.

Lea, J. 1979. Discipline and capitalist development. See Fine et al 1979, pp. 76–89

Lefcourt, R., ed. 1971. *Law Against the People.* NY: Vintage. 400 pp.

Lichtman, R. 1975. Marx's theory of ideology. *Socialist Revol.* 23:45–61.

Marx, K. 1970a. *Capital,* Vol. I. London: Lawrence & Wishart. 767 pp.

Marx, K. 1970b. *The German Ideology.* NY: International. 158 pp.

McManus, J. J. 1978. The emergence and non-emergence of legislation. *Br. J. Law & Society* 5:185–201

Merritt, A. 1980. The nature of law. *Br. J. Law & Society* 7:194–214

Miliband, R. 1977. *Marxism and Politics.* Oxford: Oxford Univ. Press. 199 pp.

Mullin, N. 1980. Pashukanis and the demise of law: an essay review. *Contemp. Crises* 4:433–38

Muraskin, W. A. 1976. The social-control theory in American history: a critique. *J. Soc. Hist.* 9:559–69

Neumann, F. 1944. *Behemoth: The Structure and Practice of National Socialism 1933–44.* NY: Oxford Univ. Press. 649 pp.

Neumann, F. 1957. *The Democratic and the Authoritarian State.* NY: Free Press. 303 pp.

Olsen, F. 1983. The market and the family: a study of ideology and legal reform. *Harvard Law Rev.* 96:In press

Pashukanis, E. B. 1978. *Law & Marxism: A General Theory,* ed. C. J. Arthur. London: Ink Links. 195 pp.

Pashukanis, E. B. 1980. *Pashukanis: Selected writings on Marxism and Law,* ed. P. Beirne, R. Sharlet; transl. P. B. Maggs. London: Academic

Phillips, P., ed. 1980. *Marx and Engels on Law and Laws.* Totowa, NJ: Barnes & Noble. 238 pp.

Picciotto, S. 1979. The theory of the state, class struggle and the role of law. See Fine et al 1979, pp. 164–77

Piven, F. F., Cloward, R. A. 1971. *Regulating the Poor.* NY: Vintage. 348 pp.

Polan, D. 1982. Toward a theory of law and patriarchy. See Abel 1982, pp. 294–303

Polanyi, K. 1957. *The Great Transformation.* Boston: Beacon. 315 pp.

Poulantzas, N. 1973. *Political Power and Social Classes.* London: New Left Books

Poulantzas, N. 1978. *State, Power, Socialism.* London: New Left Books. 269 pp.

Poulantzas, N. 1982. Law. See Beirne & Quinney 1982, pp. 185–95

Quinney, R. 1974. *The Critique of Legal Order.* Boston: Little, Brown. 206 pp.

Rafter, N. H., Stanko, E. A., eds. 1982. *Judge, Lawyer, Victim, Thief: Women, Gender Roles and Criminal Justice.* Boston: Northeastern Univ. Press. 383 pp.

Redhead, S. 1982. Marxist theory, the rule of law and socialism. See Beirne & Quinney 1982, pp. 328–42

Renner, K. 1949. *The Institutions of Private Law and Their Social Functions,* ed. O. Kahn-Freund. Boston: Routledge & Kegan Paul. 307 pp.

Rosenblatt, R. 1981. Health care, markets, and democratic values. *Vanderbilt Law Rev.* 34(2):1067–1115

Santos, B. D. S. 1977. The law of the oppressed: the construction and reproduction of legality in Pasargada. *Law & Society Rev.* 12:5–126

Santos, B. D. S. 1979. Popular justice, dual power and socialist strategy. See Fine et al 1979, pp. 151–63

Santos, B. D. S. 1982. Law and revolution in Portugal: the experience of popular justice after the 25th of April 1974. In *The Politics of Informal Justice,* ed. R. L. Abel, 2:251–80. NY: Academic. 338 pp.

Sharlet, R. 1978. Pashukanis and the withering away of law in the U.S.S.R. In *Cultural Revolution in Russia, 1928–31,* ed. S. Fitzpatrick. Bloomington: Indiana Univ.

Snyder, F. G. 1980. Law and development in the light of dependency theory. *Law & Society* 14:723–804

Sparks, R. F. 1980. A critique of Marxist criminology. In *Crime and Justice,* ed. N. Morris, M. Tonry, 2:159–210. Chicago: Univ. Chicago Press. 470 pp.

Spence, J. 1982. Institutionalizing neighborhood courts: two Chilean experiences. See Santos 1982, 2:215–50

Spitzer, S. 1975. Punishment and social organization: a study of Durkheim's theory of penal evolution. *Law & Society Rev.* 9:613–37

Spitzer, S. 1977. On the marxian theory of social control: a reply to Horwitz. *Soc. Probl.* 24:364–66

Spitzer, S. 1979. The rationalization of crime control in captialist society. *Contemp. Crises* 3:187–206

Steinert, H. 1977. Against a conspiracy theory of criminal law apropos Hepburn's 'social control and the legal order.' *Contemp. Crises* 1:437–40

Stone, K. 1981. The post-war paradigm in American labor law. *Yale Law J.* 90:II 1509–80

Sugarman, D. 1981. Theory and practice in law and history: a prologue to the study of the relationship between law and economy from a socio-historical perspective. In *Law, State and Society,* ed. B. Fryer, A. Hunt, D. McBarnet, B. Moorhouse, pp. 70–106. London: Croom Helm. 234 pp.

Sumner, C. 1979. *Reading Ideologies: An Investigation into the Marxist Theory of Ideology and Law.* London: Academic. 313 pp.

Sumner, C. 1981. The rule of law and civil rights in contemporary marxist theory. *Kapitalistate* 9:63–92

Taub, N., Schneider, E. M. 1982. Perspectives on women's subordination and the role of law. See Abel 1982, pp. 117–39

Taylor, I., Walton, P., Young, J. 1973. *The New Criminology.* Boston: Routledge & Kegan Paul. 325 pp.

Thompson, E. P. 1975. *Whigs and Hunters: The Origin of the Black Act.* NY: Pantheon. 312 pp.

Thompson, E. P. 1978. *The Poverty of Theory and Other Essays.* NY: Monthly Review Press. 404 pp.

Thompson, E. P. 1979. The rule of law in English history. *Bulletin of the Haldane Society of Socialist Lawyers.* London: Haldane Society. 10 pp.

Tushnet, M. 1979. Truth, justice and the American way: an interpretation of public law scholarship in the seventies. *Tex. Law Rev.* 57:1307–59

Tushnet, M. 1981. The dilemmas of liberal constitutionalism. *Ohio State Law J.* 42:411–26

Tushnet, M. 1982. Marxism and critical legal studies. Presented at Ann. Meet. Conf. Crit. Legal Stud., Boston.

Unger, R. M. 1975. *Knowledge and Politics.* NY: Free Press. 336 pp.

Unger, R. M. 1976. *Law in Modern Society.* NY: Free Press. 309 pp.

Unger, R. M. 1983. The critical legal studies movement. *Harvard Law Rev.* 96:In press

[21]

MARXISM AND LEGAL PLURALISM

Peter Fitzpatrick

Legal pluralism is indicative of persisting social fields that cannot be accounted for adequately in totalising Marxist explanation. Althusser's contribution and its relation to the family, is explored as one example of inadequacy — a provocative example because of its attempts to accommodate a plurality of social fields. Yet legal pluralism also illustrates the limits of partial explanation. The first half of the article concludes in the argument that historical materialism has to accommodate particular social fields, has to accord them a particular materiality. These fields interact integrally with a totality but cannot be reduced to that totality. The second half of the article lends some concreteness to this argument in exploring particular social fields as conditions for the emergence and maintenance of modern law. Science (the operation of the science of man and of society) is presented here as a representation of many particular social fields. Both science and law are taken as elements in a total explanation of modern society. Particularist oppressions, sited in particular social fields and organised in science, are seen as conditions for the existence of bourgeois legality in its elements of universalism and equality. Modern law depends on science and cannot enter some of science's realms. But science itself depends operatively and integrally on law. Law and science are mutually supportive and interdependent, yet the maintenance of their effectuality in this requires them to be significantly independent of and opposed to each other.

This article[1] deals with the so-called first world of advanced capitalism but it follows on from my work on the third world. Much of this work tries to show that the third world reality cannot be reduced to totalising types of explanation seen in terms of modernisation or of the capitalist mode of production. Here I have drawn on and extended theories in the tradition of historical materialism that begin to accommodate the specificity, diversity and plurality of and within third world societies. In this, state law is seen as integrally dependent on a plurality of specific particularist orders, yet it also constitutively acts on and reacts back on these particularist orders (Fitzpatrick 1980a, 1980b and in press). The present article is something of a complement to this for the first world in that its basic concern is with a plurality of "semi-autonomous social fields" (Moore 1978:ch 2) as conditions for the emergence and maintenance of state law.

Legal pluralism can serve as an initial representation of this plurality of social fields. One could use instead the revived theories of 'dualism' and 'marginalisation' including theories of the specificity of sexual and racial oppressions (see *eg* Barrett 1980; Berger and Piore 1980; Gilroy 1981). But the choice of legal pluralism serves a purpose of introducing this significant body of scholarship to historical materialism.

"In political thought and analysis," says Foucault, "we still have not cut off the head of the king" (Foucault 1981a:88-9). Exceptionally, legal pluralists have sought to "escape the system of Law-and-Sovereign" (Foucault 1981a:97). Ehrlich is perhaps the great originator here with his historically sensitive "sociology of law" (Ehrlich 1936). For him the very basis of state law was a prior "social law" or "living law" which was the "inner order of associations" (Ehrlich 1936:chs III and IV). The effectiveness of state law depended on its being in accord with this living law. What would happen if associations or bodies of living law were in conflict? What is the outcome of interactions between them? How does one explain the original effectiveness and the effect on living law that state law sometimes does seem to have? These questions Ehrlich recognised but did not answer. They are also questions which dog legal pluralism, as we shall see. One line of resolution was provided by Gierke in his so-called realist theory of corporations. Like Ehrlich he saw associations or corporate organisations having a life, a reality, of their own. The state did not create corporations; it could but recognise them. But the state wins in the end for, with Gierke's organic theory of society, the state is a corporation which includes in itself all other corporate organisations and has ultimate authority over them (Hallis 1930:140-65). A broadly similar resolution afflicts the sociologically more sophisticated theorising of those thinkers usually called the French Institutionalists (see Broderick, ed 1970). They saw society as made up of a plurality of institutions, of which the state is but one. Each institution has its own distinctive law. Coherence between institutions is secured in the realm of natural law. There is a little-recognised but potentially significant Italian branch of the institutionalist enterprise in the work of Romano (Stone 1966:ch 11). He did not find an easy coherence of legal and institutional orders in an all-encompassing state or in the convenient resolutions of natural law. Relations between institutions, including the state as one such, took diverse forms such as subordination, partial incorporation and mutual interaction. There was no grand resultant, no persistent resolution emerging from these relations.

Anthropological theories of legal pluralism have either emphasised the secondary or derivative nature of state law or been satisfied with seeing state law as one type among many without confronting questions of conflict and precedence. Hence Bohannan's famed theory where state law results from a "double institutionalisation of norms" in which some "customs" operative within "social institutions" are "reinstitutionalised at another level" as state law (Bohannan 1967:47-48). So, Pospisil contests the adequacy of seeing law and society in terms of interacting individuals and the state. He argues that society is made up of a collection of "sub-groups" with their own legal systems and law is not just the property of society or the nation as a whole (Pospisil 1971:ch 4). There are other anthropological theories but these can be taken as representative enough for present purposes (see also Moore 1978:ch 2 and Smith 1974:ch 4). Thus far, it could be said that accounts of the legal pluralists are persistently partial or the plurality of parts is subordinated in arbitrary totalities as with the organicist and natural law offerings of Gierke and the French Institutionalists.

More complex is the recent efflorescence of work on legal pluralism, mainly in the United States. This is partly a matter of the rediscovery of legal pluralism (see Galanter 1980,1981a). But it is also a matter of current developments in legal regulation that give a particular salience to legal pluralism — the recognition and emergence of informal alternatives to courts, varieties of delegalisation, schemes of decarceration and various so-called community adaptations of penal and psychiatric control (see Abel ed.1982). This recent work has added totalising perspectives to the study of legal pluralism or added, at least, perspectives that transcend the partial. Thus, this work has greatly elaborated and refined the ways in which different legal orders, including state law, interact (see *eg* Galanter 1980,1981b and Griffiths 1981). Abel's acute demystifications show that in this interaction the apparent shift from state law to informal ordering can mask an extension of state control through the state's supervision or constitution of these other orders (Abel 1980,1982). There is also some concern to explain why this legal plurality emerges. It is sometimes seen as a response to fiscal and legitimacy crises supposedly afflicting countries of advanced capitalism; informal ordering emerges because it is cheaper or, less dubiously if somewhat ambivalently, because it is a means of engendering some popular participation and thus serving to make up the deficit in legitimation (see *eg* Matthews 1979, Santos 1980 and *cf* Habermas 1976:72-3). In a related vein, involvement through informal ordering is seen in terms of the containment by the state of potentially disruptive elements (*eg* Hofrichter 1982). Or informal justice is seen as existing in some cyclical alternation with formal justice (Abel 1980). It is impossible in a brief account to do justice to such a rich and diverse literature but it is fair to say that this work does not resolve or mean to resolve questions of the coherence of a plurality of social fields. The social field is seen only in terms of some function attributed to it, such as class containment or legitimation. Or social fields are seen in terms of persistent plurality, persistent diffusion. So, to take one of Galanter's titles, the search is for "justice in many rooms" (Galanter 1981a) — in many mansions (*John* xiv, 2). But, in Noddy terms, we have to ask where is the house? What the rooms are, what they do must be affected by the total structure and operation of the house in which they are located.[2]

It should be immediately and fairly asked whether totalising explanation can do better. So far, the summary account of the legal pluralists has served to set plurality as a persistent question and to suggest a need for some totalising explanation. My sympathetic concern here will be with historical materialism as totalising explanation. Because it is provocatively apt, I will use as an example a strand of historical materialism that has sought to accommodate a plurality of social fields. In the broad strokes being used here, Althusser's contribution can be taken as representative (*cf* also Cain in press and Poulantzas 1978:28-34). Althusser's Marxism accommodates several dimensions of plurality. The dimension considered here is his grappling with institutions. Somewhat in the tradition of Gramsci, Althusser sees the state as divided between a "Repressive State Apparatus" and a collection of "Ideological State Apparatuses" (ISAs) (Althusser 1971:124-149). The ISAs function basically as ideology. They comprise a variety of institutions —

educational and religious institutions and the law and the family, for example (although law also functions in the Repressive State Apparatus). These institutions sustain and cohere in the ideology of the ruling class and ultimately function to reproduce relations of production. The state, in turn, is placed integrally within a social totality (a "structure in dominance") where it is ultimately, if sometimes obliquely but of course never vulgarly, determined by the economy.

How much can this kind of totalising explanation tell us about a plurality of social fields? To lend some concreteness to the argument, I will explore the family, one of Althusser's ISAs, in its relation to that social totality integral to the capitalist mode of production.[3] The argument could, I hope, be generalised.

Hartmann's pithy observation on feminism could be adapted here: "the 'marriage' of marxism and feminism," she says, "has been like the marriage of husband and wife depicted in English common law:marxism and feminism are one, and that one is marxism" (Hartmann 1979:1). In relation to the capitalist mode, Marxism, when it has accommodated the family, has seen it as a functional adaptation to an existent totality, a totality which not only was conceived without incorporating the family but which entailed its disappearance.[4] This is not to deny that the Marxist or neo-Marxist explanation has not told us vital things about the family in its interrelation with the capitalist mode of production, even if these things do not always transcend the banal or are not always exclusive to Marxism. Thus, to take overlapping examples, the family functions in class division in various ways; it is as well that "haven in a heartless world", that "prison of love" which mitigates the psychic injuries inflicted by capitalism; it serves in the reproduction of relations of production; it is a conduit for dominant ideology; and it creates a specific, female social identity which in turn is constitutive of a segment in the reserve army of labour (see *eg* Collins 1978). The list could go on but it would contain statements of the same type — that is, statements which describe a function that the family serves for the capitalist mode of production. Doubtless this functionality can be supportive of the family and can result in measures aimed at its conservation. But all this does not amount to an explanation of the existence of the family. Ultimately, all we are given is an explanation of an aspect of the modern family which may be partly constitutive of it.

Totalising explanation has not here accounted for the specificity of the family. But the family can only serve these functions if it remains crucially separate or apart from the capitalist mode. It cannot, for example, be a haven in a heartless world if it is absorbed indistinguishably into that heartless world. This specificity and apartness are underscored in the incompatibilities, even the antagonisms, between the family and capitalism in which the family has served as a site of resistance to capitalism (see *eg* Lasch 1977,1979). And, even granted the obvious problem with continuity in change, there is much evidence that in its specificity and separation the family must be seen as having its own particular materiality or its own history, a history that pre-dates the emergence of the capitalist mode (see *eg* Macfarlane 1978:197-198, and Middleton 1981). Further, it is not only a matter of the family being specific and apart from the social totality integral to the capitalist mode of production; it is also specific *and* a part of that totality. It is not, for example, so much that family relations function in support of relations of reproduction within the totality; family relations *are* some of those relations of reproduction. That is, in short, the family cannot be reduced to this totality or seen as only subordinate to it. There is an interaction between the two in which the family has a structured and an historically based autonomy. The modern family is doubtless dependent in significant part on the capitalist mode of production but the capitalist mode is also dependent in significant part on it. This theme of unity with opposition is the main leitmotif of the article.

Are we left with an impasse? The exploration of legal pluralism suggested a need for some totalising or, at least, some overarching explanation.[5] Yet instances of totalising explanation we considered did not seem to accommodate plurality. The impasse points to two strands of work in, or emerging out of, historical materialism. One in descent from Marx, in descent from Hegel, emphasises totalising explanation. Lukacs provides a statement that is apt here:

> the total context of the complex in question takes precedence over its individual constituents. The latter can only be understood from their concrete interaction within the complex of being involved, whilst it would be futile for us to try theoretically to reconstruct the complex of being itself from its constituents (as translated in Varga 1981:163).

There has been some dissatisfaction with this position but the dominant thrust of Marxist scholarship has been to support it. Even if it means going through an Althusserian loop or discovering a "relative autonomy" in constituent parts, the position is ultimately upheld. These journeys are never undertaken without the resolve to end up in the same place. The other strand emerges out of, or even away from historical materialism and is usually associated with Hindess and Hirst (see *eg* Hindess and Hirst 1977). It entails isolating social entities and establishing their conditions of existence. This strand poses problems of overall structuring and coherence similar to those I have raised in connection with legal pluralism.

The short point I want to make here is that the two strands should not be seen as mutually exclusive. The view from the totality can only accord essence to constituent parts in its own terms. These terms, operatively, can only be limited, unless we are laying claim to an achieved absolute totality which finally encompasses all. If we are not, then these terms can only be open, unless we are satisfied with some premature closure and the resulting totemic transformation of the parts. If we are not so satisfied then the parts cannot be wholly accommodated in the totality but have to be particularly constituted even whilst being in essential interaction with the totality. (Loosely, we can say the totality will be less than the sum of its parts.) Indeed, it will be a condition of its continued identity or particularity that the part in some ways be set against the totality. The relation between part and totality is contradictory in the sense that, to borrow Giddens' formulation, they "operate in *terms of each other* but at the same time *contravene one another*" — another Hegelian intrusion (Giddens 1979:141 — his emphasis). Historical materialism, after due exploration, has to accord particular materiality to parts often suppressed in or through Manichean totalising explanation, parts with their own histories, traditions and rationalities (*cf* Pocock 1971:234). Persisting with the family as an example, Middleton's recent historical work and Godelier's recent anthropological analysis can be taken as instancing this concern with particular materiality (Middleton 1981; Godelier 1981).

The rest of the article attempts to lend some concreteness to this argument in an exploration of parts, or particular social fields, as conditions for the emergence and maintenance of modern law. This is done *via* the contribution of people called here "the radical institutionalists" — although some could well reject the label (see Foucault 1981b:5). The radical institutionalists would include Ignatieff and Foucault in their works on the penitentiary (Ignatieff 1978; Foucault 1979a), Donzelot in his analysis of the modern family (Donzelot 1980), Doerner with his history of psychiatry (Doerner 1981) and Rothman in his "Discovery" of the insane asylum, the penitentiary and the almshouse (Rothman 1971).

The radical institutionalists chart a change from a type of power and social control marked by law, centralised sovereignty and occasional or discontinuous interventions in society to a type of power and a type of social control that is disciplinary and continuously regulative and which pervasively, intimately and integrally inhabits society. It is a type of power and control not just, or so much, grounded in prohibition but more in the positive constitution of norms and the positive shaping of individuals to fit these norms. To appropriate Milton: "discipline is not only the removal of disorder, but if any visible shape can be given to divine things, the very visible shape and image of virtue" (Hill 1958:225). This change is effected in and through institutions that either emerged or took on radically new functions in the late eighteenth and early nineteenth centuries such as the penitentiary (Foucault 1979a; Ignatieff 1978), the psychiatric asylum (Doerner 1981) and monitorial schooling (Jones and Williamson 1979). Part of the concern in this is to erect a counter to those mainstream historical accounts which see these institutional changes as humane, reforming products of the Enlightenment, or some such. Perhaps this revisionist aspect has chronologically too much compressed the explanatory basis of the radical institutionalists' work. With some justification their work has been criticised as oversimplified and as overdrawn (see *eg* Bailey ed 1981). Doubtless the change was not so sharp and dramatic (see Arthurs forthcoming). Doubtless also developments central to their thesis occurred before and after this period (Ignatieff in press; Trilling 1972). Indeed the rationalisation of political rule and the bureaucratisation of state administration were integral conditions for the operation of disciplinary power (Foucault 1979b). Also, whilst "reforms" and aspects of the great change were advocated and intimated during the period, the change in its massive operation did not come, by and large, until much later in the nineteenth century. Yet it can still be allowed that the period remains pivotal and the perception of change basically valid. If chronological restraints are somewhat loosened, then necessary account can be taken of a broad range of disciplinary institutions concerned with, for example, crime, health, urban regulation, the control of mobility and migration, recreations, morality, the operation of the factory, sexuality and race.[6] The relevant effect here is the intimidating, massively shaping effect of the interacting sum of these institutions (Ignatieff 1978:215). If one did not work another could. Thus the notes of one prison chaplain from the mid-nineteenth century observe: "No.920. George Thomas. Does not read scriptures; has no wish to repent. Says he is a free man, obviously deranged" (as quoted in Melossi and Pavarini 1981:155).

This effect has to be seen not just in terms of those immediately contained by institutions but also seen as a generalised effect operative throughout the whole of society. "We are only a few steps removed from society. After us, comes you"

(Abbott 1982:21). The institutions serve as original sites and justifications for techniques of wider-ranging inspection and control. Also, by defining and containing what is unacceptable, the institution defines what is acceptable and hence provides also guides for self-regulation. Reactively, they support wide powers of prevention, of ensuring that people do not come within their domain. In this, and generally, techniques of control and their justifications can be so formulated that they could apply or could be made to apply to anyone. Thus Samuel Johnson foreshadowed many a radical critique of psychiatry when he wrote that: "of the uncertainties of our present state, the most dreadful and alarming is the uncertain continuance of reason . . . No man will be found in whose mind airy notions do not sometimes tyrannise, and force him to hope or fear beyond the limits of sober probability. All power of fancy over reason is a degree of insanity" (as quoted in Doerner 1981:58). Integral to the emergence of disciplinary institutions were the co-emergent sciences of man and of society, sciences that were means and justifications for observing, measuring, controlling and modifying human behaviour.

I would suggest that the work of the radical institutionalists could be seen as a positing and an exploration of particular materialities. Something akin to this is not infrequently asserted by them — the materiality of, for example, technologies ordering social relations being seen as no less significant than technologies of material production (see *eg* Donzelot 1979 and *cf* Giddens 1981). There is a tendency to give precedence to the particular and on occasion some radical institutionalists reject totalising explanation. Particulars are drawn together in such terms respecting the partial as nets, grids and rhizomes. More abstracted totalising elements are involved in Foucault's somewhat mysterious notion of power and in his almost perversely provocative idea of (generalising) strategies. This idea of strategies is tied to particular social fields in a way that is evidently apt here when he formulates a "rule of double conditioning" (Foucault 1981a:99-100). This rule has it that no specific and localised exercise of power can be effective without its being incorporated into an overall or general strategy of power and, conversely, the strategy cannot work unless supported by specific or localised exercises of power. These two elements are integral yet not homogenous. One cannot be reduced to the other. Thus he provides the following instance: "the father in the family is not the 'representative' of the sovereign or the state; and the latter are not projections of the father on a different scale. The family does not duplicate society, just as society does not imitate the family" (Foucault 1981a:100).

Let me now draw on these, to me, heady insights of the radical institutionalists in exploring particular social fields as conditions for the existence of modern law. It would be impossible to accommodate any number of fields here. To lend generality to the argument I use science as a representation of a great number of particular social fields. Science is seen as the main mode of the exercise of disciplinary power in modern society and includes its constitutive fields of knowledge in various sciences of man and of society. Somewhat arbitrarily, I take science and law to be generalising strategies in Foucault's terms and, in terms of the first part of this article, I take them to be elements in a totalising explanation of modern society. In both these sets of terms, particular social fields are significantly a part of science which organises them, endowing them with a generality, uniformity and coherence of effects.

Doubtless it is an exaggeration, but modern law can be seen as one side of a great divide (*cf* Redfield 1968:32-34). Medieval law was integral to a moral order and a traditional community (see *eg* Habermas 1974:50-62). In distinctive contrast, modern law neither depends on nor contains any necessary substantive morality and is based on private, isolated legal subjects with their lonely wills — Hegel's "son of civil society" (Wellmer 1971:76).[7] "In the midst of strangers, law reaches its highest level" (Black 1976:41 and see also Dumont 1965:22). Furthermore, modern law serves to effect the divide: so Habermas says that "*bourgeois formal law* ... made it possible to release norm-contents from the dogmatism of mere tradition and to determine them intentionally" (Habermas 1976:86 — his emphasis). Prynne's assertion that "Parliament...is not tied to precedents" is but a counterpart to Milton's that "all men were born free" (see Hill 1969:200 for the quotations).[8] Crudely, the modern system is one of rule through law and sovereignty over isolated or individualised legal subjects, the old order, or the moral order, having disappeared. In the resulting void, as it were, law has also an enormous "function of legitimacy" (Poulantzas 1978:87). Indeed,theorising about modern law has had to put much emphasis on consensus without ever being happy with the notion (Hunt 1981). There are, of course, qualifications. Elements of the old order lived on, often serving in ways to legitimate the new (see *eg* Pocock 1967). Nor has the bourgeoisie ever been prepared to let justice be done 'though the heavens fall' and has been known to depart from its own standard of legality. But even with these qualifications, the work of the radical institutionalists reveals this simple picture as far from complete. Put another way, this work would give some more complex content to the element of so-called consensus (hegemony and so on).

Science served fundamentally to effect the transition from particularistic, solidary bonds to universalistic, individually-based relations — or served to account for or render inescapably factual the persistence of particularistic bonds.[9] Science served in the creation of that post-feudal individual who is the basis of the modern legal order. Science not only provided the actual or immediate controls — through psychiatric or medical science for example — but provided also and inseparably those techniques of measurement, survey and classification whereby the individual, any individual, could be rendered notable (Foucault 1979a:191-193). It is because of such particularistic and pervasive powers that law can be maintained in its aspects of universality and equality and seen as marking out fields for free action.[10] Bourgeois legality would prove too delicate for a society founded on inequality and coercive authority were not individuals pre-adapted, as it were, through science.[11] Science is the necessary "dark side" of law (Foucault 1979a: 222 and see also *ibid*:194). Given this dependence of law, and given the incompatibility in the constitutive and operative definitions of science and law, science and law have to be kept significantly separate, have to stand in a certain mutual autonomy or inviolability, unless science is to prevail at the expense of law (*cf* Thomson 1981).

Just so, at a time seen by most theorists as its beginning and incipient apotheosis, bourgeois legality seems to have been declining in the face of science's advance. "Our historical gradient," says Foucault, "carries us further and further away from a reign of law that had already begun to recede into the past when the French Revolution and the accompanying age of constitutions and codes seemed to destine it for a future that was at hand" (Foucault 1981a:89). The scenario is conveniently, if somewhat too tritely encapsulated by Lasch:

> Social science owed its very existence to the rise of new modes of social control. In former times, power surrounded itself with elaborate apologetics, philosophical defenses of the status quo. As religion gave way to law as the principal source of social cohesion, and law to social therapy, the governing classes no longer attempted to mediate their pretensions with appeals to legitimacy. They appealed only to the unmediated authority of fact. They asked not that the citizen or worker submit to legitimate authority but that he submit to reality itself (Lasch 1977:23).

Law, it would seem, could not fundamentally resist the advance of science. It was dependent on science. It had no necessary substantive content to pit against the dictates of science. It was far from a closed system resistant to isomorphic infiltration from science. Tending to undercut law's resistance to science was the unity of law and science as linked instrumental apparatuses in the institutional milieu of the modern administrative state (Foucault 1979b). Further, science was a jealous god: it was a total view, one that claimed to render everything in political life explicable or potentially explicable in its terms, leaving room for law only as technique in its cause or as one of its branches (*cf* Habermas 1974: 60-61; see *eg* Horwitz 1977:254,257-259).[12]

So law, even in its own apparent expansion, seems to serve increasingly as agent, accessory and support in the advance of science. Law, it seems, comes to be regarded as a mere technique of control (Lasch 1977:187). In this situation law can be seen as increasingly marginalised, confined to some largely symbolical or procedural oversight of the operation of science or of other orders of authority (*cf* Galanter 1980:19-22; Mayhew 1971). Although this oversight serves to mark boundaries restraining science — preserving the 'rule of law' yet legitimating science — such oversight also and thereby serves to secure boundaries within which science can operate with impunity. Let me take as an example a batch of recent English cases dealing with law's supervision of prisons (*cf* also Zdenkowski and Brown 1982: 64-88 and ch 8). The two cases first decided were hailed as an advance in prisoners' rights. They held that courts could supervise internal disciplinary proceedings to ensure prisoners got a fair hearing (*R v Hull Prison Board of Visitors, ex parte St Germain* [1979] 2 WLR 42; *R v Hull Prison Board of Visitors, ex parte St Germain and others (No.2)* [1979] 3 A11 ER 545). The limited, merely procedural nature of this intervention was more eloquent about what law could not cover than about what it could. This point was dramatised in a following case where it was held that procedural natural justice did not oblige a Parole Board to give reasons for its refusal of a prisoner's application to be released on licence *(Payne v Lord Harris of Greenwich and another* [1981] 2 A11 ER 842). This was because of "the interests of society at large, including the due administration of the parole system" (*per* Lord Denning at 846).[13] If, with Foucault, we accept that secrecy is indispensible to the operation of disciplinary power (Foucault 1981a:86), this case can be seen as one precise marker of where law gives way before science. The more general necessity for science to win out emerged in a recent interview with the governor of Winchester prison. To follow legalistic procedures for internal discipline would, he pointed out, result in "lots of acquittals". This would undermine discipline. The machinery of justice should be used as a tool of social control "because, in a prison, ultimately, authority has to win" (Phillips 1981: 13 and *cf* Zdenkowski and Brown 1982:72, 115). In an earlier case the irresistable Lord Denning had said: "If the courts were to entertain actions by disgruntled prisoners, the governor's life would be made intolerable" (*Becker v Home Office and another* [1972] 2 QB 407 at 418). The final case in the batch (*Guilfoyle v Home Office* [1981] 1 A11 ER 943) further illustrates another key aspect of law's support for the ultimate inviolability of science. This entails the infiltration of law by science. In this case the prisoner had complained of assaults on him by prison officers. These are also subject to internal proceedings. He had not succeeded in such proceedings and as a last resort wished to complain to the European Commission on Human Rights. The governor prevented the prisoner corresponding with his lawyer to this end. The Court of Appeal, on an exceedingly pedantic interpretation of the prison rules, held that the governor was entitled to do this. What is significant here is the robust humanity of Lord Denning, which appears to have informed the whole decision; he considered that the prisoner had next to nothing to complain of in any case for "it looks as if they [he and "his companions in crime" (at 944)] did get a little bit of rough handling by someone or other. They were bruised and received black eyes, but nothing more" (at 945). Thus, practical rationalities of discipline are sympathetically and protectively absorbed into the legal domain.

So far we have seen that science provides conditions for the existence of modern law. In this way law is dependent on and restrained by science and hence is vulnerable. Law can be displaced or marginalised by science. Areas of science are impervious to law — domains in the despotism that is the prison were taken as an example. If law were to overrule science in such domains, law would undercut conditions of its own existence. Law's dependence on science is thus set in their interaction. I now, and finally, want to explore the contrary perspective and, in the interaction of law and science, establish the dependence of science on law. For Foucault, as we saw, law's beginning was its end. But law was not emptied of substantive morality and rendered an instrument of science in a falling down before science's advance. Law changed rather because of science's dependence on it.

Enough has been said to show that, for the radical institutionalists, science does not flow inexorably from fact but is ultimately constituted politically. Thus Binet's I.Q. test results, not from a discovery in some pure realm, but from historically specific demands of administration (Rose 1979:50). Yet it is of the essence of science in the cause of state administration that it be perceived as 'objective' and apolitical (Habermas 1971:ch 6). But science is perpetually subject to self-revelation in particular political aspects through the application of its own epistemological standards. Even in its own terms, its particular claims to the autonomous constitution of fact must be considered contingent. Further, if science were to go beyond the voluntary adherence of its subjects — that is, go beyond the continually provisional — and if it had yet to present itself and secure its own operative effects, it could not for long avoid the revelation of its political or, especially, its coercively regulatory nature. Even short of these types of limiting revelation, there would remain areas where the dominance of science is not accepted and recalcitrants not prepared to submit to the necessity of fact.

So law, as independent of fact, empowers science, and serves to constitute it operatively. It also serves to incorporate and maintain particular social fields, such as the family, as sites for the operation of science, social fields in ways often opposed to science's intervention (see *eg* Allott 1980:ch 8). It defines the abnormalities justifying science's intervention or empowers some practitioner of science to define them. It empowers officials and practitioners to intervene coercively to subordinate the legal subject to science and to override other authorities, such as the family head. It provides mechanisms of ultimate enforcement of science's dictates if the scientific subject proves less than cooperative. With convenient necessity, bourgeois legality would require that these coercive interventions and restraints be justified in law and apparatuses of legal supervision exist to enforce law's apparent primacy in all this. Thus science is invested with an aura of right and draws support from the general effects of law. Power is presented through law generally as a negative constraint leaving a measure of freedom intact and so the coercive operation of science is masked and the exercise of disciplinary power rendered acceptable (Foucault 1980:104; 1981a:86,144). Law has also to deal with the failures of science and for some of science's branches failure which, in the terms of science, is endemic. Take the now close to egregious case of the failure of the penitentiary. For that branch or constellation of science to operate, for it to be and remain a site and justification for a diversity of general social controls, it needs its basis in crime, and so not only does it fail to eliminate criminality but it goes further and positively creates and sustains criminality (Foucault 1979a:264-92; Igantieff 1978:210-11). Because of its pervasive necessity for science, law serves also as a field of cohesion and coalescence for the general operation of science. In somewhat abrupt summary, law and science are mutually supportive and interdependent, yet the maintenance of their effectuality in this requires them also to be significantly independent of and opposed to each other.

I will end with some few practical suggestions arising out of the relation between law and science and out of the wider theme of contradiction that has run through this article. These are suggestions only because more is involved in them than this relation and contradiction. We should reject, I suggest, the common perceptions and foretellings of the demise of law in the advance of science. We should also reject the common view that law is intrinsically a foe and potential tamer of science which should be readily resorted to if we wish to reform, transform, or counteract science or its effects.[14] Law is supportively at one with science, integrated into a "scientifico-legal complex" (Foucault 1979a:23). Yet law is significantly independent and controlling of science (and not, as Foucault would have it, utterly subordinated in the "scientifico-legal complex" (Foucault 1980:107-108)). Law is at once both these opposed things, hence the complexity in all this and the need, in practice, for a difficult discrimination. We could, I think, develop our discrimination in this by further exploring the vision of the radical institutionalists that, in the complex of science and law, so much of what has been presented over the last 200 years as humane or even liberating reforms have been intimations of an increasingly refined repression. Perhaps above all we should more closely seek the origins for modern society of that power we call legal and try to render these origins palpable: "...the struggle of man against power is the struggle of memory against forgetting" (Kundera 1980:3; and *cf* Pocock 1971:291).

56 *Australian Journal of Law & Society* *Vol. 1 No. 2, 1983*

Endnotes

1. Earlier versions of this article were presented at Osgoode Hall Law School in the lecture series "Law and Society" on 27 January 1982 and at the Law School, Macquarie University on 8 October 1982. I very much appreciate the valuable comments made on those occasions. Of great benefit also was the discussion following my "Protest and the Limits of Historical Materialism" (which drew considerably on the present paper), when it was presented on 18 February 1982 in the series of Political Sociology Research Seminars on "Protest and Legitimacy" organised by Chris Rootes at the University of Kent at Canterbury. In addition to all that I am indebted in an interesting lot of ways to a lot of interesting people, being Harry Arthurs, Sue Bendall, Gill Boehringer, John Buchanan, Shelby Fitzpatrick, Brian Simpson and David Sugarman.
2. One way in which the relation between particular social fields or particular legal orders and state law is dealt with is by denying significance to state law. For Galanter, state law is a symbol or deception, a mystifying professional ideology (Galanter 1981a, 198b). Ehrlich asserts that "...one might reasonably maintain that society would not go to pieces even if the state should exercise no coercion whatsoever" (Ehrlich 1936:71). The opposite tack is to accord state law some ultimate supremacy (Hooker 1975:4).
3. There are difficulties with the term "family" which are not considered here (*cf* Barrett 1980:199).
4. The point about disappearance is not pursued in the text. The 'early' Marx saw the family as passing with the abolition of private property (Marx 1971:149). Marx, with Engels agreeing, in the Communist Manifesto saw that with the development of capitalism "differences of age and sex have no longer any distinctive social validity for the working class" and both the bourgeois and the proletarian family "will vanish with the vanishing of capital" (Marx and Engels 1970:42,50). But if, as the text argues, the family cannot be reduced to the capitalist mode of production, then a dynamic related solely to the capitalist mode of production cannot necessarily eliminate the family. We would have to study the family and the capitalist mode and study them interacting before beginning to ascribe such a solvent effect to capitalism. One would need at least a much clearer and a much more comprehensive idea of the society we are moving towards than Marx and Engels provide before it can be said so assuredly that such a tenacious social field as the family would have no part in it.
5. "Suggested" only, because it could be retorted, in the tradition of Hume, that parts explain parts.
6. Explorations in these areas may reveal much about resistance to the imposition of ordering categories that have since become more unthinkingly acceptable:

   > It does in fact seem that at the end of the eighteenth century and at the beginning of the nineteenth century criminality was perceived, by the proletarians themselves, to be a form of social struggle. By the time that struggles take the form of combinations criminality no longer has quite this role; or, rather, breaking the law, the transitory and individual overturning of power and order which criminality represents can no longer have the same meaning, nor the same function in struggles (Foucault 1980:20).
7. Poggi notes:

   > ...it seems to me that within Western culture, at any rate, the principle of the depersonalisation of power — which I have suggested is entailed in the Weberian notion of legal-rational legitimacy — does possess a distinctive moral significance, and thus a true, if perhaps weak, legitimising force (Poggi 1978:107).

   This may not qualify what I say in the text for, as far as law is concerned, its significance may be confined to form (and *cf* Thompson 1977:265-266).
8. I am not saying that modern law is located entirely on this side of the divide; much of it is a product of the medieval period, as Gierke's dazzling analysis should perhaps more often remind us (Gierke 1900:73-100), although these elements of continuity will be given a heightened salience with modernity and the flowering of capitalism (Habermas 1979:133-144).
9. For example, there was the birth of scientific racism in the squaring of liberalism with colonialism and the later invention of prejudice as a scientific notion to account for persistent subordination on racial lines.
10. This vision of law is bolstered also in its immediately facilitative aspects, as in contract law for example.
11. The point can be supported suggestively by considering the fate of universalistic rule in direct or unmediated relation to inequality and coercive authority. The history of imported 'western' law in the third world could provide a massive example. For a dramatically focused instance take *R v The Earl of Crewe ex parte Sekgome* [1910] 2 KB 576. Here a law of a British protectorate in Southern Africa provided specifically for the detention of a potentially restless native. An extremely enterprising counsel argued that since this measure lacked universal application, it could not be valid law and habeas corpus would apply. The argument was rejected and the rejection bolstered in such

sentiments as those best expressed by Farwell L.J.:

> The truth is that in countries inhabited by native tribes who largely outnumber the white population such acts [as the Habeas Corpus Act], although bulwarks of liberty in the United Kingdom, might, if applied there, well prove the death warrant of the whites (615).

In such places the state's "first duty is to secure the safety of the white population by whom it occupies the land" (615-616).

12. Witness the triumph of the mechanistic view in the invention of and claims for the orrery (Cronin 1981:153-155); and "in the eighteenth century an Englishman had only to see machinery to think of God" (*ibid* 155).
13. See also Lord Denning on documents revealing the secret setting up in prisons of draconic "control units" in *Home Office v. Harman* [1981] 2 All ER 349 at 364: "It was in the public interest that these documents should be kept confidential. They should not be exposed to the ravages of outsiders".
14. Both these attitudes are often held together — dirges on the death of law usually being preludes to the advocacy of law's resuscitation, so that it can slay what has just slain it.

References

Abbott, J., *In the Belly of the Beast: Letters from Prison* (1982) Hutchinson, London.

Abel, R., "Delegalization: A Critical Review of Its Ideology, Manifestations, and Social Consequences" in Blankenburg E., Klausa E. and Rottleuthner H. (eds), *Alternative Rechtsformen und Alternativen zum Recht, Jahrbuch für Rechtssoziologie and Rechtstheorie, Band VI* (1980) Westdeutscher Verlag, Opladin.

Abel, R. (ed), *The Politics of Informal Justice: Volume 1: The American Experience. The Politics of Informal Justice: Volume 2: Comparative Perspectives* (1982) Academic Press, New York.

Abel, R., "The Contradictions of Informal Justice' in Abel R. (ed), *The Politics of Informal Justice: Volume 1: The American Experience* (1982) Academic Press, New York.

Allott, A., *The Limits of Law* (1980) Butterworths, London.

Althusser, L., *Lenin and Philosophy and Other Essays* (1971) New Left Books, London.

Arthurs, H.W., "Special Courts, Special Law: Legal Pluralism in Nineteenth Century England" in Rubin G.R. and Sugarman G. (eds), *Lawyers, Courts and Industrial Society, 1850-1914* (forthcoming).

Bailey, V., (ed), *Policing and Punishment in Nineteenth Century Britain* (1981) Croom Helm, London.

Barrett, M., *Women's Oppression Today: Problems in Marxist Feminist Analysis* (1980) Verso and New Left Books, London.

Berger, S. and Piore, M., *Dualism and Discontinuity in Industrial Societies* (1980) Cambridge University Press, Cambridge.

Black, D., *The Behaviour of Law* (1976) Academic Press, New York.

Bohannan, P., "The Differing Realms of Law" in Bohannan P. (ed), *Law and Warfare: Studies in the Anthropology of Conflict* (1967) The Natural History Press, New York.

Broderick, A., (ed), *The French Institutionalists: Maurice Hauriou, Georges Renard, Joseph T. Delos* (1970) Harvard University Press, Cambridge.

Cain, M., "Gramsci, the State and the Place of Law" in Sugarman D. (ed), *Legality, Ideology and the State* (in press) Academic Press, London.

Collins, J., "Fragmentation of the Working Class" in Wheelwright T. and Buckley K. (eds.), *Essays in the Political Economy of Australian Capitalism: Volume Three* (1978) Australia and New Zealand Book Company, Sydney.

Cronin, V., *The View from Planet Earth: Man Looks at the Cosmos* (1981) Collins, London.

Doerner, K., *Madmen and the Bourgeoisie: A Social History of Insanity and Psychiatry* (1981) Blackwell, Oxford.

Donzelot, J., "The Poverty of Political Culture" (1979) 5 *I & C*, 73.

Donzelot, J., *The Policing of Families: Welfare versus the State* (1980) Hutchinson, London.

Dumont, L., "The Modern Conception of the Individual: Notes on its Genesis and that of Concomitant Institutions" (1965) VIII *Contributions to Indian Sociology*, 13.

Ehrlich, E., *Fundamental Principles of the Sociology of Law* (1936) Russell & Russell, New York.

Fitzpatrick, P., "Law, Modernisation and Mystification" in Spitzer S. (ed), *Research in Law and Sociology: A Research Annual: Volume 3* (1980a) JAI Press, Greenwich.

Fitzpatrick, P., *Law and State in Papua New Guinea* (1980b) Academic Press, London.

Fitzpatrick, P., "Law, Plurality and Underdevelopment" in Sugarman D. (ed), *Legality, Ideology and the State* (in press) Academic Press, London.

Foucault, M., *Discipline and Punish: The Birth of the Prison* (1979a) Penguin, Harmondsworth.

Foucault, M., "Governmentality" (1979b) 6 *I & C*, 5.

Foucault,M., *Power/Knowledge: Selected Interviews and Other Writings 1972-1977* (1980) Harvester Press, Brighton.

Foucault, M., *The History of Sexuality: Volume 1: An Introduction* (1981a) Penguin, Harmondsworth.
Foucault, M., "Questions of Method: An Interview with Michel Foucault" (1981b) 8 *I & C*, 3.
Galanter, M., "Legality and Its Discontents: A Preliminary Assessment of Current Theories of Legalisation and Delegalisation" in Blankenburg E., Klausa E. and Rottleuthner H. (eds), *Alternative Rechtsformen und Alternativen zum Recht, Jahrbuch für Rechtssoziologie und Rechtstheorie, Band VI* (1980) Westdeutscher Verlag, Opladin.
Galanter, M., "Justice in Many Rooms: Courts, Private Ordering, and Indigenous Law" (1981a) 19 *Journal of Legal Pluralism and Unofficial Law*, 1.
Galanter, M., Indigenous Law and Official Law in the Contemporary United States (Paper presented to the symposium *State Institutions and Their Use of Folk Law: Theoretical and Practical Issues*, Bellagio, 21-25 September, 1981b).
Giddens, A., *Central Problems in Social Theory: Action, Structure and Contradiction in Social Analysis* (1979) Macmillan, London and Basingstoke.
Giddens, A., *A Contemporary Critique of Historical Materialism: Volume 1: Power, Property and the State* (1981) Macmillan, London and Basingstoke.
Gierke, O., *Political Theories of the Middle Age* (1900) University Press, Cambridge.
Gilroy, P., "You Can't Fool the Youths . . . Race and Class Formation in the 1980s" (1981) XXIII *Race and Class*, 207.
Godelier, M., "The Origins of Male Domination" (1981) 127 *New Left Review*, 127.
Griffiths, J., What is Legal Pluralism? (Paper presented at the Annual Meeting of the Law and Society Association, Amherst, 12-14 June, 1981).
Habermas, J., *Toward a Rational Society: Student Protest, Science and Politics* (1971) Heinemann, London.
Habermas, J., *Theory and Practice* (1974) Heinemann, London.
Habermas, J., *Legitimation Crisis* (1976) Heinemann, London.
Habermas, J., *Communication and the Evolution of Society* (1979) Heinemann, London.
Hallis, F., *Corporate Personality: A Study in Jurisprudence* (1930) Oxford University Press, London.
Hartmann, H., "The Unhappy Marriage of Marxism and Feminism: Towards a More Progressive Union" (1979) 8 *Capital & Class*, 1.
Hill, C., *Puritanism and Revolution: Studies in Interpretation of the English Revolution of the Seventeenth Century* (1958) Secker and Warburg, London.
Hill, C., *The Pelican Economic History of Britain Volume 2: 1530-1780: Reformation to Industrial Revolution* (1969) Penguin, Harmondsworth.
Hindess, B. and Hirst, P., *Mode of Production and Social Formation: An Auto-critique of Pre-Capitalist Modes of Production* (1977) Macmillan, London.
Hofrichter, R., "Neighbourhood Justice and the Social Control Problems of American Capitalism" in Abel R. (ed), *The Politics of Informal Justice: Volume 1: The American Experience* (1982) Academic Press, New York.
Hooker, M., *Legal Pluralism: An Introduction to Colonial and Neo-Colonial Laws* (1975) Clarendon Press, Oxford.
Horwitz, M., *The Transformation of American Law, 1780-1860* (1977) Harvard University Press, Cambridge.
Hunt, A., "Dichotomy and Contradiction in the Sociology of Law" (1981) 8 *British Journal of Law and Society*, 47.
Ignatieff, M., *A Just Measure of Pain: The Penitentiary in the Industrial Revolution 1750-1850* (1978) Macmillan, London and Basingstoke.
Ignatieff, M., "State, Civil Society and Total Institution: A Critique of Recent Social Histories of Punishment" in Sugarman, D (ed), *Legality, Ideology and the State* (in press) Academic Press, London.
Jones, K. and Williamson, K., "The Birth of the Schoolroom: A Study of the Transformation in the Discursive Conditions of English Popular Education in the First-half of the Nineteenth Century" (1979) 6 *I & C*, 59.
Kundera, M., *The Book of Laughter and Forgetting* (1980) Penguin, New York.
Lasch, C., *Haven in a Heartless World: The Family Besieged* (1977) Basic Books, New York.
Lasch, C., *The Culture of Narcissism: American Life in an Age of Diminishing Expectations* (1979) Warner Books, New York.
Macfarlane, A., *The Origins of English Individualism: The Family, Property and Social Transition* (1978) Basil Blackwell, Oxford.
Marx, K., *The Early Texts* (ed McLellan) (1971) Blackwell, Oxford.
Marx, K. and Engels, F., *Selected Works* (1970) Progress Publishers, Moscow.
Matthews, R., " 'Decarceration' and the Fiscal Crisis" in Fine B. *et al* (eds), *Capitalism and the Rule of Law: From Deviancy Theory to Marxism* (1979) Hutchinson, London.
Mayhew, L.H., "Stability and Change in Legal Systems" in B. Barber and A. Inkles (eds), *Stability and Social Change* (1971) Little-Brown, Boston.

Melossi, D. and Pavarini, M., *The Prison and the Factory: Origins of the Penitentiary System* (1981) Macmillan, London and Basingstoke.
Middleton, C., "Peasants, Patriarchy, and the Feudal Mode of Production in England: A Marxist Appraisal" (1981) 29 *Sociological Review*, 105.
Moore, S.F., *Law as Process: An Anthropological Approach* (1978) Routledge & Kegan Paul, London.
Phillips, M., "Justice that Obeys the Prison Rules" (1981) *The Guardian*, August 19.
Pocock, J.G.A., *The Ancient Constitution and the Feudal Law: A Study of English Historical Thought in the Seventeenth Century* (1967) Norton, New York.
Pocock, J.G.A., *Politics, Language and Time: Essays on Political Thought and History* (1971) Methuen, London.
Poggi, G., *The Development of the Modern State: A Sociological Introduction* (1978) Hutchinson, London.
Pospisil, L., *Anthropology of Law: A Comparative Theory* (1971) Harper & Row, New York.
Poulantzas, N., *State, Power, Socialism* (1978) New Left Books, London.
Redfield, R., *The Primitive World and its Transformations* (1968) Penguin, Harmondsworth.
Rose, N., "The Psychological Complex: Mental Measurement and Social Administration" (1979) 5 *I & C*, 5.
Rothman, D., *The Discovery of the Asylum: Social Order and Disorder in the New Republic* (1971) Little, Brown, Boston and Toronto.
Santos, B., "Law and Community: The Changing Nature of State Power in Late Capitalism" (1980) 8 *International Journal of the Sociology of Law*, 379. See also in Abel R. (ed) *supra* Volume 1.
Smith, M.G., *Corporations and Society* (1974) Duckworth, London.
Stone, J., *Social Dimensions of Law and Justice* (1966) Stevens, London.
Thompson, E.P., *Whigs and Hunters: The Origin of the Black Act* (1977) Penguin, Harmondsworth.
Thomson, A.D.O., Law and Social Sciences — The Demise of Legal Autonomy (Paper presented to the *Conference on Critical Legal Scholarship*, University of Kent at Canterbury, 30 March — 3 April, 1981).
Trilling, L., *Sincerity and Authenticity* (1972) Harvard University Press, Cambridge.
Varga, C., "Towards a Sociological Concept of Law: An Analysis of Lukacs' Ontology" (1981) 9 *International Journal of the Sociology of Law*, 159.
Wellmer, A. *Critical Theory of Society* (1971) Herder and Herder, New York.
Zdenkowski, G. and Brown, D., *The Prison Struggle: Changing Australia's Penal System* (1982) Penguin, Ringwood.

Part VI
Law and Ideology

[22]

International Journal of the Sociology of Law 1980, **8**, 61–81

Ideological Changes and the Legal Structure: A Discussion of Socialist Experience

KÁLMÁN KULCSÁR
Institute of Sociology,
Hungarian Academy of Sciences, Budapest I, Hungary

Introduction

The term "Ideology" has many meanings as used by social scientists, and even Marxists do not always use it unambiguously. Karl Mannheim (1933) already pointed out that the concept of ideology is also subject to historical change, and he endeavoured to clarify its meaning, that is to bring out those factors that contributed to the way it has been shaped in the course of history. The most general meaning is that of the ideological or conscious superstructure, as against production and the economy, and it includes every aspect of consciousness and related institutions, including legal regulation and the whole of the legal system. This view of ideology, however, proved to be too general and further meanings crystallized in the course of time. These additional definitions, one ought to add, can also be traced back to Marx. At the opposite extreme from the meaning cited above is the meaning which associates ideology with false consciousness. A third meaning sees ideology as determined by a certain commitment of the ideational system to a class, section of society or perhaps even a group. This ideational system expresses the existential conditions of a social class, section or group within a society and in a historical situation. The ideas that have come about in that way interact in the shaping and operation of the web of norms and institutions, the organizational system that the social division of labour gives rise to etc. To quote György Lukács: "Ideology is in the first place that form of processing reality which serves to make human practice conscious and capable of action." Furthermore, and this is most important, ideology is linked to social conflict since "it is the instrument of that social struggle which is . . . characteristic of every society" (Lukács, 1976, p. 449).

0306–3208/80/010061+21 $02.00/0

Though this is not the place for a detailed discussion of the problems of ideology there is nevertheless a need to point to a number of essential features which will aid in the understanding of the interpretation here employed.

(1) Since ideology expresses the conditions of existence of a social class, social stratum or group, it is, as an ideational system, bound by interests in any event.
(2) Ideology as an ideational system is historically determined. This means that it, on the one hand, derives from a historical situation, on the other from a certain inner development of the ideas (Hauser, 1971, p. 141). As a result of this it always contains something from the past of that society as well. In certain cases these could be traditional elements.
(3) It follows from point 2 that an ideology could contain elements as well which could be considered as survivals in relation to a given situation of society.
(4) Ideology as an ideational system can however also be anticipated, to a certain degree, that is in certain of its elements, where there is foresight rooted in a given socio-historical situation, or rather where ideas are produced which have this purpose. In such cases – where there is a considerable likelihood that the real conditions of existence are evaluated in terms of a false consciousness – a consciously formulated picture of the future can be brought to bear on the present (Kulcsár, 1975, p. 176 ff).
(5) It follows from the multiplicity of interests vested in an ideology and its complex historical determination, that, in a given case, obsolete elements, or such as are derived from the formulated image of the future, are artificially kept alive, or else their validity for the present receives forced recognition.
(6) It follows from points 1 to 5 that an ideology is a carrier of values, often containing elements whose values are contradictory. As Niklas Luhmann pointed out, in a concrete situation, thanks to its functional character it can serve as the foundation of one of many variants embodying a variety of values (Luhmann, 1967).
(7) Though an ideology as an ideational system expresses definable social and particular conditions of existence (not only economic ones though undoubtedly in the last resort principally economic ones, as Arnold Hauser rightly points out (Hauser, 1971)), ideology as an ideational system has its own laws of development, which are found in certain of its specific fields as well, such as those referring to the law, which are connected with legal developments.

If the relationship between the law and ideology is to be approached from the point of view of changes in the ideology and from a consideration of the effects these changes have had on legal structure, one must establish in the first place that in general, and primarily, changes in the normative and organizational system of the law cannot be derived from ideological changes. Changes in the law in the last resort depend on changes in sociol-economic conditions, which, however, generally act in an indirect way – through a number of mediations on the normative and organizational systems of the law. Political conditions appear as the most important element of this mediation. There is no doubt however that ideological elements are present as well, and it is also beyond doubt that ideological factors also lead directly to changes in the normative and organizational system of the law. Finally, it ought to be noted that it is extraordinarily difficult to isolate these factors empirically, and it is particularly difficult to discriminate between elements of the concept of ideology as here described and accepted, and other manifestations of culture which also have their consequences for legal regulation.

Before going on to a detailed examination of the connection between ideological changes and legal regulation, it seems to the point briefly to outline what kind of ideological elements can be said to be effective in that way.

(1) In the first place generalized ideational structures are effective such as the whole of an ideological ideational system which expresses views on society, its structure, power relations, social processes, progress, "justice" etc. and which could be coloured by moral, religious etc. elements as well, or elements based on a religious foundation as is the case with, for example, Islamic law, or on explicitly political views, such as liberalism.

(2) Furthermore, ideas relating to the law and its social role have their effect on the law. These could be abstract views, like the normative theory of the law, legal ideas, or elaborated theoretical systems connected with legality, justice, etc.

(3) Finally there are elements which are part and parcel of legal development, or concealed in conventionally accepted ways used to tackle particular problems, or such as are accepted by particular branches of the law, such as opinions held on the nature of responsibility. They are in themselves ideological in the narrow sense, but, over and beyond directly reflecting social living conditions, they can also serve as intermediaries for ideology as a wider ideational system. That is why they widely differ in particular "legal cultures".

Finally, two remarks: it must be stressed in the first place that such elements can only be isolated for the purpose of analysis; in reality they live and act intertwined, and can even express contradictions within an ideological ideational system up to a point. Secondly, there is no scope within this paper for a systematic account of the relationship between ideological changes and legal regulation, not even as restricted to the socialist experience. All I am undertaking to do is to point to certain important developments in socialist society, in Hungary in particular. Even these remarks are, unfortunately, made without my having the possibility of carrying out a thoroughgoing analysis.

The Ideological Element in Law: The Problem of Ends and Means

Otto Kahn-Freund, it will be remembered, argued that society determines the ends, and the legal tradition the means (Kahn-Freund, 1966, p. 45). This statement should be completed by what Gyula Eörsi had to say about "social changes being the major tests for traditions, just as traditions are tests for social change" (Eörsi, 1975, p. 446). One can however only go along with Kahn-Freund up to a point since, within certain limits, the law itself – and therefore the legal traditions that are built into the normative and organizational system of the law – can have an aim-determining role. On the other hand factors that are part of ideology also contribute to the choice of means, in the first place, for example, in deciding what sort of ends can best be served by using the law as a tool. In general the law serves ends that are outside itself, but when it is so used as an "instrument", the ideological element which is thus linked to it can certainly not be considered as passive. In reality the aims themselves can bring about changes, though perhaps not in a manifest manner, in the mechanism of legal regulation (Kulcsár, 1977). It seems to be reasonable to reject a one-sided cause and effect relationship in which ends and means remain in an unchanging relationship, and the law appears as the product of a defined ideology (Luhmann, 1967, p. 532). But even a relationship between aim and instrument considered to be invariable entails that the service of changing aims, which could be accompanied by changes in the function of law, could have a major effect on ideological elements embodied in the law as well. Thus legal regulation connected with social planning, which is growing in scope, could create modifications in the particular character of the law itself as well, which would be considered to be permanent (Kulcsár, 1977). In this way legal regulation could induce more general changes in certain elements of the ideological ideational system.

It follows that ideological elements can be found in the aims to which the law must adjust, though not perhaps in an entirely passive way, in the law looked on as an instrument, and in the choice of legal instruments. (Today ideological elements are largely effective in determining, for example, whether or not a state accepts capital punishment as a legal sanction.)

The determination of aims, ideology, and the law

The ideological element is most important in the social determination of the aims to be served by the law – simplifying this highly complex relationship for the moment – particularly if these are designed to produce change. This is understandable if we bear in mind the indirectness manifest in the relationship between law and society but it also follows from the nature of ideology. Ideology "as the instrument of the fight to the finish of social conflicts, emphatically strives for practice" (Lukács, 1976, p. 505). Ideology therefore is not indifferent to reality, and these aims expressing themselves as social change, or directed towards producing it, must be formulated in the political sphere if they are to receive the support of legal instruments. The manifestation of ideology in this respect is also shaped by the peculiarities of politics. Political practice has a double character: on the one hand, due to its nature, it is necessarily pragmatic, being directed towards the effective manipulation of the real situation in its everyday sense. On the other hand, as György Lukács stresses, "the ideological substance of these political decisions is certainly not neutral" (Lukács, 1976, 488 ff). It is not neutral because long term political principles are shaped ideologically, and, what is more, a single political decision can also have more general ideological consequences.

The determination of aims, and the connection between ideology and law, could be depicted thus:

Socio-economic – political system
↓
general ideological premises
↓
socio-historical situation
↓
power relations
↓
politics
↓↑
ideological elements
↓
legal regulation

It is essential that none of the factors is passive in the process of aim-determination. I have only so far outlined things in an abstract way. An analysis is not easy, not even for periods or societies where the factors appear in a relatively simple form, as during revolutionary change when for example the socialist societies took shape. In the wake of the Russian October Revolution for example, major basic changes received priority, leaving little room, particularly at first, for legal means. What happened as well was that, in connection with what a concrete situation demanded, objectives had to be defined which in themselves had an emphatically ideological character, while laying down a defined political line, such as the decree on land, or the decree on peace. In those cases the legal norm defined an objective, and its instrumental character barely came into evidence. In the course of later developments as well, however, we come across objectives expressed in legal form which were not yet required by the given standards of production. They reflected long established ideological norms to an even greater extent, and concurrently, political considerations as well. Equality between the sexes is an example.

One might well ask to what extent the transformation of the legal structure as a whole can be directly derived from the basic changes that took place in the socio-economic system as such, and to what extent it depended on ideological considerations, that were of course made possible by the basic changes. What is obvious, owing to the nature and social role of ideology as described above, is that the basis of the ideological effect that made itself felt in the legal structure as a whole must be sought in the basic social change that had taken place. Though it is true that "nothing can occur in social existence in whose conception ideology does not have a decisive role" (Klenner, 1957, p. 453) the chance that an ideology should become really effective in the shaping of society, particularly in its power relations, depends on basic social change. Let us look at just one example in the legal structure, and not even the most important one, that is, the dialectics of social and ideological effects as they find expression in the legal structure. The mature socialist legal structure clearly differentiates between family law and civil law. The basis of this was, it appears, originally ideological and had its roots in the view that family relations in a socialist society are based not on the property relations, that is, property relations linked to family relations do not determine the latter . . . in socialist conditions marriage and family rights are liberated from domination by property relations, acquiring an independent moral substance . . . (Szabó, 1963, p. 415). It is obvious that social change was needed, and a new social structure had to come into existence, potentially creating conditions where such a changed character of marriage and the family could come true before such a basic principle could be formulated and made effective. Laying down this changed character of the family as a fact (as against accepting, also as a fact, on the part of bourgeois society, that marriage and the family be determined by property rights), is in the first place an ideological factor. This factor was given a basis allowing it to be realized by the general replacement of private ownership based property relations by the dominance of social property, as regards the means of production. Laying the foundations of family law as an independent branch of the legal system in itself showed legal regulation carrying out an ideologically determined aim-defining function. This question has to be further examined however: to what degree does the extension of legal regulation of family ties, and state social political intervention in family affairs – in which there is only a quantitative difference between the legal systems of socialist and capitalist societies, but none of essence – permit a comprehensible differentiation of branches of the law according to whether or not property rights dominate? In a certain sense the rejection, by socialist legal thinking, of the difference between public and private law can be derived from the same ideological element. It is common knowledge that in many places, as a consequence of liberal legal ideology, this differentiation was a basic characteristic of bourgeois legal thinking, though even in Roman law there were signs of this differentiation. Nor did the law of all liberal capitalist societies accept it: the Common Law never did, to give an example, and current capitalist legal developments tend to obliterate it. It was peculiar that, as against the duality of public law and private law, socialist theories of law for a long time argued from a particular ideological angle, that of the rejection of the principle of private interests, while the real source of this unity was the increasingly comprehensive nature of state activity in relation to the economy and society in general. Legal theory there worked with *a priori* propositions of the kind condemned by Engels, though, in his words, what is involved is an economic reflex.

The ideological aspects of objectives to be brought about by legal regulation appear in a much more basic manner precisely in the coming into being and development of socialist societies. György Lukács, writing over half a century ago, argued that, as against capitalist society, in pre-capitalist societies legal forms intervene in a constitutive manner in economic relations, and economic and legal categories are intertwined in a manner inseparable in substance (Lukács, 1968). This is not the place to discuss the possibility of separating the two categories in capitalist society. Nor may one discuss the extent to which Lukács's view that legal forms were the mere recording of relations that functioned in a purely economic way has remained valid in spite of the changes in capitalist society that have taken place since the 1920s. What is clear, however, is that in the course of the development of socialist society the constitutive effect of legal forms on the shaping of economic conditions once again became important. Perhaps I am not mistaken if I presume to see a connection between the importance of legal forms and the nature of the earlier history of the socialist countries of East Central Europe. These countries, with the possible exception of Czechoslovakia (a relative exception at most since what later became Czechoslovakia belonged to the Austro-Hungarian Monarchy up to 1918), in many respects preserved certain elements of their feudal character, and with them the constitutive function in economic relations exercised by the state and the law. I therefore feel that, in view of the historical circumstances of the step across from the old type of society, which was a long way from being purely bourgeois, to the new one, this constitutive role of the state and the law was not something strange in the new kind of society. This is so in spite of the fact that the ideological conditions and social structures were entirely different, and that the activity of law and state appeared in socialist society in a qualitatively new mode. More precisely, it did not cause as large a break as it might have done in a society where purely liberal capitalist conditions prevailed. This constitutive role of the state and the law made itself felt as a restraining force as well. In Hungary, for example, the state and the law's constitutive role in the nascent capitalist situation was not purely positive when it intervened with unusual effectiveness in the economic life of nascent capitalism starting at the end of the nineteenth century, that is, at a pretty late stage by Western standards. What the ruling political system did – and the state and the law as part of it – was to restrain to a considerable degree the new trends that were making their presence felt, in order artificially to maintain certain retrograde elements that had taken shape thanks to peculiarly

Hungarian social developments. As a result, in the course of socialist transformation, those using state and legal instrumentalities in the service of changed aims – the substance of which were naturally constituted by the changed power relations – could rely on sources of power which would not have been available in a more advanced bourgeois society. On the other hand, the constitutive character of law was demonstrated in the economy where new laws liberated trends that had earlier been restrained, and later shepherded these into the sort of legal fold which determined the direction of progress, and permitted conscious economic development. A good example was the law on agricultural reform, which abolished the old feudal system of land-property, together with its peculiar labour-relations, opened a new way of development for agriculture and provided the labour force needed by developing industry.

Granting this constitutive importance of legal instrumentalities in socialist society then, though the (non-determinist in the technical philosophic sense) determination of social developments by the economic basis is beyond doubt, it is all the same clear that the ideological impact of legal regulation becomes particularly important. In such a case, the constitutive effect, on the one hand comes to full flower, taking off from long-term ideas of social reconstruction, which appear in socialist societies as parts of a defined ideological ideational system; on the other, as I have already pointed out, ideological elements may manifest themselves in the course of implementation using legal instrumentalities, perhaps even modifying the original, which could well make the originally elaborated system of objectives more complex. This is particularly likely if the objectives approached by legal regulation are defined too vaguely or in an overgeneralized way, since the factors involved in the definition of objectives can be complex indeed, and the concrete situation, as well as the policy which expresses it perhaps ambiguously but nevertheless in practice, therefore becomes very important. It is also clear that even a policy which is highly consistent ideologically, or one which does its best to be that, could be forced, transitionally at least, to define targets that do not in every respect reflect the basic ideology. In the case of the long term objectives of equality in socialist society already referred to, legal rules increase the difference between the salary (and income) of different positions in labour, or according to the quality of work really done. In such cases the constitutive power of legal regulation that serves such aims usually manifests itself; its ideological character, however, tends to fade. (It seems to make sense to judge the economic legislation of the NEP period in the early years of the Soviet Union from this point of view, as well as that of household plot farming in the socialist societies in general.) In these cases legal regulations were developed which were not altogether consistent with abstract ideological principles. In the latter case these legal rules did not merely survive but grew stronger, obeying the needs of a defined situation. Legal regulation – in spite of being basically determined ideologically, or rather in spite of the fact that objectives are there expressed as mediated by ideology – may well manifest political considerations that perhaps temporarily deviate from the ideological ideational system. But this ideological structure itself undergoes transformation, in certain cases because of a reaction to such legal regulation, although (despite some exceptions in socialist countries) the demands of practice cannot be said directly to shape ideologies in most cases.

The law as an instrument and the ideological effect

The law as an instrument, that is once again simplifying the ends/means relationship, as the instrument which implements a defined policy, in a double sense carries the consequences of ideology and of ideological change. On the one hand the position maintained in a given society concerning the place of law, and its social role, is ideologically determined, or at least possesses certain ideological aspects, on the other the law in its phenomenological aspects includes ideological relations, more often than not past elements that are inbuilt in legal regulation itself, in the guise of legal traditions.

As regards the first, I am referring to the different ways of evaluating the role of law in the progress of socialist societies. Many a scholar is puzzled by the fact that though Marxist social theory speaks of the withering away of the state and the law in a manner refined by the classics, as a future prospect in the post-revolutionary period, and the law is relegated into the background in pre-revolutionary ideas, and even in the practice of the first year or two after the revolution, later developments nevertheless saw the strengthening of the state apparatus, and the growing weight of legal regulation in the Soviet Union as well. The other socialist states in Europe right from the start leant heavily on legal instrumentalities while giving shape to the new society. At first sight it seems only obvious to explain things, as E. H. Carr does (Carr, 1970, p. 78), in terms of a changed attitude towards the law being the natural consequence of every revolution. The revolution attacks the existing legal order, wishing to put an end to it. Following its victory it soon wakes up to the fact that it needs a legal order of its own. The challenger and opponent of the law thus turns into a legislator who maintains it. This, however, is a partial truth only, since, for a start, Marxist ideology opposes not only bourgeois law, though that as well, but in the long term, every kind of law. One could add that though legislation of a new kind (the exception here being criminal law) took place after the October Revolution, Reissner, Stuchka and Pashukanis continued to argue that all law was bourgeois law, and opposed it as such, or at least its normative character.

Once again here is an interesting example of the often ambivalent relationship between ideology and the concrete socio-historical situation. This anti-legal ideology flourished precisely during that first decade of the Soviet State when important legislative work was done. It is true of course that this was not free of contradictory ideological elements, such as, for example, the influence of the consequences of a "created image of the future" interpreted as present reality, as in the case of the family. After stormy debates and political struggles, however, the manner of socialist construction, given historic Russian conditions, was precisely outlined, and thus objectives were defined which were primarily of an economic nature, or connected with the chosen economic policy, but which also enlisted legal instrumentalities in their service (Kulcsár, 1977). The system of plan-directives, extensive industrialization, and the collectivization of agriculture, linked with the centralization of public administration, unbelievably multiplied the quantity of instruments of legal regulation. It can also be established that the stress on law enforcement, which in that particular socio-historical situation indicated qualitative change, was accompanied by changes in those aspects of ideology that referred to the social role of law. The requirements of practice that sprang from the concrete socio-historical situation found expression in an extreme normative variant of the Marxist theory of law, as taught by Vishinsky. It ought to be mentioned, however, that such extreme normative theories were a long way indeed from Marx's, or Engels' early expressed views concerning the normative aspects of the law, what law could achieve in the social context, and the limitations to which it was subject (Marx & Engels, 1976).

It is specially interesting from the angle of the present paper that this ideology about the social role and scope of law was, in the first place, the fruit of the period in which a socialist economy and society were being constructed, and only became stressed as part of the political practice of the thirties. Because of the particular historical conditions, this ideology was even further pronounced in the socialist countries that came into existence after the war. It was only natural that this ideology should be present in these societies. This was the result, on the one hand, of somewhat similar conditions under which extensive economic development took place; on the other it was due to the Soviet regulatory and organizational model being present as a pattern for a socialist legal system. Specific historic conditions as well must, however be looked to for an explanation of the further strengthening of this ideology and practice of law, in addition to the political factors. In Hungary, for example, the law's scope was always accepted as great, and the legal profession enjoyed a high social status. Furthermore, as the effect of factors which cannot be discussed in detail within the scope of this paper, the so called "hard" social sciences, such as sociology, economics – apart from a number of outstanding personalities – and certainly jurisprudence exemplifying a sociological approach, shared a traditionally poor standard. Social problems were more likely to be reflected in literature, or in journalism. The result was that remedies were looked for in non-scientific modes of thought or even in cultural policy. It is clear of course that the exaggerated, and even voluntarist, exploitation of legal instrumentalities, which is fed by a faith in the power of normative prescription, furthers attitudes that rely solely on influencing consciousness, or on influencing behaviour directly through consciousness. That is an approach which transposes the solution of deeply embedded social and economic problems to the conscious level, and thus to the level of faith in the power of voluntaristic legal instrumentalities. To give just one example: when a socialist society was being constructed in Hungary, internal labour migration was very high, in keeping with the specific nature of extensive industrialization. Based on the above-mentioned ideological consideration attempts were made to erect legal barriers, including criminal sanctions, in the way of such population movements, which naturally failed, instead of studying the contributing factors, and taking the appropriate measures. The ideological element present in taking the law to be a means thus led to the reduction of social problems to the level of consciousness, or social-economic policy problems to the level of cultural policy. Merely apparent and momentary effectiveness – long-term effects were always left out of account – lent additional strength to this view. I mention, and not as a matter of interest only but as one of the important aspects of this problem, that this process took place in Hungary at a time when the social status of the legal profession declined catastrophically, when the number of students of law was radically reduced, and when the drafting of legislation itself, at least in the economic field, was taken away from lawyers.

The emphasis on the extreme normative theory of the law as an ideological element, led to further consequences for its ideological foundations. Central attention was given for example to the principle of legality, already powerfully stressed by Lenin in the post-revolutionary period. Let there be no misunderstanding; legality is truly the foundation of the legal order, and its role was particularly important in the period of socio-economic and political stabilization which had formulated its own legal regulations. But one should not forget either that stressing legality as the, as it were, most important fundamental principle (Szabó, 1963) functionally occurs when (a) major changes take place in legal regulation as a whole, when, that is, one must reckon with the continued effect of the old law; and (b) when legal regulation is necessarily enfeebled as a result of voluntarism, and the use of the law as an instrument in a manner that is contrary to its own specific instrumental nature. (Gyula Eörsi rightly notes that great economic power concentrated in the hands of the state may well feed voluntarist illusions (Eörsi, 1975, p. 407) which are then expressed as faith in an almighty law.) In such cases the emphasis on legality as a basic principle of first importance is connected with the further presupposition that the effectiveness of legal norms depends on subjective factors, and that, if it fails, the trouble must be sought in the "stupidity of the world", as Marx put it – in the German Ideology – referring to the attitude of King Frederick William IV of Prussia. The voluntarism that springs from this concentration however leads to further consequences as well. One example is a stress on legislation in the normative theory of law, designed to eliminate the legislative function of courts, reducing judicial interpretation to a merely mechanical act. The bureaucratization (in the neutral sense of that term) which generally accompanies excessive centralization (as discerned by Max Weber) necessarily places the emphasis on the executive organs in the process that leads from voluntaristic regulation to the implementation of the law, and this also contributed to the replacement of economic management by public administration, strengthening the process where it was already present.

The ideology which exaggerated the social role and scope of the law, focusing on the normative aspects of the law as a matter of course, and the practical consequences of this view, naturally influenced legal regulation in socialist society as it developed further. An ideology that becomes flesh and muscle as a system survives the circumstances that gave rise to it. This more or less can still be felt today, in socialist societies, though the socio-historical situation has significantly changed. However, the voluntarist legal ideology does not appear with equal force in every one of them. I am not however as yet in a position to undertake a discussion of the ideological consequences of recent socio-economic developments, or of the inter-connected effect of the political element tied to a concrete situation and of changes taking place in legal regulation.

I have already pointed to the fact that principles and ideas embodied in the law *qua* instrument are of far from minor importance in the connection between law and ideology, particularly in the form of conventions embodying ways in which the law copes with a situation. Principles and ideas that are part of the living law, and conventions and traditions that are also part of it, do not always appear on the same level. More abstract ideas are generally of a more directly political character, as, for example, the consequences of a liberal political ideology, while those elements that are usually called legal traditions or conventions tend to be produced in a more direct way by legal developments themselves. Following hundreds of years of development, major ideological elements found their way into the law *qua* instrument, and to a major degree, they can be considered as technical elements. Such kinds of ideological elements in contemporary legal systems, be they socialist or capitalist, largely go back to the political ideas of the rising eighteenth century bourgeoisie. It is certainly true for instance that equality before the law (and what I have in mind is not equal treatment by the organs administering justice which has not come true anywhere yet, but that legislation should neglect the articulated nature of the social structure) is an element which can be traced back to liberal bourgeois ideology which, in present planned societies often has disfunctional consequences for the implementation of social policy. Thus, in certain cases, it negatively influences the efficiency of the law as a social-policy serving instrument. One can reach similar conclusions in connection with other ideological elements that can be traced back to the eighteenth century or even to earlier periods (Kulcsár, 1977). Let me only mention the problem of the duty of familiarity with the law. It is common knowledge that the principle of *ignorantia iuris* is basic to the operation of every legal system. Today, however, when sociological research has shown how differentiated familiarity with the law is, being largely non-existent; when, what is more, the importance of legal regulation has largely increased as a result of the growing planned character of social management, something which particularly stresses the need for familiarity with the law; in these circumstances merely relying on the principle – which is actually a fiction – that a proclaimed law must in fact be known, is hardly sufficient in itself (Kulcsár, 1967).

As regards legal traditions that appear on the technical level – neglecting for the moment the problem of national legal traditions – I should like to refer to one only . It is common knowledge that, for centuries, or even millenia, legal norms directly addressed individuals, thus determining their structure and other specific features. Today, however, at a time of large-scale and growing organizedness of society, the majority of legal norms only address human beings indirectly, inasmuch as organizational activity itself is only realized in human behaviour, the organizations themselves being addressed in the first place. Though it is a new feature of the law *qua* instrument that the effectiveness of legal norms should be largely determined by organizational phenomena, there has nevertheless been just about no change in conventional legal techniques (Kulcsár, 1978*a*).

The ideological effect present in the application of the law is an important aspect there. The application process of legal rule is able to carry social change into the law, but when what is needed is precisely the legal implement of much change which cannot, perhaps for ideological reasons, be made effective directly and promptly through constitutionally determined legislative organizations, law-applying organizations decide in accordance with these social changes in confrontation with the prevailing ideology (Kulcsár, 1971, p. 493). It is well known, for example, that in Hungary during the last decades the number of cohabitations without marriage increased, which caused a lot of property problems after the dissolution of such type of cohabitation. Since the Constitution and the Family Code consider the marriage and family as a basic value in society, the courts – starting out from this ideological premise – were not in the position of being able to apply, for instance, the legal principle of community property normally applied between married couples. Therefore the Hungarian Supreme Court "considered" this cohabitation legally as "association" (in the sense of civil law) and decided the property problems according to this consideration. The reason for this decision was purely ideological because it is clear that the nature of cohabitation is much closer to marriage than to civil association.

The impact of legally relevant ideological elements, or such as are part and parcel of the law, naturally manifests itself in a variety of ways. I shall try and outline six types basing my argument on thirty years of socialist experience, in Hungary in the first place.

Types of Ideological Change and their Effect on the Structure of Law

1.Theirst type of adequate ideological mediation of the consequences of real social change is perhaps the most general type in the period when one social system replaces another, and even when there are essential socio-economic changes within a particular system. This is primarily present in constitutional legislation which generally reflects, and expresses in ideological terms as well, basic socio-economic changes, and therefore also such changes as occurred in power relations. One ought to note, however, that it may well happen that they do not merely mediate changes, but formulate universal principles which have not, or not yet, come true in the given situation. Therefore we can witness a constant discussion of the so-called, programmatic (mostly ideological) or legal elements of socialist constitutions. This discussion is connected precisely with the extreme normative attitude, and the demands of a socio-historical situation, sometimes of a directly political nature, which gave birth to the normative position. Programmatic or "political" norms, with an expressly ideological emphasis, lay the foundations of certain future changes.

This type of ideological impact appeared in perhaps its purest form apart from constitutional provisions in legal arrangements designed to protect social property. The social ownership of the means of production was clearly one of the basic conditions for the coming into being of a socialist society. Thus, in connection with means of production, a large proportion of goods and chattels became social property. It is obvious that their great social importance required a stress on their social protection, especially in the early years of socialist society, when one had to reckon with deliberate attacks on social property on the part of the former owners and the remnants of the old ruling class. That is why the socialization legislation itself contained penal clauses, even before comprehensive regulation of the subject was undertaken within the framework of the criminal law. One ought to add that in Hungary, and very likely in the majority of the socialist countries, the attitude of most people to state property which had taken shape in the earlier age of private property differed from that to private property. The legal position was the same, but in the minds of people, particularly the peasantry and the working class, offences against state property, if considered such at all, were judged to be venial. The severity of the law defending social property therefore made practical sense, over and above its ideological importance. It is an open question, however, whether the Draconian character of the penal clauses concerned, and their over-zealous carrying out at one time was due to the socio-economic and ideological importance of social property, or to the political consequences of a subjectively interpreted specific situation. I am inclined to take the latter view, though crime statistics suggest that the historically produced gap between attitudes to social and private property is closing. In Hungary the proportion of crimes against social property within crimes against property in general has steadily declined from 43% in 1965 to 35% in 1975.

Time was certainly needed to make the laws protecting social property effective, not merely the passage of time, but the growth of those social-economic conditions which created a basis for the effectiveness of the legal norm and for a well-balanced law-enforcement policy. At the time when a start was made on running the economy in a socialist way, the state will, expressed in decrees designed to introduce a strictly controlled economy, was seriously handicapped by the absence of certain economic preconditions, by inflation, war damage, a lack of management experience and expertise etc. The criminal law was not the proper instrument for neutralizing these, and economic stability was finally produced by economic events and measures. The real implementation of a legal norm depends on social conditions even when these changes are a matter of apparent indifference to it (Kulcsár, 1978*a*).

2. *The ideological overvaluation of the effect of social change brought about by legal regulation* can lead to undesirable consequences on a society-wide scale. Miklós Világhy is right in many respects when he argues that "every phenomenon of civil law, and every one of its basic institutions, derives in the last resort from the commodity relation, as a material basis, and its legal reflection. . . ." I interpret this as saying that the most important institutions of civil law are genetically linked to commodity relations. One can similarly interpret the conclusion, with certain reservations that "in socialist conditions, all those insecurities and debates which have so far centred on the place of civil law in the legal system, and its basic institutions, can be fundamentally traced back to the insecure place of commodity relations in the socialist social order (Világhy, 1968, p. 472). The reservation here could well result from the insecurities in the interrelationship of social property and commodity relations. To understand the problem one must be aware that Marxist economics, going back to Marx, has considered commodity relations as a defining characteristic of capitalist society, arguing that commodities are the universal form of capitalist production since in a capitalist society just about everything is up for sale, and can be bought (Világhy, 1968, p. 446). Though economists have hardly managed to clear up this problem for socialist societies, a trend could be later discerned in Marxist ideology which restricted commodity relations to capitalist society, not recognizing that commodity relations exist in a socialist society as well, or else not granting this circumstance sufficient importance. In other words the transitional stage of socialist society, including commodity production, is a long drawn out historical process.

Thus legal regulation as well started with the implicit, and often explicit, ideological premise that commodity production is at the very least not characteristic of socialist society. Pashukanis, who without further ado identified civil law and capitalist law, and argued that, if there are commodity relations in socialist society, they must necessarily be of a capitalist character, and survivals of capitalist conditions, expressed the extreme manifestation of this ideological position. Though there can be no doubt that commodity production has been a part of the economic reality of every European socialist society right from the start, though commodities were not always the final product, this was not sufficiently recognized by the ideology or the law. The question is curiously connected with economic activity based on central plan directives. These, by prescribing figures, and thanks to the compulsion contained in plan-contracts, actually made commodity relations between enterprises merely formal. Moreover, as a result of various emergency situations and industrialization a part of consumer goods at least were treated as subject to a central distribution system, rather than as genuine commodities.

As I mentioned, the importance and the nature of commodity relations in a socialist society cannot as yet be considered to have been clarified by economists. The connection, for example, between effects deriving from the anarchic nature of commodity relations and the consequences of the potentialities of economic planning in a socialist society has not been properly studied yet. Nor is it clear in what ways, if any, recent developments in capitalist society have affected the anarchic nature of commodity relations in that society. As a result there is continued uncertainty about the instruments of socialist economic management and other devices which are still awaiting use. This ideological confusion – which arises from the absence of properly worked out theoretical foundations of political economy in the socialist societies – may give scope for an ideological judgement of a specific situation, based on particular interests, or imagined interests. It also encourages the ideological rationalization of decisions taken. All this creates further uncertainty in the development of the legal instrumentalities of economic management, contributing even to a still unfinished debate amongst socialist lawyers concerning the nature of business law.

3. This takes us to the third issue which could perhaps be formulated as a question. *To what extent can ideological elements handicap overdue social change, or connected legal regulation?* A number of formulations are possible. One is to what extent do identical conditions in two differing social systems, that is, socialist and capitalist society, in spite of differing ideological foundations create a substantial identity, that is one that is not based merely on similar *formal* solutions? Gyula Eörsi argued there, in connection with convergence theories, that the identity of forces of production, the presence of commodity relations, and contacts deriving from the coexistence of the two societies, as well as the consequences of the class struggle, can produce substantial identities in many respects. These identities, however, do not in the last resort affect those fundamental relations which divide the law of the two systems, creating two types of law, since capitalist society is compelled to adjust to forces of production that have far transgressed beyond the bounds of private property, while the socialist state does not merely intervene in the economy, but comprehensively directs and manages it (Eörsi, 1975). In this interplay of identities and differences are the productive relations and structure of power of the two social systems, though these, of course, have their own ideological consequences. (One such specific problem of an ideological nature, which took shape as a result of a variety of mediations, is that of the "rule" of subjective responsibility in socialist law.)

Such far-reaching problems cannot be discussed here and convergence itself was only brought in by way of example. This is true of the next problem as well, which is the second possible formulation of the basic problem. It is common knowledge that reforms of varying depth were carried out in the system of economic guidance and management in the socialist countries of Europe when the period of extensive economic development came to a close. Since the economic theories on which they were based differed, so also were the legal measures taken. It is clear that this divergence, which occurred given identical social and economic, and in the last resort, ideological foundations, cannot be explained away by referring to specifically national features in the development of law, or to different socio-economic experiences. Ideological elements were manifested in and contributed to the way such experiences were judged and evaluated and such ideologically influenced judgements are clearly connected with consequences that derive from the political situation of the country concerned. These consequences, as I pointed out earlier, can strengthen a general basic feature of the joint ideological system, but they can fit new elements into that system as well, in keeping with the political aspects of the concrete socio-historical situation.

A third approach, close to the previous one, concerns the social and ideological conditioning of the creation and effectiveness of the legal norms that serve economic planning. The problem really manifests itself as that of specifying the triple interrelation of economic, social, and legal rationality (Kulcsár, 1977).

This means that, since the decisions of economic planning are implemented in a social medium which includes both political conditions and ideological elements, economic decisions that appear to be rational in themselves are in their realization exposed to influences deriving from this political and ideological environment. These can distort the decision, even in the process of its realization through legal norms, and its social consequences could well become disfunctional. Thus, in Hungary, economically highly important efforts to increase labour productivity are conditioned by the ideological and constitutional requirement that there be full employment. This then renders unpredictable the effect of a number of legal norms which appear otherwise to be perfectly rational.

National traditions in the development of law are essentially similar conditional factors. These do not merely affect the professional activity of legislators and law enforcement agencies but are able to influence, in differing directions, the effectiveness of legal regulation that accords with, or differs from, the tradition, precisely because the tradition has become part of the consciousness of ordinary people.

4. Finally, I wish to refer briefly to those *purely ideological considerations which, perhaps outliving their usefulness, or else being too far ahead, project back an ideologically conceived picture of the future,* and so make an impact on legal regulation. It can even happen, and this to a certain extent is connected with the historical circumstances under which socialist societies exist, that surviving, and back-projected, elements can make their joint presence felt in a particular legal norm.

Thus, following the October Revolution, the first socialist courts had a formally lay character as well. Later, and this practice still prevails, courts of first judgement in the Soviet Union were constituted of a professional judge and two peoples' jurors. This system, with minor or major modifications, was naturalized in the European socialist countries as well. The importance of the lay element remained undiminished as a matter of principle (Kulcsár, 1971). Sociological research in a number of countries has shown however that lay participation was primarily of an ideological character [1]. The problem however goes beyond lay participation in the work of courts, extending to the socialization of state duties, that is, the direct participation by working people in the carrying out of state duties. Attempts to deal with the real problem in the present situation, both in its well-founded and in its as yet foundation-less aspects, manifest an interpretation, brought up to date, of the presupposition that the state and the law will wither away. The withering away of the state and the law as a historic process has tempted many a thinker, working within the Marxist tradition, to take this future prospect to be a principle that ought to show its effects in the contemporary world as well. This has led to efforts designed to achieve socialization, that is, measures taken to ensure that voluntary organizations take over certain state duties which involve administering particular legal provisions. In Hungary, for example, the trades unions handle social insurance, including pensions. The result has been a bureaucratic organization, naturally employing officals, within the trades unions, much like the state bureaucracy, only perhaps working less efficiently and more bureaucratically, with powers that can be described as legislative (law-creating) in a certain sense, using state methods, and the fact that it works under the supervision of a non-state body, the National Council of Trades Unions, does not make much of a difference.

Ideological elements projected into the future were particularly demanding in the first stage of development of socialist society, as regards legislative practice. Such were, for example, the institution of *de facto* marriage in Soviet family law, and the almost complete liquidation of the law of inheritance. Responsibility under civil law in socialist societies showed a peculiar amalgam of a presumed future projected back onto the present and of the political consequences of a given era. The principle of objective responsibility in Civil Law, in the objective responsibility of employers for accidents at work, was linked with socialism as a result of the struggle of the working class movement. Nevertheless, in the development of socialist civil law, emphasis was given to subjective responsibility, though not from the start (Sólyom, 1975), in many cases for ideological and political reasons. "There is much to the argument that this general idea of subjective responsibility directly ensues from the identification of legal and moral requirements, and the harmonization of the basis on which responsibility rests in civil and criminal law, and from the proposition that legal offences in socialist society have no objective basis, but are rooted in subjective backwardness, that is, a backward consciousness"

(Sólyom, 1975, p. 281). I have already pointed to the connection between such ideological elements and a defined political situation. Since the effect of that situation has lessened, signs of change have appeared in the ideological aspects of responsibility in civil law, and the view no longer prevails that offences in socialist society can have no objective aspects, and that they can all be derived from backward thinking. In other words a presumed image of the future is no longer taken as being present fact.

Summing Up

Though I was unable to probe the depths of the relationship between ideology and the law, and even less so the effects of ideological change on legal developments, it can at least be established that this relationship is ambivalent in all its complexity. There are historical precedents of actual social and legal changes occurring in spite of the domination of an ideological ideational system that remained unbroken for a time. It is enough to refer, with Thurman Arnold, to the growth of the large monopolies in the shade of an official ideology of free competition (Arnold, 1940, pp. 207, 211).

There have been similar examples, up to a certain point, in the growth of socialist societies, such as the growth of a centralized state administration, and of the law, in spite of an abstract ideology proclaiming the withering away of the state and the law, and the socialization of state duties in general. However complex the mediating mechanism may be, naturally allowing for many different variations, the law either sooner or later adjusts to the ideational system of the ruling ideology, or else the ideological elements suffer changes that bring them into line with the requirements of the actual socio-historical situation, even in cases where, on a level of much higher abstraction, and perhaps only temporarily, the ideological system appears to be unbroken.

The basic question is whether the ideology which is in the dominant position in a given society accords with objective social processes, that is, does it mediate the sort of effects of legal regulation which are important for the effectiveness of law and which harmonize with the demands of objective social processes? A legal norm has to be realized as part of human behaviour which is affected by many other factors as well. The law is, and can only be, one of these factors. The chances of realization therefore depend primarily on other social conditions. A great number of examples could be cited from the practice of socialist states, and capitalist ones as well. I shall, however, confine myself to one. Hungarian family law, at an early stage of socialist development, included prescriptions which correctly expressed social processes, and this was true though these norms, at that time, owed their existence to ideological considerations (Kulcsár, 1962, p. 145 ff). As against this, and also in the field of family law, the dissolution of marriages, as established in the practice of the 1950s for a time, which was also largely due to ideological factors, no longer paid proper regard to the conditioning power of social circumstances, leading to disfunctional consequences, which finally resulted in changes in divorce practice.

The experience of socialist societies thus largely confirms Friedmann's views (Friedmann, 1947, p. 415). Though I have certain reservations about the way he formulates them Friedmann argued, when discussing legal aspects of the industrial revolution, in opposition to those who stressed the importance of ideology in shaping legislation and social conditions, that the direction in which the law has to move ultimately depends on the basic political ideology unless solid social foundations no longer support the extreme consequences of an ideology.

This proposition focuses attention on the basic nature of ideology which I indicated as a functional relationship with the interests and efforts of sections of society and social groups, something that crops up again and again in all kinds of definitions (Wiatr, 1968). This functional element which is given by it being bound to interests, suggests an approach critical of ideology, the basis of which must be on the one hand a study of ideology in relation to the affected class and other interests, as well as social processes and phenomena and the trends they show, and on the other hand a comparison between the initial ideology and the process of realization of the institutions, norms, and practices based on that ideology. When it comes to the law, which is itself replete with ideological elements, there is a special need for such an operation. György Lukács, following Engels, also refers to the specifically ideological characteristics of the law, which leads – largely due to the professional interests of those who practise law – to exaggerating its importance, and to the law being increasingly diverted from economic reality (Lukács, 1976). And since in the long run, economic reality puts up barriers to prevent legal regulation from being effective, the study of socio-economic reality, of specific class interests, and of the mechanisms that are effective in the relationship between ideology and legal regulation, is extraordinarily important. This is even more the case when the problem is that of social reconstruction and planning, and the use of "the law" to expedite social change.

Notes

1 In Hungary, the 1972 Law on the Organization of Courts endeavoured to define the duties of lay assessors in keeping with their true importance.

References

Arnold, Thurman (1940) *The Folklore of Capitalism* 9th ed. New Haven.

Carr, E. H. (1970) *Socialism in One Country*. Vol. 1. Penguin Books: Harmondsworth.

Eörsi, Gy. (1957) Tervszerzödések. *Plan-contracts*. Akadémiai Kiadó: Budapest (in Hung.).

Eörsi, Gy. (1975) Osszehasonlitó polgári jog. *Comparative Civil Law, Types of Law, and the Ways of Legal Development*. Akadémiai Kiadó: Budapest (in Hung.).

Friedmann, L. (1972) Einige Bemerkungen über eine allgemeine Theorie des rechtlichen Verhaltens. – Zur Effektivität des Rechts Zur Effektivität des Rechts. Herausg. Rehbinder, M. und. Schelsky, H. Düsseldorf.

Friedmann, W. (1967) *Legal Theory*. Columbia University Press: Columbia.

Hauser, A. (1971) Propaganda, Ideology, and Art. In *Aspects of History and Class Consciousness* (Mészáros, I., Ed). Routledge and Kegan Paul: London.

Kahn-Freund, Otto (1966) Comparative law as an academic subject. *The Law Quarterly Review* **82**, January.

Klenner, H. (1957) Zur ideologischen Natur des Rechts. – Staat und Recht im Lichte des Grossen Oktober. Berlin.

Kulcsár, K. (1967) La connaissance du droit en Hongrie. *A'Année Sociologique* **18**.

Kulcsár, K. (1971) A népi ülnök a biróságon. (*The lay judge in courts*). Akadémiai Kiadó: Budapest (in Hung.).

Kulcsár, K. (1972) Sozialer Wandel und die Mitwirkung des Laienelements in der Rechtspflege. In *Zur Effektivität des Rechts*. Herausg. von Rehbinder, M. und Schelsky, H. Düsseldorf.

Kulcsár, K. (1975) A történetiség jelentösége a társadalomépitésben. (Historicity in shaping society) *Szociológia* No. 2 (in Hung.).

Kulcsár, K. (1976) *A jogszociológia alapjai*. (*The foundations of the sociology of Law*) Közgazdasági és Jogi Könyvkiadó: Budapest.

Kulcsár, K. (1977) Social planning and legal regulation. *Acta Iuridica* Academiae Scientiarum Hungaricae. Tom. 19. (3–4).

Kulcsár, K. (1978*a*) Social factors in the effectiveness of law. In *Hungarian Society and Marxist Sociology in the Nineteenseventies* (Huszár, T., Kulcsár, K., Szalai, S., Eds.) Corvina Press: Budapest.

Luhmann, N. (1967) Positives Recht und Ideologie. *Archiv für Rechts- und Sozialphilosophie* No. 53, 540–541.

Lukács, Gy. (1968) Geschichte unf Klassenbewusstsein, Neuwied, Luchterhand.

Lukács, Gy. (1976) *A társadalmi lét ontológiája*. (*On the ontology of social existence*) Vol. II. Budapest (in Hung.).

Mannheim, K. (1933) *Ideology and Utopia*. Harvest Books Edition: New York.

Marx, K. & Engels, F. (1976) *The German Ideology*. *Collected Works* Vol. 5. Lawrence and Wishart: London.

Sólyom, L. (1975) "Miért uralkodik a szubjektiv kárfelelösség a szocialista jogban?" Why does the principle of subjective responsibility dominate in socialist law? *Állam és Jogtudomány*. *XVIII*. No. 2 (in Hung.).

Szabó, I. (1963) *A szocialista jog*. (*Socialist Law*.) Közgazdasági és Jogi Könyvkiadó: Budapest (in Hung.).

Világhy, M. (1968) Á viszony és polgári jog (Commodity relations and civil law). *Állam és Jogtudomány XI*, No. 3 (in Hung.).

Wiatr, J. (1968) *The Twilight of Ideology?* Warsaw (in Polish).

Date received: January 1979

[23]

THE IDEOLOGY OF LAW: ADVANCES AND PROBLEMS IN RECENT APPLICATIONS OF THE CONCEPT OF IDEOLOGY TO THE ANALYSIS OF LAW

ALAN HUNT*

In this paper I note the growth of analyses of law that focus upon its ideological character and content, and I identify problems and difficulties manifest in the ideological analysis in recent critical and Marxist texts. The paper argues that work focusing upon the ideological character of law realizes significant advances over that produced by the more orthodox approaches within the sociology of law and jurisprudence employing normative analysis. It is possible to make ideological analysis more rigorous. The paper outlines the elements of a theory of and methodology for the ideological analysis of law.

I. INTRODUCTION

The application of the concept "ideology" to the analysis of law has been one of the distinctive features of the strand of critical legal studies that draws upon the Marxist tradition. My objectives in this paper are:

i) to situate the "ideological analysis of law" within contemporary Marxism,
ii) to locate its relevance to the current concerns of the sociology of law and of critical legal studies,[1]
iii) to explore the substantive contribution of work written under the imprint of "the ideological analysis of law" and to identify its major variants,
iv) to show that theoretical and methodological clarification of both the components and scope of the ideological analysis of law is needed, and
v) to outline some elements of a theory of ideological analysis.

* This paper was originally delivered as the George Lurcy lecture at Amherst College, Amherst, Massachusetts, in September 1983. I would like to thank Piers Beirne, Maureen Cain, Jeremy Cooper, Steve Redhead, David Sugarman, and Ronnie Warrington for valuable comment and criticism.

[1] For my present purpose I distinguish "critical legal studies" as a trend of analysis that, while drawing significantly on the Marxist tradition, is primarily identified by the political project of intervening in the scholarship and practice of legal education.

LAW & SOCIETY REVIEW, Volume 19, Number 1 (1985)

12 THE IDEOLOGY OF LAW

There is an extensive literature that refers variously to "the ideology of law," the "ideological dimension of law," or "legal ideology." Behind the apparent homogeneity of this writing lie diverse conceptions of ideology and even greater diversity in the way these conceptions are used. Its effects are regularly taken for granted when they should be treated as problematic, and its heuristic potential for the analysis of law is often thwarted by the vagueness and imprecision that one encounters in probing apparently sophisticated conceptualizations. "Ideology," like "dialectics," is all too often invoked as an evasion rather than a solution. If the concept of ideology is poorly used by many of those who write in the Marxist tradition, it is hardly used at all by those who approach the study of law from other perspectives. In the major texts on the sociology of law, both old and new, the concept "ideology" is noticeable by its absence. While no single concept provides a magic key to the mysteries of law, the idea of ideology is important in understanding legal life. There is no concept within the sociology of law that plays the role that is given to ideology within the Marxist tradition. Thus, the ideological analysis of law is not only significant in its own right, but it provides an instructive point of differentiation between Marxist analyses of law and mainstream sociology of law.

Perhaps the closest alternatives to "ideology" within mainstream sociology of law are the concepts "symbolic,"[2] as used by Gusfield (1963) and later by Carson (1974), and "legitimation," as used within the Weberian tradition (Weber, 1966). Neither of these alternatives has, however, either the breadth or the specificity provided by the concept "ideology." If we aspire, as I do, to break what Trubek has aptly characterized as "the stifling debate between instrumental Marxism and liberal legalism" (Trubek, 1977: 553), we must explore the potential utility of the Marxist concept "ideology," not to show the superiority of one tradition over another but to advance the explanatory power of social theory in its application to the analysis of law.

---

[2] This paper does not discuss the concept of "symbolism" further. It is, however, important to note the existence of important strands of work which, drawing on the symbolic-instrumental dichotomy, have brought the focus on the symbolic dimensions of law into increasingly close proximity with the concerns of ideology analysis. Such an exploration would require an extended discussion of such diverse authors as Foucault (1977), Ignatieff (1978), and Habermas (1976).

II. MARXISM AND IDEOLOGY

We must, at the outset, recognize that a "correct definition" of ideology cannot be discovered from a search of Marx's texts. Marx used the concept in a variety of ways. Sometimes ideology refers to all ideas, sometimes it refers only to those ideas that are deemed unscientific ("false consciousness"), and sometimes it refers to those ideas that serve the interests of dominant classes, "class beliefs" (cf. Williams, 1977: 66). Not only is the concept open in its texture, but it is also multidimensional. Nevertheless, there are a number of uses of the concept that must be eliminated because they make a definitional assumption about the relationship between "ideology" and "class."

My objective is to use the concept to explore the connection between ideas, attitudes, and beliefs, on the one hand, and economic and political interests, on the other. We can thus ignore ideology as "Ideology," which refers only to a systematic and totalized world view (*Weltanschauung*). Consistent world views may exist, but they must be treated as special or exceptional cases. Second, the idea that ideology necessarily entails some sort of "false consciousness" should also be discarded because it removes the empirically important issue of the association between ideas and interests. For similar reasons we should reject the view that ideology necessarily has a class designation or derivation. For example, the idea that "nationalism" is necessarily traceable to the interests of the "petty bourgeoisie" is empirically problematic and should be replaced by an approach that sees such connections as raising empirical rather than conceptual issues.

While the concept of ideology has often been misused in the ways we describe above, there have been important advances toward a theory of ideology in recent Marxist writing. Our next step is to identify these advances and to relate them to the analysis of law as ideology.[3]

The concept of "ideology" has played a key role for Marxist theorists who make up the "Western Marxist" tradition that

[3] To undertake this task systematically would require a thorough study of the historical development of the Marxist theory of ideology. Much of this work has already been undertaken with a greater or lesser degree of success; of particular interest is the work of the Birmingham group (Centre for Contemporary Cultural Studies, 1977), Ernesto Laclau (1977), and Larrain's wide-ranging history of ideology (1979). The decisive intervention of Althusser is to be found in his major texts (Althusser, 1969; 1971) and has been the subject of critical analysis by Hirst (1979) and McLennan (McLennan *et al.*, 1977). The impact of semiology on the theory of ideology is investigated by Coward and Ellis (1977) and Sumner (1979).

has sought to liberate Marxism from the ossification of orthodox "Marxism-Leninism." Central to this project has been the need to reformulate Marxist theory in a way that avoids the related deficiencies of "economism" and "reductionism." If social institutions and ideas are not a simple reflex of economic or class interests and yet are linked to such interests, a sophisticated concept of ideology is needed to explore such linkages in a thorough, empirically grounded manner.

It is thus no accident that the more recent development of a Marxist theory of law, a subject that had previously received little attention, should follow close on the heels of developments in Marxist theories of ideology. Law is interesting and important because it is both close to yet distinct from the state and is, at the same time, the bearer of important ideological values. Albrow characterizes the development within Marxist theory as a movement "from a Gramscian interest in politics to an Althusserian interest in ideology and finding in law a bridge between the two" (Albrow, 1981: 127).

The main thrust of the renewed concern with ideology has been directed towards elaborating a conception of ideology that plays more than the epiphenomenal or marginal role attributed to it within Marxism-Leninism. This goal reflects a political agenda that sees the need to grapple with the persistence of capitalism, while, at the same time, elaborating non-insurrectionary political strategies for socialist transformation within the advanced capitalist democracies. Theorists have realized that to do this ideology needs to be understood in its role of preserving and reproducing capitalist social and economic relations. While much of the debate has often taken an abstract and theoretical form, these real and pressing political concerns are very much present.

As an example of the recent developments in the theory of ideology, consider the use made of the concept of "relative autonomy." The term "relative autonomy" refers to the partial independence of different social elements, such as the legal, political, and ideological, both from each other and, more importantly, from the general interests of a dominant class. This concept serves the interests of the new Marxism because it acknowledges the fundamental importance of the economic base (albeit "in the last instance") while allowing the ideological realm to be treated as an arena of struggle that is not simply the reflex of economic class conflict. This places a heavy theoretical and political burden on the fragile shoulders of the concept, and despite the attractiveness of the idea of "relative autonomy" difficult theoretical problems remain. The primary problem is to achieve what Althusser (1969) described as the necessity of holding on to "both ends of the chain" at the same time; that is, to encompass both the relative autonomy of ideology (or law or state) and the determination of ideology (or law or state), in the last instance by economic relations. There are those within the Marxist tradition who argue that the concept "relative autonomy" cannot overcome such theoretical hurdles and that "there is no middle way" (Cutler *et al.*, 1977: I, 172).

Nevertheless, some real and important advances have been made during the course of the debate on ideology. These achievements can best be illustrated if we look separately at three major issues that Marxist scholars have explored with the aid of the concept of ideology.

A. *Ideology and Human Subjectivity*

A major but insufficiently recognized thrust of the Althusserian tradition was to develop a theory that could at once accommodate the traditional socio-economic concerns of Marxism and a concern for human subjectivity. While this results in some of the most difficult and opaque discussion in Marxist theory, one element is especially important for the analysis of law. The human being according to the Althusserian tradition has three "instances": as a biological being, as a "subject," and as a participant in social relations. For Althusser the "subject" is created by and through a range of different discourses. For example, political discourse produces the individual as "citizen," with its consequent images of atomized but equal citizens existing in a common relationship to the state. Legal discourse transforms both human beings and social entities; for example, corporations become "legal subjects." Legal subjects as the bearers of rights and duties are the primary constituents of the "form of law," which will figure large in my subsequent discussion. The creation of legal subjects involves the recognition of "the law" as the active "subject" that calls them into being. It is by transforming the human subject into a legal subject that law influences the way in which participants experience and perceive their relations with others. Thus, legal ideology provides a constituent of what Althusser called the "lived relation" of human actors (Althusser, 1969: 233). One important implication is that we are encouraged to view law not merely as an external mechanism of regulation but as a constituent of the way in which social relations are lived and experienced. This approach radically changes the role accorded ideology in social life. Ideology is perceived not as a form of consciousness, which is the conventional view, but as a constituent of the unconscious in which social relations are lived. Once this possibility is appreciated, we have in ideology a new and powerful tool for exploring the relationship between "the Law," legal subjects, and social relations.

B. The Determination of the Content of Ideology

Theorists have been concerned both with the generation of specific elements of ideology and with the patterning or structuring of these elements into more or less coherent and integrated systems that make it possible to employ the concept of "bourgeois legal ideology." Here my earlier rejection of the view that every ideological element has a necessary class designation is important. The class dimension of ideology is not an intrinsic property of words or concepts, but instead arises from the way in which ideological elements are combined and interrelated. Ideologies are not to be treated "as if they were political number plates worn by social classes on their backs" (Poulantzas, 1975: 202). Therborn expresses this particularly well:

> [i]deologies actually operate in a state of *disorder*. . . . ideologies operate, constantly being communicated, competing, clashing, affecting, drowning, and silencing one another in social processes of communication (Therborn, 1980: 77, 103).

Thus, an ideology is not a unitary entity. It draws its power from its ability to connect and combine diverse mental elements (concepts, ideas, etc.) into combinations that influence and structure the perception and cognition of social agents. Colin Sumner (1979) expresses something of this approach with his suggestion that ideologies act as grids which select, sort, order, and reorder the elements of thought. This view of ideology is particularly salutary in the field of legal analysis since it counsels us not to assume the coherence and consistency of legal discourse but to search out the resonances of the social, economic, and political struggles that reside behind the smooth surface of legal reasoning and judicial utterance.

The general thrust of the concern with the determination of ideology is the insistence that ideology is a social process that is realized in and through social relations. At the same time ideologies have their own distinctive characteristics, the most important of which are an internal discourse such that the elements of an ideology are not reducible to a mere reflection of economic or social relations. It is this internal dimension of an ideology that semiotics seeks to grasp through the concept of "sign" and its derivatives.

C. *Functions of Ideology*

The third important issue within the theory of ideology concerns the *functions of ideology*; attention is directed towards the role of ideology as an essential element in the process of legitimation and hence in the reproduction of the prevailing social relations. This concern is particularly pronounced in Poulantzas, who, building on Gramsci's metaphor of ideology as the "cement" of society, proposes the general thesis that: "Ideology, which slides into every level of the social structure, has the particular function of *cohesion*" (1975: 207). Poulantzas is of special significance with regard to the ideology of law because his analysis leads him to the view that juridico-political ideology is the "dominant region" within the dominant ideology within capitalist modes of production. From this he concludes that in capitalist societies law fulfills "the key function of every dominant ideology: namely, that of cementing together the social formation under the aegis of the dominant class" (1978: 88). I do not subscribe to the view that to speak of "function" is to lapse into functionalism; rather we must distinguish between function and functionalism and reject the latter. Functionalism assumes that there are necessary functions that must be fulfilled and then proceeds to search for the agency that realizes or fulfills each function. The deficiency of functionalism is that functions are reified. Their existence is assumed and all social practices and institutions must be classified in terms of them. Poulantzas' cement metaphor and his designation of the state as fulfilling "the particular function of constituting the factor of cohesion between the levels of a social formation" (1975: 44) come perilously close to functionalism. This danger can be avoided if we treat the metaphor as an hypothesis about the *effectivity* of ideology. The concept *effectivity* seeks to draw attention to the effects or results of ideology while at the same time leaving open the issue of whether or the degree to which a possible function of ideology is fulfilled. Thus, with respect to law, we should abandon any *a priori* views about its integrative or legitimating functions and treat them as open questions relating to the specific effects or consequences of legal regulation and legal ideology.

Distinguishing among these three different issues within the theory of ideology allows us to identify the significant advances that have been achieved in the recent debate. But these advances have extracted their own price. The most important price has been that in order to establish the "specificity" (distinctive characteristics not reducible to the economic base) of ideology, the Althusserian tradition posited the existence of conceptually distinct "instances" of economic, political, and ideological practices. So pervasive has this tendency been that in many texts these conceptual distinctions are assumed to represent real separations. But there is no location inhabited by ideology; there is no realm of the ideological (Jones, 1982). Nor are all social, political, and economic institutions necessarily associated with specific ideological practices. Much more helpful is Althusser's (1971) suggestion of a distinction between "sites" that "produce" ideology and those that "transmit" ideology. Certain institutions such as the media and the university are identified with the ideological realm because they both "produce" and "transmit" ideology, whereas schools, the family, sports, and the like are primarily transmitters of ideology. Applying this distinction to legal systems, we can immediately identify both the creation and dissemination of ideology and proceed to investigate the extent to which these two activities are separated.

A second deficiency within the theory of ideology is the persistence of the *reflection* metaphor, by which I mean the persistent assumption that there exists an objective social world that is "reflected" in thought and in the process is to a greater or lesser extent distorted. This metaphor is ubiquitous as a means of asserting the determination of ideology by material relations and of expressing the divergence between a "real concrete"—that is, some objective ideology-free reality—and its representation in ideology. This imports a dubious epistemology derived from naive materialism. More significantly, the metaphor has its own logic which leads to notions of ideological "distortion" or, more seriously, "inversion" of the real world. Thus, ideologies are discussed in terms of their truth or falsity, which implies that there is a social reality independent of consciousness and that thought simply corresponds to a greater or lesser extent to this given reality. The dubious nature of the implication is never confronted. While the idea of "reflection" raises the question of how ideology is determined, it does not provide any assistance in pursuing this line of inquiry. As Stuart Hall and his colleagues comment:

> As is often the case in those areas where Marxism is not yet fully developed, the simple formulae are often too simple, too reductive for our purposes. The idea for example, that, broadly speaking, legal norms and rules in a bourgeois society will reflect and support bourgeois economic relations, . . . may provide the first, basic step in such a theory, but it remains, too general, too abstract, too reductive, too sketchy (Hall *et al.*, 1978: 196).

The most important figure in the development of the theory of ideology has been Antonio Gramsci. He has profoundly influenced not only the questions asked but also the general direction of contemporary Marxist discussions. In particular, Gramsci's concern with "hegemony," the processes through which the dominance of capitalist power is secured within civil society, provides both the theoretical and political framework for the ongoing Marxist debate. The issues raised by the idea of "hegemony" go to the very heart of the problems facing the Marxist analysis of law in that this concept poses as a central issue the dialectic of coercion and consent.

The earliest Marxist writings on law, which I have characterized as the "oppositional stage," sought to combat conventional notions of the consensual character of law and strove to demonstrate its repressive or coercive character (Hunt, 1981a). In contrast, most contemporary Marxist writings on law have sought to demonstrate and explore the real significance and deep consequences of the dual character of law as coercion and as consent. Not only is this attempt to grasp and to integrate the elements of coercion and consent a central *leitmotif* of Marxist legal theory but, as I have argued elsewhere, its theorization presents major problems. Moreover, if my argument is correct, the same difficulties are encountered by the non-Marxist sociology of law (Hunt, 1981a).

III. THE IDEOLOGICAL DIMENSIONS OF LAW

A concern with the ideology of law is at the heart of all recent Marxist treatments of law. In this section, I shall examine some of this recent theoretical work in the light of the preceding discussion. I hope to show how some of the ideas advanced above have been fruitfully employed, and I shall point to a number of unproductive features that remain. There has, however, been such an explosion of Marxist, neo-Marxist, and critical theory of law over the past few years that I am forced to be selective. I will concentrate my attention primarily on four recent texts.

These are *The Politics of Law* (Kairys, 1982a), which is especially significant as the first collective presentation of the Critical Legal Studies movement; *Marxism and Law* (Beirne and Quinney, 1982), a collection that brings together some of the more important of the previously published contributions to Marxist debate on law; *Reading Ideologies* (Sumner, 1979), which is the most closely related to my concerns because it focuses on the applicability of the Marxist theory of ideology to the analysis of law; and *Marxism and Law* (Collins, 1982), which sets out to examine the total theoretical field and gives the relationship between law and ideology a crucial role in the attempt to set forth a general Marxist theory of law. As we shall see, a number of the problems that arise are common to all the texts, which in itself suggests the importance of the issues under consideration.

A. *Mystification, Distortion, and All That*

The most general feature of ideological analysis is that it starts from the proposition that there is no direct or necessary correspondence between the realm of "knowledge" and that of "the real." As I have already noted, the most pervasive embodiment of the theory of ideology in Marxism is to be found in the metaphor of "reflection." The merit of the metaphor is that it succeeds in combining two central propositions: (a) the known and the real are not identical, and (b) the real is the "object" that produces or determines the "image." The metaphor of reflection captures the most basic feature of Marx's materialist dictum: "It is not the consciousness of men that determines their being, but on the contrary their social being that determines their consciousness" (Marx, "1859 Preface"). It is thus not surprising that the metaphor of "reflection" and its derivatives are frequently invoked.

In all four of the texts under discussion a reflection theory of ideology is a dominant motif. The linguistic variants are many, but the most frequently employed are: "mirrors," "distorts," "illusion," "fantasy," "facade," "mystifies," and "reifies." The problem that I wish to highlight is that these terms are used in such a way as to imply a theory about the relationship between knowledge and its object, a taken-for-granted "social reality." Propositions such as "law distorts" and "law reflects" are used as if there were some pre-given relationship between the real and its ideological representation. The alternative I propose is that the nature of the relationship between reality and its ideological representation should be seen as "the problem," or object of analysis, without prejudgment as to the way in which the relationship can be captured or portrayed.

For an example of the limitations of reflection theory, consider the essay in Kairys' collection by Nadine Taub and Elizabeth Schneider (1982) on the role of law in the subordination of women. Taub and Schneider argue that the legal distinction between public and private reflects, in a distorted fashion, an actual distinction between the nondomestic and domestic social realms. In so doing the legal distinction functions ideologically and "camouflages the fundamental injustice of existing sexual relations" (1982: 124). This readiness to attribute causality to the legal distinction between public-private leads Taub and Schneider to ignore the question of whether this distortion results from legal ideology or from some other mechanism. For example, no consideration is given to the role of other discourses concerning the family—thus precluding, without discussion, the possibility that the law is largely passive and merely gives effect to an ideological separation between public-private that is produced elsewhere.[4] Now I do not hold any strong view about whether this is the case, but I do wish to suggest that the metaphor of reflection distracts attention from such issues and for that reason should not be invoked as if it were a conclusion.

In contrast, the essay by Peter Gabel on reification in Beirne and Quinney examines the process of legal reasoning in great detail and concludes that "reification" is a result determined by the process rather than a pre-given necessity (Gabel, 1982).[5] In the course of this analysis Gabel makes the important point that we need to distinguish between (a) the processes that create the ideological characteristics embedded

[4] For a stimulating discussion of the public-private dichotomy as it relates to family law, see the article by Frances Olsen (1983), which has the great merit, in contrast to "reflection" approaches, of isolating the complex and shifting boundary between the public and the private and, consequently, its tortuous history in legislation.

[5] In the case of reprinted papers, which occur primarily in the Beirne and Quinney collection, I cite the reprint rather than its original publication.

in the law and (b) those consequences flowing from law that have a particular ideological content. With this in mind, we can see a hitherto unrevealed distinction in the usages "mirrors," "distorts," etc., which are often used interchangeably. Some terms (e.g., mirrors, reflects, reifies) have as their primary referrent the process by which the "real" is transformed into an ideological form (see, e.g., Gabel and Feinman, 1982) while others (e.g., mystifies, illusion) focus on the results or consequences of the ideological form (see, e.g., Kennedy, 1982). Ideological analysis should separate, as distinct methodological and expository stages, the analysis of the production of legal ideology from the analysis of the effectivity of legal ideology.[6]

B. *The Form of Law*

It is generally agreed that the ideological character of law can be identified at a number of different levels. I shall specify, at least provisionally, three different levels for analysis since this allows me to explore the interrelationship among them. They are:

(a) the ideological content of concrete legal norms;
(b) the ideological content of what are conventionally referred to, most explicitly by Dworkin (1978), as "principles";
(c) the ideological content of the "form of law."

At the core of any attempt to understand ideology is the question of its material determination. Distinguishing these levels allows us to address the important question of whether legal ideology is primarily the resultant of one of them. There is an unexplored and perhaps unconscious polarization in the texts under consideration. It is possible to identify two broadly distinguishable positions.

The first I call *Concrete Determination.* This position argues that the ideological content of law is largely manifest in the content of specific laws, whether judicial rules or specific legislative enactments. This position emphasizes the role of "struggle" in the formation of legal ideology.

---

[6] Note that the reflection theory of ideology is not the only one available within the Marxist tradition. Another version is that derived from Marx's application in *Capital* of the essence/appearance distinction. We should be cautious about assuming a simple continuity between reflection theory and essence/appearance theory. Frequently, these two approaches are conflated in the texts under consideration. The further exploration of the ideological dimension of law requires attention to the issue of Marxist epistemology and the need to challenge the simple empiricist model of both reflection and essence/appearance that characterizes much of the recent discussion of the ideology of law (Hindess, 1977; Cutler *et al.*, 1977).

The second I call *Form Determination*. This perspective sees in the form of law the key to law's ideological role. The concrete level gives effect to the necessary and inescapably general ideological content inscribed in the form of law.

Frequently, the position taken by an author arises naturally from the object of analysis: where the object of analysis is concrete, as with a specific statute or series of cases, the discussion tends to focus on concrete determination (Kairys, 1982b; Horwitz, 1982; Tushnet, 1982; Klare, 1982a; Freeman, 1982). Where the interest is at a more general theoretical level, form determination comes to the fore (Gabel and Feinman, 1982; Picciotto, 1982; Poulantzas, 1978; Rifkin, 1982). But this is not a simple empirical versus theoretical divide; some of the most powerful work operates at all three levels (Klare, 1982b; Hay, 1982).

The distinction among the three levels of analysis not only involves important theoretical questions, but it is also related to political differences and debates. Marxists perennially argue over the extent to which law can be harnessed and mobilized to the advantage of subordinate classes or groups, a question that Collins appropriately calls "the radical predicament" (Collins, 1982: Ch. 6). Those who give priority to form analysis typically deny that the bourgeois form of law can contribute much, apart from defense, to struggles against the capitalist order. As Mark Tushnet puts it, the form of law "serves as an additional barrier to the organisation of the under-dog to upset existing social arrangements" (Tushnet, 1977: 102). On the other hand, those who focus their attention on concrete determination tend to see particular legal outcomes as the results of struggles that depend on the balance of forces involved. This issue is at the heart of the important current controversies concerning the "politics of law." There is significant disagreement among "progressives" about the extent to which struggles over the creation and enforcement of legal rights are politically significant and potentially worthwhile. These questions are currently being raised in the internal debates within the Conference on Critical Legal Studies (Hutchinson and Monahan, 1984; Munger and Seron, 1983; Sparer, 1984; Trubek, 1984), and they continue to be debated in Britain under the insistent prodding of E.P. Thompson (1975; 1980; see also Adlam, 1981; Hunt, 1981b).

Leaving aside these broader political questions, I want to focus attention on questions concerning the form of law. An emphasis on the form of law is attractive in that it provides an escape route from the difficulties of instrumentalist versions of

Marxist theory, which focus on the law as an instrument of the will of the dominant class. The form of law is seen not as a manifestation of the will of a dominant class but as a necessary and inevitable consequence of the very nature of capitalist economic relations. Hugh Collins (1982) suggests that there exist economistic and class instrumentalist versions of the theory. In my view both the "economistic" and "instrumentalist" trends are inherent within classical Marxism, and they come to the fore with the ossification of orthodox Marxism. The common problem of both variants is that of "reductionism"; the difference is that class instrumentalism merely adds another step in the reductive logic since class relations are treated as directly derivable from and so reducible to economic relations.

The discussion of the form of law in recent Marxist literature is heavily influenced by the renewed interest in the writing of the early Soviet jurist Evgeny Pashukanis (Beirne and Sharlet, 1980). Pashukanis' influence has focused discussion on the question of whether a *single* form of law is characteristic of capitalist society (cf. Balbus, 1977; Redhead, 1978; Hirst, 1979; Cotterell, 1980; 1981; Warrington, 1981; Picciotto, 1982). This discussion has typically proceeded at a high level of abstraction, concerning itself with the general and abstract capitalist mode of production rather than with the situation in actual capitalist societies. Analysis at this level views capitalism as a simple totality of exchange relations and leads to the identification of a single form of law, the bourgeois legal form.

If, however, the level of analysis is changed and we focus our attention on concrete social formations (that is, historically given societies), we need to identify more than a single form of law. Capitalism has undergone massive changes and development. It exists within widely different political and state structures, and its internationalization has profoundly affected the relations among nation states. While mainstream sociology of law has for some time been concerned with the phenomenon of legal pluralism (Galanter, 1981), Marxist writers have only more recently paid serious attention to this question (Fitzpatrick, 1983). As David Sugarman argues, studies of the contribution of law to the development of capitalism, from Weber (1966) through E.P. Thompson (1975), Atiyah (1979), Horwitz (1977), and others, can only lead to the conclusion that

> there was no single "capitalist" form of law—whether we call it contractual, commodity form or absolute private property. It is more accurate to view each as one of several *forms* of capitalist law which co-existed over long periods, complementing and conflicting with one another (Sugarman, 1983: 256).

What remains to be done is to identify systematically the various forms of law and to study the general conditions affecting their interaction.

However, the general trend in the texts we are treating as representative of recent critical and Marxist scholarship is either to assume a simple, single form of law or to slip between the singular and plural. The apparently sophisticated concept "the form of law" tends to be invoked as a rhetorical device that points to some underlying uniformity of legal phenomena that remains unexplored. When the form of law is identified, it is by reference to general values or what Balbus calls "abstract universals" (Balbus, 1977: 580). But in listing abstract universals, the distinction between form and content becomes blurred. If the concept of "legal form" or "forms of law" is to advance our understanding of the relationship between law and economy, there is an urgent need for conceptual clarification.

My proposals in this regard are modest. I suggest that when we restrict the concept "form of law" at a high level of abstraction to denote the logically necessary characteristics of a legal order within a specified economic or political order, this makes it possible and, indeed, necessary to address the co-existence of forms of law when analyzing specific societies. With regard to law in capitalist societies, the form of law is characterized by (i) "reification" (separation of the juridico-political realms from the economic), (ii) legal subjectivity (separation of legal status from political or economic status), and (iii) the legal subject (a human or organizational entity vested with legal rights) (Hirst, 1979).

I also believe that the form of law has no *necessary* ideological characteristic or content. Instead, certain ideological values have, to borrow Weber's idea, an elective affinity or homologous relationship to the legal form. Hence, values such as individualism, equality, and private property become universal and preponderant values under capitalism and come to function as if they were the form of law itself. The close association between the concept of law and these values means that these values come to legitimate the existing forms of social relationships. Thus, the legitimating potential of law is shared or taken over by values the law only contingently embraces.

I have not included in my definition of "the form of law" the much emphasized element of "formalism." I am uncertain whether formalism inheres in the form of law or is an ideological value preponderantly associated with law in capitalist society. This uncertainty derives from my reflections on Horwitz's work. What Horwitz brings out most powerfully is the essentially contested character of formalism, a contest between impersonal Weberian legal rationality and the class facilitative character of the transformation of American law (Horwitz, 1975; 1977).

Treating legal formalism as a problematic feature of the legal form has the virtues of not universalizing the ideological values most characteristic of law in capitalist society and of directing attention to struggles that surround all ideological elements. This approach reminds us that the most pervasive values that may be subsumed under the label "ideological forms of law" (universality, certainty, etc.) are subject to contradiction and interact in complex ways in the course of legal disputes. My approach alsc reflects reservations I have about following the realist methodology of starting with legal values and subsequently comparing them to "reality." The viability of this position depends on the questionable assumption that legal values have an existence independent of the concrete legal rules in which they are embedded.

The foregoing analysis of the form of law throws into relief an important problem which I wish to mention but do not have the space here to pursue. The "discovery" of the ideological dimension of law by the Marxist and critical traditions tends towards a conceptualization of law itself as an *ideological phenomenon*. The danger is obvious: the materiality of the law—that is to say, law's real impact on real people and real relations—tends to be ignored. In seeking to establish the extent to which all social practices are suffused by ideology, we must not lose sight, to paraphrase Marx, of "the dull compulsion" of legal regulation, particularly in the spheres where law operates relatively unproblematically to give effect to the existing forms of social, economic, and political relations. If we are to grapple with real world problems, we must not retreat into idealistic theories of ideological determination.

C. *The Function and Effectivity of Legal Ideology*

One of the most distinctive features of the contemporary Marxist and critical trends is the powerful historical scholarship which has been its most notable achievement to date. In Britain there has been the major impact of the project that produced *Whigs and Hunters* and *Albion's Fatal Tree* (Thompson, 1975; Hay *et al.*, 1975) and *Policing the Crisis*, a "contemporary history" study of the "mugging crisis" of 1972-73 (Hall *et al.*, 1978). The latter work is of particular interest because of its self-conscious attempt to integrate theoretical and historical analysis. And in the United States there has been a similar interest in revisionist legal history, spearheaded by Morton Horwitz. These critical legal histories share a common concern with the effectivity of legal ideology as it operates in conjunction with the material and coercive instrumentality of law. Douglas Hay's powerful analysis of the combined impact of "justice," "terror," and "mercy" is a good example of work that focuses on this conjunction (Hay, 1982).

The two most important strands present in this tradition are best characterized by the distinction between "function" and "effectivity." Attention to "function" yields formulations of a general theoretical character about the role of legal ideology at the level of either the abstract modes of production (e.g., Althusser's "ideology secures the reproduction of the social relations of production," 1971: 141) or, more concretely, with respect to historical epochs (e.g., Poulantzas' "juridical ideology written into law becomes the dominant area of ideology in a mode of production in which ideology no longer plays the dominant role," 1978: 88). A concern for "effectivity," on the other hand, leads to a focus on the causal role of legal ideology in specific historical circumstances; e.g., Klare's (1982a) study of the influence of judicial ideology on the formation of labor relations in the U.S.A. before World War II.

The distinction between "function" and "effectivity" rarely appears in pure form. Instead, we frequently find either an oscillation between these foci of inquiry or a conflation of the two levels. This is unfortunate. In the analysis of legal ideology one must keep firmly in mind the different *levels of abstraction* of these related but distinguishable perspectives. Thus, it is perfectly proper to treat a possible function of legal ideology as an hypothesis to be evaluated through concrete historical investigation and discarded, amended, or qualified in the movement from one level of abstraction to another. It is a mistake, however, to treat a possible function of law as given or proven and to use history to "reveal" the operation of this essential or assumed function. It is equally unacceptable to arrive through concrete historical analysis at a conclusion concerning the effectivity of legal ideology and then to pronounce this a "function" fulfilled by law during a particular historical epoch.

As an illustration of the second of these questionable procedures, consider E.P. Thompson's thesis that "the rule of law itself, the imposing of effective inhibitions upon power and the defence of the citizen from power's all-intrusive claims, seems to me to be an unqualified human good" (Thompson, 1975: 266). Thompson arrives at this conclusion from his compelling study of "The Black Act" of 1723. The Act itself and its enforcement are interpreted as a conflict between the "new" landowning Whig gentry and the customary rights of farmers and forest-dwellers. Thompson demonstrates that in the period after the 1688 constitutional "revolution," when the structures and supports for the legal order were still weak, the rule of law had a significant impact on the manner in which this draconian legislation was enforced. But Thompson moves, without further argument, from his historically specific study to a generalization about the function of legal ideology in modern capitalist society.[7] I have considerable sympathy with Thompson's insistence on the contemporary significance of the rule of law, but not with the means by which he arrives at it, for Thompson ignores important differences in levels of analysis.

Having clarified the different levels of analysis involved in the distinction between "function" and "effectivity," we need to consider the risks inherent in functionalist modes of analysis. One such danger is the temptation to lapse into a naive instrumentalism which posits a single dominating function expressed, for example, in theses such as "law reproduces the social relations of capitalist society" or "law legitimates capitalist social relations." Such single function theses are themselves attributable to the ideological reification of law. In such theories law is presented as "the Law" and is discussed as if it were a totally coherent and integrated process. A valuable corrective against tendencies to see law in this way is found in modern Marxist and critical legal theory: the idea of "contradiction." This concept focuses attention on the limits of

[7] The historical studies in the two collections of texts are peppered with less serious and less controversial examples. Genovese in his otherwise very convincing account of the role of law in the slave states asserts, as a given, the hegemonic function of law (Genovese, 1982). In so doing he comes perilously close to the functionalist circle of specifying a necessary function and then showing it revealed in practice. Janet Rifkin (1982), in advancing an abstract, necessary connection between law as hegemonic ideology and the ideology of patriarchy, similarly builds an unnecessarily functionalist account of the rule of law in perpetuating male dominance.

doctrinal coherence and on the variable operation of different legal procedures and institutions.

One of the most important contributions of radical legal historiography has been to breathe life and substance into the abstract category of "contradiction." At the outset this enterprise involves distinguishing between *internal* and *external* contradictions. The shift to a more empirical level of analysis, one of the hallmarks of the Critical Legal Studies movement, has allowed scholars to highlight the contradictory character of legal development; and it has helped them to avoid the pitfalls of instrumentalism. There is, however, a tendency within critical legal studies to focus one-sidedly on either internal or external contradictions. Thus, some work that examines doctrinal development stresses its internal incoherence while another strand emphasizes contradictions arising from the interplay of classes, class fractions, and other social and political forces as they struggle over the creation and practice of law. Both strands of research could be improved if they worked with a more systematic model of internal and external contradictions.

This is not the place to develop such a model, but I want to mention three considerations. First, with respect to both internal and external contradictions different "levels" need to be distinguished. Looking at internal contradictions, for example, we can distinguish among: (a) juridical reasoning and its ideological forms, (b) the ideologies embodied in the policy aspects of legal doctrine, (c) different legal institutions (e.g., types of courts), and (d) the professional ideologies of different kinds of legal actors. Such distinctions involve no profound theoretical insights, but they do provide a checklist of the sources and forces involved in the ideological determination of law. Second, the internal and external dimensions of legal ideology are not watertight compartments, and the interface between the two is a significant location of contradiction. Models of internal and external contradictions must take this into account and allow for some permeability. Finally, I would stress the practical significance for intervention in the politics of law of a careful analysis of contradictions since these pinpoint areas in which the subordinate classes have their greatest potential for effecting change. This speaks to the political importance of the model-building enterprise rather than to how it should be done.

Thinking about contradictions highlights problems with two widespread features of contemporary Marxist writings.

The first is a tendency to overemphasize the independence or autonomy of the internal ideology of law. A clear example is found in Karl Klare's conclusion from his study of the Wagner Act that law-making because of the impersonal, antiparticipatory, suprahistorical forms of thought and procedures involved "is governed by the process of alienation" (1982a: 168). This analysis does not give due weight to the pressures and contradictions that constantly press upon the judicial process and disrupt the calm of formal judicial logic in ways that Klare's substantive analysis demonstrates. I also question the conclusions that Klare draws from this line of argument. His preferred alternative requires "a quest for justice in each concrete historical setting" and the abolition of the rule of law (1982a: 168). In my view the call for individualized justice is not self-evidently a progressive demand. I remain convinced that the most important lesson for legal politics that may be drawn from our experience of "actual socialism" in the Soviet Union and other states is the necessity of retaining formalized and entrenched rights, the core of the rule of law, to protect citizens and social institutions against political usurpation by the state and the bureaucracy.

The second feature of the recent critical literature that my analysis calls into question is what I see as an overemphasis on the autonomy of the general ideological function of law, variously expressed by the legitimating or hegemonic function. Let me take as my example Colin Sumner. His analysis is in many respects parallel to the position I have advanced, but I believe he overstates the general function of legal ideology. "The Law," he argues,

> lies hidden beneath a heavy shroud of discourse, ritual and magic which proclaim the Wisdom and Justice of the Law. . . . Once this shroud is torn into tatters that hegemonic bloc of classes and class fractions which sustain the rule of capital is in trouble because inequality and domination can *only* be justified mystically and that is precisely the ideological function of law (Sumner, 1979: 277; emphasis added).

Now if the ideology of "The Law" is as effective as Sumner suggests, it is difficult to imagine how this shroud could ever be "torn into tatters"; this is a case of pure verbal militancy. More important is the contention that legal ideology provides the *primary* justification for inequality and domination. This is, in my view, quite simply wrong. Capitalist systems employ a wide range of ideological justifications which are used (a) differentially over time and (b) in different combinations.

These include such important legitimating ideas as "economic efficiency," "freedom," "democracy," and "national interest." The significance of legal ideology lies in its articulation along with other nonlegal ideological bases of legitimation. This point is made by Sumner but then seemingly forgotten.

> . . .The effectiveness of law as an ideological force, as a means toward ruling class hegemony, depends upon its ideological encapsulation of a consensus *constructed outside itself* in other economic, political and cultural practices (Sumner 1979: 264; emphasis added).

This point is nicely illustrated in *Policing the Crisis* (Hall *et al.*, 1978). The authors show that it was the combination of legal ideology with other elements, including appeals to moral consensus, the nation, and ethnicity, that made the shift to a more authoritarian mode of governance possible. While it is appropriate to stress the importance of legal ideology in contemporary capitalism, we must avoid any tendency to think that law is the only structure other than naked violence that props up the capitalist social order. It follows that our analysis of legal ideology, and its relationship to the production and reproduction of hegemony, must pay close attention to the way legal ideology is articulated in conjunction with economic, political, and cultural ideologies.

IV. CONCLUSION

Martin Albrow in a perceptive but critical review of recent Marxist texts on law expressed doubt as to whether "a general critique of law as ideology can lead into the scientific study of social relations underpinning and generating law, i.e., the sociology of law" (Albrow, 1981: 127). I hope that the above discussion has gone some way to demonstrate that Albrow is both right and wrong. He is right in castigating a "*general* critique of law as ideology"; but he is wrong in suggesting that the investigation of legal ideology cannot contribute substantially to the sociology of law.

Ideology is and will remain a difficult, slippery, and ambiguous concept, and there is little to be gained by searching for a "better" definition. Problems cannot be avoided, for ideology involves issues that go to the heart of the puzzling interrelationship between human subjectivity and social action. Yet, handled with care, the concept "ideology" provides an indispensable and irreplaceable tool of analysis.

If the potential utility of the concept is to be realized, it is necessary that we attend closely to two separate but related sets of distinctions. The first is between the concrete particular and the concrete totality. The transition from one to the other is not a movement from micro to macro levels. This can be illustrated by taking, for example, the methodology involved in the study of a piece of legislation. The concrete particular focuses attention on the immediate or proximate influences, for example, doctrinal developments in that area of law, the particular "problem" addressed by the legislators, or the internal dynamics of the commission or inquiry proposing legislative action. The concrete totality retains the focus upon the legislation itself but seeks to situate that process in the context of wider economic, social, or political determinants. Understanding the relationship between the particular and the totality requires attention to the existence of distinct levels within the legal framework. We need to distinguish, for example, between the ideological elements present in the substance of the legislation, the legal form in which legislation is cast, and the way in which the form and substance of the law relate to the dominant ideological features of the legal system. These levels within the legal system are in turn related to the different levels of social relations, which means that the next step is to investigate the connections between "legal relations," on one hand, and "social relations," on the other. This involves turning our attention from the specific sets of social relations affected by the projected legislation to broader social forces rooted in economic, political, and other practices and to institutions that affect the creation and application of the legislation.

The second set of distinctions that must be maintained is between more abstract and more concrete conceptualizations. The need to distinguish between levels of abstraction is a theme found both in Marx's own methodological writings (Carver, 1975) and in the recent methodological debate (Echeverra, 1978; Sayer, 1979). What follows from this distinction is that concepts must be appropriate to different levels of abstraction. This implies that the unitary conceptions of the "form of law" derived from an abstract conception of the commodity relation are poorly suited to the analysis of the "forms of law" within historically specific legal systems. More generally, when the object of investigation is a specific legal system, more concrete concepts are needed than those that can be derived from an examination of the relationship among economic, political, and ideological practices at the abstract level of "the capitalist mode of production."

The implications of these two sets of distinctions underline one general theme of this paper: namely, that the ideological analysis of law must be understood as operating at a number of different levels, and that these different levels are both conceptual and empirical.

Colin Sumner suggests a distinction between "ideology" as basic or simple elements and "ideological formations" as complex systematizations of ideologies (Sumner, 1979: 20). I suggest that we can improve upon this scheme if we define "ideological elements" as the constituents of any text or speech act (for example, a legal norm or judicial pronouncement) but depart from Sumner by insisting that these elements are far from "basic" or "simple." Despite their apparent protean quality they involve already complex determinations. Ideology has no primary units or building blocks, for concepts do not themselves have any necessary ideological content; this is only acquired as they are employed in specific discourses. From this it follows that no word, however sensitive and emotive its connotations, has any necessary class content or implication; "equality," "fairness," "democracy," and the other key verbal labels only acquire ideological characteristics in their use.

I would retain Sumner's term "ideological formation" for those phenomena that link different ideological elements. This use allows for inconsistencies and tensions within legal discourse but does not assume any necessary systematization. In a legal system the degree of systematization is an issue for empirical inquiry. Additionally, I suggest the term "ideological form of law" to designate configurations of ideological elements where there has been conscious systematization.

The distinctions that the three concepts defined above allow have a significance with regard to legal phenomena which we can illustrate by contrasting a simple conversation with the judgment of an appellate court. While the former will consist of "elements of ideology," the appellate judgment may either involve an "ideological formation" linking discrete elements or may achieve a more rigorous systematization as "an ideological form of law." This makes the "reading" of legal ideology more complex. In my view it restricts the applicability of semiotic analysis, with its emphasis on discourses reducible to primary units of "signs," because in judicial discourse there is already present a more complex structure derived from the modes of legal reasoning.

The second implication of my classification of legal ideology is that we must be wary of assuming a single function derived from an analysis of the form of law at a high level of abstraction. This means that we should not uncritically accept as proven conceptions of the legal order that seek to identify it in essence as a locus of such phenomena as "mystification," "legitimation," or "alienation." Rather, it is likely that research will disclose a considerable degree of variation in the function and effectivity of different types of legal practice.

The advance of Marxist and critical analyses of law which has been characterized by a special interest in ideological analysis has had a dual impetus. On the one hand, there has been a growing dissatisfaction with the methods and results of traditional legal scholarship and education. On the other hand, there has been a growing consciousness of the need to overcome the limitations and weaknesses of instrumentalist versions of Marxist theory. But the invocation of the concept "ideology" has in its turn necessitated a deepening awareness of both the pitfalls and potential of ideological analysis. This essay has been directed to an exploration of some problems posed by the use of this concept and to advancing some suggestions for the further development of ideological analysis. In it I have tried to stress the need for a greater theoretical self-consciousness in employing the concept of ideology and at the same time to underline the general shift in critical and Marxist studies towards a more concrete historical and empirical analysis of law.

Finally, to avoid any possible misunderstanding of the nature of my current project, I should acknowledge the importance of issues that I have not discussed. I have had nothing to say about the important questions associated with the investigation of the material or social determination of law and legal relations. Nor have I concerned myself with the other side of the same problem: the extent to which law and legal regulation are themselves constitutive of social and economic relations. The omission of these questions should not be read as denying their importance in the analysis of law. The issues involved in the harnessing of the concept "ideology" to the analysis of law are themselves of sufficient importance to merit the specific focus of this essay.

REFERENCES

ADLAM, Diana (ed.) (1981) *Law, Politics and Justice: Politics and Power*, 4. London: Routledge & Kegan Paul.

ALBROW, Martin (1981) ". . . law, ideology, law, ideology, law, ideology . . . sociology?" 32 *British Journal of Sociology* 127.
ALTHUSSER, Louis (1969) *For Marx*. Harmondsworth: Penguin.
——— (1971) "Ideology and the Ideological State Apparatuses," in *Lenin and Philosophy*. London: New Left Books.
ATIYAH, Patrick (1979) *The Rise and Fall of Freedom of Contract*. Oxford: Clarendon Press.
BALBUS, Isaac (1977) "Commodity Form and Legal Form: An Essay on the 'Relative Autonomy' of the Law," 11 *Law & Society Review* 571.
BEIRNE, Piers and Richard QUINNEY (eds.) (1982) *Marxism and Law*. New York: John Wiley & Sons.
BEIRNE, Piers and Robert SHARLET (eds.) (1980) *Pashukanis: Selected Writings on Marxism and Law*. London: Academic Press.
CARSON, W.G. (1974) "Symbolic and Instrumental Dimensions of Early Factory Legislation," in R. Hood (ed.), *Crime, Criminology and Public Policy*. London: Heinemann.
CARVER, Terrell (1975) *Karl Marx: Texts on Method*. Oxford: Blackwell.
CENTRE FOR CONTEMPORARY CULTURAL STUDIES (1977) *On Ideology*. Birmingham: CCCS.
COLLINS, Hugh (1982) *Marxism and Law*. Oxford: Clarendon Press.
COTTERELL, Roger (1980) "Review of Beirne and Sharlet 'Pashukanis: Selected Writings on Marxism and Law'," 7 *British Journal of Law & Society* 317.
——— (1981) "Conceptualizing Law: Problems and Prospects of Contemporary Legal Theory," 10 *Economy & Society* 348.
COWARD, Rosalind and John ELLIS (1977) *Language and Materialism: Developments in Semiology and the Theory of the Subject*. London: Routledge & Kegan Paul.
CUTLER, Antony, Barry HINDESS, Paul HIRST and Attar HUSSAIN (1977) *Marx's 'Capital' and Capitalism Today*. London: Routledge & Kegan Paul.
DWORKIN, Ronald (1978) *Taking Rights Seriously*. London: Duckworth.
ECHEVERRA, Rafael (1978) "Critique of Marx's *1857 Introduction*," 7 *Economy & Society* 333.
FITZPATRICK, Peter (1983) "Marxism and Legal Pluralism," 1 *Australian Journal of Law & Society* 45.
FOUCAULT, Michel (1977) *Discipline & Punish: The Birth of the Prison*. London: Allen Lane.
FREEMAN, Alan (1982) "Legitimizing Racial Discrimination Through Antidiscrimination Law," in P. Beirne and R. Quinney (eds.), *Marxism and Law*. New York: John Wiley & Sons.
GABEL, Peter (1982) "Reification in Legal Reasoning," in P. Beirne and R. Quinney (eds.), *Marxism and Law*. New York: John Wiley & Sons.
GABEL, Peter and Jay FEINMAN (1982) "Contract Law as Ideology," in D. Kairys (ed.), *The Politics of Law: A Progressive Critique*. New York: Pantheon.
GALANTER, Marc (1981) "Justice in Many Rooms: Private Ordering and Indigenous Law," 19 *Journal of Legal Pluralism* 1.
GENOVESE, Eugene (1982) "The Hegemonic Function of Law," in P. Beirne and R. Quinney (eds.), *Marxism and Law*. New York: John Wiley & Sons.
GUSFIELD, Joseph (1963) *Symbolic Crusade: Status Politics and the American Temperance Movement*. Urbana: University of Illinois Press.
HABERMAS, Jürgen (1976) *Legitimation Crisis*. London: Heinemann.
HALL, Stuart, Chas CRITCHER, Tony JEFFERSON, John CLARKE and Brian ROBERTS (1978) *Policing the Crisis: Mugging, the State and Law and Order*. London: Macmillan.
HAY, Douglas (1982) "Property, Authority and the Criminal Law," in P. Beirne and R. Quinney (eds.), *Marxism and Law*. New York: John Wiley & Sons.
HAY, Douglas, Peter LINEBAUGH, John RULE, Edward THOMPSON and Cal WINSLOW (1975) *Albion's Fatal Tree: Crime & Society in Eighteenth-Century England*. Harmondsworth: Penguin.

36 THE IDEOLOGY OF LAW

HINDESS, Barry (1977) *Philosophy and Methodology in the Social Sciences.* Brighton: Harvester.

HIRST, Paul (1979) *On Law and Ideology.* London: Macmillan.

HORWITZ, Morton (1975) "The Rise of Legal Formalism," 19 *American Journal of Legal History* 251.

——— (1977) *The Transformation of American Law 1780-1860.* Cambridge, MA: Harvard University Press.

——— (1982) "The Doctrine of Objective Causation," in D. Kairys (ed.), *The Politics of Law: A Progressive Critique.* New York: Pantheon.

HUNT, Alan (1981a) "Dichotomy and Contradiction in the Sociology of Law," 8 *British Journal of Law and Society* 47; and P. Beirne and R. Quinney (eds.), *Marxism and Law.* New York: John Wiley & Sons.

——— (1981b) "The Politics of Law & Justice," in D. Adlam (ed.), *Law, Politics and Justice: Politics and Power,* 4. London: Routledge & Kegan Paul.

——— (1983) "Marxist Legal Theory and Legal Positivism," 46 *Modern Law Review* 236.

HUTCHINSON, Alan and Patrick MONAHAN (1984) "Law, Politics and the Critical Legal Scholars: The Unfolding Drama of American Legal Thought," 36 *Stanford Law Review* 199.

IGNATIEFF, Michael (1978) *A Just Measure of Pain: The Penitentiary in the Industrial Revolution, 1750-1850.* New York: Pantheon.

JONES, Kelvin (1982) *Law and Economy: The Legal Regulation of Corporate Capital.* London and New York: Academic Press.

KAIRYS, David (ed.) (1982a) *The Politics of Law: A Progressive Critique.* New York: Pantheon.

——— (1982b) "Freedom of Speech," in D. Kairys (ed.), *The Politics of Law: A Progressive Critique.* New York: Pantheon.

KENNEDY, Duncan (1982) "Legal Education as Training for Hierarchy," in D. Kairys (ed.), *The Politics of Law: A Progressive Critique.* New York: Pantheon.

KLARE, Karl (1982a) "Judicial Deradicalization of the Wagner Act and the Origins of Modern Legal Consciousness 1937-1941," in P. Beirne and R. Quinney (eds.), *Marxism and Law.* New York: John Wiley & Sons.

——— (1982b) "Critical Theory and Labor Relations Law," in D. Kairys (ed.), *The Politics of Law: A Progressive Critique.* New York: Pantheon.

LACLAU, Ernesto (1977) *Politics and Ideology in Marxist Theory.* London: New Left Books.

LARRAIN, Jorge (1979) *The Concept of Ideology.* London: Hutchinson.

McLENNAN, Gregor, Victor MOLINA and Roy PETERS (1977) "Althusser's Theory of Ideology," in Centre for Contemporary Cultural Studies, *On Ideology.* Birmingham: CCCS.

MUNGER, Frank and Carol SERON (1983) "Critical Legal Studies versus Critical Legal Theory." Mimeo.

OLSEN, Frances (1983) "The Family and the Market," 96 *Harvard Law Review* 1497.

PICCIOTTO, Sol (1982) "The Theory of the State, Class Struggle and the Rule of Law," in P. Beirne and R. Quinney (eds.), *Marxism and Law.* New York: John Wiley & Sons.

POULANTZAS, Nicos (1975) *Political Power and Social Classes.* London: New Left Books.

——— (1978) *State, Power, Socialism.* London: New Left Books.

REDHEAD, Steve (1978) "The Discrete Charm of Bourgeois Law," 9 *Critique* 113.

RIFKIN, Janet (1982) "Toward a Theory of Law and Patriarchy," in P. Beirne and R. Quinney (eds.), *Marxism and Law.* New York: John Wiley & Sons.

SAYER, Derek (1979) *Marx's Method: Science, Ideology and Critique in 'Capital'.* Brighton: Harvester.

SPARER, Ed (1984) "Fundamental Human Rights, Legal Entitlements and the Social Struggle: A Friendly Critique of the Critical Legal Studies Movement," 36 *Stanford Law Review* 509.

SUGARMAN, David (ed.) (1983) *Legality, Ideology and the State.* London and New York: Academic Press.

SUMNER, Colin (1979) *Reading Ideologies: An Investigation into the Marxist Theory of Ideology and Law*. London: Academic Press.

TAUB, Nadine and Elizabeth SCHNEIDER (1982) "Perspectives on Women's Subordination and the Rule of Law," in D. Kairys (ed.), *The Politics of Law: A Progressive Critique*. New York: Pantheon.

THERBORN, Göran (1980) *The Ideology of Power and the Power of Ideology*. London: New Left Books.

THOMPSON, Edward P. (1975) *Whigs and Hunters: The Origin of the Black Act*. London: Penguin and New York: Pantheon.

——— (1980) *Writing by Candlelight*. London: Merlin.

TRUBEK, David (1977) "Complexity and Contradiction in the Legal Order: Balbus and the Challenge of Critical Social Thought about Law," 11 *Law & Society Review* 529.

——— (1984) "Where the Action Is: Critical Legal Studies and Empiricism," 36 *Stanford Law Review* 575.

TUSHNET, Mark (1977) "Perspectives on the Development of American Law: A Critical Review of Friedman's *A History of American Law*," 1977 *Wisconsin Law Review* 81.

——— (1982) "Corporations and Free Speech," in D. Kairys (ed.), *The Politics of Law: A Progressive Critique*. New York: Pantheon.

WARRINGTON, Ronnie (1981) "Pashukanis and the Commodity Form Theory," 9 *International Journal of Sociology of Law* 1.

WEBER, Max (1966) *Max Weber on Law in Economy and Society*, ed. Max Rheinstein. Cambridge, MA: Harvard University Press.

WILLIAMS, Raymond (1977) *Marxism and Literature*. Oxford: Oxford University Press.

[24]

THE PLACE OF LAW IN THE MARXIAN STRUCTURE-SUPERSTRUCTURE ARCHETYPE

ALAN STONE*

Law occupies a critical place in a Marxist theory of society. Yet Marx and Engels did not provide a coherent and detailed discussion of law. Subsequent writers in the Marxist tradition have either developed simplistic versions of the unsustainable thesis that the capitalist class dominates the legal apparatus in a capitalist society, or they have virtually abandoned Marxism as a framework for analysis of the law. This paper examines leading texts of Marx and Engels and employs them to provide the outlines of a plausible Marxist theory of law that can embrace the rich complexity of legal activity in a modern capitalist society.

I. INTRODUCTION

Law was clearly a subject of interest for Marx and Engels, as an excellent collection of their writings on the subject attests (Cain and Hunt, 1979). Yet while they devoted considerable attention to particular laws that were the focus of intense political debates (such as the English 1834 Poor Law Amendment and the Corn Laws) and mentioned law in discussions of the structure (or base) superstructure dichotomy, they provide no comprehensive discussion of law within the context of historical materialism. The legal system is only addressed as part of more general analyses of the movement of history and the economy's interface with society (Marx, 1911; Marx and Engels, 1976). Their statements are often only a few sentences long and raise more questions than they answer.

Nevertheless, many writers within the Marxian tradition have sought to construct a coherent theory of law's place within the capitalist system. Renner (1949) made the first major attempt in 1904, but the theorist whose work is widely held to be the most brilliant and imaginative was Pashukanis (1978),

* I want to thank Richard Lempert, the *Law & Society Review*'s anonymous reviewers, my colleagues Bob Carp and Tom Dumm, Josh Cohen (M.I.T.) and, especially, Joel Rogers (Rutgers) for their invaluable criticisms and suggestions.

once the Soviet Union's leading legal theoretician. Pashukanis' principal work on law was published in 1924, but it fell out of fashion in the Soviet Union (Pashukanis himself was killed in the Stalinist purges of 1937) and was not rediscovered until the 1970s, this time by Western Marxists and others outside the Marxist tradition. Even before Pashukanis' rediscovery, however, Western Marxists had begun to focus on the possibility of developing a Marxist theory of law. This interest is manifest in an outpouring of recent scholarship. Like any corpus of work, the more recent efforts range from the shoddy to the first-rate. In the latter category one would clearly include the efforts of Collins (1982), Fraser (1976; 1978), and Tushnet (1978; 1983).

As different as the cited examples are, they share a disdain for the simple (if not simple-minded) view that law is nothing more than a capitalist confidence game designed solely to cover up the exploitation of the masses. That simplistic perspective characterizes the worst work, which develops the image of an instrumentalist criminal law used by an elite to subjugate the masses. We may readily dispose of this perspective. First, the criminal justice system is in large measure mobilized by and serves the needs of ordinary people who suffer from crime. Second, the criminal law is far less important to the maintenance and functioning of the capitalist social order than parts of the civil law. As Sparks succinctly observed, criminal law is important "at the margins of social life; . . . in day-to-day affairs it is not at all that important to the maintenance of late industrial capitalism's social order. . . . the most generally useful laws are likely to be the ones that define ownership and control" (Sparks, 1980: 159). In what follows, I critically review some of the more important Marxist expositions of law and then set forth my own additional contribution. But initially it is important to note what can and cannot be expected of a Marxist theory of law.

II. MARXIST THEORY

A Marxist theory of law cannot be expected to yield specific predictions about such mundane things as the content of specific legal rules or whether, where, or when specific laws will be enacted.[1] The propositions underlying Marxism are too

[1] For example, consider *Swift v. Tyson*, one of the most important American cases on commercial law. The Supreme Court upheld a rule allowing a good faith holder of a bill of exchange to recover from a defendant who had been defrauded into giving the bill of exchange. While the Court

general to yield unequivocal predictions at an operational level. Thus, no crucial tests are available that can falsify Marxist theory, and in this limited, "Popperian" sense Marxist theory is unscientific (Popper, 1959: 40-43; Tushnet, 1983: 283).

Marxism, however, has a good deal to offer those who seek to understand the legal system. Marxism is methodological in that it provides a way of ordering concepts that relate diverse facts. Marxism is also heuristic in that its central formulations (such as the connection between structure and superstructure) provide a coherent picture of the connections among *apparently* discrete realms, such as technology, the economy, law, and class structure. Law, politics, economics, sociology are, under Marxism, ways of approaching a larger whole rather than disciplines focusing on natural divisions in social life that are capable of being understood as self-contained systems. In this Marxism is consistent with the general approach of law and social science (Lempert, 1983). At the same time Marxism illuminates our views of particular areas of study because we can perceive their connections to other areas. None of this, of course, requires us to throw away the findings of specialized studies or to renounce statistical or other techniques of empirical inquiry. Far from being a substitute for such inquiry, Marxism can build on it. In short, even if Marxism cannot deterministically explain or predict specific events or outcomes, it can provide a shape or structure to revealed relationships that is sensitive to "notions of individual action, natural causes and 'accidental' circumstances" (McLennan, 1981: 234). Understood in this way and stripped of: (1) the temptation to engage in specific prediction, (2) frequent diatribes (of which Marx was often guilty), and (3) the conflation of ideals of distributive justice with reasoned analysis, Marxism can be a powerful tool in understanding the social world and the place of law in it (Moore, 1980).

---

couched its decision in the need to facilitate the use of negotiable instruments, and thereby promote capitalist development, some states did not follow the federal rule. Also, as Gordon has observed: "The Swift rule may have made it more secure for people like the plaintiff to take commercial paper in payment of or as security for debts, but it made it less secure for people like the defendant to use such paper as a medium of exchange, because they were liable on their paper to subsequent holders even if they got nothing for it" (Gordon, 1980: 224). Thus, although negotiable instruments are essential in a capitalist scheme of production, a choice for either of the rules available to the Court in *Swift* and the state legislatures could be interpreted as consistent with Marxist theory. If this is the case in an area as central to the capitalist system as negotiable instruments, consider the even greater difficulty of developing a Marxist theory that would yield a falsifiable explanation of the different "pre-no fault" rules governing divorce in the various American jurisdictions.

III. THE ECONOMIC-LEGAL CONNECTION: RENNER AND PASHUKANIS

Two major figures—Renner and Pashukanis—are important in recent Marxist discussions about the law, although in Renner's case references are often critical. The reasons for this are not hard to find. Renner was a member of the Austro-Marxist group which, from the beginning of this century to the 1930s, sought to update Marxism to take account of the dramatic economic and social changes that had occurred since Marx's time, such as the growth of large-scale corporate enterprises, the rise of the welfare-service state, and changes in the class structure, including, especially, the emergence of a broad-based middle class (Bottomore, 1978: 1-44). This effort was in part a defensive response to the intellectual attack on Marxism that arose from Marx's failure to anticipate trends that would begin just a few years after his death. The Austro-Marxists adopted the crucial theoretical view that the economic structure and the superstructure interact with each other; they thereby virtually abandoned *any* notion of economic primacy, a crucial concept in Marx's Preface to the *Critique of Political Economy* (Adler, 1978: 259-61).

Renner's work on law follows the same path. Avoiding any serious attempt to probe Marx's structure-superstructure language, Renner found only a weak connection between economic development and law (1949: 252-60). Law cannot cause economic development or change, according to Renner, but can be gradually modified to meet changed economic conditions. For example, the contract, a device employed in connection with real and personal property, was adapted to the employer-employee relationship. Laws change "steadily, continuously, imperceptibly, like the growth of grass, according to the law of all organic development" (1949: 252-53). Thus, Renner concluded, fundamental social changes can occur "without accompanying alterations of the legal system" (1949: 252).

While Renner had acute perceptions about the durability and adaptability of such legal concepts as contract, he failed to grasp an important part of what he had shown. On the one hand, *laws* change, but, on the other hand, what I shall call *essential legal relations*, such as contract or property, are at once durable and adaptable. Renner's failure to grasp the distinction between law in general and the fundamentals of the legal order is what compelled him to the view that there is only a weak relationship between the economic system and its changes, on the one hand, and the legal system and its changes, on the other. With this view of the empirical situation, it is natural to slight the problem of what compels laws to be consistent with the requirements of the economic system. So long as crude notions of capitalist domination of law prevail, either directly through force or indirectly through a consciously constructed ideological system, the problem is not interesting for the answer is obvious, and Renner's inattention to this problem does not count heavily against his theory. But for the more sophisticated group of contemporary Marxist scholars, Renner's failure to deal adequately with this problem and his virtual abandonment of Marx's hypothesized connection between economic structure and superstructure are fatal flaws that make his work of little more than historical interest (see, e.g., Bierne and Quinney, 1982).

Pashukanis' work, on the other hand, is an intellectual starting point for many Marxists currently interested in the law. His views must be understood in the context of the major problem he sought to address. Writing in 1924, well before Stalin's consolidation and its accompanying terror, Pashukanis sought to determine the place of law in a future communist society. His conclusion—that law, like the state, was associated with a class society and would accordingly wither away with the development of classless society—was, even when it was written, familiar Marxist dogma and is the least interesting aspect of his work. What was ingenious was the general Marxist "theory" of law that Pashukanis devised as a route to this conclusion. The principal connection that Pashukanis saw between the capitalist economic structure and its legal superstructure is that the latter reflects and corresponds to the former. That is, the conceptions that Marx employs to elucidate the inner workings of the capitalist economic system have conceptual parallels in the capitalist legal system.

In developing his argument, Pashukanis distinguishes between technical rules (such as train timetables which regulate rail traffic) and legal rules (such as the liability of railroads toward consignors of freight). In the former case he sees a unity of purpose since technical rules can benefit everyone in similar ways, but in the latter case "differentiation and opposition of interests begin" (1978: 81) since legal rules systematically advantage particular parties in particular transactions. A capitalist system, Pashukanis tells us, involves the production and distribution of commodities (goods intended for sale in the market rather than for personal consumption).

This characteristic, in turn, implies an atomistic economy in which private economic units (including collaborative units such as corporations and trade unions) compete and bargain with one another in product, service, and labor markets (1978: 85).

The dynamics of competition and bargaining, which drives the economic system in capitalist society, is for Pashukanis rooted in the conflicting interests of parties involved in social relationships. With conflict the key motivating force, individuals (including corporate "persons"), who are the key actors in the system, are inevitably drawn into disputes with others. This gives rise to legal action. The legal system is thus another arena for pursuing economic conflict, but it is not the same as the economic system. Its central actor is not the economic man/woman of the marketplace, but the judicial one.

Capitalist law (exemplified by contract law) reinforces an ideology that embraces individualism, private autonomy, and material self-interest but which, at the same time, affirms mutual obligation and obedience to external authority (1978: 97). Just as the commodity acquires an exchange value independently of the will of the producer, so also "man acquires the capacity to be a legal subject and a bearer of rights. . . . He is simply the personification of the abstract, impersonal, legal subject, the pure product of social relations. . . ." (1978: 112, 113). Social relations between persons assume a doubly mysterious form. "They appear as relations between things (commodities) and . . . as relations between the wills of autonomous entities equal to each other—legal subjects" (1978: 117). The state, through the judicial machinery, *appears* to be the impartial guarantor of obligations and arbiter of disputes between rival claimants and forces (1978: 147), but behind this it is "the organized power of one class over the other" (1978: 150). Thus, the rules of law, imposed by the state to clarify and stabilize social relations, are rooted in and mirror the relations of production.

This portion of Pashukanis' analysis deals primarily with contract and property. With the exception of criminal law, he does not probe other legal areas. But his treatment of criminal law may be analogized to many other areas of law. In essence, Pashukanis argues that capitalist social relationships and the legal relationships that parallel them in the paradigm case of contract law are transplanted into other areas. For example, in a criminal prosecution, the state appears both as plaintiff (public prosecutor) and judge. The prosecutor asserts a claim, demanding satisfaction from the defendant in the form of a high price (a severe sentence). The offender pleads for leniency—a discount. The court determines the guilt and intention of the *individual*. The question of whether the act was caused intentionally, negligently, or accidentally reinforces the concept of the autonomous subject (1978: 177, 178). Finally, the whole of the criminal proceeding is affected by the principle of "equivalent recompense"—making the value of the punishment, be it "time" or "money," equal to the value of the costs imposed by the criminal (1978: 186). Clearly, most of the same points could have been made with respect to tortious conduct as well.

As the foregoing shows, Pashukanis' "theory" of the connection between the capitalist economic structure and legal superstructure is an elaborate one. It is primarily concerned with the forms of law rather than with the particulars of substance; indeed, it is virtually silent on substance or the ways in which rules change over time. Thus, it yields no operational predictions and so is not scientific in the Popperian sense, but as with Marxism generally, this is not a fatal flaw.

The great merits of Pashukanis' analysis are, first, its attempt to draw important connections and parallels between the economic structure and the legal superstructure. One need not accept his commodity theory of law to accept its insights into the legal subject, individual responsibility, and the structure of the legal system generally. Second, the analysis allows for the domination of the legal system by the dominant classes but avoids a crude instrumentalism in which members of the dominant classes always prevail. Third, in drawing the distinction between legal and technical rules, Pashukanis' analysis helps to differentiate in a rudimentary way between the rules that sustain and define social relationships and those that aid a society's functioning. All societies want their trains to run on time.

There are, however, serious problems with Pashukanis' approach. As Collins (1982) has shown, Pashukanis' attempt to explain all legal rules as reflections of commodity exchange is crudely reductionistic. While his views on criminal law are insightful, Pashukanis, as Collins argues with respect to the law of assaults, "seems to ignore its [the criminal law's] role as vindicator of the dominant values and standards of a community" (Collins, 1982: 109). Thus, Pashukanis' approach does not explain why the state, and not the victim or his or her relatives, is the plaintiff in criminal cases.

More fundamentally, Pashukanis' discussion of public law is confused and fails to consider important components of capitalist legality. Despite an extended discussion of the *forms* of capitalist legality, Pashukanis does not show how judges, formally independent of class pressures, act to promote capitalist interests. "How then does the coincidence between law and ruling class interests come about?," Tushnet asks (1983: 281). The problem is especially acute when one looks at administrative regulation and the many laws that operate to restrain capitalist interests (e.g., environmental laws). Indeed, the administrative structure of the modern regulatory state, in which a governmental unit is frequently the moving party and the goal is more often rule-making than the assignment of culpability or the assessment of damages, eludes Pashukanis' analysis.

Law has many functions in contemporary capitalist society. While one can divide these functions in many ways, I will employ Habermas' typology (Habermas, 1973: 53, 54). Habermas divides laws into: (1) those that constitute the mode of production (e.g., property, contract) and promote the economy; (2) those that complement the market by adapting the legal system to new business arrangements (e.g., much commercial law); (3) those that replace market activities (e.g., public utility law and occupational licensure); and (4) those that respond to politically effective reactions to economic dysfunction (e.g., minimum wage or environmental laws). Pashukanis' theory, with its narrow focus on the legal forms, cannot explain the range of law in the modern state.

I believe that the structure-superstructure formulation of Marx and Engels suggests an attractive alternative to Pashukanis' approach. It allows us to develop a theory that can embrace the variety of law in the modern capitalist state without discarding what is most attractive about Pashukanis: his insight that law can reinforce capitalist domination although judges and administrators are neither capitalist conspirators nor automatons in service to a capitalist elite. Indeed, the theory I shall propose allows considerable room for official independence and the ability of judges and administrators to engage in honest, critical reflection and to draw differing conclusions from similar factual episodes. The first step toward this theory is to examine closely Marx and Engels' structure-superstructure formulations.

IV. STRUCTURE AND SUPERSTRUCTURE

The starting point for any Marxist conception that seeks to relate law to the economic structure of society is Marx's famous 1859 Preface to *The Critique of Political Economy*, in which he stated:

> In the social production which men carry on they enter into definite relations that are indispensable and independent of their will. These relations of production correspond to a definite stage of development of their material powers of production. The sum total of these relations of production constitutes the economic structure of society—the real foundation, on which rise legal and political superstructures and to which correspond definite forms of social consciousness. The mode of production in material life determines the general character of the social, political and spiritual processes of life. It is not the consciousness of men that determines their existence, but, on the contrary, their social existence determines their consciousness (Marx, 1911: 11, 12).

Some preliminary observations are in order. First, as the above quotation indicates, the term "superstructure" includes a wide range of human activities—indeed, virtually every facet of life not specifically located in economic production; that is, every facet of life except "the totality of the operations aimed at procuring for a society its material means of existence" (Godelier, 1976: 60). Thus, superstructure includes the beliefs of persons operating within a given society, cultural artifacts such as works of art, and the institutional rules such as laws that guide conduct within a society. It is fair to ask whether Marx's claim here is that the mode of production can be shown to determine religious preferences, styles of music, and the particular laws governing domestic relations in some direct, mechanistic manner. If so, the wide variety of cultural, religious, intellectual, and other differences among contemporary capitalist societies would require us to reject Marx's hypothesis out of hand, "for such a position implies that the economic base is ultimately (if not immediately) self-sufficient and that its spontaneous development is the sole determinant of social evolution" (Jessop, 1982: 11).

This simplistic view (known as economism) was common among many prominent Marxists in the period following the death of Engels in 1895 and for this reason has been attributed by some to Marx and Engels. But, as we will see, a very different construction of the language is possible.

Second, the quoted language in the above text appears to be inconsistent with other Marx-Engels texts insofar as it applies to law, and it is even inconsistent with other language in the 1859 Preface. Later in the same paragraph Marx asserts: "At a certain stage of their development, the material forces of production in society come in conflict with the existing relations of production or—*what is but a legal expression for the same thing*—with the property relations within which they had been at work before" (1911: 12; emphasis added). Some scholars, comparing the two quoted portions of the 1859 Preface, have suggested a confusing and, perhaps, inconsistent dualism (Tushnet, 1983: 281; Plamenatz, 1955: 30, 31). Is property law part of the superstructure and consequently an effect of the economic structure, or is it simply a "legal expression" of the economic structure? While one must admit that the text is ambiguous, a closer examination of this and other Marx-Engels texts, together with the introduction of certain additional concepts, can clarify the apparent ambiguity and, more importantly, provide a framework that reveals connections between the law and economy that make for an underlying unity in the law of capitalist states.

How can one reconcile language that suggests a "legal expression" is synonymous with a part of the "economic structure" with language that suggests that all elements of the superstructure are separate from and somehow caused or shaped by the "economic structure"? Some Marxists have thrown away the dichotomy as it applies to law, claiming it is untenable (Thompson, 1975: 261). To do so implies that Marx and Engels were intellectually confused not only in the Preface to the *Critique of Political Economy* but in many other places as well. Indeed, the structure-superstructure dichotomy is one of the cornerstones of both the Marxist view of society in stasis and the Marxist conception of historical change. As O'Hagan has observed, the dichotomy is critical to Marxism for several reasons. The superstructure helps to "maintain a stable system in which power over production and enjoyment of products is thus unequally allocated. . . . [Superstructures] . . . impose a level of unity, cohesion and integration 'over and above' the disunited and indeed antagonistic interests of the classes composing the society" (O'Hagan, 1981: 86). They both present particular interests as the general interests of society and provide sets of enforceable rules.

It is possible to reconcile the apparently inconsistent formulations on law when we turn from the rather compressed

Preface to other texts which suggest that the notion of legal superstructure contains two quite distinct, but related, concepts. In his 1888 essay, "Ludwig Feuerbach and the End of Classical German Philosophy," Engels distinguishes "essential legal relations" from the law (or judicial practice). The former phrase embraces those essential legal conceptions that are central to a capitalist economic order, such as property, contract, and credit. Essential legal relations must be distinguished from the particular laws that are based upon them (Engels, 1959: 235, 236). Thus, the underlying notion of credit must be distinguished from the particular provisions of the Uniform Commercial Code, and the underlying concept of property must be distinguished from local landlord-tenant laws.

Although they employ different terminology, other Marx and Engels texts supply further support for this interpretation. *The German Ideology* of 1845-46 provides several such examples:

> Private property is a form of intercourse necessary for certain stages of development of the productive forces; a form of intercourse that . . . cannot be dispensed with in the production of actual [capitalist] material life. . . . Because property . . . as in all epochs is bound up with definite conditions, first of all economic, which depend on the degree of development of the productive forces and intercourse—conditions which inevitably acquire a legal and political expression (Marx and Engels, 1976: 355, 356).

While not very artfully framed, the ideas are akin to those of Engels quoted above. The forms of intercourse (or essential legal relations) are integrally connected with the economic system; these in turn give rise to particular legal and political rules and institutions. Elsewhere in *The German Ideology* Marx and Engels refer to the "productive forces and . . . the intercourse corresponding to these" as conditioning particular conceptions, laws, etc. (1976: 36). Again, "All [production] relations can be expressed in language only in the form of concepts. . . . These general ideas and concepts are looked upon as mysterious forces . . . [and] are further elaborated and given a special significance by politicians and lawyers" (1976: 363).

In exploring the distinction between production relations and the concepts that refer to them, I will use the method employed by Marx in developing his structure of capitalism—the method of abstraction (Marx, 1973: 100-108). Marx began by provisionally assuming away all social relations except those that he viewed as fundamental (capital and labor), developing abstract categories that were intended to elucidate the fundamentals of that relationship, and then gradually reintroducing other relationships and facts (Sweezy, 1942: 11-20). My approach is the same.

I begin with "essential legal relations," by which I mean the legal relations that mirror and legally define the fundamental economic relationships in a society. In a capitalist society these would include property and contract. Thus, one must employ these essential legal relations to comprehend the commercial, industrial, and employment relationships of a capitalist society—any capitalist society. As we will see, the concept of essential legal relations facilitates the understanding of linkages between the economy, on the one hand, and such lower order legal concepts as lease or easement as well as particular legal rules and decisions, on the other. And while one must be alert to the danger of reifying such essential legal relations as contract or property, one must be equally alert to the danger of disregarding the subjective content of action which is ordinarily expressed in conceptual terms. These concepts are parts of actors' meanings as they undertake action; they are not simply categories imposed by an observer (Weber, 1977: 109-15).

The concept of essential legal relations also addresses one of the criticisms raised by Kamenka in his review of Marxist discussions of the law. He criticizes the incapacity of many Marxists to distinguish laws that are central to a legal system from laws that could be changed tomorrow without affecting the character of the legal system (or economic system, one may add) (Kamenka, 1981: 476). In other words, not all laws and legal concepts—even in such areas as contract or property—are of equal importance. The question is which are most fundamental. We will see that, starting from the concept of essential legal relations, it is possible to structure legal concepts and rules in order of importance despite the mass of particulars. First, however, we must examine the concept of essential legal relations, beginning with a discussion of the economic base—in this case capitalism.

V. CAPITALISM AND ESSENTIAL LEGAL RELATIONS: PROPERTY AND CONTRACT

The term "capitalism" is traceable to nineteenth-century socialist theoreticians, of whom Marx was the most important. Although Marx did not attempt to fully define the term, his writings form the basis for a broad consensus on the essential characteristics of capitalism. The most important of these characteristics, according to Marx, is that "the owner of the means of production . . . finds the free worker available, on the market, as the seller of his own labour" (Marx, 1977: 274). These relations give rise to one class that owns the means of production, including factories, mines, mills, raw materials, and machines, and another class that sells its labor power to the former in a free market. This relationship between classes is to be distinguished from one in which one class legally controls the persons of others for laboring purposes (slavery), or in which certain obligations (or mechanisms for remission) are owed from one to another as a result of tradition or status (feudalism), as well as from many other sorts of arrangements.

Capitalism, as Marx conceived it, is inescapably tied to certain ideas and arrangements that are realized in and guaranteed by law. The first of these is contract. The essence of a contract consists of a promise by one party to do something in return for a specific act or promise on the part of another party. It is a voluntary arrangement, "freely" entered into by both parties, and so stands in sharp contrast to obligations owed as a result of either one's status or enslaved condition. The relationships between the capitalist and the laborer, seller and buyer, and creditor and borrower are contractual at their core. A prerequisite for capitalism in the realm of the labor bargain as well as in other areas of commercial life is the recognition and enforceability of contracts by the state.

The second distinguishing feature of capitalism that cannot thrive without law is the private *ownership* of the means of production. Prior to the sixteenth century in Britain and elsewhere, the notion of property was quite different from the one developed in conjunction with capitalism. The feudal concept of "property" embodied both common and private property, a sense of social obligation requiring the performance of duties, and a sense of stewardship in the use of personalty and land. But with the coming of capitalism, the idea of a communal interest in property withered away, as did the senses of stewardship and social obligation (Larkin, 1969: Chs. 1 and 2). Under capitalism "property is equated with private property—the right of a natural or artificial person to exclude others from some use or benefit of something. . . . Whereas in pre-capitalist society a man's property had generally been seen as a right to a revenue, with capitalism property comes to be seen as a right in or to material things" (MacPherson, 1975:

105). The conceptual change is reflected in the fact that property became more freely alienable and open to more uses, with the principal restrictions on the use of property being those assumed by contractual agreement and those imposed by the obligation not to interfere with other property owners in the enjoyment of their rights (Holdsworth, 1946: 105).

The essential legal relations of contract and property came to cover more and more of the social relationships in evolving capitalist society. As Marx observed, "Whenever, through the development of industry and commerce, new forms of intercourse have been evolved (e.g., insurance companies, etc.) the law has always been compelled to admit them among the modes of acquiring property" (Marx and Engels, 1976: 92). To which we might add that they are also subject to the contract relationship. Thus, stock certificates, commodities futures, options, and an array of other devices employed in commerce and industry have come to be embraced within the essential legal relations of contract and property. These are, in Habermas' terminology, "necessary to constitute the mode of production and maintain it" (Habermas, 1973: 53). Their usefulness in ordering the many kinds of activities and transactions that help establish the economic foundations of capitalism renders them essential to the system.

VI. CAPITALISM AND ESSENTIAL LEGAL RELATIONS: CREDIT AND COMBINATION

But capitalism requires still more. Specifically, capitalism requires credit and the capacity to enlarge capital by combining with other sources of wealth. Credit and combination, both contractual relationships, are essential legal relations that enable capitalism to expand.

Most production in a capitalist society is not for the personal use of the producers but is instead for sale at a profit. The capitalist engages in the processes of manufacture, distribution, and sale to turn a profit. In Marx's direct language, the production of goods simply for their utility "must therefore never be treated as the immediate aim of the capitalist; nor must the profit on any single transaction. His aim is rather the unceasing movement of profit-making" (Marx, 1977: 254). There are two important aspects to this description. First, the capitalist is interested in the continual repetition of the profit cycle and not simply in a single instance of profit-making. General Motors does not seek to sell its 1985 automobiles so that it can distribute the proceeds to its employees and shareholders and then exit from business. Rather, it arranges its activities so that it can produce and sell its products in continuous cycles of profitability, symbolized by Marx's "M-C-M'." The capitalist uses money (M) to purchase commodities such as labor power, raw materials, machines, and the like (C), intending the cycle to result in more money than the amount originally expended (M'). And the cycle repeats.

Credit, as Veblen noted, may be divided into two subcategories: "(a) that of deferred payments in the purchase and sale of goods . . . and (b) loans or debts. . . ." (Veblen, 1932: 49). The need for credit follows from the M-C-M' cycle, with its goal of ever-increasing profits. Unless credit is employed in the M-C part of the cycle, barter and available cash constitute the only means of payments, sharply limiting profit-making opportunities. Credit also aids those with profit-making potential who do not have immediate access to the resources needed to realize this potential. Most directly, credit can increase the size of M, allowing more commodities (C) to be purchased in any particular cycle, with the concomitant potential of an M' of greater magnitude. Credit also aids the unceasing quest for profit-making since it can speed up each cycle by providing money for additional investments before earlier investments have been fully paid off.

In short, the *unceasing* pursuit of profit-making requires the establishment and development of a credit system for a variety of reasons. Credit, then, constitutes a third essential legal relation, and with the rise of capitalism became a regular institution of economic life rather than the exceptional phenomenon it had been (Mandel, 1968: 217).

For many of the same reasons, combining with others is central to capitalism. The institution of contract allows one to reach an agreement not only with an adversary (e.g., buyer-seller or capitalist-employee) but also with those who share an interest in collaboration. Both types of combination are important, but the former is defined almost entirely by contractual agreement, while the latter, although rooted in contract, extends beyond it. Indeed, Coase (1937) has shown that the organizing authority and integrative activity of a business firm reduce the costs of negotiating and entering into many individual contracts, while Williamson (1975) suggests that the complete absorption of one business organization by another, the ultimate in combination, is a way to avoid the uncertainties of contractual relationships.

Because of the enhancement of capital, skill, and market power that combinations allow, it is natural in capitalism to seek allies in the pursuit of greater wealth. One special form of combination, the investment stock company, dramatically expands the ability of people to participate in the ownership of the means of production and provides the capitalist a means of greatly enhancing the available resources. Of course, combinations such as guilds, religious orders, monasteries, and towns existed in the pre-capitalist era (Davis, 1961: Chs. III and IV; Carr, 1909: 161, 162). Indeed, these earlier forms of combination supplied many of the key ideas essential to combinations that arose under capitalism, including perpetual succession and management by elected representatives (Kramer, 1928). Nevertheless, these early forms of combination had characteristics antithetical to those that make the later forms part of the essential legal relations of combination under capitalism. Early corporate forms were rife with: (1) restrictions on which activities could be pursued, (2) membership qualifications, (3) training requirements, and (4) restrictions on the ability of members to deal with non-members (Scott, 1951: 1-6).

Thus, the idea of essential legal relations, which, I argue, is the starting point in understanding Marx and Engels' theory of the relationship between economic structure and superstructures, refers to the legal expressions or images of the central components of the capitalist economic structure. The essential legal relations pervade subsidiary concepts (i.e., sale or mortgage) as well as other aspects of the legal order. For example, many crimes (burglary, robbery, fraud, etc.) and torts (trespass, strict liability) are premised upon the essential legal relations in that concepts like contract and property are essential to an understanding of what is wrongful about these acts. Similarly, other legal rules may modify or erode essential legal relations (such as environmental regulations or minimum wage laws). Notwithstanding these tensions, which constitute much of the politics of modern capitalist societies (and which I discuss later), the fundamentals of essential legal relations remain. For otherwise capitalism as a system could not survive. This is true almost as a matter of definition. The economic and legal concepts are that close.

VII. THE STRUCTURE OF HIERARCHY

In seeking to understand the Marxian conception of structure-superstructure and the law's place within it, it is important to note first that there are many segments of the superstructure (philosophy, religion, culture, law, politics). While it is appropriate for some purposes to distinguish between structure and superstructure as two separate and distinctive spheres, such a sharp bifurcation obscures linkages. Although essential legal relations are in one sense superstructure, in another sense they are the reflection of structure ("a legal expression" for "relations of production"). As such they can be linked not only to the structure but also to other elements of the superstructure, such as the arts and politics, and to less essential aspects of the legal culture, such as decisions in particular cases. In all cases the linkages are hierarchical, for superstructural elements and their included aspects may be conceived of as relatively further from the structure or nearer to it. We determine the "distance" from the structure by the number of intermediate links and the centrality of the particular superstructural segment or included aspect to the functioning of the base.

To take a simple example, high culture is far less critical to the functioning of the economic base than are essential legal relations. Capitalism can function effectively under a wide variety of cultural arrangements without significantly impeding its daily operations, but a breakdown of such essential legal relations as property or contract will destroy the basis for fundamental capitalist operations. Similarly, capitalism can accommodate its operations to a variety of specific laws on a particular subject, but the range of acceptable variations in essential legal relations is far more limited. Certainly, Marx in giving preeminence to the structure meant no more than that the productive state and social relations of society influence or color the activities in distant areas of superstructures, such as the artistic aspects of culture (Marx, 1973: 110, 111). A particular violinist, for example, may accept, reject, or be indifferent to the mode of production with virtually no effect on the health of the capitalist system. It is perhaps true that the mode of production may ultimately frame his or her discourse, experience, and understanding but if so, it allows for a wide range of thought and behavior that can be exhibited within the system's constraints. This room for human discretion applies to other superstructural segments (including law) as well.[2]

[2] The capitalist structure, because of its individualistic competitive base, may allow substantially more room for discretion than other economic structures. For example, to hold people to a feudal economic system may

Let us return now to the Preface, which *apparently* stated that the legal superstructure is determined by the structure but also told us that property relations are but the legal expression of the relations of production. The key to clearing up the apparent inconsistency is understanding that Marx was referring to different things. In the first instance he was speaking about the legal superstructure, while in the second instance the reference was to the essential legal relations to which the legal superstructure is linked. The apparent confusion, as G.A. Cohen acutely observes, stems from the fact that there was simply "no attractive alternative" to describing production relations except in legal terms (Cohen, 1978: 224, 230). Cohen goes on to note that the economic system requires a specified, orderly set of essential legal relations in order to function and maintain itself on a continuing basis. The economic structure and essential legal relations are connected without intermediation. In that way essential legal relations are but an expression of the economic structure, even though they are at the same time part of one of the superstructural segments. A person undertaking an act, such as entering into a business contract, may simultaneously experience the process as an economic, legal, ideological, and perhaps even religious activity, but while structure and superstructure are thus simultaneously cojoined, they are also separate since the objective institutions, associative relationships, and legitimation structures of each segment are different (Godelier, 1976: 62, 64; Weber, 1968: Pt. 1, Chs. I and II).[3]

---

require far greater constraints in other superstructural segments to maintain the legitimacy of the order than those required by capitalism.

3 Contrast the construction that Collins offers in his admirable book. Addressing the constitutive problem (law as a reflection of structure, yet superstructure), Collins argues that legal rules "subsume existing customs leaving them redundant as guides to correct behavior" (Collins, 1982: 88). The customs, in turn, originate in the practices necessary to the mode of production and the mechanisms needed to control deviance. The content of the law, Collins goes on, is thus superstructural because it is determined by the "dominant ideology as it is represented in customary standards of behavior," but it is also part of the structure "to the extent of being the sole institution giving [relations of production] concrete form and detailed articulations. Thus law is superstructural in origin but because of its metanormative quality it then may function in the material base" (1982: 88, 89).

Collins' argument, although solving the constitutive problem on a theoretical plane, leaves too much unresolved. The idea of a "dominant ideology" does not help us to specify doctrines and laws for examination, whereas the concept of essential legal relations does. Moreover, although Collins' view concedes a hierarchy and elaboration of law, the concept of "dominant ideology" provides no guidance about how to organize such a structure. The concept of essential legal relations, as I shall show shortly, does. Furthermore, merely giving the concept of dominant ideology a central

VIII. MEDIATION AND DERIVATIVE SUBRELATIONS

Our next task is to move from essential legal relations to the particulars of legal decision-making. This will be done in two steps. The first is to show how particular decisions and doctrines are derived from essential legal relations. The second is to show how public law and judicial rulings that conflict with the accumulation interests of the capitalist class fit in.

Engels has written:

> Still higher ideologies, that is, such as are still further removed from the material economic basis, take the form of philosophy and religion. Here the interconnection between conceptions and their material conditions of existence becomes more and more complicated, more and more obscured by intermediate links. But the interconnection exists (Engels, 1959: 237).

Implicit in this statement is the idea that if we are to understand the "higher ideologies," we must attend to the intermediate links. An important set of links may, consistent with Marx's scheme, be called "derivative subrelations." In the legal sphere the derivative subrelations are legal conceptions that fall between essential legal relations and particular rules. Thus, property is an essential legal relation. Under it are such derivative subrelations as easement, lease, and the like. Derivative subrelations of credit include security, bankruptcy, lien, etc. From these derivative subrelations flow particular legal rules and further subrelations. In both cases distance from the economic structure is a function of the number and quality of mediating subrelations.[4] For example, assignment is a derivative subrelation under contract, but delegation of performance is a derivative subrelation under assignment in descending order from the structure. Particular legal rules (i.e., where personal performance is required under a contract, a substitute's performance does not discharge the contractor's duty), in turn, flow from the lower derivative subrelations.

---

role does not help elucidate the linkages between the economic structure and daily judicial and administrative decisions. Nor does it help us to understand how ideas in conflict with the dominant ideology, like environmentalism, arise, and how these ideas are translated into legal rules. As we will see in the discussion of public law below, the concept of essential legal relations helps us to place such laws in the context of a capitalist legal order.

[4] I do not wish to be understood as saying that distance is *necessarily* inversely related to importance to the structure. It is entirely consistent with my formulation that a change in something distant from the economic structure can have a major impact on the structure. For this reason I use the word "quality" in the above sentence.

One merit of this view is that it accords with the manner in which the Anglo-American judicial system works. Essential legal relations, the expression of economic structure, give rise to derivative subrelations. Courts, confronted with particular matters, accept the essential legal relation, consider the functions and purposes of the derivative subrelation, and then seek to render a best decision consistent with the derivative subrelation's principal function. Since there is room for differences in judgment in this process, different courts can adopt different particular rules, as the example of *Swift v. Tyson* discussed in footnote 1 shows. Moreover, this dynamic accords with the differences that exist in human behavior. Judges are not omniscient. They can be stupid or wrong, just as they can be farsighted and brilliant. They are not constrained by a "dominant ideology" or by more direct influences of economic interest to reach those specific decisions that will *best* constitute and maintain the mode of production. And the system for its part can tolerate suboptimal and even occasionally antagonistic decisions at the case level.

This system of transmission from economic structure to the decisions of individual judges shows a structure of causation that is, at once, complex and flexible yet constraining. The fundamentals—essential legal relations—are set and nearly universally accepted, part of the "taken for granted" social order.[5] If they should become widely questioned, this would indicate that the economic structure itself is being widely questioned. From these essential legal relations, judicial and legislative officials seek to derive consistent subrelations to meet particular problems or resolve particular cases. So long as the essential legal relations are taken as the starting point, those actors who create the derivative subrelations and the

[5] The processes by which the fundamentals are taken for granted are complex and would require a separate paper to explore fully. Here I shall simply mention some of the important considerations. First, the essential legal relations are encountered as part of our early socialization in much the same way that table manners, habits of dress, and so on are inculcated. An adult settling a dispute between two children battling over a toy will reward it to one of them, announcing that it "belongs to X." The word "property" is not used, but the concept and attributes are (Levi-Strauss, 1967: 19). Such instruction continues onward from childhood through adulthood, and in most cases the essential legal relations become ingrained. Second, a capitalist society invests considerable effort in developing a coherent ideology regarding the importance and fairness of the essential legal relations. Courts, law schools, and the elites in these and other institutions exert pressures and guide others to work with (i.e., accept) the essential legal relations. Finally, we should not underestimate the high costs of replacing the essential legal relations with others. Most people are unwilling to incur the effort required to supplant existing essential legal relations.

particular legal rules under them will develop a jurisprudence compatible with the structurally defined system although they act neither conspiratorially nor consciously on behalf of a class or ruling group.

Not only can the system allow creative and flexible decision-making within the framework set by the essential legal relations, but it can also tolerate the mistakes, the inefficiencies, and the conscious or unconscious attempts at subversion that are inevitable when decisions are entrusted to a multitude of variously motivated human agents. For example, the developing law of business corporations in nineteenth-century America displayed many twists and turns before ultimately abandoning size limitations, restrictions on indebtedness and the consideration for which stock may be given, and other provisions that limited corporate growth and capital accumulation. Despite these restraints and inefficiencies, the system was nevertheless capitalist, and eventually the principles of liberal general incorporation were reached (Dodd, 1936: 38). Similarly, as Engels observed, the different ways in which legal rules from older societies are adapted to capitalist ones can result in more or less efficient coordination between the structure and legal superstructure (Engels, 1959: 235, 236; Hall, 1977: 57, 58).

To summarize thus far, paying attention to the Marxian idea of structure and superstructure allows us to understand how the economic structure and the activities of judicial decision-makers are linked to the making of specific decisions that constitute and maintain the mode of production. Linkages move along the following path:

structure
↓
essential legal relations
↓
derivative subrelations
↓
particular rules

This does not mean that particular rules may not alter or modify derivative subrelations, for they may. But most legal activity occurs in a routinized pattern in which the category hierarchically above is not questioned. A judge rendering a decision on a question of negotiable instruments does not ordinarily challenge the derivative subrelation of negotiability and will certainly not question the essential legal relation of contract. Thus, without resorting to crude instrumentalism, this construction shows how legal agents act to support capitalist social relations, and at the same time it accords with the manner in which legal decisions are made. Moreover, it allows us to detect signals indicating that the mode of production is being seriously challenged. When an economy's essential legal relations are openly challenged, we know that this is the case.

Such a challenge occurs when the "justice" of the allocative biases inherent in essential legal relations is subject to question. The conception of contract, for example, includes the notions that people are "free" to enter into them and that, with only certain exceptions, the terms arranged by the parties must not be upset by courts. An alternative ethic which is inimical to the capitalist system would have the state determine the "correct" terms for every bargain in the context of some theory of distributive justice. Similarly, as G.A. Cohen argues, the implicit claim of the property system that it is just and proper may be challenged. "Now every actual piece of private property . . . either is or is made of something which was once the private property of no one. . . . We must ask, apart from how he in particular got it, how the thing came to be (anyone's) private property in the first place, and examine the justice of that transformation" (Cohen, 1981: 15).

But, while philosophers may sometimes ponder such questions, this is generally not done in the real world. Ordinarily, legal actors accept the underlying notions contained within essential legal relations in much the same way that table manners are accepted and employed, without rationally considering them or demanding moral justifications. In this way, through biases built into the very concepts with which the law works, essential legal relations *help* to establish and maintain social conformity as well as what Antonio Gramsci termed "social hegemony"—ruling group homogeneity in the face of a diversity of particular societal interests (Gramsci, 1971: 12, 13, 146, 195, 247, 261; Sumner, 1979: 256, 257).

IX. PUBLIC LAW AND SOCIAL CONFLICT

Now that I have shown how particular decisions and doctrines are derived from essential legal relations, it is time to turn to public law and rules in apparent conflict with the accumulation interests of the capitalist class. The sequence of discussion is intended to follow Marx's method of abstraction, starting from the most fundamental aspects of capitalist law and incorporating other aspects of the capitalist legal system in steps. For this reason I started with activities in the realm of private law that help maintain the economic system. The next step is to incorporate public law into the analysis.

I begin with the observation that capitalist societies have proved remarkably flexible and adaptive. Innumerable rules and changes over time have occurred in every capitalist society. The law of America or England that prevails in the 1980s is obviously different from prevailing law in those nations 50 or 100 years before. Nevertheless, the essential legal relations and most derivative subrelations have persisted. The problem, then, is to show how the ideas developed thus far can embrace such change and the constant core. This task requires us to examine public law and politics in capitalist society. In doing so, we must confront the fact that many rules in the modern state conflict with the direct interests of the capitalist class. Nor can we take comfort in the thesis suggested by some that every rule in apparent conflict with capitalist interests is nothing more than a concession by the capitalist class designed to assure the quiescence of their enemies. Like the crude instrumentalism that preceded it, this perspective is contradicted by a fair look at the contents and operations of modern capitalist legal systems.

Let us start with a modified reiteration of Pashukanis' view that much of the law in a capitalist society is a reflection of generalized commodity exchange, which presupposes an atomized economy of individual units engaged in trading transactions with other units (Pashukanis, 1978: 85, 93-97). An economy of this sort is characterized by legal relations between individuals involving, for example, A entering into a contract with B and then perhaps suing B for a breach of that contract. A and B may be two businessmen, buyer and seller, employer and employee, or virtually any other pair of contracting parties. The abstractness of the essential legal relationship of contract can embrace any relationship with adverse interests, as Pashukanis observes. But just as the law both facilitates and is shaped by the pursuit of individual gain, which is inherent in a capitalist society, so too it can facilitate and be shaped by collaborative efforts directed toward the same goal. A and B might, for example, enter into a partnership and together contract with C to purchase goods for less than either could have purchased them alone or, without contracting, they might agree not to compete in the same market. The two-person case, whether it involves a contract or not, can, of course, be extended to almost any number of similarly situated individuals who perceive that their well-being will be enhanced by extended collaborative efforts; for example, a trade association or a cooperative research venture.

Such collaboration produces interest groups, which are based upon the divisions in a capitalist society. Bukharin has outlined a number of dimensions along which divisions exist that commonly give rise to such groups. These include: (1) *size* (big business and small business), (2) *policy interest* (importers and exporters), (3) *vocation* (financiers and industrialists), (4) *industry* (insurance and commercial banking), (5) *firm* (A.T.&T. and I.B.M.). *Intermediate classes* (such as managers, bureaucrats, and professionals), *transitional classes* (remnants of old orders), and *declassé groups* outside the structure of production, distribution, and exchange may develop joint interests at variance with the interests of other groups (Bukharin, 1965: 276-92). Some of these divisions are more likely to be within classes than between them. Nor is the working class exempt from interest group fragmentation. For example, Marx expected the savings bank, designed to promote working-class saving and thrift, to "lead to a split between that portion of the working class which takes part in the savings banks and the portion which does not" (Marx, 1976: 427). But ties to the economic system, through savings bank deposits or other links, are not the only bases on which working-class divisions may arise. The Marxian framework can extend to the range of intra-class divisions that occur in real life, whether based on race, sex, religion, neighborhood, or some other dividing dimension. Nor is it surprising, given a Marxian framework, to find that group life mirrors the self-seeking life of the individual, for whom essential legal relations generate the central rules for the allocation of resources.

Groups, like individuals, may use the devices of private law to attain their ends. The collective bargaining agreement is a contract, just as is an individually negotiated wage agreement, and groups have the same control over their property as individuals have over theirs. In addition, groups, unlike individuals, are often able to induce the state to reallocate resources to them through legislation and/or administrative action. Indeed, groups often form for just this purpose. Thus, both public and private law are potential ways of advancing wealth in a capitalist society.[6]

[6] To treat private law as if it were completely eclipsed by public law in the day-to-day workings of a capitalist society, as some scholars have done (Tushnet, 1978: 99; Fraser, 1978: 167), is to seriously distort the larger picture. Indeed, most of a capitalist society's daily transactions, such as sales, are covered by the mundane common law rules of the private law. To suggest, as

Public law, then, under capitalism is usually not a reflection of class divisions, although some public laws such as labor legislation or those governing the distribution of the tax burden may be. More typically, interest groups representing segments of classes employ available processes before courts, legislatures, and administrative decision-makers to gain advantages over other interest groups. For example, the history of federal and state banking legislation in this country is a history of conflict, victory, failure, and compromise among local, regional, and national commercial banks, credit unions, investment banks, etc. There can be many outcomes of such battles, and it is impossible in a few sentences to present a full-scale theory that explains the variety of outcomes in the numerous public policy areas in which such conflicts arise.

Several observations, however, are in order. First, in the name of the "public interest," laws can be enacted to fulfill any of the functions described by Habermas. For example, laws affecting monetary policy can be enacted to promote the economy. Such laws can originate from either interest group activity or the public-spiritedness of public officials. Second, groups from the economically dominant class in competition with other segments of the dominant class can ally themselves with groups from other classes, to whom concessions will have to be made. For example, domestic automobile companies and the automobile workers' union may align themselves against automobile importers. Finally, it is entirely possible in a democracy for groups representing segments of inferior classes to prevail frequently in their battles with segments of the dominant classes. Divisions within the dominant class, its relative lack of concern about a subject, the threat of cost-imposing lower-class actions (such as strikes) are among the factors that can lead to this result. Yet even such defeats are consistent with capitalist domination so long as the fundamental legal relations are not challenged.

Consider utility regulation as an example. Public utilities enter into large numbers of contracts with their subscribers, who are "free" to reject the service and provide alternatives (such as a solar home heating system). Sometimes a utility can offer various grades of service from which users can select. In these respects, the contract device remains intact and the essential legal relations remain unquestioned; contracts are

---

Fraser (1978) does, that corporatism, consisting of a grand alliance of government agencies, trade unions, and corporate organizations, has destroyed private autonomy is seriously misleading.

honored and the utility's ownership of its property is not challenged. However, a utility is often an area's sole supplier of an essential service and so is in a position to extract monopoly profits. To forestall this, consumers, including other powerful capitalist interests, demand legal protection. The usual solution is a law establishing a public utility commission. Such commissions are usually given the power to affect the *terms* of the contract or the *uses* of the utility's property, but they cannot destroy or transform the essential legal relations themselves. In other words, the regulations limit the discretion of individuals or groups to make certain choices in employing essential legal relations, derivative subrelations, and particular rules. These restrictions may be relatively tight, such as the requirement that a particular rate should be charged, or they may be relatively loose, such as the Federal Trade Commission's prohibition against false advertising, which precludes certain kinds of misleading messages without specifying what must be said. Whatever the restrictions, however, the essential legal relations are at their core respected, and those aspects of the legal superstructure that are isomorphic with elements of the economic base remain to foster the accumulation of wealth under capitalism even if the segment of the capitalist class that controls public utilities cannot take full advantage of the subrelations ordinarily derived from them.

Indeed, freedom to contract or deal with property has never been absolute. There have been illegal or unenforceable contracts and limitations on the use of property for as long as these legal concepts have existed. But the fact that there are rules, exceptions to the rules, limitations, and exceptions to the exceptions does not negate the conclusion that a capitalist society's fundamental operations are based upon a chain that leads from structure through essential legal relations to particular rules. This is the glue that holds a capitalist society together. Various interest groups are able to change aspects of their positions through the legal institutions the state provides. Sometimes these efforts focus on public law and at other times private law is used to establish particular rules or decisions. The outcomes of such efforts may make the mode of production more efficient, or they may make it less efficient. They may represent the effective actions of one group or another (Habermas, 1973: 53, 54). Each effort requires separate investigation, but they all operate within a framework of essential legal relations.

We have already seen that these essential legal relations, although part of the legal superstructure, express core economic relations. It is also important to note that they are incorporated into the political superstructure as well. While an analysis of the capitalist state is beyond the scope of this article, it follows from our discussion of essential legal relations that if they are embedded in the political superstructure, the state in a capitalist society is a state of the capitalist class, even when the class loses important political and legal battles to others. The essential legal relations under capitalism, inconsistently but on balance, serve to protect and further an unequal allocation of resources in society. A challenge to the essential legal relations means that the economic order is being fundamentally attacked.

X. CONCLUSION

This article is not intended to explicate what Marx "really meant" in the Preface or at any other place in his analysis. Instead, I have sought to employ Marxism heuristically and methodologically to draw connections between the capitalist economic system—in all of its variants—and law. Under this view, law does not stand or exist outside society, but this does not mean that legal history is nothing more than a reflection of economic or social developments. One may, consistent with Marx, acknowledge the relative autonomy of the numerous judges, administrators, and other policy-makers in our legal system and thus avoid the notion that law under capitalism is nothing more than the conspiratorial product of a ruling class. The perspective offered here recognizes and puts into context the numerous judicial and legislative decisions that are adverse to the interests of political rulers or business firms. From this perspective the many sharp divisions among legal decision-makers are the natural result of human agency. They pose no necessary problems for capitalism, for they do not preclude and, indeed, usually reflect agreement on the essentials. These essentials are part and parcel of the basic economic structure, and so long as the economic structure is well-established, accord on the essential legal relations will characterize legal action, and derived subrelations will reflect the essential relations in most instances. Thus, we have a framework for understanding the extent to which the economic system determines the actions of legal officials and the limits of their discretion.

The view developed here is obviously far removed from the reductionist economic determinism of which Marxism is not infrequently accused. It conceives, rather, a complex framework involving different levels of legal action (as measured by the distance from the structural base) and various mediating laws and concepts. It also recognizes that to understand the specifics of a legal situation, one must specifically investigate the problem under consideration, but it rejects an eclecticism that sees no ultimate organizing principles applicable to the diversity of legal events. Such principles, I have argued, may be found by attention to structure, as Marx used the term, and by careful analysis of the links to and within the superstructure.

REFERENCES

ADLER, Max (1978) "Ideology as Appearance," in T. Bottomore and P. Goode (eds.), *Austro-Marxism*. Oxford: Clarendon Press.

BIERNE, Piers and Richard QUINNEY (eds.) (1982) *Marxism and Law*. New York: John Wiley.

BOTTOMORE, Tom (1978) "Introduction," in T. Bottomore and P. Goode (eds.), *Austro-Marxism*. Oxford: Clarendon Press.

BUKHARIN, Nikolai (1965) *Historical Materialism*. New York: Russell & Russell.

CAIN, Maureen and Alan HUNT (eds.) (1979) *Marx and Engels on Law*. New York: Academic Press.

CARR, Cecil Thomas (1909) "Early Forms of Corporateness," in Association of American Law Schools (eds.), *Select Essays in Anglo-American Legal History*, Vol. 3. Boston: Little, Brown.

COASE, R.H. (1937) "The Nature of the Firm," 4 *Economica (New Series)* 386.

COHEN, G.A. (1978) *Karl Marx's Theory of History*. Princeton: Princeton University Press.

——— (1981) "Freedom, Justice and Capitalism," 126 *New Left Review* 3.

COLLINS, Hugh (1982) *Marxism and Law*. New York: Oxford University Press.

DAVIS, John P. (1961) *Corporations*. New York: Capricorn Books.

DODD, E. Merrick (1936) "Statutory Developments in Business Corporation Law, 1886-1936," 50 *Harvard Law Review* 27.

ENGELS, Frederick (1959) "Ludwig Feuerbach and the End of Classical German Philosophy," in L.S. Feuer (ed.), *Marx and Engels: Basic Writings on Politics and Philosophy*. Garden City, NY: Anchor Books.

FRASER, Andrew (1976) "Legal Theory and Legal Practice," 44 *Arena* 123.

——— (1978) "The Legal Theory We Need Now," 40 *Socialist Review* 147.

GODELIER, Maurice (1976) "The Object and Method of Economic Anthropology," in D. Seddon (ed.), *Relations of Production*. London: Frank Cass.

GORDON, Robert W. (1980) "Review: Freyer's *Forums of Order*," 54 *Business History Review* 223.

GRAMSCI, Antonio (1971) *Selections from the Prison Notebooks*. New York: International Publishers.

HABERMAS, Jürgen (1973) *Legitimation Crisis*. Boston: Beacon Press.

HALL, Stuart (1977) "Rethinking the Base and Superstructure Metaphor," in J. Bloomfield (ed.), *Class, Hegemony and Party*. London: Lawrence & Wishart.

HOLDSWORTH, William (1946) *Essays in Law and History*. Oxford: Clarendon Press.

JESSOP, Bob (1982) *The Capitalist State*. New York: New York University Press.

KAMENKA, Eugene (1981) "Demythologizing the Law," *Times Literary Supplement* 475 (May 1).

KRAMER, Stella (1928) *The English Craft Gilds.* Oxford: Oxford University Press.

LARKIN, Paschal (1969) *Property in the Eighteenth Century.* New York: Howard Fertig.

LEMPERT, Richard O. (1983) "From the New Editor," 17 *Law & Society Review* 3.

LEVI-STRAUSS, Claude (1967) *Structural Anthropology.* Garden City, NY: Anchor Books.

MacPHERSON, C.B. (1975) "Capitalism and the Changing Concept of Property," in E. Kamenka and R.S. Neale (eds.), *Feudalism, Capitalism and Beyond.* London: Edward Arnold.

MANDEL, Ernest (1968) *Marxist Economic Theory,* Vol. 1. New York: Monthly Review Press.

MARX, Karl (1911) *Critique of Political Economy.* Chicago: Charles H. Kerr.

——— (1973) *Grundrisse.* Harmondsworth: Penguin.

——— (1976) "Wages," in Karl Marx and Frederick Engels, *Collected Works,* Vol. 6. New York: International Publishers.

——— (1977) *Capital,* Vol. I. New York: Vintage Books.

MARX, Karl and Frederick ENGELS (1976) "The German Ideology," in Karl Marx and Frederick Engels, *Collected Works,* Vol. 5. New York: International Publishers.

McLENNAN, Gregor (1981) *Marxism and the Methodologies of History.* London: Verso Editions.

MOORE, Stanley (1980) *Marx On the Choice Between Socialism and Communism.* Cambridge, MA: Harvard University Press.

O'HAGAN, Timothy (1981) "On the Withering Away of Superstructures," in J. Mepham and D.-H. Ruben (eds.), *Issues in Marxist Philosophy,* Vol. IV. Brighton, England: Harvester Press.

PASHUKANIS, Evgeny B. (1978) *Law and Marxism: A General Theory.* London: Ink Links.

PLAMENATZ, John (1955) *German Marxism and Russian Communism.* New York: Harper & Row.

POPPER, Karl R. (1959) *The Logic of Scientific Discovery.* New York: Basic Books.

RENNER, Karl (1949) *The Institutions of Private Law and Their Social Functions.* London: Routledge & Kegan Paul.

SCOTT, William Robert (1951) *The Constitution and Finance of English, Scottish and Irish Joint Stock Companies to 1920,* Vol. I. New York: Peter Smith.

SPARKS, Richard F. (1980) "A Critique of Marxist Criminology," 2 *Crime and Justice: An Annual Review of Research* 159.

SUMNER, Colin (1979) *Reading Ideologies.* New York: Academic Press.

SWEEZY, Paul (1942) *The Theory of Capitalist Development.* New York: Oxford University Press.

THOMPSON, E.P. (1975) *Whigs and Hunters.* New York: Pantheon.

TUSHNET, Mark (1978) "A Marxist Analysis of American Law," 1 *Marxist Perspectives* 96 (Spring).

——— (1983) "Review: Collins' *Marxism and Law,*" 68 *Cornell Law Review* 281.

VEBLEN, Thorstein (1932) *The Theory of Business Enterprise.* New York: New American Library.

WEBER, Max (1968) *Economy and Society,* 3 Vols. New York: Bedminster Press.

——— (1977) *Critique of Stammler.* New York: Free Press.

WILLIAMSON, Oliver E. (1975) *Markets and Hierarchies: Analysis and Antitrust Implications.* New York: Free Press.

CASES CITED

Swift v. Tyson, 41 U.S. (16 PET) 1 (1842).

Part VII
Final Account

[25]

CHAPTER 11

Liberty, Equality and the Conceptual Minimum of Legal Mediation

Csaba Varga

We are living in an age of social revolutions—and not for the first time in the course of the history of our century, full of calamities here in Eastern Central and Eastern Europe, but also in the wide regions of Asia and Africa, as well as of South America.

This especially holds true for the regions which are looked upon as the peripheries in relation to the centre of the world economy. The picture shows one common feature: these are societies which move along forced paths controlled by ideological and/or modernising desires. They are societies in the process of substituting democratic arrangements for self-nominated charismatic leadership believing that, because of belatedness in development, they happen to be in a kind of emergency situation, and their recognising it is the precondition of further development. Thus leadership resorts to social experimentation, subordinating the whole of society to this objective, about which Thomas Mann still held the hope in 1919—when applying to the Chancellor of Austria for Georg Lukács's life— that '[t]his possibility was one which occurred but once, as a consequence of a lost war', 'at a time when catastrophic conditions offered transitorily to social zealots the possibility of trying out their ideas experimentally on the living body of the people.[1] Each of those in power places on their banner the realisation of liberty, of equality, and of something else in accordance with their own programme, while the emergency situation referred to mostly requires their practical negation, at least transitorily. However, according to the logic of the forced path, deformation of the conditions deforms the result as well. More exactly: all the factors alien to the original objective which are incorporated into the process as a result of some concrete necessity, becoming socially irrevocable in it, may set auxiliary directions which, finally, themselves block the way towards implementing the objective. The paradox of the process may manifest itself not only in the crying contradiction between the desired objective and the paths actually followed in reality, as with the dream of the Golden Age set against the misery of the present (e.g., the tyranny of hierarchical structures, bureaucratically set in motion and devastating the basic tissues of society, causing the refeudalisation of society instead of the establishment of a classless society), but it seems as if law too is constructed in such a way that the very idea of any law and order is dying out. Or, rather, is a kind of law and order perhaps going to get constructed without any law standing behind it?

The ideas to be explored in the following are not political standpoints. Their relevance is not even to a philosophy social or historical in character. Consequently, they reflect neither committedness nor sympathies nor choices. It is simply the lawyer who stands behind them, representing a specifically homogenous aspect of social existence. In his specific role the lawyer has to represent the specific values of the specifically distinct structure and independent operation of that particular aspect of social existence. Dealing with the ontology of social existence from the point of view of law, he knows that no matter what overriding roles assert themselves in the total complex of social existence and become characteristic of individual partial complexes, they are characterised not by subordination but by being different in their ontological relationship. For the socialisation of social existence presupposes the development of partial complexes (not only the economy, or politics, but religion, morals, law, science, etc.) in accordance with their own particularities. To put it in philosophical terms, it presupposes the formation of homogeneous aspects of social existence, which are different from each other and successfully manifest their being different in their social reproduction. Alternatively, it is the lawyer who in the following is to speak about the social preconditions of the partial complex of law and its homogeneity, as well as of the possible limitations which may jeopardise this homogeneity by eliminating the particularities of this aspect of existence and, thereby, also its distinctiveness.

In all that, a variety of subjective motives may play a role; however, from the above standpoint, it may only have one objective outcome. Therefore I believe that the fortunate process of self-reflection and self-moderation ongoing in Hungary and in some other neighbouring countries makes this search not unnecessary and unfeasible but, on the contrary, timely, and enables me to carry out the analysis of causes and consequences, at least from one point of view, to the end.

I *The Dilemma of Unlawfulness and Lawfulness*

What is dramatic about the murder of a priest committed somewhere by someone? The fact that people in uniform on duty ruthlessly killed a man who happened to be a priest, for political reasons? This is obviously so if we look at the event in its tragic straightforwardness and irrevocabilty. But if the query is of more general character, directed to the relationship between power and law, behind the point which gave rise to consternation on account of having received publicity, we have to see the submerged iceberg too. We have to see the power in whose eyes law is nothing else but the ornament of its mightful '*mihi placet*' at any given time. Once it grasped a club and it has been holding this in its hands ever since and no one can tell on whom it will deliver a blow, and when. All it needs do is merely make reference to the club whenever it wishes to limit someone else.

That is exactly the reason why the problem is by no means restricted to the cases of state terrorism. If it were exclusively such things, that would be enough to awaken us from our apathy, instead of our simply having lost interest. For the institutional movement amounting to this or that kind of state-run terror can also be tame and bloodless. It may be manifested in the lack of operation of law courts, the silence of administration and the sabotage of law-enforcement.

What kind of law and order is it in which the trial of lawsuits fully founded legally can be hindered by administrative decision (as happened in Hungary, for example, in relation to lawsuits aimed at achieving a proper redivision of private animal stocks which had got mixed in the course of requisitioning performed by the occupying military after World War Two)? Or in which there can be *ab initio* an exclusion of any remedy against discretionary administrative measures taken to the detriment of basic rights (as happened in cases of decisions about nationalisation and deportation in Hungary in the late 1940s and early 1950s)? Or in which a licence can be extorted in spite of an express prohibition (as in the scandalous case, e.g., of the beer bar to be built by a functionary's relative in the protected forest of Lake Héviz in Hungary)? Or in which a licence can be refused against the terms both of a law and of a government decree, enacted to give authority for it, through the deliberate silence of the government agency (as in the matter of the permission of private book publishing)? Or in which the population of a country may be made to face, not only without its approval but without even so much as knowing about it, a *fait accompli* which inflicts on it serious financial risks (e.g., by importing dangerous wastes from neighbouring Austria to Mosonmagyaróvár and Körmend in Hungary). Or where such things may even amount to a governmental modification of a peace treaty (as by the contract for building the Czechoslovak-Hungarian hydraulic power station at Gabcikovo and Nagymaros)? Or in which the validity of a Criminal Code can be suspended by resort to a nonlegal norm (e.g., by making legal indictments dependent upon a preliminary political party decision)?

Or in which (e.g., in respect of the regulations of the Highway Code on traffic accidents) a privileged separate order gets established without any explicit public legitimation, (by and for the police and also in favour of those who exercise leading functions in the party and the state, and relatives of these) so that the man in the street does not even know whether the legal status of the prohibited act has been modified, or whether it is only a matter of selective non-implementation that regularly selects on the basis of the culprits being within the boundaries of party and state power? Or in which an overpoliticisation of society can turn into over-reliance upon authorities to such a degree that guarantees of rights become practically unheard of in whole periods of legal development (e.g., in case of the disappearance of the presumption of innocence, or of the bare idea of meting out milder punishments than those proposed by the state prosecutor, or just of the possibility of acquittal) as happened in the Soviet Union until the recent past? Or in which the political context undergoes such a dramatic deterioration that something which is still legally conceivable (such as the disciplinary dismissal of a prison officer of the highest rank in the wake of a report submitted in the official way by a political convict) may be transformed from a real possibility (such as was reported by the late Hungarian poet and essayist, Gyula Illyés, in his historical memoirs, writing of an event that had happened in the turbulent years of the so-called white terror in the early 1920s) into being an historical anecdote without any contemporary impact except as making people smile (for let us bear in mind that even in Hungary the prison Code was confidential material for decades)?

What happens in real life does not necessarily depend upon norms, just as norms do not necessarily reflect or derive from such happenings. But positing a normative sphere can only make sense provided that at the same time you posit a world of facts that can be contrasted to it. And, as is known, in social existence normativity can only play a role if it is assumed that as soon as one raises the possibility of bringing the two into relation, every actualisation of the normative is an actualisation by the other.

What else is interesting at all in these examples, the list of which could undoubtedly be continued? To bring about the legal control of those who implement the law is an ancient problem which has emerged in every effort to reduce law (ius) to a written text (lex), e.g., in the efforts of Justinian, or Ivan the Terrible, or Frederick the Great. The protection of laws against judicial sabotage is not a novel problem either; attempts have been made to take care of this problem institutionally from as early as the late Middle Ages. (In Byzantium, judges were under an obligation, in case of any ambiguity revealed while applying a law, to turn to the sovereign committee which was exclusively authorised to eliminate it; much the same was seen in the form of the *référé législatif* at the time of the French Revolution; the aim in both cases was to prevent judges taking liberties under the pretext of applying the law.)

The particularity of all this is an outcome of the claim to totality made by the revolutions of our century. The attempt to institutionalise change not only embraces the whole of society and virtually all the segments of its existence in a hitherto unprecedented way (étatisation of society as it were, largely annihilating its own existence, autarchy and reserves); it also displays a formidable accomplishment in formulating uniform hierarchical establishments and ruthlessly radiating and asserting central power (even if it is built upon competitive parallel competences as was done in Byzantium and as survived in Russia, as well as being a feature of the organisation of Nazi power in certain fields).

The social pathology embodied in these examples is not simply that execution slips out of the hands of the sovereign ruler or law-maker. What is new about them is that each of their components is organised into a single system of the all-embracing state, and that is the way they operate. For instance, in vain does ideology ascribe great importance to the separation of law-making and law-applying (*Rechtssetzung und Rechtsanwendung, création et application de droit*); what it enacts is in practice only one single input—and not necessarily the decisive one—in a process (consisting of interactions of elements not necessarily presupposing albeit undoubtedly supplementing each other) which is carried out in the name of law, and as its realisation. If enacting a law is in itself not sufficient to make the state machinery work in a uniform way, because each and every part and segment of it formulates, balances conflicting interests according to, and asserts, its own 'legal policy', then we may in the end see a state come into existence where that which is enacted in books will be accidental as compared to what will actually be made to happen. Suppose that each and every level of state machinery did not simply consider itself to be what it is and, as such to be a functioning unit of the rule of law, but acted by holding a primary responsibility for the individual realisation of the given programme of ideology or for modernisation. In such a case, what mattered would exclusively be the agency's own 'legal policy' projected into the concrete situation, or, rather, its political, tactical or strategic considerations, or prestige points of view, or just whatever personal interests may stand behind them.

'These two articles tell us everything we need to know. The rest was not intended for us. The other articles are intended for the world at large, for those who consider that what matters are the articles, as such, not the essentials.'[2] It seems as if the way of thinking hidden in such once-off trickery of political tactics came to be the main rule followed for decades. With its long-term practice and on account of its deep immorality it thoroughly undermined the validity of everything objectivated—words, writing, institutions. What was sabotaged was not a single institution or person but a complete sub-system integrated into the total system of society. The legal system itself could not but become Janus-faced, as a phenomenon internally split and built upon the negation of one of its manifestations.

All the way from children's tales up to the painful reality of today, we may encounter the myth of the good ruler whose wicked entourage is a source of mere suffering for the people. Is the assumption which projects before us the gigantic struggle of good law and bad execution the same in value? Or even more so if the Number One in the power structure qualifies the execution as unlawful too, and perhaps even names an individual as personifying the unlawful execution and has him executed too?

At this point the question must definitely be raised whether this phenomenon is indeed unlawfulness. To put it more precisely: can something which is the result of the closed operation of a closed system of law be unlawful at all?

1 *Unlawfulness or Law in Action?*

The formal reconstruction of logic manifested in the construction and operation of law[3] displays the following structure: (i) the legal system (from the Constitution through the laws and decrees up to the judgements and their enforcement in individual concrete cases) is built upon the hierarchical breakdown of the normative order into elements of decreasing generality in which each and every level (as there is no gapless definition or entailment) is qualified as *creation* within the upper level's *application*. (ii) The establishment of correspondence between a lower and a higher level (just as with the establishment of the fulfilment of any criterion within any normative system) is within the exclusive *constitutive* function of those who are responsible for its administration. (iii) Whatever has been authoritatively decided (*res judicata*) in the normative order (in the absence of a right of appeal, or after expiry of any such right) gets *incorporated* into the legal order as one of its now indelible components.

It has to be said that the legal order has an ideology and a practice of self-reference of its own. However, all that is constructed from it, is according to its own criteria, organised into a unity in a formal way—procedurally, as it were. Every step within the normative system is a constitutive function which becomes an element of the normative system through gaining legal force. Thus, at the risk of over-simplification, one may state that whatever has been posited as a part of the legal order becomes a part of it. The ideology of law and its self-certification as lawful can have variable social weight, but may even amount to no more than words.

In this sense the legal order offers no independent evaluation, separable from its formal-procedural closure: once anything has been successfully injected into the legal order as part of it, it has at the same time been made a legitmate (i.e. lawful) part of it.

The concept of validity is generally used for describing and explaining the unity of the legal system. But it follows from what has been said that validity is also the product of a constitutive function. It is not a quality inherent in acts or objects, but is the result of their getting qualified which—provided certain social and legal conditions are met—comes into being in the system's self-reference as its own qualification of itself by itself.[4] Consequently, the inference of the validity of the system from the so-called apex norm (*Grundnorm*) proves to have an ideological character too. For the system actually proceeds step by step within a contiuum in which the inference and/or transposition of validity also takes place step by step. In the alternative, and just to the contrary, validation is non-vertical as it gets carried out, in a diversity of directions, not only from above but horizontally and from below too, with various norms supporting one another in a self-renewing interaction within the continuity of the system.[5]

From this flows the necessary conclusion that normative closure is not a feature outwardly added to law, as a contingent characteristic of it, but one which belongs to a communication performed in a specific practice of reference which—(granted other social and legal conditions) establishes law. That is to say, it is that practice of reference that in a normatively closed way performs what we call 'law', and carries it as the exclusive medium of its specific motion and social existence.[6]

Thus the crux of our argumentation is procedurality and, particularly, the procedural institutionalisation of legal force. It is nothing other than the formal-procedural closure of the normatively closed systems at any given time in which the last word utterable and uttered—without further regard to what that word is or to the relationship it has to the other components of the system—becomes for all purposes a member of the system.

Consequently—and precisely with a view to the final shaping of the system—an enormous responsibility is laid on the pre-closing phase of motion within the system. This is why it is stressed that there must be feedback into the legal (sub-) system as it is at any given moment from all the other subsystems of society; and this must be internally acceptable in the legal (sub-) system.

In other words, the existence of a *remedy in law*, i.e. an *appeal*, in order to harmonise actual legal movement with desirable legal movement as socially perceived according to the 'natural meaning' of legal texts, or, in our context and terms, the establishment of the institutional and operational conditions of reconsideration, is therefore not simply and not merely the deferential begging of the subject for the self-limitation of an otherwise unlimited tyranny of power. On the contrary, the powers that be have the most urgent short-term and long-term interest in being able to identify as their own law (indelible and unmodifiable) what they have presented as such in sober state, after repeated reconsideration, with no remaining trace of the concrete-individual circumstances in space and time which may have influenced their first, primitive, reaction.

Just to repeat: as a result of formal closure, everything becomes legal in law which occurs as legal, where there is no institutionally possible and conceivable alternative.

This dilemma may become actualised in a diversity of ways—from terroristic situations to bureaucratic manipulations. It may happen, for example, that a robbery or a rape committed by a member of the occupying forces is punishable with death both on paper and in practice, yet it may be that more frequently the initiative is foreclosed by the liquidation of the victim. It may happen that those who make reports about resort by the authorities to apparently illegitimate violence, not only have no chance of a serious hearing, but face the risk of being accused of defying the authority. Routine administrative action may also produce situations allowing of no real alternatives. The silence of the administration can prove to be impossible to fight against successfully (e.g. the resistance of the governmental agency mentioned above could not be broken by those applying for a licence for private publishing for a year and a half). Similar problems flow from the arbitrariness of present-day procedure (e.g., the registration of associations, a responsibility of local councils according to the law, was practically suspended by the non-legal requirement of prior political approval by the police or the Communist Party in Hungary for years). The exercise of discretionary power can also be wholly devoid of grounding in the law in force (e.g. in a practice of police administration where the reasons officially given for imposing obligations, limitations, or prohibitions merely reiterate the general wording of the law—e.g. 'offending the public interest'). Independence of anything legal is quite obvious in cases of quasi-administrative practice where we may only speak about the one-sided abuse of a power position subject neither to legal authorisation nor to legal limitation (e.g., management of the press through the use of 'prohibited authors' lists by the government press agency, or quasi-administrative press management through the daily interventions of the local organs of the party).

What is going on here? I believe that in such situations the law is not simply distorted but is subject to a modification touching upon its basic identity. For in such cases the political motives of law-making will be reposited for a particular situation in a concretely actualised way, while the true motives are *praeter* or *contra legem* as it were, that is, not at all determined by any legalistic considerations such as those in whose name action is taken.

The outcome in such a case may be politically desirable or rationally justifiable, but from a *legal* point of view it is nothing but arbitrariness and chaos. By negating the law's principle of construction it denies the idea of law itself. Yet arbitrariness in the guise of law is certainly even worse than anything else. As long as law has any kind of prestige for those subjected to it, arbitrariness committed in the name of law is the hardest of all to defend oneself against,[7] and the harm done is not merely that of arbitrariness but also the consequential damage to the prestige and moral credit of law, so important to any future.[8] In the final analysis, law is far from being simply a rule; it is a state (no matter how evaluated) of order, issuing from the practice of rule(s).

In *Alice in Wonderland*, Alice and the others might have believed at the beginning that, in the Queen's game of croquet, croquet was really played. However, they soon had to realise from the Queen's orders and their implementation that, instead, it was only the Queen's game that was being played. And even though they may have become confused about the nature of so obscure a game, that did not change the fact that there was a game in progress, and it had rules, although there was actually but one rule reconstructable and foreseeable, namely that the Queen alone was competent to set all the further rules.[9] Rules which have been declared to have and believed to have institutional standing may be subverted completely. But then her allocation of discretion will immediately institutionalise some new one(s) in their place. Something like this was experienced by Alice *Through the Looking Glass*: 'When I use a word,' Humpty Dumpty said in a rather scornful tone, 'it means just what I choose it to mean—neither more nor less.' 'The question is,' said Alice, 'whether you can make words mean so many different things.' 'The question is,' said Humpty Dumpty, 'which is to be the master—that's all'[10]

After all, what does it mean to say that a law is unconstitutional? or that a decree is unlawful? or that a decision taken by the judiciary offends a norm? The formal reconstruction of the internal logic of law conceptualises this question in terms of conflict of norms. It accepts as an axiomatic basis that to be free from contradictions is not a logical principle of the system. Consequently, any conflict established outside the law may concern validity within the law only and exclusively (i) as the outcome of the exclusion of this conflict from the system by a measure of positive law; (ii) after its presence within the law has been constitutively established within the law.[11]

The 'fact' of unlawfulness may only be established legally by the law. What is more, establishment of it may only be made by the law where there is a procedure for eliminating from the system whatever has been qualified as 'unlawful'. In other words: unlawfulness may be established only in order to start a process of reconsideration. And this process—like any process in the law—poses a dichotomous alternative: either unlawfulness gets established and, by the same stroke, discarded, or the attempt fails and the lawful quality of what was challenged is confirmed, and its position within the system becomes unchallengeable.

This means that logic turns upside down the ideology expressed in the statement: 'the lawful is whatever is within the law', and concludes instead: 'whatever is within the law is lawful'. At the same time, it realises what follows from this consistent logic: only that can be unlawful which thereby gets placed outside the law. And with this we have reached again our starting point: in law the decisive moment is the last word utterable and actually uttered in a process, the one which gains legal force.

What the whole thing boils down to is that, from a legal point of view, the law *hic et nunc* is what cannot be appealed against in procedure. From a social point of view, it is what is imposed upon society as a legal practice without the chance of society doubting it. This is what gets institutionalised as law in society; this is what those subjected to it can adjust to as the only foreseeable and rationally calculable standard in law.

Accordingly, no matter what tragic periods have been displayed by our history, only a public opinion trusting in the 'natural' meaning of words can call them 'periods of unlawfulness'. For if I call them that as a contemporary, I only give articulation to one of the possible opinions according to which the system in question is not consistent, not coherent, nor, above all, free from contradictions. That is to say, I am arguing for the institutionalisation of something differing in content from what exists as law, even though I refer to the same text (actually: to a different interpretation of it).

The fact that law as experienced (*droit vécu*, rather than imposed) may at times be antihuman, corrupting, and even murderous, and that it may negate the sense of justice of contemporaries, or the judgement of posterity as to the 'natural' meaning of the enacted law, cannot be alleviated by the statement of its unlawfulness in retrospect, or by any kind of social, political, or legal rehabilitation. What was experienced as law by contemporaries can no longer be changed. Law can only declare change *ex nunc*—which may concern nothing but exclusively the judgement of posterity.

2 *Negation of Law or a Separate Order?*

What happens in situations which we regard as unlawful because of their contradicting our natural sense of justice and our trust in the 'natural' meaning of words? Must that which has been declared as law but which we consider unfit for living through as law be discarded from the realm of law? Or is it perhaps a kind of legal order, but one that splits, and engenders internal divisions?

The situation described above is commonly referred to as an antimony within the legal order.[12] This characterisation is obviously based upon a belief in doctrinal clarification, i.e. in the logical unambiguity of each and every statement within the law and consequently also of their interconnection. In turn, it presupposes the homogeneous formalisation of each and every component on the one hand, and the identification of meaning on the other.

In view of the fact that these situations are to a great extent confused, casual and unforeseeable, they resist formalised expression and also the identification of the original enactment, till the very end. In other words, until you have eliminated the problem you cannot define what parts to count as antinomic at all. That is why such a split is to be conceived of as particularisation or fragmentation, in which an ideal projection gets broken in practice, engendering a series of separate orders.

The only outcome of this process that can be taken for granted is a practical negation of the generality of law. But the question of what separate orders the law breaks into is only formulated in the practice of arbitrariness, contingent from a legal point of view. Law becomes unforeseeable not only because of the leeways affecting what will be declared part of it but also because so often the law as one has experienced it can also be described in retrospect only.

When speaking about particularism or fragmentation, our knowledge of history brings to mind the separate orders of the feudal social/legal structure. However, the arbitrariness now in question cannot be referred to as re-feudalisation. Let me just mention the Chinese, Aztec, or medieval European modes of regulation. They calibrated law according to personal status from the very beginning. And anything that was experienced as law was properly built into the law without the annihilation of law and its ideal, without creating a legally unmotivated split between law as declared and as experienced. Consequently, it was undertaken in a moral sense as well (just as at the end of the last century the authors of the German Civil Code, when preparing the very first civil law book common to the whole nation, drafted a special set of regulations for the imperial family, working these into the structure of the Code itself as a novel added to it). So even from the point of view of the ideals of feudalism, the arbitrariness of which I am speaking has an atavistic character.

The problem itself puts enormous weight on the responsibility of the holders of power for what they shape as law, for there lies the responsibility for resisting temptation of a direct power reaction to any given situation in favour of a transformation of power into law, with the consequent opportunity for an appeal and possible subsequent reconsideration. And when genuine consolidation is at hand, no matter how ashamed those responsible for the exercise of power are and must be of the past and present experiences, they cannot and must not shrug off the past and separate themselves from it by simply referring to what is already trodden into the past as 'the age of unlawfulness', for that was the law itself as it was experienced at that time. In other words, their responsibility for the past defines their responsibility for both the present and the future, since they never do anything in the name of the law but what they are willing also to undertake as law.

II *The Pathologies of Legal Mediation*

What may be hidden behind all that ideologically? Obviously, a concept of law instrumentalised to the utmost, having lost genuine social backing, simplified into a sterile state.

But if we are to approach the problem which is historically and politically specific to our regions, we have to see something else as well. Primarily, a self-asserting Marxism, which in its practice, by postulating a unity of the methodological principles of the historical and the logical subordinated history to its utopia of the future, i.e. re-posited it according to its wishes and felt needs, adjusted it to tactical considerations too, as a result of which even the logical could at most be manifested in a medium emptied of real past and future.

In order that something could serve as ideological background, no system of theses identified with a theory is needed. It may be sufficient to conceptualise it as the quintessence of practice.

Well, without being authorised to find any kind of scapegoat, I believe that all the simplifications related to law can at least symbolically be traced back to the wording of a political pamphlet, the *The Communist Manifesto* and I emphasise here that I am speaking about simplifications committed later in the name of theory, and not about the political and related merits of a political pamphlet: '[Y]our law is but the will of your class made into a law for all.'

Only to recall some facts of history: in Europe at the beginning of our century the spokesmen of the communist cause had to stand up against the sanctity of the law as such, in order to prepare the way for their objective, i.e. to overthrow the standing order. However, it seems that once they were in possession of power, they only learnt from Marxism—neglecting even the context of the quoted sentence[13]—that law is but state command, the will of the ruling class now represented by themselves. It is not the expression of a social integration as in sociology; it is not the basic feature of social organisation as in anthropology (*ubi societas ibi ius*); it is not the agent of mediation which makes social co-operation possible as in Lukacs[14]—it is simply a one-sided instrument aimed at enforcing the power policy of the state. Or it is like a communicating vessel in which no movement is made possible except in one direction arbitrarily; it proceeds downwards from above and is as it is. It is like a medium whose agent is narrowed down *ad absurdum*, for the ruling class will be represented by its vanguard, and the vanguard, in turn, by those acting in its name.

1 *Instrumentalisation*

In social movements inspired by ideological considerations and/or the force of modernisation, usually two influences compete. On the one hand, one may identify in them a deep mistrust of any spontaneity, together with a mentality driving them to institutionalise every change in a compulsory way, radiated downwards hierarchically by legal decrees and the compelling force of state machinery. On the other hand, in the long run, the only legal reforms which can be implemented are those which re-assert reforms already achieved socially or initiate their implementation by offering desirable alternatives. To bring about a social reform by proclaiming a mere text to be a law is bound to fail.

This is a general dilemma of any undertaking which tries to come to grips with modernisation, and the wide regions of Eastern Central Europe are not an exception here. As a matter of fact, belatedness in development, with every step bound to forced paths issued in a specific practice long ago, namely that of relying exaggeratedly upon law and upon the state's having the only hand in shaping law. In the orbit of socialism, one finds the inheritance of voluntarism asserting its prejudices and proclaiming social utopias in the disguise of revolutionary committedness.

It has had a final result, as to substance, in the following characteristics: 1, the 'inference' of each and every practical step from a 'philosophy of history' approached quasi-normatively as an axiomatic theorem for deduction and, correspondingly, 2, the irrelevancy of all kinds of pragmatic consideration and empirical feedback; and, as to form, 3, the gapless etatisation of law and its treatment as mere command, in which 4, whatever is posited by the state as such will become the decisive factor and is implemented, on behalf of the ruling class and representing its vanguard, by anyone who just happens to be at the top.

However, such an extreme instrumentalisation cannot be without retribution in the long run. Making law arbitrary socially generates its own failure in that law becomes socially arbitrary. For the limitation of genuine reforms to an overproduction of arbitrary changes puts into operation a self perpetuating inflationary spiral which results in a further narrowing of an already limited scope of action. The fact is that problems accumulated as a result of the dysfunctional effects of non-organic interventions become increasingly more difficult to handle. This necessarily pushes towards solutions in which actual social reform comes to be replaced by the mere enactment of reform texts, accompanied by accumulating inefficiency and loss of credit. And the result can be nothing else but unavoidable defeat: the irrevocable devaluation of both the instruments and the ideologies behind them.

2 *Reduction to a one-faced, one-directioned medium*

The harms done by instrumentalisation primarily appear in the reduction of law to a one-faced, one-directioned medium. This follows from the tendency of power-holders to be aware of nothing else in law than solely the significance in power politics of their dominion over it. Their horizons are reduced to embracing only their potentiality for assertion of tyranny in dominating law, i.e. their ability to shape law and manipulate its operation as they like. The idea of legal mediation—admitting that law is not simply the ornament of their mightful '*nobis placet*' at any given time but a form of institutionalised bondage which, once established, binds all parties involved as sharing partners in the common enterprise of law—has hardly been developed in it. To an even lesser extent has the readiness evolved which would allow law to gain ground against mere power in situations where it might limit interests whatever they are—if they are proclaimed, or just sensed by those involved, as enjoying political protection.

As a matter of fact, there is hardly any law existing here. What is claimed to be law exists in inconsistent, one-sided allusions. It exists only in allusions to what they want and do and what is good for them; but the same may happen not to be good any longer if it turns out to serve the good of others, to 'their own' disadvantage.

This weakness of law is no more than an outcome of the similarly rudimentary character of politics. Politics can only subordinate law to its daily business because of the extremist concentration of power, which, in the long run, hinders politics also from functioning genuinely. Whatever has not developed is defective. What is characteristic of such politics is a one-sided manifestation of will and its implementation by all means at any price—sometimes by means of law (if possible), at other times through any other means as may seem expedient there and then.

What is it we are faced with conceptually in law? To put it in the language of ontology: fulfilment of the function of social mediation (*Vermittlung*). This means that law ought to be institutionalised as the medium of orderly interaction in society. It ought to be a filter which channels social action into given directions. It gets incorporated into the totality of motion as a filter which, growing into a genuine social institution defines a framework of action and sets standards to all its addressees, i.e. it is to function as a specific established agent of social mediation so as to make the co-operation of social sub-systems and the interaction of all its individual participants orderly and possible—in such a way that, as a special sub-system of society itself, it preserves and reproduces its own autonomy of heterogeneity by its closedness in its self-reproductive function and its openness towards being set in motion.[15]

In other words, mediation has at least two conceptual components which are *sine qua non*: (a) it ensures interaction (b) which is to go on in an orderly way. Ensuring interaction presupposes at least two parties in social commerce who, from the point of view of the chances of movement within the system (and, accordingly, from the point of view of the chance of exerting actual influence through the system), are equivalent. A one-sided filter operating in a single direction is therefore excluded from this. Interaction is incompatible with the existence of anyone who can come into contact with the filter but still is not bound by it. Ensuring orderliness refers to the closedness of the system. This is what gives sense to its existence as a system and makes it operate according to the precepts that posit its closedness as well. In consequence, an operation made up exclusively of the exercise of discretionary power is excluded from it—i.e. an operation in which the only orderly component is the allocation of competence to exercise; for this has the result that the supposedly final dispositions of law are not operating according to their own terms but have undergone discretionary replacement by mere arbitrariness acting as a 'casual separate order'.

As a result of the want of orderliness, such law can act neither as a mediator nor as a transmission (for even transformation no matter how onesided it is, displays some orderliness). Such a phenomenon reminds me at best of a club in possession of, and used at will by, mere Might (which must not be misnamed as 'power', as this term, reminiscent of *potestas* may be coupled with legitimating overtones). Just as you cannot call it a 'boxing' match if one party has no gloves and cannot return the other's, so I cannot call 'law' the club which is not accessible to everyone under the same rules and with the same chances.

To put it again: it is an abuse even to posit to or characterise something as a legal system if it does not work so as to mediate in the sense of facilitating an orderly interaction. For the only long-term effect of such a practice is the destruction of the distinctiveness, heterogeneity, dignity and prestige proper to law and thereby to block the chances of any further development as well.

Perhaps those involved in the communist cause have failed to notice that their revolutionary breakthrough was crowned with success, that they actually took over power, and that it was their own law that they started ruining with the ruthlessly ambitious practice of their contnued revolution breaking through everyday life? Perhaps they have not had confidence in their own enactments, or, admittedly, these have only been intended as results of a transitory compromise 'for the world at large'? For power annihilates its own law if it is not willing to filter its own measures through law; if it considers law to be applicable only to whatever extent it happily coincides with its own interests, otherwise acting almost freely through developing and asserting a casual 'legal policy' of its own; if power rejects law's being called up and put into operation when it happens to be at the other side of the match. For the law in which what is clothed in the robe of law is non-legal or overtly illegal, according to how the huge social majority understands that same law can be nothing but a mere façade.

Legality? It seems as if the revolutionising programme according to which '[as] motive forces they must sink to the status of matters of complete indifference,'[16] has been implemented in a way which proves all too successful. It is just the Lukácsian dilemma and prognosis stated in the above quoted *Legality and Illegality* of 1920. As if excluding the very idea that the revolution would ever establish itself, its uncertainty and mistrust would push it towards handling its own institutions in the old 'revolutionary' manner, as if from outside, with practical indifference towards form. For according to political conventions still accepted in Hungary, the sign of dedication is if someone achieves with all the means accessible (i.e. arbitrarily from a legal point of view, not bearing the law in mind as a criterion) what he believes to be the interest of socialism (and what may of course be of purely personal interest as well, if assertable within the system). For if everyone is a revolutionary, getting their mandate from the movement's monopoly of legitimacy in building the future, there is no wonder that in justice, parliament and government as well, attempts at realising the particular values of law are looked upon as suspicious means aimed at unidentified objectives. Appeals to law are seen as a quasi-neutral expression of marked hostility, in any case as something inadequate and, therefore, worthy of disdain. This was a fact of common experience in the recent past.

These tendencies are present in every radical movement as a basic dilemma;[17] to restrict the ideology of the 'emergency situation' to cases of genuinely forced paths is everywhere problematic.

At the same time, the variety of historical–regional contexts defines particular features as well. What happened in Hungary, for example, followed on defeat in war. The country was occupied in the name of the Big Four by one of them which, there and then, also represented the Stalinist model of socialism. A fight then started for the primacy in and the exclusiveness of power. By getting hold of the key positions in police, army, home and foreign offices, the winners substituted for rule of law patterns the direct political utilisation of state machinery. Every sort of abuse and short-sighted dissipation of the national wealth occurred in the management of oil and other fields designated for filling up the treasury of the winning party. In order to 'support' the elections, the state printing house was used for fraudulent manipulation of the ballot. The only judiciary for public law issues, the Administrative Court, was dissolved because (as we were able to learn recently from the Hungarian monthly review of juridical science in Hungary) it lost its sense of time and referred to the law not realising that something else was at stake then. The political essayist István Biho, fighting for the establishment of political and legal culture, i.e. for there to be rules of the game in (and in spite of) the struggle, was put down by the communist ideologist Georg Lukács. That seems to have 'sorted out' the fate of law but not for only one day. As Lukács, near the time of his death, might have said, this fact was irreversible, in the sense of having been built into the social processes as a factor which became immanent in them.[18]

After all, can ruining a homogeneous medium be a politically justified function at all? Especially if thereby law is to slip back into the undifferentiated heterogeneity of the crudenesss of the clenched fist? I believe that notwithstanding the facts shown above, the answer is still positive. It can be justified, obviously under certain conditions, in cases when breaking through needs also discontinuity, providing that it immediately starts laying down the bases of its own continuity. For if it fails to do so, it strangulates its own future with its own hands.

3 *Loss of Contents*

Instrumentalisation also appears whenever law is conceived as law empty of contents. This means that, discarding all traditions and past experiences, law becomes synonymous with whatever of what is just those at the top want it to be. Practice is still strongly inclined to reduce law into a means which, in possession of power, can be shaped and applied quite freely. But to do this is to forget that it is only texts and hierarchical organisations that can be organised by a stroke of the pen, while it is impossible in that way to build society, or to participate in the advantages which stem from legal mediation.

For, socially, law has an optimum content and level of utilisation at any given time. Certainly this is not so in the sense of the possibility of defining or determining it; not even in the sense that it could be inferred. But it is true in the sense that a well-designed interference is conceivable. This means that, in retrospect, you can always establish when and to what extent there was optimal proportionality of functional effects and dysfunctional side-effects resulting from the given interference. This can only be done in retrospect, approaching the desired evaluation of the result from the angle of scoring for degrees of error. However, by revealing the steps on the road to the negative result, it defines bases of exclusion.[19]

At the same time it is to be noted that no matter how conservative the instruments of law are and no matter how strongly legal development is characterised by the re-adaptation of old instruments instead of inventing new ones,[20] new situations always mean new sets of conditions, and human creativity is manifested in proper adaptation. For instruments in themselves are neutral, displaying their features and potentials exclusively in a concrete context. No matter how much experience and invention is compressed into a pair of forceps used in obstetrics, for instance, in relation to eye surgery it probably does not even count as being a medical instrument.

III *Law and the Question of its Conceptual Minimum*

The generally accepted view of law does not essentially differ from what is traditionally attributed to German legal positivism: it is what it is. Nor did Marxism offer any new criteria as it degenerated into a kind of socialist normativism: law is what is enacted and/or enforced by the state. In contrast to that, what we call law on account of certain contents may at the most be natural law (or, to use a Marxist phraseology, only law according to its own ideological self-assertion). Although there is no excuse for theories becoming shallow, in the case of such a dichotomic polarisation, I believe, there is presumably also something more and else at stake. I have in mind the development of modern formal law as an institutional set-up defining itself by its own postulates both in the validity of its construction and the legality of its operation,[21] and, thereby, the claims about the law's self-reference, self-organisation and self-constitution, apparently of a systems-theoretical relevancy only, gaining genuine ontological significance.[22] To admit that makes it possible to justify theoretically a concept of law which separates from itself as non-law everything that it does not define as law.

At the same time, we confront numerous problems contemporary society is expected to cope with. All over the world our century has prolifically produced crises, atavisms, primitivisms, moral poverty and a great many other forms of inhumanity that have led—especially since World War Two—to increasing efforts at, and claims for, asserting a new natural law. In law proper this may assume a diversity of expressions.

Attempts have been made to introduce directly the values of democracy, freedom and equality as minimum conditions into law. Material preconditions of law and order, that is to say, of legality, have been defined. A catalogue of human rights has been established in order to make it a *sine qua non* component. Under the auspices of legal culture, everything desirable has been put into words. Well, no matter how outstanding results all this may have brought in challenging theory and in popular/professional mobilisation and practice too, it could not amount to a theoretical renewal, since it has failed to substantiate the concept of law theoretically. (Theoretically it has been bound to fail as it has actually failed at transcending the level of the presentation of mere desires. Still, at the same time it has been successful in provoking an enormous breakthrough as a result of the codification of human rights and of the underlying conditions of law and order. It has promised an international law to which, in the long run, *volens nolens* each domestic law and order will have to conform. This, however, even in a case of full satisfaction will not result in the theoretical substantiation of the concept of law but, instead, as it may be hoped for, it will, finally and at least, result in a practical standard leading to more humanness in the institutions of human kind.)

Within legal philosophy too there have been several attempts at defining the minimum contents of law. In West-European, South-American and British-American legal cultures, theories of natural law, justice and ethics have developed significant traditions which, having in view their starting point, i.e. value-orientation and cultural dependency, are at their best in formulating axiologically oriented theories, bound to given cultures, but not laying down general ontological foundations.[23]

Other trends are towards defining, from an anthropological, ontological or sociological standpoint, the minimum contents of law which are necessary for social reproduction; or the minimum conditions of average obedience to the law and the exceptionality in principle of the need to actually resort to compulsion, which are the minimum conditions of the self-reproduction of law as systems of norms that are asserting themselves in society.[24] Such and similar claims can be and are theoretically justified even in a framework free from any value-boundness. However, in the final analysis, they testify to the conditions of the chances in the long run not so much of law but rather of its successful societal self-reproduction.

Finally, there are attempts far from any kind of direct substantiation, formulating nothing but formal-technical requirements as basic conditions of the 'morality' which 'makes law possible' (enactment of rules, their publicity, non-retroactivity, understandability, freedom from contradictions, realisability, stability, implemetation according to their actual wording); attempts which make the purposefully formulated internal coherence of law and its consequentiality the basic condition of the law-maker's achieving any moral credibility at all; and, finally, theoretical reconstructions which interpret law as a process within a continuity of changing density, which continuity is made up as the result at any given time of the continuous interaction between the factors of positing law as law, enforcing law as law, and socially complying with law as law.[25] Although due to their formal-technical approach and freedom from values, these are the theories which come closest to the possibility of offering a general theoretical answer, nevertheless, they also miss the point as they do not answer what is now the question. For, instead of the minimum conditions of law, one of them delineates the basic conditions of the technology of how to make the law function in a socially effective way, the second speaks about its underlying social embeddedness, while the third touches upon the components of any legal operation (including its pathologies as well), i.e. the characterisation of its genuine dynamism.

At this stage, one may well wish to ask the question: is there no chance of transcending the purely formal interest of legal positivism? of supplementing the systemic closedness of the self-definition of law with minimum conditions pointing beyond this systemic closedness? of limiting the arbitrariness already present in the formation and implementation of law—at least in theory, on the level of conceptualisation, by defining law in terms also of a conceptual minimum?

The answer is difficult to give—for we are here to bear in mind the failure of prior attempts. Anyway, in the light of past experience it is doubtful whether we can introduce directly a material criterion directly into the concept of law. At the same time, it seems that certain features of substance can be incorporated in it, due to their formal-procedural aspects as technical-technological equivalents. The question arises: if I define the ontological minimum of normative mediation by reference to the criteria of orderly interaction, shall I not arrive at the formal expression of a quasi-material minimum?

Whatever the answer might be, it is obviously quasi-material since the formulation of legal contents is free from any restriction from this point of view too: it is 'a great mystery', as the formal reconstruction of the normative system has characterised the act of law-making, situated at the borderline of the transubstantiation between 'Is' and 'Ought'.[26] However, once law making has taken place, all the political motives behind it, and all the sociological setting for it revert to being completely irrelevant. What should now exclusively matter is what has been posited as law in law: there is no 'up' and 'down' any longer. However, if there is no 'up' and 'down' any more, the moment of the quasi-material is immediately transformed into a material one in the sense that legislation defines a kind of equality in function of the posited legal text. We learn from historical experience that any degree of equality (no matter how low it be even in limiting-cases) is at the same time a degree of practical freedom. (According to the myth,[27] at least the Law of the Twelve Tables in Rome could figure as the first example of a legal revolution fought about a mere form. The direct objective may have been the public recording of the law as it was already meted out by the patricians; but it was known that this in itself meant the democratisation of legal knowledge, i.e., a degree of equality which, up to the level of this degree, resulted in a certain freedom as well.) It is perhaps a conceivable and feasible solution to describe law as mediation in the ontological sense, and thus through its connotations to insert also a minimum of equality and, thereby, freedom, into the very concept of law.

We have to accept that, in the final analysis, the game of the Queen is also law. Thus law is also this purely arbitrary unlimited discretion, in which the only moment reminiscent of legality is that discretion is allocated, i.e. that the momentary caprice referred to as law is practised by the Queen. But it is far from being full-fledged; it is defective, faulty, and inferior. Since it does not provide orderly interaction, its ontological existence is not that of a mediating complex in social existence. Therefore it is open to question whether, in an ontological sense, we should be better to call it a state of pre-law instead.

In consequence, it seems that, even though with several transpositions, equality, and, as a function of it, freedom, is also a part of the law, just as medical interference needs something more than the bare belief of the medicine-men, the lancet, incision, blood, and suffering. As recovery seems to be related to genuine healing, I guess, a part of the law should be its taking itself seriously too.

NOTES

1 Antal Mádl and Judit Györi (eds), *Thomas Mann und Ungarn; Essays, Dokumente, Bibliographie* (Budapest: Akadémiai Kiadó, 1977) pp. 339–40; cf. Csaba Varga, *The Place of Law in Lukács's World Concept* (Budapest: Akadémiai Kiadó, 1985) p. 56.

2 Quoted as an interpretation given by the president of the revolutionary tribunal in Chita, Siberia, by Endre Sik, *Próbaévek* [Years of Trial and Error] (Budapest: Zrínyi, 1967) p. 762. Following the half decade of the practical annihilation of law, one of its preconditions for avoiding bankruptcy and allowing capital flow into the country was that a Criminal Law be introduced in the Soviet Union. Lenin proposed (unusually for a post-feudal state) that the court be authorised to consider anything to be a crime on the basis of two general clauses, namely, (1) what was regarded as socially dangerous, and (2) what it found to be analogous to any category of crime defined in the Criminal Law. Cf. Csaba Varga, 'The Formation of a New, Socialist Type of Codification' in *Acta Juridica Academiae Scientiarum Hungaricae* 17 (1975) 1–2, pp. 113–14 and Csaba Varga, 'Lenin and Revolutionary Law-making', *International Review of Contemporary Law*, 1/1982, pp. 48 f.

3 Hans Kelsen, *General Theory of Law and State* (Cambridge, Mass: Harvard University Press, 1946), *The Pure Theory of Law*, trans. Max Knight (Berkeley: University of California Press, 1967), and *Allgemeine Theorie der Normen* (Vienna: Manzsche 1979) as interpreted in Csaba Varga, 'Kelsen's Rechtsanwendungslehre', in *Rechtstheorie* 18 (1986) in press.

4 Cf. Csaba Varga, 'Heterogeneity and Validity of Law: Outlines of an Ontological Reconstruction' In Csaba Varga and Ota Weinberger (eds) *Rechtsgeltung* (Stuttgart: Steiner, 1986) [*Archiv für Rechts- und Sozialphilosophie*, Beiheft 27].

5 Cf. e.g. Aleksander Peczenik, 'The Structure of a legal System', *Rechtstheorie* 6 (1975) 1, and, just in the sense followed in the text, Werner Krawietz 'Die Lehre vom Stufenbau des Rechts—eine säkularisierte politische Teleologie?' in Werner Krawietz and Helmut Schelsky, eds, *Rechtssystem und gesellschaftliche Basis bei Hans Kelsen* (Berlin: Duncker und Humblot 1984) [Rechtstheorie Beiheft 5].

6 This is the point stressed in several recent papers by Niklas Luhmann (cf. primarily his 'The Self-reproduction of Law and its Limits' in Gunther Teubner (ed) *Dilemmas of Law in the Welfare State* (Berlin and New York: de Gruyter 1986) and his 'The Unity of the Legal System' in Gunther Teubner, ed., *Autopoieteic Law* (Berlin and New York: de Gruyter 1988). Cf. also Csaba Varga 'Judicial Reproduction of the Law in an Autopoietical System' [an invited

paper to be published in the proceedings of the 13th World Congress on Philosophy of Law and Social Philosophy].

7 See the differentiation between state and law 'simply accepted as unproblematic' and those which 'count merely as a power factor' according to Georg Lukács in 'Legality and Illegality' (1920), reprinted in his *History and Class Consciousness: Studies in Marxist Dialectics* (trans. Rodney Livingstone, Cambridge, Mass: The MIT Press, 1971).

8 Cf. e.g Kálmán Kulcsár 'Politics and Law-Making in Central- East-Europe' in Zoltán Péteri, ed., *Legal Theory—Comparative Law Studies in Honor of Professor Imre Szabó* (Budapest: Akadémiai Kiadó, 1984).

9 Quoted by Antony Allott in *The Limits of Law* (London: Butterworths, 1980) pp. 255–6 as a positive answer to the question raised by Aleksander Solzhenitsyn in his *Gulag Archipelago*, namely whether all things considered Soviet law is law at all.

10 Lewis Carroll *Through the Looking Glass* [1872] (Puffin Books edn, p. 274).

11 Cf. note 3 and, in particular, Kelsen *Allgemeine Theorie der Normen*, ch. 29, p. 101.

12 Cf. Carlos E. Alchourrón and Eugenio Bulygin *Normative Systems* (Vienna and New York: Springer, 1971) pp. 123ff and Ch. Perelman, ed., *Les antinomies en Droit Dialectica* 69/62, 18 (1964) (Brussels: Bruylant, 1965).

13 'Your very ideas are but the outgrowth of the conditions of your bourgeois production and bourgeois property, just as your jurisprudence [Recht] is but the will of your class made into a law [Gesetz] for all, a will, whose essential character and direction are determined by the economic conditions of existence of your class.' K. Marx and F. Engels 'The Manifesto of the Communist Party' [1848] in their *Collected Works* VI (Moscow: Progress, 1975). Cf. Varga *The Place* pp. 96–8.

14 For Lukács, language and law are special part-complexes mediating among the individual components of the total social complex which in turn is nothing else but the state of the interaction of complexes at any given time (cf Varga *The Place*, ch. 9.1). At the same time, 'the need [for] . . . legal regulation of social activities emerges at a relatively low level of the social division of labour', no matter how elementary this division of labour is (e.g. 'beaters and hunters in the hunt'). Geörgy Lukács, *A társadalmi lét ontológiájáról* [Towards the Ontology of Social Being] II (Budapest: Magvetö, 1976) p. 208.

15 Cf. Niklas Luhmann *The Autopoiesis of Social Systems* (Florence: European University Institute, 1985 [Colloquium Papers 81].

16 Lukács, *History and Class Consciousness*, p. 264, 'Where the total, communist, fearlessness with regard to the state and the law is present, the law and its calculable consequences are of no greater (if also of no smaller) importance than any other external fact of life with which it is necessary to reckon when deciding upon any definite course of action. The risk of breaking the law should not be regarded as very different from the risk of missing a train connection when on an important journey.'

'Where this is not the case, where it is resolved to break the law with a grand gesture, this suggests that the law has preserved its authority—admittedly in an inverted form—that it is still in a position inwardly to influence one's actions and that a genuine, inner emancipation has not yet occurred.' (Lukács, p. 263).

17 In the Hungarian Soviet Republic, for instance, the legally free scope of action of so-called 'revolutionary legality' was, even during the 133 days of its whole

existence, supplemented by a wish for law and order and also for its codificational foundations. Cf. Béla Sarlós *A Tanácsköztárság jogrendszerének kialakulása* (Budapest: Közgazdasági és Jogi Könyevkiadó, 1969). In contrast to this, in China, for instance, the struggle to achieve legal consolidation was at the same time fought out in the clash between the indigenous tradition (the unfixed, flexible *li* of Confucianism, which is a guide to moral decision-making) and the western pattern of modernisation (the *fa*, in its fixed and inflexible character reminding one of the imperial repressive laws, even though it was under Soviet influence that this was being received). Cf. Varga 'The Formation' pp. 129–32.

18 E.g. Lukács *A társadalmi lét* . . . III, pp. 172 and 359 and, as to irreversibility applied to the preservation of past facts in the collective memory of society, II, pp. 189–90.

19 This evidence in sociology, having but a negative proof, is mostly developed in case-studies. Cf. S. B. Burman and B. E. Harrell-Bond, eds, *The Imposition of Law* (New York: Academic Press, 1979). For a more general formulation, see Allott, *The Limits of Law*; Maria Borucka-Arctowa, 'Can Social Sciences Help us in Determining the Limits of Law?' in E. Kamenka, R. S. Summers and W. L. Twining, eds, *Soziologische Jurisprudenz und realistischen Theorien des Rechts* (Berlin: Duncker und Humblot, 1986) [*Rechtstheorie*, Beiheft 9].

20 Cf. Alan Watson, *Legal Transplants: An Approach to Comparative Law* (Edinburgh: Scottish Academic Press, 1974).

21 Cf. Csaba Varga, 'Moderne Staatlichkeit und modernes formales Recht' in *Acta Juridica Academiae Scientiarum Hungaricae* 26 (1984) 1–2.

22 Since the publication of his *Rechtssoziologie* (Hamburg: Rowohlt, 1972), the most radical representative of this idea has been Niklas Luhmann.

23 Just to mention one or two items from the huge bibliography on the topic: Heinrich Rommen *Die ewige Wiederkehr des Naturrechts* (Leipzig: Hegner, 1936) and Leo Strauss *Natural Right and History* (Chicago: The University of Chicago Press, 1953); Otto A. Bird *The Idea of Justice* (New York: Praeger, 1967) and John Rawls *A Theory of Justice* (Cambridge, Mass.: Harvard University Press, 1971); David Lyons *Ethics and the Rule of Law* (Cambridge: Cambridge University Press, 1984).

24 E.g. Maria Borucka-Arctowa 'Koncepcja "natury ludzkiej" wspolczesne problemy oceny prawa' *Etyka* 1970/6 and 'A természetjog jelenkori problémái és a jogtuda kérdése' [The Contemporary Problems of Natural law and the Question of Legal Consciousness] in Csaba Varga, ed., Vendégeloesdások a jogelmélet köréböl [Guest Lectures in Legal Theory] I, (Budapest: Eötvös Loránd Tudományegyetem, in preparation); Lukács *A társadalmi lét*. . . II, pp. 213 and 485f, III p. 18, etc., or Varga *The Place of Law* pp. 193ff. The third topic having a wide range of literature, suffice it here to cite M. J. Detmold, *The Unity of Law and Morality* (London: Routledge and Kegan Paul, 1984).

25 E.g. Lon L. Fuller *The Morality of Law* (New Haven and London: Yale University Press, 1964) ch. 2 and, as a critique in the sense above, Csaba Varga's note in *Acta Juridica Acadamiae Scientiarum Hungaricae* 12 (1970) 3–4, pp. 449–50; Csaba Varga lReflections on Law and on its Inner Morality' in *Rivista Internazionale di Filosofia del Diritto* 62 (1985) 3 and Csaba Varga 'Law as a Social Question' in *Festschrift Zygmunt Ziembinski* (Poznan: in preparation), or, for some arguments taken from it, Csaba Varga 'Law, Language and Social Mediation' in the proceedings of the IVR Special Conference in Reykjavik in 1986

(in preparation); Csaba Varga *Anthropological Jurisprudence? Leopold Pospíšil and the Comparative Study of Legal Cultures* (Budapest: Institute of Sociology of the Hungarian Academy of Sciences 1986); for a revised version see *Law in East and West*, published by the Institute of Comparative Law of Waseda University) Tokyo: Waseda University Press, 1988.

26 Hans Kelsen *Hauptprobleme der Staatsrechtslehre* (Tübingen: Mohr, 1911) p. 411.

27 Livy [Titus Livius] *History of Rome* III, 9–57, cf. Csaba Varga *A kodifikáció mint társadalmi jelenség* [Codification as a Social and Historical Phenomenon] (Budapest: Akadémiai Kiadó, 1979) ch. 2, para 2 [English translation in press].

Name Index